INSIDE U.S. BUSINESS
A Concise Encyclopedia of
Leading Industries

INSIDE U.S. BUSINESS

A Concise Encyclopedia of Leading Industries

Philip Mattera

DOW JONES-IRWIN
Homewood, Illinois   60430

We recognize that certain terms in this book are trademarks, and we have made every effort to print these throughout the text with the capitalization and punctuation used by the holder of the trademark.

This publication is designed to provide accurate and authoritative information in regard to the subject matter covered. It is sold with the understanding that the publisher is not engaged in rendering legal, accounting, or other professional service. If legal advice or other expert assistance is required, the services of a competent professional person should be sought.

From a Declaration of Principles jointly adopted by a Committee of the American Bar Association and a Committee of Publishers.

ISBN 0-87094-950-0

Library of Congress Catalog Card No. 87–70392

Printed in the United States of America

1 2 3 4 5 6 7 8 9 0 DO 4 3 2 1 0 9 8 7

ACKNOWLEDGMENTS

Given the broad range of topics covered in this book, I had to depend a great deal on other published sources of business information. I made use of innumerable articles in the business press, especially *The Wall Street Journal, Business Week,* and *Fortune.* In the case of the latter magazine, I learned an enormous amount as a member of the staff and as a reader of the publication.

Among the hundreds of other written sources I consulted, including books, reports, pamphlets, and press releases, there are several that should be mentioned, as I drew on them for nearly every chapter. *Everybody's Business: An Almanac,* edited by Milton Moskowitz, Michael Katz, and Robert Levering (Harper & Row, 1980), was of enormous assistance. That volume's success in making business narrative readable and compelling was part of the inspiration for *Inside U.S. Business,* which in part tries to do for industries what *Everybody's Business* did for individual corporations. In the general discussions of industries, I also made great use of Standard & Poor's Industry Surveys and *U.S. Industrial Outlook,* published annually by the Commerce Department. The sections on labor relations for each industry take a great deal of their historical information from *Labor Unions,* edited by Gary M. Fink (Greenwood Press, 1977). And assembling the Source Guide in each chapter was made easier by consulting Lorna M. Daniells' *Business Information Sources* (University of California Press, rev. ed., 1985).

As for human assistance, I would like to thank my agent Timothy Seldes for his faith in this project. My family, especially my parents and grandparents, and friends such as Randall Dodd, John Downing, Ash Corea, David Kirkpatrick, and Key Martin provided essential support. But the greatest debt is owed to Donna Demac, my live-in editor and a whole lot more. Her encouragement, indulgence, criticism, and inspiration were indispensable.

Philip Mattera

CONTENTS

PART TWO
CONSUMER GOODS AND SERVICES

PART THREE
ELECTRONICS

PART FOUR
ENERGY

PART FIVE
FINANCE

PART SIX
HEAVY INDUSTRY AND TRANSPORTATION

Walter Wriston, former chairman of Citicorp, has stated that "information about money has become as important as money itself." America's preoccupation with business in the 1980s is also a preoccupation with business information. Everyone from young professionals to investors to public-interest activists wants to know what is going on in management, finance, and the like.

Yet most people have a problem knowing how to begin. Even if they have studied business, the gap between what is learned in school and the current state of things is often quite wide. *The Wall Street Journal* and the rest of the business and trade press provide up-to-date information, but the reader who is new to the subject is usually given too little background to understand fully the latest developments.

Getting oriented to a subject can require an enormous amount of background reading—a luxury that is often simply not available in the business world, where all too many research projects are assigned on an "I need the answer yesterday" basis. And even when there is the time it is often difficult to find the appropriate information.

Inside U.S. Business has been written to fill the gap. Each chapter provides a succinct but wide-ranging introduction to a major industry. The reader is given a general orientation to the field and a survey of the history of the industry, including its triumphs and failures, its achievements and scandals. Special attention is paid to the transformations of industries in the 1980s brought about by new technologies such as genetic engineering and satellites as well as by upstart companies such as Apple Computer and People Express.

The narratives take the reader right up to the current competitive situation of each industry and the major technological and regulatory issues it faces. There are also thumbnail sketches of the most important companies and surveys of the industry's labor relations, especially in such cases as coal mining, where workers have played a central role in the history of the industry.

Each chapter also includes a Source Guide, which directs the reader to the best people, organizations, and publications that can provide additional information. This includes the names of leading experts and analysts, trade associations and unions, specialized data sources and directories, trade publications, and major books and reports on the industry. Many of these sources are not widely known outside of the individual industries.

Because of the complexity and rapidly changing nature of American commerce, *Inside U.S. Business* cannot pretend to provide definitive accounts of the industries it covers. Nevertheless each chapter was thoroughly researched and was written to include discussion of all the major issues one needs to know about in getting oriented to an industry. The chapters are certainly not the last word on the subjects, but they do prepare the reader to engage in further research more efficiently.

Inside U.S. Business does not cover all aspects of the commercial world. The 25 industries chosen are those that, in the opinion of the author, are of the greatest importance for the American economy in the 1980s and that are integrated enough—unlike, say, construction and real estate—to be discussed in fairly general terms.

Business outside the United States is for the most part beyond the scope of this book. The focus of the chapters is on commercial activities within the United States, though the overseas operations of U.S.-based companies and the foreign trade situations faced by American firms are also covered when they are crucial to understanding an industry.

Inside U.S. Business was written with the widest possible audience in mind. Technical details of scientific and financial issues were kept to a minimum, and as little business jargon as possible was employed. The information provided was the most current available as of the time this book went to the printer in early 1987. The author hopes that people at all levels of business sophistication will find this volume a useful tool as well as interesting reading.

Communications

Book Publishing

Book publishing is a schizophrenic business. On the one hand it is a sizable industry with revenues surpassing $11 billion a year and constituting an important part of the giant media/information/entertainment sector. Yet book publishing, more than its brethren in that sector, is also an intellectual endeavor. Because it is a major disseminator of ideas, the industry has sometimes been called a "guardian of culture." The conflict between these two roles has been intensifying in recent years as one part of the industry has plunged headlong into commercialism and another has stubbornly sought to remain faithful to literary ideals.

As a business, book publishing has some peculiar economics and practices. First of all, it is a relatively small industry as big business goes. If all publishers were combined into one, the resulting firm would rank only 30th or so on the Fortune 500. While a small number of major houses account for the lion's share of publishing revenues (especially for paperbacks), there are an extraordinarily large number of producers, variously estimated at 15,000 to 20,000 in the United States alone.

Publishing is also unique in producing such an immense number of different products; more than 40,000 new titles are issued each year. Unlike other consumer goods, for which consumption is somewhat predictable, the demand for any given title cannot be easily projected. Brand loyalty does not exist in this sector, and each product must be marketed and promoted individually.

Hardcover publishers lose money on most of their titles and depend greatly on a few best-sellers and the proceeds from the sale of paperback rights. In many cases books are treated like perishable goods: if titles don't sell quickly they are taken off the shelves by booksellers, who can return them to the publishers for full credit within a certain period.

Publishing is characterized by a rather old-fashioned method of distribution. Publishers' sales representatives and booksellers negotiate over each and every title. Given the continuous flood of new volumes, many books are given little opportunity to find their readership; some barely appear in shops at all. Wholesalers (the largest is Ingram Book Co. of Nashville) deal mainly with libraries and play a limited role for bookstores.

Leonard Shatzkin, a veteran of the publishing industry, lambasted this system a few years ago in his book *In Cold Type* and proposed a merchandising system (such as that used for greeting cards) in which the publisher would determine how many copies of each title to provide to the bookseller within a specified inventory value. There has been minor movement in this direction, but distribution by negotiation is still the rule.

What has happened at the retail end is an enormous growth in influence of the chain stores. The two leading chains are B. Dalton, consisting of about 800 stores, and Waldenbooks, owned by K mart Corp., with some 1,000 stores. Together they account for more than $1 billion in sales.

Publishers go to great lengths to please the chains. There are stories of houses changing covers and titles that didn't appeal to Dalton and Walden buyers consulted in advance of publication. The size of orders from these chains can make or break a title. Competition among the chains is intense, and Dalton and Waldenbooks have recently joined with others such as Barnes & Noble and Crown Books in discounting best-sellers. In late 1986 Barnes & Noble agreed to purchase the larger B. Dalton chain from Dayton Hudson Corp.

CULTURE AND COMMERCE

Before World War II the publishing business was stodgy and in many ways not much more than a cottage industry. Some major trade publishing houses dated back to the early 19th century:

Harper & Row had its origins in 1817, Houghton Mifflin in 1832, and Little, Brown in 1837. They and others played an influential role in the development of American culture but remained largely untouched by the corporate modernization that began in the latter part of that century. A study of the industry by O. H. Cheney in the 1930s found many antiquated practices.

The development that began to shake up the business was the rise of the paperback. There had been brief experiments with softcover volumes in the 1830s and 1880s, but they did not endure. In 1939 Robert de Graff persuaded Simon & Schuster to invest in a venture designed to follow the lead of Penguin Books, established in England four years earlier. The resulting enterprise, called Pocket Books, brought out a series of successful paperbacks priced at 25 cents each. The acceptance of paperbacks by both regular readers and people who had not previously read books was stimulated during World War II, thanks to the distribution of large quantities of "Armed Forces Editions" to the troops.

After the war, paperback publishing took off, with new houses such as Bantam and New American Library entering the business. Established booksellers shunned this new, inexpensive product, so paperbacks were distributed in an entirely different way from hardcovers: by magazine and independent distributors that simply supplied an assortment of titles rather than negotiating with the retailers, which were drugstores, newsstands, cigar stores, and later supermarkets.

These titles, mainly popular fiction with lurid covers, came to be known as mass market paperbacks and in 1985 accounted for $960 million in revenues, according to the Book Industry Study Group, compared with $1.5 billion for adult trade (general-interest) hardcovers. The mass market business is much more heavily concentrated than hardcover publishing. The leading houses are Avon (owned by Hearst), Ballantine (Newhouse), Bantam (the German company Bertelsmann), Berkley (MCA), Dell (Doubleday), Penguin, Pocket Books (Gulf & Western) and Warner Books (Warner Communications).

During the early 1950s Jason Epstein convinced his superiors at Doubleday that there was also a market, especially among college students, for inexpensive paper editions of the classics and the more serious titles that had been issued by the trade publishers.

Doubleday went along with the idea, and the Anchor list, first issued in 1953, was a great success. Other trade houses such as Alfred A. Knopf (Vintage Books) and Beacon Press jumped on the bandwagon that came to be called quality paperbacks. Known since the early 1970s as trade paperbacks, this segment accounted for $741 million in revenues in 1985.

During the late 1950s and 1960s, publishing also prospered because of the rapid growth of the textbook business, a result of soaring educational enrollment. This business is especially attractive to publishers because it is considerably less precarious than trade books: Demand for individual titles is higher and more predictable; manufacturing and marketing costs are much lower, as are discounts to retailers; and a title can sell for many years. The record probably belongs to Paul Samuelson's *Economics*, which has gone through 12 editions in 37 years and has greatly enriched both Professor Samuelson and McGraw-Hill. The textbook business did suffer somewhat during the 1970s, as college enrollment slipped, but has since recovered. Texts for elementary, secondary, and college students together accounted for $3 billion in revenues in 1985.

CONGLOMERATION AND CONCENTRATION

The growth of publishing in the 1950s and 1960s forced many houses to abandon the genteel operating practices that had existed for more than a century. The need for capital for expansion prompted houses such as Houghton Mifflin and Random House to go public. This put the firms under much greater public scrutiny and forced publishers to pay greater attention to financial results. Bennett Cerf, cofounder of Random House, wrote that after the company went public, "We were publishing with one eye and watching the stock with the other."

The industry also elicited a great deal of attention from the large electronics and media firms, which regarded book publishers as key to the burgeoning educational market. The result was a frantic acquisitions binge in publishing throughout the 1960s. ITT bought Bobbs-Merrill; Litton Industries bought Van Nostrand Reinhold; RCA bought Random House; CBS bought Holt, Rinehart & Winston; Raytheon bought D. C. Heath; and Time Inc. bought Little, Brown. A latecomer to the party was Gulf + Western, which acquired Simon & Schuster in 1975.

Although some of these buyers later sold off their publishing assets when the fast bucks were not forthcoming, conglomerate ownership became a significant controversy. Groups such as the Authors Guild charged that parent companies were forcing publishers to reduce the variety of titles and to concentrate on potential best-sellers. While many parent firms have maintained a hands-off posture, there have been some egregious cases of meddling. For example, ITT told Bobbs-Merrill in 1978 to drop fiction from its list and to concentrate on cookbooks and self-help. (Even that did not help the troubled house, which was purchased by Macmillan in 1985 and dissolved.)

The fear and loathing of conglomerate ownership were intense enough among Houghton Mifflin authors to prompt a public protest when that venerable house was the target of a takeover attempt by Western Pacific Industries in 1978. Writers such as Archibald MacLeish and John Kenneth Galbraith denounced the bid, and Western eventually decided to abandon its effort.

The defenders of conglomerate ownership argued that the new parent companies injected much-needed capital into publishing operations and forced them to be more sophisticated about finance. They also pointed to the steady growth in the number of publishers as evidence that diversity was not endangered. (In fact, there has been a flowering of small presses in recent years. Notable examples include California houses such as Ten Speed Press, North Point Press and Black Sparrow Press.)

While conglomerate ownership does have its drawbacks, the main tendencies of publishing in the past 15 years—increasing commercialization and concentration of ownership—have proceeded even among those houses that were untouched by the conglomerate invasion.

The new merger wave which hit publishing beginning in the late 1970s has taken place mainly "within the family." Houses have been buying up each other at an accelerating pace. Harper & Row bought both Crowell and Lippincott; the Dutch publisher Elsevier purchased Dutton, which was later acquired by an investment group that turned around and sold the house to New American Library, which was later purchased by Britain's Penguin Publishing; Viking merged with Penguin; Putnam bought Grosset & Dunlap; Macmillan bought Scribner's as well as Bobbs-Merrill; Gulf + Western purchased Prentice-Hall and textbook publisher Esquire Inc.; the West German Holtzbrinck Group bought Holt, Rinehart's trade division and renamed it Henry Holt & Co.; Time Inc. purchased leading textbook publisher Scott, Foresman; Germany's Bertelsmann acquired Doubleday.

Some publishers have joined in the diversification game themselves. Doubleday acquired the New York Mets, and Harcourt Brace Jovanovich bought the Sea World chain of marine parks as well as a couple of television stations in Minnesota.

THE BLOCKBUSTER COMPLEX

Publishers, merged and unmerged, have also been succumbing to what has been termed the blockbuster complex. In his book by that name, Thomas Whiteside placed the origin of modern commercialism in publishing in 1957, when Art Linkletter used his television show to plug his book *Kids Say the Darndest Things* all the way to the best-seller list.

By the 1970s the links between books and television and films had been cemented, and publishers were putting more and more emphasis on surefire categories such as pulp fiction, self-help, diets, and celebrity biographies; virtually anything else had to be by a "brand name" writer. These popular authors were becoming celebrities, appearing regularly in the gossip columns and even more so on the TV talk shows, where they shamelessly promoted their books.

Thanks to superagents such as Scott Meredith, Irving "Swifty" Lazar, and Morton Janklow, film and TV deals became major elements in negotiations between authors and publishers. Richard Snyder, chairman of Simon & Schuster, has remarked, "In a sense we are the software of the television and movie media." The promise that a book would become a major multimedia property prompted publishers to offer huge amounts, especially for paperback rights.

In 1968 Fawcett paid $410,000 for the paperback rights to Mario Puzo's *The Godfather*. By 1976 Avon was willing to pay $1.9 million for Colleen McCullough's *The Thorn Birds*. The peak was reached in 1979, when Morton Janklow arranged an auction for the rights to Judith Krantz's best-seller *Princess Daisy* in which the bidding *began* at $1 million; Bantam ended up paying $3.2 million.

Although the slump that hit the industry in the early 1980s slowed down this escalation, publishers have recently been shelling out huge amounts to a favored few authors. In 1985 the rage was for political memoirs: David Stockman received an advance of $2 million from Harper & Row to tell his story, and Jeane Kirkpatrick, Geraldine Ferraro, and Tip O'Neill each got about $1 million from other houses. Random House paid $3 million for an authorized biography of Ronald Reagan.

The fact that one of these advances (to Ferraro) was paid by Bantam, a traditional paperback house, indicates the changing relationships between hardcover and softcover publishing. During the 1970s several trade houses acquired mass market paperback publishers, and now paperback houses such as Bantam and Warner Books are branching into hardcover trade publishing. In 1986 Hearst Corp., owner of trade publisher William Morrow and paperback house Avon, paid $5 million for hard- and softcover rights for James Clavell's novel *Whirlwind*.

LABOR RELATIONS

Publishing was traditionally a poorly paid and nonunion industry. In the 1970s many employees, especially women in clerical jobs, began to challenge that state of affairs. Several hundred employees of Harper & Row went on strike in 1974 for 17 days and managed to win substantial pay increases. Soon afterward District 65 of the United Automobile Workers union launched an organizing drive among publishers and succeeded in signing up houses such as Harper & Row and Viking-Penguin. Yet most of the 75,000 people who work in the industry are still unorganized.

The 10 Largest U.S. Book Publishers: 1985 Revenues ($ Millions)

1. Simon & Schuster	$921.5
2. Reader's Digest Books	550.0
3. McGraw-Hill	460.2
4. Time Inc. (Time-Life Books; Little, Brown; Book-of-the-Month Club)	420.0
5. Macmillan	405.6
6. Harcourt Brace Jovanovich	401.3
7. Random House	385.0
8. Doubleday Publishing	380.0
9. SFN (formerly Scott, Foresman)	379.9
10. Encyclopaedia Britannica	345.0

Source: *BP Report*, August 25, 1986.

LEADING COMPANIES

For the 35 years following its founding in 1945 **Bantam** was known as the leader of the paperback industry. The company, which went through a series of owners ending up with Bertelsmann Publishing of West Germany, has paid record amounts for the paperback rights for best-sellers, including the all-time high of $3.2 million for Judith Krantz's *Princess Daisy* in 1979. In the 1980s Bantam entered the hardcover trade market and brought out a succession of major hits such as the autobiographies of Lee Iacocca, test pilot Chuck Yeager, and actress Shirley MacLaine. By the mid-1980s it was challenging Simon & Schuster for the role as the "hottest" house in the industry.

Doubleday was for many years the lumbering giant of the industry. Frank Doubleday, who founded the house in 1877 with S. S. McClure, developed close relationships with writers such as Rudyard Kipling and Joseph Conrad, while his son Nelson, who took charge in the late 1920s, had no literary pretensions. Nelson, Jr. took over the company in 1978 and, overcoming his reputation as a bon vivant, confronted the growing financial crisis of the publishing operation. After some severe cost cutting, including the shutting down of Dial Press in 1985, the business began to turn around. In late 1986 the publishing operation was sold to West Germany's Bertelsmann publishing group for an estimated $500 million.

Harcourt Brace Jovanovich, founded by Alfred Harcourt and Donald Brace in 1919, had its first success with a book by John Maynard Keynes and went on to publish authors such as Sinclair Lewis, Carl Sandburg, and T. S. Eliot. William Jovanovich took over the company in 1954 and was still running it in the mid-1980s. An author himself, Jovanovich diversified the house into areas such as Sea World marine parks and moved its headquarters to Orlando, Florida, in 1983. In 1986 Harcourt agreed to purchase CBS Inc.'s educational and professional book publishing operations for $500 million.

Random House has lost its top spot among U.S. book publishers but remains one of the most prestigious, with imprints such as Alfred A. Knopf and Pantheon as well as Random House itself. The firm was founded in 1925 when Bennett Cerf bought the Modern Library series from his employer Horace Liveright and went into business with Donald Klopfer. The company made a name for itself by challenging the obscenity laws and winning the right to publish James Joyce's *Ulysses* in the 1930s. Random House was purchased by RCA during the conglomerate mania of the 1960s and was sold to the Newhouse publishing empire in 1980.

Simon & Schuster has emerged in the 1980s as the most aggressive of the big trade publishers. Under the leadership of Richard Snyder since the house was purchased by Gulf + Western in 1975, S&S has epitomized the unabashed commercialization of book publishing. Concentrating on big-name authors and investing heavily in promotion, Snyder turned S&S into the largest and perhaps most successful trade publisher. He has been aided by S&S editor-in-chief Michael Korda, who cultivated major authors and was himself author of several books celebrating ruthlessness in business. With the purchase of textbook producer Esquire Inc. in 1984, S&S became the largest U.S. book-publishing company.

SOURCE GUIDE

LEADING STOCK ANALYSTS AND EXPERTS

John Dessauer, industry statistician and director of the Center for Book Research, an industry-sponsored center at the University of Scranton.

Oscar Dystel, former head of Bantam and now a consultant based in White Plains, New York; an expert on the paperback business.

J. Kendrick Noble, analyst at Paine Webber.

TRADE ASSOCIATIONS AND UNIONS

Association of American Publishers, New York.

American Booksellers Association, New York.

District 65, United Automobile Workers, New York.

DATA SOURCES AND DIRECTORIES

American Book Trade Directory, an annual directory of booksellers in the United States and Canada (New York: R. R. Bowker).

Book Industry Trends, an annual statistical volume (New York: Book Industry Study Group).

The Book Publishing Annual, a survey of the industry prepared by the staff of *Publishers Weekly* (New York: R. R. Bowker).

The Bowker Annual of Library and Book Trade Information, a review of the industry and compilation of statistics (New York: R. R. Bowker).

Industry Statistics, issued annually (New York: Association of American Publishers).

Literary Market Place, an annual directory of U.S. book publishers, agents, associations, suppliers, and other individuals and organizations in the trade (New York: R. R. Bowker). Companion volume *International Literary Market Place* covers 160 other countries.

Publishers' Trade List Annual, a set of volumes that reproduces the catalogs of publishers (New York: R. R. Bowker).

Publishers, Distributors & Wholesalers of the United States, directory (New York: R. R. Bowker).

TRADE PUBLICATIONS

American Bookseller, monthly.

BP Report, weekly.

Publishers Weekly.

BOOKS AND REPORTS

Cheney, O. H. *Economic Survey of the Book Industry 1930–1931.* Reprint. New York: R. R. Bowker, 1960.

Coser, Lewis, Charles Kadushin, and Walter W. Powell. *Books: The Culture and Commerce of Publishing.* New York: Basic Books, 1982.

Dessauer, John. *Book Publishing: What It Is, What It Does.* 2d ed. New York: R. R. Bowker, 1981.

Shatzkin, Leonard. *In Cold Type: Overcoming the Book Crisis.* Boston: Houghton Mifflin, 1982.

Tebbel, John. *A History of Book Publishing in the United States.* 4 vols. New York: R. R. Bowker, 1978–1981.

Whiteside, Thomas. *The Blockbuster Complex.* Middletown, Conn.: Wesleyan University Press, 1981.

CHAPTER TWO

Broadcasting and Cable

There is little doubt that electronic media have become the most important influence on the imagination of the American people. A significant portion of the population spends more time with radio and television than with any other activity, including working and sleeping. The most important influence that program purveyors hope to have on audiences is on buying habits. Although newspapers still command the largest dollar share of total advertising expenditures, television plays the leading role in the dissemination of ads for national companies. TV networks took in an estimated $9.2 billion in ad revenues in 1985, while station owners directly received another $12.1 billion. Radio's share was an estimated $6.3 billion, and cable television got some $600 million. Taking into account cable subscription fees, the total TV and radio business had some $35 billion in revenues.

Yet the media industry is no longer a simple money machine. The emergence of a variety of competing program delivery systems—from cable to satellite to microwave—has turned the business upside down more than once. The players are changing with dizzying speed, and the previously invincible networks have been losing audience share and finding themselves up for grabs in the takeover wave. The upheaval has been encouraged by the Reagan administration's Federal Communications Commission, which has moved eagerly to undo 50 years of regulation.

A WIRELESS WORLD

The discovery of radio waves by Heinrich Hertz in the late 19th century inspired numerous experiments with wireless forms of telephone and telegraph. The first to perfect the technology for transmitting Morse code through the air was a young Italian named Guglielmo Marconi. His device took the world by storm and opened up a new industry in Europe and abroad. In 1899 the Marconi Wireless Company of America was formed to provide communications for ships at sea.

The technology was improved in the United States by Reginald Fessenden, whose work led to the first wireless voice transmission in 1906, and by Lee De Forest, who invented the audion vacuum tube that served as the basis for radio receivers. By the 1910s there was lively activity in radio by hobbyists, the military, and a few corporations (such as United Fruit, which used it to communicate with its banana boats going to and from Central America).

Radio's first great moment came in 1912, when a young operator for American Marconi picked up a distress signal from the Titanic and stayed at the receiver for 72 hours straight, relaying information. That operator, incidentally, was David Sarnoff, who went on to become one of the preeminent figures in American broadcasting as head of RCA.

During this time the advance of radio was impeded by the conflicting patent claims of American Marconi, De Forest, AT&T, and others. The problem was eased during World War I, during which time the federal government ordered companies—including light-bulb makers General Electric and Westinghouse—to produce radio components without regard to patent rights. At the end of the war, the U.S. Navy was lobbying heavily to get Congress to make radio a government monopoly under the navy's control. This particular plan was shot out of the water, but the idea of monopoly remained alive.

In 1919 the federal government was alarmed at the attempt of American Marconi, as the subsidiary of a foreign firm (British Marconi), to purchase certain essential patents owned by General Electric. As an alternative the Wilson administration worked with GE to create a new company called Radio Corporation of America

(RCA), which absorbed the assets of American Marconi. RCA, essentially a subsidiary of GE with a large minority interest owned by AT&T, was the vehicle by which a small group of companies attempted to dominate the new industry through the pooling of patents—so much so that soon after Westinghouse Electric entered the arena, it was invited to join the combine (as was United Fruit).

It was Westinghouse's establishment of the first commercial broadcasting station in Pittsburgh in 1920 that gave rise to a mass mania over radio. After KDKA went on the air, would-be listeners rushed to purchase the few receivers on the market (produced by Westinghouse) or more often badgered hobbyists they knew to put together simple crystal devices. Westinghouse expanded to Newark, New Jersey, with station WJZ, which made a splash by broadcasting the 1921 World Series.

During 1922 hundreds of new stations were licensed by the Department of Commerce, which ran out of three-letter designations and had to switch to four. The largest number of stations were run by companies (especially radio manufacturers and dealers) for publicity reasons. Many others were established by newspapers or educational institutions. All were assigned the same frequency, which meant that they had to alternate transmission times in some areas. The initial programming was sparse and unpolished, but a new age of communications had begun.

Corporate harmony was not part of the new era. The greatest tension was between AT&T and its partners in the radio combine. An agreement concluded in 1922 gave the phone company the exclusive right to produce and sell radio transmission equipment, while receiving apparatuses would be manufactured by GE and Westinghouse and marketed by RCA.

Yet AT&T sought to expand its domain through the promotion of radiotelephony (i.e., allowing people to buy time for their own broadcasts over the air). AT&T established several such toll broadcasting stations, including WEAF in New York and WCAP in Washington. It also claimed extensive rights over all broadcasting because of its patents in the field of transmission technology. The situation was clarified considerably in 1926, when AT&T agreed to quit broadcasting and sell its stations in exchange for a monopoly on wire connections between stations.

THE RED AND THE BLUE

At the same time, a new entity called National Broadcasting Company (NBC) was formed to operate AT&T's former stations and RCA's outlets. It was agreed that NBC—50 percent owned by RCA, 30 percent by GE, and 20 percent by Westinghouse—would pay AT&T generous rates for guaranteed access to land-line connections.

NBC began its network broadcasting with a November 1926 gala production originating at the old Waldorf-Astoria Hotel in New York City and at other sites. By early 1927 NBC had two radio networks: NBC–Red, fed by WEAF, and NBC–Blue, which originated with WJZ.

That same year, the Columbia Phonograph Record Co. joined with a struggling operation called United Independent Broadcasters to form a serious rival to NBC. The venture nearly went under but was rescued by a group of investors including the owners of the Congress Cigar Co. of Philadelphia. William Paley, the 26-year-old son of one of the partners in Congress Cigar, ended up as president of what had become known as the Columbia Broadcasting System (CBS).

Although CBS would later dominate the broadcast industry, in the late 1920s NBC reigned supreme. But the comfortable arrangement of the radio combine was shaken in 1930, when the Justice Department brought antitrust charges against RCA, GE, and Westinghouse. The industry was stunned but worked out a consent decree they could live with. The final deal was for GE and Westinghouse to give up their ownership interests in RCA. The latter was allowed to keep its radio manufacturing facilities, and GE and Westinghouse would be allowed to compete in that business after a 30-month interval.

After taking office the Roosevelt administration made clear its intention of creating a comprehensive regulatory framework for radio and the emerging technology of television. FDR personally affirmed the importance of radio with the inauguration of his "Fireside Chat" broadcasts in 1933.

Federal oversight of broadcasting started back in 1912 with a law—prompted by the Titanic disaster—establishing strict requirements for ship radios. In the 1920s the Commerce Department held a series of National Radio Conferences to deal with the chaos caused by the sudden appearance of hundreds of stations on the air. Following the 1923 conference, Commerce established rules for different classes of stations (depending on transmission power), placing them on different frequencies. Legislation passed in 1927 created a Federal Radio Commission, which expanded the regulatory structure; but the delicate issue of controlling advertising on the new medium was sidestepped.

In 1934 the Roosevelt administration succeeded in getting Congress to approve legislation that overhauled federal regulation of broadcasting as well as telephones (on the latter, see Chapter Five). The legislation established the Federal Communications Commission (FCC) and charged it with overseeing the airwaves with a view to promoting the public interest, which was said to include a diversity of programming at both the local and the national level. Stations were to be licensed for no more than three years, and it was made clear that broadcasters were simply being given temporary rights to use a public resource.

The FCC was not allowed to directly censor programming or advertising, but the commission soon realized that its license renewal power gave it great sway over broadcast policies. When it wanted to discourage practices such as radio lotteries or liquor advertising, the commission simply issued a statement saying such things might not be in the public interest. This so-called raised-eyebrow approach got the message across to broadcasters, who usually complied without a direct order.

By the late 1930s radio was in full flower. More than 25 million American homes were equipped with the large receiving consoles, and listening to comedians such as Jack Benny and serials such as "The Green Hornet" had become part of the ritual of daily life. The first major broadcast demagogue Father Coughlin was on the air, and radio was beginning to supply dramatic reports on the growing crisis in Europe. In 1938 the power of the medium was made alarmingly clear as a Halloween Eve dramatization of "The War of the Worlds," aired over CBS by Orson Welles' Mercury Theater, caused widespread panic until people realized that a martian invasion was not actually taking place.

By this time the networks were firmly in control of the business. NBC led the field with its Red and Blue networks, followed by CBS and the even smaller Mutual Broadcasting System, launched in 1934. There were also some 20 regional networks.

The growing degree of concentration of broadcasting power began to generate concern at the FCC. In 1938 the commission launched an antitrust investigation. The result was the *Report on Chain Broadcasting*, which raised questions about NBC's ownership of two national networks and about the CBS "network option" policy of being able to preempt local programming at any time. The report also suggested it was not appropriate for the networks to own artist bureaus (in effect, talent agencies), since their role as users of performers was seen as creating a conflict of interest.

The networks moved quickly to divest themselves of the artist bureaus but resisted the other changes. They brought pressure to bear on FCC chairman James Fly through conservative members of Congress. Fly fought off the attacks, and the reforms were implemented and upheld by the Supreme Court. The NBC Blue Network was put up for sale and was purchased for $8 million by Edward Noble, a candy manufacturer of Lifesavers fame. Noble revamped the operation and renamed it the American Broadcasting Company.

But critics of the industry were not satisfied. There was still the issue of what many regarded as the excessive amounts of commercials and recorded music on the air; local stations were not living up to their responsibility to provide a diversity of programming. A 1946 report for the FCC by Charles Siepmann and Dallas Smythe, entitled *Public Service Responsibility of Broadcast Licensees* and more commonly known as the Blue Book, proposed stricter standards for limiting advertising and promoting discussion of public issues and local live programming. The industry attacked the report ferociously, and the commission did little to implement the Blue Book's proposals.

In fact the commission backtracked by reversing the so-called Mayflower decision, which barred broadcasters from editorializing without due regard for balance. It also rescinded the AVCO ruling, which called for competitive bids in license transfer cases. Then, in 1952, the industry got Congress to pass legislation prohibiting the FCC from considering applicants other than the proposed transferee. In the view of some analysts, these actions tended to move away from the spirit of the 1934 act and pushed broadcast channels closer to private property.

TELEVISION TAKES HOLD

As soon as World War II was over, RCA moved ahead aggressively in the development of television. Experiments in TV technology dated back to the 1920s, and RCA's Sarnoff was the most enthusiastic promoter. Commercial television had its debut in a transmission from the 1939 World's Fair in New York; but the industry developed slowly, and expansion was brought to a halt by the war.

RCA's bullishness on television was not shared by the entire broadcast industry. Some people felt that the rise of TV would spell the doom of radio. Matters were complicated further by the efforts of Edwin Armstrong to win favorable treatment for his invention of frequency modulation (FM) radio. FM broadcasting, which Armstrong pushed as a superior technology to AM, had been approved on an experimental basis but found itself in competition with television for certain parts of the frequency spectrum. In 1945 the FCC opted for the RCA position, giving a full-speed-ahead signal for television. Armstrong entered into a drawn-out lawsuit against RCA and ended up killing himself in 1953.

By 1948 the FCC had licensed about 100 television stations. It then instituted a freeze, saying that the interference problem had to be studied. At the same time, the network system took firm hold in the TV industry. NBC took the lead, while CBS held back awaiting the outcome of a dispute over competing methods of color broadcasting. When it did jump on the bandwagon, it had to buy most of its allotment of stations rather than establishing new outlets.

ABC struggled to keep up with its stronger rivals, and a shortage of capital forced it to merge with United Paramount Theaters. (The exhibition arm of the Paramount movie studio, it had been spun off as an independent company as a result of a federal antitrust case.) The fourth national network, Dumont, had great difficulty getting affiliates; in 1955 it disbanded the network and sold off the stations it owned to Metromedia.

During the 1950s television took hold of the American imagination to an even greater extent than radio did in the 1930s. When a TV station began operations in a city, theater and movie attendance, nightclub patronage, and even use of taxicabs declined markedly. By 1952 there were some 15 million sets in use in 64 cities, and countless people were already addicted to programs such as the "Texaco Star Theater" (with Milton Berle, "Mr. Television"), "I Love Lucy," and "Your Show of Shows."

TV was also assuming growing importance in the political process, as seen in Eisenhower's commercials during the 1952 presidential race and his running mate Richard Nixon's televised "Checkers" speech, in which he denied charges of financial impropriety. Broadcasting also played a central role in the witch-hunts of the period. A group calling itself Aware Inc. published lists of purported "subversives" working in the industry. Network executives succumbed to intimidation, firing many producers and writers and instituting a blacklist.

Yet television also played a role in the downfall of McCarthyism. Edward R. Murrow and Fred Friendly of CBS took on the Wisconsin senator in a series of "See It Now" programs and did much to change public opinion. The televising of McCarthy's 1954 hearings to investigate supposed subversion in the army also swayed people by providing a close up view of the senator's unsavory methods.

By the late 1950s, however, TV programming had to a great extent shifted away from public affairs and serious drama. There was a great craze for quiz programs until the revelations that many of them were fixed. Live programs became a rarity, replaced by telefilms produced by Hollywood studios seeking new revenue sources to substitute for the declining movie business. During the same period much of commercial radio abandoned any semblance of diversity and adopted formula formats such as Top 40 hits.

This new direction for TV was strongly encouraged in the early 1960s by CBS, whose president James Aubrey encouraged less-sophisticated programs. In a famous memo, he called for more "broads, boobs, and busts." This is precisely what CBS dished up in the form of comedy series such as "The Beverly Hillbillies," "Petticoat Junction," "Mr. Ed," and "The Munsters."

Things reached such a state that President Kennedy's FCC chairman Newton Minow decried what he called the "vast wasteland" of television programming. Minow encouraged the expansion of educational TV—promoted since the early 1950s by the

Ford Foundation—and paved the way for the creation of the Corporation for Public Broadcasting in 1967 and the Public Broadcasting Service in 1969.

The 1960s also witnessed the flowering of the public-interest movement in broadcasting. Activists, seeing the growing influence of mass media in American life, began demanding that broadcasters pay more attention to minorities and issues of social change. In 1964 one of the pioneering organizations, the Office of Communication of the United Church of Christ, working with local groups, began monitoring the output of TV stations in Jackson, Mississippi.

The organization found that the white-owned stations ignored the black population, which made up 45 percent of the viewing area, as well as the civil rights movement sweeping the South. On that basis the group petitioned the FCC to deny license renewals to the stations. The FCC claimed that public-interest groups had no standing to intervene in such cases because they had no economic stake. A federal appeals court overruled the commission and established that organizations such as the United Church of Christ could indeed intervene. During this period public groups succeeded in getting the FCC to regulate the equal employment practices of broadcasters.

Television station owners and the networks also found themselves under increasing criticism because of the amount of advertising on the air (particularly the commercials aimed at children), the increasing amount of violence (especially in the action-adventure programs that ABC came to specialize in), and the portrayal of women and minorities. In 1969 the Supreme Court, in what is known as the Red Lion decision, affirmed the responsibility of broadcasters to air conflicting views on public issues.

In 1970 the FCC continued its efforts to limit the power of the networks by restricting the role the networks could have in the production and syndication (selling old series for rebroadcast) of programming.

THE WIRED NATION

Within a few years the issue for the networks was no longer how much power they would be allowed to amass but rather the question of how they would cope with the rise of competing TV delivery systems: cable television and various forms of pay-TV.

Cable, formerly known as community antenna television, started out as a technique for delivering broadcast signals to areas that could not be reached by regular transmissions. A powerful antenna would receive the signal and relay it to households via cable. The first community antenna was erected in 1949 to allow a group of residents in Astoria, Oregon, to pick up weak TV signals from Seattle. The first cable television company was formed the following year in Lansford, Pennsylvania.

For many years cable remained a relatively insignificant element of the television business, though broadcasters frequently complained that cable operators were making money out of receiving their signals and selling them to households. The FCC approached the issue of cable regulation gingerly, given that the business did not involve broadcasting and was not conducted across state lines. In the absence of FCC rules many local authorities asserted jurisdiction over cable, demanding that operators obtain franchises.

As cable began to grow in importance, expanding out from remote areas, the FCC began to pay more attention. In 1965 the commission finally acted, issuing rules that required cable operators to deliver signals of any broadcast stations within 60 miles (what became known as the must-carry rule) and that limited the cable transmission of programs being shown over local stations. The commission, concerned that the growth of cable would inhibit local broadcasting (especially UHF stations), issued a series of other rules that restricted the industry's development. The industry was also tainted in 1971 when Irving Kahn of Teleprompter, a leading promoter of cable, was convicted of bribing local officials in Johnstown, Pennsylvania, to obtain a franchise.

The vitality of the cable business began to improve in the late 1970s. The FCC relaxed a number of its rules, and a new kind of programming was appearing on cable systems: pay services providing uncut movies, sporting events, and other features not available on broadcast stations.

The notion of pay television—as opposed to free (i.e., advertiser-supported) TV—first arose when the medium was developing in the late 1940s. A major proponent was Zenith, which tested a "phonevision" system in which scrambled broadcasts were unscrambled via signals transmitted over telephone lines. The idea did not catch on, but various subscription TV schemes came and went in the following years, usually eliciting an angry reaction from theater owners, who feared the medium could lead to their demise. To appease both motion picture and broadcast interests, the FCC adopted rules limiting the spread of pay-TV systems.

In the mid-1970s cable and pay-TV were joined in a novel programming service created by Time Inc. In 1972 Time had started Home Box Office as a pay service for the company's cable system in New York. HBO was soon offered to other cable operators and began spreading at a modest rate. The turning point came in 1975, when HBO began distributing its program via satellite rather than microwave. The service was thus able to market its programs nationwide. This gave a tremendous boost both to HBO and to the cable systems it was supplying.

HBO's success inspired other programmers to turn to satellites. Broadcaster Ted Turner used the technology to turn his Atlanta TV outlet WTBS into the first "superstation" beamed to cable systems across the country. He later supplemented this with an all-news service called Cable News Network. Turner's services were advertiser supported and were included in the price of a basic cable subscription, whereas HBO and competing pay services such as Showtime that soon emerged required an additional monthly fee. By the late 1970s the once sleepy cable industry was one of the hottest businesses around. A sign of the times was the $650 million Westinghouse agreed to pay in 1980 to acquire Teleprompter.

As companies rushed to wire the more attractive communities (mainly wealthier urban and suburban areas) they found themselves up against local authorities eager to get the best possible terms in the franchise agreement. Cable companies often had to form alliances with local public figures and make generous service commitments. Promises of state-of-the-art systems with 100 or more channels (including noncommercial ones for public access) and with interactive capabilities led to rapidly escalating construction costs for systems, especially in areas where the cable had to be placed underground.

By about 1983 the bloom was off the cable business. Operators, in addition to being bogged down in franchise disputes and heavy capital costs, discovered that subscriptions were not growing as fast as earlier forecasts had suggested. A disturbing number of subscribers were canceling services. This process, called "churning" in industry jargon, became a particular problem for the pay services.

Moreover cable was being confronted with the emergence of a variety of competing "wireless" delivery systems, including DBS (direct broadcast satellite: beaming of programs from satellites to receivers in the home), MDS (multipoint distribution systems: transmissions via microwave to special rooftop antennas), and SMATV (satellite master antenna television: systems in which an apartment building or complex receives satellite signals through a common earth station and distributes them to individual households via wire).

As it turned out, none of those technologies ended up as a major challenger. DBS all but disappeared, and the others remained limited in scope. There was some suggestion, however, that an improved version of MDS—a multichannel rather than the usual single channel—could be more successful.

By 1985 analysts were predicting a rosy future for cable. The optimism was partly inspired by the passage of the Cable Communications Policy Act of 1984. The law gave the FCC a defined mandate for regulating cable but also decreed an end to cable rate regulation beginning in 1987. Then in July 1985 a federal appeals court struck down the must-carry rule, freeing cable operators to convert more channels to lucrative pay services. The ruling was widely interpreted as an affirmation of the cable industry's claim, based on First Amendment arguments, that it should be immune from the regulatory strictures of the 1934 Communications Act. In August 1986 the FCC adopted a more limited must-carry rule that represented a compromise between the demands of cable operators and broadcasters.

By 1986 some 40 million households subscribed to cable, representing nearly 45 percent of U.S. households with television. Some 30 million of these were pay-cable subscribers. The industry had improved enough so that leading operators Tele-Communications Inc. and American Television and Communications (ATC, a Time Inc. subsidiary) were talking with Ted Turner about the possibility of creating a national network for the distribution of original programming to cable systems.

While technologies such as DBS failed to live up to their claims of supplanting cable, another innovation of the 1980s emerged as a more serious contender: private earth stations, more commonly known as satellite dishes.

DISHES AND PIRATES

Back in 1979 these dishes were still an amusement for the wealthy; the Neiman-Marcus catalog offered one for $36,500. But in the following years the price dropped sharply, and people in remote areas not served by cable began buying the devices to supplement the limited broadcast programming they were able to receive. The dishes turned famine into feast. People in the most isolated areas were able to pluck dozens of channels out of the air, including pay services and even raw feeds (unedited transmissions).

Once earth stations reached a certain presence, pay-TV providers such as HBO began to complain that dish users were in effect stealing their signals. Thus began the great debate over "signal piracy." The term often also encompassed people who tapped into cable lines without subscribing and those who used illicit converters to receive pay services via the cable. In 1983 police in Pennsylvania arrested a man calling himself "The HBO Kid," who ran a million-dollar operation selling such converters.

By the early 1980s the cable industry, estimating the losses from piracy at $500 million a year, began to fight back. HBO and other services stepped up legal actions against pirates and announced plans to begin scrambling their signals at the source. At the same time, owners of earth stations banded together—led by a group called SPACE (Society for Private and Commercial Earth Stations)—to affirm their right to receive satellite signals.

The issue found its way to Congress, where Senator Barry Goldwater sponsored a bill that became part of the 1984 cable act. The provision represented something of a compromise between the two sides. It legalized the ownership and use of dishes for the purpose of receiving *unscrambled* signals. Programmers were supposed to develop plans for providing converters so that dish owners could view decoded scrambled signals at a reasonable fee.

The law stimulated rapid growth in earth station sales, and the number of dishes in operation by 1986 was estimated at 1.5 million. Yet after HBO finally began scrambling its signal in Janu-

Leading Cable and Pay-TV Services

	Number of Subscribers (in Millions)
Cable operators (as of June 30, 1986)	
1. Tele-Communications Inc.	3.78
2. ATC (Time Inc.)	2.76
3. Group W	2.00
4. Storer Cable	1.57
5. Cox Cable	1.33
6. Warner Amex	1.26
7. Continental Cablevision	1.20
8. United Cable Television	1.02
9. Newhouse	.94
10. Times Mirror Cable	.89
Pay-TV services (as of April 30, 1986)	
1. HBO	14.5
2. Showtime	5.1
3. Cinemax	3.7
4. Movie Channel	3.0
5. Disney Channel	2.6

Source: Paul Kagan Associates, Carmel, Calif.

ary 1986, the tensions between programmers and dish owners heated up again, and dish sales cooled off. Earth station users charged that cable operators and programmers were conspiring to monopolize the sale of decoding equipment. In the spring of 1986 the Justice Department indicated that it was looking into the

Leading Advertiser-Supported Cable Services (as of July 1986)

	Company	Programming	Homes Reached (in Millions)
1.	ESPN	Sports	37.1
2.	WTBS	Superstation	36.3
3.	Cable News Network	News	33.7
4.	USA Network	Entertainment	31.9
5.	Christian Broadcasting Network	Family programs	31.1
6.	Music Television (MTV)	Music video	29.3
7.	Nickelodeon	Children	26.8
8.	Nashville Network	Country music	25.9
9.	Lifetime	Health	25.0
10.	Weather Channel	Weather	20.7

Source: Nielsen Television Index, Coverage Tracking Report.

charge. In the meantime, dish owners were slow to purchase the $400 decoders and pay the monthly fees that were also required to view scrambled programming.

One irate dish dealer in Florida made his position known by interrupting an HBO transmission with an antiscrambling message. This new form of hacking, by someone who identified himself as Captain Midnight, panicked the satellite industry. But there was a bit of relief when the culprit, who also worked as a satellite engineer, was tracked down and persuaded to plead guilty to a charge of unauthorized transmission of an interfering signal.

DEREGULATION AND MERGER MANIA

While these new technologies were going through their growth pains, the television networks began to experience a decline in viewing levels. The network share dropped from around 90 percent of the prime-time audience in the early 1970s to 76 percent in 1984. Advertisers started to get concerned and were beginning to spend some of their money on cable networks. But even this did not help once videocassette recorders began invading American homes, allowing people to tape programs and then "zap" commercials (fast-forward through them) while viewing the shows later. These factors contributed to a slowdown in network revenues, which unfortunately occurred while production costs for programming were rising rapidly. The result of all this was a squeeze on ABC, NBC, and CBS.

There was, however, good news for the networks and other broadcasters coming from Washington. After taking office in 1981, the Reagan administration embarked on a crusade to dismantle much of the regulatory structure that had been built since 1934. While some deregulatory moves were made under Carter, Reagan's FCC chairman Mark Fowler argued that the advent of new technologies had made the premise of regulation—the need to protect a scarce resource—obsolete.

With unbridled laissez-faire zeal, Fowler went after the commission's key regulatory bases. Starting in 1981 the FCC:

- Eliminated limits on commercial time for radio and television and ended requirements for minimum amounts of public affairs programming.

- Relaxed rules governing children's television.
- Abolished the requirement that stations keep program logs open for public inspection.
- Lifted the requirement that license holders must operate a station for at least three years before reselling it.
- Reduced detailed renewal procedures to the point that a licensee could seek a renewal simply by sending in a postcard.
- Attempted to abolish all ownership limits but reached a compromise with Congress under which the old 7–7–7 limit (7 TV stations and 7 AM and 7 FM radio stations) was raised to 12–12–12, though Congress insisted that the potential audience of the 12 TV stations could not exceed 25 percent of the total TV households in the United States.

The commission also attempted to repeal the rules that limit network participation in program production and syndication; but apparently Hollywood got to President Reagan, and Fowler was told to back off. The commission has also publicly criticized the fairness doctrine, which requires broadcasters to air opposing points of view on controversial public issues. In addition, in 1981 Congress extended the traditional three-year license period to seven years for radio and five for television stations.

Among these changes, the expansion of the ownership limits probably had the most far-reaching effect. In fact it can be seen as a major factor in the extraordinary wave of media mergers that occurred in 1985. In that one year an estimated $30 billion worth of electronic media properties (including two of the networks) changed hands, with the blessing of the FCC. The largest transactions announced during the year were:

- General Electric purchased RCA for $6.3 billion.
- Capital Cities purchased ABC for $3.6 billion.
- Kohlberg, Kravis, Roberts (KKR) took Storer Communications private for $2.3 billion.
- A group led by Tele-Communications Inc. and ATC agreed to purchase Group W Cable for $2.1 billion.
- Rupert Murdoch purchased seven independent TV stations from Metromedia for $2 billion, later selling off one of them for $450 million.
- The Tribune Company purchased Station KTLA in Los Angeles for $510 million, the most ever paid for a single broadcast outlet.

The acquisitions by Murdoch and the Tribune Company represent more than picking up attractive properties. Each deal was an element in the race to create a fourth television network. Murdoch, working through the Twentieth Century-Fox film studio, which he also bought in 1985, planned to use the Metromedia stations as the basis for affiliating currently independent TV outlets around the country. Murdoch intended to integrate such an operation with his Sky Channel satellite service in Europe. Tribune Company, which owned six stations after buying KTLA, was after the same goal.

The quest for a viable fourth network has been around years. Dumont attempted to play that role after the war but could not attract enough affiliates. Other companies such as Paramount and Metromedia have made stabs at the goal but have not gotten far.

The new interest in a fourth network is based in part on the growth and vitality of the independents, which have increased from 73 in 1972 to some 260 in 1986. The UHF stations among them have benefited from the spread of cable, which makes them more accessible (though revision of the must-carry rule may change this). The power of the stations owned directly by Murdoch and Tribune Company is seen in the postmerger figures compiled by *Broadcasting* magazine on the penetration by the leading ownership chains:

Network	Penetration of TV Households
Capital Cities/ABC	24.39%
GE/NBC	20.94
CBS	19.45
Tribune	18.60
Fox	18.13

During this period, radio has been going through an upheaval of its own. Most dramatic has been the rapid decline of AM. Whereas more than two thirds of the radio audience went to AM in 1970, FM had more than 70 percent by 1985. The brassy, jingle-laden sound of AM has lost its appeal to many people. Some AM stations have responded by seeking FCC approval to begin broadcasting in stereo, but there were no signs this would be enough to save AM. Along with this has occurred a revival of radio networks. Companies such as Satellite Music Network provide 24-hour-a-day feeds in several different formats to mostly small and medium-sized stations around the country.

Overall, the trend in broadcasting has been toward a concentration of ownership and a further shift away from local programming. Even cable, which was supposed to make television available for community needs, has moved more and more toward the type of programming provided by the networks and the independents. The new technologies have provided a variety of delivery methods but relatively little in the way of diversity of programming.

LABOR RELATIONS

Workers in the radio industry responded eagerly to New Deal labor legislation by organizing to improve the poor working conditions that characterized the industry. In 1937 the American Federation of Radio Artists (AFRA) was formed, and in a few years the union was widely recognized as the bargaining agent for broadcasting talent. As for other radio workers, the Association of Technical Employees was formed in 1934 as a management-dominated union. But within a few years it began to operate independently, and in 1940 it changed its title to the National Association of Broadcast Engineers and Technicians (NABET). The union found itself in jurisdictional disputes with the International Brotherhood of Electrical Workers, but in 1951 it received a CIO charter giving it jurisdiction over the broadcasting industry. Consequently the union substituted Employees for Engineers in its title.

In 1952 AFRA merged with the Television Authority, a federation of four performers' unions, to form the American Federation of Television and Radio Artists (AFTRA). The performers' union also had jurisdictional problems—with the Screen Actors Guild (SAG), which repeatedly rejected AFTRA's merger overtures. Finally the two unions made a pact under which SAG would bargain for filmed television performers and AFTRA would represent performers on live or videotaped programs. During the 1950s some AFTRA officials were involved in promoting the blacklist; but the group was voted out in 1955, and AFTRA joined the forces opposing the blacklist.

AFTRA called its first national strike in 1967, forcing the networks to show reruns. The walkout was settled after 13 days, just in time for ABC to broadcast the Academy Awards ceremony.

Later that same year, NABET struck ABC for two months. The union also struck NBC in 1976 and ABC again in 1977.

In 1982 AFTRA filed for Chapter 11 after a federal judge refused to stay a $10 million antitrust judgment against the union. Although unions are usually considered immune from antitrust laws, a jury found AFTRA guilty of restraint of trade for pressuring advertising agencies not to give business to a nonunion company that wrote music and jingles for commercials. The case was settled out of court.

In the 1980s the broadcast unions have been under intense pressure as a result of cost-cutting measures instituted by the networks. The new owner of ABC, Capital Cities, has a history of taking a hard line with labor. Both CBS and General Electric, the new parent of NBC, have also adopted harsh policies.

LEADING COMPANIES

The **American Broadcasting Company** was created in 1945 after NBC was required by a court ruling to divest itself of one of its two radio networks. ABC struggled along, lacking the capital necessary to make a serious entry into television. To improve its resources the company merged with United Paramount Theaters in 1953. Leonard Goldenson, who headed United Paramount, ended up running the network for 30 years. Through the 1950s ABC remained a perennial also-ran in the ratings game. The network began to receive some serious audience shares in the 1960s and came close to being acquired by ITT in the latter part of the decade. In 1976 ABC suddenly leaped to first place in the prime-time ratings, thanks to the efforts of the gifted programmer Fred Silverman (known as "the man with the golden gut"). The network also became a leader in news programming. ABC had a series of disappointments in cable programming efforts but in 1984 purchased ESPN, the sports network and the largest cable service. In 1985 it was announced that ABC would be acquired in a friendly transaction by Capital Cities.

CBS, the last remaining independent network, was formed in the late 1920s through the rescue of a small network that had been set up as a competitor to NBC. William Paley, the son of one of the owners of a cigar company that invested in the network, became head of CBS and tenaciously held on to that position for nearly 60 years. CBS was for many years the "class act" in the broadcasting business, especially with its superior news and public affairs programming. It was the invincible leader in the ratings until dislodged by ABC in 1976. In 1985 the network was shaken, first, by an effort by a group of conservatives to change what they considered to be the liberal bias of the network. Then Ted Turner announced an audacious plan to take over CBS in a $5 billion deal that involved no cash at all. CBS defeated Turner by repurchasing 21 percent of its stock for nearly $1 billion, a tactic that ballooned the company's long-term debt. As further protection, CBS chairman Thomas Wyman asked Loews Corp. to raise its stake in the company as high as 25 percent. In September 1986 Wyman lost the support of the board, and Paley and Loews chairman Laurence Tisch stepped in to take over management of CBS on an interim basis. They ended up staying indefinitely.

The **National Broadcasting Company** was the first broadcast network—in fact it was two networks until the federal government insisted that one be divested in 1943. NBC was formed in 1926 as part of a complicated arrangement between the Radio Corporation of America and AT&T. As part of the larger RCA organization, NBC was always financially stronger than its rivals. "General" David Sarnoff, who ran the company from its earliest days to his retirement in 1966, was the leading proponent of television in the 1930s and 1940s. He also diversified RCA into electronics and other fields. After Sarnoff's departure RCA went through a period of managerial instability that came to an end with the arrival of Thornton Bradshaw in 1981. Grant Tinker, hired by Bradshaw to head NBC, turned the languishing network around. In the 1985–86 season NBC for the first time came out on top in the ratings. The network and the rest of RCA was acquired by General Electric—its original owner—for more than $6 billion in 1986. Later that year GE named one of its executives, Robert Wright, to replace Tinker.

Viacom was formed in 1971 out of the syndication business CBS had to spin off in response to an FCC ruling forcing the networks out of that part of the business. Under president and chief executive Terrence Elkes, Viacom emerged as one of the fastest-growing companies in the television business. Aside from syndication, it got into programming (starting Showtime in 1976 as a rival to HBO), cable system operation, and broadcast station ownership. In 1985 it went on a buying spree, acquiring (as leader of an investment group) a 15 percent interest in the Orion Pictures film studio, paying Warner Amex Cable $690 million for the MTV and Nickelodeon cable services and the 50 percent of Showtime it did not already own, and acquiring CBS's St. Louis station for $122 million. In September 1986 an investment group led by Viacom's chief executive offered to take the company private in a deal worth $2.7 billion.

SOURCE GUIDE

LEADING STOCK ANALYSTS AND EXPERTS

R. Joseph Fuchs, media analyst at Kidder Peabody.

Paul Kagan Associates, leading cable and pay-TV experts, Carmel, California.

Dennis Leibowitz, media analyst at Donaldson, Lufkin & Jenrette.

Richard MacDonald, media analyst at First Boston.

John Reidy, media analyst at Drexel Burnham Lambert.

TRADE ASSOCIATIONS AND UNIONS

American Federation of Television and Radio Artists, New York.

Association of Independent Television Stations, Washington, D.C.

National Association of Broadcast Employees and Technicians, Bethesda, Maryland.

National Association of Broadcasters, Washington, D.C.

National Cable Television Association, Washington, D.C.

Screen Actors Guild, Hollywood, California.

DATA SOURCES AND DIRECTORIES

Broadcasting/Cablecasting Yearbook, a wide-ranging compilation of data and listings (Washington, D.C.: Broadcasting Publications).

Cable TV Financial Databook, an annual directory and data source (Carmel, Calif.: Paul Kagan Associates).

International Television Almanac, an annual compilation of data on networks, producers, group stations owners, etc. (New York: Quigley Publishing).

Television and Cable Factbook, a two-volume directory of broadcast stations, cable operators, and programmers (Washington, D.C.: Television Digest).

TRADE PUBLICATIONS

Broadcasting, weekly.

Cablevision, fortnightly.

Channels, monthly.

Multichannel News, weekly.

Television Digest, weekly.

BOOKS AND REPORTS

Barnouw, Erik. *A History of Broadcasting in the United States.* 3 vols. New York: Oxford University Press, 1966, 1968, 1970.

Bergreen, Laurence. *Look Now, Pay Later: The Rise of Network Broadcasting.* Garden City, N.Y.: Doubleday Publishing, 1980.

Sterling, Christopher, and John Kittross. *Stay Tuned: A Concise History of American Broadcasting.* Belmont, Calif.: Wadsworth, 1978.

Film and Video

For more than three quarters of a century motion pictures have been central to popular culture in America. They have created enduring images of life in the United States and have both reflected and shaped the changing social and political values of the country. While films in the postwar period have faced stiff competition from television, they remain a primary expression of American reality and fantasy.

Movies are also a big business. From the earliest days of Hollywood, films have been an unabashedly commercial endeavor. It is a rather unstable industry, however. The major movie-producing studios swing from boom to bust and back at an unsettling pace. The reason is a preoccupation with producing blockbuster films, which by their nature lead to either feast or famine. The huge windfalls created by successes such as *The Sound of Music* in the 1960s and *Star Wars* and *E.T.* in more recent years keep the studios chasing after the next rainbow.

This perennial problem has been made more complicated in the 1980s by dramatic changes in the patterns of film viewing. Box office receipts—about half of which go to the owners of the country's 20,000 movie theaters—slipped to $3.7 billion in 1985 from the record level of $4 billion the year before. Annual ticket purchases continued to hover around the 1 billion mark, where they have remained for more than 20 years. The reason for the lack of growth is the challenge from videocassettes and pay-TV. By mid-1985 some 23 percent of U.S. homes were equipped with videocassette recorders, and some 38 percent were pay-cable subscribers. While pay-TV growth has leveled off, use of videocassettes has been booming. An estimated 50 million prerecorded cassettes were sold in 1985, many of them to video shops that rent the tapes over and over again.

These new outlets, once minor considerations for the studios, have become major rivals for audiences. But they are also increasingly important sources of revenue for the moviemakers. Unsure whether the rise of video spells salvation or doom, Hollywood is scrambling to find its place in this new entertainment scheme, just as it did 35 years ago when television first started substituting the living room for the neighborhood movie palace.

FROM THE KINETOSCOPE TO THE SILVER SCREEN

Toward the end of the 19th century, inventors in the United States and Europe started working on devices to produce and project moving pictures. The process was made practical by the work of Thomas Edison and his assistant William Dickson in the late 1880s, following George Eastman's creation of the first celluloid roll film.

Although Edison took out a patent for his devices, he seemed to regard moving pictures as little more than a novelty. His backers, on the contrary, saw great commercial potential, and the wizard of Menlo Park was persuaded to produce short films. This was no easy task. Edison's camera, called a kinetograph, was a large, immobile device that had to be operated indoors in a specially constructed structure (nicknamed "Black Maria" because it looked something like the police wagons that went by that name). Edison's operation first focused on animal acts and then moved on to human subjects such as boxer Jim Corbett and Japanese dancers.

The first public establishment featuring Edison's viewing device, called Kinetoscope, opened in New York in 1894. The machine was a large box inside which light was projected through a reel of film. Viewers, one at a time, looked through a peephole to see action. Before long, people were calling it a "peep show."

Other innovations came quickly. The Lumière brothers in France perfected a portable camera, and Thomas Armant in the United States developed methods for projecting films to an entire audience at once. Edison's Kinetoscope Company bought the rights to Armant's work and kept him in the background. In 1896 Koster and Bials' Music Hall in New York presented the first public performance of a motion picture, using what was called Edison's Vitascope.

American Mutoscope and Biograph Company emerged as the first serious rival to Edison, both in peep shows and in theatrical movies. The company claimed that its devices were different enough from Edison's to avoid patent infringement. Edison disagreed and launched what became a perennial campaign to protect what he saw as his exclusive rights to motion picture technology.

By the turn of the century, peep shows had gained enormous popularity; they were the leading form of entertainment for immigrants and others of the working class. Theatrical films took off when a strike of vaudeville actors in 1900 prompted theater owners to find an alternative to live shows. The process was also assisted by the efforts of Edwin Porter to transform motion pictures from short amusements into longer, more serious works of art. Inspired by the French cinema pioneer George Méliès, Porter produced the first U.S. feature film *Life of an American Fireman* in 1903.

As motion picture theaters, generally known as nickelodeons, spread across the country, the film industry became big business. In order to supply the exhibitors, a middleman system arose in which distributors formed companies called film exchanges that purchased or leased films from producers and rented them to theater owners.

By this time a slew of companies were defying Edison's patent claims relating to both the production and exhibition of movies. In 1908 Edison and his leading rivals decided it was better to cooperate rather than attack one another in the courts. They boldly established what they intended to be a production monopoly, the Motion Picture Patents Company, which claimed the right to license film exchanges and extract $2-a-week royalty payments from all exhibitors. Two years later Edison and his partners established the General Film Company, which set out to take over the distribution business.

These would-be monopolies had as little success as Edison had previously had in trying to keep competitors out of the business.

Independent producers remained in business and challenged the trust, as did a number of major film exchanges that resisted being bought out. By the beginning of World War I, the monopolies had crumbled, and the independents were growing in number and power in the industry.

Among the leaders of this new wave was Carl Laemmle, whose Independent Moving Picture Company established the "star system." Edison and his associates deliberately did not publicize the names of their players, in order to deny the actors too much bargaining power. Laemmle correctly assumed that audiences would be drawn in when they knew their favorite player would appear in a film. Laemmle was also one of the first to set up shop in Hollywood, the Los Angeles suburb where many producers went to be far away from the East Coast–based trust.

Another independent, Adolph Zukor, who like many producers came from an immigrant background, created a middle-class audience for movies after he imported the French production *Queen Elizabeth*, which starred prominent stage actress Sarah Bernhardt.

The rising costs of film production—a result in part of escalating salaries of star players such as Mary Pickford and star directors such as D. W. Griffith—led to the independents' consolidation into the studios that would dominate the industry for decades.

In 1920 Marcus Loew, a leading exhibitor, entered production with the purchase of ailing Metro Pictures. After a big success in 1921 with *The Four Horsemen of the Apocalypse* (starring Rudolph Valentino), Loew purchased Goldwyn Pictures, founded in 1916 by Samuel Goldfish (who later changed his name to Goldwyn). Loew then acquired the operations of a rising young producer named Louis Mayer, and the result is what became known as Metro-Goldwyn-Mayer. The other majors emerged in more or less the same manner.

Even before the start of the 1920s leading players and directors were growing frustrated with the power of the studio moguls. In 1919 four of the biggest stars in the business decided to break away and produce films on their own. Mary Pickford, Douglas Fairbanks, Charlie Chaplin, and D. W. Griffith established United Artists as a vehicle for distributing films they intended to produce on their own. The studios were initially amused—one executive

remarked that "the lunatics have taken charge of the asylum"—
but UA became an important force in the industry.

THE MOVIES LEARN TO TALK

No sooner had the business achieved some structural stability
than the film world was turned upside down by the arrival of a
new dimension: sound. Experiments in combining images with
sound had gone on since Edison invented the phonograph in
1877, but it was not until the 1920s that the technique was perfected by engineers at AT&T's Western Electric subsidiary.

The studios were initially resistant to the new technology, but
the Warner Brothers studio, founded in 1923, eventually came
around. After investing in Vitaphone Corp. (the company set up
to market AT&T's technology), Warner brought out *Don Juan* in
1926 with an operatic sound track. But the big sensation came the
following year, when the Warner production of *The Jazz Singer*
with Al Jolson included the first spoken dialogue. The enthusiastic reception received by this film prompted the other studios to
rush into the production of talking films. The Silent Era quickly
came to an end.

The advent of sound certainly caused dislocation for the industry—and for those players who had poor stage voices—but it also
made the medium more varied. MGM, for instance, specialized in
lavish musical extravaganzas, while Warner made a name for
itself with films of social realism.

The 1930s were a difficult time for the industry, which by this
time was clearly dominated by a group of eight major studios.
The "Big Five"—vertically integrated firms with a major presence
in distribution and exhibition as well as production—were
Warner Brothers, MGM, Paramount, Twentieth Century–Fox,
and RKO. The "Little Three" were Universal and Columbia (involved solely in production and distribution) and United Artists
(distribution only).

The slump in the business during the height of the Depression
forced several studios into temporary bankruptcy, and in 1938 the
Justice Department began what would be a long-term effort to
prosecute the major studios for antitrust violations.

Like the rest of the economy the movie business rebounded
with the mobilization for war. Hollywood eagerly produced films

that fit in with the fighting spirit of the time, and in the 1940s the industry reached what was perhaps its pinnacle of influence in American culture. In 1946 weekly movie attendance reached an all-time high of 90 million, and industry profits were also at record levels.

Those halcyon days did not last for long. The first blow came with the political witch-hunts of the postwar period. In 1947 the House Un-American Activities Committee opened an investigation of Communist influence in the film business. Attention became focused on a group of individuals, mainly screenwriters, who were accused of leftist associations and subpoenaed to appear before the committee. The Hollywood Ten, as they came to be known, were cited for contempt after they denounced the hearings and refused to answer questions or name names. Industry leaders bowed to the committee and collectively vowed not to employ persons "believed to be Communists." Thus was the blacklist created.

The next ordeal was the culmination of the Justice Department's antitrust crusade against the industry. The government won its case, and the studios lost their appeals. By the late 1940s the five major integrated companies were forced to start divesting themselves of their theater chains. Practices such as block booking (requiring theater owners who wanted any of a studio's films to take all of them) and the fixing of minimum admission prices also went by the boards. The likes of Loew's, RKO, and Warner no longer held absolute sway over the movie business.

The third and most serious challenge to the studios was the increasing popularity of a new form of entertainment known as television. Starting in the late 1940s TV sets were invading U.S. homes at a dizzying rate, and the small screen quickly won the cultural loyalty of America. The film producers soon felt the results in declining box office receipts. The industry fought back with gimmicks such as CinemaScope and 3–D films, but it was a futile battle. Motion pictures were no longer the country's premier leisure activity.

HOLLYWOOD IN THE AGE OF TELEVISION

Columbia was the first studio to realize that television could be turned into an opportunity. In the early 1950s the company's

Screen Gems subsidiary began producing "telefilms" for TV. Some of these were scaled-down versions of theatrical films, while others were entirely new productions. Warner jumped on this bandwagon in 1955, and the other studios soon followed suit. By the 1960s television production was a major income-producing activity for the film companies, especially for Universal. The studios, led by RKO (which passed from Howard Hughes to General Tire and Rubber in 1955 and soon exited the production business), also generated revenue by selling the TV rights to their film libraries.

The income derived from television helped the studios survive but not necessarily prosper. Things got particularly bad in the late 1960s after a series of expensive flops. Filmmaking virtually came to a halt, and there were shake-ups in both the ownership and management of many of the leading movie companies. Transamerica bought United Artists, MCA purchased Universal, and Gulf + Western acquired Paramount. The old-line Hollywood moguls were steadily replaced by a new generation of business-oriented executives.

By the late 1970s the industry was looking a lot more healthy, thanks largely to such blockbusters as *Jaws, Grease,* and *Star Wars.* Although critics often sneered at the juvenile orientation of the films of George Lucas, Steven Spielberg, and their followers, movies such as *Return of the Jedi* were box office smashes. With the number of older filmgoers apparently in decline Hollywood went all out for the youth market.

The movie business looked attractive enough so that in 1982 Columbia, just after being purchased by The Coca-Cola Company, formed a joint venture with CBS and Time Inc.'s Home Box Office (HBO) subsidiary to create the first new major studio in decades. The venture, called Tri-Star Pictures, was the most successful of a series of projects put together by different sectors of the entertainment business.

This flurry of activity reflected the upheaval in the industry wrought by the rise of new entertainment media. In the early 1980s the powerhouse was pay-TV. Cable television was invading American homes at a rapid rate, and analysts were predicting the virtual demise of the theatrical film business at the hands of pay services. HBO, the leader of those services, was becoming a major force in Hollywood by financing films in exchange for pay-TV rights. Studios resented this intrusion, but many producers could not turn down the seductive deals HBO was offering. For instance, HBO was able, thanks to its position, to get early rights to a movie like *On Golden Pond* for $3.5 million. Given the box office success of the film, HBO would have had to pay at least four times that amount if the deal had been struck after the theatrical run.

By the mid-1980s, however, pay-TV came back down to earth. Growth in subscriptions leveled off as many viewers found themselves dissatisfied with the few hits and lots of filler being offered by the services. People also came to realize that videocassettes offered a much wider range of choices. VCRs, which were first offered in the mid-1970s and received a moderate response, took off in the 1980s. VCR shipments to dealers, which had been stuck below 2 million units a year, soared in 1983, and reached about 14 million in 1986.

Videocassettes suddenly became a major factor in movie studio calculations. While access to videos was certainly eating into box office receipts, the rights to videocassette versions of films were becoming a significant revenue source for the studios. Although many in the industry viewed the rise of video rentals—from which the industry gets no share—as a threat, it turned out that consumers would be willing to purchase prerecorded videos of hit films.

The success of videos such as *Raiders of the Lost Ark* proved this point and also helped to push prices for video rights up to unprecedented levels. *The Empire Strikes Back* went for an astounding $12 million. Some of the major studios have set up their own subsidiaries to market video versions of their films. Even when the rights are sold to others—the leading independent is Vestron Video—the studios make out much better with videos than they do with pay-TV. In 1984 *Fortune* reported that the studios received about $1 per cassette viewer, taking rentals into account, but only 5 or 10 cents per pay-TV viewer.

The video business became all the more appealing to the studios when it turned out that a number of box office flops (*The Cotton Club*, for instance) turned into hits in cassette form. By 1985, revenues from video rights just about equaled what the studios earned from theatrical showings.

One significant pitfall in the videocassette business was the growing practice of piracy. Hollywood had long been plagued by the sale of unauthorized prints of feature films, but the problem was generally not a major one. The advent of videocassettes made illicit duplication much simpler. Pirates simply transferred film prints onto videocassettes, which are easily reproduced. Copying of films released on videocassette could be done by anyone with a pair of VCRs.

By the early 1980s counterfeit copies of hundreds of films were being produced in massive quantities around the world. In some countries in the Middle East and Africa the pirates were said to control nearly all of the videocassette market. The situation was summed up in a 1983 headline in the trade newspaper *Variety:* "WORLD VID PIRACY AT $1–BIL MARK: MORALITY CAN'T KEEP PACE WITH TECHNOLOGY."

Hollywood has desperately sought technical solutions to combat the problem. The industry had hopes that videodisks, which were much more difficult than cassettes to reproduce, would save the day, but the disks did not catch on with consumers. The producers of videocassettes, worried about the development of VCRs with two recording heads, began experimenting with techniques of making cassettes copyproof. In April 1985 Embassy Home Entertainment released cassettes of *The Cotton Club* equipped with a device that prevented copying by impairing the automatic gain control of the VCR, but professional pirates were able to overcome the obstacle. In 1986 Warner attacked the problem by putting secret markings on each print of Sylvester Stallone's film *Cobra,* so that pirated cassettes could be traced back to a particular theater.

The studios' heightened concern about the losses from piracy was a reflection of the financial crunch of the industry. Yet with the average production cost of films made by the major studios continuing to rise—the figure surpassed $15 million in 1985—Hollywood was doing more than trying to maximize its returns from the videocassette business. For instance, the studios began seeking greater control of the other outlets for their products. Despite old antitrust problems, studios such as Columbia made investments in theater companies, and Twentieth Century–Fox and Universal's parent MCA purchased television stations. This

Market Share of the Major Studios in 1985

	Box Office Receipts	Film Rental Revenues*
1. Warner	16.5%	18%
2. Universal	15.4	16
3. Paramount	10.8	10
4. Fox	10.0	11
5. Columbia	9.7	10
6. Tri-Star	9.1	10
7. MGM/UA	7.6	9
8. Orion	5.6	5
9. Disney	3.5	3

* Film rental revenues are what is left over after theater owners take their share, usually about half, of box office receipts.
Source: *Variety.*

was in addition to Warner and Disney's direct involvement in cable. All of which suggests that the upheaval in the entertainment business is far from over.

LABOR RELATIONS

The decision by the early film studios to move from the East to the West Coast was not only because of the climate. Being in Hollywood gave the industry access to the labor market of the country's largest nonunion city, Los Angeles. Organizing among studio workers began as early as 1918, when a strike of craft workers led to wage increases but no contract. After agitation resumed in the 1920s, the studios formed the Association of Motion Picture Producers mainly for the purpose of developing a united policy toward labor. Two years later they signed the Studio Basic Agreement with five unions representing craft workers.

Creative personnel were slower to organize, despite the efforts of the Actors' Equity Association. In 1927 the studios tried to ward off unionization with the creation of the Academy of Motion Picture Arts and Sciences, a management-dominated entity that was supposed to represent directors, actors, writers, and technicians. After the studios tried to impose large wage cuts in 1933, the talent began seeking true union representation. The Screen Actors Guild (SAG) was formed, and the Screen Writers Guild (established in 1920 but which had become dormant) was revived. After a protracted battle the producers relented in 1937, and unionization for actors was established. But management resisted recognizing the Screen Writers Guild for several more years.

In 1960 the Screen Actors Guild struck the industry for six weeks in order to win compensation for actors when films were sold to television. Similar walkouts occurred in 1980 and 1981 over the issue of remuneration when films were put on videocassettes or pay-TV. The Writers Guild of America (which the Screen Writers Guild became part of in 1954) struck over related issues in 1981 and 1985.

Within the Screen Actors Guild there was controversy in the early 1980s over the political views of president Ed Asner, an outspoken critic of Reagan administration policies in Central America. (Reagan, incidentally, was president of the guild for six terms beginning in 1947.) Conservative union members led by Charlton Heston waged a campaign against Asner, and though they failed to unseat him, in 1984 they did defeat an Asner-supported measure to merge SAG with the Screen Extras Guild. Asner was succeeded in 1985 by Patty Duke, who defeated conservative candidate Ed Nelson.

LEADING COMPANIES

Columbia was started in the 1920s as a small independent producer by Harry Cohn, his brother Jack, and Joe Brandt. The company, which pioneered the practice of shooting scenes out of sequence in order to keep down production costs, specialized in low-budget features but also prospered from the social-minded films of Frank Capra. Columbia—run by Harry Cohn, the quintessential ruthless studio boss, until his death in 1958—was the first studio to move into television production. In the late 1970s Columbia was embarrassed when it was revealed that its hotshot film head David Begelman had forged more than $60,000 of company checks for personal use. The investment house of Allen & Company, which had bought a controlling interest in the studio in the early 1970s, thwarted a takeover by financier Kirk Kerkorian in 1981 by purchasing his shares. But the Allens turned around and sold their interest at a great profit to The Coca-Cola Company in 1982.

MCA, which began as a small talent agency in 1924 and grew into one of the leading entertainment companies, got into the film business in 1962 with its purchase of Decca Records, which at the time owned Universal studios. Universal, which emerged in the 1920s as one of the second-tier major studios (it did production and distribution but owned no theaters), did not have many big stars under contract before 1940 and originally made its name by creating the horror genre with films such as *Frankenstein* and *Dracula*. After being purchased by MCA, Universal took the lead among film studios in television production. By the mid-1970s it was producing more than 25 percent of the prime-time programs. In 1986, with longtime president Lew Wasserman in his 70s, the company was reported to be seeking a merger with another large entertainment company.

MGM/UA Entertainment was established in 1981 as the merger of two of Hollywood's old-line studios: Metro-Goldwyn-Mayer and United Artists. Soon after Ted Turner completed purchasing the company in 1986 from Kirk Kerkorian, he sold the United Artists portion of it back to Kerkorian for $480 million. MGM, the product of the merger of three early film operations, was until 1959 owned by Marcus Loew's giant theater chain. With its roaring-lion trademark and motto *Ars Gratia Artis* (Art for Art's Sake), MGM produced many of the musical extravaganzas of Hollywood's Golden Era—above all, *The Wizard of Oz*. The company went into decline after World War II and suffered numerous management shake-ups. Financier Kirk Kerkorian bought control of the studio in 1969 and began selling off assets such as the prop and costume collections. Turner had difficulty putting together the financing for his acquisition and ended up with an extraordinary debt load after the $1.6 billion deal was completed. He sold MGM's real estate and film lab to Lorimar-Telepictures and kept the asset he was mainly interested in: MGM's valuable film library.

Paramount, formed by a combine of five independent regional distributors in 1914, was run with an iron fist by Adolph Zukor for decades. The company was often shaky, and its films had less of a distinctive identity than those of MGM or Warner. In 1966 the studio was acquired by conglomerate Gulf + Western, whose boss Charles Bluhdorn fired most of the management and made himself president. In 1984 the studio lost two of its top executives—Barry Diller, who went to Fox, and Michael Eisner, who left to head Disney—leaving company veteran Frank Mancuso to pull the studio back together.

Twentieth Century–Fox dates back to Fox Film Corp., an independent producer that challenged the Edison monopoly early in the century. The studio, which merged with Twentieth Century Pictures in 1935, was ruled by Darryl Zanuck for more than a quarter of a century. For many years it churned out a succession of B movies (inexpensive formula films designed to fill out double bills). After being purchased in the early 1980s by Denver oil tycoon Marvin Davis, the studio languished. Half of the company was sold to press baron Rupert Murdoch in early 1985 and the remainder later in the year.

United Artists was established in 1919 by four of Hollywood's leading creative personalities in an attempt to escape the control of the big-studio moguls. The founders—Mary Pickford, Douglas Fairbanks, Charlie Chaplin, and D. W. Griffith—used UA as a distribution vehicle while producing their films independently. The company, which also worked with other independent producers, went public in 1957 and was sold to the Transamerica conglomerate in 1967. Arthur Krim and Robert Benjamin, who had taken over UA in 1951, were not happy with life under Transamerica, and they left in 1978 to establish a new production company called Orion. In 1980 UA had the distinction of producing *Heaven's Gate*, one of the most spectacular fiascos in the industry's history. The studio has since weathered being absorbed into Kirk Kerkorian's MGM/UA, which was then sold to Ted Turner, and then sold back separately to Kerkorian.

Walt Disney Productions has sought to carry on the work of its legendary founder, who died in 1966. Although the unquestioned leader for many years in animated features, the company never became a major studio. By the 1970s Disney lost the youth market to the likes of George Lucas and Steven Spielberg. Under the leadership of Michael Eisner, Disney has focused in recent years on reaching an older audience with films such as *Splash* and *Down and Out in Beverly Hills*, the company's first R-rated feature. In 1984 Disney fought off a takeover bid by Saul Steinberg and then thwarted Irwin Jacobs with the help of the Bass Brothers.

The film business of **Warner Communications** is based on the Warner Brothers studio, which was founded in the 1920s by four sons of a Polish immigrant couple. Warner, which produced the first talking feature film, gained a reputation for movies with social and political themes, though the studio also did its share of musicals. The studio went into decline in the 1950s and 1960s, and in 1969 it was acquired by Kinney National Service Corp., a conglomerate built by Steven Ross beginning with funeral parlors and parking lots. Under its new parent, which renamed itself Warner Communications in 1971, the studio rebounded with hits such as *The Exorcist* and *All the President's Men*. In the mid-1980s the parent company rode an earnings roller coaster after acquiring video game producer Atari and then fought off a takeover by Rupert Murdoch. The studio emerged as one of the most stable and best run in the industry.

SOURCE GUIDE

LEADING STOCK ANALYSTS AND EXPERTS

David Londoner, entertainment analyst at Wertheim & Co.

Art Murphy, film industry expert who teaches at the University of Southern California and writes for *Variety*.

Harold Vogel, entertainment analyst at Merrill Lynch.

TRADE ASSOCIATIONS AND UNIONS

Alliance of Motion Picture and Television Producers, Sherman Oaks, California.

Motion Picture Association of America, New York.

Screen Actors Guild, Hollywood, California.

DATA SOURCES AND DIRECTORIES

International Film Guide, published annually (London: Tantivy Press and New York: New York Zoetrope).

International Motion Picture Almanac, a compilation of data on the industry, issued annually (New York: Quigley Publishing).

The Motion Picture Guide, a 12-volume directory of films, with an annual supplement (New York: Cinebooks; distributed by R. R. Bowker).

Variety International Show Business Reference, an annual compilation of entertainment-world data (New York: Garland Publishing).

TRADE PUBLICATIONS

Hollywood Reporter, daily.

Variety, published daily in Hollywood; weekly in New York.

Video Week.

BOOKS AND REPORTS

Griffith, Richard, and Arthur Mayer. *The Movies.* Rev. ed. New York: Simon & Schuster, 1970.

Litwak, Mark. *Reel Power: The Struggle for Influence and Success in the New Hollywood.* New York: William Morrow, 1986.

McClintick, David. *Indecent Exposure: A True Story of Hollywood and Wall Street.* New York: William Morrow, 1982.

Schwartz, Nancy Lynn. *The Hollywood Writers' Wars.* New York: Alfred A. Knopf, 1982.

Shipman, David. *The Story of Cinema.* New York: St. Martin's Press, 1982.

Stanley, Robert H. *The Celluloid Empire: A History of the American Movie Industry.* New York: Hastings House, 1978.

CHAPTER FOUR

Newspapers and Magazines

Like book publishing, the newspaper business (and to a lesser extent magazines) has a dual identity. On the one hand it is very much a commercial endeavor, often a quite profitable one. Yet the press is also a quasi-public institution. Newspapers are vital to the political, social, and economic life of communities. This role becomes most apparent when it is interrupted; newspaper strikes such as the one in Philadelphia in 1985 create great dislocations in cities.

Newspaper publishing is also like the book industry in that it has been steadily changing from a collection of small, family-run enterprises, each bearing the mark of its founder, into a branch of big business. Attracted by the benefits of owning unregulated monopolies in the hundreds of one-paper towns, large media corporations have been gobbling up newspapers at a steady rate. Faced with tough challenges from the rise of the electronic media and the growth of the direct-mail business, newspapers have nonetheless prospered in recent years. America's 1,700 newspapers continue to receive the largest portion of advertising spending (some 27 percent) among the media, and the total advertising and circulation revenues of the industry have climbed to more than $33 billion.

Magazine publishers also have weathered the threat from television but have experienced frequent fluctuations in advertising demand. The 11,000-title industry, which had revenues of about $15 billion in 1985 (including about $5 billion for consumer publications), has also had to confront a shift in reading tastes from general to special-interest publications.

FROM THE PENNY PRESS TO THE CHAINS

Newspapers in America date back to the late 17th century, and the tradition of a free press is rooted in the success of John Peter Zenger in the 1730s in defying censorship. Newspapers became significant as a business beginning with the rise of the *New York Sun* and other penny papers in the 1830s. The industry expanded rapidly after the Civil War, thanks to inventions such as the Linotype, web-fed rotary presses, and the typewriter. The late 1800s and the early years of the 20th century were the heyday of the great press barons, particularly Joseph Pulitzer and his *St. Louis Post-Dispatch* and *New York World* and William Randolph Hearst (the master of yellow journalism) and his *San Francisco Examiner* and *New York Journal.* The latter part of that period also saw the expansion of the wire services—the United Press and the International News Service joined the Associated Press, which had its origins in the 1840s—and the rise of the first newspaper chains, led by those of Hearst and E. W. Scripps. The creation of the *New York Daily News* in 1919 gave rise to the tabloid format.

The period between the world wars also witnessed the development of magazines into a medium of mass communications. Henry Luce perfected the form with the introduction of *Time* in 1923 and even more so with *Life* in 1936. In between he brought out *Fortune* in order to show that business was civilized.

The social changes after World War II eventually created conditions that undermined the weakest segment of the newspaper business: the afternoon dailies. The PMs, as they are called, traditionally appealed to blue-collar workers who finished their day shifts early enough to spend some time with a paper after returning home and before eating dinner. The office workers and professionals, who grew rapidly in number during the same period, were more inclined to look at a morning paper over breakfast. The PMs have also suffered from a tendency on the part of advertisers to concentrate their spending on the one paper in town with the highest circulation. Another blow, also felt by morning papers, has been the increasing importance of suburban publications.

Some PMs prospered by switching to all-day publishing schedules, but many simply gave up the fight. Among the more prominent casualties were the *Washington Star* in 1981 and the *Philadelphia Bulletin* and *Cleveland Press* the following year.

Between 1950 and 1985 the number of afternoon papers dropped from 1,450 to 1,220 nationwide, while morning papers increased from 322 to 482. The latter year's figures also include 26 all-day papers. Total circulation of dailies increased steadily after World War II, but it has been flat (at a daily average of 60 to 63 million copies) for the past two decades.

Over the past 50 years a number of financially weakened papers, both PM and AM, have stayed alive through arrangements known as joint operating agreements (JOAs). Devised during the Depression, JOAs are arrangements in which competing papers in a city consolidate their financial and production facilities to reduce costs while keeping their editorial operations separate. For the first few decades these schemes had a precarious existence, since they could easily be struck down by the federal government as violations of the antitrust laws.

A legal challenge to the JOAs in the 1960s and the prospect of a Supreme Court decision outlawing the arrangements prompted the industry and its supporters in Congress to act. Their efforts were successful, and in 1971 President Nixon signed into law the Newspaper Preservation Act. This provided a legal basis for JOAs, though only a few new arrangements have been added to the two dozen that were established before the legislation took effect. The most recent of these was a proposed linkup of the *News* and the *Free Press* of Detroit, announced in 1986.

Although there have been periodic rumblings, Congress has taken no action in response to the steady growth of the newspaper chains. By the late 1970s about 50 independent papers a year were succumbing to the tantalizing offers being made by the media giants. Independent dailies declined from some 1,400 in 1945 to 490 at the end of 1985. At that latter point there were 156 chains, which owned a total of 1,186 dailies with a combined circulation of more than 48 million copies a day.

The chains are especially attracted to cities with only one newspaper, a monopoly situation that gives the publisher enormous freedom in setting ad prices. Or else they like to own both of the "competing" papers in town. Today only about 150 American localities have more than one paper, and in many of those cases a single chain owns both publications.

Defenders of chains argue that they bring more professional management and needed capital to smaller newspapers while permitting cost reductions through practices such as large-scale newsprint purchases. Critics of concentration of ownership, such as Ben Bagdikian, express concern about the political consequences of having such a large portion of these vital institutions controlled by a few large corporations that are far removed from the concerns of local communities.

Gannett, the largest chain, has not only bought up smaller publications but has also created a national daily that is being viewed with alarm by many papers. *USA Today*, which started publication in 1982, aims to be the first truly national general-interest newspaper. (*The Wall Street Journal* is somewhat specialized, the *Christian Science Monitor* is limited to a circulation of less than 200,000, and the *New York Times* has never succeeded in achieving large-scale national distribution.) *USA Today*, with its bite-sized articles, has been derided by many journalists as a "fast-food newspaper"; but its daring use of color and charts, extensive sports coverage, and local news from around the country have prompted many papers to make similar changes to protect their circulation.

There is considerable disagreement on the extent to which chain ownership has affected the editorial policies of newspapers. There is no question, however, that the acquisition of papers has accelerated the technological transformation of the industry. In the 1970s many newspapers made the leap from hot type, the molding of letters out of blocks of lead using clattering Linotype machines, to cold type, in which copy is generated on computer terminals and printed via photocomposition and offset presses. While traditionalists have bemoaned the passing of the old system, the new technology has permitted papers to publish cleaner-looking pages much faster.

Some of the national papers, especially *USA Today* and *The Wall Street Journal*, have employed satellite technology to transmit pages from a central editorial office to local printing plants around the country. Another new technique being adopted by papers is computerized layout systems. These are terminals that permit editors to plan and modify pages—including text, photographs,

The 10 Largest Newspaper Chains (as of July 31, 1986)

	Daily Circulation (in Millions)	Number of Dailies
1. Gannett	5.72	91
2. Knight-Ridder	3.64	27
3. Newhouse	2.99	26
4. Times Mirror	2.64	9
5. Tribune Co.	2.62	7
6. Dow Jones	2.54	23
7. New York Times Co.	1.83	26
8. Scripps-Howard	1.52	20
9. Thomson Newspapers	1.48	94
10. Cox Enterprises	1.30	21

Source: John Morton Research, an affiliate of Lynch, Jones & Ryan, Washington, D.C.

and even ads—on a single screen, thus allowing much faster and more careful creation of the paper. The leading company in providing computerized copy systems to newspapers (and some magazines) is Atex, a subsidiary of Eastman Kodak. It is facing an aggressive challenger in System Integrators Inc. of Sacramento, California.

THE STATE OF THE MAGAZINE BUSINESS

Magazines, like newspapers, have defied those doomsayers who predicted the demise of print media as a result of the rise of television. Rather than competing with other advertising media, they tend to battle with one another, especially in key arenas such as supermarket checkout racks.

The consistent leader of the business has been Time Inc., with its stable of money-makers such as *Time, People,* and *Sports Illustrated.* But other media companies have been expanding their magazine activities, leading to a fairly hot market in magazine acquisitions during the 1980s. Real estate developer Morton Zuckerman purchased *The Atlantic* in 1980 and four years later bought out the employee-owners of *U.S. News & World Report,* vowing to make the stodgy newsmagazine an effective competitor of *Time* and *Newsweek.* In 1984 Rupert Murdoch's News America Publishing and CBS each bought half of the Ziff-Davis magazine empire of 24 publications for a combined price of more than $700 million.

There have also been a large number of start-ups. A handful of these have been general-interest publications, including the new *Vanity Fair,* launched by Condé Nast (owned by Newhouse), and *Picture Week,* which Time Inc. began test-marketing in 1985 but abandoned the following year.

Yet the vast majority of new magazines has been aimed at more specialized audiences—now considered the most promising path to success in the business. As a result, magazines today are usually discussed by category. Among the main genres of recent years have been the following.

Computer Magazines. With the boom of personal computers in the early 1980s a number of publishers, both established and new, went after a market of PC users frustrated with impenetrable instruction manuals and hungry for clear explanations of how their new acquisitions worked. Some issues of publications, such as *Byte* (McGraw-Hill), were so thick and heavy with ads that mail carriers complained about delivering subscriber copies. By 1984, with the end of rapid growth in the PC market, there was also a shakeout in the computer magazine business, and many of the dozens of PC publications have disappeared.

Fitness and Health. Taking advantage of another trend, publishers have brought out dozens of new magazines devoted to exercise, sports, nutrition, and general well-being (one is called *Self*). The overcrowding suggests that a shakeout may be in the making here as well.

The 10 Leading Magazine Companies, by 1985 Magazine Revenue
($ Millions)

1. Time Inc.	$1,482
2. McGraw-Hill	676
3. Triangle Publications	648
4. Hearst Corp.	569
5. International Thomson Holdings	560
6. Advance Publications	510
7. Dun & Bradstreet	406
8. CBS Inc.	385
9. Washington Post Co.	326
10. Meredith Corp.	228

Source: *Advertising Age,* June 30, 1986.

Affluence.   A new crop of magazines celebrates wealth, conspicuous consumption, and success in business. Some publications are aimed only at wealthy readers. *Avenue* magazine in New York is delivered by limousine to its readers, all of whom must live in Manhattan's Upper East Side. New and old magazines such as *Town & Country, Architectural Forum, Gourmet,* and *GQ* are prospering by focusing on expensive homes, expensive food, and expensive clothes. *Manhattan, inc.* gushes over the movers and shakers of New York.

LABOR RELATIONS

The largest union in the newspaper business, the International Typographical Union (ITU) is also one of the oldest in the U.S. labor movement, having roots in the 1830s. Efforts to organize the editorial employees of newspapers remained tentative until the industrial union drives of the 1930s. The immediate impetus for the establishment of the Newspaper Guild was a column—actually a call to arms—published by Heywood Broun in the *New York World-Telegram* in 1933. As a result of abysmal pay levels in the industry and the encouragement of the National Recovery Administration, unionization of the country's large newspapers (along with *Newsweek* and Time Inc.'s magazines) spread rapidly.

After the war, the guild's growth slowed down, and the union's power varied greatly around the country. The biggest showdown between publishers and the combined forces of the guild and the craft unions came in New York in the early 1960s. In 1962 the printers at several of the city's seven dailies walked out, and publishers of the others shut down. The strike/lockout lasted for 114 days, during which time the papers suffered heavy losses; several did not survive long even after the dispute ended.

In the 1970s unions found themselves under attack from publishers seeking to modernize their operations and cut costs. The switch to cold type made possible a sharp reduction in staff levels, which the craft unions tried mightily to resist.

One of the bitterest labor situations during that decade arose at the *Washington Post.* After several short strikes in which the guild and the craft unions did not honor one another's picket lines, the printers walked out in October 1975 in what became a 137-day strike related to the introduction of new technology. In part because of some sabotage of presses just before the strike began, many editorial people once again refused to join the walkout.

Management, meanwhile, had in anticipation of the strike secretly sent supervisory employees to a school in Oklahoma to learn how to take over union jobs. As a result the paper missed only one issue, and publisher Katherine Graham succeeded in defeating the strike. After the walkout ended, the guild brought charges against some of its members for crossing the picket line. A group of those people tried to decertify the guild, and the union only barely won the representation election that was held in 1976.

That same year magazine and book employees of Time Inc. went out on strike over the demand for guaranteed rather than merit raises. The strike ended in defeat in less than three weeks, after managers and strikebreakers succeeded in putting out the magazines without interruption.

Another major confrontation at the big New York papers took place in 1978, prompted mainly by disputes involving work rules. After the press operators walked off the job, the publishers locked out the other employees, and the *Times* and *News* did not publish for 88 days (Murdoch made a deal that allowed the *Post* to resume after 56 days). More recently, in 1985, newspapers in Philadelphia were shut down for 46 days, and printers at the *Chicago Tribune* walked off the job but the paper kept publishing.

Unions in the newspaper business have responded to their weakened state by joining forces. While a number of mergers have gone through smoothly, the attempt of the ITU to find a new partner was a long-running soap opera. An effort to join with the Newspaper Guild collapsed in the early 1980s, and ITU president Joe Bingel started flirting with the Teamsters. But that attempt fizzled out after Bingel lost a reelection bid. Finally, in late 1986, the ITU membership voted to merge with the Communications Workers of America.

Magazines making use of free-lancers have been confronted in recent years by a new form of labor organization. Frustrated by low payment rates and poor treatment at the hands of editors, free-lancers established the National Writers Union in 1983. Although its members technically are independent contractors rather than employees, the union has succeeded in winning contracts at publications such as *Ms. Magazine, The Nation,* and *Columbia Journalism Review.*

LEADING COMPANIES

Known to most people as the company the famous stock average is named after, **Dow Jones** is one of the leading players in the business information industry. Its biggest money-maker is *The Wall Street Journal*, the bible of business that also has the highest circulation of any daily in the country. The *Journal* has been in the enviable position at times of having so much advertising it had to turn some away. Editions of the paper are also published in Europe and Asia. The paper's reputation was tarnished somewhat in 1984 when it was revealed that one of its stock market columnists was giving market-sensitive information to traders before it was published in the *Journal*. The company, which is run by former *Journal* reporters Warren Phillips and Ray Shaw, also produces the Dow Jones News Service (the "broadwire" that the financial world depends on for speedy information) and Dow Jones News/Retrieval, a business information data base. Aside from the *Journal*, the company publishes *Barron's*, a weekly for investors, and about two dozen small newspapers. It also owns a large share in the *Far Eastern Economic Review*, a weekly based in Hong Kong. The *National Observer*, a general-interest weekly created by the company in 1962, folded in 1977.

Under the reign of Allen Neuharth, chief executive from 1973 to 1986, **Gannett** grew from a chain of small-town newspapers into one of the premier media companies in the United States. Now the largest chain in terms of both total circulation and number of papers owned, Gannett shook up the newspaper world in 1982 with the creation of *USA Today*, a national daily. In 1985 the company accelerated its buying binge, acquiring the *Des Moines Register*, *Family Weekly* (a Sunday supplement), and the *Detroit News*. In 1986 it acquired the *Courier-Journal* and *Times* of Louisville, Kentucky. Right after that deal was announced Neuharth made the surprise announcement that he would relinquish the CEO's job but remain as chairman.

McGraw-Hill is the publisher of *Business Week* as well as some 60 trade publications, ranging from *Coal Age* to *Electronics*. The company, founded by James McGraw and John Hill around the turn of the century, moved from books to magazines to data. Standard & Poor's, the bond-rating and information service, was acquired in 1966, and economic forecaster Data Resources Inc. was purchased in 1979. Under Joseph Dionne, who took over as chief executive in 1983, the company began using its vast data base of business information to create a variety of new products, especially on-line services.

The **New York Times Company** is mainly known, of course, as the publisher of the *New York Times*, considered by many to be the best paper in the country and certainly the most influential. Transformed from a mediocre daily into a newspaper of record by Adolph Ochs in 1896, the *Times* has been controlled ever since by Ochs and Sulzberger family members. In 1976 the company responded to sagging readership by unveiling what it dubbed the "new *New York Times*." This involved the creation of daily sections (Home, Living, and Weekend) meant to make the paper more appealing to an upper-middle-class suburban readership while retaining a serious commitment to news. Although the "lifestyle" emphasis has often been criticized by traditional journalists, it turned out to be a great business coup. The *Times* has prospered in the past decade, and its new sections were used as models by many other papers. The company also publishes more than two dozen small papers and magazines such as *Family Circle*.

The **Newhouse** publishing group began in 1912, when Samuel Newhouse, Sr. (still in his teens), took over the *Bayonne Times* in New Jersey. He bought the *Staten Island Advance* in 1922 and proceeded to assemble an immense newspaper and magazine empire. The founder died in 1979, and control of the privately owned business fell to his sons Si and Donald. By 1986 the Newhouses had 26 dailies, and under the name of Advance Publications they owned the Condé Nast group of magazines (*Vogue, Glamour, House & Garden*, etc.). In 1980 they bought Random House from RCA, and in 1985 they purchased the *New Yorker*. The family's wealth has been estimated by *Forbes* magazine at $2 billion.

News America Publishing is the parent company of Rupert Murdoch's American operations. Murdoch was a major press baron in Australia and Britain when he invaded the United States in the early 1970s. He started quietly with two papers in San Antonio, Texas, but went on to create the *Star* as a challenger to the lowbrow tabloid *National Enquirer*. He then embarked on a string of media purchases, including the *New York Post, New York* magazine, the *Village Voice*, the *Boston Herald-American*, and the *Chicago Sun-Times*. To his newly acquired daily tabloids Murdoch has brought the kind of sensationalized journalism, mixed with conservative politics, that made him infamous abroad (a classic *Post* headline: "HEADLESS BODY FOUND IN TOPLESS BAR"). In 1984 Murdoch bought 12 trade publications from Ziff-Davis, and in 1985 he became a broadcasting and film mogul by purchasing seven TV stations from Metromedia for $2 billion and the Twentieth Century–Fox film company for $575 million. In 1986 an investment group led by the publisher of the *Chicago Sun-Times* agreed to purchase that paper from Murdoch.

Time Inc., the quintessential media octopus, was founded by Henry Luce in the 1920s. Luce, the son of a missionary, unabashedly used *Time, Life,* and *Fortune* to promote his conservative view of the world. Through these publications Luce, who proclaimed this to be the "American century," became one of the most influential men in America. After Luce died in 1967, Time Inc. became a more traditional though far from stagnant corporation. Time expanded its book-publishing operation with the purchase of Little, Brown. In the 1970s, video—including a group of cable TV companies and the HBO and Cinemax pay-TV services—became the fastest-growing part of the company. But the magazine business grew as well: *Money* was launched in 1972, *People* in 1974, and *Discover* in 1980. The weekly *Life*, shuttered in 1972, was revived as a monthly in 1978. While all of these new ventures (with the exception of *Discover*) have been successful, Time Inc. has also had a string of conspicuous failures. With much fanfare the company bought the *Washington Star* in 1978, only to close it down three years later. Time spent nearly $50 million on a publication called *TV–Cable Week*, which was terminated after five months. A teletext project was also dropped. In the early 1980s, as the cable business declined, Time set up a magazine development group to explore possibilities for new publications. The main result of the group's work, a new magazine called *Picture Week*, was abandoned after about a year of market testing. In 1985 Time also broke out of its tradition by buying established magazines from others. It spent $480 million to purchase Southern Progress Corp., publisher of *Southern Living* and other publications. In 1986 the company purchased and shut down *Science 86* and *Science Digest* to reduce the competition faced by *Discover*.

Times Mirror is the parent company of the *Los Angeles Times*, 7 other newspapers, 11 magazines, and other media properties. The *Times*, controlled by the Chandler family, was a provincial and virulently reactionary publication until Otis Chandler took over in 1960. It is now one of the country's leading papers and, with its huge number of ad pages, is the most profitable daily after *The Wall Street Journal*. Times Mirror, whose chief executive is now Robert Erburu, has purchased a number of leading papers. In 1970 it bought *Newsday*, the Long Island daily that is considered the country's leading suburban paper, and the *Dallas Times Herald*. In 1979 the company bought the *Hartford Courant*, in 1980 the *Denver Post*, and in 1986 the *Baltimore Sun*. In that latter year the company agreed to sell off the Dallas paper, while *Newsday* was making an aggressive push into New York City.

The best-known properties of the closely held **Tribune Co.**, built by Colonel Robert Rutherford McCormick, are the *Chicago Tribune* and the *New York Daily News*. While the *Tribune* has done consistently well the *News* has fallen on harder times, losing its first place (in circulation) among dailies to *The Wall Street Journal*. In 1980 the *News* sought to grow by putting out an evening edition called *Tonight*; but the effort, although impressive in journalistic terms, failed to find an adequate audience and was terminated after a year. Soon afterward the Tribune Co. management, led by Stanton Cook, put the paper up for sale but ended up keeping it after obtaining union concessions.

Washington Post Co., the publisher of the country's second most important paper, has been run by Katherine Graham since 1963, when her husband Philip died. After being given control of the paper by Katherine's father Eugene Meyer in 1946, Philip Graham helped lift the paper from its status as a poor third to the *Star* and the *Times-Herald* (which the *Post* bought in 1954). He also purchased *Newsweek* in 1961. His widow continued the improvement of the paper, though other acquisitions (such as the *Trenton Times*, bought in 1974 and sold in 1982) have been less successful. Katherine Graham's son Don took over as publisher of the *Post* in 1979, when his mother became chairman of the parent company.

SOURCE GUIDE

LEADING STOCK ANALYSTS AND EXPERTS

Edward Dunleavy, analyst at Salomon Brothers.

R. Joseph Fuchs, analyst at Kidder Peabody.

James B. Kobak, a leading magazine consultant based in Darien, Connecticut.

John Morton, a leading analyst of the newspaper industry who has his own research firm affiliated with Lynch, Jones & Ryan, Washington, D.C.

J. Kendrick Noble, Jr., analyst at Paine Webber.

TRADE ASSOCIATIONS AND UNIONS

American Newspaper Publishers Association, Reston, Virginia.

Magazine Publishers Association, New York.

National Writers Union, New York.

Newspaper Guild, Washington, D.C.

DATA SOURCES AND DIRECTORIES

Editor and Publisher International Yearbook, a volume published by the leading trade journal of the newspaper business, includes statistics and a directory of newspapers in the United States and abroad, as well as other organizations and companies (New York: Editor and Publisher Inc.).

The Folio: 400, a special issue of *Folio* magazine that includes rankings of the top magazines overall and by category.

IMS/Ayer Directory of Publications, an annual directory of newspapers and periodicals in the United States, Canada, and Puerto Rico (Fort Washington, Penn.: IMS Press).

Magazine Industry Market Place, an annual directory of periodicals arranged by category and other companies and organizations involved in the magazine business (New York: R. R. Bowker).

Newspaper Advertising Bureau, New York. An association that collects information on newspaper advertising.

Publishers Information Bureau, New York. An association that collects information on magazine advertising.

Standard Periodical Directory, a biennial directory of more than 65,000 American and Canadian publications (New York: Oxbridge Communications).

Standard Rate and Data Service, a series of monthly volumes providing information on the circulation, advertising rates, and other commercial information on newspapers and magazines (Wilmette, Ill.: National Register Publishing).

Ulrich's International Periodicals Directory, a comprehensive annual directory of some 128,000 periodicals from around the world (New York: R. R. Bowker).

TRADE PUBLICATIONS

Editor & Publisher, weekly.

Folio: The Magazine for Magazine Management, monthly.

Media Industry Newsletter, weekly.

BOOKS AND REPORTS

Bagdikian, Ben H. *The Media Monopoly*. Boston: Beacon Press, 1983.

Bryon, Christopher. *The Fanciest Dive*. (on Time Inc.) New York: W. W. Norton, 1986.

Halberstam, David. *The Powers that Be*. New York: Alfred A. Knopf, 1979.

Hynds, Ernest C. *American Newspapers in the 1980s*. New York: Hastings House, 1980.

Leab, Daniel J. *A Union of Individuals: The Formation of the American Newspaper Guild, 1933–1936*. New York: Columbia University Press, 1970.

Patten, David A. *Newspapers and the New Media*. White Plains, N.Y.: Knowledge Industry Publications, 1986.

CHAPTER FIVE

Telecommunications

The telecommunications industry has undergone a remarkable transformation during the 1970s and 1980s. What was once an industry dominated by a giant, regulated telephone monopoly and a few other carriers has become something of a free-for-all. Extensive deregulation and the breakup of the Bell System have given rise to a new generation of companies and new lines of business for the traditional carriers. There is also a technological upheaval as satellites, fiber optics, and other systems battle for supremacy in the $103 billion telecommunications service industry and the $17 billion telecommunications equipment market.

FROM SMOKE SIGNALS TO THE TELEPHONE

The sending of messages over great distances dates back to early civilizations. Smoke signals and semaphores remained the state of the art until the early 19th century, when the first electrical telegraphs were devised. In the United States, Samuel F. B. Morse pioneered the use of the electromagnet in telegraphy and developed a code of dots and dashes to represent the letters of the alphabet and numerals.

Morse's original device consisted of a pen that electric currents caused to make marks on a moving strip of paper. At the suggestion of his assistant Alfred Vail, Morse changed the design to one that resembled a doorbell. He patented the sounding device in 1840 but failed to attract investor interest.

Three years later Congress appropriated $30,000 to build a test line between Washington and Baltimore. Sitting in the Supreme Court chamber of the Capitol in 1844, Morse transmitted the now legendary message "What hath God wrought." After this well-publicized event, telegraphy caught on quickly, especially with newspapers. Dozens of telegraph companies were formed, and in 1856 a group of them combined to form Western Union. The rapidly growing company completed the first transcontinental telegraph line in 1861, which promptly put the Pony Express out of business. The first transatlantic cable was laid in 1866.

As telegraphy was coming into its own, various researchers began exploring the possibility of transmitting voices in the same manner that the telegraph conveyed electric currents. One of the more successful of these men was a speech therapist by the name of Alexander Graham Bell. Backed by the wealthy fathers of two of his students and assisted by Thomas Watson (no relation to the IBM Watson), Bell hit on a promising technique in 1876, and one of his backers rushed a description of it to the U.S. Patent Office on February 14.

Coincidentally it was later the same day that rival inventor Elisha Gray of Chicago filed a "caveat" with the Patent Office, warning that he was working on a speaking telephone. Those few hours of difference would be decisive for Bell. The timing ended up being more important than the fact that Bell's application did not even mention telephones. It spoke of improvements in telegraphy; and the crucial element, a variable-resistance transmitter, was inserted in the margin as an afterthought.

Despite the conflicting patent claims, no one had actually succeeded in transmitting a human voice. That came on March 10, when Bell, having adopted the variable-resistance idea, succeeded in sending the message "Mr. Watson, come here; I want you" after he spilled some acid on himself.

Bell's telephone gained fame later that year with a demonstration at the Centennial Exposition in Philadelphia. Even then there was skepticism about the practical applications of the device. So much so that when one of Bell's backers offered all rights to the telephone to the president of Western Union for $100,000, he was turned down.

Attitudes changed after commercial service was initiated by the Bell Telephone Company in 1877. Western Union, realizing that it had missed a big opportunity, made a deal with Elisha Gray and formed the American Speaking Telephone Company. The firm commissioned a promising young inventor named Thomas Edison, who built an improved transmitting device. Western Union decided that with its extensive wire network it was the ideal company to develop the telephone business.

Bell and his colleagues were not about to knuckle under, even in the face of a challenge from behemoth Western Union (the first truly national corporation). Led by Theodore Vail, a former telegraph operator, the Bell company launched a legal assault against Western Union. The telegraph company, inhibited by the fact that it found itself the object of a takeover campaign by financier Jay Gould, consented to a settlement in 1879. Western Union agreed to abandon the telephone business in exchange for 20 percent of the Bell company's phone rental receipts over the 17 years of Bell's patents.

The Bell company fought hundreds of other patent suits; and while it always prevailed, one case went to the Supreme Court and was decided in favor of Bell by a margin of only one vote. Although its legal rights were firmly established, Bell had difficulty financing the expansion of the system. The firm resorted to licensing others to build telephone operations in various places, and the main company went through a series of financial and management reorganizations. In 1899 the headquarters of the company were moved from Boston to New York, and the name American Telephone & Telegraph was adopted.

The Bell monopoly moved to dominate long-distance service and equipment manufacturing as well. Intercity service was initiated in 1881 with the connection of Boston and Providence, and Bell set up a long-lines subsidiary in 1885. To expand its output of equipment, Bell in 1881 purchased a controlling interest (later expanded to full ownership) in the Western Electric Co.—founded by Bell rival Elisha Gray—and made it the system's sole supplier.

But it was not long before the Bell monolith began to totter. Public discontent over Bell's rates (15 cents a call) escalated, and in 1885 there was the first attempt at government regulation of the business. The Indiana legislature passed legislation limiting basic phone charges to $3 a month. (The law was repealed three years later.) In the 1890s, as Bell's original patents began to expire, hundreds of independent phone companies were established.

Not long after becoming AT&T, the Bell company was the object of a takeover battle that ended in 1907 with victory for a group of bankers led by J. P. Morgan. Theodore Vail, who had left the company in 1887, was called back to rebuild the sagging monopoly. Vail promoted the idea of public service and welcomed government regulation. What he abhorred was competition. He refused to connect Bell long-distance facilities to other phone companies, and with the financial backing of Morgan he succeeded in taking over many of the independents. In 1909 AT&T even managed to win control over Western Union. Vail regarded telecommunications as a natural monopoly and intended to have AT&T run the business.

THE KINGSBURY COMMITMENT

The rest of the industry had a different view, of course, and persuaded the Justice Department to begin investigating whether AT&T was violating the antitrust laws. AT&T decided to compromise rather than fight and in 1913 reached a settlement. Making what became known as the Kingsbury commitment (named after an AT&T executive), the Bell system agreed to divest itself of its Western Union holdings, purchase no more independents without the consent of the Interstate Commerce Commission, and connect with other phone networks.

Although Vail's dream of a comprehensive national monopoly was dashed, AT&T still enjoyed many local monopolies as well as control over the long-distance business. By the 1910s state regulation of the local monopolies was spreading rapidly, and on a national level the Mann-Elkins Act of 1910 extended the jurisdiction of the ICC to telephone, though the commission ended up doing little in that direction.

In the period leading up to World War I, calls for government involvement went even further. In 1913 the Wilson administration's postmaster general began advocating nationalization (the actual term was postalization) of the phone system, as had occurred in all other major nations. Congress finally heeded this cry in 1918, and the president was empowered to take control of the country's telephone and telegraph systems. This was a strange kind of nationalization in that industry executives remained in place and shareholders continued to receive dividends.

Although federal control helped the Army Signal Corps during the war, the government had to raise phone rates and ended up with a substantial deficit. The experiment in nationalized telecommunications was terminated after a year, and the companies were returned to private hands. Private ownership under monopoly conditions was affirmed again in 1921 with the Graham Act, which exempted telephone mergers from the antitrust laws, thus allowing AT&T to consolidate local companies.

During the 1920s AT&T felt confident enough to dabble in new areas such as radio broadcasting (which it abandoned in 1926; see Chapter Two) and the development of sound systems for motion pictures (see Chapter Three). Bell Laboratories also did some early research on television.

By this time telephones were firmly established as part of everyday life for most Americans. AT&T did experience some falling off in business in the early years of the Depression, but it did not last long. At the end of 1937 the Bell system stood at a record 15.3 million phones.

THE UNIVERSAL SERVICE PRINCIPLE

The 1930s did, however, present a challenge to the phone industry in the form of more extensive federal regulation. The Communications Act of 1934 established the Federal Communications Commission and gave it jurisdiction over both broadcasting and common carriers. The latter consists of services such as telephone and telegraph that are obliged to provide access to anyone on a first-come, first-served basis. With regard to telephone, the nation's policy was to be that of providing the widest possible service at the lowest possible price.

There were many in Congress who wanted not simply to regulate the telephone giant but to reduce its size as well. The greatest criticism was leveled at AT&T's ownership of Western Electric, since it was alleged that the prices charged the parent company by Western served to inflate phone service rates. In 1935 Congress ordered the FCC to explore these charges, and a massive investigation of AT&T was launched. The resulting Walker Report advocated direct regulation of Western Electric's prices, but the full commission took a softer line.

The Bell System remained intact and retained its dominance. In 1939 it controlled some 83 percent of all telephones, 98 percent of long-distance wires, and 100 percent of transoceanic radio telephony. The 16.5 million Bell phones generated 90 percent of all U.S. phone industry revenues. The largest of the independents was General Telephone, founded in 1926 and now known as GTE.

After World War II, telephone usage grew at unprecedented rates—helped by the fact that most of the Bell System had been converted to direct dialing, and the use of operators in long distance started to be phased out as well. AT&T also took up the old problem of developing transatlantic cable service, since radio telephony across the ocean (inaugurated in 1927) remained interference prone and unreliable. The task, which required sophisticated repeater devices to amplify voices through the line, was accomplished; cable service was launched in 1956.

The glory of this period for AT&T management was marred by a revival of federal legal action against the company. In 1949 the Justice Department filed an antitrust suit against the Bell System, seeking divestiture of Western Electric. After years of legal maneuvering AT&T signed a consent decree in 1956 that allowed it to hold on to Western but confined the subsidiary to manufacturing equipment for the Bell System (except for military work) and prohibited the parent company from entering any business other than common-carrier communications.

Although there was criticism to the effect that the Eisenhower administration let "Ma Bell" off too easily, the consent decree restriction on entering new businesses turned out to be a major impediment for AT&T in the emerging new telecommunications industry.

HUSH–A–PHONE VERSUS THE "BLACK BEAUTY"

AT&T's battle with the forces of competition began with the issue of customer equipment. In the 1950s a device called Hush-a-Phone, which allowed someone speaking into a phone to avoid being overheard by others in a room, was approved by the FCC and put on the market. Ma Bell, which had built an equipment as well as a service monopoly, was horrified. It was taken as a matter of faith that only Bell-produced equipment should be used in the Bell System. The idea of standardization extended to matters of style. Like Henry Ford, AT&T allowed its customers to have any kind of phone they wanted—as long as it was the standard one known ironically as the "black beauty."

Although AT&T got a federal appeals court to overrule the FCC on Hush-a-Phone, various retailers, led by Ben Jamil of New York, began selling antique and foreign phones to customers tired of the standard model. Ma Bell fought hard against these incursions, both in court and by finally introducing a slightly larger variety of models from Western Electric. But it was too late. More companies entered what became known as the interconnect industry and clamored for legitimacy. The matter was resolved in 1968, when the FCC issued its ruling in the Carterfone case.

Thomas Carter of Texas had invented a device, which he called Carterfone, that could couple a telephone handset to a mobile radio transmitter. AT&T threatened to disconnect any customers who used the device, and Carter sued. The case was referred to the FCC, which decided not only to permit the Carterfone but also to abolish all rules prohibiting the attachment of nonsystem, customer-owned equipment.

At first, however, AT&T was allowed to insist on installing (for a fee) a protective device on all such equipment, supposedly to prevent damage to the system. The FCC soon decided that these devices were superfluous and that any equipment produced by a certified manufacturer could be directly installed. The interconnect industry was off and running.

The 1960s also saw the beginning of a challenge to Ma Bell's dominance in the long-distance business. A venture called Microwave Communications Inc. (MCI) applied to the FCC in 1963 for permission to furnish private-line service via microwave between Chicago and St. Louis. While this application was being fought by AT&T, another proposal was submitted by Texas entrepreneur Sam Wyly, who wanted to offer a digital data transmission service through a company called Datran. In 1970 the FCC decided to authorize such specialized carrier operations. AT&T responded by developing its own digital service, but the FCC's green light to the specialized carriers meant that Ma Bell was not going to have a clear field in the emerging technologies.

Moreover the Justice Department once again took aim at AT&T, filing an antitrust suit in 1974 that sought to break up the Bell System. The suit was based on charges that since the 1956 consent decree, Ma Bell had deliberately blocked the interconnection of competing equipment and had sought to prevent the establishment of specialized carriers.

The level of frustration among AT&T executives during this period reached new heights. Assailed by antitrust charges in its core business and restricted by the 1956 decree from entering new ones, Ma Bell had the worst of both worlds: being regulated as a monopoly yet losing the immunity that legitimate monopolies expected from antitrust prosecution and competition. Meanwhile upstart companies like MCI were going after the most profitable part of the business, with none of the Bell System's responsibility for maintaining a comprehensive network for providing universal service.

The new and lucrative markets emerged as a by-product of the computer age. By the 1960s U.S. business was heavily computerized, and the transmission of digitized data was becoming as important as voice connections in the communications activity of corporations.

In 1961 Bell began leasing the DataPhone, which was supposed to address the computer industry's transmission needs. But the data processing people were not pleased with the product, and others began pressing for the right to provide alternatives. The dispute forced the FCC to take up the thorny problem of deciding where data processing left off and communications began. In its various computer inquiries, which stretched for years, the commission never fully answered the question, but it was firm in its restrictions on AT&T. The fear was that Ma Bell could use revenues from monopoly businesses to subsidize unregulated ones and thereby gain an unfair advantage over its rivals.

BABY BELL AND THE ROAD TO BREAKUP

Pressure from AT&T finally caused the FCC to abandon this position in 1980. The commission decided that, starting in 1983, Ma Bell could enter some unregulated businesses as long as it did so through an "arm's-length," unsubsidized subsidiary—which the business press immediately dubbed Baby Bell.

Neither the Justice Department nor AT&T's competitors were happy with this arrangement and sought to block it in court. Charles L. Brown, chairman of AT&T, decided that the mess could not be straightened out until the cloud of the antitrust suit was lifted. He and the rest of Bell management began to accept the idea that the only way to do this would be to agree to the severing of the 22 Bell operating companies that provided local service around the country. Once the Reagan administration took office in 1981 the chances of such a settlement—which would avoid a complete dismembering of the Bell System—were greatly improved. By the end of the year, an agreement was reached; and on January 8, 1982, the Justice Department announced that the suit would be dropped. On the same day, the government abandoned its antitrust case against IBM.

Whereas IBM got off scot-free, AT&T had to divest itself of the operating companies by January 1, 1984. Under the terms of the divestiture, drawn up and implemented under the supervision of federal judge Harold Greene, AT&T was allowed to hold onto Western Electric, the long-distance business, and Bell Laboratories and was given the right to enter unregulated businesses via Baby Bell. That subsidiary was originally called American Bell and then renamed AT&T Information Systems.

The operating companies were reorganized into seven regional holding companies (RHCs) that remained as regulated monopolies and were supposed to focus on providing local service. Judge Greene allowed them to retain the profitable Yellow Pages business and the exclusive use of the Bell name and logo in the United States. He also barred AT&T from entering electronic publishing.

The Bell divestiture—by far the largest corporate breakup in U.S. history—involved such daunting tasks as dividing up some $150 billion in assets and nearly 1 million employees among AT&T and the seven RHCs. While from a managerial standpoint this went rather smoothly, it caused unprecedented disruptions for customers. Complaints about deterioration of service skyrocketed, and delays in the installation of equipment reached unprecedented levels.

There was also an upheaval in phone rates, stemming from the fact that divestiture meant the end of the traditional Bell practice of keeping long-distance rates artificially high to subsidize local service. Under the new arrangement the charge for each call was to be determined by the cost of providing it. Thus local rates shot up while AT&T's long-distance fees began declining. The United States was divided into about 160 local access and transport areas (LATAs), with AT&T and its competitors in long distance handling calls from one LATA to another while the RHCs handled local calls.

LONG–DISTANCE SERVICE

The success of MCI and Datran in getting the FCC to authorize specialized carrier service opened up the long-distance business to widespread competition in the 1970s. Companies such as MCI built their own transmission facilities, while others leased lines from AT&T and retailed the capacity. Not having the fixed costs and the regulatory restraints of Ma Bell, these competitors were able to provide long-distance service at substantially reduced rates. The growth of these competitors was limited by customer complaints about poor connections and the fact that users had to dial a string of extra digits. By 1983 the competing long-distance companies—of which there were dozens, led by MCI and Sprint—still had well under 10 percent of the market.

After the divestiture plan was put into motion, AT&T began fighting hard to see that its long-distance business, now the main revenue producer of the streamlined corporation, remained dominant. AT&T was particularly worried what would happen after the introduction in September 1986 of "equal access," the elimination of the extra digits that users of competing long-distance providers had to dial. To pay for the conversion to equal access and the loss of the old Bell subsidy from long distance, the RHCs were allowed to begin collecting local access charges of several dollars per month from each subscriber.

This was in addition to the fees already paid by the long-distance carriers themselves to the RHCs for each connection. One reason why MCI and the other upstart carriers were able to underprice AT&T was the fact that the FCC allowed them to pay much lower fees of this sort. Since these fees were the biggest element of cost, the raising of the fees for the upstarts in the period leading up to equal access forced them to raise their rates.

As various local phone companies began converting to equal access, customers were asked to choose among the competing long-distance carriers. The companies sought to influence these choices with an extraordinary marketing blitz. Phone subscribers were bombarded with endless TV commercials, newspaper and magazine advertisements, direct mail solicitations, and phone pitches. Some $500 million was spent in these activities in 1985 alone.

It soon became clear that AT&T would remain dominant, if only because many users were too bewildered to choose and many local companies assigned such people to AT&T by default. Many of the smaller carriers had to drop out of the business or merge. In late 1986 MCI remained the leading upstart, with about 10 percent (including Satellite Business Systems, which it took over in 1985 as part of an arrangement with IBM) of the $50 billion long-distance market. U.S. Sprint, which GTE purchased from Southern Pacific in 1983 and spun off into a joint venture with United Telecommunications in 1986, trailed with 4 percent but was investing heavily to challenge MCI for second place. AT&T had about 85 percent of the market.

THE EQUIPMENT BUSINESS

The failure of AT&T to block the use of non-Bell equipment allowed the interconnect industry to flourish, both in the residential phone market and the business equipment segment. In the 1970s, once subscribers were able to purchase their own phones, an astounding range of products flooded the market. Many of these were electronic "smart phones," which could store frequently called numbers, dial them automatically, and perform other feats. While many of these devices were sold, it turned out that most subscribers were satisfied buying the phone they had been leasing from AT&T.

Businesses meanwhile were growing more and more enamored of sophisticated private branch exchanges (PBXs—i.e., switchboards) that allowed internal phone systems to perform equally amazing tricks. AT&T had been facing competition in this market since 1977, when Canada's Northern Telecom introduced the first electronic digital PBX. Ma Bell responded with its Dimension switchboard, but many customers found it lacking and turned to the competition. By the early 1980s AT&T had lost a majority of the PBX market. The introduction of a more advanced System 85 in 1983 did not reverse the trend. In 1985 the leaders in the $3.4 billion PBX market were Northern Telecom with 21.2 percent, AT&T with 18.9, Rolm with 18.4, Mitel with 10.2, and Japan's NEC with 6.9 percent.

The rise of foreign competition in the business equipment as well as residential phone market caused the U.S. balance of trade in telecommunications gear to plunge into the red in 1983. The U.S. position was further eroded in 1986 when ITT abandoned its effort to develop a digital switching system for the American market and agreed to sell its European telecommunications business to France's state-owned Compagnie Générale d'Electricité.

NEW TECHNOLOGIES: SATELLITES

The traditional method by which the Bell System provided service was through an immense network of copper wires strung between telephone poles or buried under streets and roads. Later, coaxial cables were added to the grid. The last 20 years have also witnessed the rise of technologies that have served both as new links in the established phone system and as techniques for bypassing it. The approach that has probably generated the greatest interest was the use of orbiting microwave relay stations, otherwise known as satellites.

The idea of using artificial satellites as a means of facilitating telecommunications dates back to an article published by Arthur C. Clarke in 1945. Long before it was technically feasible, Clarke envisioned extraterrestrial relays placed in a geostationary orbit (the orbit, 22,300 miles above the equator, that would keep a satellite in a fixed position relative to a part of the globe) that could serve as receivers and retransmitters of radio signals beamed up from earth.

In 1946 the U.S. Army succeeded in bouncing a radar signal off the moon, and in later years the navy used the moon as a passive relay for signals sent from Washington to Hawaii.

American space activity accelerated after the Soviet Union's dramatic Sputnik launching. By the beginning of the Kennedy administration, the use of satellites was a hot issue, and the debate centered around the control of this new resource. AT&T considered the technology a mere extension of the phone system and sought exclusive rights from NASA to develop satellites for communications. Ma Bell's request was turned down, partly because some members of Congress felt that satellites should remain under government control.

AT&T nonetheless moved ahead with its plan to launch about

50 satellites in low-altitude (i.e., nongeostationary) orbit. The low-altitude approach was less efficient for communications, since the satellites did not remain in fixed positions relative to the earth and thus had to hand off signals to one another as they orbited.

The advantage, however, was that the shorter distance the signals traveled created less of an echo on the line. Some critics of AT&T suggested that it pushed the low-altitude approach only because its leading satellite competitor Hughes Aircraft was far ahead in the development of geostationary techniques.

While the debate in Congress on satellites was still in progress AT&T got the FCC to grant permission in 1961 for the launching of Telstar I, the first privately owned "bird." AT&T timed the launching carefully and worked its publicity machine overtime. The festivities included the first satellite telephone conversation; the participants were AT&T president Fred Kappel and U.S. Vice President Lyndon Johnson.

Congress ended up legislating a compromise. The Communications Satellite Act of 1962 created a national monopoly in the form of the Communications Satellite Corporation (Comsat), which was to be sponsored by the U.S. government and owned half by communications carriers and half by private investors. Comsat also became the U.S. representative to and a primary shareholder in Intelsat, an international satellite consortium formed in 1964.

It was not long before Comsat's monopoly was questioned. In 1965 ABC applied to the FCC for the right to establish a private satellite network. The commission returned the application, saying it had to take some time to study the matter, given the novel legal and policy questions that were raised. Finally in 1970 the agency put aside the objections of Comsat and ruled that any qualified applicant could enter the domestic satellite business. This so-called open-skies policy prompted a major expansion of private satellite services, led by Western Union, RCA, and Hughes. The move was also aided by a subsequent FCC decision to deregulate the use of receive-only satellite earth stations.

IBM jumped on the satellite bandwagon in 1975 by creating a joint venture with Comsat and Aetna Life & Casualty called Satellite Business Systems. SBS was intended to provide sophisticated, high-volume digital transmission services covering voice and data. The operation launched its satellite in 1980 and signed up its first customer the following year. Unfortunately for the partners, which ended up sinking hundreds of millions of dollars into the venture, other customers did not follow in great numbers. In the early 1980s SBS switched its emphasis to the consumer, entering the long-distance sweepstakes. It failed at this too, and in 1985 the operation was handed over to MCI as part of a major investment by IBM in the leading upstart carrier.

The satellite business turned out to be somewhat more lucrative for the companies that focused on customers such as cable television networks. Turner Broadcasting and Home Box Office led a move to satellites that included many TV programmers and other media operations such as *The Wall Street Journal*, which used the technology to transmit pages to printing plants around the country.

To get around FCC rate regulations on common carriers, Hughes Aircraft started a trend toward selling the transponders (the relay devices on the satellites) rather than leasing them. But by the early 1980s there were signs of a transponder glut, and some carriers had difficulty selling their satellite condominiums.

The tendency toward a surfeit of transponders continued into the mid-1980s, and in 1985 the satellite services business was still under $2 billion. There was some excitement over the use of the super-high-frequency Ku band, which generates more-powerful transmissions, allowing the signals to be received by smaller, less expensive antennas. But the future of the technology was clouded by the development of a rival system called fiber optics.

FIBER OPTICS

The development of modern telecommunications and calculating equipment has been based on the manipulation of electrons. Yet as early as the 1870s Alexander Graham Bell explored the use of light as an alternative to electricity, though the approach remained impractical. The development of the laser in the early 1960s revived the quest.

Companies such as Corning Glass, ITT, and AT&T began experimenting with the use of glass fibers through which voice and data are transmitted in the form of bursts of light. One of the advantages of glass fibers is that they save an enormous amount of space. Copper wires permit about 48 conversations at a time—with electromagnetic interference and "leakage" as frequent problems—while the fibers can handle hundreds of times as many. Fibers also make possible vastly greater transmission speeds than copper wires. The glass fibers also avoid the problem of corrosion and do not require the repeater devices needed every mile or so on copper wire lines. The drawback of what came to be called fiber optics is that photons cannot be easily switched. They work well in transmitting from Point A to Point B but not if other connections have to be made.

As fiber optics techniques were refined in the early 1980s, various companies rushed into the market. AT&T announced plans to install a cable along the East Coast between Boston and Richmond, Virginia. Various railroad lines joined the party by offering their rights of way for the laying of the fiber cables. By 1984 the business press was full of predictions that fiber optics would make satellites obsolete by reducing the cost of land-based communication to a pittance.

However, it was not long before the signs of excess capacity appeared here as well. A number of companies scaled back their construction plans, and the outlook for the industry became more sober. U.S. Sprint nonetheless remained bullish on fiber optics. In 1986 it was heavily promoting its 6,500-mile system in TV and newspaper ads and was still planning to expand the network by 23,000 miles.

BYPASSING THE GRID

The traditional phone companies have employed satellites and fiber optics, but those technologies are also being used by rival telecommunications providers and their customers to avoid all or part of the phone system and thereby obtain higher-quality and/or lower-cost services. This practice, known as bypass, was pioneered by MCI's microwave proposal of the early 1960s. After being authorized by the FCC, it and other specialized carriers began offering a variety of new services.

For residential customers, this mainly meant bypassing AT&T's long-distance network by using the independent facilities of MCI, Sprint, SBS, and others. For business users the choices, more sophisticated and varied, included:

- Private lines that enabled companies to bypass the local telephone company in gaining access to long-distance carriers.
- Private lines—involving coaxial cables, microwave relays, and satellites—that permit companies to bypass both the local phone companies and the long-distance carriers.
- So-called value-added networks, such as Tymnet and GTE Telenet, that not only permit high-quality data transmission but also include services such as error checking, data storage, and procedures such as packet switching that permit lower-cost transmissions.

Some bypass is taking place through facilities called teleports that by the mid-1980s were being planned for some 20 cities around the United States. Teleports give companies access to satellite, microwave, and fiber optics facilities outside the control of the phone companies. One of the largest was a joint venture by Merrill Lynch, Western Union, and the Port Authority of New York and New Jersey.

The rise of bypass has represented a particular threat for local phone companies, which were estimated to be losing more than $100 million a year in revenues from the practice in the mid-1980s. Even AT&T was promoting local bypass and in 1985 got FCC permission to follow the procedure in connecting business customers to WATS and 800 services. All of this has fueled the desire of the regional holding companies to go beyond the limits placed on them in the course of the AT&T breakup.

THE GROWING ASPIRATIONS OF THE RHCs

Not long after they were set off on their own, the regional holding companies spun off from AT&T decided they were not satisfied with an existence limited to the relatively unexciting business of providing local telephone service. The very names that some of the RHCs adopted were meant to convey a dynamic high-tech or at least nontelephone image: Nynex (New York and New England), Ameritech (the Midwest), Pacific Telesis (California and Nevada) and U.S. West (Rocky Mountain and northwestern states). The other three—Bell Atlantic (mid-Atlantic), Bell South, and Southwestern Bell (Texas, Oklahoma, Kansas, Missouri, and Arkansas)—kept the Bell name but were equally aggressive in wanting to branch out.

The RHCs (or Baby Bells, as they came to be called) entered fields such as computer retailing, software, real estate, and financial services. Several of them even placed bids on contracts to help the Chinese government expand its telephone system. By the end of 1986 the RHCs had spent an estimated $3.5 billion to purchase additional businesses and a large but undetermined amount to start new ventures from scratch.

Judge Greene, who retained authority over the RHCs in the aftermath of divestiture, frowned on these outside activities. He ruled that the RHCs could engage in some of the proposed businesses only if they got permission for each venture and did not allow them to account for more than 10 percent of revenues. The regionals have submitted to these restrictions reluctantly and have kept the pressure on Judge Greene. In early 1986 some of the RHCs began pushing to enter the long-distance business, and Ameritech won permission to produce telecommunications equipment overseas. Later that year a federal appeals court reversed one of Judge Greene's decisions and allowed the RHCs to market specialized services outside their geographical areas. The Baby Bells by this point were optimistic that they would be able to branch out as they pleased.

CELLULAR TELEPHONES

One business that the RHCs were allowed to enter from the start was a new form of mobile telephone service. The combination of telephones and automobiles dates back to 1946, when the first mobile radiotelephone service was inaugurated in St. Louis. More widespread service was established in the 1960s. The problem with the traditional kind of mobile phone service was the limitation on the number of channels—23 per city. This meant that users often had difficulty obtaining a dial tone, and even when calls were completed the service was often poor.

Back in the late 1940s telephone researchers figured out that capacity could be greatly expanded if the same frequencies could be used simultaneously in different areas. This required a shift from a single-transmitter/receiver system to an arrangement of multiple antennas, each operating at lower power and covering a limited range. As an automobile moved from one area, or cell, to another the call would be "handed off" from one system to the next.

It was not until the 1970s that advances in electronic switching equipment made this technique possible. AT&T set up the first trial system in Chicago in 1978, and it proved a great success. In 1982 the FCC began accepting applications for cellular telephone licenses in the 30 largest cities. The plan was to allow two competing systems in each market, one of which would be awarded to a phone company.

Dozens of companies joined the cellular gold rush; when the FCC opened up the next 60 largest markets some 150 firms filed about 1,000 applications. The commission decided to adopt a lottery system rather than comparative assessments in granting the licenses, and in 1984 the FCC allowed the applicants for the second 60 markets to form a giant consortium to divide up the business among them. In 1986 Southwestern Bell agreed to pay some $1.2 billion to purchase most of the cellular operations of Metromedia.

THE FUTURE

The trend among all telecommunications suppliers is toward the complete digitization of transmissions. In the mid-1980s the catchphrase was integrated services digital network (ISDN). This notion, pushed particularly by AT&T, involves a single system for transmitting (via phone lines) voice, data, video, and anything else that could be put in digital form. The speeds envisioned by the ISDN planners are astonishing—128,000 or more bits of information a second. ISDN represents an attempt by phone companies to reestablish their grid as an all-purpose transmission medium. Its success will require the adoption of technical standards that rival the networks being developed by the computer companies, led by IBM. Whatever approach prevails, there is no question that the development of methods of sending more and more information of different sorts at faster and faster speeds will continue to dominate telecommunications.

LABOR RELATIONS

Communications workers have the distinction of being in one of the few relatively high tech industries that are extensively unionized. As a result they, among all union workers, have probably had the most experience in dealing with technological change and automation. The leading company in the industry, AT&T, was until its breakup the largest private employer in the United States.

From the earliest years, telephone workers have tended to fall into two categories: electrical craftsmen and less skilled phone operators. At first, teenage boys were employed as operators, but they proved too unruly. They were replaced by adult women, and the job remained a pink-collar ghetto until the 1970s.

Labor organizing in the phone industry started slowly but accelerated after the founding of the International Brotherhood of Electrical Workers in 1891. A male-dominated craft union, the IBEW ignored the operators until a wave of militancy began in Boston around 1912. The union reluctantly offered some assistance to the operators and ended up taking them into the organization, but only in a separate, second-class department.

The IBEW had some success after World War I, but telephone management moved to create company unions that remained in place until the early 1930s. Even the fact that AT&T cut many jobs during the early years of the Depression while keeping the dividend intact did not lead to serious unrest. It was the passage of the Wagner Act that revived independent unionism in the industry, and in 1939 the National Federation of Telephone Workers was formed.

The organization remained highly decentralized and rather weak. As a result, pay for telephone workers fell behind other industries. Amid the postwar labor militancy in 1946 the NFTW threatened a strike and got AT&T and the operating companies to bargain on a national level for the first time.

The following year the federation sought another big raise, but management declined to resume national bargaining. This time the strike was carried out. More than 300,000 workers around the country walked out in what was the most widespread strike in U.S. history. The NFTW had not prepared adequately for the action, and after several weeks the strike began to crumble. Local unions began settling with individual operating companies for small wage increases. Later that same year the NFTW decided to reorganize itself into a more centralized body and to change its name to the Communications Workers of America.

The CWA conducted a number of regional strikes in the 1950s, including a 72-day walkout at Southern Bell in 1955. In the 1960s the union had to fight off raids from the Teamsters and contend with the spreading automation of the system.

In the 1970s the threats to the CWA were from an organizing offensive by the IBEW, especially in the interconnect industry, and the uncertainty of what would happen if and when the Bell System was broken up. The union won a substantial wage increase after a weeklong national strike in 1971, and three years later AT&T agreed to national bargaining. The CWA sided with Ma Bell in its battle against competition, but after divestiture was announced the union set out to minimize the impact on AT&T's workers. There were signs that the RHCs would resist national bargaining and that a less regulated AT&T would be harder to deal with.

The latter proved true in 1983, when AT&T sought to hold the line and the CWA ended up calling a national strike. The walkout lasted about three weeks and ended with an 8.5 percent wage increase over three years.

The CWA has worked hard to adapt to the new environment created by deregulation and the breakup of the Bell System. In 1981 the union created a Committee on the Future, which examined changes in the industry and recommended bargaining strategies such as an emphasis on retraining. Recognizing that its domain had to extend to the entire information industry, the union vowed in 1985 to organize IBM. In the great long-distance wars of the 1980s, the CWA spent several million dollars promoting AT&T because it continued to use operators while the upstart carriers were completely automated.

This cooperative approach did not stop AT&T from announcing in August 1985 that it planned to eliminate 24,000 jobs in its Information Systems unit. A strike over the action was narrowly averted when the CWA and AT&T reached an agreement limiting the layoffs and restricting the use of subcontracting.

The union also had to confront the fact that several of the RHCs were setting up nonunion subsidiaries and were indicating they would take tough stances when CWA's contracts expired in 1986.

Things turned out to be no easier with AT&T after the union and the company agreed to complete their negotiations before talks began with the RHCs. The CWA rejected the company's offer of an 8 percent wage increase over three years and initiated a national strike. AT&T stood fast and made its pitch directly to workers through newspaper advertisements. The two sides reached a settlement that included the same wage package but also had special provisions for job retraining, and the strike ended after 26 days.

A few weeks later CWA talks with some of the RHCs broke down, and some 70,000 workers went on strike for about a week until settlements were reached.

LEADING COMPANIES (APART FROM AT&T AND ITS OFFSPRING)

GTE has long been the largest among the independent telephone companies that control the small sector of the industry that was never absorbed into the Bell System. Founded as General Telephone in 1926, GTE later got into the telecommunications equipment and electronics businesses, the latter through the purchase of Sylvania in 1958. The company acquired the Telenet data communications network in 1979 and the Sprint long-distance service in 1983. Sprint, which had a hard time competing with AT&T and MCI, was spun off into a joint venture with United Telecommunications in 1986. During the same year, GTE took on Siemens as a partner for its switching-equipment operation.

IBM saw the increasing fusion of data processing and communications as an opportunity to invade some of AT&T's traditional markets. IBM led a joint venture called Satellite Business Systems that failed to attract enough high-volume users of data transmission systems. SBS was also a disappointment in the long-distance business, and the operation was handed over to MCI in 1985 when IBM took an equity position in that company. IBM also had difficulty achieving results after its 1984 purchase of Rolm, a leading telecommunications equipment producer.

MCI (or Microwave Communications Inc. as it was originally called) has played a major role in introducing a greater degree of competition to the telecommunications business. The company was founded by John Goeken, owner of a mobile-radio business, who applied to the FCC in 1963 for permission to construct a microwave radio system between Chicago and St. Louis. AT&T fought the idea, but the company persevered, especially after William McGowan took over in 1968. The FCC finally allowed MCI and others to provide private-line service as well as discount long-distance calling in competition with AT&T. MCI, which became the only serious rival to AT&T (though a distant second) in the long-distance business, was bolstered in 1985 when IBM purchased an 18 percent stake in the company.

Northern Telecom Inc., the U.S. subsidiary of Northern Telecom Ltd. (which in turn is 52 percent owned by Bell Canada), has emerged as a leader in the telecommunications equipment business. It introduced the first digital switchboard in the United States and took first place in the PBX market.

SOURCE GUIDE

LEADING STOCK ANALYSTS AND EXPERTS

John Bain, analyst at Shearson Lehman Brothers.

Eastern Management Group, Parsippany, New Jersey.

Edward Greenberg, analyst at Morgan Stanley.

Robert La Blanc, La Blanc Associates, Ridgewood, New Jersey.

Robert Morris, analyst at Prudential-Bache.

Northern Business Information, New York.

Yankee Group, Boston.

TRADE ASSOCIATIONS AND UNIONS

Communications Workers of America, Washington, D.C.

North American Telecommunications Association (interconnect industry), Washington, D.C.

U.S. Telephone Association, Washington, D.C.

DATA SOURCES AND DIRECTORIES

AT&T, *The World's Telephones*, an annual compilation of statistics (Morris Plains, N.J.: AT&T).

U.S. Federal Communications Commission, *Statistics of Communications Common Carriers*, published annually.

U.S. Telephone Association, *Annual Statistical Volume* (Washington, D.C.: U.S. Telephone Association).

TRADE PUBLICATIONS

Communications Daily.

Communications Week.

Data Communications, monthly.

Satellite Communications, monthly.

Telecommunications, monthly.

Telecommunications Reports, weekly.

Telephony, weekly.

BOOKS AND REPORTS

Brock, Gerald W. *The Telecommunications Industry.* Cambridge, Mass.: Harvard University Press, 1981.

Brooks, John. *Telephone: The First Hundred Years.* New York: Harper & Row, 1976.

Brooks, Thomas R. *The Communications Workers of America.* New York: Mason/Charter, 1977.

Demac, Donna A., ed. *Tracing New Orbits: Cooperation and Competition in Global Satellite Development.* New York: Columbia University Press, 1986.

Goulden, Joseph C. *Monopoly.* New York: G. P. Putnam's Sons, 1968.

Green, James Harry. *The Dow Jones–Irwin Handbook of Telecommunications.* Homewood, Ill.: Dow Jones-Irwin, 1986.

Kahaner, Larry. *On the Line: The Men of MCI.* New York: Warner Books, 1986.

Kleinfield, Sonny. *The Biggest Company on Earth: A Profile of AT&T.* New York: Holt, Rinehart & Winston, 1981.

Schacht, John N. *The Making of Telephone Unionism, 1920–1947.* New Brunswick, N.J.: Rutgers University Press, 1985.

Tunstall, W. Brooke. *Disconnecting Parties: Managing the Bell System Breakup—An Inside View.* New York: McGraw-Hill, 1985.

U.S. Congress, House Committee on Energy and Commerce. *Telecommunications in Transition: The Status of Competition in the Telecommunications Industry.* Washington, D.C., 1981.

U.S. International Trade Administration. *A Competitive Assessment of the U.S. Fiber Optics Industry.* Washington, D.C., 1984.

U.S. National Telecommunications and Information Administration. *Issues in Domestic Telecommunications: Directions for National Policy.* Washington, D.C., 1985.

PART TWO

Consumer Goods and Services

CHAPTER SIX

Beverages

Americans are a thirsty people: The year-round demand for ice-cold beverages that are either sweet or alcoholic or both seems insatiable. Drinks are often used like medicines: People consume them to perk up or calm down, when they are busy or when they are relaxing. The satisfying of this need was once taken care of through home brews or the concoctions at the local druggist or soda fountain.

Today the packaged beverage industry—including $25 billion in soft drinks and $66 billion in alcoholic beverages—is very big business, and American products such as Coca-Cola have changed the drinking habits of people around the world. The authors of a book called *The Cola Wars*, noting the extraordinary spread of soft drinks to all kinds of societies, have declared: "Aside from physiological and biological similarities, the human race may not have a more common denominator than these drinks."

"THE PAUSE THAT REFRESHES": SOFT DRINKS

The soft drink business in the United States emerged out of the tonics and elixirs that druggists used to prepare for customers in order to cure a variety of ailments. One popular formula combining coca leaves and the kola nut was invented in 1886 by Atlanta druggist John Styth Pemberton. The rights to the product, Coca-

Cola, were acquired by Asa Griggs Candler, who proceeded to market it in syrup form to soda fountains around the country.

Candler was not interested in the idea of bottling the product for direct sale to consumers, and in 1899 he sold the rights to do so to a group of Tennessee businessmen for $1. Candler ultimately turned out to be more concerned with politics than commerce, and control of The Coca-Cola Company was acquired by Georgia financier Ernest Woodruff in 1919. His son Robert, who took over in 1923, remained chief executive until 1955 and continued to exercise great influence over the company until his death in 1985.

Thanks to aggressive marketing, Coca-Cola came to assume a prominent place in American life. As it was introduced around the world, Coke became a leading symbol of the United States, and the company went to great lengths to cultivate this status. Incidentally the company resisted the nickname Coke for many years because of the association with cocaine. The small trace of the drug in the original Coca-Cola formula was eliminated in 1903.

Right after Pearl Harbor, Woodruff vowed to make Coca-Cola available to everyone in the military. Thanks to Eisenhower's fondness for the drink, dozens of bottling plants were set up around the world, often right behind the frontline troops.

While Coke, in its familiar green bottle, dominated the soft drink market up to and through the 1940s, a serious competitor was slowly gaining ground. Pepsi-Cola was invented by North Carolina pharmacist Cabel Bradham in the 1890s. The Pepsi-Cola company grew rapidly around the turn of the century but later ran into serious financial difficulties, falling into bankruptcy several times and passing through a variety of owners. The company got a boost during the Depression, when it started selling Pepsi in 12-ounce bottles for the same nickle price as Coke's 6-ounce serving.

Still, Pepsi remained a distant second until the 1950s, when the company turned to what would later be called "lifestyle" advertising, associating the drink with young "sociables." The company scored a major coup in 1959 when Khrushchev was photographed drinking Pepsi at an exposition of American products in Moscow. After that point Pepsi was a true contender; and Donald Kendall, the executive who arranged to have Khrushchev drink the product, was promoted to chief executive of the company. Kendall's friendship with Richard Nixon helped Pepsi get the first foothold in the Soviet market in the early 1970s. (The company now supplies Pepsi in exchange for the right to sell Stolichnaya vodka in the United States.) Coke later used its contacts with Jimmy Carter (through Atlanta lawyer Charles Kirbo) to get the first shot at the Chinese market.

Beginning in the 1960s Coke and Pepsi escalated their rivalry with a succession of advertising campaigns aimed at tapping into the changes in the American psyche and getting people to associate one or the other cola with one's personal identity. In the place of traditional slogans such as Coke's "The pause that refreshes" and "Pepsi-Cola hits the spot," the companies spent millions on promoting notions such as "You've got a lot to live, and Pepsi's got a lot to give" and "Coke is the real thing."

Until the early 1960s the two leading companies had only one soft drink brand apiece. A much smaller competitor Royal Crown then paved the way to a giant new market by bringing out the first major sugar-free soft drink. The Coca-Cola Company brought out Tab in 1963, and Pepsi-Cola soon followed with its own low-calorie brands. The two big companies also launched assaults on the market of their much smaller competitor, The Seven-Up Co., by pushing their own lemon-lime drinks: Coke's Sprite and Pepsi's Mountain Dew.

BRAND PROLIFERATION

The introduction of new brands continued into the 1970s but really took off in the early 1980s. The impetus was a challenge by The Seven-Up Co. on the issue of caffeine. Unlike colas 7UP contained no caffeine, but for many years this distinction seemed to make little difference to consumers.

Seizing on the health consciousness of the 1980s, Seven-Up began emphasizing the caffeine issue in order to bolster its flagship brand and to generate interest in a new caffeine-free cola called Like that the company was introducing.

At first the majors dismissed the caffeine controversy, but Pepsi soon got scared and decided to introduce its own Pepsi Free. (This was in addition to Pepsi Light, a lower-calorie, lemon-flavored version brought out in 1977.) Soon The Coca-Cola Company, which had just introduced the sugar-free Diet Coke, went with the tide and brought out caffeine-free versions of Coke, Diet Coke, and Tab. These six cola varieties were joined by Cherry Coke in 1985.

In the intensified battle for supermarket shelf space (the industry term is *facings*), Pepsi began to give Coke the most serious competition ever. In the 1970s Pepsi had begun challenging Coke on taste rather than on the traditional price basis, using a series of taste-test ads. By the 1980s this "Pepsi Challenge" was paying off as Coke's market share slipped. The corporate share for The Coca-Cola Company was bolstered by the tremendous success of Diet Coke; but when regular Coke's share plunged several percentage points from 1983 to 1984, the company began to run scared.

The people in Atlanta were prompted to make the most radical decision in the history of the company. In April 1985 chief executive Roberto Goizueta announced that the company would make the first major change in the formula of Coke in the 99-year history of the product. The new Coke was to have a smoother, sweeter taste that some people decided was much closer to that of Pepsi.

The company had spent more than four years evaluating a change in formula and was convinced that new Coke would be a hit. It soon became clear, however, that consumer loyalty to the old taste was much stronger than the company had anticipated. The majority of consumers not only expressed their dislike of the new Coke, they began organizing to get the company to return to the traditional taste. Organizations such as Old Coke Drinkers of America were formed and began talking of filing lawsuits against the switch.

In July, only three months after the fanfare of the introduction of the new Coke, Goizueta in effect admitted defeat. He announced that the company would resume selling the old Coke, to be dubbed Coca-Cola Classic, alongside the new Coke. This brought the company's cola line up to eight permutations and created a marketing nightmare. The new Coke was to remain the company's flagship brand, yet results began to come in showing that the Classic version was selling better in many parts of the country. As McDonald's and other leading restaurant chains abandoned the new Coke, the company was struggling to keep the brand alive.

As the Coke and Pepsi lines slugged it out for market dominance, their smaller competitors such as Royal Crown and Dr Pepper often suffered as a result of the ensuing price war. The two majors also stepped up the pressures on their bottlers—which, aside from those few that are corporate owned, are independent companies—to carry more of their products. 7UP was a particular victim of this process. The bottlers were barred from directly distributing competing products, but many had handled 7UP, for instance, rather than Sprite or Teem, another lemon-lime brand brought out by Pepsi-Cola.

The heightened competition hurt the smaller cola producers, as well as Dr Pepper (which is technically not a cola). In addition a good deal of the action in soft drinks began shifting to new markets. One of the fastest-growing areas was soft drinks containing fruit juice. The Pepsi-Cola company took the lead here with its Slice brand, which even seized market share from 7UP.

Some other large companies have attempted to claim a portion of the lucrative soft drink market. In 1980 Proctor & Gamble acquired Orange Crush and Hires root beer. Four years later R. J. Reynolds, the tobacco giant, purchased Canada Dry (leading producer of mixers such as ginger ale) as well as Sunkist (leader in the orange drink market). In 1986, after a disappointing experience in the business, Reynolds announced the sale of its soft drink operation to Britain's Cadbury Schweppes.

The power of the industry's Big Two would have gotten much greater if the companies had been allowed to proceed with deals announced in 1986. PepsiCo planned to purchase Seven-Up for $380 million, and Coca-Cola was ready to pay $470 million for Dr Pepper. Both mergers were blocked by the federal government for antitrust reasons. The domestic business of Seven-Up was instead purchased in a leveraged buyout by Hicks & Haas of Dallas, which had earlier acquired Dr Pepper in the same manner.

Coca-Cola did, however, go ahead with the acquisition of two of its largest independent bottlers for a combined price of more than $2 billion. The company then sold 51 percent of the bottling operation to the public through a stock offering.

According to figures from *Beverage Industry* and analyst John C. Maxwell published in Standard & Poor's Industry Survey, the market shares of the leading brands in 1985 were as follows:

1.	Coke (new and Classic)	21.2%
2.	Pepsi	17.4
3.	Diet Coke	6.6
4.	Dr Pepper	5.6
5.	7UP	4.7

The corporate totals were Coca-Cola 38.6 percent, PepsiCo 27.4 percent, Dr Pepper 7.1 percent, Seven-Up 6.3 percent, and R. J. Reynolds 4.6 percent.

ALCOHOLIC BEVERAGES

The production of intoxicating beverages has been an important U.S. industry since the earliest days of the country. Alcoholic beverage consumption reached a peak in the early 19th century, when the hard-edged pioneers of the West guzzled large quantities of whiskey.

German immigrants arriving in the middle of the century brought with them the brewing skills of Europe; before long, beer became the most popular drink among Americans. Consumption of hard liquor along with beer remained high enough to inspire a dogged temperance movement, which succeeded by 1919 in having the production of all forms of alcoholic beverages banned. If anything, Prohibition probably increased the demand for liquor, and after repeal in 1933 the business boomed. Seagram was the first company to establish national liquor brands and thus secured a position at the top of the industry.

The first major shift in drinking habits came after World War II as many consumers switched from "brown goods" of the whiskey family to "white" drinks such as vodka and gin. Another upheaval began in the 1970s. Alcohol consumption stopped growing at its usual healthy rate, and large numbers of people switched from liquor to wine. The beer business remained healthy, but only because companies such as Miller introduced lower-calorie "light" brands. By the 1980s the talk was of the "new abstinence," and the most dramatic beverage growth was seen in sparkling water, of all things.

The industry was put on the defensive by a new temperance movement that succeeded in getting the drinking age increased to 21 in many parts of the country and that began seeking federal legislation to ban beer and wine ads from radio and television (the networks voluntarily prohibit commercials for liquor). While resisting restrictive laws, the industry has also jumped on the sobriety bandwagon by pushing less-intoxicating sweet drinks such as wine coolers and even nonalcoholic beer and wine.

THE BEER BRAWL

Back in the 19th century most beer was consumed in taverns or by sending a youngster to the bar to fill a tin pail and bring it home. The beer was produced on the tavern's premises or in a nearby brewery. Producers gradually grew larger, but many brewers were wiped out by Prohibition. After repeal the beer industry was dominated by small, regional, often family-owned brewing companies. A few companies such as Anheuser-Busch and Schlitz sold on a national basis, but the business remained a distinctly sleepy one.

The event that shook things up was the purchase of Miller Brewing by the tobacco giant Philip Morris in 1970. The aggressive marketers of Philip Morris instilled new life in what had been the seventh-ranked brewer by improving the quality of the product and launching the now famous "Miller Time" ad campaign. Picking up early on the increased calorie consciousness of the population, the company led the way in the light segment with the introduction of Miller Lite.

Miller's aggressiveness propelled the company into second place behind Anheuser-Busch, which was forced to adopt similar marketing tactics. A–B brought out a light version of Budweiser, the number one brand, along with a variety of other products across the price spectrum. By 1980 the two companies had established a solid hold over the industry, sharing 50 percent of the market between them.

During the early 1980s A–B continued its climb toward its stated goal of a 40 percent share, while Miller faltered. The latter's flagship brand Miller High Life began sinking and was surpassed by the company's own Lite brand.

In the meantime there was an intensifying battle among the second tier of producers. Regional brewers, such as Heileman in the Midwest, began buying up their weaker brethren as consolidation appeared as the only alternative in a business beset by declining levels of demand. Stroh bought F. & M. Schaefer and

Joseph Schlitz. Pabst bought Olympia and was then itself the subject of a drawn-out and complicated takeover battle.

Industry leader Anheuser-Busch kept the heat on by competing in terms of price as well as quality and by moving quickly into the low-alcohol segment, bringing out a brand called LA (for low alcohol) in 1984. Competition has also been heightened by the increasing popularity of foreign brands such as Heinekin, Molson, and Beck's. Imports rose from 1.1 percent of the U.S. market in 1975 to 4.3 percent in 1985. According to figures from *Impact* and *Modern Brewery Age* published in Standard & Poor's Industry Survey, the shares of the domestic beer market of the top U.S. producers in 1985 were as follows:

1.	Anheuser-Busch	38.2%
2.	Miller Brewing	20.8
3.	Stroh Brewery	13.1
4.	Heileman	9.1
5.	Coors	8.3
6.	Pabst	5.0

Despite the increasing concentration of the industry there has been a renaissance of small, quality brewers in recent years. Led by Fritz Maytag's revival of Anchor Brewing in San Francisco in 1970, the new breed includes Hibernia Brewing in Eau Claire, Wisconsin, and Old New York Brewing, which opened the first new brewery in New York City in many years. In 1986 there were about 50 "microbreweries"—those producing fewer than 15,000 barrels a year—in operation.

THE SOBERING PICTURE FOR LIQUOR

For much of its history America was a hard-drinking country. Even Prohibition and the poor quality of much of the bootleg products did little to depress consumption levels. Tastes changed after World War II, thanks to Heublein's aggressive promotion of drinks such as Bloody Marys and screwdrivers that just happened to require the company's leading product, vodka.

Yet it took the health obsession of the 1970s to put a serious dent in liquor consumption. White wine or nonalcoholic beverages replaced scotch-on-the-rocks and martinis as the status drinks. Brown goods of the whiskey family are on their way to becoming extinct as younger people's tastes change.

The industry's leaders have responded in several ways. First, they have put more emphasis on premixed sweet and flavored drinks, such as Seagram's Captain Morgan Spiced Rum, that have been growing in popularity. They have also moved further into the faster-growing wine business. Seagram, which already produced Paul Masson wines, purchased Coca-Cola's Wine Spectrum division in 1983; and in 1985 Brown-Forman Distillers acquired the leading company in the wine cooler business.

Seagram has also sought to improve the image of liquor with an ad campaign arguing that the alcohol content of liquors is not disproportionately high in relation to beer and wine. Other producers, such as Jack Daniels (owned by Brown-Forman), went after new markets such as women who might be induced to switch over to harder drinks. According to *Business Week* (June 16, 1986), the leading brands in 1985 were:

Brand	Cases Sold (in millions)
1. Bacardi rum	7.65
2. Smirnoff vodka	5.67
3. Seagram's 7 Crown	4.50
4. Canadian Mist	3.70
5. Jim Beam bourbon	3.37
6. Jack Daniels bourbon	3.15
7. Popov vodka	2.80
8. Seagram's V.O.	2.77
9. Windsor Supreme	2.67
10. Seagram's Gin	2.55

SOURING GRAPES FOR THE WINE BUSINESS

Until the 1930s wine production was an underdeveloped industry in the United States. In the years following repeal the business began to grow—especially in California, where the industry was aided by the expert research conducted at the University of California at Davis. The liquor company Schenley (now part of Rapid-American Corp.) bought two wineries in the state in 1939, and Seagram purchased Paul Masson in 1946.

But the real powerhouse in the industry was the operation established in 1933 by two brothers, Ernest and Julio Gallo. Through tireless marketing and bold modernization after the war, Gallo went on to become the giant of the industry and helped to create a significant national market for wine.

The industry took off like a rocket in the 1970s as people began switching from liquor, and even the likes of The Coca-Cola Company jumped in. By the early 1980s the bloom was off, due partly to a shift in tastes away from alcoholic beverages entirely and partly to rising import penetration. By 1982, shipments of U.S. wineries were flat after a decade of 10 percent average annual growth.

Just as the industry was worrying it would end up in the same boat with the liquor business, salvation came in the form of a simple idea: wine mixed with citrus juices. These drinks, dubbed coolers, were invented in the 1970s by Californian Michael Crete to enliven beach parties. Crete eventually turned his idea into a business, California Cooler, which he sold to Brown-Forman for about $150 million. Other beverage companies such as Stroh Brewery and Seagram also jumped into wine coolers, and the business zoomed to some $1.2 billion in 1985.

According to figures from *Impact* reported in *Fortune* (September 1, 1986), the leading wine producers in 1985 were Gallo with 26.1 percent and Seagram with 8.3 percent. All other domestic producers were below 6 percent each, and imports accounted for 23.4 percent.

LABOR RELATIONS

The most controversial labor issue in the soft drink industry was an international one. After workers at the Coca-Cola bottling operation in Guatemala organized a union in the 1970s, the organization suffered attacks from right-wing death squads, which resulted in the deaths of more than a dozen people. An international campaign led by the International Union of Food & Allied Workers Associations prompted The Coca-Cola Company to put pressure on its Guatemala franchisee to see to it that the union's rights were recognized. There was some improvement in the situation, but the plant was closed in early 1984. The workers occupied the facility for more than a year, and then Coca-Cola arranged to keep the operation going under the control of a new set of investors.

Coca-Cola has frequently been charged in the United States with allowing migrant workers employed by its Minute Maid orange juice subsidiary to live in miserable conditions. In 1985 the company caused a controversy with American unions when it introduced a line of Coca-Cola clothes that were produced overseas. Following protests, the company agreed to switch to U.S. production for all clothes sold in the United States.

The main labor controversy in the beer industry has concerned Coors. Unions and civil rights groups have accused the company of discriminatory hiring practices and of intimidating employees with lie detector tests. The Brewery Workers Union went on strike at Coors in 1977 over these issues, and the AFL–CIO organized a boycott of the company's products. After the strike stretched out for more than 18 months, Coors workers voted to decertify the union.

Other brewing production employees, such as those at Anheuser-Busch, are members of the Teamsters Union. A–B suffered a three-month strike in 1976.

The United Farm Workers scored a major victory in 1967, when it signed a contract with Gallo. But in 1973 the giant winemaker made what the UFW charged was a sweetheart deal with the Teamsters Union. The UFW, after challenging an election that certified the Teamsters as the representative for Gallo workers, launched a national boycott of the company's products that lasted until 1978. In 1980 other workers at Gallo and at United Vintners represented by the Distillery, Wine and Allied Workers Union staged a 17-day strike, the first in the union's 35-year history. In 1986 the union agreed to wage concessions but went on strike against a dozen wineries to resist industry efforts to reduce benefits and change work rules. The walkout ended abruptly after eight weeks when the wineries threatened to bring in permanent replacement workers.

LEADING COMPANIES

Anheuser-Busch, whose Budweiser brand has long been the country's leading beer, is by far the leading brewing company in America. Built by Adolphus Busch in the late 19th century and run ever since by members of the Busch family, A–B weathered a strong challenge from Miller Brewing in the 1970s and emerged all the stronger for it. Under the leadership of August Busch III the company has modernized its marketing and management techniques and made some diversification moves. Thanks to a strong line of beers across the price spectrum, Busch has steadily gained market share, approaching its stated goal of 40 percent.

The Coca-Cola Company was the pioneer in the soft drink market and for many years had a commanding lead over the business. The company jealously guards the secret formula for Coke's flavoring ingredients, code-named Merchandise 7X, going so far as to abandon its operation in India when a court in that country ordered the company to hand over the secret to the local bottlers. The company branched out into other parts of the beverage business in 1960 when it acquired Minute Maid, the pioneer in the frozen orange juice field. The company bought Taylor Wines in 1977 and developed a sizable presence in the wine business. But the operation did not meet the company's profitability standards, and the business was sold to Seagram in 1983. Coca-Cola has also gotten into the entertainment field through the purchase of Columbia Pictures in 1982. Roberto Goizueta, who has been chief executive since 1981, scored a big success with Diet Coke in 1982 but was forced into an embarrassing position in 1985 when a change in the formula of Coke proved a flop.

Coors is the most controversial of the major beer companies. Founded by Adolph Coors in the 1870s, the ultraconservative members of the Coors family running the company came into conflict with unions and civil rights groups in the 1970s. The company's product, produced in a single brewery in Golden, Colorado, for years held a kind of cult status in many parts of the country. This was in part because the beer was not sold east of the Mississippi, a marketing policy necessitated by the fact that Coors, being unpasteurized and containing no preservatives, had a limited shelf life. The management of the company, which introduced Coors Light in 1978 and began national distribution, passed in 1985 to a new generation of Coors family members.

Dr Pepper has long been a favorite in the south and has a respectable following elsewhere in the country. In 1980 it overtook 7UP as the third-ranked soft drink but was later surpassed by Diet Coke. The company purchased mixer maker Canada Dry in 1982 but sold the business to R. J. Reynolds in 1984. The Dr Pepper Company was taken private in a $512 million leveraged buyout in 1983. After a proposed purchase by Coca-Cola was nixed by the federal government in 1986, the company was sold to a private investment group, Hicks & Haas.

Gallo is the behemoth of the wine industry. Founded by brothers Ernest and Julio Gallo in the 1930s the secretive, privately held firm has led the way in the modernization of wine production in the United States. The Gallos have always had a good sense of changing tastes. They developed Thunderbird for the ghetto market, Boone's Farm for the late 1960s "pop wine" boom, and in the 1970s started placing greater emphasis on higher-quality table wines. In 1985 they brought out Bartles & Jaymes, which became the leading wine cooler.

The **G. Heileman Brewing Co.** of La Crosse, Wisconsin, ranked 31st among U.S. brewers in 1960, went on to acquire a series of weaker competitors and claw its way up to fourth place by the mid-1980s. Chairman Russell Cleary has fought Anheuser-Busch and Miller in its midwestern stronghold while expanding nationally. The company engaged in a long battle for Pabst Brewing, from which it ended up with some of that company's assets. In the mid-1980s it bucked the tide of overcapacity in the industry by announcing plans to build a new brewery in Milwaukee.

The roots of **Heublein** date back to the 1870s in Connecticut. The company bottled the first prepared cocktails in the 1890s and survived Prohibition by pushing A–1 Steak Sauce. Heublein bought the rights to Smirnoff vodka in 1939, at a time when the drink was largely known in the United States. Heublein skillfully created a market for the stuff after the war with promotion of new mixed drinks containing vodka and an ad compaign that stated that vodka left the drinker "breathless." The company got into the wine business with the purchase of United Vintners in 1969 and then took a plunge in fast food with the acquisition of Kentucky Fried Chicken in 1971. In 1982 Heublein was acquired by cigarette maker R. J. Reynolds.

PepsiCo, the parent company of Pepsi-Cola, has evolved from a perennial also-ran into a serious challenger to industry leader Coca-Cola. Through savvy advertising and risks such as entering the caffeine-free market, the company has risen to within a few points of Coca-Cola's market share. Chief executive Donald Kendall began diversifying the company in the 1960s, buying Frito-Lay foods as well as businesses outside the food and beverage field. During the mid-1980s Kendall began shedding acquisitions of the latter sort, including North American Van Lines and Wilson Sporting Goods. Kendall was succeeded by D. Wayne Calloway in 1986.

Philip Morris, the leading cigarette producer, entered the beverage field in 1970 with the purchase of ailing Miller Brewing Co. The master marketers at Philip Morris shook up the 115-year-old beermaker and brought out the hugely successful Lite beer, thus making Miller one of the great Cinderella stories of the 1970s. The company lost its luster during the 1980s, largely as a result of a drop in popularity in the flagship brand Miller High Life. Philip Morris tried to work the same earlier magic with Seven-Up after the company was acquired in 1978. But it was not to be. The lemon-lime drink continued to lose market share, and a caffeine-free cola called Like that Seven-Up introduced in 1982 never received wide acceptance. In 1986, after an attempt to sell Seven-Up to PepsiCo was blocked by federal antitrust regulators, the domestic operations of Seven-Up were sold to Hicks & Haas.

Royal Crown has been the leading innovator in the soft drink field but has not had the resources to market in a manner comparable to Coca-Cola and Pepsi. In the early 1960s the company brought out Diet Rite, the first national diet soft drink, and in 1980 it introduced the first caffeine-free cola RC 100. In 1984 the company was taken private by financier Victor Posner.

Seagram is the largest producer of liquor in the world, selling 150 brands of spirits as well as 200 brands of wine. The company is based in Montreal but does two thirds of its business in the United States. Seagram's distilling business was built by brothers Sam and Allan Bronfman beginning in the 1920s. Much of their Canadian-produced liquor ended up in the United States during Prohibition, and after repeal the company kept on selling in grand proportions. The company developed the first national liquor brands with the introduction of Seagram's 5 Crown and 7 Crown, blended whiskies that were lighter and smoother than the rye and bourbon Americans previously drank. Under the autocratic control of "Mr. Sam" Bronfman, the company kept its control of the brown-goods market but was slow to follow the move to white goods such as vodka and gin. Sam's son Edgar, who took over in 1971, expanded Seagram's presence in the wine business by buying Coca-Cola's Wine Spectrum subsidiary in 1983 and ventured into the soft drink business with the introduction of a line of mixers in 1983. The company enjoys substantial revenue from its 22 percent ownership of Du Pont, which it ended up with as a result of an unsuccessful battle with the chemical giant for the Conoco petroleum company in 1981.

Stroh Brewery Co., a family-owned and -operated business since its founding in the 1850s, emerged in the 1970s as one of the faster-growing beer producers. Under the leadership of Peter Stroh, the company acquired F. & M. Schaefer in 1981 and Joseph Schlitz Brewing Co.—once the country's largest beermaker—in 1982. Known for its "fire brewing" process, the company has expanded its national advertising and distribution and entered new markets such as low-alcohol beer and wine coolers.

SOURCE GUIDE

LEADING STOCK ANALYSTS AND EXPERTS

Emanuel Goldman, analyst at Montgomery Securities.

Gomberg, Fredrikson & Associates, San Francisco–based consultants to the wine industry.

John C. Maxwell, Jr., veteran analyst now at Furman, Selz, Mager, Dietz & Birney.

Jesse Meyers, publisher of the newsletter *Beverage Digest*, Old Greenwich, Connecticut.

Marvin Shanken, editor and publisher of *Impact*, a leading newsletter for the alcoholic beverage industry, New York.

Robert S. Weinberg, a leading consultant to the beer industry, based in St. Louis.

TRADE ASSOCIATIONS AND UNIONS

Distilled Spirits Council of the U.S., Washington, D.C.

Distillery, Wine and Allied Workers International Union, Englewood, New Jersey.

National Soft Drink Association, Washington, D.C.

U.S. Brewers Association, Washington, D.C.

Wine Institute, San Francisco.

DATA SOURCES AND DIRECTORIES

Annual Statistical Review, a volume of data on the liquor, beer, and wine industries (Washington, D.C.: Distilled Spirits Council).

Brewers Almanac, a statistical volume published annually (Washington, D.C.: U.S. Brewers Association).

Business Week publishes an annual survey of liquor brands selling 500,000 cases or more, in June.

Liquor Handbook, an annual volume of data on the market for liquors (New York: Gavin-Jobson Associates).

Modern Brewery Age Blue Book, an annual directory and compilation of statistics (Norwalk, Conn.: Business Journals).

Soft Drink Industry of the United States: Statistical Profile, published annually (Washington, D.C.: National Soft Drink Association).

TRADE PUBLICATIONS

Beverage Digest, semimonthly.

Beverage Industry, semimonthly.

Beverage World, monthly.

Impact, semimonthly.

Modern Brewery Age, weekly.

Wines & Vines, monthly.

BOOKS AND REPORTS

Cahalan, Don, Ira H. Cisin, and Helen M. Crossley. *American Drinking Practices.* New Brunswick, N.J.: Rutgers University Center of Alcohol Studies, 1969.

Cavanagh, John, and Frederick Clairmonte. *Alcoholic Beverages: Dimensions of Corporate Power.* New York: St. Martin's Press, 1985.

Dietz, Lawrence. *Soda Pop: The History, Advertising, Art and Memorabilia of Soft Drinks in America.* New York: Simon & Schuster, 1973.

Enrico, Roger, and Jesse Kornbluth. *The Other Guy Blinked: How Pepsi Won the Cola Wars.* New York: Bantam Books, 1986.

Jacobson, Michael, Robert Atkins, and George Hacker. *The Booze Merchants.* Washington, D.C.: Center for Science in the Public Interest, 1983.

Kahn, E. J., Jr. *The Big Drink: The Story of Coca-Cola.* New York: Random House, 1960.

Louis, J. C., and Harvey Z. Yazijian. *The Cola Wars.* New York: Everest House, 1980.

Newman, Peter. *King of the Castle.* On the Bronfmans and Seagram. New York: Atheneum Publishers, 1979.

Oliver, Thomas. *The Real Coke, The Real Story.* New York: Random House, 1986.

CHAPTER SEVEN

Cigarettes

The cigarette industry is one of the most controversial and most profitable areas of commerce. For decades its products have been denounced as health risks, yet Americans still consume some 600 billion cigarettes a year. The business is dominated by six companies, which have been trying since the early 1970s to stimulate growth by introducing a dazzling array of new brands, ranging from "designer" cigarettes to no-name generics. Despite repeated predictions of doom the cigarette industry remains very much alive. Yet the Big Six have hedged their bets, investing large sums in nontobacco enterprises.

TOBACCO'S ROAD

The tobacco industry in America began with the leaves that some of the natives of the New World presented to Columbus (who initially thought them worthless). The production of the plant that the Indians loved to smoke became an important enterprise in the colonies and remained so after independence. George Washington and Thomas Jefferson were among the prominent growers of their day.

For a long time the main form of tobacco consumption in America was chewing, with cigars and pipes being common only among the more "respectable" strata of society. The smoking of hand-rolled cigarettes gained some popularity in the first half of the 19th century, but that habit remained socially suspect.

The rise of the cigarette as the dominant tobacco product was ushered in by the development of large-scale rolling machines in the 1880s. One man who recognized the potential of mechanization and mass production was James Buchanan "Buck" Duke, the young proprietor of a tobacco enterprise in North Carolina. Duke signed James Bonsack, the inventor of one of the more promising rolling machines, to an airtight contract. Duke used his control over Bonsack's machines to take over most of the tobacco industry and in the process turn the United States into a country of cigarette smokers.

A ruthless competitor, Duke either drove his rivals out of business by undercutting their prices or else seized control of their companies through purchase of majority interests in their stock. By the end of the century Duke had turned his American Tobacco Company into what outsiders called the Tobacco Trust, which controlled some 90 percent of the cigarette production—and much of the rest of the tobacco industry—in the entire country.

Duke soon turned his sights abroad, plotting an invasion of the British market. Knowing the trust's power, the independent producers in Britain banded together in defense, creating the Imperial Tobacco Co. They then fought Duke by threatening to invade his comfortable domain in the United States. The enemies decided cooperation was more prudent than all-out competition. They agreed not to poach on one another's markets and set up the British-American Tobacco Co. to sell jointly to the rest of the world.

Buck Duke was on his way to achieving quite literally a monopoly of the U.S. tobacco industry, but the sentiments of the Progressive Era eventually undermined his empire. In 1911 the Supreme Court ordered the dismemberment of the Tobacco Trust into a number of independent firms, including American Tobacco, R. J. Reynolds, Liggett & Myers, and Lorillard (the latter three being companies that the trust had earlier gobbled up).

As separate companies these four continued to dominate the industry. The popularity of cigarette smoking increased rapidly during and after World War I, and the big producers sought to create national brands. The first product to fit this description was Reynolds' Camels, introduced in 1913. American's Lucky Strikes followed suit beginning in 1916. Liggett's Chesterfields completed what stood as the Big Three of the business for more than 30 years.

SELLING THE IMAGE

The success of the leading brands was in large part a result of the heavy advertising of the tobacco companies. Slogans such as "I'd walk a mile for a Camel" and "Reach for a Lucky instead of a sweet" were constantly drummed into the national consciousness and resulted in increased sales. Even today, despite the ban on radio and television commercials, cigarettes are the country's most heavily advertised product. More than $2 billion a year are spent on appealing to smokers and potential smokers.

The reasons for the heavy promotion are, first, the fact that there is basically very little product differentiation among the various little white tubes filled with leaves; winning over a customer in most cases means selling the image that the producer chooses to associate with a particular brand. The other reason is that cigarette companies are peddling a product that is not terribly healthy, and there is always the danger that people may start taking the health warnings too seriously if their habits are not constantly reinforced by ads.

Concocting illusory product differentiation and responding to the health alarms have been the twin preoccupations of the cigarette industry in the postwar period, especially since the 1952 publication of an article in *Reader's Digest* that alerted people to the dangers of smoking. Although there had been some earlier reports of the problem, it was that article and follow-ups in the magazine that received enormous media attention and generated public concern. Cigarette sales began to drop for the first time, and the industry began to worry.

But it also found an appropriate—and lucrative—way to respond. The manufacturers started promoting filter-tip cigarettes as a safer version of what were already known as "coffin nails." Existing but obscure filter brands were given new life, along with newly developed filter products such as Winston, which went on to become one of the perennially best-selling brands in the United States.

The greatest marketing coup of the era was undoubtedly the relaunching of a minor brand called Marlboro by Philip Morris, a cigarette maker founded in Britain in the 1840s but "Americanized" in 1919 that grew into one of the leading firms. Working with advertising wizard Leo Burnett, Philip Morris turned what was previously a "woman's brand" into a macho product by associating it with that quintessential image of American virility—the cowboy. The evocation of "Marlboro Country" (the rugged West) created a giant success for the brand and eventually helped Philip Morris attain the largest market share of the cigarette producers.

ON THE DEFENSIVE

Having survived the *Reader's Digest* assault of the 1950s, the tobacco industry was able to breathe easily until the early 1960s, when the health controversy broke out once again. In 1962 the British Royal College of Physicians published a study arguing that smoking was unequivocally linked to lung cancer and other diseases. The U.S. surgeon general followed suit in 1964 with a report that scared large numbers of smokers into giving up the habit, at least temporarily, and prompted Congress to pass legislation requiring warning labels to be printed on every package of cigarettes.

The surgeon general's report also brought about a public-policy debate on smoking that continues to the present. Antismoking forces gained strength after 1964 and succeeded in getting Congress to ban cigarette advertising on radio and television beginning in 1971. In the 1970s federal transportation agencies established rules requiring separate smoking sections in airplanes and intercity buses.

President Carter's secretary of health, education and welfare Joseph Califano launched a major federal assault on smoking in 1978. But intense pressure from tobacco state politicians such as Jesse Helms of North Carolina swayed Carter and contributed to Califano's removal in 1979.

In the Reagan administration the antismoking rhetoric has been somewhat subdued, though Surgeon General Dr. C. Everett Koop has spoken out strongly on the hazards of cigarettes and has argued that smoking, rather than occupational health hazards, is the main cause of cancer among American workers. At other levels of government some 10 states and 150 municipalities had by 1986 passed laws limiting smoking in workplaces.

In addition the controversy over cigarette advertising continues. In December 1985 the American Medical Association's policymaking body voted to support a ban on the advertising of tobacco products in any medium.

On another front, the cigarette industry has had to confront a rapid rise in the number of product liability suits brought against it. Despite the tilt toward plaintiffs in that general area of law, the industry received favorable rulings in two major cases in late 1985 and maintained its unbroken record of success in the legal arena. In April 1986 a federal appeals court ruled that the warning labels on cigarette packages protected the industry from claims that consumers were not adequately alerted to the dangers of smoking.

SELLING THROUGH THE STORM

The tobacco industry has stood firm in the face of the criticism. On the health issue the industry has tirelessly argued that there is no "absolutely certain" causal link between smoking and lung cancer and other diseases. The cigarette companies no longer imply, as they did back in the 1920s and 1930s, that smoking is healthy; they simply shield themselves behind the agnostic statement that "no one knows for sure" whether cigarettes are dangerous. Until it is proved to their satisfaction that there is a cancer link, they are perfectly willing to go on selling their product.

And a profitable product it is. Cigarettes provide one of the highest returns on sales of any industry, and most of the six major U.S. producers continue to generate healthy earnings despite the stagnant level of demand.

One of the sources of prosperity for some time was the low-tar-and-nicotine segment of the market—what the industry refers to as high-filtration or "hi-fi" brands. In the 1970s this market did for the industry what filters accomplished in the 1950s. In the intense battle for market share, the industry began producing dozens of new hi-fi as well as full-flavor (i.e., high-tar-and-nicotine) brands as segmentation became the rule of the day.

During the past dozen years, the industry has tried almost every imaginable variation and gimmick to stimulate sales. These range from "prestige" brands such as Philip Morris' Players and Reynolds' designer brand Ritz (which is emblazoned with the Yves St. Laurent name) down to the generic products that were pushed heavily by Liggett beginning in 1980. To respond to the popularity of generics, other producers began offering packages containing 25 rather than 20 cigarettes for the same price; they also created discount brands priced to be competitive with the generics. By 1986 off-price cigarettes accounted for about 8.5 percent of the market.

The biggest challenge for the industry in recent years was to recover from the drop in demand brought about by the doubling (to 16 cents a pack) of federal excise taxes that took effect in 1983. This first rise in levies since 1951 raised the price of a pack to more than $1 in major cities.

Cigarette consumption has been declining, but higher prices—along with foreign growth, especially in the third world—have allowed the industry to increase its aggregate revenues, which reached some $30 billion at the retail level in 1985. The battle for position among the six major producers has remained intense. The big successes at either end of the spectrum have been Philip Morris, which passed longtime leader Reynolds in 1983, and last-place Liggett, which has doubled its share thanks to generics. In 1985, according to the annual *Business Week* survey (December 23, 1985), the rankings by market share were as follows:

1.	Philip Morris	35.7%
2.	R. J. Reynolds	32.0
3.	Brown & Williamson	11.7
4.	Lorillard	8.2
5.	American Brands	7.4
6.	Liggett	5.0

Although the cigarette business remains attractive for the moment, the leading producers are hedging their bets. Actually the diversification began after the surgeon general's 1964 bombshell. American Tobacco got into biscuits and bourbon and in 1970 changed its name to American Brands. Reynolds bought businesses involved in food, shipping, and packaging; in 1970 it too took "Tobacco" out of its name and replaced it with "Industries." Philip Morris bought Miller Brewing and Seven-Up.

More recently the two industry leaders have taken additional giant steps into the food business: Reynolds bought Nabisco Brands for $4.9 billion, and Philip Morris purchased General Foods for $5.7 billion. The chairman of Philip Morris, Hamish Maxwell, stated in a letter to stockholders: "While the company does not share a common concern about the future of tobacco, we believe the best step we can take is to . . . broaden our earnings base."

LABOR RELATIONS

Beginning with the Tobacco Trust, the cigarette industry was not a great friend of organized labor. The Tobacco Workers International Union, formed at the turn of the century, had its main organizing successes with smaller producers. It was not until after the Supreme Court ruled favorably on the constitutionality of the National Labor Relations Act in 1937 that several of the major companies signed with the TWIU. R. J. Reynolds held out and remains nonunion to this day.

A more radical alternative to the TWIU was chartered by the Committee for Industrial Organization in 1937. The union, which eventually took the name of the Food, Tobacco, Agricultural and Allied Workers Union, concentrated on organizing agricultural workers. The FTA faced strong opposition to its attempt to bring black and white workers together in one organizational structure, as opposed to the segregated locals formed by unions such as the TWIU. The FTA was expelled from the CIO in 1949 because of Communist Party influence in the union, which ended up merging with the Distributive, Processing and Office Workers of America.

The ranks of cigarette production workers have declined steadily in recent years as a result of mechanization and plant closings by the weaker producers. The number of hourly employees in the industry in 1985 was about 38,000.

LEADING COMPANIES

American Brands is the descendant of the company that Buck Duke used to corner the tobacco business in the late 19th century. Divested (by a 1911 Supreme Court ruling) of the other cigarette companies it had acquired, American went on to produce Lucky Strikes, one of the top national brands for many years. American was slow to jump on the filter bandwagon in the 1950s and ended up losing a major chunk of its market share. Yet it remained profitable in its less dominant role in the industry. The company made major moves into nontobacco businesses in the 1960s and 1970s, acquiring companies such as Jim Beam Distilling, Sunshine Biscuits, and Swingline staplers. In late 1986 American Brands made an unsuccessful offer for Chesebrough-Pond's, a producer of health and beauty aids and packaged food.

Brown & Williamson has been a subsidiary of British-American Tobacco (now BAT Industries) since 1927. B&W had a big success with Kool menthols but remains one of the less exciting companies in the industry. The parent company is the world's largest cigarette maker, with revenues of $13 billion and sales operations around the world. It began diversifying in the 1960s, buying cosmetics companies, department stores such as Saks Fifth Avenue, and other businesses.

Liggett Group (formerly Liggett & Myers) began as a snuff manufacturer in the 1820s. In 1899 it was swallowed up by the Tobacco Trust and reemerged in 1911. Its major brand for many years was Chesterfield, one of the three leaders along with Camels and Lucky Strikes. After World War II the company began a steady slide to last place among the major producers. Liggett showed some renewed life in the 1980s, when it led the push into generics. The company was acquired by Grand Metropolitan PLC of Britain in 1980.

Lorillard is the country's oldest tobacco company, with its origins back in 1760. The company was part of the Tobacco Trust from 1899 to 1911. It enjoyed some success in the 1950s, thanks to Kent, one of the first filter cigarettes, and in the 1970s, thanks to several low-tar brands. The company was acquired by Loews Corp. in 1968.

Philip Morris, one of the leading U.S. marketers, had its roots in a London cigar and cigarette maker established in the 1840s. The company entered the U.S. market in 1902 and was taken over by American shareholders in 1919. Thanks to the phenomenally successful relaunching of Marlboro in the mid-1950s, the company rose to the top ranks of the tobacco industry and took the number one spot in market share in 1983. A favorite of Wall Street, Philip Morris also turned Miller Brewing, which it bought in 1970, into the country's second largest brewer. In 1981 the company outmaneuvered R. J. Reynolds to purchase a 22 percent share of Rothmans International, the tobacco arm of the South African–based Rembrandt Group. In 1985 Philip Morris purchased General Foods for nearly $6 billion. The company has worked hard to overcome the image problems associated with tobacco by spending large sums for cultural and artistic donations.

R. J. Reynolds, the king of the North Carolina tobacco business, emerged from the Tobacco Trust in 1911 and turned Camel into the country's first national brand. The company led the way to the filter era with the introduction of Winston, still the number two seller, in 1954. Reynolds began diversifying in the 1960s, buying companies such as Chun King foods, Del Monte, and Sea-Land shipping. In 1982 it bought Heublein and in 1985 Nabisco Brands. Confident in the future of the cigarette industry, Reynolds spent $1 billion in the early 1980s constructing the world's largest cigarette factory—with an annual capacity of 5 billion packs—near Winston-Salem, North Carolina. In early 1987 the company, renamed RJR Nabisco, agreed to sell Heublein to Grand Metropolitan for $1.2 billion.

SOURCE GUIDE

LEADING STOCK ANALYSTS AND EXPERTS

Emanuel Goldman, analyst at Montgomery Securities.

John C. Maxwell, Jr., veteran analyst now at Furman, Selz, Mager, Dietz & Birney.

TRADE ASSOCIATION

The Tobacco Institute, Washington, D.C.

DATA SOURCES AND DIRECTORIES

Business Week publishes an annual survey of cigarette industry market shares by brand and by company, in December.

Tobacco Industry Profile, an annual statistical publication (Washington, D.C.: Tobacco Institute).

World Tobacco Directory, an annual volume listing manufacturers, dealers, associations, and others in the industry (Redhill, Surrey, England: International Trade Publications).

TRADE PUBLICATIONS

Tobacco International, fortnightly.

Tobacco Reporter, monthly.

BOOKS AND REPORTS

Finger, William R., ed. *The Tobacco Industry in Transition*. Lexington, Mass.: Lexington Books, 1981.

Sobel, Robert. *They Satisfy: The Cigarette in American Life*. Garden City, N.Y.: Anchor Press, 1978.

Taylor, Peter. *The Smoke Ring: Tobacco, Money and Multinational Politics*. New York: Pantheon Books, 1984.

CHAPTER EIGHT

Drugs and Health Care

Over the past few decades, health care has emerged as one of the largest spheres of activity in the United States. By the early 1980s more than 10 percent of GNP was devoted to the treatment of illness. Of the estimated $425 billion spent in 1985 the largest share (some $167 billion) went to hospital care.

From a strictly commercial point of view, the main business involved in health care has traditionally been the production of drugs, which by 1985 was a thriving $32 billion industry yet one tarnished by a long list of products that turned out to be harmful. In recent years private enterprise has also been expanding its presence in health care by taking over hospitals and other institutions from the public and nonprofit sectors. What has emerged is a "medical-industrial complex" that is exercising ever more influence over the practice of medicine.

FROM SNAKE OIL TO ANTIBIOTICS

The use of botanical substances in the treatment of illness dates back to early civilizations. Apothecary shops have been in existence in Europe for at least 900 years. While some traditional herbal remedies were effective, treatment was often a hit-or-miss proposition.

Modern pharmacology might be said to begin with the English physician Edward Jenner, who in 1796 discovered a way to vaccinate people against smallpox. In the early 19th century researchers learned how to isolate drugs such as morphine and quinine from plants. But it was many decades before drug production started to become scientific.

In the interim, traditional pharmacy was becoming more commercial. The first U.S. drug manufacturing operation was established in Carlisle, Pennsylvania, in 1778 to supply medicines to George Washington's troops. The industry that developed in the 19th century was often less than respectable. For decades it was dominated by so-called patent medicine producers, who sold a variety of extracts, tinctures, syrups, and other concoctions. (Actually very few of these products were patented, since that would have required disclosure of their contents. They are more properly designated as proprietary drugs.)

The patent medicine men made elaborate claims for their products, often listing on the label dozens of ailments that would supposedly be cured quickly and cheaply. Some of the nostrums were merely ineffective solutions made up mainly of water. Yet others contained quantities of addictive substances such as opium or were poisonous.

By making their pitch directly to users, patent medicine companies came into conflict with the medical profession. The American Medical Association warned the public about the dangers of self-medication and in the process also came to the aid of its physician-members who prepared their own medicines. Yet some doctors saw that there was money to be made in large-scale production of legitimate pharmaceuticals. Companies such as Abbott Laboratories, Miles Laboratories, and Upjohn were established by physicians in the 1880s. During the same period, a variety of pharmacists, chemists, and entrepreneurs also began creating "ethical" drug houses such as Eli Lilly, A. H. Robins, and G. D. Searle. At the time, "ethical" referred to producers who revealed the contents of their products and sold to doctors rather than consumers. Today ethical drugs are those sold by prescription, while proprietary ones are those sold over the counter.

Despite advances such as the introduction of aspirin by the German company Frederich Bayer in 1899 and the development of a typhoid vaccine at about the same time, drug production was not put on a scientific basis until the work of the German biochemist Paul Ehrlich. He pioneered the idea that different bodily tissues have a selective affinity for specific chemical substances. He also built on the earlier work of Louis Pasteur that established the role of living organisms called bacteria in illness and other biological processes. Ehrlich paved the way for the development of sulfa drugs and antibiotics that fought against particular forms of bacteria, and he himself produced the first chemotherapeutic drug, which was used to treat syphilis.

In the following years advances in the discovery and production of drugs came much more frequently. Research in endocrinology led to the identification of insulin, and in 1928 the British physician Alexander Fleming discovered penicillin, the first of the great antibiotics but one that was effective for a limited range of diseases.

THE AGE OF WONDER DRUGS

In the late 1940s the creation of a series of antibiotics capable of fighting a broad spectrum of diseases ushered in what became known as the era of the "wonder drug." Newly prominent drug companies were frantically searching for new substances to turn into disease fighters while also devising methods for producing them in large quantities.

The pace quickened even more in the 1950s. The next wave of products consisted of tranquilizers such as Librium and amphetamines such as Dexedrine that were hailed as major advances in the treatment of mental illness. In 1954 Jonas Salk produced a vaccine for poliomyelitis. This period also saw important developments in research on hormonal chemistry. A small company in Mexico called Syntex found a way of producing large quantities of the female sex hormone progesterone from yams and synthesized a substance called norethiserone that controlled ovulation. Researchers for G. D. Searle separately produced a similar substance. While Searle and Parke-Davis (working with Syntex) put these discoveries on the market in 1957 as drugs to treat menstrual disorders, they realized they had the basis of an oral contraceptive. Parke-Davis was reluctant to market what was then a controversial product, but Searle brought out Enovid—the first version of what became known as "the pill"—in 1960. Within several years there was evidence linking Enovid with problems such as thrombophlebitis (inflammation of a clotted vein), but

Searle managed to convince the Food and Drug Administration (FDA) the pill was safe enough to remain on the market.

Although drug companies had become the darlings of Wall Street, they were considerably less popular in other quarters. No sooner had the pharmaceutical industry risen to fame with its miracle drugs than it was the subject of increasing criticism regarding both the safety and the pricing of its products.

The safety issue actually stemmed back to the late 19th century, when Dr. Harvey W. Wiley led a 25-year battle against the harmful quack medicines of the era. His efforts helped bring about the Pure Food and Drug Act of 1906 and the creation of the FDA. Unfortunately the Supreme Court interpreted the law as prohibiting only mislabeling. The Sherley Amendment of 1912 forbade false and fraudulent therapeutic claims. But the courts decided that fraudulent intent had to be proven—a difficult matter—so there was still no effective legislation against harmful medicines.

The turning point came in the 1930s. The Roosevelt administration was pushing for stricter regulation, which the industry as usual was fighting. Then came the case of the S. E. Massengill Company of Bristol, Tennessee. The firm was producing Elixir of Sulfanilamide, the first liquid version of an effective antibiotic. The product was not tested, and it turned out that the substance the active ingredient was dissolved in had a devastating effect on the kidney. More than 100 users suffered a slow, agonizing death before the cause was discovered. The outcry over the Elixir case helped bring about passage of the Food, Drug and Cosmetic Act of 1938, which established much stricter safety standards and rules for testing.

Although the industry grumbled about the cost of the testing procedures and the delays in FDA approval, it was widely thought that the days of harmful medicines were over. That notion began to dissolve with the case of Chloromycetin, an antibiotic that was introduced by Parke-Davis in 1949 and believed to have fewer side effects than other drugs of the sort. Although the drug was originally supposed to be used for typhoid fever, Parke-Davis promoted it heavily, and by the early 1950s it was being prescribed for a wide variety of less serious ailments. Soon the drug was being linked to severe and irreversible anemia. Parke-Davis defended its product, and after an investigation the FDA allowed it to remain on the market with a warning label.

The industry also came under fire for the high costs of its products. This stemmed in part from changes in the marketing practices of the industry. Traditionally drug companies dealt mainly with pharmacies, and doctors made out their prescriptions according to generic names. With the rise of the wonder drugs, physicians began specifying brand names. The industry started spending huge sums encouraging this practice. Armies of "detail men" (sales representatives) were sent out by the drug houses to visit doctors to familiarize them with the latest products and make pitches for their own brands. The companies also spent large sums advertising in medical journals and mailing out free samples and lavishly printed brochures to doctors.

The industry also encouraged brand name consciousness by labeling new products with catchy, easy-to-remember brand names and cumbersome, hard-to-remember generic designations. For example the Swiss company Hoffman-La Roche's popular tranquilizer Librium was generically called chlordiazepoxide hydrochloride. This practice meant that once a drug's 17-year patent protection expired, doctors would be likely to go on prescribing the brand name even if cheaper generic equivalents had come on the market.

All of these practices inflated the expenses of the big drug houses and along with high research costs were reflected in their prices. Some felt the process had gotten out of hand, and in 1959 Senator Estes Kefauver of Tennessee opened hearings on the subject. The senator kicked up a storm and in 1961 issued a report concluding that prescription drug prices were unreasonable in relation to production costs.

Kefauver's proposed legislation to remedy this and other problems relating to the industry was going nowhere when another drug tragedy occurred. This time it was the linking of the sedative thalidomide to serious birth defects in the children of women who took the drug while pregnant. Approval to sell thalidomide in the United States had been refused by the FDA, but after reports on its hazards appeared abroad, there was concern about the thousands of U.S. patients who had been given the drug on an experimental basis.

Amid the scare, Congress revived and passed Kefauver's bill but without the pricing provisions. The 1962 legislation set stricter standards for manufacturing and rules for reporting to the

FDA, made it easier for the government to stop the sale of drugs found to be harmful after approval, required certification of each batch of antibiotics, and required that drugs be effective as well as safe. The pricing issue was brought up again by Senator Gaylord Nelson of Wisconsin in 1967 hearings and at other times but never resulted in restrictive legislation. Allegations of improper testing and lax FDA enforcement were also persistent, particularly later during the Reagan administration.

THE SEARCH FOR "MAGIC BULLETS"

By the early 1970s the drug business was under a cloud. The number of new drugs had been steadily declining, falling from more than 300 in 1959 to fewer than 100 in 1973. Companies that had grown fat on various wonder drugs of the early postwar period were facing patent expirations. Federal government impatience with the rising cost of medicine had prompted plans to require medicaid and medicare patients to use the cheapest available form of drugs—low-priced generics rather than the brand name products that brought healthier profits to producers. The FDA and the Federal Trade Commission were also getting tougher on the advertising claims made for over-the-counter products.

It was not long, however, before some rays of sunshine began to appear for the industry. Advances in molecular biology and biochemistry were promising a new generation of highly effective drugs for specific ailments. Researchers, who were systematically studying thousands of possible chemical structures in the search for "magic bullets," began to achieve impressive results.

The most successful of the new wave of drugs to reach the market was Tagamet, a major breakthrough in the treatment of peptic ulcers. Developed and sold by SmithKline and French (now SmithKline Beckman), Tagamet's virtue was that it did not merely help the body deal with the effects of an ulcer but actually stopped the production of acid. The drug became one of the most widely prescribed pharmaceuticals in the world and propelled the formerly sleepy SmithKline to the upper ranks of the industry.

Tagamet also prompted an industry scramble—dubbed "Tagamania"—to find similar superdrugs. Companies started escalating their research budgets, which in the aggregate increased from about $1 billion in 1976 to $4 billion in 1985. The buzz phrase was "custom-designed drugs," meaning those that interacted with specific cellular processes in the body. Taking advantage of new knowledge concerning "receptors" (complex proteins on cell surfaces, where reactions with drug molecules take place), researchers started with the chemistry of the tissue and then tried to devise an appropriate drug. There was also a move toward drugs that did not simply treat the symptoms of disease but actually attacked the cause of the problem at the cellular level.

The areas of greatest activity included cardiovascular drugs ("beta blockers" and calcium antagonists to prevent angina and hypertension), drugs to treat arthritis, and anti-inflammatory drugs.

While some observers were comparing these breakthroughs to the wonder-drug era of the 1940s, the reputation of the industry was being marred by a series of controversies over the safety of its products. Among these were:

Copper-7: An intrauterine contraceptive device introduced by G. D. Searle in 1974. Hundreds of lawsuits linking use of the device to problems such as pelvic infections and infertility prompted Searle to take Copper-7 and its other IUD product off the market in 1986.

Dalkon shield: A contraceptive device sold by A. H. Robins from 1971 to 1974. Many users ended up having problems with infertility and sometimes fatal infections. By the mid-1980s the company had been hit with more than 10,000 lawsuits. Deciding that it did not have the resources to handle all the settlements, the company filed for Chapter 11 protection in 1985.

Darvon: A painkiller introduced by Eli Lilly in 1957 as a nonnarcotic alternative to morphine and codeine. The drug had a huge success, but it was later accused of being less effective than aspirin yet quite addictive. Despite many calls to ban the drug, the FDA simply criticized Lilly for inadequate warning labels and allowed it to keep Darvon on the market.

DES (diethylstilbestrol): A drug originally synthesized in 1938 and used by women to prevent miscarriages. Despite evidence that it caused cancer in animals, the product was marketed by several companies. By the 1970s daughters of women who had used DES were reporting complications including vaginal and cervical cancers.

Depo-Provera: A long-lasting contraceptive that is injected into a woman. The product was never approved in the United States despite years of effort by its producer Upjohn. Yet it has been marketed aggressively abroad (especially in the Third World), where it has been linked to serious side effects and birth defects.

Oraflex: An antiarthritis drug introduced with great fanfare by Eli Lilly in 1982. There were soon reports linking the drug to internal bleeding and kidney and liver problems. In 1985 Lilly pleaded guilty to charges that it had failed to inform the FDA about four deaths and other illnesses related to use of the drug.

Despite these setbacks, the drug business in the mid-1980s was riding high. Impressive new drugs continued to come out of the research pipeline, and demographic trends—namely the increasing elderly proportion of the population—suggested a growing demand for the industry's wares. Companies even made the best of the rise of generics, which reached about 20 percent of the market, by selling so-called branded generics: versions of drugs priced midway between brand name products and those from generic producers. New diseases such as AIDS, while a tragedy for thousands of victims, represented lucrative potential markets for the industry; in the mid-1980s numerous companies were searching for an effective AIDS vaccine.

Drug companies were also benefiting from the rapid growth in the market for home diagnostic kits, a market that reached an estimated $200 million in 1985. Companies such as Hoffman-LaRoche and Syntex that produced drug-testing kits also stood to gain from the trend toward the testing of employees to detect the presence of illegal drugs.

The industry has also had success on Capitol Hill. In 1982 Congress passed legislation that provided increased tax incentives for companies to devote research efforts to so-called orphan diseases, those for which the potential number of users is too small to make it commercially attractive to develop drugs. The law also gave companies producing orphan drugs (defined as those needed by fewer than 200,000 patients) exclusive marketing licenses for seven years when the substances do not qualify for patent protection.

In 1984 President Reagan signed a landmark drug bill that represented a compromise in the conflict between brand name and generic producers. The law directed the FDA to expedite the approval process for generic versions of approved drugs, while allowing for branded drugs patent extensions of up to two years to make up for time taken up in the approval process.

In 1986 Congress passed a bill permitting the export of drugs not yet approved for sale in the United States. The law also set up a federal program to compensate children injured by vaccines.

THE BIOTECHNOLOGY REVOLUTION

Another cause for optimism in the drug industry stems from the rise over the past decade of an advanced form of biochemistry. Called genetic engineering or biotechnology, this new field involves the manipulation of DNA molecules to produce miraculous new drugs.

The story of biotechnology is basically that of the combination of scientific and entrepreneurial instincts. As biochemical researchers grew more sophisticated in their ability to rearrange genetic material, some of them quickly appreciated the commercial implications and acted on them. Cetus Corp., the oldest biotechnology firm, was established in California in 1971 by microbiologist Ronald Cape. Biotechnology pioneer Herbert Boyer of the University of California at San Francisco joined with venture capitalist Robert Swanson in 1976 to form Genentech, which went on to become the industry leader. Biogen was established in 1978 by an international group of scientists.

In the early years these companies did little more than research, so it was a sensation when Biogen announced in 1980 that it had succeeded in genetically restructuring bacteria to produce interferon, a highly effective disease-fighting agent found naturally in the body but only in very small amounts. Interferon was widely considered a potential cure for some forms of cancer as well as a variety of viral diseases.

A Supreme Court decision in 1980 was the Magna Charta for the industry. The Court ruled that new forms of life are eligible for protection under the patent laws. The new status of the industry made it more attractive to established companies. The limited investment in biotechnology by large corporations developed into a new gold rush. Some bought into the existing ventures, while others—among them numerous drug companies—set up their own biotechnology operations.

One of the industry's successful products has been a variety of monoclonal antibodies, copies of the body's disease-fighting agents. These substances were initially most effective as diagnostic devices, allowing people to test themselves for pregnancy or illness through methods that were much simpler and faster than traditional laboratory techniques. Similar results were being achieved with substances called DNA probes.

By the mid-1980s the biotechnology industry had come of age. In the United States several hundred companies were making use of about $2.5 billion of invested capital. The industry had succeeded in synthesizing human insulin and was awaiting FDA approval for interferon. Research was also proceeding on a new generation of safer and more effective vaccines as well as a substance called tissue plasminogen activator that dissolves clots that block arteries during heart attacks. Most exciting was the report from the National Cancer Institute in late 1985 that a substance called Interleukin-2, synthesized by Cetus, was showing impressive results in treating cancer patients.

From its earliest days biotechnology has been the subject of major controversy over safety. Critics have charged that the industry's practice of gene-splicing—the separation of DNA molecules and recombination of genetic material from different sources—could create dangerous organisms that, if accidentally released, could have disastrous health consequences.

Congressional efforts to establish new safety laws were inconclusive, and in 1978 the Department of Health, Education and Welfare asked the FDA and the Environmental Protection Agency to regulate the field through existing laws and National Institute of Health guidelines.

The safety crusade on biotechnology has to a great degree been the work of one man, Jeremy Rifkin, working out of a small organization in Washington called the Foundation on Economic Trends. Since the mid-1970s Rifkin has been warning of the hazards of genetic engineering and has effectively used the political and legal systems to carry on his crusade. In 1986 he forced the Agriculture Department to suspend the license of a small firm, Biologics Corp., whose genetically engineered vaccine for pigs was just beginning to be used by farmers. The license was restored, but Rifkin had made front-page news.

Rifkin was also the leading critic of a set of guidelines issued by the Reagan administration in 1986 for the supervision of biotechnology by five government agencies.

In July 1986 the FDA approved the first genetically altered vaccine for human use. Designed to protect against hepatitis B, the vaccine was developed by Chiron Corp. and was to be marketed by Merck. The industry sold only about $200 million worth of goods in 1985 but was expected to grow to more than $1 billion by the beginning of the 1990s.

THE RISE OF THE HOSPITAL

While drug production in the United States has always been a commercial endeavor, the institutional treatment of the ill has taken several different forms. Starting in the late 1960s the nearly extinct for-profit hospital began to make a dramatic comeback. While the growth in the new "hospital industry" started to slow down in the mid-1980s, corporations have staked out a major role in the practice of health care.

The role of hospitals of any kind in systematic health care is less than a century old. Before the late 19th century, hospitals were indistinguishable from almshouses, serving mainly as repositories for the ailing poor—what Paul Starr has called "places of dreaded impurity and exiled human wreckage."

Health care was largely performed by individual physicians in their offices or in the home of the patient. Since surgery was limited and health technology was primitive there was little need for large institutions aside from those sheltering victims of chronic diseases.

This situation began to change after the Civil War, the result to a great extent of the professionalization of nursing, the widening use of anesthesia, and the adoption of Joseph Lister's antiseptic techniques. The latter encouraged a greater range of surgical procedures by reducing the chances that the patient would die of infection.

Many of the early hospitals were established as profit-making endeavors by physicians with the backing of wealthy sponsors. Larger hospitals were set up as "voluntary" institutions, meaning they were supported by religious or philanthropic groups rather than by the government. As hospitals came to assume a more and more dominant role in the health care system in the 20th century, it was these nonprofit institutions that prevailed. Of the 4,306 U.S. hospitals in 1928, 1,889 were voluntary, 1,877 profit-making, and the remainder public. By 1960 there were only 856 for-profits, while the voluntaries had grown to 3,291. The growth of the nonprofits was aided by the Hill-Burton Act of 1946, which provided federal subsidies for their construction.

At the same time, the entire health system grew more and more complex. The voluntary hospitals set up Blue Cross private health insurance plans beginning in the 1930s. These were joined by Blue Shield plans, set up by medical societies to cover doctors' fees for hospital treatment. Various attempts to create a national insurance system were unsuccessful, though in the 1960s the federal government created health programs for the elderly (medicare) and the poor (medicaid).

In fact it was these programs, which brought enormous amounts of federal funds into health care, that stimulated the revival of profit-making hospital companies. Starting in the late 1960s companies such as Hospital Corporation of America (HCA) and Humana Inc. began purchasing nonprofit hospitals or else taking over their management.

Many hospital administrators welcomed this trend. In a period of rapidly rising costs and complicated government regulations, they found they could no longer manage effectively. Many joined nonprofit chains to take advantage of lower-cost purchasing and other economies of scale. Yet particularly in the West and Southeast, administrators turned to the private sector.

Calling themselves proprietary or investor owned, chains such as HCA introduced businesslike practices in the institutions they took over—so much so that critics charged that they were eroding the quality of health care. The pattern of the private chains, it was charged, was to "skim off" the most profitable patients, those fully insured people who needed short-term treatment not involving expensive procedures. Those without coverage or those requiring long-term care tended to be shunted off to public or nonprofit hospitals. The private chains are also accused of reducing staffing to inadequate levels and charging higher prices than nonprofit institutions.

Despite the controversy HCA and the others grew at rapid rates for two decades. By 1984 about 1,700 of the nation's 6,800 hospitals were investor owned. The industry talked boldly about seeking to introduce brand name consciousness into health care by setting up their own insurance plans or health maintenance organizations, so that a company would be associated with all aspects of care.

What brought the halcyon days to an end was the decision by the federal government finally to do something to control the problem of galloping hospital costs. In 1983 Congress established a prospective payment system for medicare. This involved the creation of some 470 diagnostic related groups (DRGs) and the setting of fixed reimbursement levels (adjusted for different regions of the country) for them. A medicare patient who entered the hospital had to be categorized according to a DRG, and the hospital would be reimbursed no more than the amount fixed for the DRG. If the institution could provide the care for less than the fixed amount, it could keep the difference.

At the same time, the attempts by corporations to cut down on employee health costs by raising deductibles and otherwise restricting medical insurance plans tended to reduce the amount of care people were seeking. Simultaneously there was an accelerating trend toward outpatient treatment for ailments that were previously handled in hospitals. Private companies began building freestanding clinics and emergency rooms (so-called Docs-in-the-box) to handle these procedures. The spread of health maintenance organizations—both nonprofit ones and for-profit chains such as Maxicare Health Plans—also reduced hospital visits by concentrating on preventive medicine. Consequently hospital utilization rates began to fall, reaching 62 percent in late 1985 compared with 75 percent at the beginning of the decade.

All of this spelled trouble for the private hospital companies. In October 1985 HCA, the biggest of the chains, announced that its earnings would probably be flat in 1986. The next day American Medical International, another leading chain, reported a fourth-quarter earnings drop of 38 percent. Wall Street, used to much more favorable news from the industry, panicked and began dumping hospital stocks. The companies as a group lost some $1.5 billion in market value in a single day. In addition the attempts by the industry, led by Humana, to set up their own insurance programs were having disappointing results.

Although troubled, the private hospital industry will surely survive. So will nonprofits, but many of them have adopted private-sector techniques such as advertising and product differentiation (luxury suites and other amenities) to attract patients. Hospitals have all but abandoned their traditional role as providers of vital public services and have leaped headlong into the medical-industrial complex.

LABOR RELATIONS

The growth of hospitals has been accompanied by the creation of a large nonprofessional labor force characterized by low status and low pay. Some union organizing began in San Francisco–area hospitals after World War I, but it was not until the late 1950s that the movement began to grow. One major obstacle to overcome was the fact that in 1947 nonprofit hospitals had succeeded in getting Congress to exempt them from the provisions of federal labor law.

The new wave of hospital organizing was closely linked to the civil rights movement in that minority workers were heavily represented in the industry. The spearhead of the drive was New York's District 1199 of the National Union of Hospital and Health Care Employees, a small union representing mainly drugstore workers. The union staged a 46-day strike against seven hospitals in 1959, winning improvements in wages and working conditions but not recognition. The union struck again in 1962, and the impasse was resolved only when Governor Nelson Rockefeller agreed that if the walkout was ended, he would press the state legislature to provide labor law protection for employees of nonprofit hospitals.

The law was passed, and District 1199 was firmly established as the collective bargaining representative in the voluntary institutions. Meanwhile, District Council 37 of the American Federation of State, County and Municipal Employees organized workers at the city's municipal hospitals, and Local 144 of the Service Employees International Union signed up employees at many of New York's proprietary institutions.

The organizing successes in New York spurred campaigns in other parts of the country. By 1967 some 8 percent of the country's hospitals had unions for all or some of their workers, compared with less than 3 percent in 1961. Outside of large northern cities successes did not come so easily. In Charleston, South Carolina, it took a 110-day walkout, including massive demonstrations and a threat by longshoremen to shut down the port, to win recognition.

Organizing was helped by the decision of Congress in 1974 to extend national labor law protection to workers at voluntary hospitals. Yet management in many parts of the country—including the Sun Belt regions, where the new private chains concentrated their activity—fought hard against unionization. Hospitals were among the most aggressive users of antiunion management consultants. By the mid-1980s the industry was still only about 20 percent organized.

In 1984 the National Union of Hospital and Health Care Employees separated from its parent, the Retail, Wholesale and Department Store Union, with which it had been on unfriendly terms for some time. However, District 1199 in New York, which accounted for about half of the hospital union's 150,000 members, remained with the parent union. District 1199, which had struck New York's voluntary hospitals in 1976, staged another militant strike of 47 days in the city in 1984.

Unionized workers in the pharmaceutical industry are represented mainly by the Oil, Chemical and Atomic Workers Union and the International Chemical Workers Union. The most notable confrontation of recent years occurred at industry leader Merck, which in 1984 locked out 730 workers in New Jersey, precipitating a strike at several Merck plants and a corporate campaign against the company. The strike was settled after three months.

LEADING COMPANIES

Abbott Laboratories was founded in 1888 by Dr. Wallace Abbott, who pioneered the use of pills consisting of only active ingredients rather than fluid extracts of entire plants. Abbott, an aggressive promoter, ran into trouble with the American Medical Association over his sale of shares in the company to doctors. In the following years the company devised products such as sodium pentothal (the so-called truth serum) but in the 1970s had repeated difficulties in its production of intravenous solutions and was the subject of the FDA's largest product recall.

Genentech became the leader of the biotechnology industry that emerged in the 1970s. Founded by a leading biochemist and a venture capitalist, the company came to epitomize the excitement of genetic engineering in the minds of the general public. When Genentech went public in 1980 there was a scramble to buy shares, which on the first day more than doubled from the initial price of $35. The company succeeded in synthesizing human insulin and a growth hormone called Protropin and is a leader in the development of interferon. In 1986 analysts were predicting that Genentech's blood clot dissolver could be a billion dollar a year product by the 1990s.

Hospital Corporation of America is the McDonald's of the private hospital business. It was established in 1968 by Dr. Thomas Frist of Nashville, his son Dr. Thomas Frist, Jr., and Jack Massey, one of the founders of Kentucky Fried Chicken. HCA became the largest of the commercial chains, and in 1986 it owned 258 institutions and managed 219 others. A 1983 attempt to acquire American Hospital Supply, a controversial deal because of that company's dominant role in its field, was defeated by a rival bid from Baxter Travenol Laboratories.

Eli Lilly & Co., one of the grand old names in the drug business, has been plagued in recent years with safety problems. Its Darvon analgesic was accused of being less effective than aspirin yet highly addictive. It was one of the producers of the estrogen DES, which has been linked to cancer in the daughters of women who used it. In 1985 Lilly admitted that it failed to inform the FDA about several deaths and other illnesses linked to its antiarthritis drug Oraflex. Lilly was founded in 1876 in Indianapolis by Eli Lilly, inventor of a process for coating pills with gelatin to make them easier to swallow. In the 1920s the company made its mark through the sale of insulin (extracted from animals) and was later a major producer of penicillin and Salk vaccine. From 1930 to 1960 it was usually the leader in the prescription drug business.

Merck & Co., the 1980s leader of the ethical drug industry in the United States, is a descendant of a German pharmaceutical house dating back to the 17th century. U.S. operations began around the turn of the century and became independent of the German Merck during World War I. Merck, one of the most highly regarded drug companies, was a leader in the development of vitamins and antibiotics and since the mid-1970s has brought out a variety of new drugs. In 1983 the company bought a majority interest in Banyu Pharmaceutical Co. of Tokyo.

Pfizer started out as a chemical company in the 19th century and achieved recognition as a drug house in the 1940s thanks to its successes in improving the production of penicillin. Pfizer was the first drug company to use aggressive marketing techniques, which shook up the genteel traditions of the industry but ended up being adopted. Pfizer developed a good reputation, but in the mid-1980s there were reports linking its antiarthritis drug Feldene to sometimes fatal internal bleeding.

G. D. Searle & Co., purchased by Monsanto for $2.7 billion in 1985, was founded in the Midwest in the 1880s. Searle became a full-line manufacturer and starting in 1949 enjoyed a great success with Dramamine, a drug for treating motion sickness that was turned into an over-the-counter product in 1954. In 1960 the company introduced the first oral contraceptive Enovid. Management of the firm was taken over by former Defense Secretary Donald Rumsfeld in 1977, and the Searle family sold off its interest in 1984. By the mid-1980s the company was facing hundreds of lawsuits based on harmful effects suffered by users of its Copper-7 intrauterine contraceptive device.

SmithKline Beckman, or SmithKline and French, as it used to be known, is one of the oldest U.S. drug houses. Founded in Philadelphia in the 1830s, the company produced a wide range of products and was the first regularly to send free samples to doctors. After World War II SmithKline was a leader in the development of tranquilizers and amphetamines. After a slump in the 1960s the company achieved a phenomenal success with Tagamet, an antiulcer medicine that was one of the most prominent of the custom-designed drugs that started to appear in the 1970s. In 1982 SmithKline spent $1 billion to purchase Beckman Instruments.

SOURCE GUIDE

LEADING STOCK ANALYSTS AND EXPERTS

Peter Drake, biotechnology analyst at Kidder Peabody.
Frederic Greenberg, drug analyst at Goldman Sachs.
John Hindelong, hospital analyst at Smith Barney.

Linda Miller, biotechnology analyst at Paine Webber.
Ronald Nordmann, drug analyst at Paine Webber.
Ronald Stern, drug analyst at First Boston.

TRADE ASSOCIATIONS AND UNIONS

American Hospital Association, Chicago.
Association of Biotechnology Companies, Washington, D.C.
Federation of American Hospitals (for-profits), Washington, D.C.
Industrial Biotechnology Association, Rockville, Maryland.
National Union of Hospital and Health Care Employees, New York.
Pharmaceutical Manufacturers Association, Washington, D.C.

DATA SOURCES AND DIRECTORIES

American Drug Index, an annual listing (Philadelphia: J. B. Lippincott).

The Biotechnology Directory, an annual guide to products, companies, research, and organizations, edited by J. Coombs (New York: Nature Press).

Drug and Cosmetic Catalog, an annual directory (New York: Harcourt Brace Jovanovich).

Genetic Engineering and Biotechnology Firms Worldwide Directory, an annual volume (Kingston, N.J.: Sittig & Noyes).

Investor-Owned Hospitals and Hospital Management Companies and *Statistical Profile of the Investor-Owned Hospital Industry*, both annual directories (Washington, D.C.: Federation of American Hospitals).

Physicians' Desk Reference, an annual guide to prescription drugs (Oradell, N.J.: Medical Economics).

Prescription Drug Industry Factbook, triennial (Washington, D.C.: Pharmaceutical Manufacturers Association).

TRADE PUBLICATIONS

BioTechnology, monthly.
Drug and Cosmetic Industry, monthly.
Drug Topics, fortnightly.
Genetic Engineering News, eight times a year.
Health Care Financing Review, quarterly.

Healthcare Financial Management, monthly.

Hospitals, fortnightly.

McGraw-Hill's Biotechnology Newswatch, fortnightly.

Modern Healthcare, monthly.

BOOKS AND REPORTS

Braithwaite, John. *Corporate Crime in the Pharmaceutical Industry*. Boston: Routledge & Kegan Paul, 1984.

Egan, John W., Harlow N. Higinbotham, and J. Fred Weston. *Economics of the Pharmaceutical Industry*. New York: Praeger Publishers, 1982.

Kotelchuck, David, ed. *Prognosis Negative: Crisis in the Health Care System*. New York: Vintage Books, 1976.

Mahoney, Tom. *The Merchants of Life: An Account of the American Pharmaceutical Industry*. New York: Harper & Row, 1959.

Mintz, Morton. *By Prescription Only*. Boston: Beacon Press, 1967.

————. *At Any Cost: Corporate Greed and the Dalkon Shield*. New York: Pantheon Books, 1985.

National Academy of Sciences. *The Competitive Status of the U.S. Pharmaceutical Industry*. Washington, D.C.: National Academy Press, 1983.

National Institute of Medicine. *The New Health Care for Profit*. Washington, D.C.: National Academy Press, 1983.

————. *For-Profit Enterprise in Health Care*. Washington, D.C.: National Academy Press, 1986.

Starr, Paul. *The Social Transformation of American Medicine*. New York: Basic Books, 1982.

U.S. Congress, Office of Technology Assessment. *Commercial Biotechnology: An International Assessment*. Washington, D.C.: January 1984.

Wohl, Stanley. *The Medical Industrial Complex*. New York: Harmony Books, 1984.

Yoxen, Edward. *The Gene Business*. New York: Harper & Row, 1983.

CHAPTER NINE

Food and Agriculture

Agriculture was the root of all commerce, and despite the Industrial Revolution, food production remains one of the largest spheres of business activity. Yet this production is no longer limited to what is grown or raised on the farm and brought directly to market. To a great extent, supplying the means of sustenance has become simply a branch of manufacturing. Large, corporate-type farms have taken over the land, and foodstuffs go through extensive processing and packaging before they reach the consumer. Modern farming, food processing, and the industries that provide the inputs they require—tractors, seeds, fertilizers, additives, and the like—together constitute a megasector of the economy known as agribusiness. In 1985 Americans spent some $300 billion on food for consumption at home.

FROM CANNING TO FREEZING

While societies have for at least a millenium preserved food through techniques such as drying, salting, and smoking, the origins of large-scale food processing are to be found in the 19th century. The development that began to free people from the constraints of time and distance regarding food consumption was the invention of vacuum packing. A Frenchman named Nicholas Appert is credited with having devised the process in 1809, but for what would today be called national security reasons it was kept secret. Similar techniques using tin cans rather than jars emerged in the United States in the 1820s.

Canning started developing into an important industry with the invention in the 1850s of equipment to produce the cans automatically. The use of canned foods by both armies during the Civil War gave a further boost to the industry, as large numbers of Americans grew used to tins and came to enjoy the consumption of exotic foods as well as familiar ones out of season.

It was during this period of the late 19th century that other food production techniques were devised. Gail Borden invented a meat biscuit for people on expeditions (unfortunately it had no taste) and went on to create a more successful product in condensed milk, which he patented in 1856. Wheat farming spread throughout the prairies and plains, and the great milling empires of the Washburn and Pillsbury families were established in Minneapolis. John Dorrance perfected condensed soup, and his employer Campbell Soup began marketing the product aggressively. Henry Heinz began establishing the first national brands for prosaic products such as pickles and catsup.

The meat industry also arose during this time. Cattle raising spread through the West, and once rail lines were completed Chicago became the center of the slaughtering trade. In the 1870s Gustavus Swift and Philip Armour established companies that went on to become the giants of meatpacking. Using assembly-line techniques and newly devised refrigerator cars, Swift and Armour extended the markets for their meat products across the country. But their operations did not always adhere to the most sanitary practices. The uproar caused by the publication in 1906 of *The Jungle*, Upton Sinclair's exposé of unhealthy conditions in meatpacking, prompted Congress to enact the first Pure Food and Drug Law.

The rise of factory food elicited a backlash in the form of evangelical-type nutrition movements. One of the crusaders was Mother Ellen White of the Adventist Church, who established a sanitarium in Battle Creek, Michigan, in 1866. Under the leadership of Dr. John Kellogg, the establishment became famous for having its patients eat dry, brittle food. The cereal concoctions served at Battle Creek were soon being marketed to a receptive public by, among others, William Kellogg (brother of the head of Battle Creek and founder of the Kellogg Company) and Charles

Post (a former patient at the sanitarium who called his version Grape-Nuts).

THE RISE OF THE FOOD ENGINEERS

Like the Civil War, World War II served to advance the food processing industry. Special packaging techniques used to feed the troops were later adapted to civilian use. The reluctance of women, who had gotten a taste of work outside the home during the war, to return to drudgery in the kitchen encouraged the invention of all sorts of prepared products, many of them in frozen form (the freezing of food was perfected by Clarence Birdseye, a sometime explorer, after World War I).

The creation of "instant" versions of food required a great leap forward in chemistry. Manufacturers had long grappled with the problem of making processed food more appetizing. In earlier periods this was done by adding sugar, salt, and vegetable colors. By the 1950s hundreds of chemical additives with unpronounceable names were devised and used to advance what came to be called food engineering. These included stabilizers and emulsifiers to maintain consistency, preservatives to prevent spoilage, and artificial flavors and colors to enhance taste and appearance.

Perhaps the leading paradigm of the rise of food engineering was the quest for a substance that would substitute for the cream used in coffee. In the early 1950s chemists devised an instant powdered version, dubbed Pream, that had the desired characteristics: it did not need to be refrigerated, and it was immune from spoilage. The problem was that it had the wrong taste. The Carnation Company improved on it with the introduction of Coffee-Mate in 1961. This product more convincingly imitated cream, and it stimulated an entire array of nondairy coffee "lighteners."

The notion of completely synthetic foods as the solution to world hunger enjoyed a vogue in the 1960s, along with great hopes for soybeans and fish protein concentrates. While completely lab-produced food did not advance very far, food engineering marched on. Convenience foods overwhelmed the nation's supermarkets, and it required an increasingly sophisticated knowledge of chemistry to understand the labels on foodstuffs. By the late 1970s genetic engineering was added to the industry's bag of tricks. For instance, companies such as Campbell Soup and Heinz have sponsored research aimed at developing "supertomatoes" with tough skins allowing them to be picked mechanically and shipped to soup and catsup factories with less damage. Some experiments have tried to create square tomatoes that would be even more efficient to process. Taste, of course, ends up being something less than super. By 1984 about $1 billion a year was being spent on food research and development.

ROLLER COASTER PRICES

Whereas technology was the preoccupation of the food industry in the 1950s and 1960s, the following decade saw the laws of economics return to center stage. In the early 1970s food prices changed their traditional behavior and shot ahead of other elements of the cost of living. The sharp price increases, especially for meat, in the early 1970s turned out to be linked to a huge sale of grain to the Soviet Union. Public resentment was increased as people began to realize the extent to which food production and distribution had been taken over by a behemoth known as agribusiness. As a result of the Soviet deal some public exposure was for the first time given to the giant grain trading companies such as Cargill and Continental Grain.

While farmers were certainly enjoying higher income in these years, the accusatory finger came to be pointed at the food processors and distributors, which were said to keep 60 cents of every dollar Americans spent on food. While food processing became one of the most profitable of industries, the prosperity on the farm was short lived.

By 1976 farm prices were sinking, and farmers with medium and small operations grew restless. The insurgent American Agricultural Movement, founded in 1977, called for a farmer's strike (which did not succeed) and organized a tractor blockade of Washington in 1978. The movement's demand was for an improvement in the federal government's price support program.

That program dates back to the Agricultural Adjustment Act of 1933, which sought to remedy the perennial problem of American farmers: overproduction and the consequent downward tendency of the prices they receive for their output. The 1933 law put the government in the business of providing subsidies and controlling acreage devoted to six basic crops. While the Agriculture Department paid out substantial sums each year to farmers—often on the condition that they not farm—the program did not protect them from severe economic crunches. In the late 1970s the farmers' rallying cry was for complete parity—an esoteric concept that meant a guarantee of supports that would keep farm prices in the same relationship to production costs as existed in the golden era of 1910–1914.

The farm movement never succeeded in winning its full agenda in Congress but managed to keep the price support program alive even while the Reagan administration was slashing subsidies of all sorts. In part this has been a result of the severe crisis of the farm sector in the 1980s, stemming from factors such as President Carter's embargo on grain sales to the Soviet Union, high interest rates, and sinking commodity prices.

The troubles in the farm sector have tended to accelerate the concentration of ownership; bigger operations are better able to weather the crisis. Of the 2.3 million farms still in existence in 1985, those with more than $100,000 in sales generated almost 70 percent of farm income and received 66 percent of government subsidies. Smaller family farmers had by 1985 fallen into desperate enough straits to warrant a charitable media event—Farm Aid—along the lines of the concerts organized for the starving people of Africa. The plight of the farmer was also worsened by the growing level of food imports. By 1986 the United States was reaching its first trade deficit in food since 1959.

The suffering of the farm sector has also brought grief to the industries that supply it, especially the farm equipment producers. Industry leaders such as International Harvester and Caterpillar Tractor have been saddled with heavy losses. Harvester—which came close to bankruptcy, suffered a six-month strike in 1979–80, and experienced a succession of management shake-ups—dropped out of the business in 1985. It sold its agricultural equipment line to Tenneco subsidiary J. I. Case and devoted itself to producing trucks under the new corporate name of Navistar International. Caterpillar, hit with major strikes in 1979 and 1982–83, moved more than half its production abroad. In 1985 Deere & Co. had about 50 percent of the depressed market and Case-Harvester about 25 percent.

UNCERTAINTY AND CONSOLIDATION AMONG THE PROCESSORS

Low farm prices spell prosperity rather than despair for the big food processors; for them it means reduced raw materials costs. The food industry has, however, faced a challenge in keeping up with the changing demographics and tastes of the great consuming masses.

The push toward convenience that occurred right after World War II returned with much greater force in the 1970s. The entry of millions of women into the waged labor market brought about a demand for foods that could be prepared in even less time and with appliances such as microwave ovens. But the new consumer requirements had other dimensions. There was much greater concern about nutrition and weight watching, while at the same time people were growing more sophisticated and adventuresome in their tastes.

These trends have prompted food companies to move in two major directions. On the one side they have been furiously developing products with reduced levels of sugar, salt, cholesterol, fat, and artificial ingredients. Adopting terms such as "natural" and "lite," the processors have given consumers the appearance if not always the reality of healthier foods. (There are no federal rules governing the use of these terms.)

The other move has been toward "upscale" products that may be more pleasing to the palate but work against the health trend. For instance, superpremium ice creams, which have greatly elevated levels of butterfat, were one of the success stories of the late 1970s and early 1980s. Once-specialized items such as croissants are produced and consumed on a mass level. Stouffer's Lean Cuisine line of frozen entrees represented an attempt to exploit both of these trends.

While hustling to keep up with the often contradictory desires of consumers, the food industry has also had to cope with the fact that the business has simply not been expanding at a torrid rate. Demographics have kept growth to 1 or 2 percent a year.

Companies have responded in several ways. One has been an intensification of the battle for market share. When a hot new area comes along (such as granola bars a few years ago) the big firms all jump in and heavily promote their versions. The pace of new-product introductions has accelerated, reaching more than 2,200 in 1985, though it must be noted that many of these were simply modifications of existing offerings. Another element of the market share battle has been the introduction of national brands to products (such as pasta) that were previously sold regionally or ones (such as fruits and vegetables) that were not sold by brand at all.

The other approach has been to grow by buying someone else's business. The once sleepy food industry has become a hotbed of merger activity. Acquisitions have come in three phases. Starting in the 1960s many companies responded to the first signs of slower growth by diversifying into other businesses. One popular area was toys: General Mills bought Parker Brothers, and Quaker Oats acquired Fisher-Price. Meatpacker Esmark generated lots of bad jokes when it acquired Playtex, a leading producer of women's undergarments, in 1975.

Many of the food companies were not successful as conglomerates, so the second wave of acquisitions was focused on the food industry itself. Following the early lead of Beatrice, which had been snapping up hundreds of small food producers since the 1950s, other processors began hunting for firms that would fit with their existing operations. Campbell Soup entered the dog food and pickle businesses; General Foods bought Entenmann's bakers; Heinz swept into the low-calorie market with the purchase of Weight Watchers International; Hershey acquired several pasta makers; and Pillsbury adopted Green Giant.

The third and most recent wave has been the most dramatic. Rather than simply acquiring relatively small producers, the food giants have become engrossed in a spectacular series of billion-dollar mergers—the largest outside of the oil industry. This phase may be said to have begun with the merger of Nabisco and Standard Brands in 1981. While that was billed as a consolidation of equals (the combined company was named Nabisco Brands), the following deals were more in the line of takeovers.

In 1984 Swiss food giant Nestlé offered to buy Carnation for $3 billion. The following year the big cigarette makers, seeking to diversify further out of tobacco, got into the act. R. J. Reynolds (which had already bought Del Monte in 1979) arranged to acquire Nabisco Brands for $4.9 billion. A few months later Philip Morris made a deal to take over giant General Foods for $5.6 billion.

The 10 Largest Food Companies, by 1985 Food Sales ($ Billions)

1.	General Foods	$9.022
2.	Beatrice	8.122
3.	Dart & Kraft	6.800
4.	IBP	6.755
5.	Anheuser-Busch	6.743
6.	Coca-Cola	6.479
7.	Nabisco Brands	6.253
8.	PepsiCo	5.716
9.	R. J. Reynolds	4.698
10.	Archer Daniels Midland	4.540

Source: *Food Processing*, December 1985.

Perhaps more remarkable was the series of deals that began with a 1983 attempt by David Mahoney, chief executive of Norton Simon, to take his food-based conglomerate private through a leveraged buyout. Mahoney was thwarted when the company was instead acquired for $977 million by Esmark (the name adopted by meatpacker Swift & Company in 1973). A year later Kohlberg, Kravis, Roberts & Co. tried to take Esmark private through an LBO, only to be outbid by Beatrice, which paid $2.7 billion. In 1985 the Kohlberg firm turned around and proposed an LBO of industry octopus Beatrice. This time the buyout went through, for a final price of $6.2 billion.

THE CRISIS OF THE MEATPACKING INDUSTRY

While many food processors look attractive to tobacco companies, one segment of the business has been mired in crisis for some time. The once powerful meatpacking industry has been crippled by changing patterns of consumption and high costs.

Actually there are two segments to the industry. The old-line producers have had the most difficulties. Some of their tribulations were caused by the rise in the 1960s of a new generation of meatpackers—especially Iowa Beef Processors, now owned by Occidental Petroleum and called IBP—that set up their slaughterhouses right in the cattle-raising areas, thus enjoying much lower costs than the companies stuck with facilities in Chicago and other cities.

Most of the older packers ended up being acquired or going through other transformations: Greyhound bought Armour (and later sold it to ConAgra); General Foods bought Oscar Mayer;

Swift became Esmark, and its meatpacking business was later spun off as Swift Independent Co.; and Wilson Foods, purchased by LTV in 1967, was spun off in 1981 and went into Chapter 11 in 1983. The industry is consolidating, and the survivors are concentrating on the more profitable processed products rather than simple slaughtered meat.

STEPS TOWARD DEREGULATION

The initial Pure Food and Drug Law inspired by Upton Sinclair's revelations about meatpacking was followed in 1938 by the Food, Drug and Cosmetic Act. While this law provided for additional regulation of food production, it put the burden on the Food and Drug Administration to prove that any substance used in processing was unsafe.

The cancer scares of the 1950s helped bring about a series of amendments in 1958 that shifted the burden of proof to manufacturers to show that substances were safe. The 1958 legislation also included a provision, known as the Delaney clause, that put an absolute ban on the use of any additive found in laboratory tests to cause cancer in animals or humans. The law did, however, allow manufacturers to continue employing additives already in use and "generally regarded as safe." Some of these, including the artificial sweetener cyclamate, were later found to be carcinogenic, and the FDA began the long process of testing them all.

There has for many years been heated debate on the use of food additives. The industry has defended the substances as safe and essential to providing the variety of foods American consumers want. Critics have warned of possible health risks. The FDA has wavered between strong action and indulgence of the industry, delaying for many years the implementation of a ban on a group of artificial colors. The public has been perplexed.

In 1985 FDA commissioner Frank Young began taking steps to loosen regulation. Young explicitly said that the agency would adopt an unorthodox view of the Delaney clause: that substances posing only a *small* risk of cancer could be authorized. Young put this into action in late 1985, when the agency permitted the use of the carcinogen methylene chloride in decaffeinating coffee.

The FDA has also moved to drop barriers to the controversial practice of food irradiation. The process, developed in the 1950s, is said to be a superior form of preservation because less heat is used than in other techniques. Irradiation is permitted in a number of other countries, but opponents in the United States argue that the long-term health effects of the practice are not known. Irradiation was given a boost in 1984 after the Environmental Protection Agency halted the use of the pesticide ethylene dibromide on stored grain. In 1985 the FDA gave approval for Radiation Technology of Rockaway, New Jersey—a leader in the business—to begin irradiating pork and later authorized wider use of the process.

LABOR RELATIONS

The creation of large-scale agricultural operations in California in the late 19th century brought with it the first farm labor organizing. The miserable conditions under which the mostly Chinese and Japanese immigrant labor force toiled made the big farms a focus of agitation by the Industrial Workers of the World in the early years of the 20th century. But the group's Agricultural Workers Organization fell prey along with the rest of the IWW to the repression of radicals during and after World War I.

Militancy in the fields arose again in the 1930s especially among Mexican workers, who had become the largest immigrant group in the California farm labor force. The Communist party set up the Cannery and Agricultural Workers Industrial Union, which won some strikes in the early 1930s but found organizing difficult after California became flooded with desperate Dust Bowl refugees. Tensions between rival AFL and CIO organizers also limited the organizing progress of the period.

Greater success was achieved in Hawaii. Harry Bridges' International Longshoremen's and Warehousemen's Union made an impressive effort in the 1940s to organize the multiethnic labor force of the sugar and pineapple plantations of the islands. The ILWU won passage of legislation that sanctioned organizing among Hawaiian plantation workers—a right denied their brethren on the mainland. After a series of major strikes the ILWU was firmly entrenched, and the Hawaiian farmworkers got some of the best wages and conditions of agricultural laborers anywhere.

Back on the mainland there was a resumption of farm organizing after the war, but it was complicated by the establishment of the *bracero* program, under which growers were allowed to bring in (low-wage) workers from Mexico to toil in the fields. Established unions were once again unable to overcome their rivalries, and the major advance in farmworker organizing did not come until the 1960s, when a Chicano organizer named Cesar Chavez put together an association closely tied to the Roman Catholic Church.

Chavez's National Farm Workers' Association joined with Filipino workers in a mid-1960s strike against grape growers in Delano, California. Taking advantage of the fact that farmworkers were exempt from federal labor law and thus were not constrained by the ban on secondary actions, Chavez expanded the strike to a consumer boycott, particularly against the products of Schenley Industries. Chavez gained the support of political figures such as Senator Robert Kennedy, and after a 230-mile *peregrinaciones* (pilgrimage) to Sacramento to request action on farm labor by the governor, the union was recognized by Schenley. Chavez's organization, which became the United Farm Workers, continued its campaign against other producers of table grapes and won contracts with the major growers in 1970.

The UFW then moved on to the California lettuce and strawberry fields, but the union ran into increasing competition from the Teamsters, who increased their foothold in agriculture by offering sweetheart deals to the growers. The two unions signed an agreement in 1977 that defined separate jurisdictions, but rivalry continued (and in 1984 the Teamsters declined to renew the pact).

Chavez scored a major victory in 1975 when he got the California legislature to enact a collective bargaining law for farmworkers. The UFW made good use of the law, especially in a drawn-out but largely successful strike against lettuce growers in 1979. But the future of the UFW remained threatened by two forces: an internal rebellion in the union against the autocratic leadership of Chavez and the march of mechanization in the fields. The union also faced a less sympathetic figure in the California statehouse after George Deukmejian succeeded Jerry Brown as governor in 1983.

The UFW never expanded its organizing efforts much beyond California, so it was another group, calling itself the Farm Labor Organizing Committee, that took up the plight of the migrant laborers who picked tomatoes and cucumbers in Ohio and Michigan. The committee organized a strike against the growers (who mainly supplied Campbell Soup) in 1978 and a boycott of Campbell products in 1979. Finally in 1986 the workers triumphed, getting both the growers and Campbell to sign a contract.

The other major area of labor confrontation in the food industry has been meatpacking. Unionism among butchers began after the Civil War as the big meatpacking operations were formed. The Amalgamated Meat Cutters union was chartered by the AFL in 1897. The union suffered major strike defeats in 1904 and 1922, and in the 1930s it saw the rise of a rival CIO union, the United Packinghouse Workers of America. The two bodies finally merged in 1968.

In the early 1980s the major meatpackers launched an all-out assault on labor costs. Companies successfully pressured the United Food and Commercial Workers (formed by the 1979 merger of the Meat Cutters and the Retail Clerks International union) to grant wage concessions. In some cases plants were closed down and then reopened under new management that renounced previous labor agreements, as happened after Armour shut down its operations and sold them to ConAgra. An even more drastic approach was taken by Wilson Foods. In 1983 the company, claiming that its labor costs were unbearable, entered Chapter 11 for the purpose of abrogating its union contracts. After doing so, Wilson slashed wages by as much as 50 percent and kept operating.

Wage cuts and bankruptcy were also the fate of Rath Packing, whose owners decided to sell the business to the employees in 1980. The crisis of the industry made it difficult for this experiment in worker ownership to succeed. In late 1983 the management of Rath followed Wilson's lead by filing for Chapter 11 and getting a bankruptcy judge to set aside the labor contract. Despite the bitterness this caused, Rath's workers made further concessions; but it was not enough, and the company headed for liquidation.

The national leadership of the foodworkers' union has tolerated concessions as an alternative to additional plant closings. But some locals have adopted a more militant posture. The leading example was Local P–9, which called a strike against Hormel (a leading pork processor and one of the last independent firms in the industry) after the company unilaterally cut wages more than 20 percent in 1984. The local hired consultants Ray Rogers and Ed Allen, who began a corporate campaign against Hormel and urged the strikers to pursue their battle, even after the union's national leaders denounced the walkout as "suicidal" and ordered it to end. When Local P–9 kept up its defiance, the UFCW took over the local and negotiated a new contract with Hormel.

LEADING COMPANIES

Beatrice is the lumbering giant of the food industry. Founded in Nebraska in 1894 as a middleman operation for dairy and poultry products, the company grew into a large dairy producer in the first half of the 20th century. Starting in the early 1950s Beatrice went on a dazzling buying spree, acquiring several hundred food companies. Beatrice itself kept a low profile and allowed its many businesses to operate quite independently. The obsession with growth came under some criticism in the 1970s, and after James Dutt won a boardroom battle for control of the company in 1979, he set out to sell a number of money-losing and even some successful businesses. He later reorganized the company and launched a campaign to make the Beatrice name known to consumers. Dutt ran afoul of the company's board and was ousted in 1985. A few months later, Kohlberg, Kravis, Roberts & Co. arranged to take the company private for more than $6 billion. The position of chief executive was given to Donald Kelly, former head of Esmark (bought by Beatrice in 1984). Kelly then embarked on a process of selling off chunks of the company.

Campbell Soup was built on the invention of condensed soup in the 1890s by chemist John Dorrance, who worked for his uncle's canning company. The firm had a big success with the product, making Campbell into one of the first national food brands. The firm bought Pepperidge Farm, a producer of premium baked goods, in 1961 and in the 1970s diversified into businesses such as pickles, chocolate, dog food, and restaurants. Campbell has pursued growth through acquisition into the 1980s, with purchases such as Mrs. Paul's Kitchens, a leading frozen-fish producer.

Cargill is the largest of the highly secretive half-dozen companies that dominate the world grain trade. Privately held Cargill was founded in the 1860s by Will Cargill, who along with Frank

Peavey soon dominated the U.S. grain business. Under the leadership of the Cargill and MacMillan families, the company gained a reputation as a "faceless giant." It along with the other big trading companies got some unwelcome attention in the 1970s because of their role in arranging the controversial Soviet grain sales. In recent decades Cargill has branched out into a variety of other businesses, including salt mining, barge construction, and sugar. In 1978 it acquired meatpacker MBPXL. The company's staggering size was revealed in late 1985, when it made one of its infrequent disclosures of financial results: For the year ending May 1985, revenues were more than $32 billion, making Cargill the country's largest private company.

General Foods has for many years been the leading innovator in the food industry. The company dates back to the cereal business started by Charles Post after his time at the Battle Creek Sanitarium. Postum Cereal later merged with the Jell-O Company and Clarence Birdseye's frozen-food operations. General Foods has long been a leader in coffee roasting, frozen vegetables, and other segments. During the early 1980s the company sought to reduce its dependence on mature products by acquiring companies such as Entenmann's bakers, the Ronzoni pasta company, and meatpacker Oscar Mayer. GF also scored with new products such as Crystal Light powdered beverage and Jell-O Pudding Pops. In 1985 the company was acquired by Philip Morris for more than $5 billion.

General Mills was put together in 1928 by Minneapolis miller James Bell and half a dozen other big millers from across the country. The company became a major figure in the cereal (Wheaties, Cheerios) and flour businesses. In the 1960s it diversified into areas such as toys and clothing, but the nonfood businesses were spun off in 1985.

H. J. Heinz has been a leader in the production of pickles, relishes, sauces, and condiments for more than a century. It is perhaps best known for its catsup and its 57 Varieties slogan (an arbitrary number from the start). Heinz bought the Ore-Ida frozen-potato business in 1965 and Weight Watchers foods in 1978. Under chief executive Anthony O'Reilly the company has emphasized cost controls and has sought to expand its already extensive foreign operations.

Kellogg, the leader in the breakfast cereal market, has resisted diversification. Founded by William Kellogg to sell what was then a health food—wheat flakes—the company survived a long Federal Trade Commission antitrust action against the leaders of the cereal industry in the 1970s. After becoming chief executive in 1979, William LaMothe launched a campaign to increase market share and discouraged a takeover by buying back 20 percent of the company's stock.

Kraft had its origins in the cheese business that James Kraft started in Chicago in 1903 and in a group of dairy companies. Functioning as a subsidiary of National Dairy Products, Kraft produced processed favorites such as Velveeta cheese spread and Miracle Whip salad dressing. In 1980 the company merged with Dart Industries, maker of Tupperware products, Duracell batteries, and other items. Six years later Dart and Kraft decided to go their separate ways, with Kraft keeping the food businesses and Duracell, and Dart holding onto everything else.

Pillsbury was founded in 1869 by Charles Pillsbury, who went on to become one of the pillars of the Minneapolis milling business. Known mainly as a producer of flour and other baked products (its Doughboy is one of the more famous advertising characters), the company got into the restaurant business in the 1960s with the purchase of Burger King. William Spoor, who ran Pillsbury from 1973 to 1985, arranged the acquisition of Green Giant (the largest packer of peas and corn), Haagen-Dazs ice cream, and Van de Kamp's (a specialty food producer).

Quaker Oats was formed in the late 19th century by a group of oatmeal millers; the Quaker name was adopted in 1901. The company became the leader in hot cereals and also was one of the early producers of pet food. Starting in 1969 the company branched out into other food areas, such as Celeste frozen pizza and Stokely Van Camp, maker of pork and beans and Gatorade drink. In 1986 Quaker purchased Anderson, Clayton & Co., best known as the producer of Gaines dog food.

RJR Nabisco was the result, first, of the 1981 merger of Nabisco and Standard Brands and then the 1985 purchase of the combined company by R. J. Reynolds. Nabisco itself was born of the merger of two rival baking groups in 1898. The company developed the first brand name cracker (Uneeda) and went on to dominate the cookie and cracker market with brands such as Ritz, Oreo, and Fig Newton. Standard Brands was built on Fleischmann yeast and gin, Royal baking powder, and Chase & Sanborn coffee. Reynolds entered the food business with the 1966 purchase of Chun King Chinese foods.

SOURCE GUIDE

LEADING STOCK ANALYSTS AND EXPERTS

George Abraham, a leading meatpacking consultant, of Abraham & Associates, Sarasota, Florida.

William Leach, food industry analyst at Donaldson, Lufkin & Jenrette.

William Maguire, food industry analyst at Merrill Lynch.

Emanuel Melichar, an economist at the Federal Reserve who is an expert on agricultural economics.

TRADE ASSOCIATIONS AND UNIONS

American Frozen Food Institute, McLean, Virginia.

American Meat Institute, Arlington, Virginia.

Grocery Manufacturers of America, Washington, D.C.

National Food Processors Association, Washington, D.C.

United Farm Workers of America, Keene, California.

United Food & Commercial Workers International Union, Washington, D.C.

DATA SOURCES AND DIRECTORIES

Agricultural Statistics and the *Handbook of Agricultural Charts*, annual volumes (Washington, D.C.: U.S. Department of Agriculture).

Food Engineering's Directory of U.S. Food Plants, published biennially (Radnor, Penn.: Chilton).

Hereld's 5,000—The Directory of Leading U.S. Food, Confectionary and Beverage Manufacturers, published semiannually (Lawrenceville, N.J.: Hereld Organization).

TRADE PUBLICATIONS

Agricultural Outlook (U.S. Department of Agriculture), monthly.

Food Engineering, monthly.

Food Processing, monthly.

Food Technology, monthly.

Frozen Food Age, monthly.

Meat Industry, monthly.

Milling and Baking News, weekly.

National Food Review (U.S. Department of Agriculture), quarterly.

National Provisioner, weekly.

BOOKS AND REPORTS

George, Susan. *Feeding the Few: Corporate Control of Food.* Washington, D.C.: Institute for Policy Studies, no date.

Marsh, Barbara. *A Corporate Tragedy: The Agony of International Harvester Co.* Garden City, N.Y.: Doubleday Publishing, 1985.

Meister, Dick, and Anne Loftis. *A Long Time Coming: The Struggle to Unionize America's Farm Workers.* New York: Macmillan, 1977.

Morgan, Dan. *Merchants of Grain.* New York: Penguin Books, 1980.

Root, Waverly, and Richard de Rochemont. *Eating in America: A History.* New York: William Morrow, 1976.

U.S. Congress, Office of Technology Assessment. *Technology, Public Policy and the Changing Structure of American Agriculture.* Washington, D.C.: March 1986.

_____

CHAPTER TEN

Restaurants, Hotels, and Casinos

Restaurants and hotels have traditionally been among the most entrepreneurial of businesses in the sense that the barriers to entry are relatively minor. Inns, taverns, and other public places have been around for centuries and have represented the easiest route for enterprising souls who want to escape from the laboring classes. Proprietors of restaurants and small hotels work long, hard hours and put their personal mark on the establishment. This form of commerce is the quintessential small business.

Yet in early 20th century America a new approach to the business of feeding and lodging was beginning to take shape. In 1919 a man named Conrad Hilton bought and renovated a small hotel in Cisco, Texas. In 1925 Howard Johnson took over a money-losing drugstore in Quincy, Massachusetts, and made a hit selling homemade ice cream. In 1927 John Willard Marriott opened a root beer stand in Washington, D.C. and then branched into spicy Mexican food during the winter months.

From such unlikely beginnings these three men built empires that have changed the landscape of the country. Joined by McDonald's hamburger stands and Holiday Inns in the mid-1950s, these franchised and corporate-owned hotels and restaurants have replaced smaller, locally owned establishments and turned food and lodging into major industries.

THE FAST-FOOD REVOLUTION

The man who deserves the most credit or blame for transforming the eating habits of America is Ray Kroc. A sometime piano player and paper cup salesman, Kroc was 52 and the distributor of Multimixer milkshake machines when he had what amounted to a religious experience in 1954. It occurred while he was visiting a major customer, the McDonald Brothers, who operated a roadside hamburger stand in San Bernardino, California.

Kroc was overwhelmed by the volume of business the McDonalds were enjoying by serving up bags of burgers, french fries, and milkshakes with factorylike efficiency. While the brothers were satisfied with their modest gold mine, Kroc immediately envisioned a string of such establishments across the country. He made a deal with the McDonalds under which Kroc got the right to use their name and methods in franchising the concept and the brothers would get a bit more than a quarter of the 1.9 percent of the franchisee's gross to be collected by Kroc.

The McDonald's concept spread like a brush fire: The number of stores jumped from dozens to hundreds, and the number of hamburgers sold—displayed on a sign below the golden arches—soared into the billions. Kroc established rigid standards by which the stands had to be operated; in fact he turned the management of a McDonald's into a sort of science, the precepts of which are taught to aspiring store managers at an institution called Hamburger University.

Kroc's system essentially involved the industrialization of food service: the use of equipment and procedures that were so defined that a totally inexperienced teenager—the preferred employee—could be inserted in the system and function with no difficulty. The result was a perfectly tuned machine turning out utterly predictable food in a wholesome and unthreatening environment. Kroc summarized his approach as Quality, Service, Cleanliness, and Value.

The remarkable rise of McDonald's served as the catalyst for the emergence of a national fast-food industry. The diners and greasy spoons that lined the country's roads were steadily replaced by the familiar outlets of a small number of major chains. The pattern of the hamburger business was repeated in other sectors such as fried chicken (Kentucky Fried Chicken), pizza (Pizza Hut), fish (Arthur Treacher's), and even restaurants with more extensive menus (Denny's).

The go-go atmosphere of fast food in the 1960s brought the business to the attention of large corporations. Pillsbury acquired Burger King in 1967, General Foods bought the Burger Chef chain in 1968, and Heublein purchased Kentucky Fried Chicken in 1971. Later PepsiCo acquired Pizza Hut and Taco Bell, and Hershey Foods bought Friendly Ice Cream Corp.

The industry continued to grow in the 1970s, helped by demographic changes such as the movement of women into the waged labor market and by economic changes such as the sharp rise in the cost of food used to prepare meals at home. Aided by extensive marketing and advertising expenditures, the chains turned fast-food "dining" into a socially acceptable way for a family to feed itself.

Using devices such as the Ronald McDonald character, McDonald's in particular won the loyalty of children, who became increasingly important in determining where a family was going to eat out. In 1972 McDonald's reached $1 billion in total store sales and surpassed the U.S. Army as the nation's biggest dispenser of meals.

The supremacy of McDonald's in the hamburger business began to be challenged in the 1970s. After initially holding back the necessary investment in Burger King, Pillsbury gave its subsidiary the resources to compete more effectively with the industry leader. Meanwhile an executive of Arthur Treacher's Fish & Chips decided to establish a chain that would serve higher-quality and more-substantial burgers than the ones purveyed by McDonald's. R. David Thomas named the firm after his daughter, and Wendy's eventually became one of the largest chains in the country.

By the 1980s both Wendy's and Burger King were prepared to challenge the predominance of the McDonald's empire. Burger King introduced successful nonhamburger menu items and in 1982 initiated the aggressive advertising campaign that came to be known as the Battle of the Burgers. Later Wendy's joined the fray with its now famous "Where's the beef?" commercials, which exploited the fact that McDonald's had traditionally been stingy with the portion of meat in its hamburgers. McDonald's was shaken by these assaults but continued to grow at a handsome rate, thanks in part to popular new offerings such as Egg McMuffins (which opened the breakfast market to the chains), Chicken McNuggets, and later the McD.L.T., a burger with lettuce and tomato served in such a way that the meat remained hot and the vegetables cool until the thing was ready to be consumed.

Today the hamburger business remains the dominant force in

The 10 Largest Restaurant Chains, by 1985 Systemwide Sales ($ Billions)

1.	McDonald's	$12.520
2.	Burger King	5.085
3.	Kentucky Fried Chicken	3.286
4.	Wendy's	3.150
5.	Hardee's	2.814
6.	Marriott Food Service Management	2.290
7.	Pizza Hut	2.150
8.	Dairy Queen	1.693
9.	Domino's	1.550
10.	Taco Bell	1.351

Source: Reprinted by permission from *Nation's Restaurant News*, August 11, 1986. Copyright Lebhar-Friedman, Inc., 425 Park Avenue, New York, N.Y. 10022.

the franchise restaurant industry, which had sales of some $49 billion in 1985 ($18 billion of that from corporate-owned stores and $31 billion from franchise outlets). This in turn represents nearly a third of the $153 billion market in commercial feeding.

Yet there have been a number of reports suggesting that the burger business may not be able to keep up its customary rate of growth. There are signs that the chains have simply saturated the market and that customers are getting tired of the same old fare. The increased concern about nutrition and the revival of sophisticated dining among yuppies and other groups have cast a fair amount of disrepute on fast food.

The chains are dealing with the saturation problem by seeking new markets, including the placement of stores in institutional settings such as military bases, museums, and schools. Burger King went so far as to create a fleet of mobile restaurants in 1985 to capture potential customers such as workers at remote construction sites who could not get to a regular store.

As for the change in tastes, the chains seem to be banking on the appeal of convenience and relatively low cost. Nearly half of all money spent on food is now spent eating out in the country's 260,000 or so restaurants, and the chains are fighting to keep their share.

THE RISE OF THE LODGING INDUSTRY

Small, locally owned hotels and motels went the same way as the mom-and-pop restaurant; they were replaced by the chains. Conrad Hilton branched out from Texas to sites across the country (and eventually abroad, until the international business was sold off). At the lower end of the business, Memphis real estate developer Kemmons Wilson set out in the 1950s to transform the motel from a disreputable rendezvous for lovers to a family institution. The company created by Wilson, Holiday Inns (renamed Holiday Corp. in 1985), went on to become the largest lodging company in the world.

The industry enjoyed steady growth until the early 1980s, when it was especially hard hit by the recession and high interest rates. Nevertheless the building boom continued, and many cities ended up with gluts of hotel rooms. By the mid-1980s new rooms were being constructed at a rate of more than 160,000 a year, and occupancy rates slipped to about 64 percent, down from about 73 percent in the late 1970s.

Many of the lodging companies found they could no longer remain in their traditional market niches. They had to pay much greater attention to marketing and to developing new services.

The pressures on the $42 billion lodging industry led to an increasing segmentation of the business. Hoteliers moved up and down the scale in the search for new business. Companies such as Marriott went after the luxury market with the establishment of special concierge floors or all-suite hotels. In order to attract guests, hotels began offering services such as computers in rooms and teleconference facilities; there was even a willingness to cut prices, especially for conventions and other group functions.

At the same time there was a movement to less-expensive ac-

The 10 Largest U.S.-Based Hotel Chains In 1985

	Rooms	Hotels
1. Holiday	318,608	1,685
2. Sheraton (owned by ITT)	134,455	488
3. Hilton Hotels	96,101	270
4. Ramada Inns	96,000	570
5. Quality Inns International	91,000	800
6. Marriott	65,072	147
7. Days Inn of America	46,000	325
8. Motel 6	45,000	401
9. Hyatt Hotels	44,000	80
10. Hilton International	34,774	90

Source: *Hotels & Restaurants International*, July 1986. Hotels and Restaurants International, A Cahners Publication, Newton, Mass., USA.

commodations. Budget facilities such as Motel 6 prospered, and Holiday Corp. and Marriott built facilities that were attractive but inexpensive.

GAMBLING ON GAMING

Several of the large hotel chains have also diversified into casinos, and companies such as Hilton and Holiday Corp. now get nearly 40 percent of their profits from gaming.

The lucrative though not risk-free casino business began back in 1931 when the state of Nevada legalized gambling. Because state rules required each owner of a company to be licensed, public companies were effectively excluded. Instead the industry came to be infiltrated by a fair amount of organized crime money. It was mobster Bugsy Siegel, in fact, who constructed the Flamingo, the first plush casino in the state, soon after the end of World War II.

The 1969 Corporate Gaming Act allowed public companies to enter the business, and the image of the industry gradually improved. Yet there continued to be reports of mafia associations of some casino executives, and there have been a number of cases of skimming of profits.

Nevada retained its geographic monopoly on casino gambling until 1976, when the voters of New Jersey approved a referendum permitting the establishment of casinos in Atlantic City. Resorts International took a chance and purchased the biggest hotel in town before the vote took place. Its gamble enabled it to open its casino before anyone else, in May 1978, and to have the market to itself for a year.

Then the influx began. By the end of 1981 there were eight other casinos in town, built by Caesars World, Bally Manufacturing, Holiday Corp., Ramada, and others. For a while it seemed that there was business enough for everyone. The gross win in Atlantic City—house wins minus house losses at the tables and the slots–grew at a phenomenal average rate of 68 percent a year.

This did not necessarily mean nirvana for the casino owners. They were saddled with heavy debt from the expensive construction of their properties, and they had to offer inducements (free bus service, free chips, etc.) to bring in the masses. By 1985 the 10 casinos in Atlantic City had gross winnings of some $2 billion, greater than that of the more than 50 casinos in Las Vegas. Yet the growth rate in Atlantic City had started to slow down significantly.

Analysts attributed the phenomenon to the limited hotel space and poor transportation system of the city, which meant that most visitors were day-trippers who tended to wager less than the Las Vegas conventioneers and vacationers, who dropped greater sums during their visits averaging four to five days.

As these realities became clear, several companies abandoned partly constructed casinos in Atlantic City, while some of those in operation experienced losses. Elsinore Shore Associates, owner of the Atlantis Casino Hotel, filed for bankruptcy in November 1985.

Other operators were betting on a brighter future for Atlantic City. Resorts International proceeded with construction of a second casino in town; Showboat Inc., a Las Vegas veteran, was also building in Atlantic City; and New York real estate developer Donald Trump, already partner in one casino with Holiday Corp., opened a second property in 1985.

Meanwhile things began looking up in Las Vegas. The "city that never sleeps" started increasing its gross winnings by worrying less about the high rollers and placing greater emphasis on the "grinds," the less affluent visitors who lose less per capita but who exist in much greater numbers. The grinds' futile dreams of easy money go a long way in enriching the bottom lines of the casino operators.

LABOR RELATIONS

The predominant sector of the restaurant industry, fast food, has remained almost entirely nonunion. Companies such as McDonald's and Burger King have gone to great lengths to maintain full control of their underpaid work force. McDonald's has employed what it calls rap sessions, discussions that serve both to allow workers to air their gripes and to allow supervisors to get a reading of the attitude of the troops.

There have been some serious organizing drives among fast-food workers, though few have been successful. When McDonald's sought to open its first stores in San Francisco in the early 1970s, the company found itself confronted by unions and local politicians who were opposing city approval because of the labor policies of the company. It took a long court battle before McDonald's prevailed. In the late 1970s the fast-food chains faced an intensive campaign in Detroit by an independent group called the Fastfood Workers' Union.

Aside from fighting unions, McDonald's has long lobbied for a lower minimum wage for teenagers, who make up the large majority of the company's labor force. However, by the mid-1980s, with demographic trends reducing the size of the teenage labor force, McDonald's and other chains began hiring older workers.

Other parts of the feeding and lodging industry are unionized, the largest union being the Hotel Employees and Restaurant Employees International Union. This organization is widely suspected of having mob connections; in 1984 a Senate subcommittee charged that the union was under the "substantial influence" of organized crime interests.

The union has been challenged both by employers (demands for concessions led to a bitter 75-day strike at Las Vegas hotels and casinos in 1984) and by a much smaller rival union, the United Industry Workers, that has convinced a number of groups of workers to switch their affiliation. The larger union staged a 27-day strike in New York City in 1985 that resulted in a 25 percent wage increase over five years. Hotel workers at eight of Atlantic City's casinos staged a one-day walkout in 1986.

LEADING COMPANIES

Bally Manufacturing prospered for decades as the country's leading producer of slot machines and pinball machines and later arcade games such as Space Invaders and Pac-Man. The company's bid to expand into casino ownership in Atlantic City resulted in a ruling by New Jersey's tough-minded Casino Control Commission that founder William O'Donnell had to resign because of suspected associations with organized crime. Bally, under the leadership of chairman Richard Mullane, prospered by going after the low rollers. In late 1985 the company announced it would purchase MGM Grand Hotels, the owner of two casinos in Nevada, for $440 million.

Burger King, a subsidiary of Pillsbury since the 1960s, has engaged in a perennial battle with industry leader McDonald's. The company suffered frequent management changes in the late 1970s and early 1980s, but it emerged as an aggressive challenger to McDonald's, especially in the advertising arena. While McDonald's took great pains to appeal to children, Burger King found greater receptivity among adults. Parent company Pillsbury's food service operations also included restaurant chains such as Steak & Ale, Bennigan's and J. J. Muggs.

Caesars World (owner of the high rollers' favorite spot in Las Vegas, Caesars Palace) was founded by Clifford Perlman and his brother Stuart. The New Jersey Casino Control Commission required the brothers to dissociate themselves from the company, which proceeded to fall into a financial mess because of credit losses. The company has experienced a turnaround in recent years, thanks to effective management by Henry Gluck.

Golden Nugget's young chief executive Stephen Wynn caused a stir in 1985 when he made a bid for Hilton Hotels Corp. Although the bid was unsuccessful it added to the reputation of Wynn, who was already respected for having made Golden Nugget one of the most successful of the Atlantic City casino owners.

Hilton Hotels Corp. originated with the $5,000 purchase of a hotel in Cisco, Texas, by Conrad Hilton in 1919. Hilton went on to acquire the Statler chain and prestigious individual hotels such as the Waldorf-Astoria in New York City and the Palmer House in Chicago. The foreign properties of the company expanded rapidly in the 1950s and 1960s, but the Hilton International operation was sold to Transworld Corp. in 1964 at the urging of Conrad's son Barron, who now runs the company. In the 1980s Hilton got into the casino business but suffered a major disappointment in 1985 when the New Jersey Casino Control Commission denied a license to the company to operate the $320 million casino it was building in Atlantic City. The casino was sold to real estate developer Donald Trump. In 1985 the company fought off a takeover attempt by Golden Nugget.

Holiday Corp. is the new name of Holiday Inns, the lodging empire founded by Memphis real estate developer Kemmons Wilson in the early 1950s. Franchises and company-owned properties spread rapidly across the United States and abroad. In 1980 the company bought Harrah's casinos and by the middle of the decade was receiving 37 percent of its revenues from gambling.

Chief executive Michael Rose pushed the company upscale through the creation of Crowne Plaza and Embassy Suite Hotels while also courting the budget market through the Hampton Inns chain.

Kentucky Fried Chicken originated in the supposedly unique recipe for fried chicken developed by Colonel Harlan Sanders in the late 1930s. The company started franchising in the mid-1950s; it was bought in 1964 for a mere $2 million by Kentucky business-man (and future governor) John Y. Brown, Jr. Brown built the business into a $250 million chicken empire, which he sold to Heublein Corp. in 1971. The business faltered and ended up be-ing a drain on Heublein's profits from vodka and other products. In 1986 PepsiCo agreed to purchase the company from Heublein's parent RJR Nabisco for $850 million.

Marriott Corp. had its origins in a root beer stand established by John Willard Marriott in Washington, D.C., in 1927. Marriott built a string of Hot Shoppes in Washington and went on to amass a food service empire that now includes the Roy Rogers and Bob's Big Boy chains as well as a large airline catering busi-ness. In 1957 the company opened the first of a chain of hotels concentrated in suburbs and airports. Since the mid-1970s the company, under the leadership of J. W. "Bill" Marriott, Jr. (his father died in 1985), has financed much of its growth by selling off ownership of hotels to investor groups and collecting hefty man-agement fees for running the properties. The company spent $400 million on the massive New York Marriott Marquis in Times Square and in late 1985 purchased the Howard Johnson Company for $300 million.

McDonald's, the pioneer of the business, is still leader of the fast-food industry. Under the leadership of Fred Turner, presi-dent since 1968 and chief executive since 1977 (Ray Kroc died in 1984), the company has continued to break all records in the food service business. Its rate of expansion—some 500 restaurants a year—is astounding. In 1984 the company reached the landmarks of 8,000 stores and 50 billion burgers sold. Having conquered the suburbs and small towns, McDonald's has in recent years focused on cities and foreign sites. In 1985 more than one fifth of its 8,500 stores were abroad, accounting for 23 percent of its $3.4 billion in revenues. McDonald's continued to spend massive amounts on advertising—some $567 million in 1985, making it the ninth-biggest advertiser in the United States. The company has reached a new level of status in sociological and business terms: In 1985 the original McDonald's set up by Kroc in Des Plaines, Illinois, was turned into a museum, and the shares of McDonald's Corp. were added to the elite group that makes up the Dow Jones Industrial Average.

Pizza Hut, founded by Frank and Daniel Carney in Kansas in 1958, grew rapidly in the 1960s and 1970s. Purchased by PepsiCo in 1977, the chain helped stimulate a transformation of the pizza business from a mom-and-pop one to a major segment of the franchise industry. In the late 1970s and early 1980s there was a wave of popularity of pizza franchise restaurants that entertained diners with singing robots and video games. Created by Atari founder Nolan Bushnell, Pizza Time and its imitator ShowBiz Pizza Place eventually lost their appeal. In recent years the Godfather's Pizza chain, now owned by Pillsbury, has enjoyed rapid growth by serving deep-dish pizza.

Resorts International, originally a paint manufacturer, is one of the most controversial of the casino companies. Founder James Crosby used his relationship with an official of the Bahamian government to get permission to build a casino on Paradise Island in 1967. Resorts opened the first casino in Atlantic City in 1978, but in 1985 it barely convinced the Casino Control Commission to renew its license. The chairman of the commission and the state attorney general argued that Resorts was not fit to retain the license because of some company funds that ended up in the pocket of the prime minister of the Bahamas. The company denied any wrongdoing. Following Crosby's death in 1986 several parties began bidding for the company.

Wendy's International was founded by R. David Thomas, a fast-food executive, in 1969. Its stores used a turn-of-the-century motif and higher-quality food to appeal to a more mature clientele. Wendy's has gained enormous attention in recent years—and solidified its hold on the adult hamburger market—with its "Where's the beef?" commercial and another controversial ad that implicitly linked McDonald's with totalitarianism by using a mock Russian fashion show to make a point about the lack of real choices provided by Wendy's competitors.

SOURCE GUIDE

LEADING STOCK ANALYSTS AND EXPERTS

Stephen W. Brener, a hotel consultant with his own firm in New York City.

Michael Culp, a fast-food analyst at Prudential-Bache.

Lee Isgur, a casino analyst at Paine Webber.

Daniel Lee, a hotel and casino analyst at Drexel Burnham Lambert.

Harold Vogel, a casino and hotel analyst at Merrill Lynch.

TRADE ASSOCIATIONS AND UNIONS

American Hotel and Motel Association, New York.

Hotel Employees and Restaurant Employees International Union, New York.

National Restaurant Association, Washington, D.C.

DATA SOURCES AND DIRECTORIES

Directory of Chain Restaurant Operators, an annual listing of chains (New York: Business Guides, a subsidiary of Lebhar-Friedman).

Hotel and Motel Red Book, an annual directory of over 10,000 hotels and motels in the United States (Walnut Creek, Calif.: PacTel Publishing).

Hotel and Travel Index, a quarterly directory of some 33,000 hotels and motels around the world (New York: Murdoch Magazines).

Laventhol and Horwath, an accounting and consulting firm in Philadelphia, publishes several annual statistical volumes, including *U.S. Lodging Industry* and *Study of Financial Results and Reporting Trends in the Gaming Industry*. It also publishes with the National Restaurant Association the annual *Restaurant Industry Operations Report*.

Trends in the Hotel Industry, published annually by a Texas accounting and consulting firm (Houston: Pannell Kerr Forster).

TRADE PUBLICATIONS

Cornell Hotel and Restaurant Administration Quarterly.

Gaming Business, monthly.

Hotel and Motel Management, monthly.

Hotels and Restaurants International, fortnightly.

Nation's Restaurant News, biweekly.

Restaurant Business, monthly.

Restaurant Hospitality, monthly.

Restaurants and Institutions, fortnightly.

BOOKS AND REPORTS

Boas, Max, and Steve Chain. *Big Mac: The Unauthorized Story of McDonald's*. New York: Mentor Books, 1976.

Emerson, Robert L. *Fast Food: The Endless Shakeout*. New York: Lebhar-Friedman, 1979.

Kroc, Ray. *Grinding It Out*. The autobiography of the founder of the McDonald's empire. Chicago: Contemporary Books, 1977.

Love, John F. *McDonald's: Behind the Arches*. New York: Bantam Books, 1986.

Luxenberg, Stan. *Roadside Empires: How the Chains Franchised America*. New York: Viking Press, 1985.

CHAPTER ELEVEN

Retailing

The buying and selling of goods has played a major role in most societies. The coming together of merchants and customers in marketplaces such as the ancient Greek agora and the Middle Eastern bazaar has allowed for the intermingling of peoples and to some extent the growth of civilization.

In more modern times the central place of commerce is seen most clearly in the United States. The growth of the great department stores starting in the mid-19th century ushered in the era of mass consumption. And the sprouting of shopping centers and malls after World War II redefined the social landscape of much of the country. Today retailing, with its annual sales of $1.4 trillion, is the largest business sector in the United States, encompassing nearly half of all enterprises.

FROM YANKEE PEDDLERS TO MERCHANT PRINCES

The growth of retailing in the United States followed the overall development of the country. As significant numbers of settlers moved inland starting in the early 1800s, they were followed by traveling merchants. These entrepreneurs sold pioneer families items such as housewares and notions that they could not obtain from the land.

The Yankee peddlers, as they came to be known, satisfied vital needs of the frontier people, and many were willing to exchange goods for pelts, honey, or other homemade items. Yet the peddlers also had a reputation for dishonesty—for passing off inferior or counterfeit products on unsophisticated country folk. Phrases such as "Don't take any wooden nickles" emerged from these practices. Many peddlers retained their less than scrupulous ways when they settled down in one place and opened a general store. The growth of the mail-order business later in the century was stimulated by the dissatisfaction of rural people with their local merchants.

Back in urban areas retailing was also undergoing a transformation. As cities began growing rapidly in the early 19th century, some merchants began expanding traditional specialty shops into grander emporia with greater selections of dry goods. Eventually all sorts of other products were added, and by the late 19th century huge establishments known as department stores sought to satisfy every conceivable material need. There is considerable dispute about what was the first true department store in the United States—the term was not used until the 1880s—but the leading pioneers undoubtedly were A. T. Stewart, Rowland Macy, and John Wanamaker.

Stewart, an Irish immigrant who arrived in the United States in the 1820s with a stock of linens and laces, soon opened the country's largest store in lower Manhattan. The Marble Dry Goods Palace was also unusual in that it was the first store to establish fixed prices, thus ending the traditional practice of haggling between salesclerk and customer.

Macy, a veteran of several unsuccessful stores in Massachusetts, adopted a similar fixed-price policy and also sold exclusively on a cash basis when he opened a large store in New York City in 1858.

Wanamaker, who began operation in Philadelphia in the 1860s, sought to upgrade the quality of ready-made clothing and also pioneered the money-back guarantee. In 1896 Wanamaker branched out to New York, taking over the business of Stewart, who had died in 1876.

By the end of the 19th century these establishments and others such as Marshall Field's of Chicago had dramatically altered the way urban Americans shopped. Department stores in the major cities elevated the mundane activity of buying goods into something exalted; lavish emporia were the temples of consumption. Goods were displayed in ways that stimulated demand rather than simply responding to it. Leading stores had amenities such as stools for customers to sit on while considering their purchases and "silence rooms" to allow overwrought shoppers to regain their composure and go on buying.

Department stores were all the more marvelous to customers because they were the first establishments to install newly invented devices such as elevators, electric lighting, telephones, and cash registers. The stores also pleased customers with free home delivery via great fleets of horse-drawn (and later motorized) carriages.

The late 19th century saw other retailing developments that involved the shifting of business away from small, local merchants to larger enterprises. The most significant of these for what was still a largely rural population was the growth of the mail-order business. Although some limited purchasing by mail existed earlier, the father of this business was certainly a former country storekeeper and traveling salesman by the name of Aaron Montgomery Ward. Knowing the dissatisfaction of farmers with their local country stores, Ward began selling goods by mail in 1872. The response to Ward's catalogs, which came to be known as "wish books," was strong, and the company grew rapidly.

Another pioneer of mail order, Richard Sears, got into the business accidentally in the 1880s. While working as a railroad station agent in Minnesota, Sears ended up with a COD shipment of watches that a local jeweler refused to accept. Sears made a deal with the supplier to sell the watches himself. This worked out so well that Sears quit the railroad, opened a mail-order watch business in Minneapolis, and later moved to Chicago. By the 1890s he and partner Alvah Roebuck were selling a wide variety of products through the mail, and before long they surpassed Ward.

Aided by the enactment of rural free delivery in 1896, both companies continued to prosper, building strong bonds with millions of families. The catalogs produced by the two companies helped to shape U.S. consumption patterns and are now considered classic Americana.

The great mail-order houses did not please everyone. Local merchants, seeing their livelihood endangered, fought back. They organized public catalog burnings and promoted smear campaigns that accused Sears and Ward—which were given unfriendly nicknames such as Rears and Soreback and Monkey Ward—of selling inferior merchandise. The companies took great pains to disprove these charges; Ward's went so far as to give a committee of farmers the run of its warehouse, allowing the group to tear open large numbers of packages and compare the contents against what was advertised in the catalog. The committee reportedly found nothing amiss.

The small-merchant lobby also struggled against another of the retailing developments of the period: the rise of the chain stores. The chains emerged in two kinds of shops: variety stores and groceries. The pioneer in chain selling of food was George Huntington Hartford, who along with George Gilman opened an ornate store in lower Manhattan in 1859 to sell tea. Hartford, who later adopted the grandiose name of Great Atlantic & Pacific Tea Company, added coffee and spices and later a full line of groceries to his stores. By keeping prices low A&P gained a loyal customer following, and by 1876 there were 67 A&P stores stretching from Boston to St. Paul, Minnesota; in 1915 the number had risen to 1,000.

Low prices were also the appeal of the variety stores that Frank Woolworth began opening in the 1870s. Limiting his goods to ones selling at 5 or 10 cents each, Woolworth built an empire that by the time of his death in 1919 included more than 1,000 stores with total sales of $119 million. Woolworth's major competitor was James Cash Penney, who opened his first store in Wyoming in 1902. Penney, who called his early shops Golden Rule Stores, expanded across the West and after 1913 began growing at a phenomenal rate across the country. By 1933 there were nearly 1,500 Penney stores.

The growth of the Hartford, Woolworth, and Penney empires and other chains gave rise to an intense antichain-store movement that culminated in the 1930s. Led by Representative Wright Patman of Texas the antichain forces tried to halt the march of the national retailers through discriminatory legislation. The battle was played out in a series of dramatic congressional hearings, and in the end the power of the chains prevailed. Not only did the national corporate merchants retain their empires, but many local department-store powerhouses ended up as parts of national retail holding companies such as Federated Department Stores and Allied Stores.

THE MALLING OF AMERICA

In the postwar period, chain stores and department stores were entrenched enough in American commerce to serve as the anchors of what became the predominant new style of retailing, the shopping center. The oldest planned shopping center is reputed to be Country Club Plaza, built near Kansas City in 1922. But it was only during the 1950s that these collections of stores began to transform the American landscape.

Drawing on precedents such as Milan's Galleria (built in the 1860s) and the Old Arcade that was constructed in Cleveland in 1936, developers soon began enclosing the shopping centers and calling them malls. Like the early department stores, malls sought to immerse customers in an all-encompassing shopping environment. Climate was carefully regulated, security and cleanliness were attended to obsessively; in short, nothing was allowed to stand in the way of the urge to consume.

In replacing traditional commercial districts, malls have in many places become the main arenas of social life. People come to them not only to shop but to seek the company of others and even to engage in civic activities. Political organizations have used malls for disseminating leaflets, and when courts in some states upheld the right of mall owners to ban such activity, the rulings were denounced as major impediments to free speech.

While suburban malls have often been criticized for causing the decline of downtown areas, the transformation of historic structures into enclosed shopping centers has contributed to the revival of many urban districts. Beginning with Fanueil Hall in Boston, the Rouse Co. and other developers have carried out projects such as The Gallery in Philadelphia, the Grand Avenue Complex in Milwaukee, South Street Seaport in New York, and Union Station in St. Louis.

By the mid-1980s the spread of malls had slowed down, largely because of saturation in many parts of the country. Yet developers in Minnesota announced plans in 1985 for constructing the largest (10 million square feet) mall in the country. The project was expected to cost $1.2 billion.

The postwar period also saw a dramatic transformation of the food retailing business. Groceries were traditionally sold in small shops in which clerks waited on each customer. The rise of chain stores such as A&P affected the ownership but not the operating style of the shops. A Memphis grocer named Clarence Saunders is credited with being the first to break out of the mold. His Piggly Wiggly stores, the first of which opened in 1916, introduced self-service.

This concept caught on in places, but the major leap occurred in 1930 when a large cash-and-carry store called King Kullen's opened in the Jamaica, Queens, area of New York City. This was the birth of the supermarket, and in the years after World War II these food palaces rapidly replaced traditional grocery stores. A&P transformed its shops accordingly though not fast enough, and other chains such as Safeway and Kroger rose to the top ranks of retailers.

THE DISCOUNTERS' CHALLENGE

The comfortable prosperity that many of the country's large retailers enjoyed in the 1950s did not last for long. Although retailing was never a high-margin business, efficient stores made respectable income by selling goods at manufacturers' list prices. Discounting was limited to special sales or particular departments such as Filene's famous Automatic Bargain Basement.

During the late 1950s there appeared on the scene a group of retailers who sold all their goods all of the time at discounted prices. The first wave came with the factory outlet stores that were set up in abandoned textile mills in New England. Building on the principles of low overhead, high turnover, and customer self-service, the discounters began to spring up everywhere. They won the right to sell goods such as appliances below list price, and they defied local "blue laws" banning Sunday hours.

The man who came to epitomize the discounting revolution was Eugene Ferkauf. A one-time luggage dealer, Ferkauf built a national chain called E. J. Korvettes that caused an upheaval in the department store business. Ferkauf, known as the Duke of Discounting, enjoyed shaking up the stodgy retail trade with gestures such as the 1962 opening of a discount store in New York's snobbish Fifth Avenue shopping district.

Ferkauf left the company in 1968, and in 1979 Korvettes was purchased by the French retailer Agache-Willot. The new owners could not stem what was already a serious cost-control problem, and in 1981 the company filed for bankruptcy.

Another major player in the early discounting era has survived and is stronger than ever. Back in 1962 the S. S. Kresge Co. plunged into discounting with the establishment of a chain called K mart stores. These stores, which now number 2,200, have been a phenomenal success, propelling Kresge (which changed its name to K mart in 1977) from a sleepy variety store chain into the second-largest retailer in the United States.

During the 1980s discounting has become more important than ever. There has also been an expansion from traditional discounting into other forms of low-price selling. Discounters buy at wholesale and cut their retail prices through low overhead and high volume. A new variation, known as off-price stores, involves purchasing their goods at below wholesale prices by accepting manufacturers' overruns, end-of-season goods, and other irregular lots. The off-price retailers enjoy about $200 per square foot in annual sales (almost twice the level of traditional department stores) and turn over their stock nine times a year (compared with a normal level of three times). Some of the more successful off-price chains are Syms, T. J. Maxx, and Marshalls.

By the mid-1980s off-price stores numbered more than 10,000 and accounted for about 5 percent of sales in clothing, accessories, and footwear. Some traditional department stores have threatened to stop buying from manufacturers who sold to off-price retailers, who in turn have charged department stores with price-fixing.

Most recently the off-price segment has been undercut by even more heavily discounted goods. The latest rages are wholesale cash-and-carry clubs and gray-market dealers (who obtain brand name goods through unauthorized channels).

Some traditional retailers have responded to the discounters not by fighting them but rather by joining the game. None has been so successful as Kresge's K mart venture, but a number of chains have even experimented with off-price stores.

Yet this is only one of a number of directions the big chains have pursued in response to an increasingly precarious competitive situation. Following the early lead of Macy's, mass retailers such as J. C. Penney and Sears have been trying to improve their fashion image and attract a more "upscale" clientele. Other chains such as Woolworth, Federated, and Dayton Hudson have been opening smaller specialty-type stores instead of full-line department stores.

Food retailers have also been responding to the simultaneous pressures to go upscale and downscale. On the one hand they have gone along with the demand for low prices through the stocking of generic products and no-frills practices such as reducing selections, selling out of shipping cartons, and charging for bags. On the other hand, many supermarkets have responded to increased food sophistication by adding salad bars, gourmet departments, and other amenities.

RETAILING WITHOUT STORES

Another challenge facing the big chains is the rise of alternative forms of distribution that do not involve stores. The most important of these is also one of the oldest forms of retailing: mail order. While purchasing goods from a catalog was long the practice of rural families, it has in recent years become more popular among all segments of the population. Catalog sales surpassed $24 billion in 1984.

One old-line catalog seller, Sears, has benefited from this surge, while the other major player, Montgomery Ward, could not stem the losses in its mail-order operation. Ward discontinued its catalog business in 1985, and the retailer's parent Mobil Corp. announced plans to sell off the entire company.

The main beneficiaries of the mail-order boom have been specialized suppliers who sell everything from rare fruits to jewels. Yet as the number of catalogs proliferated (reaching some 6,000) direct-mail companies began to complain that the competition was eating into their profits.

Besides the great catalog glut, mail-order houses have also come under pressure for their tax practices. Thanks to the wording of state sales tax regulations, companies selling by mail to out-of-state customers are not required to collect sales tax. The customers are theoretically required to come forward and pay on their own, but few do. Now state officials are seeking legislation that would close what they see as a legal loophole depriving their coffers of countless dollars of tax revenues.

The other main form of retailing without stores is electronic shopping. Although bold predictions have been made regarding the extent to which families will make their purchases via home computers and cable television devices, the reality has so far been undramatic.

A series of videotex experiments carried out by companies such as Warner Amex, Times Mirror, and CBS have discovered some but not overwhelming interest on the part of consumers to shop electronically. A few systems have gone into limited commercial operation in locations such as Coral Gables, Florida, and Orange County in California. A service of longer tenure is Comp-U-Card. This is a buying service for subscribers who have access to computerized information on some 250,000 products through their PCs. The products can be ordered on line with a credit card. In operation since 1973 the service at the end of 1985 had 50,000 subscribers via computer and another 2 million who gain access to the information by telephone.

Another form of high-tech shopping is the electronic kiosk. These are devices placed in stores that give the user computerized information on a wider range of goods than is displayed and allow the customer to place orders electronically.

TOO MANY STORES?

In 1985 analysts of the retail industry began to question one of the basic assumptions of the business: that the construction of more stores led to an overall increase in the level of retail sales. A report published by the Marketing Science Institute presented a discouraging forecast regarding growth of retail sales during the remainder of the 1980s. The study raised doubts about the wisdom of the expansion strategy and gave ammunition to those who argue that the United States already has too many stores.

Advocates of the "overstoring" thesis noted that average annual sales per square foot of retail space—the traditional measure of a merchant's success—declined in real terms from the mid-70s to the mid-80s. Some retailers have been responding to this situation by closing or consolidating existing stores or reducing the size of the new ones that are opened. They are also fighting harder for increased market share.

SHOPLIFTING

Retailers are also responding to the crunch they are in by getting tougher with that group of "customers" who erode what is already a narrow profit margin: shoplifters. Theft has been a problem for large stores since their earliest days, with shoplifting levels tending to increase during economic downturns. In recent years some security experts have claimed that 1 of 10 customers is a thief and that the value of shoplifted goods can amount to 5 percent of a store's gross profits. The guesstimate of the total volume of shoplifting in the United States is anywhere from $10 to $30 billion a year.

Over the past decade stores have transferred some of their security measures from watching the customers to protecting the goods (though cameras, two-way mirrors, and other forms of surveillance are still very much in use). The approach involves attaching to goods plastic devices that can only be removed by a salesclerk; if they are not removed they set off an alarm at the door. These tags, made by companies such as Sensormatics, are beginning to be used in supermarkets as well as department stores.

While these devices have been effective some chains have supplemented them with the controversial practice of broadcasting

The 15 Largest Retailers, by 1985 Retail Sales ($ Millions)

1. Sears, Roebuck	$26,552
2. K mart	22,420
3. Safeway	19,651
4. Kroger	17,124
5. American Stores	13,890
6. J. C. Penney	12,634
7. Federated Department Stores	9,978
8. Lucky	9,382
9. Dayton Hudson	8,793
10. Wal-Mart	8,451
11. Southland	8,055
12. Winn-Dixie	7,774
13. A&P	6,615
14. F. W. Woolworth	5,958
15. Montgomery Ward	5,388

Source: Reprinted by permission from *Chain Store Age Executive* (August 1986). Copyright Lebhar-Friedman, Inc., 425 Park Avenue, New York, N.Y. 10022.

subliminal messages ("Don't steal") along with the store's background music.

LABOR RELATIONS

Although working in a store was for a long time considered a sort of white-collar job and thus preferable to toiling in a factory, retail employees have experienced more than their share of mistreatment. In the early days the main grievance was the long hours. Workweeks of as much as 80 or 90 hours prompted retail workers to form "early-closing societies" aimed at reducing the number of hours shops remained open and thus the amount of time clerks were expected to be on the job. The societies evolved into unions, and by 1890 the Retail Clerks National Protective Association (later shortened to the Retail Clerks International Association) was chartered by the American Federation of Labor.

The RCIA continued its battle over the workweek and later turned to wages as well. The problem the union had in organizing was that the retail work force was characterized by seasonal employment and high turnover. Some of the large employers, such as Sears, Penney, and Filene's of Boston, discouraged unionization by adopting paternalistic policies, including profit sharing plans and grievance procedures.

During the labor upheaval of the 1930s, militant locals in the RCIA, especially in New York, grew tired of the conservative leadership of the union and eventually broke away and formed the Retail, Wholesale and Department Store Union. In 1979 the RCIA and the Amalgamated Meat Cutters merged to form the United Food and Commercial Workers (UFCW).

During World War II Montgomery Ward was involved in one of the more famous incidents in U.S. labor history. When Ward's president Sewell Avery defied an order from President Roosevelt to renew a union contract, FDR ordered the company seized by the army under his wartime powers. When Avery refused to cooperate with the army he was forcibly removed from his office.

After the war the retail work force expanded enormously, but the unions failed to keep up their organizing pace, especially at the new chains. In recent years the main labor relations battle in the retail field has involved supermarket workers.

For many years unionized workers at the big chains enjoyed

relatively good pay, benefits, and working conditions. But as competition from nonunion chains intensified in the late 1970s, companies began efforts to reduce their labor costs.

Safeway went through some bitter strikes in 1978 over the company's use of computerized time and motion work rules. The Winn-Dixie chain was the target of a national AFL–CIO boycott because of its attempt to vacate labor agreements. Kroger, traditionally a paternalistic employer, began to get tough with the UFCW. In regions such as Pittsburgh, Cleveland, and southern Michigan the company warned that unless the union agreed to concessions, stores would be closed—and Kroger made good on that threat in numerous places. At the end of 1985 some 10,000 UFCW members struck seven supermarket chains in the Los Angeles area. Despite staying out for eight weeks, the workers had to take a pay cut.

A different way of dealing with labor costs was devised by the UFCW and A&P after the chain closed 70 of its stores in the Philadelphia area in 1982. The union got the company to agree to a plan under which many of the stores were reopened with lower wage rates. This was not unusual, but A&P also agreed that if labor costs in the stores were kept to 10 percent of sales, the company would contribute 1 percent of sales to a special fund out of which bonuses would be paid to the employees. The union also helped employees of two of the other closed A&Ps reopen them under worker ownership and management.

LEADING COMPANIES

Batus Inc., a subsidiary of the London-based tobacco giant BAT, is the holding company for Gimbels, Saks Fifth Avenue, and other retail properties that BAT began purchasing in the United States in the early 1970s. Gimbels was founded in the 1850s as a trading post in Indiana. It merged with Saks in 1923. The Marshall Field chain, the great Chicago retail empire, was acquired in 1982. Batus has been disappointed in Gimbels' performance in recent years, as the mass merchandiser faltered while its traditional rival Macy's moved upscale. It came as no surprise in early 1986 when Batus announced plans to sell Gimbels and some other stores while holding onto fashionable Saks, Marshall Field, and other properties.

Carter Hawley Hale had its origins in the small dry-goods store Arthur Letts opened on Broadway in Los Angeles in the late 19th century. What was originally known as The Broadway grew steadily in the West and merged with Hale Brothers stores in 1950. The company became a leader in upscale retailing after acquiring Neiman-Marcus in 1968 and Bergdorf Goodman in 1972. Neiman-Marcus, best known for the unusual and extremely expensive items in its catalog, was founded in Dallas in 1907 and in recent years has expanded across the country. Bergdorf, the high-class women's clothing store in New York, had its origins in a 19th century tailor shop. In 1977 Carter Hawley Hale (it adopted the name in 1974) made an unsuccessful attempt to acquire Marshall Field but the following year purchased the historic but ailing Wanamaker empire of Philadelphia. In 1984 the company defeated a bold takeover attempt by The Limited. Two years later, faced with another bid by The Limited and a partner, Carter Hawley Hale spun off its specialty retailing business.

Dayton Hudson was formed in 1969 by the merger of two old-line department store companies—Hudson's of Detroit and Dayton's of Minneapolis. Dayton's, a fashion trendsetter, also founded the large B. Dalton bookstore chain in the 1960s. Dayton Hudson has made various forays into discounting but sold its chain of Plum's off-price stores.

Federated Department Stores is an amalgam of more than a dozen retail groups, including famous names such as Bloomingdale's, Filene's, I. Magnin, and Rich's of Atlanta. Federated was set up in 1929 as a holding company under the leadership of the Lazarus family of Columbus, Ohio, though the groups have always kept considerable autonomy. Filene's, for instance, retained its famous Automatic Bargain Basement, where generations of Boston shoppers have fought over special shipments of goods at extremely low prices. Bloomingdale's, founded in 1872, made a name for itself with dazzling and hip displays of goods, showing in the process how a department store could be a fashion leader. For many years Federated had fallen behind its competitors in innovation, but in the 1980s some new life was injected by Howard Goldfeder, who took over as CEO in 1981. The company's biggest effort in recent years has been the MainStreet chain of smaller, soft-goods stores for middle-income consumers.

The Great Atlantic & Pacific Tea Company may not be so great any longer, but the company refuses to die. The A&P empire began as a tea store opened by George Huntington Hartford in the late 1850s. Hartford branched out from tea to coffee and spices and eventually to a full line of groceries. A&P stores began sprouting up like mushrooms everywhere, each laid out identically. The company went along with the supermarket revolution starting in the late 1930s but was slow to modernize after the war. Still, at the end of the 1960s the company was the biggest retailer in the United States. In the early 1970s the company pushed a campaign called WEO (originally Warehouse Economy Outlet, later Where Economy Originates) in which goods were sold at the cheapest possible levels. This set off a price war that hurt A&P more than its competitors, and WEO was dropped in 1973. A&P lost considerable ground in the 1970s, and in 1975 new CEO Jonathan Scott began closing hundreds of stores and eliminating thousands of employees. The company was purchased by the West German Tengelmann Group in 1979, and in 1980 James Wood was brought in to attempt another rescue job. Wood had disappointing results with a group of Plus Stores (no-frills stores with limited selections), but he managed to stop the decline. By the mid-1980s the company was in stable financial health and was expanding and upgrading its stores. In 1986 A&P purchased the Shopwell and Waldbaum supermarket chains.

K mart is the result of one of the most dramatic success stories in modern retailing. In the early 1960s the S. S. Kresge chain of variety stores recognized the potential of the discounting movement and began opening K mart stores. The experiment grew like mad and eventually took over the company in importance as well as name. K mart reached the number two spot among retailers in the early 1980s and by 1985 was gaining quickly on industry leader Sears. The company, which purchased the large Walden Books chain from Carter Hawley Hale in 1984, also embarked on a process of upgrading its "polyester" image.

Kroger Co. surprised the retail world by shooting ahead of Safeway in 1984 to be the leading food retailer, based on U.S. sales alone. (Safeway does considerable foreign business.) Founded by Barney Kroger in the 1880s, the company has traditionally been strong in the Midwest but has expanded across the country. In recent years Kroger has been ruthless in the battle for market share, playing hardball with its unions and pulling out of markets where results were not satisfactory. Kroger does a large amount of its own manufacturing through several dozen food processing plants.

The Limited, a women's clothing empire founded by Leslie Wexner in the 1960s, has been the fastest-growing retailer of the past two decades. From the mid-1970s to the mid-1980s the company grew to 100 times its original size, and Wexner's large personal stake in the company rose in value to about $1 billion. The company has achieved its record through both its own stores and the shops of the Lane Bryant chain (acquired in 1982) and Lerner stores (bought in 1984). That same year Wexner shocked the retail world by attempting a takeover of Carter Hawley Hale. The bid was eventually dropped, but Wexner went on in 1985 to acquire the high-class New York specialty shop Henri Bendel. The following year Wexner joined forces with a large real estate developer in another run at Carter Hawley.

R. H. Macy & Co. began as a dry-goods shop opened by Rowland Macy in Manhattan in 1858. Promoting the practices of fixed prices and payment in cash, Macy was also one of the first merchants to branch out into a wide variety of goods. After being taken over by the Straus family in the 1880s Macy's kept to its cash-only policy, guaranteeing prices 6 percent lower than those in stores that sold on account. Macy's bought the Bamberger's chain in 1929 and began opening stores in New York's suburbs and around the country in the 1950s. In the 1970s Macy's, under the leadership of Edward Finkelstein, pioneered the "upscale" movement by creating boutiques and specialty departments within the larger stores. The company experienced a sharp decline in 1984, and a number of top executives departed. In 1985 a group of the remaining managers, led by Finkelstein, offered to take the company private in a $3.6 billion leveraged buyout.

Montgomery Ward, one of the two great catalog companies, was founded by Aaron Montgomery Ward in 1872. Through his "wish books" Ward made available a wide variety of goods to farm families and allowed them to reduce their dependency on often unscrupulous local merchants. In the 1920s the company began opening stores where catalog goods were put on display. Customers put so much pressure on Ward's to sell goods on the spot that the company began opening retail outlets. The company was slow to modernize after World War II and barely survived a takeover attempt by Louis Wolfson in the early 1950s. Ward's had a turnaround in the 1960s and in 1968 merged with Container Corp. of America to form Marcor, which was bought by Mobil Corp. in 1974. Ward's has not kept up with the times since then, experiencing slow growth and losses. The catalog business was suspended in 1985, and Mobil announced it was trying to sell the company. In 1986 Ward revealed a plan to convert many of its stores into specialty outlets, but the survival of the chain was still in question.

J. C. Penney is one of the leading mass merchandisers in the United States. The chain was founded by James Cash Penney with a tiny, cash-only dry-goods store in Wyoming in 1902. Penney bought out other chains and opened more stores at a rapid rate; he had nearly 1,400 by 1929. Penney traditionally sold mainly clothing and footwear but in the early 1960s introduced full-line stores. The company began returning to its old specialty in the mid-1970s and during the early 1980s began seeking to improve its fashion image and attract a more affluent clientele. The company set aside $1 billion for a modernization drive, but by the middle of the decade there were still no solid financial signs of success, and the company was having second thoughts about its move upscale.

Safeway Stores emerged from the West to surpass A&P in the 1970s as the nation's biggest supermarket chain. Founded as a cash-and-carry grocery in Idaho in 1915, Safeway has based much of its growth on private-label sales. Starting in the 1970s it moved decisively to reduce overhead and increase sales by emphasizing nonfood items. In 1980 the company started opening no-frills Food Barn stores. Following a hostile tender offer from the Dart Group in 1986, Safeway agreed to be taken private in a $4.2 billion leveraged buyout.

Sears, Roebuck & Co. is the world's leading retailer, though K mart is coming up fast. The company started out as a mail-order house for watches, founded by Richard Sears, a former railroad station agent in Minnesota. Seeing the success of Montgomery Ward, Sears and his partner Alvah Roebuck branched out into a general line of merchandise. The company soon overtook Ward's in sales, thanks in part to Sears' extremely efficient method for fulfilling mail orders. The system, involving conveyor belts and pneumatic tubes, helped to inspire Henry Ford's automobile assembly line. The company began opening retail stores in the 1920s. Under the autocratic control of General Robert Wood, the U.S. Army quartermaster during World War I, the company set up the Allstate auto insurance business in 1931 and began expanding abroad. Franklin Roosevelt once said that the best way to convince the USSR of the superiority of the American way of life would be to drop Sears catalogs all over the Soviet Union. During the 1980s the company has plunged into the financial services game by acquiring the Dean Witter brokerage house and the Coldwell Banker chain of real estate agencies. Sears also introduced a hybrid credit and financial services card called Discover, but many observers believed that the company's attempt to become a financial supermarket was far from being realized. On the retail side, the company has moved somewhat upscale in its appeal and launched a program to remodel 600 of its 800 stores and turn many of them into "stores of the future." However, in the mid-1980s, with competition from discounters escalating, the company's retail revenues were flat.

Southland Corp., the owner of the 7–Eleven chain, is the leading convenience store retailer. The convenience store was born in the 1920s in Dallas, when the manager of an ice dock owned by Southland Ice Co. began to sell eggs, milk, and bread during his long opening hours. The availability of essential foodstuffs at hours when grocers were closed proved to be popular, and Southland began opening stores at a rapid pace. Originally called Tote'm Stores, the chain was christened 7–Eleven in 1946 to reflect what were then the hours of business. By the beginning of 1986 the company had more than 7,500 stores, better than a third of them franchised. In 1983 Southland bought the Citgo refinery, and in 1984 the company was found guilty of setting up a slush fund to pay bribes to New York State officials to fix sales tax cases. The company in recent years sought to upgrade its stores and got involved in developing a $1 billion office complex in Dallas.

F. W. Woolworth Co. played a major role in retailing by popularizing the five-and-dime variety store. Founded by Frank Woolworth in the 1870s, the company rapidly moved to the top ranks of American merchants—which Woolworth emphasized by erecting a headquarters in 1913 that was the tallest building in the world. The company was slow to modernize after World War II, and an attempt to follow Kresge into the discounting business through a chain of Woolco stores was a failure. That chain was shut down in 1982. In the mid-1980s, however, Woolworth found success in a batch of specialty shops—selling goods such as stationery or jewelry—that do not carry the Woolworth name.

SOURCE GUIDE

LEADING STOCK ANALYSTS AND EXPERTS

Joseph Ellis, analyst at Goldman Sachs.

Jeffrey Feiner, analyst at Merrill Lynch.

Management Horizons, a retail consulting firm based in Dublin, Ohio.

TRADE ASSOCIATIONS AND UNIONS

Association of General Merchandise Chains (variety and discount stores), Washington, D.C.

International Association of Chain Stores (food chains), Alexandria, Virginia.

National Grocers Association (independents), Reston, Virginia.

National Mass Retailing Institute (discounters), New York.

National Retail Merchants Association (department and specialty stores), New York.

Retail, Wholesale and Department Store Union, New York.

United Food and Commercial Workers International Union, Washington, D.C.

DATA SOURCES AND DIRECTORIES

Directory of Department Stores and *Directory of Discount Stores/Catalog Showrooms*, both published annually (New York: Lebhar-Friedman).

Financial and Operating Results of Department and Specialty Stores and *Merchandising and Operating Results*, both annual statistical volumes (New York: National Retail Merchants Association).

Fortune, as part of its Service 500, publishes an annual ranking of the fifty largest retailers, in June.

"$100 Million Club," an annual listing of the top retail companies, published in the August issue of *Chain Store Age Executive*.

Operating Results of Self-Service Discount Department Stores and the Mass Retailers' Merchandising Report, published annually (New York: National Mass Retailing Institute).

Phelon's Discount Stores, a biennial directory of more than 2,000 discount and self-service stores and their key personnel (Fairview, N.J.: Phelon, Sheldon & Marsar).

Sheldon's Retail Directory, an annual listing of major department stores, chains, and other retailers and their key personnel (Fairview, N.J.: Phelon, Sheldon & Marsar).

Thomas Grocery Register, an annual three-volume work listing information on some 62,000 U.S. and Canadian firms involved in food distribution (New York: Thomas Publishing).

TRADE PUBLICATIONS

Chain Store Age, monthly (published in several editions).

Discount Merchandiser, monthly.

Discount Store News, fortnightly.

Progressive Grocer, monthly.

Stores, monthly.

Supermarket News, weekly.

BOOKS AND REPORTS

Bluestone, Barry, Patricia Hanna, Sarah Kuhn, and Laura Moore. *The Retail Revolution*. Boston: Auburn House, 1981.

Hendrickson, Robert. *The Grand Emporiums*. Briarcliff Manor, N.Y.: Stein & Day, 1979.

Kowinski, William. *The Malling of America*. New York: William Morrow, 1985.

Mahoney, Tom, and Leonard Sloane. *The Great Merchants*. Rev. ed. New York: Harper & Row, 1974.

May, Eleanor G., C. William Ress, and Walter J. Salmon. *Future Trends in Retailing*. An influential study of the industry. Cambridge, Mass.: Marketing Science Institute, 1985.

Weil, Gordon L. *Sears, Roebuck, U.S.A.* Briarcliff Manor, N.Y.: Stein & Day, 1977.

CHAPTER TWELVE

Textiles and Apparel

Spinning, weaving, and clothesmaking are among the oldest productive activities of the human race, and these businesses continue to be important to the economy of nearly every country on earth. They are also the center of the most bitter trade controversy between developed countries and less developed ones. The U.S. textile and clothing industries, shaken by steadily rising imports, have responded with a campaign for protectionist policies along with a wave of automation, new marketing strategies, and a slew of acquisitions and buyouts. Leaders of the two sectors, each of which had shipments worth about $57 billion in 1985, say they are fighting for survival.

THE LEGACY OF SLATER'S MILL

The growth of the textile industry was virtually synonymous with the Industrial Revolution in England and America. Eighteenth century Britain witnessed a series of inventions—such as the flying shuttle, the spinning jenny, and the water frame—that turned spinning and weaving from domestic crafts into mass production.

The introduction of this technology into the New World was accomplished by Samuel Slater, a former mill supervisor in England, which in the late 18th century had strict prohibitions on the export of textile know-how. Receiving backing from merchants in Rhode Island, Slater constructed from memory a small mill based on the design of British inventor Richard Arkwright. This operation, opened in 1790, can be seen as the beginning of American industry.

In the following years small spinning mills proliferated in Rhode Island and Massachusetts, but the creation of a true factory system was brought about through the efforts of Francis Cabot Lowell starting in 1813. After spending several years studying the British system, Lowell returned to New England with a plan to consolidate the various phases of textile production— spinning, weaving, dyeing, and printing—under one roof.

Lowell established the Boston Manufacturing Company and opened a mill in Waltham, Massachusetts, to realize this plan. The Waltham system caught on and helped to stimulate the growth of the textile industry throughout New England, including the town of East Chelmsford, which was renamed Lowell in honor of the textile magnate. The supply of the raw material, cotton, had by this time been greatly increased by Eli Whitney's invention of the cotton gin in 1793.

In its early decades the textile industry was supplying fabric that was sold in the dry-goods stores that were springing up throughout the cities and towns of the United States. The only ready-made clothing was that produced in "slop shops" and sold to sailors in waterfront outlets. This began to change with the introduction of the treadle-powered sewing machine by Isaac Singer in the 1850s. Westward expansion and the California gold rush created a demand for durable, ready-to-wear apparel for hardworking landlubbers. It was during this time that German immigrant Levi Strauss built a business in San Francisco selling tough trousers to forty-niners.

The clothing industry was given a further impetus by the large government contracts awarded for the production of army uniforms during the Civil War. As immigration accelerated in the latter part of the century, the menswear industry grew in stature and made use of this new labor pool. The shirt industry developed after World War I (during which men in the army were first exposed to shirts with attached and unstarched collars), when Arrow Shirts (owned by Cluett, Peabody) introduced the process of Sanforizing, which prevented shrinking.

The women's apparel industry developed more slowly. It was not until the early years of the 20th century that a significant degree of mass production replaced custom tailoring for this type of clothing. The trend began with undergarments and silk kimonos and then spread to shirtwaists and later to cotton dresses.

In the 1920s a group of real estate developers in New York erected buildings on Seventh Avenue designed to house workrooms and showrooms for apparel companies. The 16-block area became the center of the women's garment trade in the United States. After American fashion began to escape the grip of French haute couture in the 1930s, the garment district emerged as a design as well as production and marketing center.

SOUTHWARD, HO!

While the clothing industry remained concentrated in the Northeast, the dominance of the New England textile mills began to erode in the late 19th century. The traditional center of the industry reached its pinnacle of power with the large textile complexes in Fall River, Massachusetts (which called itself "Spindle City"); New Bedford, Massachusetts; and Manchester, New Hampshire. But during the Reconstruction era mills began to pop up in the South, particularly in the Carolinas.

After World War II the South became the center of the manufacturing end of the textile business. Faced with increasing unionization and rising costs, many of the New England producers simply packed up their bags—their capital, that is—and transferred production below the Mason-Dixon line.

One of the more notorious practitioners of this policy was Royal Little, the founder of Textron, who got into the synthetic yarn business in the 1920s and made a killing from the vogue for rayon. After receiving government contracts in the 1940s for parachutes and jungle hammocks, Little began buying up New England competitors, including giant American Woolen. He shut down many of the mills, selling off their assets in order to set up operations in the South and to get into other lines of business. Similar moves were also made by J. P. Stevens, which laid off many thousands of workers in the North and then fought a bitter battle when unions tried to follow the company to the South.

Although labor costs and the general business climate in Dixie were hospitable to the textile mills and to the many clothing producers that also relocated there, the industry did not remain placid. First of all, there was a major upheaval in the making with the spread of manmade fibers. Rayon, which was invented in 1891, was synthetic in the sense that it derived from cellulose rather than cotton or wool. Yet the bigger change came from the use of inorganic materials.

This path was blazed by Wallace Carothers, a research scientist who began working for Du Pont in 1927 in an effort to create an artificial substitute for silk. It took Carothers seven years to find the right compound and Du Pont another four to figure out how to produce the substance efficiently. But when nylon was put on the market in 1940 in the form of women's hosiery, public acceptance was immediate. Du Pont sold 64 million pairs of nylons the first year alone.

After the war, synthetic fibers based on petrochemicals began to assume a major place in the textile and apparel business. By the 1960s material such as polyester was being used in the majority of clothing, and chemical companies such as Celanese, Monsanto, and of course Du Pont had become leading fiber producers.

No sooner were the textile and apparel industries adjusting to this sea change than they faced a challenge from another quarter: foreign competition. The first significant signs of this threat came in the 1950s, when Japan, having recovered from the war, began exporting heavily to the United States. The Eisenhower administration persuaded the Japanese to accept voluntary trade restraints in 1957, but by the early 1960s imports were mounting from other Asian countries.

The problem continued to grow, and by the early 1970s both the United States and other developed countries were eager to do something to protect textile and apparel producers from what was seen as predatory Third World competition. The result was the Arrangement regarding International Trade in Textile, more commonly known as the Multifiber Agreement (MFA).

The MFA, which took effect in 1974, essentially represented a way for the developed countries to get around the free-trade provisions of the General Agreement on Tariffs and Trade in order to shield what was considered a vulnerable sector of their economies. Under the agreement, developed countries were able to negotiate specific import limits with Third World producers. Revisions to the MFA in 1977 and 1981 gave importing nations even more latitude.

Although the MFA gave some relief to U.S. producers, the textile and apparel industries faced a worsening crisis in the 1970s and early 80s. The textile sector was plagued with serious overcapacity, cutthroat competition among domestic manufacturers, and fragmentation of production. Aside from howling for more protectionist trade policies, the industry responded to its predicament in several ways.

STRATEGIES FOR SURVIVAL

One tack was to move away from the traditional focus on commodity products and emphasize instead more profitable and distinctive items, such as designer towels and sheets. Fieldcrest Mills was a leader in this strategy, succeeding in foreign as well as domestic markets. Industry leaders Burlington and J. P. Stevens jumped on the bandwagon with upscale home furnishings. There was also a push in specialized new fibers used in products such as snakebite-proof pants and better bulletproof vests.

The other major strategy of the large textile companies was a massive investment in new plant and equipment. The aim here was not to increase overall capacity but to modernize old facilities and reach new levels of efficiency. The industry spent large sums—reaching about $2 billion in 1985—on new technologies such as direct-feed carding in yarn production, open-end spinning, and various kinds of shuttleless looms for weaving. This surge of automation did significantly increase productivity, but it also accelerated the decline of employment levels in the industry.

Most of the 15,000 firms in the clothing sector were too small to make major capital investments, though some of the larger companies did adopt laser cutting devices and other computerized equipment. A nonprofit operation called Tailored Clothing Technology Corporation (referred to as TC^2) was set up in the early 1980s by a group of clothing and textile firms to research further innovations.

Nonetheless apparel remains a highly labor-intensive industry, and wage costs continue to be decisive. The major producers, especially the big blue-jeans makers, have dealt with this imperative by seeking out cheaper labor wherever it might be found. Levi Strauss, for instance, has shifted a great deal of production abroad, taking advantage of Tariff Item 807, which allows a U.S.

company to do some aspects of production overseas and then import the semifinished items back home and pay duties only on the value added abroad. Many of the foreign facilities are located in export processing zones, in which tariffs and other government regulations are relaxed and labor is strictly controlled.

In the United States some aspects of production can be farmed out to subcontractors known as jobbers, who frequently make use of sweatshop or home labor to get the work done. Even in the unionized Northeast, garment workers continue to be paid less than their counterparts in any other industry.

By the early 1980s the clothing business was suffering both from a sharp drop in demand during the recession and from a general decline in the popularity of designer jeans and other brand name apparel. Jeans sales reached a record level of some 600 million pairs in 1981—a result, so it is said, of the film *Urban Cowboy*—and then began declining.

The upheaval in the textile and clothing industries has also brought about a wave of changes in ownership of major firms. After some leading corporate raiders showed interest in these sectors, a batch of companies rushed to go private in order to remain independent. Dan River used an employee stock ownership plan (ESOP) to accomplish this in 1983 as did Cone Mills and jeans producer Blue Bell the following year. In 1985 Levi Strauss was taken private in a leveraged buyout by the Haas family, descendants of the founder.

Becoming private was also the fate of Cannon Mills, which succumbed to a takeover by financier David Murdock in 1982. Cannon was then sold to Fieldcrest Mills in late 1985. At about the same time, Springs Industries agreed to acquire M. Lowenstein, and West Point–Pepperell said it would purchase Cluett, Peabody. In 1986 VF Corp. (maker of Lee, the third-ranking brand of jeans) announced it would purchase Blue Bell (producer of second-ranking Wrangler). As a result of mergers, buyouts, and bankruptcies the number of publicly held apparel companies dropped from 125 in 1976 to 54 in 1985.

All this restructuring, technological change, and marketing emphasis did not change the fact that imports were capturing a steadily increasing share of the U.S. textile and clothing markets. In 1985 textile imports approached $4 billion, triple the 1972 total. Apparel imports meanwhile soared above $15 billion in 1985, more than seven times the 1972 level.

This trend fanned the fires of protectionist sentiment in Congress. There was particular concern over reports that certain exporting countries were arranging for their products to pass through other nations in order to get around the MFA import limits. The result was legislation that took aim at what were regarded as the prime offenders—Hong Kong, South Korea, and Taiwan—by cutting their import allowances by about 30 percent and reducing levels for other countries by lesser amounts.

The Textile and Apparel Trade Enforcement Act passed both houses of Congress in late 1985 but was vetoed by President Reagan in December. The House narrowly upheld the veto the following summer. Meanwhile the trade debate continued, with the industry insisting on the need for better protection and its opponents (major retailers, for instance) arguing that legislation like the 1985 bill would raise domestic clothing prices and that automation, not imports, was mainly responsible for the loss of hundreds of thousands of jobs over the past decade. Nevertheless the leading textile and apparel firms, along with their unions, established the Crafted with Pride in the USA Council, a body that worked to convince the public of the need to "buy American."

LABOR RELATIONS

Just as textiles were central to the development of American industry, so were the workers employed in the mills key figures in U.S. labor history. The Lowell "factory girls" were the first Americans to be exposed to the rigors of mass production, and they were among the earliest workers to act collectively to further their lot. The first strike in the mills took place in 1824 in response to attempts by the owners to extend hours and reduce wages. The workers ended up returning to work on management's terms, but an era of labor militancy in the mills was opened.

By the late 19th century the labor force in textiles as well as clothing was changing rapidly, becoming the domain of new immigrants from Europe. Unions had been formed, but they were mostly limited to skilled native workers. By the early years of the 20th century the low-paid and overworked immigrant labor force began organizing to improve their lot.

In the mills the decisive events included the Fall River strike of 1904 and the large-scale walkout in Lawrence, Massachusetts, in

1912. The latter event, which occurred after the American Woolen Company tried to cut wages, was a bitter 63-day affair that ended in victory for the workers and wage increases throughout the New England textile industry.

Around the same time there was upheaval among clothing workers, who were concentrated in New York. Major strikes of shirtwaist makers in 1909 and cloakmakers in 1910 resulted in the Protocol of Peace, an accord that abolished home work and inside subcontracting, limited the workweek to 54 hours, and created an arbitration process for grievances (in exchange for giving up the right to strike). The following year the deaths of 146 young women workers who were caught behind locked doors during a fire at the Triangle Shirtwaist Company brought public attention to sweatshop conditions and led to various reforms.

By World War I the International Ladies Garment Workers Union, formed in 1900, was one of the more influential U.S. labor organizations. In 1914 the Amalgamated Clothing Workers of America was formed in the men's clothing industry as a more aggressive alternative to the United Garment Workers, which was oriented to skilled tailors and cutters.

The movement of both textile and clothing firms to the South was in large measure aimed at escaping unions. The firms that established those industries in the South had set a paternalistic (though low-wage) and fiercely antiunion tone in the region. When organizers arrived in the new center of the industries after World War II, mill owners were willing to defy the law in the attempt to remain union free.

After workers at Deering-Milliken's plant in Darlington, South Carolina, voted in 1956 for the Textile Workers Union of America (a CIO union formed in the 1930s), the company closed the operation and spent years fighting the unfair-labor-practice charges brought against it. It was not until 1980 that the company agreed to pay $5 million in compensation to the workers who had lost their jobs.

Another epic labor battle took place at J. P. Stevens. In 1963 the Textile Workers began an organizing drive at the company's plants throughout the South. Although the union won a number of representation elections (including one that inspired the film *Norma Rae*), Stevens refused to negotiate a contract. Eventually the Amalgamated Clothing and Textile Workers Union (formed by the 1976 merger of the Textile Workers and the Amalgamated Clothing Workers) adopted a strategy proposed by Ray Rogers that involved pressuring the company's outside directors and lenders. This "corporate campaign" helped bring about a 1980 agreement in which Stevens agreed to recognize the union at facilities where workers had voted in favor of representation.

Despite the J. P. Stevens settlement, unionization of southern textile mills has not progressed much further. A key election at Cannon Mills in 1985 resulted in a dramatic defeat for the union.

Clothing workers' unions have also been in a weakened condition because of rising imports and the decline in jobs. Production workers in apparel declined from 1.2 million in 1973 to just over 1 million in 1985. During the same period, textile production employment fell from 863,000 to 619,000. The clothing unions have tended to put their greatest energies in "buy American" campaigns and have not pushed too hard to end the low wage scales of the industry. The unions have also not had much success battling the resurgence of sweatshops and home labor.

The last major labor battle in the clothing industry took place at Farah Manufacturing in the early 1970s. The workers, mostly Chicano women, at the pants producer's El Paso and San Antonio plants walked out in 1972 to protest the company's refusal to recognize the union they had voted for in 1970. After 22 months and a lot of public support, Farah finally agreed to negotiate a contract.

LEADING COMPANIES

Burlington Industries, the world's largest textile company, got started as a producer of rayon in North Carolina in the 1920s. During the Depression the company began gobbling up other mills in the South and became the leader in the commodity end of the business. By the 1980s Burlington was shaking off its stodgy reputation by investing heavily in modern equipment and bringing out designer products.

Hartmarx, formerly known as Hart, Schaffner & Marx, is one of the oldest names in the men's clothing business. It got started as a Chicago retail clothing store in 1872 and later moved into the wholesale end of the business. It ran the first national clothing advertising and became the leading producer of men's suits. In the 1980s the company has remained strong while producers of less expensive clothing have been buffeted by imports.

Levi Strauss, the leading apparel company, is famous the world over for its blue jeans. The company was founded by a German immigrant who set up a dry-goods business in San Francisco in the 1850s. A Nevada tailor named Jacob Davis approached the company in 1872 with his idea for using rivets to reinforce workpants. Strauss embraced the idea and brought out a product, the 501 Double X blue denim waist overall, that remained virtually unchanged for more than a century. Levi Strauss rode the wave of popularity of blue jeans in the 1960s and 70s but stumbled in its attempts to diversify into other lines of apparel.

Milliken & Company of Spartanburg, South Carolina, is the largest privately held textile firm (estimated 1985 sales of $2 billion) and certainly the most secretive. Formerly known as Deering-Milliken the company pioneered the use of modern equipment and has been one of the most ardent opponents of unionization. President Roger Milliken stepped into the spotlight in 1985 by becoming the chief spokesman for the Crafted with Pride in the USA Council.

During the 1970s **J. P. Stevens** became known to most Americans as the premier corporate opponent of unionization. The company made its peace with the Amalgamated Clothing and Textile Workers Union in 1980 and then sought to improve its image and its competitive position by moving aggressively into designer home furnishings. Joining forces with designer Ralph Lauren, Stevens got leading department stores to install special boutiques carrying an extensive line of its luxury products, ranging from sheets to stemware to furniture. Stevens, which started out as a New England woolen mill and moved its manufacturing to the South after World War II, has also been spending large sums to modernize its production facilities.

SOURCE GUIDE

LEADING STOCK ANALYSTS AND EXPERTS

Margaret Gilliam, textile and apparel analyst at First Boston.

Edward Johnson, textile and apparel analyst at Prescott Ball & Turben, New York.

Jay Meltzer, textile and apparel analyst at Goldman Sachs.

Kurt Salmon Associates, a textile and apparel consulting firm based in Atlanta, Georgia.

TRADE ASSOCIATIONS AND UNIONS

Amalgamated Clothing and Textile Workers Union, New York.

American Apparel Manufacturers Association, Arlington, Virginia.

American Textile Manufacturers Institute, Washington, D.C.

International Ladies Garment Workers Union, New York.

DATA SOURCES AND DIRECTORIES

Davison's Textile Blue Book, an annual directory of more than 18,000 companies in the textile industry (Ridgewood, N.J.: Davison Publishing).

Fact File: The Textile/Apparel Industries, a compilation of statistics issued annually (New York: Fairchild Publications).

Focus: Economic Profile of the Apparel Industry, a biennial compilation of statistics (Arlington, Va.: American Apparel Manufacturers Association).

Textile Organon, a monthly compilation of statistics on manmade fibers (Roseland, N.J.: Textile Economics Bureau).

TRADE PUBLICATIONS

Daily News Record.

Textile Industries, monthly.

Textile World, monthly.

Women's Wear Daily.

BOOKS AND REPORTS

Chapkis, Wendy, and Cynthia Enloe, eds. *Of Common Cloth: Women in the Global Textile Industry.* Amsterdam and Washington, D.C.: Transnational Institute, 1983.

Clairmonte, Frederick, and John Cavanagh. *World in Their Web: Dynamics of Textile Multinationals.* London: Zed Press, 1981.

Conway, Mimi. *Rise Gonna Rise: A Portrait of Southern Textile Workers.* Garden City, N.Y.: Doubleday Publishing, 1979.

Dunwell, Steve. *The Run of the Mill*. Boston: David R. Godine, 1978.

National Research Council. *The Competitive Status of the U.S. Fibers, Textiles and Apparel Complex*. Washington, D.C.: National Academy Press, 1983.

Stein, Leon, ed. *Out of the Sweatshop*. New York: Quadrangle Books, 1977.

Toyne, Brian, ed. *The Global Textile Industry*. London: Allen & Unwin, 1984.

Waldinger, Roger D. *Through the Eye of the Needle: Immigrants and Enterpise in New York's Garment Trades*. New York and London: New York University Press, 1986.

PART THREE

Electronics

CHAPTER THIRTEEN

Mainframes and Minicomputers

In the mid-1950s the process of handling data took a major technological leap with the spread of electronic computing devices. Computers, which were initially devised for military and scientific purposes, soon swept the business world, shaping the way in which corporations kept their records and did their planning. The computer industry grew into one of the major sectors of American business and provided its customers with ever more powerful and efficient processors. By the mid-1980s the industry was shipping hardware with a total value of more than $50 billion. About 30 percent of this represented large-scale devices known as mainframe computers that usually sell for more than $1 million each; another 43 percent consisted of smaller machines called minicomputers and other electronic office equipment. These segments are the subject of this chapter. Personal computers, peripheral equipment, software, and semiconductors are discussed elsewhere. Labor relations in the entire electronics industry are discussed in the chapter on semiconductors.

FROM ABACUS TO ENIAC

The urge to count is a fundamental human trait; and as soon as the numbers involved exceeded fingers and toes, people turned to mechanical computational aids. Until the 17th century, devices such as the abacus sufficed, but then men of science such as Blaise Pascal and Gottfried Wilhelm von Leibniz began devising machines that could take over the tedious chores of arithmetic. In the mid-19th century British inventor Charles Babbage advanced the concept with his project (never realized) of building an "analytical engine." Several decades later in the United States Herman Hollerith invented punch cards and mechanical tabulators suitable for serious computation.

Hollerith started out producing his machines for the Census Bureau but found there was an enormous demand for the devices in the business world. Yet Hollerith was a better inventor than he was entrepreneur, and in 1910 his company was taken over by financier Charles Flint. A pioneer in promoting what would later be called synergistic mergers, Flint combined Hollerith's firm with several others to form the Computing-Tabulating-Recording Company, more commonly known as CTR.

In 1914 CTR hired a talented young marketing man named Thomas Watson to serve as general manager. Watson had been working for National Cash Register (NCR), where he rose to prominence as an aggressive disciple of John Patterson, the king of the cash register business. Patterson's ruthless tactics against the competition resulted in an antitrust suit naming him and Watson among the defendants. The original guilty verdict was overturned on appeal after Patterson made extensive use of company resources to help Dayton, Ohio (where NCR was based), recover from a devastating flood.

By the early 1920s Watson was running CTR, promoting aggressive salesmanship to turn the company into the leader of the tabulating industry. Through paternalism and a strong dose of what today is called corporate culture—there were among other things company songs and the ubiquitous slogan THINK—Watson built one of the best-managed organizations in American business. In 1924 he changed the name of the company to International Business Machines.

While IBM was swallowing the punch-card business, work was going on in various research centers with the aim of developing more sophisticated counting machines. At Bell Labs in the late 1930s mathematician George Stibitz hit on the idea of using electric switches to represent the zeroes and ones of the binary number system. Howard Aiken, a graduate student at Harvard who was doing similar work, ended up getting some funding from IBM, which was more interested in the prestige of being associated with a Harvard project than in the practical results. Watson was skeptical of electronic computing devices and remained so until the early 1950s. When Aiken unveiled his machine—the automatic sequence controlled calculator, or Mark I—in 1944 he barely mentioned IBM, which outraged Watson and probably contributed to his resistance to computers.

A separate research project at the Moore School of Electrical Engineering of the University of Pennsylvania resulted in the device that paved the way for the computer industry. Following an approach often credited to John Atanasoff of Iowa State College, John Mauchly and J. Presper Eckert assembled a machine based on electronic vacuum tubes. The huge contraption, dubbed the Electronic Numerical Integrator and Computer (ENIAC), was first demonstrated publicly on February 14, 1946—a date that could be called the birth of the modern computer age.

Eckert and Mauchly recognized the commercial potential of what they had created and sought to keep the patents in their own names. A dispute over this issue led to their departure from the Moore School and the establishment of a private company to produce ENIAC-like computers under the name of UNIVAC. The two men lacked business finesse as well as adequate capital, so in 1950 they agreed to sell the business to Remington Rand, a large office-supply outfit.

The new owners soon scored a coup when they made a deal with CBS to use UNIVAC to predict the outcome of the 1952 presidential election. The computer forecast a landslide victory for Eisenhower by 9:00 P.M. on election night, but officials were skeptical of the result and refused to air it until a much larger percentage of the actual voting results had come in. Nevertheless Walter Cronkite helped to introduce millions of Americans to these electronic marvels, and the name UNIVAC became synonymous with computers.

THE RISE OF IBM

In the next few years other companies joined Remington (which merged with Sperry Corp. in 1955 to form Sperry Rand) in the computer business, the most important of these new entrants being IBM. Thomas Watson, Jr., who became president of the company in 1952, had none of his aging father's hesitation about electronic computers. The younger Watson gave the go-ahead for development of a scientific computer that became known as the defense calculator, or the 701. With this product and its commercial version, the 702, IBM let loose its formidable sales machine on the computer business. In fact it was this marketing prowess that made 702 into a huge success despite the fact that it was technically inferior to UNIVAC. IBM quickly moved on to the 705, which incorporated magnetic core memory. By 1956, only three years after the introduction of the 701, IBM had seized 85 percent of the computer market, leaving Sperry far behind with a 10 percent share.

IBM's lead was solid enough so that the company could take its time joining the rest of the industry in the move from vacuum tubes to transistors. Then, as integrated circuits were perfected and put into use, IBM began planning its major technical initiative. The results of this preparation were announced with much fanfare in April 1964. At simultaneous press conferences in 62 U.S. cities and 14 foreign countries, IBM unveiled its 360 Series—a range of computers that were supposed to address any kind of data processing need. The $5 billion that IBM risked on this entirely new generation (the industry's third) of machines represented one of the greatest business gambles ever.

There was some stumbling, but the 360 turned out to be a great success and established IBM as the unquestioned leader of the business. In fact, analysts started referring to the industry as "IBM and the Seven Dwarfs," the latter consisting of Sperry, Control Data Corp., Honeywell, RCA, NCR, General Electric, and Burroughs. IBM's dominance allowed it to set the standards for the industry and gave the company's salesmen enormous leverage over the people in corporations responsible for computer-buying decisions, many of whom were persuaded that purchasing data processing equipment from anyone but IBM was an unacceptable risk.

IBM's hard sell—which often included promises of new, improved products that were far from completed—put its competitors at a severe disadvantage. After Control Data was burned by what it considered a very premature announcement of an IBM model, CDC's founder and chief executive William Norris began complaining to the Justice Department. Getting no action, Norris finally filed a private antitrust suit against IBM in late 1968, charging the industry leader with advertising "paper machines and phantom computers." Soon afterward, on the very last day of the Johnson administration, the Justice Department brought its own case against IBM.

IBM fought back against CDC but ended up settling out of court in a 1973 accord under which IBM sold its Service Bureau Corp. subsidiary to CDC at asset value and agreed to pay out about $100 million over several years. (IBM had been forced to create the Service Bureau as an arms-length operation as part of the 1956 consent decree it signed to resolve antitrust charges brought by the Justice Department with regard to the tabulating business.) But perhaps the most important element of the settlement was the provision for destroying the computerized index CDC had compiled of the 75,000 pages of internal IBM documents it had obtained during the discovery phase of the case. The Justice Department had been hoping to get its hands on that index to aid its case against IBM (which stretched through the 1970s and was finally dropped by the Reagan administration in January 1982).

The dominance of the 360 Series had a negative as well as a positive effect on IBM's competitive position. Two new sets of rivals emerged. One group purchased IBM mainframes and leased them out to customers at better rates than IBM offered to rental customers. Another set of companies, such as Mohawk Data Sciences and Telex, began producing peripheral equipment that worked with IBM systems (the industry jargon is "plug compatible") but that was cheaper and more efficient than comparable devices made by IBM.

Big Blue, as IBM was nicknamed, fought back with various tactics, including the introduction of the 370 Series in 1970. It priced this new line of products to the disadvantage of the leasing companies and made some design changes that complicated life for producers of what came to be called plug-compatible peripherals.

These moves against the upstarts resulted in yet more litigation against IBM. Big Blue prevailed in a case brought by Greyhound Computer Leasing but lost the initial verdict in the suit brought by Telex. The federal appeals court overturned the verdict, and after Telex vowed to go to the Supreme Court the two parties settled. But IBM's legal woes mounted as about a dozen other small competitors sought their day in court. *Fortune* described the experience as "IBM's travails in Lilliput."

As if this was not enough, Big Blue was also confronted by a direct assault in its core business: the production of large-scale, general-purpose mainframe computers. IBM never quite had this market entirely to itself, but the group of competitors known as the Seven Dwarfs (who were renamed the BUNCH, an acronym for Burroughs, the Univac division of Sperry, NCR, Control Data, and Honeywell, after GE and RCA dropped out of the business in the early 1970s) were perennial also-rans. Then in 1970 Gene Amdahl, a leading IBM engineer who had designed the 360 Series, left the company with the intention of producing mainframe computers that were superior to IBM's but ran on the same software.

Amdahl's vow was initially laughed off by Big Blue, but the new company obtained funding from Fujitsu (which wanted access to the technology) and American venture capitalists. Overcoming the odds, Amdahl brought out its 470 V/6 in 1975 and began luring away some of IBM's major customers, who were impressed by the better price-performance ratio of Amdahl's machine. Before long there was a rush into the IBM-compatible mainframe business by companies such as Itel, Two Pi, and Magnuson Systems.

On another front IBM was threatened by the increasing popularity of smaller systems that allowed easier and more flexible data processing operations. This segment of the business was created back in 1957 by a young MIT engineer named Kenneth Olsen. Several years later the firm, called Digital Equipment Corp., brought out a system for $120,000 while the cheapest mainframes were going for well over $1 million. These inexpensive systems (soon labeled minicomputers) found many willing customers, and DEC experienced a breathtaking rate of growth. But it was in the 1970s that minis, by then also being produced by companies such as Data General and Hewlett-Packard, came into full flower.

In all, the 1970s were a period of discomfort for IBM. Its overall market share dropped from about 60 percent to 40 percent over the decade, and its profit margins slid several points from the typical 1960s range of 24 to 28 percent. For the first time Big Blue seemed less than invincible.

BIG BLUE TRIES TO BOUNCE BACK

At the end of the decade IBM unleashed a plan to regain dominance. The industry had long been awaiting Big Blue's next major step. In 1975 the company abandoned work on something called Future System, which was supposed to replace the 370 Series. IBM's planners decided that an entirely new generation of machines would be too disruptive and instead opted for an evolutionary change. In fact it was this slower pace that gave breathing room to the leasing companies and IBM-compatible manufacturers.

In 1979 Big Blue changed the rules of the game. IBM announced the 4300 line—a new generation of medium-scale mainframes that were priced far below existing levels. The cost per megabyte of memory plunged from $75,000 to $15,000. This bargain elicited orders by the truckful. In only three weeks IBM had requests for 42,000 machines, more than twice what the company had planned to produce over the life of the series. Delivery schedules were stretched out over four years.

The overwhelming demand created problems for IBM. Customers were upset at the long waiting periods for delivery, and some of these turned to the IBM-compatibles instead. Many large-scale users, anticipating big price cuts to match the bargains on the smaller 4300 machines, canceled previous purchase orders and switched to leasing while waiting for announcements regarding high-end models. IBM got caught in a financial squeeze and suffered both earnings and stock price declines.

IBM's delays in bringing out new high-end machines created a new opening for the plug-compatible mainframe producers, who soon gained a total market share exceeding that of the BUNCH. By the early 1980s Big Blue appeared to abandon its previous attempts to eradicate this form of competition, and the likes of Amdahl (no longer run by Gene Amdahl) became a permanent if still unstable factor in the mainframe business.

This is not to say that the 1980s brought a repetition of the woes that the 1970s had visited on IBM. In fact Big Blue became more aggressive than ever, especially after the Justice Department dropped its long-standing antitrust suit in January 1982. IBM eagerly adopted tactics such as volume discounts that it previously had shunned and brought charges against Hitachi and National

Advanced Systems for theft of trade secrets. IBM also bought a share of Rolm (later expanded to full ownership) to improve its position in the communications end of the business, and it purchased a chunk of Intel to gain better access to advanced semiconductor technology.

In 1985 IBM finally launched the first of its new generation of high-end mainframes. Code-named Sierra during the development process, the 3090 Series represented a less than earthshaking improvement over the 3080 Series. In fact the lack of a big leap–along with the price cuts IBM offered on the 3080 machines—prompted some users to decide they would be better off buying used mainframes from the older series. In addition there were announcements of competing machines from Amdahl, Burroughs, Honeywell (a mainframe built by Nippon Electric and using Honeywell software), and National Advanced Systems (a distributor of plug-compatible machines made by Hitachi).

All of the industry suffered from the sharp falling off of growth in the computer business in the mid-1980s. The effect on behemoth IBM was most pronounced, with the company's earnings and stock price declining sharply.

THE FUTURE OF MAINFRAMES

The boom in personal computers in the early 1980s caused some observers to predict a decline in the market for mainframe and minicomputers. While desktop machines have taken over some processing functions previously done by larger systems, those bigger machines are still quite essential for allowing PCs to communicate with one another. Local area networks run by minis or mainframes are the rage—particularly for office automation— and IBM gave this technology a boost in late 1985 with the introduction of its own version of the network.

The future of the mainframe business may also revolve around what has been called fifth-generation technology. The Japanese computer industry, with aid from the government, has been conducting research for several years on machines that would allow users to operate them without complicated programming. Many American companies are still skeptical about this approach, which will require great advances in the field of artificial intelligence.

What American computer makers are more excited about is the development of what are known as supercomputers. These are the systems capable of handling the huge number of computations involved in sophisticated scientific and engineering applications. The supercomputer market is essentially owned by Cray Research. By the end of 1984 there were 130 supercomputers in place worldwide, and Cray had supplied 88 of these.

The Cray-2, introduced in 1985, offered performance in the mind-boggling range of 600 to 1,200 MFLOPS (millions of floating-point operations per second). Founder Seymour Cray then turned to the Cray-3, which was supposed to achieve a much more amazing performance of 16,000 MFLOPS through the use of gallium arsenide chips. The market for supercomputers, estimated at $300 million in 1985, was forecast to grow to $1.5 billion by 1990. Other players in the business include Control Data and Japanese producers Hitachi, Fujitsu, and NEC, which by 1985 had still not achieved much of a presence in the United States.

LEADING COMPANIES (APART FROM IBM)

Burroughs has been one of IBM's most persistent competitors in the mainframe business since the 1950s, gaining a reputation for the simplicity and power of its programs. The company got into

The Top 15 Computer Companies Worldwide, by 1985 Data Processing Revenue ($ Millions)

1. International Business Machines	$48,554
2. Digital Equipment	7,029
3. Sperry	4,755
4. Burroughs	4,685
5. Fujitsu	4,309
6. NCR	3,885
7. NEC	3,761
8. Control Data	3,679
9. Hewlett-Packard	3,675
10. Siemens	3,265
11. Hitachi	2,885
12. Olivetti	2,518
13. Wang Laboratories	2,428
14. Xerox	1,959
15. Honeywell	1,951

Source: From the Datamation 100, reprinted with permission of *Datamation*® magazine, ©Copyright by Technical Publishing Company, a Dun & Bradstreet Company, 1986, all rights reserved.

the computer business early in that decade, after making a name for itself in adding and accounting machines. But Burroughs did not have the marketing finesse to go along with its technical prowess. W. Michael Blumenthal, President Jimmy Carter's first treasury secretary, was brought in to run the company in 1980. He rescued the company from a nosedive, bought memory-device maker Memorex in 1981 and in 1985 introduced a new series of mainframes to compete with IBM's Sierra line. In 1986 Burroughs acquired rival mainframe maker Sperry for $4.4 billion and the combined company was named Unisys. Sperry's ancestor Remington Rand was the leader of the industry in its early days after it took over the company founded by computer pioneers John Mauchly and J. Presper Eckert. But soon the firm's UNIVAC machines fell victim to IBM's superior salesmanship and became a distant second. In 1971 Sperry bought the computer business of RCA and resisted diversifying out of mainframes.

Control Data Corp. (CDC) was formed in 1957 when a group of engineers led by William Norris broke away from a subsidiary of Sperry Rand to produce sophisticated scientific computers on their own. Norris decided to mount a legal challenge to IBM in the late 1960s over pressure tactics used by Big Blue to discourage customers from buying a CDC system. A settlement of the case in 1973 allowed CDC to buy IBM's computer service operation at a bargain price. In the following years Norris placed more emphasis on the service business and the production of peripheral equipment while also sinking many millions of dollars in a computer-based learning system called PLATO. He also made a name for himself as a leading exponent of corporate social responsibility. At the beginning of 1986 Norris finally stepped down, and his successor Robert Price set out to clear up the company's financial problems.

Cray Research is the undisputed leader of the supercomputer business, the production of the fastest mainframes for advanced technical applications. The company was established in 1972 by Seymour Cray, a brilliant engineer who pioneered supercomputers while working for Control Data.

Digital Equipment Corp. (DEC) was the originator of a segment of the mainframe business consisting of smaller, more flexible machines known as minicomputers. Founded in 1957 by young MIT engineer Kenneth Olsen, DEC experienced phenomenal growth until the early 1980s, becoming the second-largest company in the computer industry. Facing a slowing of growth in minicomputers Olsen then moved to improve the company's marketing ability. Since the late 1960s DEC has been in a heated contest with Data General, a rival formed when DEC engineer Edson de Castro struck out on his own. The development of a new mini called Eagle at Data General was chronicled in Tracy Kidder's popular 1981 book *The Soul of a New Machine.*

Hewlett-Packard, the premier instruments company, has been trying for years to break into the big leagues of the computer business. Founded in a Palo Alto, California, garage in 1938 by William Hewlett and David Packard, the company first got into the minicomputer business in 1968 and remained one of the leading players in that segment. Under the leadership of John Young the company has faltered in expanding its presence, especially in the PC and computer-aided engineering areas.

Honeywell's roots go back to A. M. Butz's invention of the thermostat in 1883. The company got into the computer business in 1955 by buying an operation from Raytheon. In 1963 Honeywell pioneered the concept of IBM-compatibility with the introduction of its H–200, a product that prompted Big Blue to accelerate the announcement of its pathbreaking 360 Series. The company's presence in the industry took a leap after the purchase of General Electric's computer business in 1970, but Honeywell faltered and remained one of the less dynamic of the mainframe producers. By the mid-1980s Honeywell was pulling back from the production of general-purpose mainframes and concentrating on factory automation. In late 1986 Honeywell's computer operations were turned into a joint venture with France's Groupe Bull and Japan's NEC.

NCR Corporation, the modern incarnation of the old National Cash Register empire, entered the computer business in the early 1950s but was slow at integrating it into the rest of the company. NCR retained a foothold in the mainframe business by selling to its faithful customers in the retail and financial areas. Charles Exley, who took over as president in 1976, established a strategy of aiming at specialized markets, but the company remained a weak player in the industry. In 1986 NCR introduced its first new mainframes in seven years.

Wang Laboratories, founded by An Wang in 1951 as a producer of custom-built electronic components, grew during the 1970s into the leading producer of word-processing systems. The company's ascent faltered in the early 1980s, when the rise of personal computers reduced the appeal of Wang's dedicated terminals. A spate of problems involving new products and financial controls further weakened the firm, but by 1985 the founder was engaged in a personal campaign to revive the company.

SOURCE GUIDE

LEADING STOCK ANALYSTS AND EXPERTS

Datapro Research Corp., Delran, New Jersey.

Dataquest Inc., San Jose, California.

Gartner Group, Stamford, Connecticut.

International Data Corp., Framingham, Massachusetts.

Seybold Consulting Group, Boston.

Ulric Weil, veteran analyst now with his own firm in Washington, D.C.

Frederic Withington, veteran analyst at Arthur D. Little, Cambridge, Massachusetts.

Yankee Group, Boston.

TRADE ASSOCIATION

Computer and Business Equipment Manufacturers Association, Washington, D.C.

DATA SOURCES AND DIRECTORIES

Computer and Business Equipment Industry Marketing Data Book, an annual volume of statistics (Washington, D.C.: Computer and Business Equipment Manufacturers Association).

Datamation 100, an annual ranking of the leading computer companies, in June (New York: *Datamation*).

Gartner Group Top 100 DP Almanac, an annual statistical review of the leading data processing firms (Stamford, Conn.: Gartner Group).

TRADE PUBLICATIONS

Computer Decisions, fortnightly.
Computers and People, bimonthly.
Computerworld, weekly.
Datamation, semimonthly.

BOOKS AND REPORTS

Brock, Gerald. *The U.S. Computer Industry*. Cambridge, Mass.: Ballinger, 1975.

Fishman, Katharine. *The Computer Establishment*. New York: Harper & Row, 1981.

McClellan, Stephen. *The Coming Computer Industry Shakeout*. New York: John Wiley & Sons, 1984.

Shurkin, Joel. *Engines of the Mind: A History of the Computer*. New York: W. W. Norton, 1984.

Sobel, Robert. *IBM: Colossus in Transition*. New York: Times Books, 1981.

Weil, Ulric. *Information Systems in the 80s*. Englewood Cliffs, N.J.: Prentice-Hall, 1982.

CHAPTER FOURTEEN

Microcomputers and Software

At one time computers were large, forbidding devices locked in temperature-controlled rooms and tended to by a priesthood of specialists. For most people they were mysterious and marvelous machines that were becoming an increasing force in their lives yet were still hidden from view. Even computer students and aficionados could only gain access to the data processing power of mainframes via remote terminals and time-sharing arrangements. Until the early 1970s companies and institutions, not individuals, owned all the computers in existence.

Starting in 1975 this state of affairs began to change at a remarkable pace. Small computer systems, or microcomputers, appeared on the scene and were eagerly purchased by people seeking direct and personal access to data processing and what became a new form of entertainment. The industry that grew up around this phenomenon expanded at a rate rarely seen in the history of American business. Despite a slowdown in the early 1980s the industry had by the middle of the decade reached a revenue level of some $21 billion for hardware and software combined. What was once the exclusive domain of youthful entrepreneurs—a number of whom are now multimillionaires—is now a developed industry dominated by IBM, the traditional giant of the computer industry.

HISTORY OF A YOUNG INDUSTRY

The pioneering company in the microcomputer industry was a now defunct firm called Micro Instrumentation Telemetry Systems (MITS). Formed in 1968 by a group of Air Force officers/ electronics buffs stationed in Albuquerque, New Mexico, MITS started out producing radio transmitters for model airplanes. A few years later Ed Roberts, who had bought out his partners, got into calculators, and after the disastrous price war in that business he hit on the idea of producing kits that would allow hobbyists to make use of the recently developed microprocessors, the so-called computers on a chip.

Encouraged by Les Solomon, an editor at *Popular Electronics*, Roberts had the prototype ready in early 1975 when it was announced to the world on the cover of Solomon's magazine. The product was called Altair, a name suggested by Solomon's 12-year-old daughter because it was the destination of the Starship Enterprise in an episode of *Star Trek*. Pathbreaking though it was, the Altair was primitive by later standards. It had no keyboard or display screen, and after the circuit board was assembled programming could only be introduced through a series of switches.

But what excited the electronics hobbyist world was that it was indeed a computer, built on an Intel 8080 chip and capable of being programmed. It was that capability that interested two young men named Bill Gates and Paul Allen, who had been programmers since their early teens. Seeing the issue of *Popular Electronics* announcing the Altair, the two called MITS and offered to produce a version of the popular computer language Basic to run on the machine. Roberts was interested, and after Gates and Allen delivered the program six weeks later, they and MITS developed a close working relationship. Gates and Allen set up a company called Microsoft that became one of the premier software houses. Another early programmer was Gary Kildall, an instructor at the U.S. Naval Postgraduate School who wrote the operating system CP/M, which became the standard for the first generation of micros.

The Altair was a great success among hobbyists, and MITS was soon joined in the micro business by a slew of other small companies, including IMSAI, Processor Technology, and North Star. All these producers emerged out of the alternative computing scene of the San Francisco Bay area and Silicon Valley. This was the milieu of young "hackers" who were committed to making computers more accessible to noninstitutional users and were suspicious of those who attempted to make a big business out of micros. They were particularly unsympathetic to people like Gates and Allen who were making money from software. The prevailing ethic was that software should be freely shared, and pirating of programs was commonplace. (For more on the issue of software copyright see Copy Protection and Piracy later in this chapter.)

Some micro buffs were more explicitly political and talked of "computer lib" as a means of social change. Lee Felsenstein initiated a project called Community Memory to provide free computerized information services to the public. Both the politicos and the techies came together with the budding entrepreneurs in a group called the Homebrew Computer Club.

SETTING UP THE APPLE CART

Two of the participants in Homebrew meetings were a pair of friends named Steven Jobs and Stephen Wozniak. The two Steves had been involved in electronics since their teens. In the early 1970s they were drawn into "phone phreaking," the production of devices called blue boxes that allowed one to make long-distance phone calls without paying for them.

Jobs, who dabbled in Eastern religion, ended up working for Nolan Bushnell at Atari. At the time, Bushnell was already a Silicon Valley success story, thanks to his invention of Pong (an electronic version of table tennis that was the first video arcade game). Pong started a video game mania, and Atari (which means "check" in the Japanese game of Go) grew like mad, especially after the introduction of home versions of Pong and other amusements.

Jobs was more interested in computers than in games. After Bushnell turned down his proposal for a micro, he urged his friend Wozniak to build one independently. Wozniak, a brilliant engineer and an inveterate prankster, took on the challenge while remaining in his job at Hewlett-Packard. The resulting product, built first in Jobs's parents' house and then the proverbial garage, was christened Apple®.

After the 50 copies of the primitive Apple I were well received, Jobs and Wozniak managed to persuade Mike Markkula, a former marketing wizard at Intel who was comfortably retired in his mid-30s, to help the fledgling company get off the ground. Jobs also convinced leading Silicon Valley publicist Regis McKenna to take on the firm as a client. In the meantime Woz was designing an improved version of the system.

The Apple II, which Jobs insisted be as easy as possible to use and have an attractive and unforbidding design, was an instant hit. More than any other product, it helped to bring micros out of the hobbyist world and to a wide range of the general population. One of the elements of this success was the availability on the Apple II of the first financial analysis program for micros, Visi-Calc®.

The machine also brought rapid growth to Apple Computer, whose operating revenues leaped from $8 million in 1978 to $117 million in 1980. The initial expansion was made possible by $517,000 in venture capital that Markkula arranged to obtain from Venrock Associates (the venture capital arm of the Rockefeller interests), Don Valentine, and Arthur Rock in early 1978. This investment paid off handsomely. When Apple went public in December 1980 the $517,000 was suddenly worth about $200 million, and the shares owned by Jobs, Wozniak, and Markkula made them centimillionaires. Thanks to the company's generous stock options, many other employees hit the jackpot as well.

Along with the success of the Apple II the micro market exploded. Dozens of start-up companies jumped into what was hailed as a new gold rush. Analysts made bold predictions about the spread of micros into virtually every household; the sky was said to be the limit.

Several companies soon rose to the top of the heap. These represented the two leading strategies of the time. Commodore International, a former typewriter company, led the push into the home market. Led by Jack Tramiel, Commodore brought out the low-cost PET (named after the pet rock fad of the time). But after the company got a poor reputation for service, its sales effort was focused in Europe. In 1981 Tramiel, convinced of the demand for cheap computers in the United States, brought out the VIC 20 and priced it at $299. Tramiel's persistence made Commodore a success even while other home-computer makers got pummeled in the intensely competitive market.

By the early 1980s Jobs's skepticism about the market for home computers seemed to be justified; the greatest demand lay in business and professional users. One company that established a strong foothold there early on was Tandy Corp., parent company of the Radio Shack chain of electronics stores. Tandy's TRS–80 Series won a loyal following among serious but not necessarily hobbyist users, and the Model 100 (one of the first laptop devices) became the standard for journalists and others who needed to write or record data while on the road.

The most spectacular rise and fall in this segment was that of Osborne Computer. Adam Osborne got into the micro scene in the mid-1970s after he self-published *Introduction to Microcomputers* and started writing columns for publications such as *Info-World*. Osborne expanded his book-publishing operation and was successful enough so that McGraw-Hill bought the business in 1979. He then decided to produce his own systems.

Introduced in 1981 the Osborne 1 was an impressive if not attractive machine. It was a no-frills micro that had disk drive, monitor, and keyboard, all built into a portable package; several software programs were also thrown in for the price of $1,795. The Osborne took off, and by its second year the company was doing $70 million in sales. Yet in September 1983 Osborne Computer went into Chapter 11, the victim of poor management. Osborne himself disclaimed responsibility and placed the blame on Robert Jaunich, the former president of Consolidated Foods who had been brought in to run the company. Whoever was the culprit, it seems that Osborne Computer was a classic case of a company soaring too high too fast.

Osborne was not the only disaster in the business and professional segment. Dozens of small companies came and went, and neither Hewlett-Packard nor Xerox was able to make much of a splash. Apple hoped to have a clear field for a more sophisticated and expensive office system it was developing with the code name of Lisa. But that was not to be.

ENTER BIG BLUE

By 1980 planners in computer behemoth IBM had become impressed with the growth of the micro market. Although Big Blue had traditionally concentrated on selling large mainframe systems and had been slow to enter even the minicomputer market, IBM was confronting the 1980s with an aggressive posture, hoping to overcome the frustrations of the 1970s (see Chapter Thirteen for more on that period). An operation called Entry Level Systems (later Entry Systems Division) was set up in Boca Raton, Florida, to develop an IBM machine to compete with the micros produced by entrepreneurs who were not yet born when Big Blue got into the computer business in the early 1950s.

The IBM PC, introduced in August 1981, took the world by storm. While it was no technological leap forward—the components were standard ones supplied by outside vendors—the machine did have the IBM cachet, and that made all the difference. Big Blue did make some smart moves: The PC had an open software system, which encouraged the production of many compatible programs by independent firms, and the leap from an 8-bit to a 16-bit processor came at the right time for the industry.

IBM's machine was announced around the time the Apple III was suffering from engineering problems (which had led to major recalls) and poor marketing. IBM was able to charge ahead in the office and professional segment, matching Apple's market share only a year after the introduction of the IBM PC. In 1983 Big Blue gained more ground as Apple's new entry for the business market, the $10,000 Lisa®, failed to win widespread acceptance because of its limited software and inability to communicate with other computers, especially IBM mainframes. By October 1983 *Business Week* was able to proclaim: "The battle for market supremacy is suddenly all over, and IBM is the winner."

Meanwhile at the low end of the market a fierce price war was in progress. Atari was slugging it out with Coleco and Mattel in the game-player segment, while Texas Instruments and Atari were losing ground to Commodore and Coleco in the home-computer area (defined as machines costing less than $1,000). Prices for basic home computers dropped to $99 (after rebates), causing a string of fatal losses for several producers. Among the victims in the shakeout of 1983 were Texas Instruments, Mattel, and Timex, which was selling the "minimicrocomputer" created by British inventor Clive Sinclair.

Starting in 1984 Apple, having brought in John Sculley of PepsiCo to serve as president, launched its counterattack against IBM. The campaign included a new version of Lisa and a less expensive but impressive system called Macintosh®. Sculley and Jobs hoped to pitch the Mac—which offered a more powerful (32-bit) processor, excellent graphics, and a handheld input device (a mouse)—to smaller companies and university students.

Yet by 1985 Apple was abandoning its quest to rout IBM from the personal computer market, realizing it was more realistic to introduce devices that would make Macintoshes compatible with IBM office networks. (In 1986 Microsoft Corp. released a program enabling Macintoshes and IBM PCs to share some forms of data.) With Sculley completely in charge—he forced Jobs out in late 1985—Apple improved its margins but continued to slip in market share. Yet Sculley kept promoting the Macintosh.

Part of the reason for Apple's slide was a new force in the micro market that was challenging Big Blue as well: producers of IBM-compatible PCs. Just as happened in the mainframe and peripheral markets, a group of companies saw an opportunity in producing micros that worked on the same software as the venerable IBM PC but were better or cheaper than the machines put out by IBM itself.

The most outstanding of the clone producers was Compaq Computer, a company that racked up the amazing figure of $111 million in sales for its first year in operation (1983). Compaq started out producing portable models, and it trounced the IBM "luggable" introduced in 1984. (IBM also went nowhere with its PC Jr., a scaled-down version of the PC introduced in 1983 and discontinued in 1985.) Compaq then brought out desktop machines that competed with the basic PC as well as the higher-performance AT and XT machines.

By 1986 several Asian producers also brought out IBM clones. The most promising of these was the system sold by Leading Edge and built by Daewoo of South Korea. Microcomputer imports began to edge up. The combined pressures from foreign and domestic clone-producers set off a price war, and IBM saw its share of the market drop substantially.

SOFTWARE TAKES CHARGE

The direction of the microcomputer software industry was to a great extent determined in 1980 when a group of pin-striped representatives of IBM visited young Bill Gates of Microsoft. Big Blue was looking for a programming language for its then secret personal computer project and was impressed with Microsoft's work. IBM also ended up asking Gates to provide an operating system for the PC. The program, called MS–DOS® (Microsoft disk operating system) by Gates and PC–DOS® when sold by IBM, quickly became the dominant standard as the IBM PC and its clones seized a large chunk of the micro market.

Thanks to the PC's open architecture and IBM's encouragement of independent producers, the range of PC-compatible applications software expanded rapidly. For business users, integrated financial packages (ones that combined spreadsheets and graphics) were the rage, and Lotus Development's 1–2–3® (designed for the PC) soon dethroned VisiCalc, the pioneer in this field. As a result Lotus became the largest independent software producer.

By the mid-1980s, as micro hardware reached a certain level of sophistication, industry analysts began saying that the future of personal computing depended much more on advances in software. The new wave of novice users needed more-accessible programming, while those with more experience required software with greater versatility and sophistication.

These conflicting goals sometimes caused problems. Lotus brought out an advanced integrated program in 1984 called Symphony®, which was technically impressive but which many users found too difficult to use. The same problem plagued Ashton-Tate, another of the top software houses, with its dBase III® database management program.

The software industry has also come under pressure to do something about its prices. While the cost of micro hardware has steadily declined, software prices generally have not budged. Large corporate users have grown frustrated at having to pay near retail prices even when buying large quantities of programs, and in 1985 they started hounding the software houses to allow volume purchase discounts.

One of the reasons for the sticky prices is the distribution system of the highly fragmented software industry. With some 5,000 developers having more than 25,000 programs on the market, stores can only stock a small number of the most popular ones, and this discourages discounting. Some smaller producers have sought to sell cheap programs through the mail, but they find it hard to get attention while the Big Three—Lotus, Ashton-Tate, and Microsoft (which branched out from systems to applications software)—loudly tout their wares.

The problems of the smaller producers have given rise to a

wave of consolidation in the industry. The more than 200 mergers in 1985 included Ashton-Tate's $22 million acquisition of Multimate International, a leading word-processing program producer. The configuration of the industry is bound to change further with the transition from text-based to more versatile graphics-based software.

COPY PROTECTION AND PIRACY

One of the main reasons software companies gave for their high prices were the heavy losses they incurred from the unauthorized copying of programs. Analysts estimated those losses at several hundred million dollars a year in the early 1980s.

The problem for the industry was that software is extremely easy to copy; in fact, copying the contents of a floppy disk onto another (blank) disk is one of the first operations a PC user learns. Moreover, many of the young hackers who made the PC revolution happen regarded software as tools that should be freely available to anyone who wanted to use them.

As software companies grew larger and left the hacker mentality behind they started spending a considerable amount of time and money to "copy-protect" their products.

Yet clever hackers were able with little difficulty to break the protection codes and distribute copies to friends. By the early 1980s there were special programs such as Locksmith that automatically circumvented protection codes and allowed one to make copies of protected software. "Liberated" software often ended up on electronic bulletin boards from which PC users could download it through the phone lines onto disks.

Software makers fought back by developing new devices for preventing unauthorized copying. The first advanced protection device was Vault Corp.'s Prolok system, introduced in the early 1980s. This involved the placement of a tiny hole in the disk that must be in the proper place for the software to run. Later, software companies developed "lock and key" combinations of hardware and software devices to deter piracy.

While many individual PC users amassed collections of pirated disks, the software industry came to realize that the pirates who were costing them the most were corporations that purchased one or several copies of expensive business programs such as

Lotus 1–2–3 and then made many additional unauthorized copies to distribute among the staff. The research firm Future Computing estimated in a 1985 study that there were as many pirate copies of business software programs in circulation as legitimate ones.

The software industry started getting tough with corporate pirates in 1984. Lotus Development charged Rixon Inc. with unauthorized copying of 1–2–3 and sued the company for $10 million. The parties settled out of court, with Rixon agreeing to make a substantial payment. In 1985 MicroPro International, producer of the popular WordStar® word-processing program, sued a subsidiary of American Brands, also winning a settlement. Later that year an FBI investigation led to a lawsuit against a Philadelphia publishing company for providing an unauthorized copy of a $4,800 database program to a New York typesetting firm.

Such actions prompted many companies to take the software copyright issue more seriously. Numerous large firms adopted strict internal policies against software copying, and some of them began arguing that the only practical solution was a system of software site licenses. Under this arrangement a vendor would sell a company a few copies of a program and the right to make a limited number of additional copies. Vendors had mixed feelings about site licenses, since they ended up receiving less in revenues for each copy of their programs in use, but the discounted proceeds were more than they received when extra copies were simply pirated.

At the same time, many corporate users began to put pressure on software producers to eliminate copy-protection features, which companies felt were making some programs less efficient. Fearing that they could lose more from reduced legitimate sales than from piracy, a number of leading software companies began abandoning copy protection in 1986.

LEADING COMPANIES

Apple Computer was not the first to produce a micro but was the pioneer in introducing personal computing to a mass audience. Founded by two young hackers Steven Jobs and Stephen Wozniak, the company attracted venture capital and professional management and embarked on a dizzying rate of growth. The world became more complicated when computer giant IBM stormed into the market. Apple stumbled with several products and allowed IBM to win over the lucrative office segment. By the mid-1980s Apple had become a billion dollar company, and Jobs's unorthodox management methods were steadily abandoned. In 1985 he was stripped of his operating authority and then ousted entirely.

Ashton-Tate had its origins in 1975, when George Tate (who was repairing stereos at the time) was inspired by the announcement of the first micro, the Altair. Tate started programming, and in 1980 he formed Software Plus with Hal Lashlee. The company prospered by selling dBase II®, a database management program devised by Wayne Ratliff. Under the leadership of Edward Esber (Tate died in 1984) the company emerged as one of the largest independent software producers.

Atari was the first Silicon Valley success story of the micro age. The company was established by Nolan Bushnell, who created the first electronic arcade game (Pong) and gave rise to the video game mania of the 1970s. Atari was purchased by Warner Communications in 1976 and for several years soared, thanks to booming sales for home video games. Poor product development, management disarray, and the decline of the game industry brought grief to the company, which Warner sold off at a bargain basement price to Jack Tramiel in 1984. Tramiel sought to revive the company with a more serious home computer called the 520 ST.

Commodore International grew up far from the magic of Silicon Valley. Founded in the Bronx in 1954 as a typewriter repair company by Jack Tramiel and Manny Kapp, Commodore first expanded into the general office equipment business and then the volatile calculator market of the early 1970s. Tramiel got into the computer business in 1976 after buying MOS Technology and the following year brought out one of the early micros, called PET. Commodore became a leader of the home-computer market through its ruthless price-cutting, but Tramiel was ousted in early 1984. The company went into a slump that Tramiel's successor Marshall Smith hoped to escape from with the introduction of a fancy home computer called Amiga in 1985.

Compaq Computer emerged from the blue in 1983 as the leading IBM-compatible micro. Starting with a portable model (actually known as a "luggable" because of its 28-pound weight) and then branching out to desktop machines to match IBM's line, Compaq achieved a breathtaking rate of growth. It reached $500 million in revenues by its third year. Launched by venture capitalist Ben Rosen and former Texas Instruments engineer Rod Canion, Compaq trounced IBM's portable model and brought out smaller and lighter luggables in 1986. Later that year Compaq introduced a new desktop machine that was the first personal computer to use Intel's powerful new 80386 microprocessor.

IBM took the micro world by storm in 1981, when the colossus of Armonk (long wedded to the market for big mainframe machines) brought out a personal computer. The PC was no technological marvel, but the IBM name brought it a healthy market share and leadership of the industry. In the following years IBM introduced a succession of more powerful PCs—the XT in 1983, the AT in 1984, and the RT in 1986—aimed at solidifying Big Blue's dominance in the office and professional market. IBM had less luck with its PC Jr. (a scaled-down version of the PC) and a portable PC, both of which went nowhere. But in 1986 IBM brought out a $2,000 laptop machine with a detachable display.

Lotus Development Corp. was founded in 1982 by Mitchell Kapor, a one-time disc jockey and teacher of transcendental meditation. In the late 1970s he got involved in programming, and after the IBM PC appeared he got venture capital from Ben Rosen to bring out an integrated financial software package called Lotus 1–2–3, which went on to become the best-selling program. Lotus, which became the industry leader, introduced a more sophisticated package called Symphony in 1984 and the following year brought out Jazz®, which was designed for the Macintosh.

Microsoft, the leader in systems software for micros, was founded in 1975 by William Gates and Paul Allen. The two young programmers produced a version of the Basic language for the first micro, the Altair, and went on to fame and fortune after being chosen by IBM to produce both the systems software and the programming language for its PC. Later Microsoft expanded into applications software with well-received products such as the Word® text-editing program, Windows®, which allowed micro users to shift more easily between different programs, and Excel®, a spreadsheet program for the Macintosh. The company went public in a well-received offering in 1986.

SOURCE GUIDE

LEADING STOCK ANALYSTS AND EXPERTS

Dataquest, San Jose, California.

Future Computing, Dallas.

InfoCorp., Cupertino, California.

Yankee Group, Boston.

TRADE ASSOCIATIONS

Association of Data Processing Service Organizations, Washington, D.C.

Software Publishers Association, Washington, D.C.

DATA SOURCES AND DIRECTORIES

Hot List, a controversial ranking of best-selling software programs produced by a major distributor (Inglewood, Calif.: Softsel Computer Products).

Microcomputer Marketplace, an annual directory of software producers and distributors (New York: R. R. Bowker).

Microcomputer Vendor Directory, a semiannual list of hardware and software suppliers (Pennsauken, N.J.: Auerbach Publishers).

The Software Catalogue: Microcomputers, a semiannual listing of programs, from information on the International Software Database (New York: Elsevier–North Holland Publishing).

TRADE PUBLICATIONS

Byte, monthly.

Computerworld, weekly.

InfoWorld, weekly.

BOOKS AND REPORTS

Carlston, Douglas G. *Software People.* New York: Simon & Schuster, 1985.

Freiberger, Paul, and Michael Swaine. *Fire in the Valley: The Making of the Personal Computer.* New York: Osborne/McGraw-Hill, 1984.

Levering, Robert, Michael Katz, and Milton Moskowitz. *The Computer Entrepreneurs.* New York: New American Library, 1984.

Moritz, Michael. *The Little Kingdom: The Private Story of Apple Computer.* New York: William Morrow, 1984.

U.S. International Trade Administration. *A Competitive Assessment of the U.S. Software Industry.* Washington, D.C., December 1984.

CHAPTER FIFTEEN

Semiconductors

It has been called the second industrial revolution, the new alchemy, a revolution in miniature, the micro millenium. It is transforming work, play, education, war, and virtually all other aspects of life. The end of its impact is far from sight. "It" is microelectronics; and even after discounting the hype, it is one of the true marvels of the modern age.

The source of this wonderment is a group of devices that combine thousands of electric circuits on pieces of silicon smaller than a fingernail. Rather than being wired together, the circuits are formed by unbelievably dense microscopic etching on the silicon, which has the useful quality of being a semiconductor of electricity. Some of these chips can store up to a million bits of information, while others have all the components of a computer.

These memory chips and microprocessors constitute the building blocks of computers, telecommunications equipment, and other "smart" machines. The $24 billion (1985) worldwide semiconductor industry is one of the most technologically sophisticated segments of business, but it is also one of the most volatile. Competition is fierce; ruthless price-cutting in the battle for market share has undone numerous companies and has become a major point of contention between the United States and Japan. At the same time, a sharp boom-bust cycle in the industry has kept producers off-balance. It is a difficult business but one that will continue to grow in importance.

HARNESSING ELECTRONS

The science and practice of electronics emerged out of research performed by Thomas Edison using one of his inventions, the light bulb. The Wizard of Menlo Park found that when a metal plate was placed in the bulb, a measurable electric current could be detected between the heated filament and the plate. The Englishman John Ambrose Fleming discovered that this device could be configured so as to detect high-frequency radio signals.

Next, in 1906, the American inventor Lee De Forest added another element to the bulb and found that it served not only to detect signals but to amplify them as well. This three-electrode audion, as improved by De Forest and others, opened up a new world of electrical communication, including radio, radio telephony, wireless telegraphy, and long-distance telephone service. These vacuum tubes also served as the main components of the first computers in the 1940s.

The next leap in electronics came during World War II, when research on radar began to focus on a class of elements known as semiconductors. These substances, particularly silicon and germanium, had the useful quality of conducting electricity more easily than insulators but not as freely as conductors and thus showed great promise as signal detectors.

After the war, scientists at AT&T's Bell Labs built on that research in an effort to find an alternative to vacuum tubes that would be less bulky and throw off less heat. In 1947 a team led by William Shockley (later to gain notoriety for his views on race and intelligence) found the answer in a tiny circuit made out of germanium and incredibly thin wires. Dubbed the transistor—short for transfer resistance—this "solid-state" device (i.e., one without moving parts) set off a process of miniaturization in electronics and brought a Nobel Prize to Shockley and the leading figures in his team, John Bardeen and Walter Brattain.

AT&T made the secret of the transistor widely available (for a price) but did not itself get into the business of making the devices, probably because of antitrust pressures from the federal government. Instead a slew of other firms obtained licenses from Ma Bell and took the leap into microelectronics. The Pentagon quickly recognized the value of the new forms of circuitry, and military research money began to flow into the industry.

Raytheon, one of the major vacuum-tube makers, pioneered the commercial consumer market with hearing aids and what were then called transistorized radios. Other entrants included older electronics companies such as Philco and Motorola, as well as a young firm called Texas Instruments that produced geophysical equipment for the oil industry. TI, having lured away a Bell Labs scientist, developed the first silicon version of the transistor and began its ascent to the leadership of the semiconductor industry.

In the early 1950s Shockley got the entrepreneurial bug and decided to leave Bell Labs to produce transistors on his own. He returned to his boyhood home of Palo Alto, California, and set up Shockley Semiconductor Laboratories in 1955. This was just at the time that Palo Alto and the surrounding area south of San Francisco Bay were emerging as a hotbed of new technology companies.

The catalyst for this was Stanford University. Starting early in the century Frederick Terman, a professor of electrical engineering and later provost of the university, encouraged his students to remain in the area after graduation and start new ventures rather than going to work for large corporations in the East. Two of his disciples were William Hewlett and David Packard, who in 1939 founded a company to sell audio oscillators and ended up creating one of the premier U.S. electronics firms.

By the early 1950s Stanford was leasing parts of its extensive property to technology companies such as Varian Associates and Hewlett-Packard. A critical mass of engineering talent began to appear in the area as companies such as Sylvania, Philco, and General Electric set up operations. Lockheed bought 700 acres in nearby Sunnyvale for its newly established Missile and Space Division. Gradually the orchards of the Santa Clara Valley began to be replaced by modern, low-rise industrial structures.

Shockley certainly picked the right place and the right time to set up shop, but it soon appeared he was not the right man to head such a venture. Although Shockley's reputation allowed him to attract some of the most talented young scientists and engineers in the country, the staff was soon put off by the boss's tyrannical ways.

Before long a group of seven key employees decided to leave and establish their own firm. In casting about for financial backing, the group took the fortuitous step of contacting the investment bank of Hayden Stone. It turned out that the Wall Street firm had a client, Fairchild Camera and Instrument, that was interested in entering the semiconductor business. The group persuaded Robert Noyce, a key figure at Shockley, to join them as head of the venture, and a deal was struck with Fairchild.

The "traitorous eight," as Shockley took to calling them, set out with the goal of trying to put together large numbers of transistors and other circuit elements into one tiny, solid-state unit. It turned out that a similar aim was being pursued by Jack Kilby at TI. In 1959 Kilby hit on a way of batch processing what amounted to miniature integrated circuits.

The news of Kilby's breakthrough mobilized Fairchild, and before long Noyce was able to announce a much better process for interconnecting circuit components. Fairchild applied for a patent for this planar process only five months after TI had filed. These events of 1959 set off both a legal battle (TI sued Fairchild) and a controversy over which company deserved credit for inventing the integrated circuit.

The courts and the historians resolved the issue in Solomonic fashion. It was decided that since TI was first but Fairchild had made refinements essential to commercial production, the two companies should share equal credit for integrated circuits. Thus Kilby and Noyce are generally regarded as coinventors, and companies that wanted to produce the devices had to obtain licenses from both TI and Fairchild.

The semiconductor industry grew steadily in the 1960s, aided by the adoption of integrated circuits by the computer industry and by the Pentagon's insatiable appetite for ever smaller and ever more sophisticated electronic components. Vacuum tubes steadily disappeared from the scene as did the old-line companies that produced them. Leadership of the business was assumed by TI, Fairchild, and Motorola.

Within Fairchild, however, there was growing instability. Many of its top people were frustrated at the relationship with the parent company; and as the firm grew larger many executives grew restless, longing to return to a more entrepreneurial atmosphere. As early as 1959 several Fairchilders acted on these feelings and left to form a company called Rheem Semiconductor. In the 1960s this pattern grew more pronounced, and soon the Santa

Clara Valley was dotted with start-up companies established by Fairchild defectors.

Many of these new ventures went nowhere, but several emerged as leading players in the semiconductor business. Fairchild manufacturing wizard Charles Sporck went to National Semiconductor, marketing man Jerry Sanders helped found Advanced Micro Devices, and most importantly Noyce departed with R&D boss Gordon Moore and process development expert Andrew Grove. Obtaining financing from venture capitalist Arthur Rock, the three set up a company called Intel.

By 1970 Intel (short for integrated electronics) had brought out several types of memory chips, which at the time had a capacity of 1K (meaning one kilobit, or more precisely 1,024 bits of information). The company also had a contract from a group of Japanese calculator producers to develop some custom chips. Faced with the difficult task of trying to cram too many chips into the allotted space, Intel engineer Ted Hoff came up with the idea of putting all the functions on a single chip.

Working with circuit designer Federico Faggin, Hoff succeeded in this effort and thereby created the first microprocessor, sometimes called a "computer on a chip." The Japanese clients were initially skeptical about the device and gave Intel the right to sell what became the 4004. The rest of the world, still caught up with the handheld calculator, also took a while to appreciate the significance of the microprocessor.

But by the middle of the 1970s the device was being heralded as the cornerstone of the microelectronics revolution. Intel's 8080, introduced in 1974 and used to create the first microcomputer, became the industry standard. In a September 1977 article in *Scientific American* Noyce noted that a microprocessor costing about $300 had more computing power than the original ENIAC mainframe, was 20 times faster, and cost only one 10,000th as much and took up only one 30,000th as much space.

What Intel had done with the microprocessor and its early memory chips amounted to a breakthrough in large-scale integration (LSI)—an industry phrase that referred to the cramming of thousands of circuits onto a single piece of silicon. Throughout the 1970s semiconductor makers achieved higher and higher levels of integration, quadrupling the capacity of memory chips every few years.

The leap from one generation to another did not always proceed smoothly. The 4K memory chip posed a number of manufacturing difficulties—a problem exacerbated by the slump that befell the industry in 1975. As semiconductor fabrication became more complex the costs of development rose rapidly. Many companies simply did not have sufficient resources to keep up.

The upshot of this was a buying spree of semiconductor companies, mainly by foreign firms seeking a foothold in a business that was still dominated by the United States. The Dutch electronics giant Philips bought Signetics, a Fairchild spin-off, in 1975. Siemens of West Germany purchased Litronix and 20 percent of Advanced Micro Devices in 1977. Northern Telecom took a minority interest in Intersil (later sold to GE), and Nippon Electric acquired a company called Electronic Arrays.

U.S. companies also got into the act. Honeywell bought Synertek (later sold to AT&T), and United Technologies purchased Mostek, a prominent spin-off from TI. In 1979 the venerable Fairchild Semiconductor, by then in decline, was taken over by the French oil services company Schlumberger, which had little luck trying to revitalize the firm that had given birth to so much of what became known as Silicon Valley.

This takeover wave generated a debate within the industry on whether semiconductor companies could survive inside large corporations. It was common wisdom that electronics giants such as RCA could not make it in the chip business because of a resistance to innovation and an inability to respond to the frequent changes of the fast-paced semiconductor market.

There was some truth to the proposition, and it is significant that the top four firms in the industry—TI, Motorola, National Semiconductor, and Intel—were independent. At the same time, there has been no evidence that IBM's purchase of 20 percent of Intel has diminished the latter's vitality. And it should be noted that large companies such as IBM produce substantial numbers of semiconductor devices for use in their own products.

More than big-business domination, the main problem for the U.S. semiconductor industry turned out to be an aggressive competitive thrust from Japan. Until the late 1970s the Americans had nothing to worry about, controlling as they did some two thirds of the world market. But the Japanese were not about to ignore this lucrative business. In the mid-1970s agencies of the Japanese government joined with five leading electronics firms—Hitachi, Fujitsu, Mitsubishi, Nippon Electric, and Toshiba—in a research and development initiative called the VLSI Project.

This effort to gain a foothold in very large scale integration paid off when the industry was moving from 4K to 16K memory chips. The demand for the denser chips was much greater than expected, and U.S. companies simply could not produce the 16Ks fast enough. This created an opening for the Japanese firms, which appeared on the scene with devices that many users found to be superior to those produced by American companies.

Led by Nippon Electric (NEC) and Hitachi the Japanese gained 40 percent of the 16K market by 1980 and were well situated to take the lion's share of the next generation of memory chip, the 64K. By this time Japanese semiconductor exports to the United States had surpassed American exports to Japan. The U.S. producers, starting to panic, formed the Semiconductor Industry Association to bring their plight to the attention of the government. An industry that had always prided itself on being aloof from Washington found itself in the position of needing federal help to overcome what it characterized as unfair obstacles American producers faced in trying to sell to Japan.

The American protestations initially had little effect. The Japanese took such a strong lead in 64K DRAM (dynamic random-access memory) chips that most American producers either dropped out of the market or never bothered to enter it. There were also signs by the early 1980s that the Japanese were better positioned for the emerging 256K generation.

All was not dismal with the U.S. semiconductor industry, however. The Americans, particularly Intel and Motorola, remained far ahead in the microprocessor market. In 1982 Intel announced what it called a micromainframe, a set of three chips that had the capabilities, including multiprocessing, of a large computer. By the mid-1980s microprocessors reached the 32-bit level (meaning they could process that many pieces of information at a time).

U.S. companies also prospered in the growing business of custom and semicustom chips. The latter involved the use of components called gate arrays that could be connected in the last stages of manufacturing to suit specific needs. Some leading commodity chip producers ignored this segment, leaving more room for a new batch of start-ups (including LSI Logic, founded by former Fairchild president Wilfred Corrigan).

The industry also kept on innovating. Devices called photo-diode arrays, or imager chips, endowed semiconductors with greater "visual" ability and allowed them to conquer one of the last vestiges of vacuum tubes: movie cameras. EPROM (erasable, programmable, read-only memory) chips made "smart" machines much more flexible. Researchers improved the performance of CMOS (complementary metal-oxide semiconductor) chips, which threw off less heat and thus reduced the cooling problems created by very dense concentrations of circuits.

American semiconductor companies also responded to the Japanese challenge through a variety of cooperative measures that sought to gain some of the advantages that Japanese firms have by being part of *keiretsu*—families of companies with great access to resources. These U.S. arrangements included joint development projects, cross-licensing of technology, and cosponsored research. Among the latter was the not-for-profit Microelectronics and Computer Technology Corp., established by a group of electronics companies to do leading-edge research. In early 1987 the industry announced plans for a project called Sematech that would focus on manufacturing techniques.

The Japanese meanwhile were not sitting still. In the mid-1980s companies such as NEC began challenging U.S. dominance in the microprocessor market. In doing so, NEC got itself in a legal battle with Intel over the issue of whether the instructions embedded in Intel's 8086 and 8088 chips amounted to a program and were thus protected under the copyright laws. As of this writing, a federal court has ruled that microcodes are so protected but has not yet decided whether NEC infringed on Intel's product.

The ruthless drive for market share by the Japanese in the 64K and 256K memory segments as well as in EPROMs also brought them legal woes. Following the disastrous year of 1985, during which U.S. producers lost more than $500 million, the Reagan administration finally responded to the complaints of U.S. producers and imposed dumping penalties against Hitachi, Fujitsu, NEC, Toshiba, Mitsubishi, and Oki. At the same time, federal courts began hearing private suits brought by U.S. producers, and the Justice Department and the International Trade Commission were investigating Japanese selling practices in the United States. These actions, along with a rise in demand and a stronger yen, helped put a halt to the steep decline in semiconductor prices.

The Top 10 Semiconductor Producers Worldwide, by Chip Sales in 1985*
($ Millions)

1.	Nippon Electric	$1,984
2.	Motorola	1,830
3.	Texas Instruments	1,767
4.	Hitachi	1,671
5.	Toshiba	1,468
6.	Philips/Signetics	1,068
7.	Fujitsu	1,020
8.	Intel	1,020
9.	National Semiconductor	943
10.	Matsushita	906

*List does not include captive operations.
Source: Dataquest.

In the summer of 1986 the United States and Japan reached an agreement allowing American chipmakers easier access to the Japanese market while discouraging Japanese producers from dumping in the United States. This led to a sharp rise in chip prices and a consequent outcry from computer manufacturers and other users of semiconductors.

The ultimate outcome of these trade issues could be decisive in setting the competitive stage for the next act in the semiconductor saga: the advent of so-called superchips, memory devices capable of holding a million or more bits of information. Along with this move to ULSI (ultra large scale integration), the industry is beginning to move away from silicon and back to gallium arsenide, which is more expensive but moves electrons faster, uses less power, operates at higher temperatures, and emits light. More daring researchers have begun investigating the possibility of chips made of organic molecules. Such "biochips" could allow much greater levels of integration and create more versatile machines.

LABOR RELATIONS

The fundamental fact about labor relations in the electronics industry is the remarkable success management has had in keeping out unions. A survey by the American Electronics Association in 1982 found that its 1,900 member companies had only 90 union contracts. And those were not at bigger, more prominent firms such as IBM, which has managed to keep its entire U.S. work force unorganized (though several unions and an independent group called IBM Workers United have been trying to change that).

The conventional view is that high-tech companies have created attractive enough conditions—workplace amenities such as hot tubs and tennis courts, generous stock options, and a general esprit de corps—so that unions lose their appeal. It is true that firms such as IBM, Hewlett-Packard, and Wang Laboratories are highly paternalistic, offering extensive benefits and in some cases declining to lay off employees even during slumps. On one level, Silicon Valley and other electronics outposts amount to a kind of worker's paradise.

The problem is that there is more than one level. The country-club atmosphere is enjoyed mainly by a narrow stratum of the total electronics work force, consisting of highly skilled engineers, top-level marketing people, and a limited number of other white-collar types. These are the people who, once they gain some experience in a leading firm, have enormous mobility. They hop from job to job, seeking higher pay and perks in exchange for what prospective bosses hope will be specialized knowledge and perhaps the trade secrets of the previous employer. It is a highly unusual sort of labor market.

Yet there is more to the electronics industry than the development, design, and marketing of products. Someone has to mass-produce the chips and computers. It is here that a different story comes to light: Electronics is basically a cheap-labor industry.

As much as the industry has fostered the image of being highly automated, there are still aspects of electronics production that remain very labor intensive. And given the intense competition of the industry, companies have gone to great lengths to keep the costs of that labor to an absolute minimum.

One strategy has been to move production overseas. The shift to what is called offshore assembly was led by Fairchild when it opened operations in Hong Kong in the early 1960s. Other companies followed suit, and by the late 1960s countries such as Taiwan, South Korea, Singapore, and Malaysia were dotted with semiconductor and other electronics factories owned by U.S. firms. Electronics became a globally integrated system of manufacturing, with low wages more than making up for the transportation costs associated with decentralized production.

These operations mainly employed young women, imposing a military sort of discipline (both in the workplace and in the dormitories in which they were housed) and paying them wages that were barely above subsistence level. Many of the plants were located in special export processing zones set up by Third World governments to lure foreign investors with tax breaks, reduced tariffs, and guarantees of labor stability. When labor costs rose slightly in these countries, electronics firms sought out new low-wage havens in countries such as Thailand and the Philippines.

Although the workers have for the most part been pushed into submission, there have been notable cases of resistance. In 1982 a group of mainly young women workers held hostage for nine hours two U.S. executives of Control Data Corp. who had come to resolve a labor dispute. Scattered strikes have also occurred in U.S.-owned electronics plants in Mexico and the Philippines.

In part because of these labor troubles and in part because of a shift to automation, American electronics firms in the 1980s began cutting back on offshore assembly and returning production to the U.S. It turned out, however, that the labor force employed back home closely resembled the one cultivated abroad. The production workers of Silicon Valley are predominantly low-paid women, and in fact many of them are recent immigrants from the same Asian countries in which offshore facilities have been located.

Whether the workers are foreign born or not, electronics companies have gone to great lengths to discourage unionization. A *Wall Street Journal* reporter who took a job (incognito) in a Texas Instruments plant found workers so intimidated that they panicked even at the mention of unions. The United Electrical workers, which started organizing in high-tech in the early 1970s, joined with other unions in cooperative drives in both California and Massachusetts, but by the mid-1980s the unions had all but abandoned what appeared to be a futile effort.

Labor organizers have insisted that once a major high-tech firm was successfully unionized, the tide would turn. Perhaps the closest a union came to such an achievement was the case of Atari. In the early 1980s workers at the home-computer and video game producer, angered over wage cuts and possible layoffs, contacted the nearest union they could find, which turned out to be the Glaziers. In early 1983, just as the union had signed up enough workers for a representation election, Atari announced that it planned to eliminate 1,700 jobs in Silicon Valley and transfer the work to low-wage operations in Asia. The action, which did a great deal to deflate the job-creating image of high-tech industry—the term *Atari Democrats* was hastily abandoned—also led to the demise of the organizing effort.

Another obstacle faced by organizers is that many of the jobs held by people they are trying to unionize may soon be obsolete. While some aspects of semiconductor assembly are still labor intensive, automation is coming rapidly. The computer makers have been at the vanguard of this trend. The facilities that Apple Computer built for producing the Macintosh were so automated that direct labor costs amounted to less than 1 percent of the total expenses of producing the machine.

THE HIDDEN HAZARDS OF HIGH-TECH

While it was growing in prominence the electronics industry gained the reputation of being a "clean" business. In place of the belching smokestacks that symbolized old-line heavy industry, the image of electronics was that of white-gowned and masked technicians in the "cleanrooms" of semiconductor facilities. It is true that some aspects of chip production have to be done in a highly purified atmosphere; it is also true that the production of semiconductors and printed circuit boards requires the use of highly toxic substances.

The first signs of health problems in electronics occurred in the 1970s with outbreaks of mysterious ailments among large groups of workers. Eventually it was determined that the symptoms, including fainting and nausea, were linked to poor ventilation in the plants. Occupational health researchers also learned that workers were being exposed to a variety of harmful substances.

These included solvents (such as trichloroethylene, or TCE) used to clean circuit boards, nitric and other acids used in photo-etching, arsine gases used in growing silicon crystals, lead oxide fumes from soldering, and radiation from substances such as Krypton-85 used to test for flaws in circuits. Some of these toxic substances were also being used by women performing home labor for electronic subcontractors.

While the high rates of occupational illness caused some concern in the industry, the public did not pay much attention to the issue of high-tech hazards until they spread outside the factory. In December 1981 the local water company in a Silicon Valley neighborhood found that a five-year-old chemical storage drum buried outside a Fairchild plant was leaking a toxic solvent into a public well. After the discovery was made public—some weeks later—local residents argued that the leaks may have been responsible for a cluster of birth defects in the area.

In 1984 the federal Environmental Protection Agency found widespread underground pollution in Silicon Valley and added a number of sites (including facilities of such prominent companies as IBM, Hewlett-Packard, and Intel) in the area to the superfund list of toxic dumps. The following year the California Department of Health Services found a high rate of miscarriages and birth defects in areas where the water was contaminated by toxic leaks from high-tech plants. There have also been incidents involving the emission of toxic gases from electronics plants.

While trade groups such as the Semiconductor Industry Association have downplayed the gravity of the health problems in and outside of the workplaces, some companies (including IBM and Fairchild) have spent large sums cleaning up toxic sites.

LEADING COMPANIES

Jerry Sanders, cofounder and chief executive of **Advanced Micro Devices,** is one of the most flamboyant characters in Silicon Valley. Sanders' showmanship, including some epic Christmas parties costing hundreds of thousands of dollars, goes along with AMD's strong emphasis on marketing. The company, a Fairchild spin-off, has prospered by focusing on three industrial markets: computing, telecommunications, and instruments.

Intel, formed by a group of defectors from Fairchild in 1968, is considered the leading technology innovator in the semiconductor business. Led by Robert Noyce and Gordon Moore, Intel pioneered the microprocessor in 1970 and has remained the preeminent firm in that segment. However, the company, along with numerous other U.S. producers, got out of the memory chip business in 1985 in the face of cutthroat Japanese competition. IBM purchased 20 percent of Intel in the early 1980s. In 1986 the company brought out its powerful 32-bit microprocessor, the 80386, which was expected to usher in a new generation of personal computers.

Motorola began life in the 1930s, producing radios for automobiles (the name is an amalgam of motor and Victrola). The company got a lift during World War II when its portable two-way radios, or walkie-talkies, were adopted by the military. Getting into semiconductors in the early 1950s the company ended up dominating the production of discrete (as opposed to integrated) devices. Although never a great innovator Motorola later emerged as the second-ranking producer of microprocessors.

The people of **National Semiconductor Corp.** are known as the "animals of Silicon Valley." Led by Charlie Sporck, the company is a dogged competitor with a fanatical obsession with reducing costs. NSC was a small and struggling producer in 1967 when its chairman, venture capitalist Peter Sprague, lured Sporck away from Fairchild to take charge. In the mid-1980s the company began putting more emphasis on its National Advanced Systems division, which distributes mainframes made by Hitachi, and its Datachecker/DTS, which makes retail checkout terminals.

Texas Instruments started out producing seismic equipment for the oil industry in the 1930s and ended up for many years as the world's largest semiconductor company. In the 1950s TI brought down the price of transistors enough to allow them to be used in radios; and in 1959 Jack Kilby, a TI scientist, invented the first integrated circuit. The company, which has traditionally focused on the commodity end of the business, became notorious in the early 1970s for ruthless price-cutting in the calculator and digital watch businesses. TI suffered heavy losses in home computers—a product it abandoned in 1983—and again in semiconductors in the 1980s. Jerry Junkins, who succeeded J. Fred Bucy as president in 1985, began trying to guide the company out of its crisis.

SOURCE GUIDE

LEADING STOCK ANALYSTS AND EXPERTS

Dataquest, San Jose, California.
Gnostic Concepts, San Mateo, California.

In-Stat, Scottsdale, Arizona.

Daniel Klesken, analyst at Montgomery Securities.

VLSI Research, San Jose, California.

TRADE ASSOCIATIONS

American Electronics Association, Palo Alto, California.

Electronic Industries Association, Washington, D.C.

Semiconductor Industry Association, San Jose, California.

DATA SOURCES AND DIRECTORIES

Electronic Market Data Book, an annual compilation of data on consumer and industrial products (Washington, D.C.: Electronic Industries Association).

Electronic News Financial Fact Book and Directory, an annual volume on the industry from the publisher of *Electronic News* (New York: Fairchild Publications).

Status (whatever year), a consultant's annual report on the integrated circuit industry that also includes a list of firms in different segments of the business (Scottsdale, Ariz.: Integrated Circuit Engineering).

Yearbook/Directory, a list of industry firms and a compilation of statistics (San Jose, Calif.: Semiconductor Industry Association).

TRADE PUBLICATIONS

Electronic Business, monthly.

Electronic News, weekly.

Electronics, weekly.

Global Electronics, a monthly newsletter from the Pacific Studies Center, Mountain View, California.

Semiconductor International, monthly.

BOOKS AND REPORTS

Early, Steve, and Rand Wilson. "Organizing High Tech: Unions and Their Future." *Labor Research Review,* no. 8 (1986).

Grunwald, Joseph, and Kenneth Flamm. *The Global Factory: Foreign As-*

sembly in International Trade. Washington, D.C.: Brookings Institution, 1985.

Hanson, Dirk. *The New Alchemists: Silicon Valley and the Microelectronics Revolution.* Boston: Little, Brown, 1982.

Malone, Michael. *The Big Score: The Billion-Dollar Story of Silicon Valley.* Garden City, N.Y.: Doubleday Publishing, 1985.

National Research Council. *Competitive Status of the U.S. Electronics Industry.* Washington, D.C.: National Academy Press, 1984.

Okimoto, Daniel, Tahue Sugano, and Franklin B. Weinstein. *Competitive Edge: The Semiconductor Industry in the U.S. and Japan.* Stanford, Calif.: Stanford University Press, 1984.

Siegel, Lenny, and John Markoff. *The High Cost of High Tech: The Dark Side of the Chip.* New York: Harper & Row, 1985.

United Nations Centre on Transnational Corporations. *Transnational Corporations in the International Semiconductor Industry.* New York, 1983.

U.S. Congress, Joint Economic Committee. *International Competition in Advanced Industrial Sectors: Trade and Development in the Semiconductor Industry.* Washington, D.C., 1982.

U.S. Congress, Office of Technology Assessment. *International Competitiveness in Electronics.* Washington, D.C., November 1983.

PART FOUR

Energy

CHAPTER SIXTEEN

Coal and Alternative Fuels

The industry once known as King Coal is now far from regal. The hope that the oil crisis of the 1970s would restore the faded glory of coal went largely unfulfilled, and the plunge of petroleum prices in the 1980s was another painful blow.

Yet the coal industry has a long history of surviving such setbacks and waiting for the next possible boom. The resilience of the coal business is a reflection of a basic fact: Coal represents America's most abundant and inexpensive source of energy. Estimated recoverable reserves in the United States represent more than 300 years of output at 1985's level of 890 million tons. A succession of presidents, beginning with Nixon, have looked at this national asset and proclaimed coal the key to U.S. energy independence.

The fundamental reason why these exhortations have not been carried out is that coal is dirty—dirty to mine, dirty to transport, and dirty to burn. The electric utility industry, the biggest consumer of coal, has been reluctant to use more coal, because to do so would exacerbate problems of air pollution and acid rain. Also, the more efficient method of extracting coal, strip mining, ravages the countryside.

The dirtiness of coal has also contributed to the tumultuous labor relations in the industry. The high risks of coal mining—including black lung disease, explosions, and cave-ins—help make miners among the most militant rank-and-file workers in the country.

In the late 1970s there was excitement in the coal industry over the revival of interest in synthetic fuels, a major part of which involved the production of oil and gas out of coal. For a few years it appeared that huge infusions of federal money would propel synfuels, and coal, into a leading role in the energy equation.

The decline of oil prices in the early 1980s put an end to those expectations, and synfuels became a dead issue. A similar fate befell the other main alternative type of energy that came into vogue at the same time: solar power. A slew of big corporations rushed into solar after the Carter administration began promoting it, and rushed out again when lower petroleum costs and Reagan budget cuts eliminated much of the appeal.

In the mid-1980s coal, synthetic fuel, and solar power all remained in the doldrums, waiting for another energy crunch to be called into center stage again.

THE ASCENT OF COAL

Although the first commercial mines were opened in the 1740s the coal industry developed slowly in America because of the abundance and greater accessibility of wood. Coal's main customers were blacksmiths and ironmakers and, during war time, the producers of ammunition.

During the second half of the 19th century coal's prospects improved steadily with the development of industry (especially steel) and the railroads. The coal used to make coke in the steel process and to burn in steam engines was the type known as bituminous. This grade of coal was softer and contained somewhat less carbon than the purer anthracite coal used for heating.

With the switch in coals came changes in both the technology of the industry and its geography. Anthracite deposits were concentrated in northeastern Pennsylvania, while bituminous reserves were scattered throughout Appalachia, the Midwest, and the northern Great Plains. The early form of mining was quarrying, or "trenching," a forerunner of strip mining. This was replaced by underground tunneling, which was more dangerous but allowed access to greater amounts of coal.

In the early days of underground mining, the coal was recovered from a solid bed with the use of only hand tools and explosives. This labor-intensive production process was also highly skilled. Miners had to learn how to undercut the coal face and insert the blasting powder in just the right way to loosen the most coal without causing a disaster. The coal then had to be loaded into baskets and dragged out, though by the mid-19th century mule-drawn carts on wooden rails were being employed.

Yet it was not until the 1930s that coal extraction began to be mechanized in a serious way. Cutting machines became more common, while mechanical loaders were slower in catching on. In the 1950s larger mining companies began to introduce huge machines called continuous miners. These devices, some 30 feet long, gouged coal out of the mine face and loaded it automatically onto shuttle cars. In the 1960s U.S. producers began using mechanized longwall systems, which functioned like continuous miners but also saved the time traditionally spent in putting up roofing, by using its own steel canopy held up by hydraulic jacks. Both systems were, in theory, much more efficient than traditional methods, but the equipment was vastly more expensive and was subject to a lot of downtime.

Coal reached its pinnacle in the first decades of the century, when it accounted for some three quarters of the country's energy needs. Yet while coal's importance in electricity generation was rising it was also being challenged by the expanding use of oil and natural gas. Coal by-products found new applications in drugs, synthetic rubber, nylons, and plastics, but coal was challenged by petroleum on that terrain as well. In 1952 petroleum replaced coal as the largest single contributor to U.S. energy consumption. By the latter part of the decade coal's future was jeopardized even more by what was then thought to be a glorious future for nuclear power. By the early 1960s coal had all but been written off.

While many of the small operators in the traditionally fragmented industry had a hard time surviving the slump, coal developed a new allure for a surprising group of investors: large oil producers and other resource companies. Continental Oil (now part of Du Pont) purchased Consolidation Coal in 1966, Occidental Petroleum acquired Island Creek Coal in 1968, and Standard Oil of Ohio bought Old Ben Coal the same year. Kennecott Copper purchased the industry leader Peabody Coal in 1968 but was later forced by the Federal Trade Commission to sell the company, which was bought in 1977 by a consortium led by Newmont Mining.

The major emphasis of the new coal barons was not the traditional deep mines of Appalachia, with their militant labor force. The focus instead was on expanding the Western open-pit extraction that emerged in the 1950s. Strip mining involved much less labor and was considerably more productive than tunneling. Much of it was done on land owned by the federal government and leased at low rates.

SEEKING SAFE MINES AND CLEAN AIR

It appeared that these investments would pay off handsomely when the rapid escalation of oil import prices in the early 1970s brought about expectations of a rush to coal as an abundant domestic source. Although coal use did expand somewhat, it fell far short of the 1 billion tons a year targeted by the federal government. The reasons for the disappointing recovery of coal are complicated, but they certainly include the following.

The reliability of coal supplies, though perhaps not as uncertain as OPEC oil, was not seen as entirely satisfactory. One problem was that of productivity, which had been steadily declining since the late 1960s. Coal operators tended to put the blame on wildcat strikes (for more, see the Labor Relations section below) and recent federal safety legislation. In 1969 Congress passed the Coal Mine Health and Safety Act, which established fairly strict rules for an industry that had a poor record (including shockingly high fatality rates) of protecting its workers. Predictably the coal operators denounced the law as too stringent, and miners criticized the Interior Department for lax enforcement (responsibility was later transferred to the Labor Department). Yet from either point of view it was undeniable that the new safety measures tended to reduce productivity while miners and their employers adjusted to the new ways of operating.

Energy customers, particularly utilities, were also hesitant to switch to coal, because of environmental considerations. The burning of coal would make it especially difficult for utilities to meet the emission standards contained in the Clean Air Act of 1970. Subsequent federal requirements on the use of emission-control devices such as scrubbers made the switch to coal a more expensive proposition. In 1981 the utility industry lobbied for and won legislation easing provisions in the 1978 Power Plant and Industrial Fuel Use Act requiring greater use of coal.

The problems were compounded by a later discovery that the burning of coal was contributing to a problem of acid rain—airborne traces of sulfuric and nitric acid that were killing aquatic life and damaging cropland.

Although the coal they produced tended to be lower in sulfur and thus less of a pollution hazard, strip miners in both the East and the West also faced environmental challenges. More militant critics pushed for a complete ban on surface mining, while others lobbied for strict laws requiring operators to restore the land to something approximating its previous state. President Ford vetoed a tough strip-mining bill in 1975, but Congress acted again in 1977 with the Surface Mining Control and Reclamation Act.

Coal operators hoped that the arrival of the Reagan administration would put an end to many of their regulatory problems, but their wishes did not quite come true. The Interior Department did move to reopen federal lands to coal leasing after a 10-year moratorium imposed by Congress. But indications that Interior Secretary James Watt was offering the lands at less than market rates prompted Congress to impose a new ban. Complaints from the Canadian government about acid rain caused the administration to restrain its deregulatory fervor regarding coal.

By the mid-1980s the emphasis was on finding cleaner ways to burn coal. Despite budget cutting in other programs, Congress in 1984 authorized $750 million for research in this field. The funds were not appropriated and came under attack from budget cutters in the Office of Management and Budget. In December 1985 Congress voted a three-year, $400 million clean-coal program, reserving the other $350 million for future use. Among the promising technologies being explored was fluidized bed combustion, which uses limestone to turn the sulfur generated by burning coal into a harmless waste product.

With the use of coal in steel production steadily decreasing, the future of coal more than ever depends on the electric utilities. Aside from the environmental issues the biggest question here may be the prospects for nuclear power. Public confidence in nukes was at a low point after the Soviet Union's Chernobyl accident in 1986, but numerous American nuclear plants were expected to go on line after long construction and regulatory delays. On the positive side, coal productivity started rising again in the late 1970s and continued the trend into the mid-1980s.

In 1974 *Fortune* depicted the coal industry as "a somewhat

The Top 10 U.S. Coal Producers, 1985

	Short Tons (Millions)
1. Peabody Coal	62.0
2. Consolidation Coal	42.7
3. Amax Coal	38.3
4. Texas Utilities	29.8
5. Anaconda	27.3
6. Exxon Coal USA	26.2
7. A. T. Massey	24.4
8. North American Coal	22.1
9. NERCO	20.8
10. Pittston	15.8

Source: *Keystone News-Bulletin*, February 1986.

frumpy middle-aged ballerina rushed out of semiretirement to fill an unanticipated gap in a show that must go on." The industry is still dancing, but the applause remains subdued.

SYNTHETIC FUELS

One of the bases for optimism in the coal industry in the late 1970s was the sudden vogue for synthetic fuels, particularly oil and gas derived from coal and oil extracted from shale. In 1979, amidst the second oil shock, President Carter proposed an $88 billion, 10-year program to produce 2.5 million barrels of synthetic oil daily by 1990.

Although at the time there were no commercial plants producing synfuel, as it came to be called, the technologies involved were far from new. Shale rock was used as a source of oil back in the 19th century. Until the 1920s "town gas," a low-grade fuel derived from coal, was used in many parts of the United States in street lamps and home ovens. Germany was a leader in the development of synthetic fuels, which were a crucial source of energy for that country during World War II.

Carter's 1979 proposal sailed through Congress, which appropriated $17.5 billion for research and created the Synthetic Fuels Corporation to administer the work. Companies such as Mobil, Texaco, and Occidental Petroleum began lining up for huge subsidies for coal gasification, coal liquefaction, and shale oil projects.

The federal government's enthusiasm for synfuels began to wane with the election of Ronald Reagan and the easing of the oil crunch. Several major projects, including a $5 billion shale oil joint venture between Exxon and Tosco Corp., were canceled. The $2 billion Great Plains coal gasification plant was built in North Dakota by a consortium of five energy companies, but its owners ended up writing off the project.

Slumping oil prices and federal budget cuts crippled the Synthetic Fuels Corporation itself, and in 1986 the agency was shut down.

SOLAR ENERGY

Whereas coal is viewed by many as a has-been technology, solar power, like synfuels, remains in the yet-to-be stage. The concept of renewable energy—solar is often defined to include wind, hydro, and other nonfossil resources—was an esoteric subject until the early 1970s. The oil crisis pushed it to a central place in the debates on the future of energy.

Solar energy advocates found they had an ally in the White House when Jimmy Carter took office. Carter got Congress to create tax credits for solar installations and to fund the Solar Energy Research Institute in Colorado. The administration also supported an event called Sun Day, held on May 3, 1978, to promote public awareness of the potential of solar power. As part of his energy plan Carter set a goal of having renewable resources account for 20 percent of the country's energy needs by the end of the century.

The heightened interest in solar was not limited to the government. As federal funding of solar research escalated, big business got into the act. Leading the move were the major oil companies, which had already hedged their bets by investing in coal and uranium. Petroleum giants such as Exxon, Texaco, Mobil, and Atlantic Richfield joined with other large companies such as General Electric and Grumman in acquiring the tiny firms that had pioneered the industry. By the end of the 1970s about half of the top 25 solar companies were controlled by billion-dollar corporations. The interest of big business was focused on the photovoltaic (the conversion of sunlight into electricity) market, while solar heating tended to remain in the hands of small entrepreneurs.

Whatever optimism had developed in the solar industry was dashed with the arrival of the Reagan administration. Reagan slashed solar research funds, which had reached a peak of $500 million in Carter's last budget, and dismissed most of the employees of the Solar Energy Research Institute. The administration insisted that solar would have to depend on private funds despite the fact that the federal government had spent countless billions of dollars on research for previous energy technologies, especially nuclear power. With the expiration of the tax credit at the end of 1985, the prospects for the solar industry grew even more cloudy.

LABOR RELATIONS

There is little doubt that the coal business has had the most contentious labor relations in American industry. While national union leaders have usually tried to maintain cooperative relations with management, the militancy of rank-and-file miners has made it impossible for those leaders to guarantee a disciplined labor force.

Union organizing among Pennsylvania anthracite miners began in the 1840s. The companies used spies and vigilantes to oppose labor militants, and workers responded with violence. In the 1870s the coal operators depicted militancy among Irish miners as a conspiracy engineered by a group called the Molly Maguires. Although some historians now question whether the conspiracy ever existed, the companies managed to get 19 miners convicted.

Bituminous miners took the lead in creating a national union. After several short-lived organizations, the National Federation of Miners and Mine Laborers was created in 1885. It ended up merging with a division of the Knights of Labor and forming the United Mine Workers of America in 1890.

The UMW had difficulty winning recognition from the operators despite a long series of strikes. The anthracite strike of 1902 brought federal intervention and a 10 percent wage increase but still no recognition. In some cases the disputes became bloody, as in the infamous Ludlow massacre of 1914. Gunmen working for the Rockefeller-dominated Colorado Fuel & Iron Co. and National Guardsmen drenched the strikers' tents with oil and ignited them while miners and their families were asleep. When the occupants rushed from the burning tents they were machine-gunned. Twenty of them were killed, including 13 children.

Worker militancy escalated after World War I, but the leader of the more conservative faction in the UMW took over as president in 1920. John L. Lewis went on to become a virtual dictator of the UMW for 40 years and a major figure in the labor movement. In his early years as president, Lewis had to contend with an unprecedented management assault that cut pay and reduced UMW representation of the industry.

In 1933 Lewis took advantage of the National Industrial Recovery Act's affirmation of collective bargaining to launch an intensive organizing drive that resulted in the signing up of more than 90 percent of the coal labor force by the end of the year. The UMW was then firmly entrenched and became a major power in the industry. During World War II Lewis staged two strikes and won concessions such as portal-to-portal pay.

After the war, Lewis pushed for pathbreaking management-funded retirement and health plans. After a 1946 strike that included a temporary federal seizure of the country's mines, the UMW won the demand. The Welfare and Retirement Fund, which provided comprehensive and free (for the miner) health care, was to be financed by a 10-cent royalty paid by the coal operators on each ton produced.

During the 1950s Lewis developed a close working relationship with George Love, president of Consolidation Coal and head of the Bituminous Coal Operators Association, an industry group set up in 1952 to bargain with the UMW on national contracts. Lewis decided that increasing productivity was necessary for the future of the industry, and for that reason he was willing to accept widening mechanization of coal production. Lewis was untroubled by the fact that this process meant declining employment levels; in fact there were reports that Lewis was lending UMW funds to smaller operators to help them mechanize. This kind of cooperation resulted in an absence of national strikes between the early 1950s and the mid-1960s.

In the latter decade the level of discontent among miners began to increase. One target was the national leadership of the UMW. Lewis retired in 1960 and was succeeded briefly by Thomas Kennedy, who resigned because of poor health and turned the union over to W. A. "Tony" Boyle. Boyle had less charisma than Lewis and was even more ruthless in crushing his union opponents. Joseph Yablonski, a reform candidate who opposed Boyle in the 1969 election for president, was later murdered along with his wife and daughter in an attack that Boyle was subsequently convicted of plotting. The Labor Department invalidated the election, and a vote in 1972 brought to power another reform figure, Arnold Miller.

In the meantime rank-and-file activism had reached high levels. Wildcat strikes in West Virginia pressured the legislature in that state to pass a black-lung compensation law in 1969. Similar pressure helped bring about a program of national compensation in the 1969 Mine Safety and Health Act.

Although miners were encouraged by the election of Miller and the triumph of the reform movement (named Miners for Democracy), the wildcats continued. The rank and file had found that such strikes were a more effective way of dealing with workplace problems than the grievance and arbitration system. The coal operators, naturally, pressed the union for strong contract language to outlaw the walkouts, and this became a major issue in the strike that began in December 1977.

In that 110-day walkout, the rank and file rejected a proposed settlement negotiated by the UMW leadership and defied a Taft-Hartley injunction issued at the request of President Carter. Most of management's retrogressions were dropped, but the operators did win the right to convert benefit coverage from the union's Retirement and Welfare Fund to private carriers.

By this time the rank and file had grown disillusioned with Miller, who among other things was accused of withholding aid that had been donated by other unions during the strike. Support for the leadership improved after Sam Church took over in 1979 following Miller's resignation for health reasons.

Most observers expected the 1981 negotiations to be resolved without a confrontation. But again the rank and file voted down a proposed settlement, this time because of a provision giving companies greater freedom to sublease mines to nonunion operators. The miners stayed out for 73 days to try to prevent a further erosion of the UMW's "share" of coal production, which had sunk to about 40 percent. After the BCOA made some improvements to its offer, including less sweeping subcontracting language, the miners accepted it.

Once again the UMW president became the scapegoat for rank-and-file discontent over contract talks. Church fell out of favor and was succeeded by Richard Trumka in 1982. In the face of poor industry conditions and rising nonunion competition, UMW members approved a 1984 contract settlement that provided the smallest wage increases since the Depression.

The next important UMW battle concerned the policies of a particular employer rather than the national contract. In 1984 a strike was called against A. T. Massey Coal Co. to oppose the firm's refusal to continue recognizing the UMW in some of its subsidiaries. After a 15-month strike that saw a great deal of violence, Massey agreed to settle National Labor Relations Board charges, and the miners went back to work.

SOURCE GUIDE

LEADING STOCK ANALYSTS AND EXPERTS

Marc Cohen, analyst at Kidder Peabody.

John Kawa, analyst at Dean Witter.

Joel Price, analyst at Donaldson, Lufkin & Jenrette.

TRADE ASSOCIATIONS AND UNIONS

National Coal Association, Washington, D.C.

Solar Energy Industries Association, Washington, D.C.

United Mine Workers of America, Washington, D.C.

DATA SOURCES AND DIRECTORIES

Coal Data and *Facts About Coal,* both annuals (Washington, D.C.: National Coal Association).

Keystone Coal Industry Manual, an annual directory (New York: McGraw-Hill).

Monthly Energy Review, Annual Energy Review, Quarterly Coal Report, Annual Outlook for U.S. Coal, and the biennial *Coal Data* (Washington, D.C.: U.S. Energy Information Administration).

Solar Energy Directory, published annually (Sharon, Conn.: Grey House Publishing).

TRADE PUBLICATIONS

Coal Age, monthly.
Coal Outlook, weekly.
Coal Week.
Keystone News-Bulletin, monthly.
Solar Age, monthly.
SynFuels, weekly.
Synfuels Week.

BOOKS AND REPORTS

Banks, Ferdinand E. *The Political Economy of Coal.* Lexington, Mass.: Lexington Books, 1985.

Braithwaite, John. *To Punish or Persuade: The Enforcement of Coal Mine Safety.* Albany, N.Y.: State University of New York Press, 1985.

Gordon, Richard L. *U.S. Coal and the Electric Power Industry.* Baltimore, Md.: Johns Hopkins University Press, 1975.

Reece, Ray. *The Sun Betrayed: A Report on the Corporate Seizure of Solar Energy Development.* Boston: South End Press, 1979.

Seltzer, Curtis. *Fire in the Hole: Miners and Managers in the American Coal Industry.* Lexington, Ky.: University Press of Kentucky, 1985.

U.S. Congress, Office of Technology Assessment. *On-site Solar Energy.* June 1978.

———. *Federal Coal Leasing Program.* May 1984.

U.S. Congress, Senate Budget Committee. *Synthetic Fuels.* Washington, D.C., September 1979.

CHAPTER SEVENTEEN

Nuclear Power and Electric Utilities

By now it is taken for granted, but electric power is one of the major blessings of modern times. The role of electricity in economic development knows no ideological boundaries; Lenin once defined Communism as "electrification plus Soviets." Lighting, heating, cooking, and the gamut of commercial and industrial activities rely on the immense network of wires that make up the electric power grid.

This system is largely under the control of the private, or investor-owned, utility industry. In 1985 these companies received revenues of $124 billion for selling some 2.3 trillion kilowatt hours of power.

This energy is produced by several means, the largest part (about three quarters of the total) coming from the burning of coal, oil, and gas. Hydro and nuclear power each contribute a bit over 13 percent. Back in the early postwar years the hope was that nuclear would provide cheap and abundant power—"too cheap to meter," the forecasts claimed. The federal government spent many billions of dollars to subsidize the effort to attain that dream.

But for the utility industry, nuclear power mainly turned out to be a nightmare. A persistent antinuclear movement challenged the claims that the technology was safe. Accidents such as the one at Three Mile Island in 1979 gave added credibility to these concerns and prompted federal overseers to impose a long list of additional regulations. Construction costs of the nuclear plants went out of control, and the projects fell years behind schedule. More than 100 orders for reactors were canceled, new orders dried up, and by the mid-1980s a number of utilities were even abandoning half-finished plants.

The nuclear quagmire, along with other woes such as a decline in the rate of demand growth, made the 1970s the worst of times for the industry. A decade later the situation had improved somewhat, and electric utilities took the surprising steps of seeking deregulation and branching out into new fields of business.

THE COMING OF ELECTRIC POWER

The electrical power industry had its roots in the breakthrough achieved in 1879 by Thomas Edison and his assistant Francis Jehl in the creation of the first long-lasting incandescent light bulb. The announcement of the device, which consisted of a carbon filament in a vacuum globe, made the stock market go crazy. The shares of gas companies, which had dominated the energy business, plummeted as investors flocked to the Edison Electric Light Company, a start-up firm established by J. P. Morgan and Western Union president Hamilton Twombly.

Edison's vision of electricity transforming commerce and the everyday life of Americans captured the imagination of the country. And Edison was determined to capture the market, both for light bulbs and for the provision of the energy to illuminate them. The Wizard of Menlo Park set up the Edison Electric Illuminating Company to build the first central-station generating plant. He shrewdly chose as his first service area a patch of downtown Manhattan that included the financial district.

After the Pearl Street station successfully started operation in 1882, competitors rushed into the new business, both to generate electricity and to produce light bulbs. Edison's poorly written patent application for the bulb was rejected, and the legal monopoly went to a rival. The rights to a refined version of that bulb were scooped up by an aggressive young inventor and entrepreneur named George Westinghouse, who also began producing generating equipment.

Despite this setback Edison's company made money expanding its service and licensing its equipment designs to others. Yet the mechanical genius was less than brilliant as a manager. He missed a number of important opportunities and insisted on using direct current rather than alternating current. The latter, adopted by Westinghouse, allowed higher voltage power to be transmitted over much longer distances. Edison held to the belief that AC was too dangerous, and as a way of highlighting the point he urged New York State to use a Westinghouse AC generator in building the first electric chair.

The battle between DC and AC was only one of the many differences in standards among the various purveyors of electricity in any given city. The desire to resolve this problem and the quest for economies of scale prompted numerous generating companies to merge with one another. J. P. Morgan, the apostle of corporate consolidation, gained control over Edison Electric and combined it with another firm to form General Electric. Edison had no place in either the name of the new firm or its management. He went back to his laboratory, and GE went on to become an industrial giant. While it and Westinghouse became the dominant figures in manufacture of electrical equipment, they were forced out of the generating business by federal antitrust pressures in the 1920s.

THE RISE AND FALL OF INSULL'S EMPIRE

The great empire builder in the utility business turned out to be Samuel Insull, a Briton who had come to the United States to serve as Edison's personal secretary. The ambitious Insull made his big move in 1892 when he went to Chicago to take over the management of the Chicago Edison Company.

Insull's approach to the business has been compared to that of John D. Rockefeller in oil: He entered a situation of chaotic competition—there were some 47 generating companies operating in Chicago alone—and ruthlessly proceeded to take over rivals and consolidate them.

Yet whereas Rockefeller's creation was eventually undone by the trustbusters, Insull managed to attain official sanction for his empire, called Commonwealth Edison. The way he did it was to embrace the notion of strict government regulation as a quid pro quo for a legal monopoly. Despite some public support for the more radical approach of government takeover, as was occurring in Europe, leading civic reformers accepted regulation, seeing it as preferable to a system of public ownership that would provide inevitable opportunities for corruption. The approach spread rapidly across the country in the early years of the century, and electric generating companies became regulated public utilities.

Insull's innovation was not limited to horizontal integration. He was also a tireless promoter of electric power and insisted that the only efficient way to provide it was through central stations rather than the on-site generators that many commercial customers preferred. He also established the first dual-rate structure: a basic charge for the first few hours and a progressively lower rate for additional demand.

With his success in Chicago, Insull set his sights higher. He assembled more powerful equipment and began expanding his service area to other parts of Illinois and neighboring states. His growing operations were assembled in a holding company called Middle West Utilities. To finance his expansion Insull broke away from the large institutional investors and sold bonds to the public. A pioneer in the use of public relations, Insull made himself into something of a folk hero in the process.

In other parts of the country, utility magnates such as John Barnes Miller of southern California were carrying out similar forms of concentration, gobbling up both private and municipal operations. Consequently by the late 1920s 10 holding companies controlled about three quarters of the country's light and power business.

At the same time, the shares of these companies became some of the most highly prized during the speculative fever of the 1920s. Holding companies changed hands at highly inflated prices. To protect his interests Insull formed an investment trust and went on expanding even after the crash of 1929.

It was in 1931 that the fragility of the economy caught up with Insull. The shares of his and other utility companies finally plunged, and before long Insull was forced out of Middle West Utilities. To escape prosecution for fraud he fled the country, later to be hunted down and extradited. While he managed to win an acquittal in his 1934 trial, Insull was a broken man.

With the advent of the New Deal, private (or investor-owned utilities, as they preferred to be called) found themselves out of favor in Washington. With support from the White House, Senator George Norris of Nebraska led a tireless crusade to promote publicly owned generating facilities. That campaign enjoyed a number of successes in the 1930s:

- The Tennessee Valley Authority, a publicly financed yet independent agency, was formed to develop hydroelectric power in the Southeast.
- In 1935 President Roosevelt created the Rural Electrification Administration to help bring electric power to the areas that private utilities had resisted wiring. The REA provided low-cost loans to cooperatives formed to produce and distribute their own power or else buy wholesale from private utilities and resell it at bargain rates.
- The Public Utilities Holding Company Act of 1935 outlawed the kind of pyramiding Insull had done and limited each utility company to owning one integrated operating system (though some exemptions were later allowed).

After World War II both privately and publicly owned utilities enjoyed rapid growth in the demand for electricity. This was due in no small part to the marketing efforts of the utilities themselves. They promoted the increasing use of electric appliances and offered inducements to builders to construct all-electric "Gold Medallion" homes. In this kind of environment expansion seemed to be a no-lose strategy and one further bolstered by the fact that new plants added to the rate base on which state regulators guaranteed a specific level of return.

THE NUCLEAR GAMBLE

In the 1950s life was secure enough for the utilities that they were willing to go along with the attempts by the federal government to promote an entirely new technology for the generation of electricity. That technology was nuclear power, and several decades later it would nearly be the undoing of the industry.

The possibility of performing nuclear fission (i.e., the splitting of the atom) and harnessing the enormous energy that resulted first emerged in the 1930s in work being done by scientists in Europe. The spread of fascism sent many of these researchers to North America, and one of them, the Hungarian Leo Szilard, became obsessed with the possibility that Germany was working on an atomic bomb. He persuaded Albert Einstein to write to

President Roosevelt and urge him to initiate an American effort to do the same.

In 1942 FDR acted on the recommendation and set up what became known as the Manhattan Project. That same year a group led by Enrico Fermi at the University of Chicago succeeded in creating the first self-sustaining nuclear reaction. Several years of intense work and a great deal of money resulted in the atomic bombs that were dropped on Hiroshima and Nagasaki in August 1945.

In 1946 the Atomic Energy Commission (AEC) was formed, and the federal agency worked hard to promote the idea that the power of the atom was not something to be abandoned now that the war was over. At the same time, a number of scientists who had worked on the Manhattan Project—including some who had regrets about the dropping of the bomb—urged that the nonmilitary uses of atomic energy be developed. The main application was to be the generation of enormous amounts of heat to create steam that in turn was to power electric generators.

The revelation that the Soviet Union had an atomic bomb of its own and the onset of the Cold War delayed the commercialization of nuclear power until the early 1950s. In 1953 President Eisenhower made an "Atoms for Peace" speech at the United Nations, in which he pledged the United States to help other countries develop civilian applications for the technology. The American private sector, which had been barred from the nuclear business by the federal government's monopoly, expressed resentment that Washington was willing to share with foreign governments information that it was keeping from domestic corporations.

In 1954 Congress heeded the plea of business and passed legislation permitting the private ownership of reactors under AEC license. The AEC welcomed the development and brought together Westinghouse and the Duquesne Light Co. of Pittsburgh for the first private project. Private is perhaps the wrong word for the deal, since the federal government was to pay most of the cost for the reactor that Westinghouse was to build for the utility at Shippingport, Pennsylvania. This plant, which started operation in 1957 and was technically owned by the AEC, was followed by half a dozen experimental reactors built by and for the private sector with the taxpayers footing most of the bill. The federal subsidies were necessary because business was not yet willing to take a risk on unproven technology. For its part, the AEC considered immediate costs secondary to the goals of demonstrating U.S. nuclear superiority and creating energy abundance: a situation in which, as AEC chairman Lewis Strauss liked to put it, electricity would be "too cheap to meter."

Although utilities were willing to gamble with Uncle Sam's money, many of them were hesitant to go further. Congress created a further inducement with the Price-Anderson Act of 1957. The law limited the damages that could be collected in an atomic accident to $560 million, with the federal government covering $500 million of that. The utilities were still slow to move, because the estimated costs for nuclear plants remained above oil- and coal-fired ones and no thoughts of fossil fuel shortages had yet entered their minds.

Commercial nuclear development thus proceeded rather slowly until the early 1960s. The turning point was the announcement in 1963 by Jersey Central Power & Light that it had determined that a large nuclear plant—its Oyster Creek plan called for 650 megawatts—would be cost competitive with coal. To make the nuclear option more attractive the leading reactor manufacturers Westinghouse and General Electric announced that they would build nuclear plants on a fixed-cost basis. The two electrical equipment giants ended up losing nearly $1 billion on the 18 turnkey plants they built on these terms. Yet they succeeded in establishing their nuclear technology—light water reactors—as the dominant one throughout the United States and most of the world. Combustion Engineering Corp. and Babcock & Wilcox (a subsidiary of McDermott Inc.) also got into the reactor business, with their own versions of the same general technology.

Utilities looked at nuclear plants in a new light and with the encouragement of Westinghouse and GE started placing increasing numbers of orders for larger and larger reactors. Thus began what became known as the "great bandwagon years."

The tone was set in 1963, when Consolidated Edison placed the first order for a 1,000-megawatt plant, which it wanted to build right in the middle of New York City. Even the AEC was nervous about locating a reactor amid such a large population center, and Con Ed was persuaded to withdraw the proposal. The 1,000-megawatt figure was soon reached again when the Tennessee

Valley Authority ordered one for Browns Ferry, Alabama. In 1972 the AEC set a limit of 1,300 megawatts despite industry talk of going as high as 8,000. The momentum continued into the early 1970s, and construction plans became so ambitious that groups of utilities joined forces to carry them out. In 1972, 16 utilities in New England combined to build two 1,150-megawatt reactors at Seabrook, New Hampshire.

THE SAFETY WAR

No sooner had the bandwagon started rolling than the nuclear industry began to be plagued by growing complaints about the safety of reactors. The AEC and the Joint Committee on Atomic Energy, which had exclusive control over atomic legislation in Congress, had long downplayed the safety issue. This was despite the fact that a study commissioned by the joint committee in the mid-1950s concluded that while the chance of a serious accident was remote, if one happened it could cause 3,400 deaths, 43,000 injuries, and $7 billion in property damage. The first serious reactor accident is believed to have occurred in 1955 at an experimental facility in Idaho, where a partial meltdown occurred.

Safety became a public issue in the late 1950s, a period of growing concern about fallout from atomic weapons. In 1956 the United Automobile Workers challenged the AEC's approval of a plan by Detroit Edison to build a nuclear plant on Lake Erie. The Fermi plant was the first U.S. commercial facility involving a liquid-metal fast breeder reactor. This technology, which creates plutonium in the process of using enriched uranium and thus produces more fuel than it consumes, was put forth as the basis of an energy nirvana. However, volatile liquid sodium rather than water is used in the breeders' cooling systems, making them much more dangerous than regular reactors. The Supreme Court ruled against the UAW, but the union's fears were seen to be justified in 1966 when the plant, only months after going into operation, suffered a serious accident that came close to a total meltdown.

The 1960s saw the emergence of an ongoing movement against nuclear power. The first target was the excess heat that plants released into the environment when disposing of nonradioactive cooling water. Critics charged that this "thermal pollution" was harming fish life in the vicinity of the plants.

Nuclear opponents refined their campaign after the passage of the National Environmental Policy Act of 1969. Taking on the Calvert Cliffs plant that Baltimore Gas & Electric was trying to build on Chesapeake Bay, environmentalists got a federal court to agree in 1971 that nuclear plants had to undergo the environmental reviews called for in the act.

Within a few years the debate shifted to the question of the reliability of the emergency core-cooling systems (ECCS) that are supposed to serve as fail-safe devices for reactors. The nuclear establishment was heartened by a 1974 report, commissioned by the AEC and conducted under the direction of Professor Norman Rasmussen of MIT, that concluded that the risk of a severe reactor accident was less than the chance of an individual being struck by a meteor.

The opposing position gained more credibility the following year, when a serious fire broke out at the TVA's Browns Ferry plant and operators temporarily lost control of the core coolant, creating a situation that some observers said could have resulted in catastrophe. The incident helped spark the growth of the national antinuclear network Critical Mass and the placement of proposals for curbing nuclear plants on ballots in seven states (most notably Proposition 15 in California) in 1976. Although all of these measures were defeated many new activists were recruited.

Antinuclear protesters then turned to direct action to try to block the construction of the Seabrook plants in New Hampshire. Starting in 1976 a group called the Clamshell Alliance staged repeated construction site blockades that slowed down work on the facility and focused national attention on the issue.

The election of Jimmy Carter in 1976 did not bring an out-and-out nuclear opponent to the White House, but it did temper federal support for nuclear growth. In 1977 Carter called nuclear energy a "last resort" and reaffirmed a ban begun by his predecessor on the reprocessing of spent nuclear fuel, in order to safeguard against the diversion of material that could be used to produce nuclear weapons.

The theoretical debate over safety became more of a real issue in the early morning hours of March 28, 1979. It was then that a serious accident occurred at one of the two Three Mile Island reactors operated by Metropolitan Edison (a subsidiary of General Public Utilities) near Harrisburg, Pennsylvania. There was no meltdown in the Babcock & Wilcox reactor, but the combination of mechanical failures, human error, and the lack of clearly defined emergency procedures in the surrounding area cast a shadow over nuclear power. More people than ever began to wonder about the wisdom of what nuclear pioneer Alvin Weinberg once called the "Faustian contract" society had made with atomic energy.

The Three Mile Island incident added another layer of trouble to an industry that was already loaded with woes. After the oil shock of 1973–74 the nuclear industry was set to step in and rescue the nation from the perils of dependence on foreign energy sources. The fly in the ointment here was that in the wake of the oil price increases, the customary postwar growth of electricity demand of 7 to 8 percent a year suddenly halted. This combined with financial problems linked to the higher costs for fossil fuels caused many utilities to abandon or delay nuclear construction plans. Power companies were also pushed in this direction by the growing delays and rapidly rising costs for the nuclear plants that were already under construction. What was once a six-to eight-year process was stretching to a dozen years or more, and the construction cost per kilowatt climbed from a few hundred dollars to several thousand. Even when nuclear plants were completed, utilities were finding that they were out of service a great deal of the time.

New orders for nuclear plants peaked at 41 in 1973 and dropped to 26 in 1974 and less than five in each of the following few years. Not a single new order for a reactor was placed in the U.S. after 1978. At the same time, cancellations of reactor orders (seen for the first time in the early 1970s) began climbing. From 1974 to 1986 more than 100 projects were scratched.

THE FUEL SQUEEZE

The major reactor builders continued to generate revenues from foreign orders and the servicing of domestic plants, but they found themselves in a bind in their role as providers of fuel. To understand how this came about, it is necessary to review how the nuclear fuel industry has been structured since 1964, when Congress passed legislation allowing private participation in what had been a government monopoly.

The first step is the mining of uranium and the conversion of the ore into uranium oxide, or yellowcake. The participants in this sector include Kerr-McGee along with leading oil (Exxon, Atlantic Richfield) and chemical companies (Du Pont, Union Carbide). General Electric entered through its 1976 purchase of Utah International.

The next step is the conversion of the yellowcake into uranium hexafluoride at one of several plants operated by Kerr-McGee and some of the other companies mentioned above. Then it is sent to one of a handful of government-owned plants for enrichment into the proper grade of uranium, a process that requires enormous amounts of electricity. The federal government has tried to privatize ownership of these plants—they are operated under contract by Union Carbide and Goodyear—but companies have not been willing to make the huge capital investment required.

The enriched uranium then goes to facilities run by Kerr-McGee and the reactor makers, where operators working by remote control solidify the uranium into small pellets and load them into metal fuel rods. The rods are then transported to the generating plant and are ready to be inserted into the reactor.

As part of their sales inducement to utilities in the 1960s, the reactor makers entered into long-term contracts to supply fuel. That was fine as long as uranium prices were stable. But in 1972 the leading international producers formed a secret cartel and conspired to raise prices. This, along with actions by the Nixon administration to raise enriched uranium prices to encourage the private-sector companies to take over the government's enrichment business, pushed uranium prices from about $10 a pound to about $35 by the mid-1970s. For a company like Westinghouse, which was obliged to supply millions of pounds of fuel, the new prices spelled major trouble. To avoid a huge loss Westinghouse reneged on its contracts and later brought an antitrust suit against the uranium companies. The drawn-out case was finally settled in 1981, with Westinghouse receiving a $100 million settlement. By the mid-1980s the uranium mining business in the United States was seriously ailing. Declining demand and cheap imports slashed both prices and output.

A SEA OF TROUBLES

In the years following Three Mile Island the plight of the nuclear industry got progressively worse:

• Efforts by the industry to accelerate the licensing process were halted, and the Nuclear Regulatory Commission issued a blizzard of new regulations. (In 1974 the AEC was abolished, and its regulatory responsibility and development efforts were placed in separate agencies. These were the Nuclear Regulatory Commission [NRC] and the Energy Research and Development Administration, which later became part of the new Department of Energy.)

• The owners of Three Mile Island, facing a $1 billion cleanup job, had to beg for help from the federal and state governments and other reactor operators. General Public Utilities also took the bizarre step of suing the NRC for not regulating the company enough; the case was thrown out of court.

• In 1983 Congress cut off funding for the Clinch River breeder reactor project in Tennessee. The demonstration project, originally authorized in 1970, had been a political football for years. Opposed by President Carter because of the risk that the plutonium produced by the breeder could be diverted for weapons production, the project was finally killed because of its rapidly rising cost.

• The finances of the Washington Public Power Supply System (informally known as Whoops) got progressively weaker and the system defaulted on $2.2 billion of its debt in 1983. The default, the largest in municipal bond history, resulted from the escalating costs of the nuclear plants being constructed by Whoops, a joint venture of 19 publicly owned utilities and four municipalities in the Northwest. The default occurred on bonds issued for the two nuclear plants (out of a total of five planned by Whoops) that ended up being canceled.

• A new NRC safety study found that the odds of a serious accident were much greater than estimated by Rasmussen and that one could be expected every 10 to 15 years.

• The Supreme Court ruled in 1983 that states could ban the construction of new nuclear plants for economic though not for safety reasons.

• There was increasing public controversy over the issue of nuclear waste. After years of debate Congress in 1982 finally passed legislation setting a timetable for the establishment of permanent underground storage sites. However, Congress avoided the issue of whether to permit the reprocessing of spent fuel into plutonium—a procedure that the Carter administration had opposed because of the danger of theft of weapons-grade material but that Reagan supported. In addition the Energy Department faced strong local opposition to any sites it considered for the storage facilities.

By the mid-1980s utilities with nuclear plants under construction found themselves facing a dilemma. Costs on the projects had gotten totally out of hand, and delays were enormous. Long Island Lighting's Shoreham plant, which was originally supposed to cost $300 million, was up to more than $4 billion and a decade behind schedule. The cost of the two Seabrook reactors in New Hampshire was estimated at more than $7 billion—eight times the original estimate—and work on one of the reactors was suspended.

The utilities had to decide whether to sink yet more money in these projects, not knowing whether they would be necessary by the time they were done. To make matters worse it became increasingly uncertain whether the utilities would ever be able to recoup their investment.

Faced with this possibility some utilities began to consider walking away from their huge investments. This was the path taken by Public Service Co. of Indiana, which in 1984 abandoned its half-finished Marble Hill plant, on which it had spent $2.5 billion.

A group of Ohio utilities took the less drastic step of converting their troubled Zimmer nuclear project into a coal-fired plant, while the state government of New York began considering a public takeover of Long Island Lighting because of the Shoreham mess.

The sorry state of the nuclear industry brought criticism from voices far removed from the antinuclear movement. One of the most dramatic statements came in a 1985 cover story in *Forbes* magazine, which declared: "The failure of the U.S. nuclear power program ranks as the largest managerial disaster in business history."

Yet another blow to nuclear power came in 1986, with the serious accident at the Chernobyl reactor in the Soviet Union. The U.S. nuclear industry hastened to point out that the graphite technology used at Chernobyl was almost unknown in the United States. Yet the incident, which caused 31 deaths in the short term and will (according to Soviet estimates) lead to 6,500 cancer fatalities, represented a serious setback for the proponents of nuclear power.

For the U.S. nuclear industry it was unfortunate that the Chernobyl accident occurred while Congress was considering renewal of the Price-Anderson law on the liability of the industry in the event of an accident. The original 1957 act's $560 million liability limit (with the federal government providing $500 million of that) was to last for 10 years. The law was revised in 1965 and 1975, with the federal government's share eventually phased out, and the maximum liability was put at the total of the industry's pooled commercial insurance coverage and assessments of $5 million that the owner of each licensed plant would be expected to make. This brought the ceiling to about $650 million by 1986. Congress was expected to raise the limit somewhat, but in the wake of Chernobyl the general sentiment was for a major increase. As of this writing, two committees have proposed a tenfold rise to $6.5 billion.

UPHEAVAL AMONG THE UTILITIES

Nuclear problems were only a part of the travails that were plaguing the electric utility industry. In the 1960s the problem was a shortage of capacity, a situation illustrated most dramatically by the huge blackout in the Northeast in November 1965. This shortfall in supply was brought on by rapid population growth and the proliferation of electric devices (air conditioners, dishwashers, etc.) in the home.

The Federal Power Commission was pressing utilities to improve transmission links between systems in order to make more efficient use of existing capacity, but the companies resisted. Instead many of them focused on increasing their own capacity by building large nuclear plants, with the results discussed above.

The slowdown in the growth of demand in the aftermath of the oil shock stunned both the utilities that were building nuclear plants and those that were relying exclusively on fossil fuels and hydro. The utilities were also hit hard by rising interest rates and the high cost of the pollution control equipment they were obliged to install in the coal-fired generating plants that the federal government promoted during the 1970s. Consumers—acting through groups such as the citizens utility boards organized in a number of states—fought against rate increases; and many state commissions, facing strong consumer protests over "rate shock," rejected utility requests or granted small increases.

More than a third of the states refused to allow the costs of construction work in progress (CWIP) in the rate base, and many state regulatory commissions were becoming resistant to allowing the bloated costs of completed nuclear projects to become permanent additions to the rate base. (The Supreme Court ruled in 1986 that utilities could not recover the cost of plants that were canceled during construction or shut down after completion.)

In the late 1970s and early 1980s the business press began to speculate whether electric utilities were still a viable business, and discussion of government takeovers was increasing among observers not usually given to talk of public ownership of industry.

The decline of oil prices and interest rates eased the crisis, and the industry began an ideological counterattack. Less rather than more government intervention was said to be the solution to the problems of utilities; the surprising new topic of debate was the possible deregulation of the industry.

This new notion was put forth as a response to changes in the way that electric power was produced and marketed. One element was the growth in the process known as cogeneration. With the rising energy costs of the 1970s many companies began making use of the intense heat that is created in many industrial processes. To the dismay of utilities these companies began using the heat to generate their own electricity. Some firms produced more power than they needed; and as a result of the Public Utilities Regulatory Policies Act of 1978 utilities were obliged to purchase this surplus power. By 1985 cogeneration was providing 2 to 3 percent of the country's energy output.

At the same time, major customers began shopping around among utilities and making better deals with distant companies than they faced with their local provider. The distant utility was able to "wheel" in the power to the user through the facilities of the local utility, which was paid a fee for this service.

The 10 Largest Electric Utility Companies, by 1985 Assets ($ Millions)

1. Pacific Gas & Electric (San Francisco)	$19,098
2. Southern (Atlanta)	16,531
3. Commonwealth Edison (Chicago)	16,285
4. Middle South Utilities (New Orleans)	13,656
5. American Electric Power (Columbus, Ohio)	13,621
6. Southern California Edison (Rosemead)	12,593
7. Texas Utilities (Dallas)	10,867
8. Public Service Electric & Gas (Newark, N.J.)	10,487
9. Philadelphia Electric (Philadelphia)	10,165
10. Detroit Edison (Detroit)	9,492

Source: *Fortune*, June 9, 1986.

Developments such as these gave rise to the argument that market forces were playing a much greater role in the electricity business, which was functioning less as a monopoly, and thus government regulation was no longer needed. Much of the assault was directed against federal regulation, which covers only the interstate transmission of power.

Utilities also insisted that they needed greater freedom to enter new lines of business to make up for the declining profitability of electric power. Lenient state regulators permitted companies, suddenly flush with cash thanks to reduced costs, to take on new activities such as oil and gas exploration, land development, banking, and cable television. In 1986 Pacific Lighting Corp. of California acquired Thrifty Corp., an operator of drug and discount stores. Yet many regulators were still concerned that the utilities were paying insufficient attention to their core business.

In all, by the mid-1980s life was much brighter for the electric utilities than in the previous decade. Lower interest rates and fuel costs and the winding down of many massive construction projects, along with a stronger economy, helped the bottom line. Yet the consequences of increasing competition, including rate reductions in some areas, were only beginning to be felt and understood. It was also unclear whether the strategy of diversification would lead to more or less stability for the industry.

LABOR RELATIONS

Initial organizing in the utility business came under the auspices of the International Brotherhood of Electrical Workers and the United Electrical, Radio and Machine Workers of America. A more concerted drive in the industry came in 1938, when the CIO formed the Utility Workers Organizing Committee. The UWOC set out to transform into true collective bargaining organizations the company unions many of the utilities had formed. After accomplishing that objective at New York's Consolidated Edison in 1945, the committee was chartered as the Utility Workers Union of America.

The UWUA grew to nearly 75,000 members when the AFL and the CIO merged in 1955, but it remained a conservative union and one weakened by the high level of automation in the industry. Nevertheless it carried out a number of strikes, the most notable being the walkouts at Con Edison in 1968 and 1983.

Labor activity related to nuclear power plants has been most tumultuous among the construction workers building them. Strikes have occurred since the building of the earliest facilities, though in 1978 construction unions and nuclear engineering companies agreed on a pact restricting strikes and lockouts on nuclear projects. Nonetheless there have been incidents of labor unrest, including wildcat actions by workers at the Seabrook project in New Hampshire in the mid-1980s.

There have also been frequent disputes at nuclear testing and fuel production facilities, especially with the Oil, Chemical and Atomic Workers. Karen Silkwood, a worker and OCAW member at a Kerr-McGee plutonium plant, was trying to expose unsafe conditions at the facility when she was killed in a suspicious car crash in 1974. She later became a heroine of the antinuclear movement.

The nuclear workers that are hardest for unions to organize are those known as "jumpers." These temporary employees are brought in to enter reactors for short periods, perhaps 10 minutes, to make a few adjustments to the equipment before they are "burned out"—that is, they get their maximum dosage of radiation.

LEADING COMPANIES

General Electric, put together by J. P. Morgan in 1892, took Thomas Edison's designs and became the leader of the electrical equipment business—a position that caused it to be a major culprit in the price-fixing case brought against the industry in the 1960s. In the 1950s it also emerged as one of the two leading nuclear reactor producers. GE received its last reactor order in

1974 but has continued to earn revenues (albeit a small portion of the giant company's total) from services and fuel for existing reactors.

Kerr-McGee started as an oil drilling company in Oklahoma in 1929 and moved into the uranium business in 1952. Founder Robert Kerr handed over control of the company to Dean McGee and entered politics, first serving as governor of Oklahoma and then becoming a powerful U.S. senator from that state. Kerr was a leading promoter of the energy business in the Senate and helped Kerr-McGee gain a position as a leading producer of uranium and nuclear fuel. The company gained national attention in connection with the case of Karen Silkwood. While documenting safety hazards at the Kerr-McGee plutonium plant where she worked, Silkwood was contaminated several times and died in a suspicious car crash while en route to meet with a *New York Times* reporter. In 1986 Kerr-McGee settled a negligence suit brought by Silkwood's estate by agreeing to pay $1.4 million. The company had been contesting a previous jury award of $10.5 million.

Westinghouse Electric has been the major rival of General Electric since the turn of the century and became the leading producer of nuclear reactors. Founded by inventor and entrepreneur George Westinghouse in 1886, the company by the mid-1980s was estimated to be earning as much as one third of its net income from nuclear activities, especially abroad. Its most controversial foreign project was a $2.2 billion reactor project started in the Philippines during the Marcos regime. Westinghouse has been accused of bribing Marcos to get the contract. After taking power, the Aquino government refused to begin operation of the plant because of safety concerns—the reactor was built near a volcano—and evidence of faulty construction. Aquino was reportedly planning to seek damage payments of several hundred million dollars from Westinghouse.

SOURCE GUIDE

LEADING STOCK ANALYSTS AND EXPERTS

Charles Benore, utilities analyst at Paine Webber.

Leonard Hyman, utilities analyst at Merrill Lynch.

Ernest Liu, utilities analyst at Goldman Sachs.

Mark Luftig, utilities analyst at Salomon Brothers.

National Economic Research Associates, a utility consulting firm in White Plains, New York.

TRADE ASSOCIATIONS AND UNIONS

American Public Power Association, Washington, D.C.

Atomic Industrial Forum, Bethesda, Maryland.

Edison Electric Institute, Washington, D.C.

International Brotherhood of Electrical Workers, Washington, D.C.

Oil, Chemical and Atomic Workers International Union, Denver.

Utility Workers Union of America, Washington, D.C.

DATA SOURCES AND DIRECTORIES

Electrical World Directory of Electric Utilities, published annually (New York: McGraw-Hill).

Moody's Public Utility Manual, an annual volume of financial data on individual utilities (New York: Moody's Investors Services).

P.U.R. Analysis of Investor-Owned Electric and Gas Utilities, an annual directory and data source (Arlington, Va.: Public Utilities Reports).

Statistical Yearbook of the Electric Utility Industry and the *Electric Power Annual Report* (New York: Edison Electric Institute).

U.S. Energy Information Administration publishes numerous statistical reports and forecasts, including *Annual Outlook for U.S. Electric Power, Electric Power Annual, Electric Power Monthly, Uranium Industrial Annual*, and the annuals *Commercial Nuclear Power* and *Nuclear Power Plant Construction Activity*.

TRADE PUBLICATIONS

Electric Light & Power, monthly.

Electric Utility Week.

Electrical World, monthly.

Public Utilities Fortnightly.

Nucleonics Week.

BOOKS AND REPORTS

Bupp, Irvin C., and Jean-Claude Derian. *Light Water: How the Nuclear Dream Dissolved*. New York: Basic Books, 1978.

Hertsgaard, Mark. *Nuclear Inc.: The Men and Money behind Nuclear Energy*. New York: Pantheon Books, 1983.

Johnson, John W. *Insuring against Disaster: The Nuclear Industry on Trial*. Macon, Ga.: Mercer University Press, 1986.

Kemeny Commission. *Report of the President's Commission on the Accident at Three Mile Island*. Washington, D.C., October 1979.

Munson, Richard. *The Power Makers: The Inside Story of America's Biggest Business*. Emmaus, Pa.: Rodale Press, 1985.

Novarro, Peter. *The Dimming of America: The Real Costs of Electric Utility Regulatory Failure*. Cambridge, Mass.: Ballinger, 1985.

Stoler, Peter. *Decline and Fall: The Ailing Nuclear Power Industry*. New York: Dodd, Mead, 1985.

Taylor, June, and Michael Yokell. *Yellowcake: The International Uranium Cartel*. Elmsford, N.Y.: Pergamon Press, 1980.

U.S. Congress, Office of Technology Assessment. *Nuclear Power in an Age of Uncertainty*. Washington, D.C., February 1984.

U.S. Department of Energy. *The Future of Electric Power in America*. Chiles Report. Washington, D.C., 1983.

U.S. Nuclear Regulatory Commission, Special Inquiry Group. *Three Mile Island: A Report to the Commissioners and to the Public*. Rogovin Report. Washington, D.C., January 1980.

CHAPTER EIGHTEEN

Oil and Natural Gas

The petroleum industry is one of the main pillars of the American economy. Its output is essential both to the country's energy needs (transportation, heating, power, light, etc.) and as a raw material for a long list of industries, including chemicals, textiles, drugs, and plastics. The value of the crude oil and natural gas produced in the United States was some $124 billion in 1985, and the products of the petroleum refineries another $169 billion. Oil companies account for more than half of the 20 largest U.S. industrial corporations, and the leader Exxon has alternated with General Motors for the top spot.

The recent history of the industry has been especially tumultuous. With the rapid increase of oil prices in the early 1970s, the industry became a favorite villain of everyone from the consumer to the president of the United States. Yet the fat days of the oil business came to an end with the slump of oil prices in the early 1980s. Once-invincible companies found themselves under attack as corporate raiders sought to dismantle some of the giants. The battle prompted companies to arrange friendly mergers that resulted in the largest deals in U.S. business history and the disappearance of some of the industry's most familiar names. Other companies adjusted to the new environment and made themselves less vulnerable to takeover by massive restructuring moves. In the mid-1980s the "oil patch" was still trying to recover from the most trying period in its history.

FROM TITUSVILLE TO SPINDLETOP

The U.S. petroleum industry began in the 1850s with the determination of a man named Edwin Drake to prove that oil, previously seen only in places where it seeped out of the ground, could be obtained directly through the drilling of wells. Drake, working with New York lawyer George Bissell, began his explorations (which were subjected to a great deal of public derision) near Titusville, Pennsylvania. On August 27, 1859, his drill struck oil and gave birth to a new kind of gold rush.

Only five years earlier the kerosene lamp had been invented, and the possibility of a new source of light, to supplant the traditional candle wax and whale oil, was realized. The kerosene in use was derived from coal; Drake's discovery promised a more accessible supply of energy. Within only a few years kerosene produced from oil almost entirely displaced the coal-derived variety.

The large number of undercapitalized entrepreneurs who rushed into the oil business and the irregularity of their output made for a very unstable industry. Prices bounced up and down as supply vacillated. As oil historians like to say, the business was ripe for consolidation.

The man who took on that task as his life's work was a young entrepreneur named John D. Rockefeller. The son of a con artist who abandoned his family and of a deeply religious woman, Rockefeller managed to combine ruthless business practices with a sense of philanthropic responsibility. In 1863 he set up a kerosene refining business with two partners in Cleveland. He soon bought out the coowners and embarked on a single-minded drive to take over as much of the business as he could—the refining and transportation aspects of the industry, that is, since Rockefeller decided that the exploration end was too risky.

Rockefeller's company went public in 1870 under the name of Standard Oil Company. For the rest of the century Standard employed every device, legal and not so legal, to dominate the industry. It grew large enough to dictate terms to the railroads and thus enjoyed freight charges substantially lower than those paid by its dwindling rivals. Rockefeller allowed competitors to operate in limited areas, but if they grew too large Standard waged unbridled price wars to keep them in place or take them over.

Standard was also far and away the leading exporter and the dominant player in the international oil market.

To get around an Ohio law limiting a corporation's ownership of shares of companies in other states, Rockefeller created an arrangement called the Standard Oil Trust, in which Standard's subsidiaries were nominally independent but were controlled by a centralized board of trustees. In 1892 the Ohio Supreme Court struck down the plan, so the holding company for the trust was converted to Standard Oil of New Jersey, a state that had adopted more liberal rules regarding out-of-state ownership.

The first challenge to Standard's domination came with the development of the Baku fields in Russia by the Nobel brothers of Sweden. Working with the Rothschilds of France the Nobels provided Europe with an alternative source of supply. Then the industry in the United States was transformed with the discovery of oil in Texas. Beginning with the 1901 gusher at Spindletop near Beaumont, the Texas wells began producing at levels far in excess of those in Pennsylvania. The dominance of the Southwest was clinched when additional finds were made in Oklahoma and Louisiana. The leading companies to emerge from the region were Gulf Oil, built with money from the Mellons of Pittsburgh, and the Texas Company, later known as Texaco.

Just as Standard's predominance began to erode a bit, public opposition to the trust reached its height, helped by muckraking books such as Ida Tarbell's unflattering history of Standard. The Roosevelt administration brought antitrust charges against the Rockefeller empire, and in 1909 a federal court ruled that the Standard Oil Trust was illegal under the Sherman Act. The case went all the way to the Supreme Court, which upheld the ruling and ordered the dissolution of Standard into more than 30 independent companies.

The distribution of stock in the new companies was done according to the ownership of Standard's shares, which raised questions as to the degree of autonomy of the firms, but there is no question that the monolithic Standard Oil was no more.

The largest of the spin-offs were Standard Oil of New Jersey (often called Jersey Standard and officially renamed Exxon in 1972), Standard Oil Company of New York (Socony, which went through several name changes until becoming Mobil in 1966), Standard Oil Company of California (Socal, which was renamed

Chevron in 1984), and Standard Oil of Indiana (which took the name Amoco in 1985).

OIL PLAYS IN THE MIDDLE EAST

By the second decade of the 20th century oil had become a strategic resource as well as a commodity. The use of motorized ground transportation, airplanes, and oil-fueled ships made petroleum crucial to the war effort. With the return of peace oil continued its rise to prominence as the fuel of the automobile age.

The importance of oil made the major international powers eager to obtain direct control over supplies of the precious black liquid. Britain, no longer able to count on its domestic supplies of coal, focused its efforts in the Middle East. The first arena was Persia, where the British backed William D'Arcy, a speculator who had obtained a 500,000-square-mile concession in 1901. After a major discovery was made in 1908, the Anglo-Persian Oil Company (renamed Anglo-Iranian in 1935 and British Petroleum in 1954) was formed.

The next move was in Mesopotamia (Iraq), which was nominally ruled by the sultan of the Ottoman Empire. A flamboyant Armenian entrepreneur named Calouste Gulbenkian gained the confidence of the sultan and paved the way for the creation of the Turkish Petroleum Company in 1912. TPC came to be controlled by the Anglo-Persian Oil Company, Deutsche Bank, and Royal Dutch/Shell (the British-Dutch firm that was established to challenge Standard Oil). For his efforts Gulbenkian got a one-20th share and came to be known as "Mr. Five Percent." With the onset of World War I Deutsche Bank's share was expropriated by the British.

By the 1920s the U.S. government grew uneasy over the British dominance of the vast reserves of the Middle East and the exclusion of American firms. This was a result at least in part of the shortage scare created by the leading producers. In 1920 the director of the U.S. Geological Survey, using data supplied by the companies, declared that American reserves were declining rapidly. The result was a sharp increase in domestic prices and the creation of the Federal Oil Conservation Board, which encouraged higher prices by restricting output, a practice that had been initiated at the state level by the Texas Railroad Commission.

Another consequence was a consensus in Washington that greater access to foreign oil was imperative.

Accordingly the U.S. government began espousing an open-door policy to the British and urged leading American producers to band together to press for a share of the Mideast action. A group of seven companies originally joined the effort, but rising supplies in the United States (the shortage turned out to be short lived) prompted most of them to drop out.

When an agreement for U.S. participation in TPC, renamed Iraq Petroleum, was worked out in 1928, only Jersey Standard and Socony remained. They and their partners, which now included the French state-owned Compagnie Française des Pétroles, agreed not to compete with one another for concessions in a huge area representing the old Ottoman Empire. To supplement what came to be called the Red Line arrangement, the heads of Jersey Standard, Royal Dutch/Shell, and Anglo-Persian met secretly at Achnacarry, a hunting lodge in Scotland, in 1928. Cooking up what became known as the As-Is agreement, the oil barons pooled the world market (aside from the United States and the Soviet Union) and divided it up according to existing shares of the major producers. Any expansion of the business was supposed to preserve those relationships. This was the first international oil cartel.

Although the architects of As-Is continued to dominate the global oil market outside the United States, they were unable to prevent competitors from expanding. Socal got a foothold in Bahrain, and Gulf Oil in partnership with Anglo-Iranian obtained a valuable concession in Kuwait. The most notable defiance came in Saudi Arabia. Socal got a vast concession from King Ibn Saud and in 1938 ended up finding the world's largest reserves. The California company had so much oil that it cut Texaco into the deal. The two firms formed the Caltex joint venture and later turned it into the Arab American Oil Co., or Aramco. In 1945 Jersey Standard and Socony joined the Saudi consortium.

Postwar demand for petroleum products increased smartly with the growth of air transport and the spread of home heating systems using oil and gas. There was also increased use of petroleum as a raw material in chemical production, including plastics and fertilizers, and in the manufacturing of products such as synthetic rubber and pharmaceuticals.

The growing market made the search for supplies a constant preoccupation of the major international producers, known collectively as the Seven Sisters: Jersey Standard, Socony, Socal, Gulf, Texaco, Royal Dutch/Shell, and British Petroleum.

THE ROAD TO OPEC

Yet it became increasingly difficult for the multinationals to exercise over Third World governments the kind of absolute control they enjoyed early in the century. The challenge to foreign companies witnessed during the Mexican Revolution appeared again in Venezuela in the 1930s and 1940s. After a large oil discovery was made in the country in 1922, the major producers had propped up the cooperative despot General Juan Vincente Gomez. When the dictator died in 1935 the government took a much harder line against the foreign oil giants. Taxes were raised, customs duties began to be enforced, and a new protective labor law for oilworkers was passed.

The most significant blow to the companies was the government's insistence on a new financial arrangement that gave it a 50 percent share of oil income, a considerably higher figure than the Seven Sisters were used to giving the host country. The Venezuelan deal inspired other oil-producing countries to demand better terms, and before long the 50–50 split was standard.

However, when the Iranian government under Mohammed Mossadegh tried to go farther and nationalize the oil industry, the West struck back: A CIA-aided coup overthrew Mossadegh in 1953. Yet the shah, who was reinstalled on the throne, proved to be difficult to control. He did initially let U.S. companies get a share of Iranian production, but in the late 1950s he asserted greater control over the country's oil operations and turned to the Italian state-owned petroleum company ENI, which offered a deal more favorable to Iran.

The terms achieved by Iran helped inspire a group of eight producing countries to meet in Baghdad in 1960 and form the Organization of Petroleum Exporting Countries (OPEC), which a dozen years later would turn the world upside down. As *Fortune* put it in 1965, "OPEC wants to do for international oil what the Texas Railroad Commission has done for U.S. oil."

The challenge to the Seven Sisters came not only from their

Third World hosts. The 1950s also saw the rise in the United States of aggressive competitors that became known as the independents. Taking advantage of a tax provision that the majors had won (which allowed U.S. companies to deduct foreign royalties from their American tax liability), companies such as Continental, Marathon, and Getty became aggressive explorers abroad. The accelerating hunt for oil by both U.S. and foreign companies brought about many new sources of supply.

The result was that while demand kept on increasing, the faster growth of supply tended to keep prices lower than the oil producers would have liked. The willingness of the independent producers to undercut the prices of the majors and sell crude to independent refiners at a discount also contributed to the trend. The flood of cheap oil into the United States worried the majors, and they turned to the federal government for help. Persuading Congress and the Eisenhower administration that the country was becoming dangerously dependent on foreign oil, the majors succeeded in getting a provision inserted in a 1955 trade bill giving the president the right to institute mandatory limits on oil imports. Critics of the program (which remained in effect until 1973) wondered how it improved national security, but there was little doubt that the import quotas boosted prices and restricted the growth of the independents.

THE GROWTH OF GAS

Another element that entered into the changing competitive situation of the energy industry after World War II was the rising importance of natural gas. The history of commercial gas usage in the United States extends back to the early 19th century, when a synthetic version derived from coal was used for lighting in various parts of the country.

Gas use waned with the growth of the oil industry. The natural gas often found along with oil or in deposits by itself tended to be burned off at the well. This was not because the gas was useless; in fact it was and is a very efficient and clean energy source. The problem was the difficulty in transporting the gas over long distances, which contributed to its low price.

In the 1920s the development of acetylene welding made possible the construction of pipelines through which natural gas could be transported over longer distances at high pressure. By the 1950s natural gas was being widely distributed around the country to both residential and industrial users. During the same period techniques were developed for freezing the gas to subzero temperatures, thus converting it into a liquid and permitting it to be transported by ship.

Natural gas was important enough by the late 1930s to prompt Congress to pass legislation regulating its pricing. Yet the wording of the Natural Gas Act of 1938 was somewhat ambiguous, and the gas-producing industry waged a battle against the authority of the Federal Power Commission to regulate wellhead prices—that is, what was charged by the producer to the pipeline operator.

In 1954 the Supreme Court upheld the FPC's jurisdiction over wellhead prices, but the producers kept fighting. Congress voted in 1956 to end price regulation. However, the revelation of attempts by an industry lobbyist to make improper payments to members of Congress caused President Eisenhower to veto the bill.

Upon taking office in 1969, President Nixon expressed some sympathy with the complaints of the natural gas industry and appointed a like-minded lawyer, John Nassikas, to head the FPC. The industry did everything possible under the law to ease regulation of the industry and allow prices to rise, but the producers hungered for complete decontrol.

The announcement by the American Gas Association of a sudden plunge in gas reserves amounting to some 5.5 trillion cubic feet was used by the industry to justify higher prices that were supposed to encourage exploration, while critics charged that the industry was fabricating the shortage to blackmail the country. This dispute became all the more fierce with the actual supply shortages that occurred at times during the 1970s, alternating with dearths of other energy products such as heating oil and gasoline.

The pressures for decontrol persisted, but when Congress finally in 1978 passed such a measure, the Natural Gas Policy Act, it embodied a compromise with the proponents of continued regulation. The law phased in decontrol of newly discovered gas over a seven-year period and in the interim subjected the intrastate sale of gas, which had previously been exempt from federal rules, to the same controls.

UPHEAVAL IN OIL

Meanwhile the oil scene had become even more tumultuous. The late 1960s saw the industry battling on fronts both at home and abroad. In 1968 an upstart company called Atlantic Richfield made a major discovery of oil in the North Slope area of Alaska. Other companies rushed in to participate in the bonanza, but the problem was how to get the oil from the frozen region where it was being drilled to a port from which it could be transported to the rest of the country.

The industry came up with an ambitious plan to construct an 800-mile-long pipeline from Prudhoe Bay down through the entire state to the port of Valdez in the south. The plan, one of the largest engineering efforts of all time, elicited loud protests from the growing environmental movement, which expressed concern over how the 48-inch-in-diameter pipeline (through which oil would travel at temperatures of around 140 degrees) would affect the delicate tundra. The environmentalists, who gained considerable support after the major offshore oil spill near Santa Barbara, California, in 1969, managed to tie up the project for years with court challenges. But in the end Congressional intervention allowed the project, redesigned to reduce ecological damage, to go through. Nonetheless the construction of the pipeline was fraught with engineering setbacks, faulty welding (some of which contractors tried to cover up), and other problems that ended up pushing the final cost to some $9 billion.

The foreign challenges came from the countries where the bulk of the world's oil was extracted. The OPEC nations had little success in the mid-1960s raising their prices. But things changed after the radical Muammar Qaddafi took power in Libya in 1969 and successfully pressured foreign companies to part with a higher percentage of their income. Other OPEC members were inspired to demand better terms for themselves. In 1971 the cartel for the first time reached agreement on raising the minimum price for a barrel of oil. The basic price, which had remained steady at $1.80 a barrel throughout the 1960s, thus began a slow ascent that brought it to a bit over $3 by late 1973.

After war broke out in the Middle East in October 1973, the Arab oil producers decided to use their oil weapon to punish U.S. support of Israel. OPEC cut back production and declared an embargo on shipments to the United States. The action lasted only five months, but the cartel also began a series of price increases that ended up quadrupling the cost of a barrel of oil.

Although evidence later came out that the United States had actually supported oil price increases to bolster its Mideast allies, the OPEC actions went much further than anticipated. The large runup in the price of oil created turmoil in the industrialized world and made the "energy crisis" a major concern of government policy for the rest of the decade.

For the oil industry the OPEC price hikes were financially a wonderful development, but they were a public relations disaster. Much of the public believed that the oil majors either had colluded with OPEC or at least were unfairly benefiting from the oil crunch. The energy crisis was often put in military terms, and the oil companies were accused by some of "war profiteering." In 1977 President Carter accused the industry of staging "the biggest rip-off in history."

The industry, of course, denied any improper actions and claimed that its high returns were necessary to pay for the exploration needed to find new energy supplies. To make its case the majors spent millions on advocacy advertising. Mobil was the most aggressive of the bunch, regularly buying space on newspaper op-ed pages to defend the industry.

The companies also noted that the American public was cushioned from the full impact of the oil cost increase by the federal price controls that President Nixon had instituted in 1971 as part of his antiinflation policies and that Congress insisted on keeping in place. However, the industry was confronted with a series of government investigations of violations of those controls. President Carter announced in 1979 that he would support the ending of price controls but got Congress to agree to subject the industry to a windfall profits tax for the transition period.

Public controversy over oil companies' actions escalated with the diversification moves that the majors began to make. Mobil completed its purchase of Marcor, owner of retailer Montgomery Ward and Container Corp. of America, in 1976. Atlantic Richfield purchased copper miner Anaconda in 1977, and other companies such as Exxon, Gulf, and Socal made major investments in mineral producers. This was in addition to earlier moves into coal and uranium.

The reputation of the oil companies was further besmirched in

the mid-1970s with revelations that a number of firms, most notably Gulf, had made large amounts of improper campaign contributions in the United States and payoffs to government officials
abroad.

The industrialized world had largely adapted to the sharp oil
price rises of 1973–74 and the slow ascent in the following years,
when another shock came in 1979. In the wake of the cutback in
oil production during the Iranian revolution, prices on the spot
market (oil not under contract) leaped as high as $40, and OPEC
hiked up its prices to as high as $23. Supply was a problem as well
as price: The United States experienced severe gasoline shortages
in the spring and summer of 1979. Long lines of angry drivers at
filling stations often erupted in violence.

GLUT AND SLUMP

The second oil shock forced individuals and corporations in the
United States to make serious changes in the way they used energy. Although many of the conservation measures proposed by
President Carter never passed Congress, energy efficiency became the order of the day. This, combined with switching to
alternative fuels and the onset of economic recession (induced in
part by high energy prices), caused the demand for oil to sink.
U.S. consumption dropped from 6.9 billion barrels in 1978 to 5.6
billion in 1982, and imports fell even faster.

A similar pattern through the rest of the industrial world
helped put downward pressure on international oil prices. By
1982 spot prices were falling rapidly, and OPEC members and
other producing countries initiated a round of price-cutting. In
1983 OPEC officially decreased its base prices for the first time in
the cartel's history.

The decline of oil prices spelled trouble for U.S. petroleum
companies. The Southwest lost its affluent Sun Belt aura and
became one of the most depressed regions of the country. Smaller
players went under, and among the larger companies there was a
dramatic period of restructuring.

The latter included a series of different processes that changed
the face of the oil patch. First, there was a wave of consolidation
as giant companies gobbled up one another. In 1981 Du Pont
emerged from a complicated takeover battle having bought Conti-

nental (Conoco) for $7.2 billion. The following year Occidental Petroleum bought Cities Service for $4 billion, and U.S. Steel (now USX) defeated Mobil in a battle for Marathon Oil, paying $5.9 billion for its prize. In 1984 Texaco bought Getty for $10.1 billion, and Mobil acquired Superior Oil for $5.7 billion. U.S. Steel completed the $3 billion purchase of Texas Oil & Gas in 1986.

The industry was also thrown into turmoil by the actions of a maverick oilman named T. Boone Pickens, chairman of the relatively small Mesa Petroleum. Charging that the managements of numerous large oil firms were not making the best use of their assets, Pickens launched a series of audacious hostile tender offers, with varying results. The assault on Phillips Petroleum led to a 1985 deal in which the company repurchased Mesa's shares at a profit for the Pickens company. But the same year, in the case of Unocal, Pickens was defeated and was excluded when Unocal management repurchased more than $4 billion worth of its shares. In the most dramatic battle, Gulf agreed in 1984 to be acquired by Chevron for $13.2 billion to escape the clutches of Pickens.

The industry has also resorted to a variety of financial moves to adjust to the slump and to prevent their stock prices from sinking too low. Firms such as Exxon, Amoco, and Standard Oil of Ohio announced common-share repurchase plans. In many cases assets have been written down or sold off, exploration efforts have been scaled back drastically, and large numbers of employees have been laid off or pressured to take early retirement. Some smaller companies such as Mesa Petroleum have turned themselves into master limited partnerships, under which their oil properties are packaged as partnerships and sold to the public.

In early 1986 the woes of the industry intensified as the decline in oil prices accelerated. Spot prices dipped below $10 a barrel for the first time in nearly a decade. Oil was becoming so cheap that the industry was warning that the United States was once again becoming dangerously dependent on foreign supplies. There was talk in Congress of instituting an import fee that would discourage use of foreign oil and help prop up domestic prices, but the Reagan administration strongly opposed the idea.

There was a change in climate in the summer of 1986, when OPEC members reached agreement on a plan to cut production about 15 percent in an effort to halt the collapse of prices.

The Top 10 U.S. Oil and Gas Producers, by 1985 Assets ($ Millions)

1.	Exxon	$69,160
2.	Mobil	41,752
3.	Chevron	38,899
4.	Texaco	37,703
5.	Shell	26,528
6.	Amoco	25,198
7.	Tenneco	20,437
8.	Atlantic Richfield	20,279
9.	Sohio	18,330
10.	Phillips	14,045

Source: *Oil & Gas Journal,* September 8, 1986.

The fall in oil prices in early 1986 exacerbated the bewildering problems of the natural gas producers. Following the second oil shock many users switched from oil to gas. This and the workings of the Natural Gas Policy Act of 1978 led to a rapid rise in prices from 91 cents per 1,000 cubic feet in 1978 to $2.60 in 1984. Gas companies and members of Congress were each divided on whether the way to deal with the situation was to tighten federal controls or to accelerate the pace of deregulation. In the meantime the decline of oil prices prompted many users to switch back to petroleum; the natural gas business entered a slump, and prices began to slide.

LABOR RELATIONS

Soon after the development of the oil industry in the late 19th century, oil field workers started organizing in Pennsylvania, the main producing area. In 1899 the various small unions were consolidated into the AFL-chartered International Brotherhood of Oil and Gas Well Workers. The brotherhood, facing strong employer resistance and an inability to keep up with the geographical dispersion of the industry, was defunct by 1905.

The birth of the oil industry in Texas brought a new round of organizing, and the unions reached a high point of power during World War I. Yet after the war the industry once again moved to enforce its open-shop policy, and the unions waned. It took the National Industrial Recovery Act of 1933 to revive union activity. The national organization Oil Workers International Union achieved a number of successes and went over to the CIO.

During the 1940s and the early 1950s the OWIU suffered from persistent internal political battles and rivalries with other industry unions. Problems continued even after a 1955 merger with the United Gas, Coke and Chemical Workers of America. The combined union, renamed the Oil, Chemical and Atomic Workers, kept a strong foothold in the industry but did not achieve much additional growth.

The OCAW faced obstacles in the increasingly automated refining sector of the industry and barely managed to keep wages rising and hold onto its members. The problem got worse with the industry slump of the early 1980s. Management began demanding contract concessions, and by early 1986 the unemployment rate among oilworkers was well above 10 percent.

LEADING COMPANIES

Atlantic Richfield was built over the past 30 years by Robert O. Anderson, a Chicago banker's son who went west to make his fortune. He became a small but prosperous refiner in New Mexico in 1941 and as a wildcatter made a major discovery in the state in 1957. He merged with Atlantic Refining in 1963 and Richfield Oil in 1966. ARCO, as the company is often called, was the first firm to succeed in Alaskan exploration in the late 1960s, and the find propelled the company to a prominent place in the industry. The company, a leading proponent of corporate social responsibility, acquired the Anaconda mining company in 1977. In 1985 ARCO announced a drastic restructuring plan that involved a $4 billion stock repurchase, the sale of a refinery, and the shutting down of all marketing operations east of the Mississippi.

Chevron, known until 1984 as Standard Oil of California, has since the breakup of the Standard Oil Trust in 1911 been one of the world's leading integrated oil producers. The company, which had its roots in the Pacific Coast Oil Co. (founded in 1879), had one of its greatest moments in the 1930s, when it got a concession to explore in Saudi Arabia and found some of the world's largest reserves. In 1984 the company acted as a white knight for Gulf Oil, which was under siege from raider T. Boone Pickens. Gulf, for which Chevron paid $13.2 billion, had its beginnings in the discovery of oil in Texas in the first years of the century. The Mellon family of Pittsburgh took over the pioneering J. M. Guffey

Petroleum Co. and turned Gulf into one of the world's largest oil firms.

Exxon, the world's largest oil company, was known until 1972 as Standard Oil of New Jersey. Its history goes back to the petroleum empire built by John D. Rockefeller in the late 19th century. The Standard Oil Trust was originally based in Cleveland, but Jersey Standard was turned into the holding company in 1892 to get around Ohio laws prohibiting a company from owning shares in an out-of-state corporation. After the Standard trust was broken up in 1911, Jersey Standard emerged as the biggest of the newly independent pieces. It moved aggressively to set up operations around the world as the leader of the major international firms known as the Seven Sisters. In the 1970s Exxon made an ill-fated attempt to diversify into office products. In 1986 amid the industry's severe slump the company consolidated many of its operations and eliminated more than a quarter of its work force. That same year the Supreme Court ruled that Exxon had to pay a fine of $2.1 billion for violations of oil price controls in the 1970s.

Mobil has been the most ideologically aggressive of the major oil companies. When the industry was under attack in the 1970s Mobil spent large sums on newspaper and magazine advertisements responding to critics. Mobil started life as the Standard Oil Company of New York, or Socony. After the dissolution of the Standard trust in 1911, Socony became one of the leaders among the spun-off producers. The company, which went through several names before becoming Mobil in 1966, made what turned out to be a disappointing diversification move in the mid-1970s with the purchase of Montgomery Ward and Container Corp. of America. Mobil lost out to U.S. Steel in a 1982 contest for Marathon Oil but purchased Superior Oil for $5.7 billion in 1985.

Occidental Petroleum was a virtually defunct company in 1956 when a wealthy entrepreneur named Armand Hammer took it over as a tax shelter. Hammer, who had made a name and a fortune trading with the Soviet Union, struck oil in California and decided to make "Oxy" into a serious business. The company went overseas in the 1960s and ended up with a major interest in Libya, a larger share of the income from which Oxy had to hand over to its host after Muammar Qaddafi took over in 1969. Hammer, who turned 88 in 1986 and was still resisting retirement, diversified the company with purchases such as Iowa Beef Processors in 1977. Oxy's Hooker Chemical subsidiary became notorious in the 1970s for its role in dumping toxic wastes in Love Canal near Buffalo, New York, where hundreds of families had to abandon their homes. The company scored a major coup with its discovery of a large oil field in Colombia in 1984.

Standard Oil of Ohio (Sohio) was the original base of the Rockefeller empire. After the breakup of the trust, Sohio remained a minor figure in the industry until it joined forces with British Petroleum in an Alaskan North Slope joint venture in the late 1960s. Sohio ended up with an abundance of crude and sold half of itself to BP in 1970 to raise capital for expansion. After a number of years of disappointing results from further exploration and the acquisition of Kennecott copper in 1981, BP ended its hands-off relationship and ousted the management of Sohio in 1986.

In 1986 **Texaco** was living under the shadow of the largest damage award ever awarded in an American lawsuit. The previous year a Texas court found that when Texaco moved to buy all of Getty Oil for $10 billion, Texaco had improperly interfered with an agreement that Pennzoil had made to acquire part of Getty. The damages and interest added up to $11 billion. Texaco appealed the verdict and was facing bankruptcy unless it obtained a reversal or a less costly settlement. Texaco started life as the Texas Company, one of the more successful producers in the early years of the oil industry in the Southwest. Texaco joined with Socal to exploit the vast reserves of Saudi Arabia in the 1930s and had what turned out to be controversial dealings with Franco and Hitler in that same decade. After World War II Texaco spread across the country and came to be regarded as one of the Seven Sisters.

SOURCE GUIDE

LEADING STOCK ANALYSTS AND EXPERTS

John S. Herold Inc., an oil consulting firm in Greenwich, Connecticut.

Walter J. Levy, chairman of W. J. Levy Consultants, New York.

John Lichtblau, president of the Petroleum Industry Research Foundation, New York.

Charles Maxwell, analyst at C. J. Lawrence, New York.
Thomas Petrie, analyst at First Boston.
Kurt Wulff, analyst at Donaldson, Lufkin & Jenrette.

TRADE ASSOCIATIONS AND UNIONS

American Gas Association, Arlington, Virginia.
American Independent Refiners Association, Washington, D.C.
American Petroleum Institute, Washington, D.C.
Independent Petroleum Association of America, Washington, D.C.
National Petroleum Refiners Association, Washington, D.C.
Oil, Chemical and Atomic Workers International Union, Denver, Colorado.

DATA SOURCES AND DIRECTORIES

Basic Petroleum Data Book, published every four months (Washington, D.C.: American Petroleum Institute).

Brown's Directory of North American & International Gas Companies, published annually (Dallas: Energy Publications Inc., Harcourt Brace Jovanovich).

Gas Facts, published annually (Arlington, Va.: American Gas Association).

International Petroleum Encyclopedia, an annual review of the industry (Tulsa, Okla.: PennWell Publishing).

U.S.A. Oil Industry Directory, an annual guide to companies (Tulsa, Okla.: PennWell Publishing).

U.S. Energy Information Administration publishes a large number of statistical reports, including *Natural Gas Annual, Petroleum Supply Annual,* and the yearly *U.S. Crude Oil, Natural Gas and Natural Gas Liquids Reserves.*

TRADE PUBLICATIONS

Foster Natural Gas Report, weekly.
National Petroleum News, monthly.
Oil & Gas Journal, weekly.
Oil Daily.

Petroleum Intelligence Weekly.

Platt's Oilgram News, daily.

World Oil, monthly.

BOOKS AND REPORTS

Adelman, M. A. *The World Petroleum Market.* Baltimore, Md.: Johns Hopkins University Press, 1972.

Anderson, Robert O. *Fundamentals of the Petroleum Industry.* Norman, Okla.: University of Oklahoma Press, 1984.

Blair, John M. *The Control of Oil.* New York: Pantheon Books, 1977.

Liscom, William L., ed. *The Energy Decade: A Statistical and Graphic Chronicle.* Cambridge, Mass.: Ballinger, 1982.

Sampson, Anthony. *The Seven Sisters.* New York: Viking Press, 1975.

Sherrill, Robert. *The Oil Follies of 1970–1980.* Garden City, N.Y.: Anchor Press, 1983.

Tugendhat, Christopher. *Oil: The Biggest Business.* New York: G. P. Putnam's Sons, 1968.

Tussing, Arlon R., and Connie C. Barlow. *The Natural Gas Industry.* Cambridge, Mass.: Ballinger, 1984.

U.S. Congress, Office of Technology Assessment. *U.S. Natural Gas Availability.* Washington, D.C., February 1985.

PART FIVE

Finance

CHAPTER NINETEEN

Commercial Banks and Thrifts

Once the epitome of security and stability, the banking industry has since the 1970s taken on a precarious new identity. Buffeted by roller-coaster interest rates and inflation levels, uneven economic recovery, and other calamities, moneylending has ceased to be a safe business. Bank failures have reached levels unknown since the Depression, and the federal government has repeatedly had to intervene to prevent the crisis from getting out of hand.

At the same time, bankers have been challenging state and federal rules governing their freedom to expand into new geographic areas and new lines of business. Congress and federal agencies have vacillated between sympathy for these aims and a sense that continuing problems among the nation's 14,500 commercial banks and 3,700 savings institutions imply the need for more rather than less supervision. The upheaval in banking is far from over.

A CENTRAL BANK OR "WILDCAT" ONES?

Banking in the United States began with the Bank of North America, chartered by the Continental Congress in 1781 to aid the young government in financing the War of Independence. Within a few years institutions such as the Bank of New York and the Massachusetts Bank were established.

Yet the first Treasury secretary Alexander Hamilton felt that a true central bank was necessary to assist in the commercial development of the nation. Congress was persuaded, and in 1791 the First Bank of the United States was established. Yet the agrarian-oriented, states' rights opponents to Hamilton's federalism carried on a battle against the bank over four decades.

After the national bank's 20-year charter was not renewed in 1811, state-chartered banks expanded without restraint. The public lost confidence in the bank notes issued by the various state institutions—the only paper currency of the time—and rushed to redeem them for "real" money, gold. Their reserves being depleted, the banks suspended payments in specie (coin) in 1814. The breakdown of the financial system revived support for a central bank; a successor institution, the Second Bank of the United States, was chartered in 1816.

Political controversy over the bank soon resumed, especially during the tenure of Nicholas Biddle as president of the bank. Biddle's aggressive promotion of the bank and expansion of its currency function prompted President Andrew Jackson, an avid opponent of institutionalized finance and tight money, to veto a bill renewing the charter of the bank in 1832.

The following three decades became known as the period of free banking, during which anyone who met minimum state requirements was able to establish a financial institution. Thousands of different kinds of bank notes circulated, most of them of dubious value outside the immediate area of the issuing bank. In fact, many notes were outright counterfeits, and others originated in "wildcat banks," so called because their offices were deliberately located in such remote spots ("out where the wildcats roam") that it was difficult for a holder of the notes to try to redeem them. Even legitimate banks came and went at an alarming rate.

The financial instability in the early years of the Civil War, as well as the government's problems in financing the war, prompted Congress to establish the first national currency in 1862. The Treasury notes were legal tender but not redeemable in specie. The following year Congress went further, creating a system under which banks would be chartered by the federal government and put under the supervision of the newly created Comptroller of the Currency.

The National Bank Act also required every bank with a national charter to redeem at full value the bank notes issued by other national banks. They were also obligated to maintain adequate reserves of gold and to deposit with the comptroller Treasury bonds equal to one third of their capital. The notes circulated by these banks, identical in size and design, were to be the nation's official currency.

To speed the conversion to this new system, Congress imposed a tax (first 2, then 10 percent) on new bank note issues by state banks. The result was not a disappearance of state banks— many still exist today—but there was a steady acceptance of the national currency and a falling-off of counterfeit and fraudulent bank notes. The financial system was more stable than in the era of free banking but not secure enough to prevent crises such as the panics of 1873, 1893, and 1907. In the latter case, which unlike the others was primarily a banking crisis, it took a special effort by leading financier J. P. Morgan to prevent a major collapse.

Events such as these shifted public sentiment once again in favor of creating a new central bank. The matter was studied, and proposals were made. In 1913 Congress created the Federal Reserve System. All national banks were required and state banks were encouraged to join the system, which consisted of 12 regional reserve banks and a central reserve board. Each member bank had to buy shares in the local reserve bank equal to 6 percent of its capital and surplus. Members had to maintain reserves on deposit and could also borrow (discount) funds from the reserve bank.

The first major test of the new system came in the 1920s, when a depression in agricultural prices seriously weakened banks in rural areas. The Fed was unable to prevent the failure or forced consolidation of thousands of these Main Street banks (as opposed to the larger money-center banks that had emerged in bigger cities to serve corporate clients). After reaching a peak of 31,000 in 1921, the number of banks in the country declined to less than 24,000 by the end of the decade.

THE NEW DEAL FOR BANKING

The stock market crash in 1929 made a bad situation worse. Banks had lent some $8 billion to brokerage houses to finance the margin selling that had fueled the speculative boom. As the effects of the crash spread, banks faced mounting loan losses from both companies and individuals, who had borrowed heavily in the 1920s for houses and automobiles.

In the early 1930s, as in the previous decade, the Fed was unable to halt the crisis. Nervous investors created runs on various banks across the country, prompting governors to declare "bank holidays." The situation deteriorated with reports that Franklin Roosevelt, elected president in 1932, intended to take the dollar off the gold standard. This caused runs on Federal Reserve banks, where people sought to exchange their currency for gold, as well as at commercial banks.

One of the first things Roosevelt did after taking office in March 1933 was to close all the banks for several days and attempt to restore confidence in the banking system. FDR made the first of his "Fireside Chat" radio broadcasts and assured depositors that those banks that were allowed to reopen (thousands weren't) would do so with an official stamp of approval as to their solvency. The panic subsided, and a later action establishing federal insurance for bank deposits further reassured the public. In the meantime Congress passed emergency legislation taking the country off the gold standard and centralizing gold ownership in the Treasury.

The emergency measure was only the first of a series of legislative actions in the mid-1930s that transformed the financial system. The Glass-Steagall Banking Act of 1933 established the Federal Deposit Insurance Corporation (FDIC) to administer the insurance program and to oversee the financial condition of participating banks. It also prohibited the payment of interest on demand deposits (checking accounts), permitted statewide branching for national banks, and mandated the separation of commercial banking and investment banking activities.

The Banking Act of 1935 required state banks with $1 million or more in assets to join the Federal Reserve System. It also broadened the powers of the Fed to regulate bank finances, created an open-market committee in the Fed (which regulates bank reserves through buying and selling government securities), and established the Board of Governors of the Fed, from which the Comptroller of the Currency and the secretary of the Treasury were excluded.

The periods during and after the war were ones of much greater stability and prosperity for the banking world. If anything, bankers were cautious to a fault. While the economy was booming and personal income was rising to unprecedented levels, commercial banks focused on their traditional commercial customers.

THE RISE OF THRIFTS AND BANK HOLDING COMPANIES

Most of the new retail business went to savings banks and savings and loan associations. These thrift institutions originated in the 19th century. The first savings banks were established in Philadelphia and Boston in 1816 in order to promote thrift among the newly emerging working class. The banks saw themselves as philanthropic institutions helping the poor attain some measure of financial security—if only to have enough saved for a proper burial. Savings banks, which as mutual institutions had no stockholders, spread mainly in the Northeast and reached a peak of 666 in 1875.

Savings and loan associations, which originated in Pennsylvania in the 1830s, were patterned after the building societies of Britain. Their members were initially limited to people who wanted to work together to finance the building of a home for each participant, though later they accepted people who simply wanted to save.

In 1932 S&Ls came under the supervision of the newly created Federal Home Loan Bank Board (FHLBB), and two years later their deposits became insured with the creation of the Federal Savings and Loan Insurance Corporation (FSLIC).

By the 1950s the thrift institutions were taking the lead in home mortgage lending, which blossomed after World War II. The S&Ls alone increased in total assets from $17 billion in 1950 to $129 billion in 1965, at which time they were some 6,200 in number.

The thrifts, however, faced a fundamental weakness in that they tended to use short-term funds to finance long-term loans, usually at low fixed rates. This was no problem as long as the spread between the interest rates on the two (that is, the difference between the cost of funds and the rates paid by borrowers) favored the banks. In the 1970s these relative interest rates turned against the thrifts, bringing about a crisis that will be discussed in more detail below (see The Interest Rate Squeeze).

Meanwhile the commercial banks had awakened from their slumber. One of the first innovations came from First National City Bank of New York (Citibank) with the introduction of negotiable certificates of deposit in 1961. Comptroller of the Currency James Saxon began liberalizing regulations governing national banks, prompting Chase Manhattan of New York to trade in its state charter for a national one. Fearing a mass defection, state regulators began to loosen up as well.

Other changes of the period included the adoption of computer systems by the larger banks and an unprecedented wave of bank mergers. The bigger banks also began expanding their presence abroad, both by entering the emerging Eurodollar market and by following major U.S. corporations to the sites of their foreign investments.

Yet perhaps the most significant event was the decision by Citibank in 1968 to transform itself into a one-bank holding company. This seemingly technical move, the first by a large money-center institution, opened a period of aggressive efforts by banks, led by the newly created Citicorp, to extend the range of their activities.

The creation of the one-bank holding company was a move designed to take advantage of a loophole in the Bank Holding Company Act of 1956. That law restricted the involvement of multibank holding companies in nonbanking businesses in order to prevent them from gaining monopolistic powers. The act excluded holding companies owning only one bank from the rule, in the assumption that they would be small and thus less threatening operations.

Instead giants such as Citicorp used the loophole to enter a wide range of new activities, such as equipment leasing, data processing services, mortgage banking, travel services, and financial counseling. The banks also began pushing for the right to expand their investment banking business, which since the Glass-Steagall Act had been limited to the underwriting of U.S. government bonds and general-obligation municipal bonds. Amendments to the Bank Holding Company Act passed by Congress in 1970 ended the distinction between one-bank and multibank entities and permitted both varieties to engage in any activity approved by the Federal Reserve.

INSTABILITY AT HOME AND ABROAD

The halcyon days for the banks did not last long. By the early 1970s there were signs that the rapid expansion of assets, in both loans and noncredit businesses, was beginning to cause instability. The strain was intensified by the tight money policy adopted by the Fed to rein in the inflation generated by the rise in oil prices.

The most dramatic result was the collapse of the high-rolling Franklin National Bank of New York in 1974. Franklin, among others, had fallen into the dangerous trap of relying on short-term funds to make longer-term loans. This trend (like many others) had been pioneered by Citicorp. But its imitators often lacked the financial expertise to pull it off; when short-term rates started escalating, it was the undoing of Franklin, Security National of New York in 1975, and others.

Federal regulators began to express concern that even giants such as Bank of America (B of A) had taken on large quantities of risky loans in the frenzy to expand assets. In 1974 the Fed rejected proposed acquisitions by B of A, Bankers Trust, and First Chicago.

The next crisis came with the downfall of the real estate investment trusts. REITs started expanding in 1960, when Congress gave these investment vehicles the same tax advantages as mutual funds. Riding the commercial building boom of the late 1960s, by the early 1970s REITs came to dominate the construction loan business. But REITs, including some established by large banks, also built up a giant pyramid of debt. The collapse of the commercial real estate market left banks with billions in bad loans.

By the mid-1970s the first stage of the banking revolution—what *Business Week* once called the "wild and woolly growth phase"—was over, brought to an end by inflation, recession, and the excesses of the banks themselves. Whereas five years earlier it was widely charged that the banks were ruining the economy with loose credit, the view now was that the economy was ruining the banks.

Yet the caution that the banks began to exhibit during the recession did not entirely prevail after the economy began to recover, even when another precarious situation emerged. This time it was the problem of Third World debt.

As part of their expansion in the late 1960s and early 1970s commercial banks took over from First World governments and international agencies the role of lending to so-called less developed countries (LDCs). When rising oil prices and the international recession (which reduced markets for Third World exports) exacerbated the LDCs' balance of payments, the volume of bank lending rose sharply. With Citicorp once again in the vanguard, the banks eagerly loaded up countries such as Mexico, Brazil, and Argentina with debt, in part to "recycle" the petrodollar deposits the banks were receiving from OPEC countries.

In 1976, as the foreign loan exposure of U.S. banks mushroomed, various voices in Congress and in the press began questioning whether the LDCs could make good on their massive obligations. The World Bank reported that from the end of 1970 to the end of 1974 LDC debt had more than doubled from $74 billion to $151 billion. The portion owed to private banks nearly quintupled from about $6 billion to $29 billion.

Bankers such as Walter Wriston, head of Citicorp, remained undaunted. They took solace in the assumption that countries, unlike corporations or individuals, could not go bankrupt. They also put their confidence in the austerity measures being promoted around the globe by the International Monetary Fund (IMF), and they insisted that an expansion of LDC export earnings would make the debt entirely manageable. Consequently the banks kept on lending, and by 1981 total LDC debt soared to more than $400 billion, of which about two thirds was held by western banks.

Whether the insouciance of the bankers was warranted or not is a matter of interpretation. While it is true that the worst did not come to pass, the world financial system had to weather a series of cliff-hanger situations. In 1982 Mexico announced that it could not pay its debt, forcing banks to scramble to arrange a new repayment schedule—a replay of a drama that had just occurred with Poland. Similar arrangements had to be made for Argentina and Brazil. While the immediate crisis passed, the fragility of the system prompted *The Wall Street Journal* later that year to publish a front-page article offering a scenario for the collapse of the world banking system over 12 days. By this time the banks had started cutting back their Third World lending.

In 1985 some LDCs began resisting the harsh measures that

were necessary to keep up with their debt obligations. Peru and Bolivia restricted their payments, and Fidel Castro was advocating Third World repudiation of foreign debt. Workers in Argentina demonstrated against repressive economic policies. Unrest over austerity was becoming more and more common.

In response to this climate the Reagan administration proposed a new approach to the debt problem. At the World Bank/IMF meeting in October 1985, Treasury secretary James Baker proposed a three-year lending increase of $29 billion, including $20 billion from commercial banks and $9 billion from the World Bank, which was to assume a greater supervisory role in LDC financial affairs.

The Baker plan shifted emphasis away from the IMF's austerity programs to a scenario based on economic growth, which was supposed to be led by the private sector of the Third World. Critics of the plan charged that it bailed out the banks and allowed them to avoid writing down the value of their LDC loans.

The new approach was applied in mid-1986 when the debt crisis flared up again in Mexico. The agreement put together by Mexico, a victim of declining oil prices, and the IMF included new loans of some $12 billion over two years (half from commercial banks) and measures designed to promote economic expansion, though a reduction in government spending was also part of the equation.

THE INTEREST RATE SQUEEZE

While the large U.S. commercial banks managed to pull through the LDC crisis, many of their smaller counterparts were not so lucky in dealing with the domestic travails of the banking industry. The major victims were the thrifts, and their major affliction was the galloping interest rates of the late 1970s.

The escalation of rates hit the S&Ls and savings banks in two ways. First, it sharply increased the cost of the funds they obtained in the money market while many of their loans were tied up in long-term, fixed-rate home mortgages at much lower levels. At the same time, their depositors were abandoning savings accounts that paid the legal limit of 5.5 percent and turning instead to the more lucrative money market mutual funds that had been created.

The latter part of the problem was addressed by Congress in 1980. The Depository Institutions Deregulation and Monetary Control Act of 1980 set in motion a program for the phasing out of Regulation Q interest rate ceilings over six years. Among its many provisions the act also:

1. Permitted all federally insured banks and thrifts to offer negotiable order of withdrawal (NOW) accounts (i.e., interest-bearing checking accounts).
2. Allowed federal thrifts to invest up to 20 percent of their assets in consumer loans, commercial paper, or corporate debt securities.
3. Preempted existing state usury ceilings on first mortgage loans and allowed states three years to enact legislation overriding the preemption.
4. Raised the limit on federal deposit insurance from $40,000 to $100,000 for each account.

The legislation slowed down the decline of the thrifts, in part by paving the way for adjustable-rate mortgages, which gave the banks greater protection in their long-term lending. But it did not reverse the process. The outflow of deposits continued, and the lifting of interest ceilings made it more expensive for the thrifts to pay for those deposits that remained. The number of federally insured S&Ls driven into merger or liquidation climbed to 24 in 1981 and 48 the next year. By 1982 Congress had to act again. It passed legislation giving federal regulators new powers to help ailing thrifts.

The FDIC and the FSLIC were authorized to exchange capital notes with troubled institutions to bolster their financial condition. The law also allowed federal thrifts as well as commercial banks to offer insured money market accounts, and it permitted S&Ls to offer checking accounts to their loan customers.

Once again congressional action had limited effect on the beleaguered thrifts. In 1984 the country's largest S&L American Savings (a subsidiary of Financial Corp. of America) avoided failure only through a last-minute government rescue. In 1985 there were runs on S&Ls in Ohio and Maryland involving institutions that were insured by private plans rather than the FDIC. The FHLBB initiated a new program of replacing the management of troubled S&Ls before they failed; 25 institutions were subjected to this process in 1985.

The 10 Largest Savings Institutions, by 1985 Assets ($ Billions)

1. American Savings (Stockton, California)	$27.3
2. Home Savings of America (Los Angeles)	26.7
3. Great Western Savings (Beverly Hills, California)	23.6
4. California Federal (Los Angeles)	18.0
5. Glendale Federal (Glendale, California)	14.1
6. World Savings (Oakland, California)	12.3
7. First Nationwide Savings (San Francisco)	11.5
8. Home Federal (San Diego)	9.9
9. First Federal (Detroit)	9.8
10. Gibraltar Savings (Beverly Hills, California)	9.4

Source: *Savings Institutions* (U.S. League of Savings Institutions), June 1986.

Yet the health of many thrifts started to show signs of improvement with the decline in interest rates. The average cost of funds for FSLIC-insured institutions, having risen from less than 6 percent in 1972 to a peak of 11.5 percent in late 1981, was down to 8.5 percent in the first quarter of 1986.

THE INTERSTATE THRUST

During the travails of the thrifts, the attention of commercial banks was directed to their crusade to break through many of the legal limitations on their activities, both geographic barriers and restrictions on their entry into certain lines of business.

The deregulatory thrust of the banks was directed at a body of law beginning with the McFadden Act of 1927, which limited branching by national banks to their home city (later extended to the rest of that one state). The Douglas Amendment to the Bank Holding Company Act of 1956 barred the purchase of banks across state lines unless the other state permitted it. While banks were free to make loans anywhere in the country, these rules severely limited their potential pool of deposits. As the big holding companies such as Citicorp became major national and international lenders, they hungered for broader sources of deposit funds. The result was a tireless quest for the legalization of interstate banking.

At the same time, commercial banks began to argue once again against the Glass-Steagall Act, which barred them from nearly all forms of underwriting, and rules that limited their other activities. The banks were concerned about the moves of Merrill Lynch, Sears, and other nonbank companies to create "supermarkets" of financial services. The fact that these competitors were not regulated gave them an unfair advantage, the bankers argued; deregulation would create what industry leaders like Walter Wriston liked to call "a level playing field."

While deregulation became a drawn-out and inconclusive drama in Congress, the banks began using loopholes, testing the limits of federal law and taking advantage of liberalized state rules to create de facto interstate banking and entry into new fields. Bank of America acquired discount broker Charles Schwab & Co. Citicorp moved its credit card operations to South Dakota to escape New York's usury laws. Various banks followed the lead of nonfinancial corporations such as Gulf + Western in setting up entities that were given the peculiar label "nonbank banks."

These institutions, which amounted to limited-service banks, took advantage of the fact that federal law prohibiting interstate banking defined banks as operations engaged in *both* lending and accepting deposits. By limiting their activity to one of the two functions (usually accepting of deposits), the creators of nonbank banks claimed exemption from the law. Federal regulators were divided on the legitimacy and desirability of these institutions, but after a period of confusion the matter was resolved by a 1986 Supreme Court ruling sanctioning their existence.

The large money-center banks also took advantage of a 1982 law that allowed out-of-state banks to purchase failing thrifts. Citicorp was the first to take advantage of the policy when it acquired a California S&L in 1982. It subsequently bought thrifts in Illinois and Florida.

Although some commercial banks were in a position to rescue failing institutions—and serve their own ends in the process—others faced their own crises. Between 1981 and 1983 some 100 banks collapsed. One of the most sensational of these was the Penn Square Bank of Oklahoma, a freewheeling institution that died from an overdose of bad energy loans. Penn Square's demise had repercussions throughout the banking industry, most notably at Chicago's venerable Continental Illinois, which had purchased more than $1 billion in loans from the Oklahoma bank.

Continental Illinois, also saddled with nonperforming real estate and energy loans of its own, experienced a panic among its major depositors in 1984. Federal regulators put together a $7.5 billion rescue package, but the bad publicity caused the run to continue. Unable to find a private buyer for the bank, the federal government in effect took over the institution. After the Continental bailout, only the fourth such government action in U.S. history, FDIC rescues became much more common.

The problems of commercial real estate, agriculture, and energy took their toll on many other banks as well. Bank of America reported huge losses—$640 million in the second quarter of 1986 alone. The failure of the First National Bank & Trust Co. of Oklahoma City that same year was the largest bank collapse since Franklin National in 1974. By the summer of 1986 some 1,400 banks were on the "problem list" maintained by the FDIC.

These difficulties did not diminish the expansionary drives of the industry. But by the mid-1980s the center of attention shifted from the bold moves of Citicorp to the emergence of so-called regional superbanks. In response to the spread of nonbank banks in their territory, a number of states began passing laws encouraging bank mergers with institutions in neighboring states. The catalyst for the trend was a regional compact established in New England. A Supreme Court ruling in 1985 affirmed the right of states to restrict interstate banking to specific regions. By 1986 the business press was suggesting that superregionals such as First Wachovia, SunTrust, and NCNB would soon become leading forces in the banking world.

By late 1986 the banks were still in transition. Some were growing progressively weaker while others were hell-bent on growth. The trend of federal regulation was also ambiguous. The Federal Reserve, concerned about bank instability, proposed to change the capital requirements from a flat 5.5 percent of assets to a system based on the riskiness of loans. In Congress there was still a tug-of-war between those seeking less regulation of banks and those wanting more. There were also moves to strengthen federal laws against money laundering, a move that was prompted to a great extent by revelations beginning in 1985 that large banks such as the Bank of Boston, Chase Manhattan, Manufacturers Hanover Trust, and Bank of America had failed to report many large cash transactions.

BEYOND LENDING

Behind the headlines about bank failures and federal regulatory policies a profound change has been taking place in the activities

The 10 Largest Bank Holding Companies, by 1985 Assets ($ Billions)

1. Citicorp	$173.6
2. BankAmerica Corp.	118.5
3. Chase Manhattan Corp.	87.7
4. Manufacturers Hanover Corp.	76.5
5. J. P. Morgan & Co.	69.4
6. Chemical New York Corp.	57.0
7. Security Pacific Corp.	53.5
8. Bankers Trust New York Corp.	50.6
9. First Interstate Bancorp	49.0
10. First Chicago Corp.	38.9

Source: *The 1986 Directory of U.S. Corporations,* which contains a reprint of the Fortune Service 500 from *Fortune,* June 9, 1986.

of the commercial banks. The 1980s have witnessed the acceleration of a shift away from traditional lending and borrowing. In the search for less expensive financing companies have turned in large numbers to the market for commercial paper (short-term IOUs issued not by banks but by nonfinancial corporations with excess cash).

The competition from commercial paper has driven down profit rates on bank lending and forced the banks to assume a new role. To an increasing extent banks are serving as middlemen in markets for financing backed by securities. This process of "securitization" turns banks from lenders (i.e., those who originate loans and keep them on their balance sheets as assets) to sellers of someone else's money (the favored term is *distribution*). Traditional corporate lending has not disappeared, but it is steadily being overshadowed by activities that look more like investment than commercial banking.

LABOR RELATIONS

In 1969 *The Wall Street Journal* wrote that in the banking industry "unions have been as welcome as Bonnie and Clyde." The situation has not changed, and the number of organized bank workers remains miniscule. In 1986 there were labor contracts at fewer than 30 of the nation's 14,500 banks. Unions such as the United Food & Commercial Workers and District 925 have had little success in the face of strong management resistance.

The most celebrated struggle of bank workers in recent times took place in Minnesota. In 1977 a group of women at the Citizens

National Bank in Willmar charged their employer with sex discrimination, organized an independent union, and sought a contract. Management refused, and eight of the women stayed on strike for years until the union was recognized in 1983. A 1980 documentary film *The Willmar 8* gave the cause national recognition.

LEADING COMPANIES

Bank of America grew from a small neighborhood bank in San Francisco at the beginning of the century to become the nation's largest bank by 1945. Led by founder A. P. Giannini, the bank built an extensive retail network throughout California. B of A was overshadowed by the more aggressive Citicorp in the 1970s, but the bank made a bold move in acquiring discount broker Charles Schwab & Co. in 1982. By the mid-1980s B of A was suffering from a large volume of bad loans in the ailing energy, real estate, and agricultural sectors. Samuel Armacost, who took over the holding company BankAmerica in 1981, came in for a great deal of criticism; in 1986 he was replaced by his predecessor A. W. Clausen. The weakened state of the bank was indicated by the takeover proposal made in 1986 (and later dropped) by First Interstate Bancorp, an institution less than half the size of B of A.

Bankers Trust, one of the New York giants, caused a stir in the late 1970s when it abandoned its consumer business and moved aggressively into investment banking activities. The bank, founded in 1903, skirted the restrictions of the Glass-Steagall Act and started a trend by acting as an agent for companies in the sale of commercial paper. By the mid-1980s Bankers was becoming an important dealmaker in areas such as mergers and takeovers.

Chase Manhattan, long known as the Rockefellers' bank, had origins in the Manhattan Co. (which started as the local water utility in New York City in 1799 and branched into financial activities) and in the Chase National Bank, which was established in 1877 and merged with the Rockefeller-controlled Equitable Trust in 1930 and then with the Bank of Manhattan in 1955. Until 1945 Chase was the country's largest bank. The bank suffered sluggish growth under the tenure of David Rockefeller and in the early 1980s suffered losses linked to the failures of Penn Square Bank and Drysdale Government Securities.

Citicorp is the largest and most aggressive of U.S. banking companies. Since the late 1960s "Fat City," as the bank came to be called, has been in the vanguard of the efforts by commercial banks to expand their activities across the country and into new fields. Led by Walter Wriston, chairman of Citicorp from 1970 to 1984, the bank branched out across the globe, becoming perhaps the only truly global financial corporation. John Reed, who succeeded Wriston after building the bank's retail business, established a somewhat more cautious style. In the early 1980s Citicorp was the subject of reports accusing it of engaging in a pattern of questionable transactions to evade foreign currency regulations.

Continental Illinois, created by a series of bank mergers in the 1920s and 1930s and one of the powerhouse banks of the Midwest, nearly collapsed in 1984 as the result of bad energy loans and a run by large depositors. Continental was rescued by the federal government, which injected new capital into the bank and in effect became the owner of the institution. By 1986 the bank was recovering and was the subject of controversy over its plan to acquire several smaller banks.

Morgan Guaranty Trust, the banking subsidiary of J. P. Morgan & Co., has long been one of the most prestigious and strongest of the New York banks. Some fifty years after it and Morgan's investment bank (which became Morgan Stanley) were separated, Morgan Guaranty was once again aiming at providing investment banking services. There were reports in the mid-1980s that the bank was even considering giving up its charter in order to be able to pursue such services without limitation.

SOURCE GUIDE

LEADING STOCK ANALYSTS AND EXPERTS

Robert Albertson, bank analyst at Smith Barney.

David C. Cates, president of Cates Consulting Analysts, New York.

J. Richard Fredericks, bank analyst at Montgomery Securities.

Jonathan Gray, thrift analyst at Sanford C. Bernstein & Co.

Thomas Hanley, bank analyst at Salomon Brothers.

Keefe, Bruyette & Woods, a bank securities firm in New York.

George Salem, bank analyst at Donaldson, Lufkin & Jenrette.

Secura Group, bank consultants, Washington, D.C.

Arthur Soter, bank analyst at Morgan Stanley.

TRADE ASSOCIATIONS

American Bankers Association, Washington, D.C.

National Council of Savings Institutions, Washington, D.C.

U.S. League of Savings Institutions, Washington, D.C.

DATA SOURCES AND DIRECTORIES

Federal Reserve Bulletin, monthly, and *Annual Statistical Digest* (Washington, D.C.: Federal Reserve Board).

International Bankers Directory, published semiannually (Skokie, Ill.: Rand McNally).

Moody's Bank and Finance Manual, an annual comprehensive collection of data on financial companies (New York: Moody's Investors Services).

National Council of Savings Institutions publishes an annual fact book.

Polk's World Bank Directory, North American edition published semiannually; international edition published annually (Nashville, Tenn.: R. L. Polk).

Sourcebook, an annual volume of data (Washington, D.C.: U.S. League of Savings Institutions).

U.S. Comptroller of the Currency publishes an annual report.

U.S. Federal Deposit Insurance Corporation publishes the annual *Statistics on Banking* and other data in its annual report.

U.S. Federal Home Loan Bank Board publishes the annual *Assets and Liability Trends* and also has statistics in its annual report.

U.S. Savings and Loan Directory, published annually (Skokie, Ill.: Rand McNally).

TRADE PUBLICATIONS

ABA Banking Journal, monthly.

American Banker, daily.

Bankers Magazine, bimonthly.

Bankers Monthly.

Banking Expansion Reporter, fortnightly.

BOOKS AND REPORTS

Balderston, Frederick E. *Thrifts in Crisis: Structural Transformation of the Savings and Loan Industry*. Cambridge, Mass.: Ballinger, 1985.

Mayer, Martin. *The Money Bazaars*. New York: E. P. Dutton, 1984.

Moffitt, Michael. *The World's Money*. New York: Simon & Schuster, 1983.

Ornstein, Franklin H. *Savings Banking: An Industry in Change*. Reston, Va.: Reston Publishing, 1985.

Roussakis, Emmanuel N. *Commercial Banking in an Era of Deregulation*. New York: Praeger Publishers, 1984.

Sampson, Anthony. *The Money Lenders*. New York: Viking Press, 1982.

Sprague, Irvine H. *Bailout: An Insider's Account of Bank Failures and Rescues*. New York: Basic Books, 1986.

Trescott, Paul B. *Financing American Enterprise: The Story of Commercial Banking*. New York: Harper & Row, 1963.

CHAPTER TWENTY

Stock Brokerage and Investment Banking

Capitalism needs capital to survive, and one of the primary ways of raising it is through the issuing of securities. This process has given rise to an industry of intermediaries that help companies plan their financing needs, bring new issues to market, and execute trades of existing securities. There are numerous functions involved in the business; some firms specialize and others do everything. Investment banks "underwrite" new securities by preparing the issue and buying it (along with other firms in what is called a syndicate) in order to resell it at a profit to investors. These firms also advise companies in mergers and acquisitions and other matters relating to finance.

Securities firms also engage in the buying and selling of equity (stocks) and debt (bonds) issues for the public. Firms such as Merrill Lynch have vast networks of retail brokerage offices to serve small investors, while other companies focus on serving institutional investors, such as pension funds and insurance companies.

The bull market of the mid-1980s has allowed the industry to prosper as never before. As the Dow Jones Industrial Average kept reaching new record levels in 1985, brokerage houses enjoyed earnings of more than $3 billion on revenues of some $35 billion. Underwriters raised a record $138 billion, and investment bank fees in takeovers reached $10 million in many large deals.

UNDER THE BUTTONWOOD TREE

The securities business in America began during the Revolutionary War as the Continental Congress and the army issued various notes and scrip. The trading of financial instruments gained some regularity in 1792, when a group of 24 brokers gathered under a buttonwood tree at what is now 68 Wall Street and established minimum commission rates and other rules. This clique, which soon moved its operations indoors, evolved into the New York Stock and Exchange Board (renamed the New York Stock Exchange in 1863).

The New York exchange adopted the airs of an exclusive private club, which was in keeping with the genteel character of the brokerage business. Security ownership was limited to a small segment of the population, and they tended to favor stability. Most portfolios concentrated on government and transportation bonds rather than stocks.

In places such as New York there was also a more rough-and-tumble side to the securities business. This consisted of ad hoc exchanges, in which speculation was more common, and "bucket shops," where customers could wager on stock movements without owning shares. These establishments came and went, while the New York Stock Exchange (NYSE) was firmly established as the leading arena for respectable trading. New York brokers excluded from the inner circle met on the street for many years—gaining the name "curbstone brokers." This curb market became more formal after World War I and changed its name to the American Stock Exchange in 1953; yet it was still regarded as a poor cousin to the NYSE.

The more rapid economic development after the Civil War stimulated growth in the investment banking side of the securities business. While some firms that could be called investment banks (including Alex. Brown & Sons and Vermilye & Co., precursor of Dillon, Read) were formed in the 1820s and 1830s, underwriting began in a serious way with the financings that Jay Cooke & Co. did for the Lincoln administration during the Civil War.

After Cooke went under in the panic of 1873, the preeminent spot was assumed by John Pierpont Morgan, whose operation epitomized the WASP-owned private banks that took deposits as well as engaging in underwriting. The other main group in the industry consisted of financiers of German-Jewish origin—most notably Jacob Schiff of Kuhn Loeb—who were excluded from commercial banking but who became important in underwriting and other aspects of corporate finance.

Both groups prospered with the wave of industrial consolidations that arose at the end of the century. The House of Morgan provided the financial wherewithal for many of the emerging industrial giants, most notably U.S. Steel, which was organized in 1901 as the first billion-dollar corporation.

Until World War I the United States was a debtor nation: Much more capital was flowing into the country from Europe than was flowing out. Morgan and the other investment banks often acted as conduits for this investment from abroad. They underwrote U.S. securities and sold them to foreign interests. When war broke out in Europe the relationship changed, and U.S. investment banks found themselves raising funds for beleaguered European powers.

After the war, the securities business expanded rapidly. Investment banks brought out issues for countless new and growing firms. The stock market went wild in the 1920s, drawing thousands of small investors who took advantage of liberal margin requirements.

The speculative bubble grew larger and larger until the end of the decade. Some cautious investors saw the warning signs and bailed out. Yet most players were caught off guard in October 1929 when, as the famous *Variety* headline put it, "Wall Street Lays an Egg."

THE DIVORCE OF BANKING

When Franklin Roosevelt took office in 1933 public resentment over the great crash and the ensuing Depression had translated into a suspicion of the financial community. The previous year the Senate Banking Committee had launched a probe—called the Pecora Hearings after the panel's chief counsel Ferdinand Pecora—of Wall Street wheeling and dealing. Given a mandate to go after the big financiers, Pecora found a variety of questionable practices relating to stock manipulation, tax evasion, and the like.

The result of congressional deliberations was the Banking Act of 1933 (or as it is commonly known, the Glass-Steagall Act). The main result of this law was the strict separation of commercial and investment banking. This forced the big banks such as Morgan to spin off or dissolve their investment banking subsidiaries, which led to the formation of firms such as Morgan Stanley and First Boston.

Congress did not stop with Glass-Steagall. Legislation passed in 1933 and 1934 established disclosure rules for companies issuing stock and created the Securities and Exchange Commission (SEC) as a federal agency to oversee the securities business.

Through the rest of the New Deal period and World War II the securities business was in a state of hibernation. The industry emerged from its sleep and became frisky in the postwar years, especially after federal judge Harold Medina dismissed an antitrust case brought by the Truman administration against 17 leading investment bankers. New York Stock Exchange president G. Keith Funston began promoting wider ownership of stock under the banner of "people's capitalism." Charlie Merrill raised the professional level of brokers (he dubbed them "account executives") and built Merrill Lynch into the leading retail firm.

In 1953 stocks took off, and the longest bull market in U.S. history was under way. Despite a setback in 1962, the rally segued neatly into what became known as the go-go years of the mid-1960s. Along with the general rise of the market there was a frenetic demand for new issues. Underwriters eagerly brought out these stocks, usually with modern-sounding technical names, even though many of them soared briefly and then collapsed. The less scrupulous investment banks paid little mind; as long as they got their profit on the initial offering, they felt the ultimate performance of the stock was the shareholders' problem.

This kind of loose ethical code was most apparent outside of the Big Board, as the New York exchange came to be known. A scandal over improper dealings at the American Stock Exchange in the early 1960s prompted President Kennedy to commission the Special Study of Securities Markets. The findings of the study led Congress to enact the Securities Act Amendments of 1964, which established stricter disclosure requirements for over-the-counter securities and more stringent rules for broker-dealers.

The national over-the-counter market consisted of thousands of firms that traded stocks outside of organized exchanges. The

Maloney Act of 1938 required OTC dealers to form the National Association of Securities Dealers (NASD) to supervise the business. In the 1960s some OTC dealers began defying Wall Street by trading securities listed on exchanges such as the Big Board, giving rise to what was called the Third Market. The large brokerage houses grumbled but did not succeed in thwarting leading Third Marketeers such as Weeden & Co.

In the meantime the NASD, prodded by the SEC, moved ahead with development of an automated trading system. Designed by the electronics firm Bunker Ramo, the automated quotation system (called NASDAQ) had its debut in 1971. Thanks to the boom in new issues and the preference of some companies to avoid the strict rules of the NYSE, the NASDAQ system has grown rapidly; and the NASD talks boldly of overtaking the Big Board in dollar volume by 1990.

While disturbed by these competitive developments the big brokerages had their hands full trying to deal with all the trades they were executing in the late 1960s. Wall Street was drowning in paperwork as volume on the Big Board jumped to more than 2 billion shares a year. The result was what became known as the back-office crisis: Old-fashioned, labor-intensive methods of processing orders could not keep up with the growth of the business. The immediate response of the leadership of the NYSE was to cut back trading hours in 1967 and 1968, and for a while trading was limited to four days a week so the back-office people could catch up on Friday. Over the longer term the crunch has forced the brokerage houses to invest large sums in computer equipment.

The market collapse of 1969–70 cooled off Wall Street but also put the squeeze on a number of the weaker firms. The Big Board leaders turned to Lazard Frères partner Felix Rohatyn—then the leading figure in corporate mergers—to act as a matchmaker for marriages between faltering securities firms and stronger ones. Some firms, which had already changed from partnerships to corporations, took the additional step of going public. Donaldson, Lufkin & Jenrette led the way in 1969, followed by many other leading firms, including Merrill Lynch, E. F. Hutton, and First Boston.

The next major turning point for the brokerage side of the securities business came on May 1, 1975 (now immortalized as Mayday), when the SEC abolished the system of fixed commis-

The 10 Largest Brokerage Firms, by Capital at Year-End 1985 ($ Millions)

1. Merrill Lynch	$2,646.9
2. Salomon Brothers	2,320.1
3. Shearson Lehman Brothers	2,251.0
4. Dean Witter	1,365.3
5. Prudential-Bache	1,259.3
6. Goldman Sachs	1,201.0
7. E. F. Hutton	1,143.4
8. First Boston	1,042.3
9. Drexel Burnham Lambert	949.3
10. Bear Stearns	811.0

Source: Securities Industry Association, New York.

sions. For the first time Big Board members had to concern themselves with price competition, both among themselves and with the discount brokerage services that were created. The discounters, led by Charles Schwab and Quick & Reilly, gained about 20 percent of the retail brokerage business by 1985.

As it turned out, commission rates for retail customers who passed up the no-frills services of the discounters and continued using the large brokers did not decline. Where the competition emerged was in the rates charged to institutional investors—pension funds, insurance companies, and the like—which trade large numbers of shares and have become the most important customers for many brokerage houses. Commissions for these investors declined from an average of 26 cents a share just before Mayday to about 10 cents at the end of the decade. In the mid-1980s the downward pressure resumed, and nickle-a-share commissions began appearing. Consequently commission income became a smaller and smaller portion of brokerage house revenues, while trading profits and investment income accounted for the lion's share.

THE RISE OF THE DEALMAKERS

While brokers were hustling to keep up their income level the investment banking side of the business heated up in more lucrative ways. The genteel practices of the bankers—both the "white shoe" WASP firms such as Morgan Stanley and the German-Jewish ones such as Goldman Sachs—and their unshakable relationships with blue-chip clients started to come unglued in the late 1970s and early 1980s. Encouraged by relaxed antitrust policies and the undervalued state of many stocks, companies became more aggressive in their merger activities. The once-disreputable practice of hostile takeovers gained legitimacy after prominent companies adopted the maneuver.

For investment banks, some of which had never done merger work of any kind, the new Wild West environment was unsettling. But the escalation of fees once the deals reached the billion-dollar level dispelled the compunctions of most firms. Some actually embraced the trend as a major new profit area. First Boston plunged into the merger field with a passion, not simply waiting for clients to come to them with merger plans but also concocting likely marriages and then trying to interest the parties. A small group of investment bankers gained the reputation of being essential to any major deal, and their fees reflected this oligopoly. In 1985 it became common for a firm to receive $10 million for working on a single large deal, and Drexel Burnham Lambert raked in $60 million for helping Pantry Pride in its successful takeover of Revlon. To earn these fees Drexel and other investment banks have also gotten involved in financing deals. First Boston, for example, made a $1.8 billion short-term loan to Campeau Corp. to help in the 1986 acquisition of Allied Stores. (For more on mergers see the Appendix to this chapter.)

Since 1982 the investment banks have also had to work harder to serve their clients, because of the adoption by the SEC of Rule 415, which allowed for something called shelf registration of securities. In line with the deregulatory vogue, the SEC decided to allow companies to forgo the customary process of preparing prospectuses each time they wanted to issue securities. Instead companies were given permission to file once for all the stock they expected to issue over two years and were allowed to keep the stock "on the shelf" until the market looked best for actually selling the issue.

Most of the major investment banks were outraged at this procedure, which they saw as potentially freezing them out of the lucrative business of underwriting. While the worst did not come to pass, Rule 415 did help to diminish the importance of syndication. The breaking up of old relationships and the desire of companies to move quickly when market conditions were best have given rise to a trend of having only one firm bring out a new

Leading Underwriters in 1985

	Dollars (Billions)	Issues
1. Salomon Brothers	$30.9	293
2. First Boston	21.6	274
3. Goldman Sachs	16.4	145
4. Merrill Lynch	15.6	189
5. Drexel Burnham Lambert	13.3	171
6. Morgan Stanley	10.1	104
7. Shearson Lehman Brothers	9.6	164
8. Kidder Peabody	3.8	83
9. Paine Webber	2.9	74
10. Smith Barney	1.6	37

Source: IDD Information Services, New York.

issue. Despite these changes, underwriters raised a record $138 billion for U.S. companies in 1985.

The investment banks have also had to contend with increased competition from major commercial banks, which have been testing the limits of Glass-Steagall and moving into new financial areas. There has been a major move into discount brokerage, especially after the Federal Reserve approved Bank of America's 1981 purchase of Charles Schwab. Leading banks are also pushing federal regulators for permission to enter markets such as municipal revenue bonds and mortgage-backed securities.

The challenges to securities firms on both the brokerage and investment banking sides, along with the need for greater access to capital, have brought about a new wave of consolidations and takeovers from outside. In 1981 alone the commodities company Phibro bought Salomon Brothers; Prudential insurance bought Bache; Sears, Roebuck bought Dean Witter; and American Express (Amexco) bought Shearson Loeb Rhoades. In 1984 Amexco turned around and added Lehman Brothers to its financial empire; General Electric purchased 80 percent of Kidder Peabody in 1986. Brokerage houses were regarded as essential elements in the plans of a handful of major companies to make themselves into financial supermarkets.

Many of those firms that survived the merger wave still needed to raise their capitalization to compete, so another batch of them decided to go public. In 1985 and 1986 firms such as Morgan Stanley, Bear Stearns, L. F. Rothschild, and Alex. Brown & Sons took that step. Among the remaining privately held firms were Drexel Burnham Lambert, Smith Barney, and Goldman Sachs (though Goldman sold a minority stake to Japan's Sumitomo Bank in 1986).

LEADING FIRMS

Drexel Burnham Lambert has catapulted to the top ranks of underwriters through its aggressive promotion of junk bonds, the high-risk securities that corporate raiders use to finance their forays against giant companies. A young trader at Drexel named Michael Milken essentially invented junk bonds in the early 1970s, and other partners at Drexel have worked directly with the likes of T. Boone Pickens and Saul Steinberg to plan their attacks. The Drexel name dates back to a prominent investment bank of the 19th century. Several partners of Drexel, which turned to commercial banking after Glass-Steagall but was soon acquired by J. P. Morgan & Co., decided to open an investment bank in the 1940s. The firm had a tough time of it until merging in 1973 with Burnham & Co. It merged again with Lambert Brussels Witter in 1976. In the mid-1980s Drexel was seeking to broaden its base in order to reduce its dependence on junk bonds.

First Boston, created in the 1930s out of the investment banking subsidiaries of the First National Bank of Boston and the Chase National Bank, developed close relationships with a number of blue-chip clients. The firm embraced the takeover mania that started in the late 1970s, and its merger specialists Bruce Wasserstein and Joseph Perella became the hottest practitioners in the field. In precarious condition in 1978, the firm was by 1985 gushing profits, earning $130 million for the year.

During the early 1980s **Goldman Sachs** emerged as the outstanding performer in areas such as block trading and risk arbitrage, as well as underwriting and mergers. The firm was founded after the Civil War by Marcus Goldman, a German immigrant who was later joined in the commercial paper business by his son-in-law Samuel Sachs. The firm was hit hard by the 1929 crash but was rescued by Sidney Weinberg, who started with the firm as a janitor's assistant and rose to the top. Weinberg and his successor Gustave Levy turned Goldman into one of the most prestigious names on Wall Street. Later the firm prospered under the leadership of Sidney Weinberg's son John and John White-head.

Merrill Lynch is the giant of the securities industry and by far the leader in the retail end of the business. Formed in 1914 by Charles Merrill and Edmund Lynch, the firm got out of the brokerage business after the crash and concentrated on underwriting. After World War II Charlie Merrill expanded his retail business, in part by improving the training of brokers and emphasizing customer relations. In the 1970s under the leadership of Donald Regan (who left the firm in 1981 to become Ronald Reagan's Treasury secretary and later White House chief of staff), the firm diversified into real estate, insurance, and other financial services. Regan also acquired the old-line firm of White Weld in 1978. Some analysts believe Merrill has suffered from spreading itself too thin in its financial activities.

Morgan Stanley, one of the top names in investment banking, was formed in 1935 by three partners of J. P. Morgan & Co. after Morgan abandoned investment banking in the wake of Glass-Steagall. The firm gained many blue-chip clients and emerged as one of the snobs of the industry, for many years refusing to participate in a stock syndication unless it was lead manager. Robert Baldwin, who ran the firm from the early 1970s to 1984, modernized operations, expanded the merger business, and finally got the firm into trading. But Morgan was slow to enter new areas such as mortgage-backed securities and by the early 1980s had lost its leading position in underwriting. The firm went public in 1986.

Salomon Brothers, founded in 1910, was primarily a dealer and trader in government bonds until the 1960s. Billy Salomon, son of one of the three founders, turned the firm into a leading underwriter in the 1960s. John Gutfreund continued the growth after taking over in 1978. Three years later he convinced his fellow partners to sell the firm to the commodities giant Phibro. Tensions between Salomon and its parent soon reached a critical level as the securities business boomed and commodities slumped. By late 1985 Gutfreund engineered a virtual dismantlement of Phibro as Salomon was being hailed as "the king of Wall Street." Perhaps the most famous figure in the firm is chief economist Henry Kaufman, for many years the leading Cassandra of the financial world (his nickname was Dr. Doom) and whose pronouncements on interest rates often moved the market.

Shearson Lehman Brothers is the result of the purchase of two of the leading securities firms by financial giant American Express in the early 1980s. The Lehman Brothers firm dated back to a cotton brokerage established by three German brothers in the South in the 1840s. It remained a commodities firm until 1906, when Philip Lehman (son of one of the founders) joined with Henry Goldman (also a founder's son) of Goldman Sachs in a series of joint underwriting ventures. Bobby Lehman, a legendary Wall Street figure, ran the firm in the 1930s, 40s, and 50s. After his death the firm went into a slump, which in 1973 former Commerce secretary Peter Peterson was brought in to remedy. Lehman prospered during the 1970s and in 1977 merged with another old-line firm Kuhn Loeb. Veteran trader Lewis Glucksman took over in 1983 and, amidst feuding among the partners, led the firm into the arms of American Express, which had acquired Shearson Loeb Rhoades (the product of a long string of brokerage house mergers) in 1981.

SOURCE GUIDE

LEADING STOCK ANALYSTS AND EXPERTS

Samuel Hayes III, professor of investment banking at Harvard Business School.

IDD Information Services (data on underwriting), New York.

Perrin Long, veteran securities-industry analyst at Lipper Analytical Services, New York.

Securities Data Co. (statistics on the industry), New York.

TRADE ASSOCIATIONS

National Association of Securities Dealers, Washington, D.C.

Securities Industry Association, New York.

DATA SOURCES AND DIRECTORIES

Deals of the Year, a list of the top 50, in a January issue of *Fortune*.

Directory of Corporate Financing, a semiannual listing of underwritings (New York: Dealers' Digest).

Directory of Wall Street Research, an annual volume listing brokerage house analysts by company and industry covered, and *Investment Decisions,* a monthly listing of analyst research reports (Rye, N.Y.: W. R. Nelson).

Fact Book, an annual compilation of statistics on the Big Board (New York: New York Stock Exchange).

Institutional Investor, a leading publication on the industry, produces M&A Deals of the Year in its January issue, a review of underwriting in its September issue, and the closely watched All-America Research Team ranking of analysts in its October issue.

Securities Industry Yearbook, a directory of key figures in the industry and data on firms (New York: Securities Industry Association).

Standard & Poor's Security Dealers of North America, an annual directory (New York: McGraw-Hill).

TRADE PUBLICATIONS

Euromoney (London), monthly.

Institutional Investor, monthly.

Investment Dealers' Digest, weekly.

BOOKS AND REPORTS

Auletta, Ken. *Greed and Glory on Wall Street: The Fall of the House of Lehman.* New York: Random House, 1986.

Block, Ernest. *Inside Investment Banking.* Homewood, Ill.: Dow Jones-Irwin, 1986.

Carosso, Vincent. *Investment Banking in America: A History.* Cambridge, Mass.: Harvard University Press, 1970.

Carrington, Tim. *The Year They Sold Wall Street.* Boston: Houghton Mifflin, 1985.

Hoffman, Paul. *The Dealmakers: Inside the World of Investment Banking.* Garden City, N.Y.: Doubleday Publishing, 1984.

Seligman, Joel. *The Transformation of Wall Street.* Boston: Houghton Mifflin, 1982.

Sobel, Robert. *Inside Wall Street.* New York: W. W. Norton, 1977. Sobel is also the author of histories of the New York and American Stock Exchanges and other books on the industry.

APPENDIX TO CHAPTER TWENTY:
MERGERS AND ACQUISITIONS

Over the past decade the U.S. business world has experienced a frenzy of takeovers and acquisitions that constitutes one of the major merger waves of American history. Virtually every issue of *The Wall Street Journal* brings news of another giant tender offer, consolidation, or leveraged buyout. In the mid-1980s company raiders such as T. Boone Pickens and Carl Icahn struck terror in the hearts of chief executives, who fought back with a variety of antitakeover devices. Yet a number of giant companies—the likes of Gulf Oil, Crown Zellerbach, and TWA—have either been taken over by raiders or forced into the embrace of more friendly acquirers known as "white knights." Other companies have re-purchased stock from raiders at big premiums, paying what is called "greenmail."

The pace and scale of takeovers reached a point at which no corporation seemed immune. By 1986 a booming stock market and legal complications dampened the hostile takeover trend, but the volume of friendly deals was still strong. In the early 1970s a deal in the $100 million range was considered big news; within a decade that figure has jumped two orders of magnitude. In 1985 there were some 3,000 corporate mergers and acquisitions with a total value of $180 billion.

However, the future of the takeover game was suddenly thrown into question in late 1986 when Ivan Boesky, a leading stock market speculator, admitted that he had made illegal use of inside information in his trading activity (see Risk Arbitrage and Insider Trading below).

BIG BUSINESS UP FOR GRABS

The turning point in the road to "megamergers" was probably the battle for Conoco in 1981. After the Canadian company Dome Petroleum bid for 20 percent of Conoco's shares in an effort to get at its Canadian oil reserves, all of Conoco ended up "in play." Seagram made an unwanted offer for a larger portion of the company, whose management turned to Du Pont as a white knight. A bidding war ensued, involving Mobil as well; after the dust settled, Du Pont was the winner with an astounding offer of $7.2 billion.

Yet the case that focused public attention—and some degree of outrage—on what was going on in the merger and acquisition (M&A) game was the Bendix fiasco of 1982. Early in that year Bendix began quietly buying shares of Martin Marietta and in August announced an offer to buy the aerospace company. Martin Marietta's management, determined to avoid such a takeover, adopted an elaborate defense in which a purchase of the company by Bendix would trigger a process in which Bendix shares in turn would be bought up by Martin Marietta. This "doomsday machine," as it was dubbed, was to be backed up by United Technologies in the role of white knight. When the confusing—and by some accounts ludicrous—process was completed Bendix was taken over completely by Allied Corp., which also ended up owning 39 percent of Martin Marietta, which was otherwise still an independent company.

No sooner had the uproar over Bendix died down than a new wave of takeovers occurred in which the billion-dollar deal rose to double digits. In 1984 Texaco deftly outmaneuvered Pennzoil to acquire Getty Oil for more than $10 billion. (That move boomeranged on Texaco when Pennzoil sued and won more than $10 billion in damages. Texaco appealed the massive award, and as of this writing the case has not been resolved.) In the meantime, Boone Pickens was pursuing an assault on Gulf Oil. Gulf fought mightily to evade Pickens and ended up agreeing to be purchased by Standard Oil of California (now called Chevron) for a staggering $13.2 billion.

Although the Gulf purchase still stands as the largest deal in history, the pace of billion-dollar mergers and acquisitions did not let up. In 1985 the leading arena switched from oil to food, with one well-known company purchasing another in mostly friendly arrangements. In what has been dubbed the "brand name merger wave," Nestle has consumed Carnation, R. J. Reynolds has eaten Nabisco Brands, and Philip Morris has devoured General Foods.

Another focus of activity has been media companies. In 1985 Capital Cities purchased ABC for $3.5 billion, Ted Turner made an unsuccessful bid for CBS, and General Electric agreed to acquire RCA for $6.3 billion.

A NEW RESPECTABILITY FOR TAKEOVERS

Hostile takeovers, which used to be considered the disreputable domain of a few unscrupulous investors, gained considerably more respectability in the early 1980s. Large corporations no longer hesitated in making unfriendly tender offers or other merger advances, and raiders were regarded in some quarters as champions of small shareholders whose investments were said to be undervalued because of poor company management.

The leading investment banks took advantage of this new climate and in some cases acted as catalysts for major deals. M&A work became a central activity for firms such as First Boston, Drexel Burnham Lambert, Morgan Stanley, and Goldman Sachs. The functions of these bankers include searching for target companies, valuing the target, and structuring the deal. They advise both acquirers and targets seeking to defend themselves.

The more aggressive investment banks did not wait for clients to come to them. The M&A departments of these firms developed their own list of potential corporate marriages and then made pitches to likely suitors. Superstars such as Bruce Wasserstein of First Boston went even further. When they heard that a deal was in the works they approached another company about becoming a rival bidder. For example, after Pennzoil announced its plan to buy a chunk of Getty, Wasserstein persuaded Texaco to come in with a better bid—a move that Texaco came to regret.

The investment banks were rewarded handsomely for their efforts. In the Gulf deal, Salomon Brothers and Merrill Lynch together collected an estimated $47 million for advising Gulf, while Morgan Stanley was paid nearly $17 million by Chevron. Some of the leading M&A operations and their main dealmakers in the mid-1980s were:

Drexel Burnham Lambert	David Kay; Martin Siegel (who was formerly at Kidder Peabody)
First Boston	Bruce Wasserstein; Joseph Perella
Goldman Sachs	Geoffrey Boisi
Merrill Lynch	Kenneth Miller
Morgan Stanley	Eric Gleacher
Salomon Brothers	Jay Higgins

The investment banks in many cases also help raise the financing for an acquisition. In fact it was a financing innovation—a device called "junk bonds"—that made it possible for raiders such as Pickens and Icahn to go after such large prey. Junk bonds are low-grade securities (rated BB or lower by Standard & Poor's or Ba or lower by Moody's) that pay 2.5 to 3.5 percentage points more interest than investment-grade bonds. The pioneer of these high-yield securities, to use their polite name, was Drexel Burnham Lambert. A young Drexel trader named Michael Milken began promoting the notion in the 1970s that some investors would be willing to buy high-risk bonds if the interest rates were made attractive enough. Eventually the raiders realized they could raise enormous sums of money through junk bonds, and Drexel became the financier for many of the largest takeover efforts. The future of junk bonds in takeovers was clouded by new Federal Reserve rules and by the insider trading scandals of 1986. But most analysts believed that the market for below-investment-grade bonds—which had grown to more than 20 percent of the corporate debt issues—would remain strong.

GOING PRIVATE

Nontraditional financing is also the basis for a different kind of deal that has grown in importance in recent years: the leveraged buyout. This is a process by which the management of a company or other investors take the firm private by purchasing the public shares with funds that are borrowed using the assets of the company as collateral. The earnings of the private company then serve to pay off the debt. When the company involved is financially strong, the leveraged buyout (LBO) group can raise huge sums of money and invest little cash of its own.

LBOs took off following the case of Gibson Greeting Cards. In 1982 Wesray Corp. (whose chairman was former Treasury secretary William Simon), took Gibson private in an $81 million deal that involved putting up only $1 million in cash. In subsequent years the size of the largest LBOs grew rapidly, reaching nearly $1 billion in the Metromedia buyout of 1984. Even larger deals followed. In 1985 the senior management of the R. H. Macy department store chain proposed taking the company private for $3.6 billion. Then Kohlberg Kravis Roberts & Co., the leading LBO dealmaker, arranged a $6.2 billion buyout of food giant Beatrice.

In 1985 the LBOs whose terms were disclosed had a total value of about $19 billion.

Aside from Kohlberg Kravis Roberts, leading LBO dealmakers include Forstmann Little, Gibbons Green, and Adler & Shaykin.

PAC–MAN AND OTHER DEFENSES

Corporations facing a takeover bid or fearing that one will occur have adopted a variety of defensive measures. The tactic employed by Martin Marietta against Bendix—that of threatening to pursue its pursuer—is called the "Pac-Man defense." Calling in a more friendly purchaser is known as seeking a "white knight," and paying a premium price to buy back the shares of a raider (but no other stockholders) is called "greenmail."

Other techniques involve changing the corporation's bylaws to make it more difficult to take control. These include so-called shark repellents, such as staggering the terms of directors so the entire board cannot be voted out at once or establishing "super-majority" requirements that up to 95 percent of the shareholders approve a merger. Another preemptive measure is to sell a block of stock, but not all of the company, to a friendly outside party to make it more difficult for a raider to gain control. This use of a "white squire" was employed by CBS when it agreed to let Loews Corp. buy up to 25 percent of its shares after the Ted Turner bid failed but other takeover attempts remained possible.

The most controversial defensive maneuver is known as the "poison pill." First used in Lenox Inc.'s resistance to a bid by Brown-Forman Distillers in 1983, the pill is an adverse financial arrangement that would take effect after a raider has successfully carried out a hostile takeover. For example, stockholders remaining after the takeover might be given the right to purchase additional shares at half the market price, thus substantially diluting the firm's equity. The more extreme forms of the pill would probably require the liquidation of the company.

Poison pills are meant to discourage raiders in the way that nuclear weapons are supposed to deter hostile action by one of the superpowers against the other. While more and more companies have adopted pills in one form or another, no one knows exactly what would happen if a pill were ever triggered. It is also unclear how effective the device ultimately is in preventing takeovers. James Goldsmith managed to evade Crown Zellerbach's pill and still win control of the company. The use of the pill was upheld in a 1985 ruling by the Delaware Supreme Court in a test case involving Household International.

Other court rulings have favored the offense. Raiders were strengthened by a decision in the Revlon/Pantry Pride case in which Revlon's arrangement to sell Forstmann Little two of the best parts of the company for a bargain price was deemed illegal. This "lock-up" arrangement to sell Revlon's so-called crown jewels was meant to make the deal more attractive to the LBO people and to discourage Pantry Pride. A similar position was handed down by a federal appeals court in early 1986 invalidating a lock-up arrangement SCM Corp. had been using to thwart Hanson Trust.

Raiders also ended up winning the battle over the "exclusionary self-tender offer," a device used by Unocal to defeat Boone Pickens in 1985. The oil company had foiled Pickens by arranging to buy back shares at a hefty premium from all shareholders except him. Although the Delaware Supreme Court sanctioned the technique, it was later banned by the SEC.

Tender offers by raiders have become less common as acquirers have made use of large-scale open-market purchases of shares to gain control. This technique, used for example by Campeau Corporation in its 1986 takeover of Allied Stores, has been facilitated by the willingness of investment banks to supply huge sums of their own money to finance the purchases.

Raiders have gotten yet more encouragement from a change in attitude on the part of institutional investors (pension funds, insurance companies, etc.), which control about 35 percent of all publicly held stock. Traditionally these investors have sided with management. But because they have a fiduciary responsibility to seek the best possible return, they have to take attractive offers from raiders seriously. Institutions have begun to oppose some of the antitakeover tactics being adopted by boards; and Jesse Unruh, California state treasurer, brought together more than 20 institutions in a group to work in opposition to some of these measures.

THE GREAT TAKEOVER DEBATE

Management adoption of extreme defensive measures fueled an already heated debate on the legitimacy of takeovers. Attitudes toward the phenomenon ranged from considering it a dangerous trend that must be controlled by government action to viewing it as a sign of a healthy, vital economy.

The financial community has been split on the matter. While many investment bankers were getting rich off the merger wave, some such as Felix Rohatyn of Lazard Frères and Nicholas Dillon, chairman of Dillon Read, worried that it was getting out of control. Many critics argued that takeovers amounted to a wasteful diversion of resources and that the vast sums being raised by raiders were putting upward pressure on interest rates and making it more difficult for companies to obtain capital for productive investments. They also noted that purchasers often ended up with dangerously high levels of debt.

Managers denounced takeovers as disruptive to companies, and labor leaders noted that takeovers accelerated plant closings and job loss. Robert Reich, a prominent public-policy analyst at Harvard University, portrayed the rise of takeovers as part of the "paper entrepreneurialism" that he saw making the U.S. economy less competitive.

The most outspoken defenders of takeovers have been laissez-faire economists such as Eugene Fama of the University of Chicago and his disciples at the University of Rochester and elsewhere. One of those disciples, Michael Jensen, published a controversial article in the *Harvard Business Review* in which he argued that allowing the "market for corporate control" to function freely was beneficial both to shareholders and the economy.

Defenders of takeovers insisted that they served to accomplish a shake-up of American industry that was necessary in the wake of disinflation, deregulation, and the decline of OPEC. While restructuring (the current buzzword in American business) may indeed be needed in some cases, it is unclear whether many megamergers do indeed contribute to greater efficiency. Surveys by *Fortune* (April 30, 1984) and *Business Week* (June 3, 1985) found that many of the large mergers of the past decade have been disasters. Examples included Mobil's purchase of Marcor, Fluor's acquisition of St. Joe Minerals, Exxon's purchase of Reliance Electric, and Sohio's acquisition of Kennecott. But there have also been notable success stories, including the marriages of American Express and Shearson, and Nabisco and Standard Brands.

WHO'S WHO IN THE TAKEOVER GAME

The takeover world has a large and colorful cast of characters. First, the raiders. There have been four leading takeover entrepreneurs in the 1980s:

James Goldsmith. The British-French food magnate and publisher has stalked a number of U.S. forest products companies in recent years. Sir James acquired Diamond International in 1981 and proceeded to liquidate the company's assets. In 1984 he collected greenmail from St. Regis and made a hefty profit on his holdings in Continental Group even when he lost his takeover bid. In 1985 he succeeded in defeating a poison-pill defense by Crown Zellerbach and eventually got himself installed as chief executive of the company. The following year he made a run at Goodyear Tire & Rubber; after a few weeks he dropped the bid and sold back his shares to the company at a hefty profit.

Carl Icahn. The former stockbroker has made plays for a long list of big companies over the past decade, including Tappan, American Can, Marshall Field, and Dan River. Although he has often been thwarted in his takeover efforts, he has usually ended up with hefty profits on his stock investments. In 1985 he made an offer for Phillips Petroleum after Pickens dropped his bid, and he also sought Uniroyal. Phillips bought back his stock, and Uniroyal ended up in a leveraged buyout; but Icahn made out well in both cases. He then turned around and initiated a dogfight for TWA. Making a deal with the airline's unions (which preferred Icahn to rival bidder Texas Air, whose chairman Frank Lorenzo is a notorious union buster), Icahn succeeded in winning control of TWA. In October 1986 he made a $7 billion bid for USX but was rebuffed by management.

Irwin Jacobs. "Irv the liquidator" started off in the closeout business but has emerged as a raider of first rank. Based in Minneapolis, Jacobs has sought but ended up selling off his holdings in companies such as Kaiser Steel, Walt Disney, Avco, and Castle & Cooke. In 1985 he succeeded in taking over sporting goods maker AMF and started selling off that company piece by piece. The following year he bought stakes in several energy companies, including Pioneer Corp., which found an unusual white knight in T. Boone Pickens. He also made a bid for Borg-Warner.

T. Boone Pickens, Jr. The chairman of Mesa Petroleum has made forays against a number of major oil companies, the most prominent being Gulf, which in 1984 agreed to be acquired by Chevron to escape Pickens. A bid by Pickens for Phillips Petroleum led to a deal in which the company repurchased Mesa's shares at a profit for the Pickens company. But in 1985 Pickens was defeated in a bid for Unocal and was excluded when that company bought back stock from shareholders at a big premium. Pickens later made several unsuccessful runs at Diamond Shamrock.

Other leading raiders include:

Bass Family. Perry Bass and his three sons have made good use of the oil fortune left by Perry's uncle Sid Richardson. The Bass family made a bid for Marathon Oil in 1981, collected greenmail from Blue Bell and Texaco, and made a friendly arrangement with Walt Disney to buy a big block of the company's stock to ward off Saul Steinberg. The family wealth has been estimated by *Forbes* at more than $3 billion.

Belzberg Brothers. The three Canadian brothers have a reputation as greenmailers (Blue Bell, Masonite, etc.), but in 1985 they purchased old-line manufacturer Scovill for $523 million. They were allied with Boone Pickens in the battle for Gulf. In 1986 the Belzbergs again made handsome profits by selling back their holdings in Potlatch Corp., Ashland Oil, and USG.

Carl Lindner. The veteran Cincinnati investor is highly secretive. Acting through his American Financial Corporation, Lindner has over the years bought and sold major stakes in companies such as United Brands, Gulf + Western, and Penn Central.

Rupert Murdoch. The international media baron has gobbled up newspapers and magazines in the United States and Britain.

In 1984 he collected greenmail from Warner Communications and made an unsuccessful bid for Champion International. In 1985 he bought seven TV stations from Metromedia for $2 billion, 12 magazines from Ziff-Davis, and all of Twentieth Century–Fox. To comply with U.S. media ownership rules he became a naturalized American citizen.

David Murdock.   The Los Angeles financier has recently acquired companies such as Continental Group, Castle & Cooke, and Cannon Mills, the last of which was later sold to Fieldcrest Mills.

Victor Posner.   The dean of raiders has been buying into old-line industrial companies since the 1960s. Operating through Sharon Steel, NVF, and other vehicles, Posner has engaged in numerous proxy battles; but in the mid-1980s his empire fell on hard times and was being stalked by other raiders.

Harold Simmons.   The Dallas financier has made passes at companies such as Pacific Southwest Air, Ozark Air, GAF, Medford (which he purchased), and Sea-Land. He was sued by the Labor Department for using pension fund assets to finance takeover bids. In 1986 he gained control of NL Industries.

Saul Steinberg.   Having grown rich from computer leasing, Steinberg first made waves in 1969 with an unsuccessful takeover bid for Chemical Bank. Operating through Reliance Group Steinberg has invested in a number of companies and has usually received quite unfriendly responses from management. In 1984 he collected greenmail from Quaker State Oil and Walt Disney. In 1986 he acquired John Blair & Co. and sold a portion of Reliance to the public.

Ted Turner.   The brash broadcasting tycoon from Atlanta made a controversial bid for CBS in 1985, and right after that failed he arranged a friendly purchase of MGM/UA for $1.5 billion. To meet his heavy debt payments he sold off most of the film company.

Other up and coming raiders include:

Paul Bilzerian.   Having made a fortune in Florida real estate in the late 1970s, Bilzerian gained national attention with a 1984 run at Syntex Corp. and 1985 bids for H. H. Robertson and Cluett, Peabody. The following year he went after Hammermill Paper, which embraced International Paper as a white knight.

Asher Edelman. The New York arbitrageur has bought into and gained control of a series of computer and other companies, usually in order to liquidate their assets. His largest coup came in 1985 when he won control of Datapoint. In 1986 he made a bid for Fruehauf Corp., which escaped him by arranging a leveraged buyout.

Charles Hurwitz. The Houston investor has taken over companies such as McCulloch Oil and Simplicity Pattern. In 1984 he greenmailed Castle & Cooke, and in 1985 he made a successful bid for Pacific Lumber.

Harvey Kapnick. The chairman of Chicago Pacific, which emerged out of the reorganization of a bankrupt railroad, has been trying to break into the big-time acquisitions league. He made a clumsy attempt for Textron in 1984, and in 1985 he acquired Hoover Corp.

Leucadia National Corp. The financial services company sought in 1984 to purchase Avco (which ended up with Textron) and then engaged in battle with National Intergroup, first seeking to block that company's merger with Bergen Brunswig and then offering to buy National. After losing a proxy battle Leucadia ended its bid and signed an accord with National.

Ronald Perelman. Having built a miniconglomerate (Technicolor, Consolidated Cigar, Pantry Pride, etc.) in his private company MacAndrews & Forbes Holdings, Perelman caused a stir in 1985 with his drawn-out but successful bid for Revlon. The following year he collected greenmail from CPC International and Gillette.

Oscar Wyatt. The founder and chairman of Coastal Corp. is one of the more controversial figures in the oil and gas world. In 1983 he bid for Texas Gas (which ended up with CSX); in 1984 he engaged in a bitter battle with Houston Natural Gas; and in 1985 he purchased American Natural Resources, which made Coastal one of the largest U.S. pipeline companies. Later that year he collected greenmail from Sonat Inc.

RISK ARBITRAGE AND INSIDER TRADING

The arbitrageurs have been called the pilot fish that swim along with sharks such as Pickens and Icahn. Once a tender offer or merger is announced the "arbs" load up on the stock of the target company in the expectation that its value will rise. The risk they take is that the deal will fall through and instead of receiving the premium price being offered by the acquirer they will end up with a bundle of stock whose value has plunged below the price they paid for it.

During the early 1980s the most prominent of the arbs was Ivan Boesky, who went to great lengths to argue that he and his counterparts were not mere speculators out for a killing. The service the arbs performed, according to Boesky, was to free small shareholders of the risk and waiting involved in the period between the announcement of a merger and its successful execution. Although arbs made many millions on deals such as Gulf and Getty, they also lost bundles on deals that collapsed, such as the Pickens bid for Phillips Petroleum and Chicago Pacific's leveraged buyout of Textron.

It was customarily assumed that the success of arbs such as Boesky was based on exhaustive research, solid analysis, and good luck. It turned out that the truth was more prosaic and sordid. In November 1986 the Securities and Exchange Commission made a startling announcement. The feds had been investigating Boesky for some time and had uncovered evidence that he illegally obtained insider information on mergers and takeovers before they were made public. Boesky admitted the crime and agreed to plead guilty to a criminal charge and pay a penalty of $100 million. He was also to be barred from the securities business for the rest of his life. At the same time, the SEC indicated that it would aggressively pursue its investigation of takeover activity.

The Boesky case was an offshoot of a wide-ranging investigation by the SEC of insider trading by Wall Street professionals. Earlier in 1986 the agency had brought charges against investment banker Dennis Levine, who cooperated with the authorities and revealed that among his other illegal activities, he had arranged to sell Boesky information on deals before they were announced. This allowed Boesky to load up on a stock with the knowledge that as soon as the deal was announced, its value was bound to soar.

Although Boesky paid for his sins, he in a sense got the best of the SEC. In the days before his indictment was made public, Boesky unloaded more than $440 million of his holdings in stocks involved in takeovers. Boesky correctly anticipated that these shares would plunge in value after the announcement that the entire takeover fraternity was being investigated. Observers called the move by Boesky to exploit the knowledge of his own legal troubles the ultimate form of insider trading.

THE LAWYERS

One prominent lawyer has said: "Corporate takeovers are analogous to feudal wars, and the lawyers are the mercenaries." In virtually every one of these wars a particular pair of mercenaries end up playing the key roles on the opposing sides. Joseph Flom and Martin Lipton are the preeminent legal tacticians in the field, and no large company feels comfortable in a merger battle without one of them on its side. Flom, of the firm Skadden Arps Slate Meagher & Flom, is the specialist in offense. His firm is paid large retainers by dozens of companies that want to be sure they can call on Skadden's services. Lipton, of the smaller firm Wachtell Lipton Rosen & Katz, is famous for devising defensive measures such as poison pills.

PUBLIC RELATIONS FIRMS

Many hostile tender offers end up as battles for the hearts and minds of shareholders, with both sides resorting to a barrage of propaganda. The orchestration of these campaigns—which involve such things as blaring full-page newspaper ads and cultivation of reporters—is the province of the public relations specialists. The two names that pop up as often as those of Lipton and Flom are Kekst & Company, led by Gershon Kekst, and Hill & Knowlton, led by Richard Cheney.

The 10 Largest U.S. Merger and Acquisition Deals (as of the End of 1986)

Transaction	Dollars (Billions)	Year
1. Chevron buys Gulf	$13.2	1984
2. Texaco buys Getty Oil	10.1	1984
3. Du Pont buys Conoco	7.2	1981
4. General Electric buys RCA	6.4	1986
5. KKR takes Beatrice private	6.2	1986
6. U.S. Steel buys Marathon Oil	5.9	1982
7. Philip Morris buys General Foods	5.6	1985
8. Mobil buys Superior Oil	5.7	1984
9. Allied merges with Signal	4.9	1985
10. R. J. Reynolds buys Nabisco	4.9	1985

Source: "Deals of the Year," *Fortune*, various years.

PROXY SOLICITORS

The job of directly winning over shareholders in proxy battles also belongs to the proxy solicitors. These companies help prepare material that will be sent to shareholders, contact individual and institutional investors with their client's pitch, and supervise the distribution of proxy material. Leading proxy solicitors include the Carter Organization, Georgeson & Co., D. F. King & Co., and Morrow & Co.

SOURCE GUIDE

DATA SOURCES

The Acquisition/Divestiture Weekly Report, a newsletter, and *Merger & Acquisition Sourcebook*, published annually (Santa Barbara, Calif.: Quality Services Company).

"Deals of the Year," an annual list of the 50 largest deals, in a January issue of *Fortune*.

"M&A Deals of the Year," an annual feature in the January issue of *Institutional Investor*.

Mergers & Acquisitions, quarterly and almanac. This leading trade publication both tracks M&A activity and publishes feature articles.

Mergers and Corporate Policy, a biweekly newsletter that serves as a supplement to *The Yearbook on Corporate Mergers, Joint Ventures and Corporate Policy* (Boston: Cambridge Corporation).

Mergerstat Review, published annually (Chicago: W. T. Grimm). Grimm is the leading M&A data source, and this volume is filled with information.

BOOKS AND REPORTS

Boesky, Ivan. *Merger Mania.* New York: Holt, Rinehart & Winston, 1985.

Davidson, Kenneth. *Megamergers: Corporate America's Billion-Dollar Takeovers.* Cambridge, Mass.: Ballinger, 1985.

Lipton, Martin, and Erica Steinberger. *Takeovers and Freezeouts.* Law Journal Seminars Press, 1979.

Nelson, Ralph. *Merger Movements in American Industry, 1895–1956.* Princeton, N.J.: National Bureau of Economic Research/Princeton University Press, 1959.

Phalon, Richard. *The Takeover Barons of Wall Street.* New York: G. P. Putnam's Sons, 1981.

CHAPTER TWENTY–ONE

Venture Capital and Initial Public Offerings

In a March 1985 speech, Ronald Reagan gave presidential endorsement to a notion that had been in the air some time. He declared: "We have lived through the age of big industry and the age of the giant corporation, but I believe that this is the age of the entrepreneur, the age of the individual. That's where American prosperity is coming from now, and that's where it's going to come from in the future."

Entrepreneurs have indeed become some of the leading heroes of the day. The legends of the electronics industry have gained the most currency: Silicon Valley is hailed as a place where the likes of Steven Jobs, cofounder of Apple Computer, can take an idea and turn it into a fortune almost overnight.

While entrepreneurs ultimately succeed or fail on the strength of their ideas, they are also dependent on financing in order to move from vision to flourishing enterprise. New ventures in emerging technologies are not the kind of risk that the average bank is willing to take; such projects must turn to a different sort of financier—the venture capitalist.

Venture capitalists are professional investors who specialize in finding and financing young companies that show promise. The VCs don't do this out of altruism. In exchange for their investment they receive substantial equity in the company, an investment that can yield enormous profits when a successful venture goes public (i.e., begins to sell its shares on the open market). Serious VCs expect an annual return of 50 percent or more for success stories, while other investments—usually the majority of the portfolio—may have to be written off entirely.

IT ALL STARTED WITH COLUMBUS

Venture capital goes back to the origins of America. Christopher Columbus was in effect an entrepreneur who was using venture capital from Queen Isabella to exploit business opportunities in distant lands. Until the middle of the 20th century, venture capital was the province of wealthy individuals who enjoyed bankrolling inventors or entrepreneurs. This is the way that pioneers in fields such as automobiles, electric power, and commercial aviation got their starts.

Beginning in the 1930s some of these patrons began to approach such investments more systematically. Laurance Rockefeller and John Hay Whitney were the leading figures in this regard, and their efforts ended up under the auspices of, respectively, Venrock Associates and J. H. Whitney & Co. Another early promoter of entrepreneurs was Harvard Business School professor Georges Doriot, who ran the American Research and Development Corp., founded in 1946.

Venture capital remained a rather specialized activity until the late 1950s, when Congress moved to encourage less-than-big business. The Small Business Investment Act of 1958 established entities called small business investment companies (SBICs). These were privately owned and operated firms that were allowed to borrow funds from the Small Business Administration and invest them in fledgling enterprises. During the 1960s there was a great surge of SBICs, but in recent years they have declined in importance, in part because of federal budget constraints.

Nearly all the rest of the venture capital industry has grown up in tandem with the development of high technology, especially the burst of advances in electronics since the creation of the microprocessor and the miniaturization of integrated circuits. The venture capitalists made Silicon Valley, and the valley made the VCs. For those who follow the financial side of high tech, venture capitalists such as Arthur Rock and Thomas Perkins are as celebrated as Steven Jobs and his fellow entrepreneurs.

Venture capital investment took off in the late 1970s, a fact that many analysts attribute to the reduction in capital gains taxes that took effect in 1979. The total funds pouring into venture capital soared from $300 million that year to $1.3 billion in 1981. The pool swelled to $4.5 billion in 1983.

THE ROLE OF VENTURE CAPITALISTS

Aside from getting rich, venture capitalists have come to play a major role in the development of new industries. By deciding which of the hundreds of business proposals that cross their desks each year are worth backing, VCs are functioning as gate-keepers of technology. They determine which products are going to be developed and marketed and which will remain dashed hopes of would-be entrepreneurs.

Venture capitalists are usually organized in the form of limited partnerships. The general partner solicits funds and manages the investments, receiving 2 to 3 percent of the value of the fund for his expenses and 20 percent or so of the profits for his trouble. That trouble can be considerable.

First of all, the general partner or partners and their staff must be experts in evaluating the large number of proposals that come their way. Once the few likely gems are separated out, there is the arcane (some would say arbitrary) process of pricing a deal involving a company that may not yet have any revenues or salable products.

Since many entrepreneurs are inexperienced in business the VC must often function as a management advisor; some actually usurp the role of chief executive, especially when a company is in trouble and the VC's investment—which usually ranges from several hundred thousand to several million dollars—is in jeopardy.

Although VCs have traditionally invested in projects that have already been incorporated and need capital to grow, in the early 1980s some investors began backing entrepreneurs in first setting up their companies. These so-called seed capitalists (such as Zero Stage Growth Fund of Cambridge, Massachusetts) offered funding in the range of $50,000 to $250,000, whereas most VCs felt that deals that small were not worth the expense of investigating.

The venture capital go-go period of the early 1980s drew new players into the field. Encouraged by liberalization of rules governing fiduciary responsibility, many institutional investors took the plunge. These included public and private pension funds, insurance companies such as Prudential and CIGNA, bank trust departments, and university endowments at schools such as MIT. Banks such as Citicorp and Bank of America joined in, as did corporations such as General Electric.

Most remarkable was the emergence of state governments as venture capitalists. About 20 states set up VC programs in order to promote job creation; some invested directly, and others gave tax breaks to state-chartered VC funds. While most state funds were small (under $10 million) Michigan, Alaska, and Wyoming have each sunk more than $30 million into such investments.

Not everyone is enchanted with the venture capital system. VCs are branded by some as "vulture capitalists" who demand majority stakes and extensive control in exchange for their financing. Critics such as Gordon Moore, chief executive of Intel, have argued that the presence of abundant venture capital entices key people away from their employers into start-ups, thus disrupting the development of technology. (Moore takes this view despite the fact that he and Robert Noyce formed Intel after leaving Fairchild Semiconductor in 1968). During the VC frenzy of the early 1980s, many observers charged that there was too much money chasing too few worthwhile projects, and as a consequence many marginal enterprises were being funded.

Whether or not the criticism was warranted, the breakneck growth of venture capital investment did come to a halt in 1984. The industry did not crash, but the total pool of venture capital declined by $300 million from 1983's record level. In 1985 the total sank further to about $3 billion. Investors became more cautious, in part because the slump in high-technology and new stock issues in general forced many companies to delay going public and instead turn to their VC backers for more funds. New entrepreneurs found they had to search longer and harder for investors.

THE BOOM AND BUST OF IPOs

In order for a venture capitalist to realize a gain on his investment he must sell his equity interest. Sometimes this is done through private placements, but the more profitable and popular method is to take the company public. Along with the boom of venture capital in the early 1980s there was a blossoming of initial public offerings (IPOs). The number of IPOs leaped from 45 in 1978, with $249 million raised, to 448 in 1981, in which $3.2 billion was obtained.

A handful of smaller investment banks emerged as the leading IPO underwriters in this period. The "four horsemen" was the label given to L. F. Rothschild Unterberg Towbin of New York, Alex. Brown & Sons of Baltimore, and Hambrecht & Quist and Robertson Colman & Stephens of San Francisco. An important role has also been played by D. H. Blair & Co. of New York.

The IPO market declined in 1982 but soared the next year to a remarkable level of 888, in which some $12.6 billion in equity was raised. The IPO frenzy of 1983 brought windfalls to both VCs and entrepreneurs such as Allen Paulson of Gulfstream Aerospace and K. Philip Hwang of TeleVideo Systems, both of whom ended up (on paper at least) as two of the wealthiest men in the country.

The following two years saw a sharp falloff in IPO activity, but the numbers of new issues and the amounts raised remained higher than at any time before the magic year of 1983. In October 1985 the initial offering of stock in Fireman's Fund brought in $900 million, far surpassing all earlier IPOs. (The previous record was held by Ford Motor Co.'s $658 million IPO in 1956.) But the following year the Fireman's offering was topped by the $1.2 billion IPO of the Henley Group, a collection of businesses spun off from Allied-Signal.

At this point the general new-issues market was beginning to heat up once again. This time the range of industries was much greater: High tech was no longer dominant, and the popular issues included everything from specialty retailers to yogurt.

LEADING PERSONALITIES AND FIRMS

Frederick Adler of Adler & Co. is a New York trial lawyer turned venture capitalist. Known for his aggressive and abrasive personality Adler is a master at taking charge of troubled companies, such as software developer MicroPro International, and turning them around.

Hambrecht & Quist has played a major role in the high-tech world, as both a venture capitalist and an investment bank, underwriting major new issues such as People Express, Apple Computer, and Genentech. Especially hard hit by the VC and new-issues slumps, the firm forced general partner William Hambrecht to relinquish many of his responsibilities to Thomas Volpe in 1985.

Thomas Perkins of Kleiner, Perkins, Caulfield, & Byers has been one of the most successful VCs. His firm's first fund, established in 1972, grew in value from $7 million to $218 million in five years, aided by major successes such as Tandem Computers and the biotechnology company Genentech.

Arthur Rock first got involved in venture capital in the late 1950s when he was working at the brokerage firm of Hayden Stone. He was contacted by a group of disgruntled engineers who wanted to quit working for William Shockley, the coinventor of the transistor, and strike out on their own. Rock helped them form Fairchild Semiconductor (as a subsidiary of Fairchild Camera & Instrument), which played a key role in the development of electronics and from which numerous people broke away and started other innovative companies with the help of Rock. His firm Arthur Rock & Co. has backed numerous other successful high-tech ventures.

Sevin Rosen Management, founded by Benjamin Rosen and L. J. Sevin in 1981, is already one of the leaders in the field, boosted by its big successes with Compaq Computer and the software company Lotus Development. Rosen is a former Morgan Stanley analyst who got involved in the early stages of the personal computer industry. Sevin founded the semiconductor company Mostek, which he sold to United Technologies in 1979.

Other prominent venture capital firms include the **Mayfield Fund** of Menlo Park, California, **Sutter Hill Ventures** of Palo Alto, California, **Hillman Company** of Pittsburgh, and **TA Associates** of Boston.

SOURCE GUIDE

LEADING ANALYSTS AND EXPERTS

Norman Fosback, publisher of the newsletter *New Issues* in Fort Lauderdale, Florida.

Stanley Pratt, chairman of Venture Economics, the leading VC consulting firm, which is based in Wellesley Hills, Massachusetts.

Securities Data Co. (data on IPO underwriting), New York.

TRADE ASSOCIATIONS

National Association of Small Business Investment Companies, Washington, D.C.

National Venture Capital Association, Arlington, Virginia.

DATA SOURCES AND DIRECTORIES

Directory of Corporate Financing, a semiannual publication with data on IPO underwriting (New York: IDD Information Services).

Directory of Operating Small Business Investment Companies (Washington, D.C.: U.S. Small Business Administration).

Pratt's Guide to Venture Capital Sources, an annual guidebook and directory (Wellesley Hills, Mass.: Venture Economics).

A. David Silver, *Who's Who in Venture Capital*. New York: John Wiley & Sons, 1984.

Value Line New Issues Service (New York: Value Line).

Venture magazine publishes a number of relevant features on a regular basis: an annual ranking of venture capital firms in June, a ranking of SBICs in October, and data on IPO activity in each issue.

TRADE PUBLICATIONS

Going Public: The IPO Reporter, weekly.

New Issues, monthly.

Private Placements, fortnightly.

Venture, monthly.

Venture Capital Journal, monthly.

BOOKS AND REPORTS

Organisation for Economic Co-Operation and Development. *Venture Capital in Information Technology*. Paris, 1985.

U.S. Congress, Joint Economic Committee. *Venture Capital and Innovation*. Washington, D.C., 1985.

U.S. Congress, Office of Technology Assessment. *Technology, Innovation and Regional Economic Development*. Washington, D.C., 1984.

Wilson, John W. *The New Venturers: Inside the High-Stakes World of Venture Capital*. Reading, Mass.: Addison-Wesley Publishing, 1985.

PART SIX

Heavy Industry and Transportation

CHAPTER TWENTY–TWO

Aerospace and Defense Contracting

Back in the 1920s the pioneering builders of airplanes were as dashing and bold as the men who flew them. Over the years the white scarfs have been replaced with pinstripes, but the $96 billion aerospace business remains one of the riskiest around. In the civilian market, companies must invest billions of dollars on new products, never knowing for sure whether by the time they are ready the airlines will still be interested in that kind of plane. This "sporty game," as John Newhouse has called it, represents a unique combination of heavy industry and advanced technology; it is both labor and capital intensive.

The military side of the business is a bit more predictable, but there is the problem of selling to an even more limited universe of buyers: the armed forces, which are subject to the vagaries of politics. Defense contractors have benefited from the tendency toward military buildup that, aside from the immediate post-Vietnam malaise, has characterized the past 50 years. While the industry is famed for producing marvelous new tools of war, it has also gained a reputation for something less than exemplary efficiency and ethics. Cost overruns on weapons systems have been a perennial problem, and numerous contractors have admitted making large amounts of illegal or questionable payments at home or abroad. In the mid-1980s there was considerable pressure on the industry to clean up its act—but that was also true a decade before. As weapons get ever more complicated and expensive and as companies continue to rely on a limited number of potential customers, it is unlikely that the aerospace business will ever function like other industries.

THE INDUSTRY TAKES OFF

The aircraft industry went through a slow ascent in the years following the Wright brothers' first successful flights in 1903. Europe held the lead in aviation until World War I, when the United States, which intended to provide about 2,500 planes for the war effort, was pressured by its allies to supply 10 times that number. Manufacturing companies came out of nowhere, and hundreds of aircraft factories were hastily established. By 1918 the output of aircraft was running at an annual rate of some 21,000 planes. The cooperation of the companies, including a pooling of patents, later prompted charges of war profiteering.

The new industrial structure collapsed very quickly after the armistice, and most of the new companies vanished. Those that survived—including Wright Aeronautical (linked to the famous brothers), Curtiss Aeroplane, and timberman Bill Boeing's firm—continued to produce mainly for the U.S. government, given that a significant commercial air transport industry had yet to emerge. Despite the limited market, there were some important newcomers to the business in the 1920s, including Douglas Aircraft, Lockheed Aircraft, and Atlantic Aircraft (an American operation set up by the famed Dutch aeronautical engineer Anthony Fokker). Henry Ford bought into the industry and went on to produce the famous Trimotor, or Tin Goose, the first successful all-metal plane.

The federal government was concerned about the underdeveloped state of the industry, and President Coolidge appointed a study board headed by Dwight Morrow to advise on what public policy should be. The board's 1925 report adopted industry recommendations such as the institution of a longer-term federal procurement policy and the recognition of proprietary designs used on government contracts. Such provisions were embodied in the 1926 Air Commerce Act, and the Pentagon set five-year procurement goals of 1,600 planes for the army and 1,000 for the navy.

During the late 1920s the aircraft industry also benefited from the aviation mania following Charles Lindbergh's famous solo transatlantic flight in 1927 and the growth of the airmail business, which the Kelly Air Mail Act of 1925 put in the hands of private contractors.

The financial wheeling and dealing of the 1920s touched the aviation business, as it did many others. Numerous aircraft producers and airlines were brought together through a series of mergers and put under the auspices of holding companies. The most powerful of these was United Aircraft and Transport Corp., which took over several transport firms and manufacturers such as Boeing, the Pratt & Whitney engine company, and Sikorsky Aviation, which at the time was doing its early work on developing helicopters.

Postmaster Walter Folger Brown encouraged consolidation in the industry in the early 1930s through his power over the granting of the all-important airmail contracts. The convenient arrangement that resulted came under attack after the Roosevelt administration took office. Senator Hugo Black led the charge, which resulted in the Air Mail Act of 1934, which instituted both a ban (that turned out to be short lived) on private transport of airmail and a more permanent requirement that aircraft producers and air transport companies be separated from one another.

The United holding company split into three independent firms: United Air Lines, Boeing Aircraft in the Northwest, and East Coast–based United Aircraft (renamed United Technologies in 1975), which included Pratt & Whitney and Sikorsky. North American Aviation spun off the Eastern and TWA airlines and continued the military aircraft business of what had been Curtiss Aeroplane and Wright Aeronautical.

Despite the Depression, the aircraft industry expanded during the 1930s, thanks to the growth of the airlines. Boeing first took the lead with the development of its 247, 60 of which were ordered by United Air Lines. But then Douglas Aircraft responded to a request from TWA and created the DC–1. This, the first of its hugely successful DC (Douglas Commercial) series, turned out to be a prototype, and the production model was the DC–2, which sat 14 passengers and had a cruising speed of 170 miles per hour, compared to 10 passengers and 155 MPH for the 247. The enlarged DC–3 (21 passengers) became even better known and more widely used.

The 1930s also saw the development of the famous "flying boats," the huge planes commissioned by Juan Trippe of Pan American to fly across oceans and alight on water where there were no airfields. The planes, dubbed Clippers by Trippe, were originally built by United Aircraft's Sikorsky Division. Beset by heavy losses United abandoned the business in 1938, and a series of other companies such as Glenn L. Martin, Consolidated Aircraft, and Boeing took over production of the flying boats.

By the end of the decade "landplanes" had also been refined considerably. The move to all-metal frames was followed by the development of four-engine planes and the quest to achieve higher altitudes, which required companies to begin work on a system of cabin pressurization.

The growing likelihood of war in Europe brought new stimulus to the military aircraft business, and Lockheed took the lead in selling abroad. The United States soon decided to expand its own fleet—especially after the German blitz of London in 1940 showed what air power could do. In May 1940 President Roosevelt startled the industry and by all accounts his own military establishment by calling for the production of 50,000 planes a year, about five times the existing capacity of the country.

The aircraft makers scrambled to increase production. Automobile companies such as Ford and General Motors were enlisted to help produce engines and later airframes (the bodies of planes) as well. After the attack on Pearl Harbor, output was stepped up even more as Roosevelt demanded 60,000 planes for 1942 and an astounding 125,000 the following year. Huge numbers of workers—including "Rosie the riveter" women joining the industrial labor force for the first time—were pulled into the factories, especially the sprawling facilities of Lockheed, Douglas, and North American in the Los Angeles area. In 1943 aircraft industry employment reached a peak of 1.3 million.

THE JET AGE

Aside from the vast numbers of propeller-driven bombers and fighters built with piston engines in the war years, the industry also developed workable jet engines during the 1940s. In 1941 the federal government formed the Committee on Jet Propulsion, which included representatives of the leading turbine companies.

One of those, General Electric, got the contract to produce a jet engine based on a British design. The first American-built jet plane was the XP–59A, which consisted of a Bell Aircraft frame and two of the GE engines; it made its trial flight in October 1942.

After the war there was an inevitable decline in military procurement, but the transition was more orderly than after the previous war, thanks to the provisions of the Contract Settlement Act of 1944. The Pentagon more gradually phased out its orders, beginning with subcontractors, and provided assistance for companies to make the conversion to peacetime production.

The major producers turned back to the civilian market, and Douglas quickly resumed its leadership. But the military business did not remain as limited as it did after the previous world war. U.S.–Soviet tensions developed into the Cold War; and the inclination of the American military, reinforced by the recommendations of the Finletter Air Policy Commission, was that air power should be the centerpiece of the U.S. military machine. This commitment led to a sharp increase in aerospace expenditures after the outbreak of the Korean War in 1950.

By the early 1950s jet engine technology was developed enough to be applied to commercial aircraft, but there was some question whether airlines would want to use the powerful gas turbines, which consumed much more fuel but permitted considerably higher speeds. Boeing, famed for its bombers during the war, decided to take the plunge. The Seattle company was rewarded in 1955, when American Airlines (previously a loyal customer of Douglas) placed a $200 million order for 30 of the 707s. Douglas suddenly realized that its hesitation on jets was mistaken and embarked on the development of a jet-powered DC–8. The company did win a considerable number of orders, but Boeing managed to take over and maintain leadership of the commercial business. The first scheduled flight of a jet plane in the United States took place with an American Airlines 707 in January 1959.

By the mid-1960s the commercial aircraft business—of the world, not only the United States—was dominated by six companies: airframe makers Boeing, Douglas, and Lockheed and engine manufacturers Pratt & Whitney, General Electric, and Britain's Rolls Royce. The early jet planes produced by these companies were noisy and heavy consumers of fuel. The technology was improved with the placement of a type of fan with 40 or so blades at the front of the engine. These resulting fan-jet engines (the first effective version of which was produced by Rolls Royce in 1960) could handle a larger volume of air and thus develop much greater thrust.

The development of fan-jets, stimulated by the Pentagon's interest in building the huge C–5A cargo planes, made possible substantially larger commercial aircraft as well. The prospect of powerful jets that could carry several times the number of passengers of existing planes was especially tantalizing to a company such as Pan American with heavily traveled intercontinental routes. Juan Trippe of Pan Am essentially decided to bet the company on the idea and enlisted Boeing to produce the plane with 350 or more seats that would become known as the 747. The purchase agreement for 25 of the jumbo jets was signed in 1966.

That same year American Airlines let it be known that it was also interested in a large jet but one not quite as jumbo as the 747. The domestic carrier was looking for a wide-bodied plane that could carry up to 250 passengers up to 2,100 miles. This sort of plane, of interest to other carriers as well, created an enticing opportunity for Boeing's competitors. Both Lockheed and Douglas, which had gone through a slump and was forced into a merger with military-oriented McDonnell Aircraft in 1967, went after the prize.

The two companies fought hard for what was called the airbus market, and each ended up getting a significant number of orders. The problem was that the airline industry could absorb only so many planes, and there was not enough business around to allow all three producers to thrive.

The weakest link among the three was Lockheed. The company was shaken when its engine partner Rolls Royce was forced into receivership and taken over by the British government. This ordeal scared off both Lockheed's lenders and customers for the L–1011 TriStar. The American company, already weakened by financial problems linked to the C–5A it was producing for the air force, nearly went into bankruptcy itself; it was saved only by a federal loan guarantee program of up to $250 million that squeaked through Congress in 1971.

The aircraft market picked up in the mid-1970s, but the rise in oil prices made airlines eager to have more fuel-efficient planes. The 747s from Boeing, the wide-bodied L–1011s from Lockheed, and Douglas's DC–10s had their place in longer, heavily traveled routes, but the carriers were looking to expand their narrow-body fleets and replace aging 707s, 727s, and DC–9s. They also wanted more efficient wide-bodies. Boeing made the biggest commitment to these markets, investing some $3 billion to develop the narrow-body 757 and the wide-body 767, each able to carry about 200 passengers on trips of 2,000 miles.

While the American producers were plunging into this new market they had to look back over their shoulder at the rising threat from abroad. In 1970 a group of French, British, West German, and Spanish aircraft companies formed a consortium called Airbus Industrie to make a foray in the international wide-body business. Their first product the A300 was a big success, and by the end of the 1970s the consortium had seized one fifth of the international commercial market.

SHAKEOUT AND RECOVERY

In the meantime it became clear that all three of the American manufacturers could not survive. With a pickup in sales of its jumbos and good prospects for the 757 and 767, Boeing became firmly established as the industry leader. So it was a question of whether Lockheed or Douglas would succumb first. For a while observers were betting it would be the latter. A series of accidents involving the DC–10 in the late 1970s undermined the reputation of the plane, and passengers began avoiding flights that used it.

But Douglas managed to recover from the DC–10 debacle and made its way in the market for smaller planes, not by investing billions, like Boeing, in an entirely new product but rather by producing derivatives of the DC–9 and DC–10. Observers were originally skeptical about the willingness of airlines to buy what was essentially old technology, but models such as the twin-engine MD–80 (based on the DC–9) proved to be successes.

Lockheed had no such luck. Sales of the L–1011 remained poor, and by December 1981 the company gave up and announced it would leave the commercial aircraft business and rely on its military contracts.

By the mid-1980s the demand for new planes had improved considerably. The plunge of oil prices bolstered the earnings of the airlines, enabling them to proceed with previously postponed expansion of their fleets. Huge orders began to be placed, such as the $3.1 billion deal announced by United and Boeing in late 1985 and Delta's $2 billion order from Douglas a couple of months later. These were topped by an announcement in August 1986 that British Airways was placing an order with Boeing that could go as high as $4.1 billion.

This favorable new climate for aircraft producers was not without its drawbacks. Having spent years and massive sums of money developing new fuel-efficient technologies, aerospace companies were now finding that the new cheapness of oil was making airlines less concerned about fuel costs. This was a particular blow for Boeing, which (along with engine maker General Electric) was spending several billion dollars developing a new type of fan-jet. The project, which Boeing called the 7J7, involved the use of an unducted fan engine (UDF). The device, which made use of external fan blades that looked suspiciously like propellers on the engine, was said to use one-third to two-thirds less fuel than existing engines. The major appeal of the technology was the fuel savings, and by 1986 it appeared that work on the new engine may have been for nought.

The 7J7 represented Boeing's delayed entry into the race for the 150-seater. The Seattle company decided to share the risk and the development cost of the plane with a group of Japanese companies, which were eager to gain access to U.S. aerospace technology.

The Big Three engine makers also approached the climate of uncertainty by spreading their risks. International collaboration became the order of the day. The trend built on the agreement by GE back in 1974 to create a joint venture with the French company SNECMA. By the mid-1980s such partnerships were the only way new engines were being developed. The biggest combination was International Aero Engines, formed in 1983 by Pratt & Whitney, Rolls Royce, and companies from Japan, Italy, and West Germany.

THE IRON TRIANGLE

Given the many uncertainties of the commercial aircraft business, many companies looked to the relatively more predictable—and usually more profitable—military side of the business. The industry enjoyed fat years during the heyday of the space program and the 1960s portion of the Vietnam War. Moreover the decline in defense spending during the period of Vietnamization of the conflict and the aftermath of the war turned out to be short lived. And by the 1970s the leading aerospace defense contractors (Boeing, General Dynamics, Grumman, Lockheed, Northrop, McDonnell Douglas, Rockwell International, and United Technologies) had developed a secure hold on the lion's share of military spending. Their close relationships with Pentagon officials and members of key congressional committees constituted what Gordon Adams has called the "iron triangle."

The story of defense contracting since the early 1970s has been one of tension between the desire of the military and Congress for the most advanced weaponry and the seeming inability of many contractors to keep the costs of producing these arms under control. Lockheed's massive cost overruns on the C–5A in the late 1960s became emblematic of the situation and contributed to the near-bankruptcy of the company. The problem has been even worse in the complex weapons systems included in the so-called triad (air, land, and sea) of strategic nuclear weapons.

The B–1 bomber, which was supposed to cost $29 million a copy when the contract was given to Rockwell International in 1970, ended up costing $200 million each. (In the interim the project, designed to replace aging B–52s, was canceled by President Carter in 1977 and kept alive by Rockwell until it was revived by the Reagan administration.) Even more checkered has been the history of the Trident nuclear submarine produced by the Electric Boat Division of General Dynamics. The management of the project was fraught with problems, and division head P. Takis Veliotis ended up fleeing to his native Greece to avoid indictment on kickback charges.

The reputations of a number of major aerospace companies were further tarnished in the 1970s by revelations that they had been making many millions of dollars in questionable payments to foreign officials to help in getting orders. Lockheed, long a leader in military exports, was implicated in payoff scandals involving the Japanese prime minister, Prince Bernhard of the Netherlands, and a cabinet official in Italy.

There were also controversies regarding the quality of the products being turned out by the industry. Pratt & Whitney, the preeminent military-engine producer, was confronted with Pentagon complaints that the company's F100 powerplant for the F–15 and F–16 fighters was stalling out and breaking down with alarming frequency.

By the early 1980s the industry was trying to put these unpleasant affairs behind it and take advantage of the trillion-dollar military buildup initiated by the Reagan administration. Aerospace companies and other contractors enjoyed a flood of new orders; observers said that the defense business could hardly have been doing better if the country had been at war. Things were so juicy in fact, with defense contractors enjoying margins about twice the average for corporations in general, that the industry began to come under unfavorable public scrutiny.

Starting in 1983 there was a series of revelations about what appeared to be wildly inflated prices the military was paying for its supplies and spare parts. The press regularly reported with indignation the $17 bolts and $600 toilet seats the Defense Department was procuring. Contractors decried what they considered a misunderstanding of the complexities of pricing in government purchasing, but the political tide was against them.

Under pressure from Congress the Pentagon began to get tougher with its suppliers. The Department of Defense started shifting from the traditional cost-plus-fee contracts to fixed-price-incentive arrangements, under which the contractor rather than the government had to shoulder increased costs. The new order of the day was competition. The navy and the air force spread their jet fighter engine business between General Electric and Pratt & Whitney to chastise Pratt for problems with the F100. In October 1985 the air force announced that it wanted seven contractors—Boeing, General Dynamics, Grumman, Lockheed, McDonnell Douglas, Northrop, and Rockwell—to compete for the contract for an advanced tactical fighter for the 1990s. The project, aimed at producing a replacement for the F–15, could be worth $45 billion. In 1986 Northrop and Lockheed were chosen to lead teams to develop competing prototypes for the new fighter.

Along with the renewed emphasis on competitive bidding, the Pentagon has demanded an end to the sloppy or dishonest billing practices of many contractors. In 1985 and 1986 prominent companies such as General Electric, General Dynamics, and Litton were suspended as authorized government contractors. Skeptics noted that these suspensions were often brief and did little to impede the companies' ongoing relationships with the Pentagon, but they once again put the industry on the defensive. As in the past Lockheed became one of the main culprits. In August 1986 the air force accused the company of overcharging hundreds of millions of dollars on the C–5B cargo plane.

In the mid-1980s the industry also had to contend with the decision by Congress to put an end to the dizzying growth of the military budget. In 1985 President Reagan reluctantly accepted the decision by the legislature, facing the need to get the budget deficit under control, to limit the increase in defense spending to the rate of inflation.

Yet for the industry there remained a major bright spot. Reagan was determined to push ahead with his controversial plan for a space-based arms system designed to neutralize incoming ballistic missiles. This strategic defense initiative (SDI), popularly known as the Star Wars plan, was from a commercial perspective one of the greatest opportunities in the history of the defense business. The cost of the project was put at $26 billion for the first five years, and that was to be just the beginning of a huge investment in developing an entirely new generation of electronic weaponry.

The large defense contractors wasted no time getting on this gravy train. According to figures compiled in mid-1986, the largest contract amount (some $620 million) had been received by Hughes Aircraft, which was acquired by General Motors in 1985. Lockheed had received $524 million, Boeing $349 million, McDonnell Douglas $319 million, and Rockwell International about $200 million. And this was just the beginning.

The Top 10 Defense Contractors, by Contracts in Fiscal Year 1985
($ Billions)

1. McDonnell Douglas	$8.9
2. General Dynamics	7.4
3. Rockwell International	6.3
4. General Electric	5.9
5. Boeing	5.5
6. Lockheed	5.1
7. United Technologies	3.9
8. Hughes Aircraft	3.6
9. Raytheon	3.0
10. Grumman	2.7

Source: Department of Defense.

LABOR RELATIONS

The entrepreneurs who pioneered the aircraft industry were none too friendly toward unions. In fact one of the reasons a group of them congregated in Los Angeles was to take advantage of the weakness of organized labor in the area. The Machinists union stepped up its efforts after the passage of the National Industrial Recovery Act, but the industry strongly resisted unionization and set up employee associations to undermine the process.

It took the 1937 Wagner Act to change the balance of power. A sit-down strike at Douglas that year brought recognition, and Lockheed signed with the Machinists after that. Companies such as Grumman continued to resist unionization.

Further organizing in the industry was divided between the Machinists and the United Automobile Workers. The presence of the UAW in the industry created a confrontation when Ford, which was still resisting unionization in its auto plants, became an aircraft subcontractor during the expansion of the industry in the late 1930s.

The open-shop policies of leading companies came under repeated attack from the unions, and the firms even defied President Kennedy in a dispute on the subject in 1962.

Labor relations in the industry were frequently turbulent in the following years, and strikes were not uncommon. In 1977 Lockheed became one of the first U.S. companies to seek contract concessions when it sought to erode seniority rights. A 12-week strike by the Machinists ended in a compromise.

The problems of the industry in the early 1980s made the companies tougher at the bargaining table. In 1983 the Machinists signed a contract with Boeing that substituted lump-sum payments for wage increases and instituted a two-tier pay structure. The pact prompted other companies to demand concessions. A UAW strike at McDonnell Douglas to resist similar givebacks collapsed after 17 weeks.

LEADING COMPANIES

Since the mid-1950s **Boeing** has been the leader of the commercial aircraft industry and a major defense contractor as well. One of the largest U.S. industrial exporters, Boeing has manufactured about one half of all the jet planes ever produced outside the Soviet bloc. The company was started as a sideline by timberman William Boeing just before World War I. For a time it was part of the United Aircraft and Transport holding company, and during World War II it became the leading producer of bombers, including the famous B–17 Flying Fortress and the B–29 Super Fortress, one of which dropped the atomic bomb on Hiroshima. In the 1950s Boeing gambled on the introduction of jet planes to the airline market and ended up displacing Douglas as the premier commercial producer. In the late 1960s the company developed the 747 jumbo jet, and in the 1970s it produced a new generation of smaller, more efficient jetliners.

General Dynamics, one of the aerospace companies almost exclusively dependent on Pentagon business, has had more than its share of troubles since the 1960s. The company, founded in 1952, experienced heavy cost overruns on the F–111 fighter, major managerial problems in the production of Trident nuclear submarines by its Electric Boat Division, and scandals regarding its billing practices. In the mid-1980s its hold over the F–16 fighter business was challenged by a cheaper plane from Northrop, but the air force decided to stick with the General Dynamics product. In 1985 a new chief executive Stanley Pace was brought in to repair the company's image.

Grumman has been a leading provider of navy aircraft since the 1930s. Founded by Leroy Grumman at the beginning of that decade, the company in more recent years has been heavily dependent on its expensive F–14 fighter. The company's E–2C Hawkeye airborne early-warning plane was used to great effect by Israel during 1982 fighting in Lebanon.

Lockheed has been one of the most controversial companies in the aerospace business. Founded by Allan and Malcolm Loughhead (who later changed the spelling of their name to Lockheed) in 1916, the company went bankrupt in 1931 and was revived the following year by Robert and Courtlandt Gross. The firm was a major aircraft producer during World War II, but it later had trouble with the performance of both its commercial jet Electra and its Starfighter planes sold to NATO countries. The company returned to the commercial business in the late 1960s by developing the L–1011 TriStar, a wide-body that competed with

Douglas's DC–10. Problems with that project and the C–5A transport it was building for the air force nearly put the company under in the early 1970s. It was rescued only by a $250 million loan guarantee from the federal government. Soon afterwards the company was embroiled in controversy following reports of some $38 million in questionable payments made to foreign officials to promote orders. In late 1981 Lockheed gave up on the commercial business and focused on military projects.

McDonnell Douglas was created by the 1967 merger of a leading military aircraft producer and a leading commercial one. James McDonnell (known as Mr. Mac) founded his firm in 1939 and during the war emerged as a major Pentagon supplier. Donald Douglas got started in airplane production in the 1920s and in the 1930s became a leader in the commercial market with his DC (Douglas Commercial) series. Douglas Aircraft was number one in civilian aircraft until Boeing brought out the first jet airliner in the mid-1950s and stole the show. Douglas went into a slump and needed the alliance with McDonnell to keep it alive. The combined company jumped into the wide-body race in the late 1960s and was doing reasonably well until its DC–10 ran into a streak of problems in the late 1970s. McDonnell Douglas opted not to follow Boeing in developing a new generation of smaller jets and instead successfully sold derivatives of the DC–9 and DC–10.

Northrop has lived for years on the inexpensive F–5 fighter that has been marketed to dozens of Third World countries. Founded by airplane designer John Northrop in 1939 after he left Lockheed, the company has been involved in a number of scandals. Chairman Thomas Jones was found guilty of making $150,000 in illegal contributions to the 1972 campaign of Richard Nixon. In the mid-1970s there were revelations that the company had regularly entertained Pentagon officials and members of Congress at a hunting lodge on the eastern shore of Maryland. In the mid-1980s Northrop, which has traditionally done more foreign than U.S. business, waged an unsuccessful campaign to get the air force to adopt its F–20 fighter over General Dynamics' F–16. Northrop was, however, chosen to lead one of the two teams developing the next generation of combat aircraft known as the Advanced Tactical Fighter. The company is also the prime contractor for the advanced technology (Stealth) bomber that may end up replacing the B–1.

Rockwell International has made its name as the largest contractor for NASA and as the producer of the B–1 bomber. Leading aircraft producer North American Aviation (a combination of several early producers) merged with Rockwell-Standard (a diversified manufacturer) in 1967, shortly after three astronauts died in an explosion of an Apollo space capsule produced by North American. The combined company adopted the name Rockwell International in 1973. It took a decade before the company could enjoy the fruits of the B–1 contract it received in 1970. The project, intended to provide a replacement for aging B–52s but seen by some as being superseded by the Stealth bomber, was canceled by President Carter in 1977 and revived by President Reagan in 1981. By the mid-1980s the company was looking ahead with dread to the sharp falloff in revenues that would occur with the completion of the 100-plane B–1 program in 1988. Rockwell's reputation was tarnished a bit when one of its space shuttles, Challenger, exploded during takeoff in 1986, but most of the blame ended up being placed on Morton Thiokol, the producer of the shuttle's booster rocket.

SOURCE GUIDE

LEADING STOCK ANALYSTS AND EXPERTS

Gordon Adams, Defense Budget Project, Washington, D.C.

Wolfgang and Christopher Demisch, analysts at First Boston.

Paul Nisbet, analyst at Prudential-Bache.

David Smith, analyst at Sanford C. Bernstein & Co.

TRADE ASSOCIATIONS AND UNIONS

Aerospace Industries Association of America, Washington, D.C.

International Association of Machinists and Aerospace Workers, Washington, D.C.

United Automobile, Aerospace and Agricultural Implement Workers of America, Detroit.

DATA SOURCES AND DIRECTORIES

Aerospace Facts and Figures, published annually (Washington, D.C.: Aerospace Industries Association).

Aviation Week and Space Technology publishes an annual directory issue with a guide to companies in the industry, in December.

Interavia ABC Aerospace Directory, an international guide to manufacturers and airlines published annually (Geneva, Switzerland: Interavia Publishing).

TRADE PUBLICATIONS

Aerospace Daily.

Aviation Week and Space Technology.

Defense Industry Report, fortnightly.

Defense Week.

Interavia (Geneva, Switzerland), monthly.

BOOKS AND REPORTS

Adams, Gordon. *The Iron Triangle: The Politics of Defense Contracting.* New York: Council on Economic Priorities, 1981.

Bluestone, Barry, Peter Jordan, and Mark Sullivan. *Aircraft Industry Dynamics: An Analysis of Competition, Capital and Labor.* Auburn House, 1981.

Gansler, Jacques S. *The Defense Industry.* Cambridge, Mass.: MIT Press, 1980.

Klare, Michael T. *American Arms Supermarket.* Austin: University of Texas Press, 1984.

Newhouse, John. *The Sporty Game.* New York: Alfred A. Knopf, 1982.

President's Blue Ribbon Commission on Defense Management (Packard Commission). *Quest for Excellence: Final Report to the President.* Washington, D.C., 1986.

Rae, John B. *Climb to Greatness: The American Aircraft Industry, 1920–1960.* Cambridge, Mass.: MIT Press, 1968.

Sampson, Anthony. *The Arms Bazaar.* New York: Viking Press, 1977.

Shaw, Linda, et al. *Stocking the Arsenal: A Guide to the Nation's Top Military Contractors.* Washington, D.C.: Investor Responsibility Research Center, 1985.

Airlines

The economic progress of the vast American continent has depended to a great extent on the development of increasingly efficient transportation. The industrial growth of the 19th century was stimulated first by the expansion of inland waterways and then by the spread of railroads. While rail lines and later trucks became the main means of transporting goods, it has been the evolution of air travel that has truly integrated American business on a national level and made possible its wide expansion abroad.

Over the past few decades air travel has changed from a novel and expensive form of transportation indulged in mainly by corporate executives and movie stars into a type of mass transit. The deregulation of the airline industry in 1978 created a free-for-all that has resulted in bargains for passengers and challenges for unions. The carriers themselves are still adjusting to the precarious new environment. Some of the familiar names have muddled through; others have been gobbled up in mergers. At the same time, a new crop of "upstart" companies has changed the face of the $48 billion industry.

FROM MAILMEN TO GLOBETROTTERS

In the years following the pioneering flights of the Wright brothers, commercial aviation was slow in getting established in the United States. The first regularly scheduled passenger line was set up to fly between St. Petersburg and Tampa in Florida in 1914, but the venture was short lived. While passenger lines were being established across Europe, aviation in America centered on the delivery of mail.

The Kelly Act of 1925 compelled the Post Office Department to open up all but transcontinental routes to private contractors. This encouraged a number of barnstormers to become entrepreneurs and stimulated the growth of commercial aviation. The business became all the more glamorous after Charles Lindbergh's historic solo flight from New York to Paris in 1927; both Main Street and Wall Street became fascinated with flying.

The late 1920s saw the emergence of a slew of companies bidding for the potentially lucrative Post Office contracts. Before long these small firms coalesced into the predecessors of what would become the major carriers, including United Aircraft and Transport, Eastern Air Transport, and American Airways. The mail carriers also began offering passenger service.

When Postmaster Walter Folger Brown took office in 1929 as part of the Hoover administration he set about to rationalize and stabilize the airmail industry. He pushed through legislation (the Watres Act) that created a system under which airlines were paid not by the actual weight of the mail they carried but by the amount of space available for mail, thus encouraging the use of larger planes. There were also bonuses for using the most advanced equipment.

Brown also pressured carriers to establish several transcontinental routes and toward that end got Western Air Express, the first successful passenger carrier, to merge with Transcontinental Air Transport, which operated a combination train and plane coast-to-coast service. The resulting company was Transcontinental and Western Air or TWA (which later changed its name to Trans World Airlines).

What seemed like a brilliant scheme to Postmaster Brown took on the appearance of a grand conspiracy during congressional hearings called by Senator Hugo Black after the Roosevelt administration took office. Brown and the major carriers were accused of carving up the airmail business in an illegitimate manner, and the resulting public outcry prompted FDR to transfer airmail transport to the army air corps.

The army pilots were not experienced in flying at night or in poor weather; and after a series of crashes Roosevelt relented and turned airmail delivery back to the more experienced private sector. The major carriers were supposed to be barred from the new system, but the Post Office restored their contracts after they made slight changes in their names and replaced some executives. American, Eastern, TWA, and United were firmly established as the Big Four of the domestic air transport business. The determination of fares and the allocation of routes in that business was placed in the hands of a federal regulatory agency called the Civil Aeronautics Board (CAB).

At the same time, another U.S. company was becoming the dominant player in the international airline field. Juan Trippe, the son of a New York stockbroker, became interested in aviation at an early age, going on to form a flying club at Yale and managing an operation that carried airmail between New York and Boston. Trippe had his eye on Cuba and set up a company with the aim of winning the airmail route between Key West and Havana. He did get the route after merging with two other companies, and the combined operation took the name of Pan American Airways.

Through's Trippe's aggressive leadership Pan Am won a rapid succession of foreign airmail contracts, which were authorized by the Kelly Foreign Air Mail Act—a piece of legislation that Trippe helped to write. By 1930 Pan Am was designated the U.S. government's "chosen instrument" for developing overseas air links, and the carrier had more than 20,000 miles of routes to 20 countries. Trippe turned his attention to transoceanic routes but was dismayed by the European carriers' demands for reciprocal landing rights in the United States.

While that political problem was being worked out Trippe had airplane manufacturer Igor Sikorsky build four-engine amphibious planes for use in the Pacific. Trippe called these flying boats clippers in honor of the old clipper ships. After having constructed facilities for stops in Hawaii, Midway, Guam, and the Philippines, Trippe inaugurated the China Clipper's mail and passenger service to Manila with much fanfare in 1935. Transatlantic service began in 1939. Throughout much of the world, Pan Am's planes became the symbol of American expansionism.

After World War II the United States emerged as the dominant force in international aviation, and Trippe sought landing rights in every corner of the globe. Pan Am lost its foreign monopoly, however, as international routes were awarded by the CAB to several other carriers, especially TWA (which was then controlled by millionaire Howard Hughes).

The late 1950s saw the introduction of passenger jets and the reduction of fares to encourage air travel among a wider section of the population. By 1957 more passengers crossed the Atlantic by air than by sea. Trippe saw the potential for mass levels of air travel and in the mid-1960s entered into an agreement with Boeing Corp. for the development of a jet capable of carrying 350 passengers. TWA followed Pan Am's lead, and thus began the age of the jumbo jet.

Mass air travel and huge planes such as the 747s that began flying in 1970 were predicated on the availability of cheap fuel. The age of the jumbo had hardly begun when that resource disappeared, and along with expensive fuel came higher interest rates and other elevated costs.

At first the airlines, protected as they were by the CAB, did not have too much to worry about. But by the mid-1970s the rigid pricing structure of the past four decades began to crack as more aggressive carriers pressed for the right to discount fares. At the same time, a deregulatory gospel started to be preached by the likes of Alfred Kahn, chairman of the CAB during the Carter administration. Before long there was serious discussion of abolishing federal oversight of the business aspects of aviation.

THE DEREGULATION FREE-FOR-ALL

This is precisely what happened after Congress passed the Airline Deregulation Act of 1978. That legislation established a schedule for the phasing out of federal regulation of routes and fares along with the abolition by 1985 of the CAB, the industry's stern but paternalistic overseer.

The major carriers lost no time in abandoning their less profitable flights to smaller cities. In the first year of deregulation about 75 localities lost all of their scheduled service. In most of those cities commuter lines stepped into the void, but they used smaller planes and had more erratic schedules.

The major, or trunk, airlines turned their attention to the more popular routes, such as New York to Miami, and the number of those flights soared. Competition in those markets led to vicious price wars, which reduced what is known as fare yield and ate heavily into the carriers' operating income. By 1980 the industry as a whole experienced its first operating loss since 1947.

In order to increase efficiency the majors (defined as those carriers with $1 billion or more in annual revenues) put more emphasis on hub-and-spoke systems. Under this arrangement commuter and regional lines brought passengers to the hub airports, from which they could fly around the country on flights of the majors. The desire to build up business in these hubs—which included Chicago and Denver for United, Atlanta for Delta, and Dallas for American—made the price-cutting all the more intense.

The early 1980s brought no relief for the industry. The recession, curtailed flights after the air controllers' strike in 1981, increased costs for fuel, interest and landing fees, and the continuing fare wars on the popular routes all prolonged the misery.

The larger carriers also saw their business eroding as a result of the emergence of small discount carriers that were able to slash prices by eliminating amenities and using nonunion labor. This approach was pioneered in the 1970s by the likes of Southwest Airlines and Air Florida. Deregulation spawned a new generation of what came to be called upstart lines. Among them were Midway Airlines, New York Air, and Muse Air. But the outstanding success story was People Express, which turned into the fastest-growing carrier in aviation history.

The evil genius of the period was Frank Lorenzo, who started with tiny Texas International Airlines and then stalked many of the leading carriers. He was defeated in his attempts to take over National Airlines (Pan Am won that battle), TWA (twice), and Frontier Airlines. But he did win Continental in 1982 and Eastern in 1986, which along with New York Air (the discounter he established in 1980) catapulted Lorenzo's Texas Air holding company into the number one spot among airline corporations. He also ended up with People Express, which by that time included Frontier.

Some of the upstarts had their own problems in the rough-and-tumble world of deregulation, and a number went into bankruptcy. While the ranks of interstate carriers jumped after deregulation, from about three dozen to some 125 in 1984, the total started to decline, reaching 96 in September 1986.

More-established lines continued to reel as a result of increased costs and discounted fares. TWA weakened, Pan Am came close to bankruptcy in 1982, and Braniff and Continental actually went into Chapter 11, although in the latter case it was mainly a ploy to abrogate labor contracts. (For more on the industry's union-management battles of this period, see the Labor Relations section below.) Other leading carriers such as Northwest, Piedmont, and USAir prospered during this period mainly by keeping out of the big brawls and serving smaller cities.

Whether prompted in a particular case by a major or an upstart, the price wars flared on a regular basis. Fare structures became so complicated that even travel agents had difficulty keeping up. The majors amassed thousands of different fares, and they used daily computer analyses to keep track of price shifts by one another. The carriers were locked into this nonstop poker game even when it had disastrous effects on earnings. The common wisdom among the majors was that it was preferable to lose income on account of discounted fares than to give up market share. Intense price competition contributed greatly to the industry's record loss of $733 million in 1982. But an improved cost picture allowed the carriers as a group to move slightly into the black in 1983 and then jump to total operating profits of more than $2 billion in 1984.

Another way in which the majors sought to come out ahead in the competitive jungle was through frequent-flyer programs. These programs originated in 1981 as the carriers sought to solidify loyalty from among those most desirable customers: the ones, usually businesspeople, who fly more than 12,000 miles a year. The airlines began offering free flights to vacation spots when a traveler amassed a certain number of miles flying on business. Corporate travel departments, which were excluded from the game, grumbled about employees who eschewed cheaper flights on certain lines in order to fly with the carrier in whose program they were enrolled. In 1986 several airlines began cracking down on the illicit market that developed to buy and sell frequent flyer coupons.

Carriers also sought to get a competitive edge through their positions on the computer systems that travel agents use to reserve the large majority of airline tickets. These systems are provided by some of the carriers themselves, and it is not surprising that the flights that tended to appear on the top of the list when a travel agent keyed in a departure time and destination were those of the supplying carrier. American's SABRE system and United's APOLLO, the two leaders in the field, have certainly bolstered the market shares of those carriers. Other lines have predictably balked at the treatment their flights receive in the systems and have tried, to little avail, to displace the leaders. In 1984 the CAB required the systems to provide unbiased displays, but a number of carriers still argued for reservation systems that were not owned by single airlines.

By the mid-1980s the competitive situation was as intense as ever, especially with the invasion by People Express of dozens of leading markets. As it turned out, People was one of the main victims of the battle. Facing a severe financial crisis in 1986, the carrier desperately tried to survive by selling off Frontier Airlines, which People had acquired only months before. A deal with United fell through because of problems with the pilot's union, and Frontier was put into Chapter 11. People, still vulnerable, succumbed to the advances of Texas Air. Lorenzo agreed to purchase People for about $122 million and Frontier for $176 million.

The purchases of People and Frontier were only one element of a dramatic process of consolidation that characterized the airline industry in the mid-1980s. In 1985 corporate raider Carl Icahn won control of TWA, United bought Pan Am's Pacific routes, and People purchased Frontier. In 1986 Northwest and Republic merged, TWA bought Ozark, Texas Air took over Eastern, and Delta acquired Western. By September 1986 the industry's new configuration, based on each carrier's 1985 business, appeared as follows:

		Revenue Passenger Miles in 1985 (in Billions)	
		Subsidiaries	Corporate Total
1.	Texas Air		66.3
	Eastern	33.1	
	Continental	16.4	
	People Express	11.0	
	Frontier	4.4	
	New York Air	1.4	
2.	United		48.0
	Pan Am's Pacific routes	6.5	
3.	American		44.1

(concluded)

		Revenue Passenger Miles in 1985 (in Billions)	
		Subsidiaries	Corporate Total
4.	Delta		40.5
	Western	10.4	
5.	TWA		35.0
	Ozark	3.0	
6.	Northwest		33.0
	Republic	10.7	
7.	Pan Am		20.6
8.	USAir		9.7
9.	Piedmont		8.2
10.	Southwest		5.3

Source: Airline Economics Inc.

LABOR RELATIONS

Unionization in the airline industry began with the associations formed by Post Office pilots in the 1920s to promote safety practices. The Air Line Pilots Association (ALPA) was established as a national union in 1931 and soon gained a solid foothold in the industry. The organization's first major test came quickly when E. L. Cord, the owner of Century Airlines and the Frank Lorenzo of his day, moved to cut pilots' pay from $350 to $150 a month, prompting a strike. ALPA garnered considerable political support, resulting in a rejection of Cord's bid for a Post Office contract. The pilots did not achieve a complete victory, but ALPA's stature was enhanced.

The first women took to the skies as stewardesses in 1930, but the unionization of flight attendants did not occur until the late 1940s. While the organization of pilots led fairly smoothly to one powerful union, the flight attendants had a more difficult time. Rivalries emerged between independent unions that were formed at United and other carriers and ALPA, which wanted to control the organization of flight attendants but resisted giving them equal status in the union. It was not until 1973 that the Association of Flight Attendants became a fully autonomous union within ALPA, but that organization represents only about half of the unionized attendants.

For many years relations between airline managements and the unions—which for ground crews included the International Association of Machinists, the Transport Workers Union, and the Teamsters—were relatively peaceful. The reason is that CAB control of fares allowed the carriers to pass along higher labor costs to passengers without competitive drawbacks.

With the advent of deregulation, this convenient arrangement was disrupted, and in some cases open warfare broke out between managements looking to cut costs and unions seeking to maintain their members' standard of living. By the early 1980s nearly every major carrier was demanding wage and work rule concessions from its employees. The unions had to face the fact that the crisis of the majors was real, which was brought home most clearly when Braniff filed for Chapter 11 in 1982.

The unions were thus willing to go along with concessions, but creative labor advisers got the unions to seek something in exchange: stock ownership for workers. Employee ownership of limited numbers of shares was nothing new, but the deals worked out by the airline unions called for the workers to receive substantial chunks of equity. Pan Am led the way in 1981 with an arrangement that gave employees 10 percent of the carrier and a seat on the company's board. Western Airlines workers got a whopping 32 percent of the carrier in 1983, and later that year Eastern gave 25 percent to its staff as well as four places on the board. Republic Airlines handed over 30 percent of its shares to employees in 1984.

In cases such as Eastern and Western, the ownership of stock initially led to improved labor relations and prompted employees to take a greater interest in efficiency. But when management demanded additional concessions, the era of good feeling ended.

The wage cuts agreed to by the unions were not always adequate to carriers hungry to reduce costs. Led by American in 1983 managements began seeking much larger reductions for future employees by pressuring unions to sign two-tier agreements that in some cases slashed pay for new hires by 50 percent (though in some cases the new hires would eventually reach parity). ALPA, many of whose members were paid more than $100,000 a year, fought hard against these arrangements but ended up agreeing to them in numerous contracts. However, ALPA struck United for a month in 1985 to limit the duration of a two-tier agreement.

Because labor represents such a high percentage of total costs (a third or more) for major unionized carriers, relations with unions were often central to the survival of the company. In fact it was the cooperation of TWA's unions that enabled raider Carl Icahn to take over the carrier in 1985.

The pressure on the airline unions has been intensified by the nonunion upstart carriers that have arisen in the age of deregulation. At People Express, pilots received a fraction of the salaries at the majors, were expected to put in more "stick time" (hours at the controls) per month, and were given ground duties when not flying.

Frank Lorenzo of Texas Air has adopted a ruthless approach to labor costs and unions. He set up nonunion discounter New York Air in 1980, and after taking over Continental in 1983, he demanded major concessions from the staff. When the unions resisted, Lorenzo pushed the company into Chapter 11, mainly to abrogate its labor contracts. While in bankruptcy Continental reduced its payroll by two thirds and chopped wages in half. A strike called by pilots to protest these actions was finally called off in defeat after two years.

As a result of the Continental affair, Lorenzo became the bugbear for airline unions, which worked to undermine his bids for TWA and Frontier Airlines in 1985. But in 1986 Lorenzo got Eastern's board to agree to a takeover after the Machinists refused new wage concessions unless Borman resigned. Once it became clear that Lorenzo would continue his antiunion policies at Eastern, the Machinists and Eastern's other unions made a last-ditch and unsuccessful effort to take over the airline themselves.

The honeymoon between TWA workers and Carl Icahn came to an end in 1986. Flight attendants went on strike in March after contract talks, in which Icahn was seeking substantial wage and work rule concessions, broke down. The company quickly shifted reservations clerks, secretaries, and others into the jobs of the strikers and kept on flying. After 10 weeks the flight attendants ended the strike but rejected the concessions.

LEADING COMPANIES

American Airlines had its origins in a batch of aviation companies that a group of Wall Street financiers began accumulating in the late 1920s. American prospered on airmail contracts, and by the end of the 1930s it was the leading passenger line. Still led by C. R. Smith, American in 1953 was the first carrier to offer non-stop, coast-to-coast service; in 1959 it pioneered the passenger jet age in the United States with the use of Boeing 707s. By that time American had replaced the Pennsylvania Railroad as the country's leading passenger carrier. Smith left the company in 1968 to become Secretary of Commerce but was called back in 1973 after his successor George Spater ran into difficulties, including the revelation of his illegal contributions to the Nixon reelection campaign in 1972. In the era of deregulation the company fared well. President Robert Crandall used a street fighter's approach to hold on to lucrative markets and resist pressure from the upstarts. By the mid-1980s Crandall was gambling on a several-billion-dollar expansion strategy that aimed at spreading reduced costs over a larger business. In late 1986 American agreed to purchase AirCal, a leading west coast carrier, for about $225 million.

Eastern Airlines began life as Pitcairn Aviation, which ran the mail between New York and Miami starting in the late 1920s. Under the leadership of World War I ace Eddie Rickenbacker, who was named general manager in 1935, Eastern became one of the Big Four domestic passenger carriers. Eastern gained a reputation for poor service but prospered thanks to its Air Shuttle service between New York, Washington, D.C., and Boston (initiated in 1961) and other lucrative routes. The company ran into financial difficulties in the early 1970s, and former astronaut Frank Borman was installed as president in 1975 to stop the decline. Borman won early wage concessions in 1977 but ran into strong opposition in the early 1980s when he sought further givebacks. Borman threatened to follow Continental into Chapter 11, but Eastern's unions (especially the militant Machinists) only agreed to further cuts after Borman agreed to giving workers 25 percent of the company's stock and four seats on Eastern's board. For a while a cooperative relationship emerged, but Borman's need for more cuts soured that. By early 1986, with Eastern facing possible default on its loans, the company's board consented to a $600 million takeover by Texas Air.

Pan American was the pioneer in international air transport and for many years was the American flagship carrier abroad. With the enterprising Juan Trippe at the controls, Pan Am established routes throughout the world, facing competition from other U.S. carriers only in the 1950s. Pan Am started experiencing problems in the 1970s, resulting in part from the costs of adding large numbers of 747s to its fleet. In 1979 the company won a takeover battle for National Airlines and hoped to recover through an expansion into domestic business. But Pan Am had difficulty operating in the deregulated environment, and losses mounted. Chairman William Seawell sold off assets such as the company's New York headquarters building and the Intercontinental Hotels chain to keep the carrier alive. In 1981 C. Edward Acker, who had made a name for himself at upstart Air Florida, took over the company and managed to win a wage cut from Pan Am's unions in exchange for 10 percent of the stock and a seat on the board. Relations with the unions remained tense, and the company was hit with a month-long strike in 1985. The walkout resulted in wage increases but two-tier provisions as well. Later that year Pan Am sold off its historic Pacific routes—inaugurated with the China Clipper in 1935—to United for $750 million. In 1986 the company inaugurated shuttle service in competition with Eastern between New York, Boston, and Washington, D.C.

People Express was the most remarkable product of airline deregulation and became the fastest-growing carrier in aviation history. Built by Donald Burr, former chief operating officer of Texas International Airlines, People challenged nearly all the major carriers with its no-frills service. The carrier established its hub at the underused airport in Newark, New Jersey, and priced its flights low enough to justify its advertising slogan: "Flying that costs less than driving." Burr, using "humanistic" management techniques, also turned airline labor relations upside down. His nonunion work force was hired at rates well below industry averages but was imbued with an esprit de corps that put teamwork before work rules and status. Each employee was required to purchase 100 shares of stock (at a heavy discount) and was asked to perform a variety of tasks. Passengers also had to get used to a new ambience, which included the end of free meals, free baggage checking, and other amenities. By late 1985 People was flying to 49 cities and had helped stimulate a series of price wars. Late that year Burr surprised the industry by acquiring Frontier Airlines for $300 million, winning the support of that company's unions, which desperately wanted an alternative to Frank Lorenzo's attempt to take over the carrier. The Frontier acquisition, along with a subsequent purchase of commuter line Britt Airways, allowed People to expand across the country. But financial problems plagued the company. In 1986, after failing to sell Frontier to raise cash, Burr reluctantly agreed to an acquisition offer from Texas Air, which then folded People into Continental.

Texas Air is the holding company for the aviation empire put together by Frank Lorenzo. Starting with the purchase of Texas International Airlines in 1972, Lorenzo used the new regulatory environment to shake up the industry. After unsuccessful bids to take over National and TWA, he established discount carrier New York Air in 1980 to compete with Eastern's Air Shuttle. Lorenzo then went after Continental and, after a drawn-out battle, succeeded in taking over the company, which had a proud history dating back to the 1930s. When unions balked at hefty layoffs and wage cuts, Lorenzo put Continental in Chapter 11 and nullified the company's labor contracts. Union opposition helped defeat Lorenzo's bids for TWA and Frontier in 1985, but in 1986 he succeeded in taking over Eastern and People Express.

Trans World Airlines started life as Transcontinental and Western Air, a 1930 merger of two of the early successful passenger lines. TWA's president Jack Frye ran into opposition from his board while attempting an expensive modernization of the carrier's fleet. Frustrated at this caution, Frye approached millionaire Howard Hughes, a longtime aviation buff, who bought control of the carrier in 1939. Hughes took over the management of the company (Frye was fired in 1947) and made it the technical leader of the industry. Hughes initially subsidized TWA with money from his Hughes Tool operation, but he later turned to outside lenders, who eventually forced Hughes to relinquish control of the firm. TWA became a formidable competitor to Pan Am in the transatlantic business, but it has been one of the weaker performers in the deregulated environment. In 1984 the carrier's holding company, Trans World Corp., which also owned Hilton International, Canteen Corp., and Century 21 Real Estate, spun off the airline. TWA came into play in 1985, and Carl Icahn snatched the company out from under the nose of Frank Lorenzo. Icahn subsequently had difficulty financing the complete acquisition, but labor concessions helped him complete the deal. In February 1986 TWA agreed to acquire Ozark Air Lines for $250 million.

United Air Lines began as the amalgamation of a large number of early aviation companies, including plane manufacturer Boeing and engine builder Pratt & Whitney, both of which were split off by government edict in 1934. William "Pat" Patterson, a former Wells Fargo banker, built United into one of the leading passenger carriers. It was first in revenues in the mid-1930s but lost that position to American at the end of the decade, only to regain it in 1961. United initially responded to deregulation by dropping routes but then joined the price-cutting wars with a vengeance. Chairman Richard Ferris, who took over in 1976, maneuvered United into one of the stronger spots among the majors. In 1985, after weathering a monthlong pilots' strike, Ferris went on a spending spree to use an accumulation of cash to turn the company into a travel industry powerhouse. He spent $750 million to buy Pan Am's Pacific routes, paid nearly $600 million to purchase the Hertz rental car business from RCA, and placed $3 billion worth of orders with Boeing for more than 100 new planes. In 1986 UAL spent nearly $1 billion to buy Trans World Corp.'s 88 Hilton hotels overseas.

SOURCE GUIDE

LEADING STOCK ANALYSTS AND EXPERTS

Michael Armellino, analyst at Goldman Sachs.

Michael Derchin, analyst at First Boston.

George James, president of the consulting firm Airline Economics Inc., Washington, D.C.

Robert Joedicke, analyst at Shearson Lehman Brothers.

Julius Maldutis, analyst at Salomon Brothers.

TRADE ASSOCIATIONS AND UNIONS

Air Line Pilots Association, Washington, D.C.

Air Transport Association of America, Washington, D.C.

International Association of Machinists and Aerospace Workers, Washington, D.C.

DATA SOURCES AND DIRECTORIES

Air Transport, an annual brochure of statistics (Washington, D.C.: Air Transport Association of America).

The Airline Handbook, an annual volume providing descriptions of the services and fleets of 2,000 carriers worldwide (Cranston, R.I.: AeroTravel Research).

The Airline Quarterly, a consulting firm's compendium of data and analysis (Washington, D.C.: Airline Economics).

FAA Statistical Handbook of Aviation, an annual volume of data on U.S. air traffic, carrier fleets, accidents, and other aviation information (Washington, D.C.: Federal Aviation Administration).

World Aviation Directory, a semiannual volume containing information on carriers, aviation services, airports, and organizations (Washington, D.C.: News Group Publications).

TRADE PUBLICATIONS

Air Transport World, monthly.

Aviation Daily.

Aviation Week and Space Technology.

Interavia (Geneva, Switzerland), monthly.

BOOKS AND REPORTS

Allen, Oliver E. *The Airline Builders.* Alexandria, Va.: Time-Life Books, 1981.

Bailey, Elizabeth E., David R. Graham, and Daniel P. Kaplan. *Deregulating the Airlines.* Cambridge, Mass.: MIT Press, 1985.

James, George W., ed. *Airline Economics.* Lexington, Mass.: Lexington Books, 1981.

Morrison, Steven, and Clifford Winston. *The Economic Effects of Airline Deregulation.* Washington, D.C.: Brookings Institution, 1986.

Sampson, Anthony. *Empires in the Sky.* New York: Random House, 1984.

Solberg, Carl. *Conquest of the Skies: A History of Commercial Aviation in America.* Boston: Little, Brown, 1979.

"Up against the Gloom and Doom: Aggressive Unionism at Eastern Airlines." *Labor Research Review,* Winter 1984. A special issue; additional articles appeared in the Summer 1984 issue.

CHAPTER TWENTY–FOUR

Automobiles

The manufacture of automobiles is emblematic both of the rise of U.S. industry through most of this century and of the crisis of the 1970s and 1980s. The auto sector pioneered modern mass production and through its relatively high wage rates helped to turn workers into middle-income consumers. The industry has given these consumers a wide range of choices in personal transportation but has been less than completely diligent in dealing with the harmful side effects of the motor vehicle age: air pollution and the carnage from highway accidents. For better or for worse, automobiles continue to play a major role in the economy. By 1984 Americans were spending to purchase and maintain their cars some $377 billion a year, one fifth of which represented new-car sales. Together with other motor vehicles the production, distribution, maintenance, and commercial use of autos accounts for some one sixth of total GNP.

THE RISE OF THE HORSELESS CARRIAGE

The quest for a self-propelled vehicle started inching toward fulfillment in the late 18th century as experiments were made with portable steam engines. Significant progress took a century to achieve, and the predominant method of propulsion came to be the internal-combustion engine. Motor vehicles in the modern sense are said to have begun with the machines constructed in Germany in the 1880s by Karl Benz and Gottlieb Daimler. By the 1890s a bona fide automobile industry was in existence in Europe.

The auto business developed more slowly in the United States. The American motor car age dates from the one-cylinder model produced by Charles and J. Frank Duryea of Springfield, Massachusetts, in 1893. The Duryea brothers had based their creation on a description of Karl Benz's car published in *Scientific American.*

During the following years scores of other inventors, including Henry Ford and Ransom Olds, jumped into the business with gasoline, steam, and even electric versions of horseless carriages. The entrepreneurs took advantage of the low capital requirements of a business in which they could buy their parts on credit and sell the finished products for cash.

Among the hundreds of entrants, the early leaders included the Pope Manufacturing Co. (the largest bicycle producer) and Olds' operation (Olds Motor Works), which started to establish Detroit as the center of the industry. In 1904 Olds split with his backer Samuel Smith and formed the Reo (for R. E. Olds) Motor Car Co.

A shadow was cast on the young industry around the turn of the century by a patent dispute. An inventor named George Selden had filed back in 1879 for a patent based on a particular kind of gasoline engine he saw at the Philadelphia Centennial Exposition in 1876. Selden engaged in legal maneuvers that resulted in the issuance of the patent being delayed until 1895— that is, until an industry that could exploit the technology had developed. In 1899 the Electric Vehicle Co. bought the rights to the Selden patent and began challenging the right of auto producers to produce gasoline-powered cars without paying a license fee.

Many automakers gave in to the pressure and in fact banded together in the Association of Licensed Automobile Manufacturers to restrict entry into the market. The association sought to undermine independents by publishing ads that warned their potential customers, "Don't buy a lawsuit with your car."

One producer who refused to recognize the claims of the association was Henry Ford, who established the Ford Motor Co. in 1903. Ford led the successful challenge to the patent cartel and also went against the industry's grain by trying to turn autos from luxuries selling at $1,000 or more into products that virtually anyone could afford.

Ford almost became part of an amalgamation of auto producers that William Crapo Durant was trying to put together. Durant had taken over the Buick Motor Car Co. in 1904 and made it into one of the more successful producers. After several deals fell through, Durant succeeded in 1908 in merging Buick, Oldsmobile, Cadillac, Oakland (later Pontiac), and some smaller companies into what he named General Motors.

That same year Ford achieved his dream of an inexpensive "car for the multitude" and introduced the Model T. After first offering the car at $850, Ford worked hard at bringing the price down, eventually getting it as low as $240. The farmers and other people of modest means targeted by Ford made the Model T an historic success. More than 15 million of them were sold over nearly two decades. The "Tin Lizzie," as it came to be called, made auto ownership into a mass phenomenon.

THE AGE OF FORDISM

The way Ford accomplished this feat was by transforming the process of production. Previously cars were manufactured in small workshops. Ford not only increased the scale of production but also invented a technique, the moving assembly line, that greatly increased the productivity of labor. He also encouraged stability in the work force by introducing the $5 a day minimum wage rate. This action shocked much of the business world—$5 was about twice the going rate for Detroit factory labor—but it was eventually seen as a shrewd move that enabled Ford workers to become Ford customers as well. Moreover Ford's wage policy was not part of a liberal approach to management. He ran the company with an iron fist; in 1928 the *New York Times* called him "an industrial fascist—the Mussolini of Detroit."

As Ford took a commanding lead in the industry, General Motors was plagued with financial problems related to its ambitious expansion plans. The company was taken over in 1910 by a banking syndicate, which brought Charles Nash and Walter Chrysler into top management. The ousted Durant then formed an alliance with race-car driver Louis Chevrolet in an effort to produce a low-cost car to compete with the Model T. Durant, an inveterate stock market operator, then began trading Chevrolet Motor Car Co. stock for GM shares; by 1916 he had regained control of GM and integrated Chevrolet and a group of suppliers, including battery maker Delco, into it. Durant also acquired the Fisher Body Co. and established the General Motors Acceptance Corp. to help customers buy on credit.

By the 1920s the industry was riding high: Annual production reached two million at the beginning of the decade, and the number of passenger cars in use climbed from 10.5 million in 1921 to 26.5 million in 1929. At the end of the decade nearly every American household owned an automobile.

Many of these customers were being drawn to the more attractive and comfortable models that Ford's rivals were putting on the market in competition with the Model T. Ford resisted the fact that the Model T was passé, and no one in the company was in a position to overrule him. Ford finally accepted the inevitable in 1927 and ceased production even though a replacement model was not ready.

Ford's stubbornness gave an opening to GM, which seized first place in the late 1920s and has never relinquished it. The rise of General Motors was also aided by the managerial talents of Alfred P. Sloan, Jr., who was president of the company from 1923 to 1937 and then chairman until he retired in 1956. Sloan, who took GM from the entrepreneurial era to the age of big business, was brought in by the Du Pont family, the major stockholders in the company, after Durant was pressured to resign amid a personal financial debacle.

While GM and Ford slugged it out at the top, countless other producers fell prey to bankruptcy and consolidation. The number of American automakers dwindled from hundreds to some 44 in 1927. The most successful of these emerged from the efforts of Walter Chrysler after he quit GM in disgust because of Durant and was then called from an early retirement in 1920 to rescue the Maxwell Motor Car Co. Chrysler turned Maxwell around, and after bringing out some successful models called Chryslers in 1924, he ended up taking over the company and renaming it after himself. After acquiring number five producer Dodge Brothers Manufacturing Co. in 1928, Chrysler joined GM and Ford in what became known as the Big Three.

The 1929 crash and the ensuing Depression burst the bubble of the rapidly expanding auto industry. Motor vehicle production peaked at 5.3 million in 1929 and did not reach that level again until 1949. While new-car sales plunged, auto registrations sank much less, indicating that while people could not afford new vehicles, they were continuing to operate the ones they already had rather than abandoning the automobile entirely. The use of the car was made more appealing by the widespread expansion of the highway system that took place during the 1930s, much of it under the auspices of New Deal public works projects.

During the war passenger car output was eventually suspended, and the automakers turned to the production of jeeps, tanks, aircraft, and other military items. Ford Motor was a bit quicker to aid the war effort than the company had been at the start of World War I, since Henry Ford (an idiosyncratic pacifist) had suffered a severe stroke in 1938 and had passed on control of the company to his son Edsel.

THE RISE AND FALL OF THE TAILFIN

The end of the war brought a tremendous demand for new passenger cars, and Detroit worked furiously to increase output. GM resumed its leading position, while Ford was in serious disarray. After Edsel Ford's untimely death in 1943, the 80-year-old founder returned as a caretaker until his grandson Henry Ford II was ready to step in. Upon assuming the throne in 1945 the 28-year-old Henry II set out to revive an operation that some analysts thought was close to collapse because of poor financial controls.

A total of nine passenger car producers were active in 1946: the Big Three, Studebaker, Packard, Nash, Hudson, Kaiser-Frazer, and Crosley. While the whole industry enjoyed the immediate postwar boom, the Korean War slump that hit the business in the early 1950s threatened the survival of the smaller firms. The result was further consolidation. In 1952 General Tire acquired Crosley and converted it to military work. Kaiser-Frazer merged with Jeep maker Willys-Overland in 1953 and ended up leaving the auto business. The following year Hudson and Nash combined to form American Motors Corp., and Studebaker and Packard joined forces. By the mid-1960s only the Big Three and American Motors remained.

The mid-1950s was another golden age for the business. Rising income levels and suburbanization made the United States an automobile-based society. And the cars that Detroit produced and consumers embraced became larger, more powerful, and embellished with tailfins and great quantities of chrome. In fact the emphasis on design represented the epitome of the strategy devised by Sloan back in the 1920s: that continual changes in styling and optional features would, despite rising prices, induce consumers to buy new cars more often.

The rise of driving at the expense of other forms of transportation was also promoted by federal policy. In 1956 Congress established the Interstate and Defense Highway System, which used excise taxes on fuel and tires in order to finance the construction of some 41,000 miles of limited-access highways throughout the country. (The system was completed by the early 1980s at a total cost of some $80 billion.)

As it turned out, the car-buying public's surrender to complete indulgence was short lived. The economic downturn of 1957–58 produced the first rush to smaller, more economical models. The problem was that Detroit had few of these to offer. In fact Ford had the misfortune of coming out during this period with its new full-sized car called the Edsel. The reception offered the car was so dismal that the term *Edsel* has entered the business vocabulary as a synonym for a new-product fiasco.

The one U.S. producer that was sitting pretty during this first small-car trend was tiny American Motors, which had a previously obscure model called the Rambler, originally brought out by Nash. Rambler sales soared in the late 1950s, and AMC president George Romney used the opportunity to denounce the typical offering from Detroit as a gas-guzzling "dinosaur."

The other beneficiaries of the trend were foreign producers. Imports, which had previously accounted for an insignificant portion of the market, jumped to 207,000 in 1957 and reached 610,000 by 1959.

By the early 1960s the bigger producers were finally bringing out their own small-car models, including "sporty" ones such as Ford's popular Mustang. Detroit's move overwhelmed the Rambler and stemmed the rise of imports, though the dirt-cheap Volkswagen Beetle retained a loyal following among the young and hip. This is not to say that the Big Three abandoned their gas-guzzlers. Full-sized cars did end up more streamlined than before, but they tended to become longer and heavier each year. At the same time, small cars became a permanent market segment.

In addition to compacts, the industry leaders introduced subcompacts in 1970—the Vega from GM, the Ford Pinto, and AMC's Gremlin.

THE NADER ASSAULT

Issues of automobile size and fuel economy became bound up with the controversy over safety that erupted during the 1960s. Many observers accuse the industry of having ignored safety issues for decades. In the late 1950s books such as John Keats' *The Insolent Chariots* brought the issue to the center of public debate, and in 1965 Senator Abraham Ribicoff held influential hearings on the subject. Yet it was publication of a book later that year by a lawyer named Ralph Nader, who had done research for Ribicoff, that galvanized public opinion on the safety issue.

Nader's *Unsafe at Any Speed*, which focused on the problems of the Chevrolet Corvair, opened with the sweeping declaration: "For over half a century, the automobile has brought death, injury, and the most inestimable sorrow and deprivation to millions of Americans." GM responded to Nader's depiction of the rear-engine Corvair as a death trap by trying to discredit the author; GM hired private detectives to spy on Nader. Instead of coming up with dirt on him, the auto giant ended up having to pay Nader $425,000 in damages and publicly apologize to him. The publicity also helped propel Nader into becoming the country's premier consumer advocate.

The uproar generated by Nader helped prompt Congress to pass the National Traffic and Motor Safety Act of 1966. The law authorized the federal government to establish safety standards for new cars, and the result was a steady decline in highway death rates for a number of years. Safety was deemphasized during the industry's economic troubles in the 1970s, and the Reagan administration sought to reverse earlier government rules such as a 1983 deadline for the installation of passive restraints (automatic seat belts or inflatable air bags) in all new cars. The deregulatory crusade ran into legal obstacles, and in 1984 Transportation secretary Elizabeth Dole offered to drop the revised 1987 deadline for passive restraints if two thirds of the states passed mandatory seat belt laws. As of mid-1986 half of the states had acted.

The mid-1960s was also the culmination of years of quiet debate over auto pollution. The link between cars and problems with air quality was first suggested in the analysis of the smog troubles of Los Angeles in the 1940s. The recognition of cars as a culprit escalated in the following decade, and in the early 1960s California established the first emission standards, which forced automakers to install blow-back devices (which controlled crankcase exhaust) on all automobiles sold in the state. Detroit, seeking to avert federal legislation, decided to put the devices on all new cars nationwide in 1963. Yet Congress acted anyway in 1965, passing the Motor Vehicle Air Pollution Act, which authorized the secretary of health, education and welfare to set emission standards and required control devices on all new cars beginning in 1968. Stricter rules were included in the Clean Air Act of 1970.

The energy problems of the 1970s prompted Congress to go even further. Legislation passed in 1975 required the National Highway Traffic Safety Administration to regulate fuel economy by requiring manufacturers to meet certain average levels for their models as a group. Each automaker was supposed to achieve a corporate average fuel economy (CAFE) of 18 miles per gallon by 1978 and 27.5 by 1985. The industry grumbled and lobbied against the rules but succeeded only in winning delays rather than abolition.

SMALL IS UNAVOIDABLE

The auto industry entered the 1970s with visions of continuing prosperity. There was some concern over a rise in imports as well as signs that the auto market was highly saturated. Auto managers were also shaken up by the unrest among blue-collar workers at places such as GM's Lordstown plant. Yet these problems were overshadowed by the expectation that a robust, even if inflation-prone, economy would keep automobile sales healthy.

This optimism was quickly and resoundingly crushed by the 1973 oil embargo. The resulting gasoline shortages panicked auto buyers just after the 1974 models had gone on sale. This, combined with a rapid series of price increases by Detroit, brought about a drop of more than 20 percent in new-car sales in 1974. Detroit was caught with product lines dominated by large, gas-guzzling cars as Americans, much more than in the late 1950s, were demanding smaller, fuel-efficient vehicles.

Surprisingly it turned out that the behemoth General Motors was quickest to adapt to the "small is beautiful" sentiment. GM brought out the tiny Chevette in a record 18 months' time (compared to the usual 36 months for new designs) and redirected billions of dollars of investment toward a new line of small, front-wheel-drive compacts. These so-called X-cars, introduced in the late 1970s, were a tremendous success and allowed GM to achieve a substantial boost in market share at the expense of slower-moving Ford and Chrysler. The smaller of the Big Three were also hit much more severely by the rise in Japanese and other imports, from 15 percent of the market in 1970 to 22 percent in 1979.

The U.S. producers resolved to meet both the Japanese challenge and the fuel economy deadlines by investing some $75 billion over a decade to accomplish what amounted to a remaking of the industry: extensive new designs and massive amounts of new plant and equipment, including a major investment in automation.

The road to revival contained a major pothole—a disastrous dive in car sales that began in mid-1979 and made 1980 into the worst year in the history of the industry. In fact the automakers' aggregate losses of more than $4 billion in net income that year constituted the worst annual performance of any American industry ever.

Chrysler, the perennial weakling of the Big Three, was the hardest hit. The company came close to bankruptcy and was saved only when its new president Lee Iacocca, hired in 1978 soon after he was fired from the same job at Ford in a dispute over strategy with Henry II, turned to the federal government for help.

Iacocca convinced the Carter administration that the collapse of Chrysler would have a disastrous effect on an already weakened economy and thus got Washington to provide the company with up to $1.2 billion in loan guarantees. The deal, which involved substantial concessions from Chrysler's employees as well as its creditors, kept the company afloat, though recovery was slow in coming.

The industry did not show strong signs of revival until some time after the 1981 decision by the Japanese government to observe "voluntary export restraints" (a euphemism for quotas) that restricted the Japanese share of the U.S. market to 1.68 million cars a year, or some 20 percent. By this time total imports had captured more than a quarter of the market.

U.S. automakers used this period of protection to cut their costs and raise their productivity drastically. The quest was to reduce what was said to be a $2,000 differential in favor of the Japanese in the cost of producing a typical subcompact car. This meant repeated efforts to get contract concessions from a sharply reduced labor force, radical changes in manufacturing techniques, and the adoption of Japanese methods such as "just in time" inventory management. The fruits of these policies were seen in things such as the automakers' break-even point; at Chrysler that figure was reduced from 2.4 million units in 1979 to 1.1 million in 1983.

Such cost controls, along with steadily increasing car prices, allowed the industry to enjoy a dramatic comeback starting in 1983. While the import challenge had not been licked, U.S. automakers were earning a bundle on those cars that they did manage to sell. Their combined earnings leaped from a token $82 million in 1982 to an impressive $5.7 billion in 1983 and an astounding $8.9 billion in 1984. Chrysler, the one-time ward of the state, started repaying its government-backed loans seven years ahead of time, and the company's dramatic turnaround made Iacocca into something of a business folk hero.

Despite the recovery of the U.S. producers, the import problem was far from solved. After declining from 21.8 percent in 1981 to 18.3 percent in 1984, the Japanese share of the market climbed up to 20.1 percent the following year as the export restraint agreement expired. Total imports in 1985 were up to 25.7 percent.

THE GLOBAL CAR

Moreover foreign competition was no longer limited to vehicles shipped from abroad. Starting in the early 1980s several Japanese producers established U.S. operations. The projects were in part a response to pressure from the United Automobile Workers (UAW) and others concerned about the decline of U.S. auto employment. The first foreign automaker to set up shop in the United States was West Germany's Volkswagen in 1978. Although VW's Pennsylvania operation ended up with a high degree of labor unrest, the Japanese followed suit. Honda began assembling Accords in Marysville, Ohio, in 1982. Nissan, which started producing trucks at its Smyrna, Tennessee, plant in 1983, expanded to automobiles two years later. Toyota got involved in both a joint venture with General Motors in California and an operation of its own scheduled to begin production in Kentucky in 1988. Mazda announced plans in 1984 to build an assembly plant in Michigan, and Mitsubishi said it would produce cars together with Chrysler in Illinois. All of this was in addition to French producer Renault's purchase of 46 percent of the common stock of American Motors in 1980.

The GM–Toyota and Chrysler-Mitsubishi joint ventures indicate that American producers have used foreign investment as an opportunity to learn the "secrets" of the Japanese success in automaking. GM and Toyota's New United Motor Manufacturing Inc. was established to produce a new subcompact using Japanese designs, methods, and labor policies. GM apparently planned to apply some of what it hoped to learn from Toyota in the wholly owned Saturn subsidiary that the company announced in 1985. Whereas both Saturn and the Toyota joint venture will recognize the UAW, the plan was to completely remake labor relations in a more cooperative mold. The attitude of the Japanese companies operating on their own in the United States toward unions has been mixed. Mazda, for instance, decided not to resist unionization at its planned Michigan facility, while problems with Honda in Ohio prompted the UAW to abandon its organizing effort at that company.

Foreign investment in the United States and joint ventures are only part of a much larger process of internationalization that has accelerated in the auto industry during the 1980s. The basic trend started some time ago. Ford established a Canadian subsidiary back in 1903 and began assembling knockdown versions of the Model T in Britain in 1911. Ford kept spreading, and by 1920 the company had operations in 20 countries; there was even a licensing arrangement with the Soviet Union.

General Motors followed suit, moving into manufacturing as well as assembly abroad. GM purchased Vauxhall Motors of Britain in 1925 and the German firm Adam Opel four years later. After World War II the two U.S. leaders, along with Chrysler to a lesser extent, became truly global companies.

With the rise to prominence of the Japanese producers in the late 1960s, the U.S. Big Three moved to get a piece of their action. In 1969 Chrysler announced that it would acquire 35 percent of Mitsubishi Motors (though it ended up buying only 15 percent). The following year GM announced a joint venture and technical cooperation with Isuzu as well as a 34 percent investment in that company. Ford revealed that it was negotiating with Toyo Kogyo (now known as Mazda), but it was not until 1979 that Ford's 25 percent investment in the Japanese company was worked out.

Another element of internationalization emerged from the decision by Ford and GM in the late 1970s to go beyond simply producing different cars in many different countries for sale in those same or neighboring nations. The first step was to standardize designs internationally so that what was essentially the same car could be marketed around the world. The leading example of this was Ford's Fiesta, introduced in 1976. The next stage involved producing what came to be called the global car. Plants in a variety of countries were used to produce components that were brought together in several centralized assembly facilities. Ford began assembling its Escort in three countries with components manufactured by Ford factories in nine nations. This technique of "global sourcing" allowed Ford to take advantage of maximum economies of scale in the component plants and also made it less vulnerable to strikes or other disruptions in any one country.

The inability of the U.S. producers to obtain strong and permanent import restrictions has prompted them to make yet another international move: getting into the import business themselves. Traditionally, American automakers produced cars for the U.S. market in the United States, and their foreign production operations were aimed at overseas markets. By the mid-1980s they were getting involved in arrangements that once would have been unthinkable. Ford announced plans to buy cars from South Korean and Taiwanese producers and sell them under the Ford name in the United States. The company also indicated that it would build a plant in Mexico to produce cars for the U.S. market. General Motors also turned to South Korea, forming a joint venture with Daewoo, and announced plans to have Japan's Suzuki produce cars that would be sold as the Chevrolet Sprint. In both cases the target market is the United States.

Such moves have begun to blur the distinction between imports and domestics and could end up undermining the "Buy American" campaigns pushed by the Big Three for many years. The trend also generated more support for a proposal, pushed by the UAW since the early 1980s, that would require any car sold in the United States to have a high percentage of American labor and components. "Domestic content" legislation twice passed the House but died in the Senate.

Yet the response from Detroit is that such arrangements are necessary in the face of the increasing competitiveness of the business and the arrival in the United States of new low-end products from countries such as Yugoslavia and South Korea. The Big Three have in effect admitted that they simply cannot produce subcompacts profitably and want to make some money selling small cars produced by others. However much this trend toward "sponsored imports" continues, it is clear that the automobile competition will continue to be waged in complicated international arenas.

LABOR RELATIONS

Collective bargaining and labor relations in the automobile industry were for much of the 20th century the pacesetter for the remainder of American industry. Tentative organizing among autoworkers began as the industry developed around the turn of the century. Such efforts were inhibited by leading companies such as Ford, which initiated the famous $5-a-day minimum wage and established a Sociological Department to regulate the personal lives of workers. Later the company used a more directly antiunion approach in the creation of an internal security force called the Service Department, led by the notorious Harry Bennett.

It was thus not surprising that the auto sector remained largely unorganized until the 1930s. Following the Roosevelt administration's affirmation of the right to collective bargaining, the AFL began halfheartedly chartering auto unions. Frustrated with oppressive working conditions and seasonal layoffs that kept annual incomes low, autoworkers responded eagerly to organizing drives.

In 1935 the AFL departed from its craft orientation and issued a limited industrial charter to the United Automobile Workers of America. Industrial union advocates were unhappy with the AFL's restrictions, and in 1936 the UAW joined the newly established CIO.

Given the rapid increase in membership, the UAW moved quickly to win recognition from the Big Three, which had been resisting federal directives on labor policy. GM was chosen as the first target. Short strikes at various sites around the country were followed by a nationwide action against the company in January 1937. The UAW successfully employed the tactic of sit-down strikes and plant occupations, most notably at the Fisher Body plant in Flint, Michigan, where an attempt by police to storm the plant was beaten back by the workers. GM capitulated in February 1937, and Chrysler followed suit later in the year.

Things were more difficult at Ford. The organizing effort was curtailed after an unsuccessful strike at the River Rouge plant, which culminated in the infamous "Battle of the Overpass," in which UAW organizers were attacked by Harry Bennett's private security force. The UAW had more success in 1941, when Ford gave in to strong government pressure and recognized the union.

In the postwar period the moderate faction led by Walter Reuther defeated left-wingers inside the union and went on to lead a number of strikes, including a critical 113-day walkout against GM in 1945–46 in which the union failed in its attempt to win a 30 percent raise to make up for wartime inflation. The union achieved only 18.5 percent, the same amount that had been awarded at other companies without a strike. Other actions against GM culminated in a 1948 agreement that systematized wage increases through annual improvement factors and cost-of-living adjustments.

In the following years the UAW won steady improvements for their members, including pioneering provisions such as supplementary unemployment benefits and company-paid pensions. The union's cooperative relationship with management averted strikes, but it heightened tension between rank-and-file workers and the UAW leadership. The result was periodic insurgencies on the shop floor, especially when a new generation of workers entered the factories in the late 1960s. Militant black workers brought the black-power movement into auto plants with the creation of the League of Revolutionary Black Workers.

This unrest had its most prominent expression in the 1972 strike against oppressive working conditions at GM's Lordstown plant. Lordstown became a symbol of the "blue-collar revolt," the frustration of young workers with the regimentation of the factory and the demand for a more humanized work environment.

The ability of the UAW to win steady contract improvements came to an end with the auto industry crisis in the late 1970s. In 1979 the union agreed to $243 million in concessions to ailing Chrysler, and the federal government insisted on another $200 million as one of the terms for the government bailout of the company. At the same time, UAW president Douglas Fraser was given a seat on Chrysler's board of directors.

By the early 1980s, with several hundred thousand autoworkers out of work indefinitely, the UAW felt it had to give in to concessions sought by GM and Ford as well as yet more demands from Chrysler. Some of this lost ground was regained when the industry rebounded beginning in 1983, a process that included a 12-day strike at Chrysler in 1985. Yet there remained a tug-of-war between company claims that the labor-cost differential with Japan had to be narrowed and worker resistance to an erosion in the standard of living.

The leadership of the UAW, taken over by Owen Bieber in 1983, dealt with the problem by promoting a more cooperative relationship with management while seeking to expand job security and worker participation. At the same time, the union sought to slow down the disappearance of auto jobs by lobbying for protectionist policies, as in its unsuccessful campaign for domestic-content legislation. The failure of this effort was highlighted in November 1986 when GM announced plans to eliminate 29,000 jobs by closing 11 plants.

The union had mixed experiences with the Japanese auto companies that were setting up U.S. operations, but GM agreed without a battle to union representation at both its joint venture with Toyota in California and its new Saturn subsidiary in Tennessee. However, in both cases the UAW granted management a greater degree of operating flexibility. The Japanese-style contract for the Saturn project has been criticized by some labor figures, including Victor Reuther (one of the founders of the UAW) because of its use of an incentive pay system.

LEADING COMPANIES

American Motors Corp., created by the 1954 merger of Nash and Hudson, has remained by far the smallest and weakest of the four U.S.-based producers. AMC's moment of glory in the small-car wave of the late 1950s was short lived, and the company only survived on the basis of the Jeep business it purchased from Kaiser Industries in 1970. AMC achieved a greater degree of stability when Renault made a major investment in 1980, but the company lost its fourth-place position among U.S.-based manufacturers to Honda of America.

Chrysler, the traditional weak sister of the Big Three, used a federal bailout starting in 1979 to help it rise from the brink of bankruptcy to reasonable prosperity by the middle of the 1980s. The company was built out of the ailing Maxwell Motor Co. in the 1920s by former GM executive Walter Chrysler. Chrysler jumped to number three with the purchase of Dodge in 1928 and held the position and managed to survive—sometimes just barely— while dozens of other companies fell by the wayside. President Lee Iacocca, who took over in 1978, made himself the personal embodiment of industrial rebirth and as a result got himself touted as a Democratic presidential candidate. Chrysler has lessened its dependence on automobiles a bit by purchasing corporate jet producer Gulfstream Aerospace, E. F. Hutton Credit Corp., and Finance America.

Ford Motor Co. was the first great U.S. auto producer. Founder Henry Ford took what was mostly a luxury item and turned it into a new mode of transportation for the masses. He also revolutionized factory production with the moving assembly line and high wages. Ford resisted phasing out his beloved Model T, and the company went into a decline in the 1920s that lasted until the founder's grandson Henry Ford II took over in 1945. The company was modernized with the help of a group of former air force systems analysts (known as the "Whiz Kids"), including Robert McNamara, who became president of Ford in the 1950s and later went on to other sorts of fame in the public sector. The company first went public in 1958. During the 1970s Ford was plagued with charges relating to safety problems with its Pinto subcompact and was also slow to respond to the shift to smaller cars following the oil crisis. The company remained very strong abroad, however, and by the mid-1980s Ford was enjoying a recovery due in part to the success of its new Taurus and Mercury Sable cars.

General Motors has led the U.S. auto industry since the 1920s. Originally formed as a merger of several early producers, GM was transformed by Alfred P. Sloan, Jr., from an entrepreneurial operation into one of the leading examples of modern corporate organization. During the 1970s GM was quick to respond to the switch in consumer preference to smaller cars, surprising observers with its new creative and aggressive stance. The company went so far as to bring out a subcompact version of the traditional luxury car Cadillac. GM invested heavily in new plant and equipment for the switchover in design, including a $5 billion commitment to create an entirely new subsidiary called Saturn to build subcompacts using advanced technology and a different approach to labor relations. Another bold move was the establishment of a joint venture with Toyota in California. In the mid-1980s the company began diversifying into nonauto businesses. GM spent $2.6 billion to purchase Electronic Data Systems (Ross Perot's computer service firm) and $4.7 billion for Hughes Aircraft. But in late 1986, after facing great difficulty integrating EDS into its operations, GM was reported to be seeking a buyer for the business. Tired of Perot's criticisms of the corporation's strategy, GM bought out his holdings in the company for $700 million and removed him from the board of directors.

SOURCE GUIDE

LEADING STOCK ANALYSTS AND EXPERTS

David Cole, director of the Office for the Study of Automotive Transportation, University of Michigan at Ann Arbor.

David Healy, analyst at Drexel Burnham Lambert.

Maryann Keller, analyst at Furman, Selz, Mager, Dietz & Birney, New York.

J. D. Power & Associates, auto market researchers, Westlake Village, California.

TRADE ASSOCIATIONS AND UNIONS

Motor Vehicle Manufacturers Association, Detroit.

Society of Automotive Engineers, Warrendale, Pennsylvania.

United Automobile, Aerospace and Agricultural Implement Workers of America, Detroit.

DATA SOURCES AND DIRECTORIES

Economic Indicators, a quarterly compilation of industry statistics; *Facts and Figures,* an annual data book; and the annual *World Motor Vehicle Data* (Detroit: Motor Vehicle Manufacturers Association).

Ward's Automotive Yearbook, an annual review of industry trends and statistics (Detroit: Ward's Communications).

World Cars, an annual guide edited by the Automobile Club of Italy (Pelham, N.Y.: Herald Books).

TRADE PUBLICATIONS

Automotive Industries, monthly.

Automotive News, weekly.

Ward's Automotive Reports, weekly.

Ward's Auto World, monthly.

BOOKS AND REPORTS

Altshuler, Alan, Martin Anderson, Daniel Jones, Daniel Roos, and James Womack. *The Future of the Automobile: The Report of MIT's International Automobile Program.* Cambridge, Mass.: MIT Press, 1984.

Crandall, Robert W., Howard H. Gruenspecht, Theodore E. Keeler, and Lester B. Lare. *Regulating the Automobile.* Washington, D.C.: Brookings Institution, 1986.

Flink, James J. *The Car Culture.* Cambridge, Mass.: MIT Press, 1975.

Katz, Harry C. *Shifting Gears: Changing Labor Relations in the U.S. Automobile Industry.* Cambridge, Mass.: MIT Press, 1985.

Maxcy, George. *The Multinational Automobile Industry.* New York: St. Martin's Press, 1981.

Moritz, Michael, and Barrett Seaman. *Going for Broke: The Chrysler Story.* Garden City, N.Y.: Doubleday Publishing, 1981.

National Research Council. *The Competitive Status of the U.S. Automobile Industry*. Washington, D.C.: National Academy Press, 1982.

Rae, John. *The American Automobile: A Brief History*. Chicago: University of Chicago Press, 1965.

———. *The American Automobile Industry*. Boston: Twayne, 1984.

Rothschild, Emma. *Paradise Lost: The Decline of the Auto-Industrial Age*. New York: Random House, 1973.

Serrin, William. *The Company and the Union*. New York: Alfred A. Knopf, 1973.

Sobel, Robert. *Car Wars*. New York: E. P. Dutton, 1984.

U.S. Commerce Department, Office of Business Analysis. *The U.S. Motor Vehicle and Equipment Industry since 1958*. Washington, D.C., 1985.

U.S. International Trade Commission. *The Internationalization of the Automobile Industry and Its Effect on the U.S. Automobile Industry*. Washington, D.C., 1985.

White, Lawrence J. *The Automobile Industry since 1945*. Cambridge, Mass.: Harvard University Press, 1971.

CHAPTER TWENTY–FIVE

Steel

Steel is one of the first examples that comes to mind when one thinks of heavy industry. A country's steel output is considered a primary indicator of its level of economic development. In the United States during the past decade steel has also been a leading symbol of industrial decline. The once powerful steel sector has been humbled by foreign competitors such as Japan, West Germany, and even Third World countries such as Brazil and South Korea. By 1986 two leading producers were operating under the protection of the bankruptcy laws. The $52 billion U.S. steel business is being rapidly transformed and with it the future of dozens of communities and tens of thousands of workers.

STEEL'S GOLDEN AGE

The development of the American steel industry proceeded in tandem with the growth of the entire U.S. economy. Rapid expansion started in the 1860s with the introduction of the Bessemer process and the widening of markets such as oil drilling and the railroads. By the end of the 19th century the United States became the international leader in steel, producing 37 percent of the world's output in 1900. At the same time, what had been a fairly fragmented industry was becoming more and more concentrated. The most significant outcome of this merger wave was the creation of the U.S. Steel Corporation in 1901. Big Steel, as it came to be known, was formed by Judge Elbert Gary and J. P. Morgan through the merger of the Carnegie Steel Co. and nine other firms, its total capital of $1,400,000,000 making it the first billion-dollar corporation. Many of the other large firms that have survived to the present, including Inland and Armco, were also formed in this period.

Years of consolidation turned steel into a classic case of oligopoly. From 1907 to 1911 the noncompetitive pricing policies of the large steel companies emerged unabashedly out of dinners that Judge Gary hosted for top executives at the Waldorf-Astoria Hotel in New York. Even after congressional antitrust pressure put an end to the Gary dinners, the industry played follow-the-leader, with U.S. Steel setting prices. The inexorable rise of steel prices frequently vexed politicians seeking to contain inflation. In 1962 an exasperated President John Kennedy publicly berated U.S. Steel for an announced 3.5 percent price increase and successfully pressured other companies to break ranks, thus giving rise to the practice known as "jawboning."

The beginning of the end of U.S. predominance in steel came after World War II, as foreign competitors rebuilt their war-ravaged plants, using modern technology. The U.S. share of world output reached 56.7 percent in 1947 and began to decline. By 1958 the figure sank below 30 percent and has remained there ever since. U.S. Steel constructed a new integrated facility (known as a greenfield site) in the early 1950s, but only one other followed in the industry. Meanwhile foreign rivals, especially Japan, invested heavily in new plants that employed basic oxygen furnaces (which are much faster than open-hearth furnaces in refining molten iron and scrap into steel) and continuous casting (a process that eliminates several steps in turning raw steel into semifinished forms). American steelmakers followed suit but at a much slower rate. Enjoying a cost advantage, foreign producers were able to underprice U.S. companies to such an extent that the share of the American market captured by imports rose from less than 1 percent in the late 1950s to more than 26 percent in 1984.

THE MINIMILL PHENOMENON

The big integrated steelmakers have also faced a domestic challenge. Abandoning the traditional "bigger is better" approach of the industry, a number of companies have prospered by selecting a niche and remaining relatively small. These producers, known as minimills, use electric furnaces and continuous casters (and often nonunion labor) to turn scrap steel into simple products such as concrete-reinforcing bars that are sold in regional markets.

During the 1970s and early 1980s, minimill operators such as Nucor and Florida Steel were hailed as success stories (along with specialty steelmakers such as Allegheny Ludlum) in an industry otherwise beset with endless tribulation. But by the mid-1980s the luster of the minimills was tarnishing as overcapacity and rising costs set in. Still, the 60 or so U.S. minimills, which accounted for some 20 percent of domestic output in the mid-1980s, are here to stay. Even a large integrated producer such as Bethlehem acknowledged their virtues by announcing in 1985 that it would turn its bar, rod, and wire unit in Johnstown, Pennsylvania, into a minimill. The specialty producers, which make noncarbon steel varieties such as stainless, account for a small portion of the industry but are much healthier than the integrated producers.

The major U.S. producers have responded to their increasingly precarious state in several ways. One of the main tacks has been to seek assistance from the government in slowing down the flow of imports. Steel executives (along with steel union officials) have been among the loudest voices calling for a protectionist trade policy, but their efforts have had mixed results.

Starting back in the Nixon administration there were programs to negotiate voluntary import limits with foreign producers. This provided some relief, but the global recession of the mid-1970s prompted steelmakers everywhere to sell more in the world's largest market. The squeeze on U.S. producers brought about major mill closings and layoffs in 1977, and the ensuing political pressure—including the formation of a 200-member Steel Caucus in Congress—prompted the Carter administration to act. Treasury undersecretary Anthony Solomon put together a trigger-price system under which dumping charges would be brought when an importer's price dropped below what was determined to be typical Japanese cost levels.

This trigger-price mechanism did not do a great deal to reduce imports, and some critics argued that it even promoted dumping by exporting countries with higher costs than Japan. The Reagan administration, with its staunch free-trade policy, initially declined to provide any relief to the beleaguered industry, but in the midst of the 1984 presidential election the political pressures were enough to get even Reagan to act. His approach was to seek a new set of voluntary-restraint agreements aimed at limiting imports of finished steel to 18.5 percent of the U.S. market. The industry, in exchange, dropped its dumping suits.

The agreements that were signed had little effect initially—import penetration dropped only slightly to 25.2 percent in 1985—but greater impact began to be felt the following year. However, stagnant demand and low prices still spelled financial trouble for the industry.

A SLEW OF STRATEGIES

The U.S. steel industry has not limited its response to crisis conditions to calling for import restrictions. The major producers have also embarked on one of the most dramatic restructuring processes ever attempted. Big Steel has taken the lead here as elsewhere. U.S. Steel (now USX) diversified to the extent that steel accounted for only about a quarter of its revenues and even less of its net income. The biggest and most controversial move the company made out of steel was its $6 billion purchase of Marathon Oil in 1982. Three years later it followed that with the announcement that it would purchase Texas Oil & Gas for about $4 billion. Other aspects of restructuring include:

Mergers.   Steel played a role in the conglomerate wave in the late 1960s as Lykes bought Youngstown Sheet and Tube, LTV bought Jones & Laughlin, and NVF acquired Sharon Steel. More recent consolidations include LTV's merger with Lykes in 1978 and LTV's purchase of Republic Steel in 1984, which made LTV the second-largest American producer. U.S. Steel sought to purchase National Steel in 1984 but was rebuffed by the Justice Department.

Joint Ventures and International Purchase Agreements.   Although the major producers howl about foreign competition, they have frequently found it convenient to make deals with their overseas rivals. Japanese companies have invested in U.S. firms, as in Nippon Kokan's 50 percent ownership of National Steel (now a subsidiary of National Intergroup) and Nisshin Steel's 10 percent interest in Wheeling-Pittsburgh. Nisshin and Wheeling had planned a joint venture for making rust-resistant steel but the plan was postponed after Wheeling entered Chapter 11. Several major companies purchase some raw steel from foreign producers, and U.S. Steel generated a major controversy in 1983 when it announced a plan (later abandoned) to purchase slabs from British Steel's Ravenscraig mill in Scotland. In late 1985 the company announced a joint venture with South Korea's Pohang Iron and Steel to produce sheet and tin products in California.

Worker Buyouts.   When National Intergroup decided it wanted to get rid of its huge Weirton operation it turned to the people with the greatest interest in keeping the mill open: the workers. In 1982 National offered to sell Weirton to the employees through an employee stock ownership plan. The 8,000 workers approved the plan though it involved wage cuts and a six-year no-strike clause. Worker ownership commenced in 1984, and so far the company has done reasonably well.

The future of the American steel industry is likely to involve more of these strategies along with further retrenchment of older and less-productive facilities. It may also involve the entry of other companies into Chapter 11, following the lead of Wheeling-Pittsburgh in 1985 and LTV in 1986.

Some observers foresee an international two-tier arrangement in which Third World countries produce the bulk of raw steel while the more developed countries focus on sophisticated spe-

The 10 Largest Steel Producers, by 1985 Raw Steel Output (Tons 000s)

1.	U.S. Steel	16,693
2.	LTV Steel	13,112
3.	Bethlehem Steel	10,440
4.	Inland Steel	6,069
5.	Armco	5,347
6.	National Steel	4,785
7.	Rouge Steel	2,753
8.	Weirton Steel	2,695
9.	North Star Steel	1,803
10.	Wheeling-Pittsburgh	1,754

Source: *Metal Statistics 1986.* Copyright Fairchild Publications, a division of Capital Cities Media Inc.

cialty steel. Whatever the exact configuration, the steel industry in the United States and abroad is bound to look very different in the years to come.

LABOR RELATIONS

Some observers of the steel industry argue that the root of the crisis of the large producers is the high price of labor. It became commonplace for steel executives, Wall Street analysts, and others to rail against what was alleged to be the $26-an-hour steelworker and to assert that labor costs had risen much faster than steel prices. Union analysts have argued that such figures ignored the increased productivity of labor and have pointed out that a comparison of the average price of a ton of steel and the wage cost per ton showed the former rising much faster. They also charged the industry with spending too little on capital improvements that would cut costs.

Labor costs and labor relations in steel are the product of a turbulent history. Organizing efforts began in the late 1850s with the creation of the Sons of Vulcan. After nearly two decades of uneven growth this group merged with other unions to form the Amalgamated Association of Steel and Iron Workers in 1876. Labor agitation increased in the 1880s, and by the end of that decade steel magnate Andrew Carnegie was trying to create a union-free environment in his mills. The conflict culminated in the violent clash of strikers and Pinkerton guards in July 1892 in Homestead, Pennsylvania. The failure of the strike ushered in a period of union decline that lasted until the 1930s.

In the 1930s the newly created Congress of Industrial Organizations established a Steel Workers Organizing Committee (SWOC), which in 1937 succeeded in negotiating a contract with U.S. Steel. Support for unionization spread rapidly among steelworkers, but independent producers (known collectively as Little Steel) refused to deal with the SWOC, prompting a series of bitter strikes. It was not until the early 1940s that Little Steel was unionized, through the intervention of the Roosevelt administration's War Labor Board. The SWOC became the United Steelworkers of America (USWA) in 1942, with Philip Murray as its president.

After the war the USWA took a leading role in enabling workers to share fully in the postwar prosperity. Industrywide strikes in 1946 and 1949 established a pattern under which the union won regular and substantial pay increases for its members. Because of steel's central role in the economy the White House took a keen interest in the negotiations and sought to discourage strikes. When contract bargaining was stalled in 1952 during the Korean War and a strike seemed imminent, President Harry Truman took the unprecedented step of seizing the steel mills with the intention of keeping them open. The Supreme Court quickly ruled his action unconstitutional, and the strike resumed until a suitable wage package was agreed upon.

The 116-day strike in 1959 was a turning point for labor relations in steel. Under the leadership of I. W. Abel, who took over the USWA in 1965, the union and the industry pursued what was called a "human relations" approach, which meant negotiating contracts without the brinksmanship of strike situations. This concept was formalized in 1973 through the Experimental Negotiating Agreement (ENA), under which the USWA gave up the right to strike in exchange for guaranteed minimum wage increases. As conditions in the industry worsened, the ENA came under increasing attack from both steel companies and rank-and-file workers. The ENA was a central issue in Edward Sadlowski's insurgent (and unsuccessful) campaign for the presidency of the union in 1977.

In 1980 industry negotiators declined to renew the ENA, so the union was free to call a strike when its contract expired in 1983. Because of the crisis condition of steel that year, the talk was not of strikes but of concessions. For the first time in the history of the union the basic steel agreement included givebacks such as a pay cut, loss of cost-of-living adjustments, and reductions in holiday and vacation time. By late 1985 the aggregate value of concessions granted by steelworkers reached $1.4 billion.

A new chapter of militancy began in 1985 at one of the weaker producers. Wheeling-Pittsburgh, after a long time on the brink, succumbed to financial pressures and filed for protection under Chapter 11 of the bankruptcy law. More than 8,000 union workers walked off the job in July to protest the company's successful petition to the bankruptcy judge to allow it to abrogate its USWA contract and demand an 18 percent wage cut. The strike brought about the resignation of Wheeling chairman Dennis Carney, but after three months the workers returned to the job with a new contract that still included a large pay reduction as well as a less generous pension plan.

At other companies the approach of the USWA under the new leadership of Lynn Williams has been one of accepting the reality of the industry's crisis but seeking something in exchange for concessions. This so-called entrepreneurial strategy has led to agreements with a division of Bethlehem Steel and Kaiser Aluminum in which workers are to participate in profit sharing plans and receive shares of stock while giving up some wages and benefits.

In 1986 the USWA, facing the prospect of more demands for concessions, entered separate contract talks with each of the steel producers; industry leaders had indicated the previous year that they wanted to abandon the coordinated bargaining that had been the rule for three decades. The union announced ahead of time that it would agree to givebacks only if a company could show it was in "dire economic circumstances." The USWA also decided to let rank-and-file workers vote on contracts for the first time in the union's history.

The first settlement was reached in March with ailing LTV, which even the union admitted was in danger of going bankrupt (as it did several months later). The USWA agreed to cut wages and benefits by $3.15 an hour in exchange for a profit sharing plan (if profits ever returned to the loss-ridden company). Then the union and National Steel reached agreement on a pact that established Japanese-style job security in exchange for concessions.

The pattern was similar at most other companies, except for U.S. Steel (recently renamed USX). There the USWA—noting the relative health of the company, suggested by its ability to spend billions on acquisitions—went on strike in August rather than accede to management demands for $3.50-an-hour cuts in labor costs. The walkout ended after six months as the union traded wage cuts for improved job security.

COMMUNITY RESPONSES TO PLANT CLOSINGS

Massive job eliminations and plant shutdowns in steel have prompted local union officials and community leaders to adopt unusual tactics in responding to economic dislocation. When Youngstown Sheet and Tube announced in the fall of 1977 that it would close its Campbell works, throwing more than 4,000 employees out of their jobs, people were moved to action. Local religious leaders banded together in the Ecumenical Coalition and initiated a campaign to keep Campbell open under community ownership—which required a $240 million loan from the federal government.

The Carter administration ended up rejecting the plan, but steel communities continued to explore public ownership as a means of saving steel operations that some experts said could be run profitably. A group called Community Steel, headed by a USWA local president, sought to buy two mills in Ohio's Mahoning Valley slated for shutdown by U.S. Steel, which refused to sell. A more radical approach was taken in the Pittsburgh area by religious figures such as Rev. Douglas Roth and local union officials such as Ron Weisen in Homestead who promoted tactics such as disrupting business at branches of Mellon Bank (accused of disinvesting in the domestic steel industry) and picketing the homes of steel executives.

The most recent effort was pursued by a group called the Tri-State Conference on Steel, which wanted to use a public authority or worker ownership to purchase the Dorothy Six blast furnace at U.S. Steel's closed works in Duquesne, Pennsylvania. Despite an energetic public campaign the initiative died after a feasibility study by the investment bank of Lazard Frères concluded that Dorothy could not be operated profitably.

LEADING COMPANIES

Bethlehem Steel was for most of the 20th century the country's second-largest steel producer. It was displaced by LTV in the mid-1980s. The company, established in 1904 by Charles Schwab, was especially strong in the structural steel used in the construction of skyscrapers. By the 1980s the firm, along with others in the industry, was suffering heavy losses. Chief executive Donald Trautlein, a former accountant, eliminated a number of less profitable operations—including the huge mill in Lackawanna, New York, which alone caused the loss of 7,000 jobs. Trautlein resigned in 1986 (against his will, according to some reports), and company veteran Walter Williams took over the difficult chore of keeping Bethlehem alive.

LTV (formerly Ling-Temco-Vought) built itself into the country's second-largest steel producer through a series of acquisitions of old-line mills. LTV was built by James Ling into one of the high-flying conglomerates of the late 1960s. The company bought a majority of Jones & Laughlin Steel in 1968, and despite antitrust problems with the federal government LTV went on to purchase the rest of Jones & Laughlin in 1975, the Lykes Corp. (parent of Youngstown Sheet and Tube) in 1978, and Republic Steel in 1984. Increased size has not enabled LTV to overcome the travails of the steel business. After suffering heavy losses for several years the company went into Chapter 11 in 1986—the largest U.S. industrial corporation to do so.

USX is the deliberately nondescriptive name assumed by U.S. Steel in 1986 to indicate the company's shift away from its traditional business. Although the firm known as Big Steel remained the leading producer in the industry, three quarters of the corporation's revenues were coming from other sources. That was the result of the purchase of Marathon Oil in 1982 and Texas Oil & Gas in 1986 for a combined price of $10 billion. Assembled in 1901 as the first billion-dollar corporation, U.S. Steel for many years epitomized heavy industry in America. In October 1986 corporate raider Carl Icahn made a $7 billion bid for the company, but USX management resisted the takeover.

SOURCE GUIDE

LEADING STOCK ANALYSTS AND EXPERTS

Charles Bradford, analyst at Merrill Lynch.

Robert Hageman, analyst at Kidder Peabody.

Peter Marcus, analyst at Paine Webber.

William T. Hogan, Fordham University economist and historian of the industry.

Robert Crandall, Brookings Institution, Washington, D.C.

TRADE ASSOCIATIONS AND UNIONS

American Iron and Steel Institute, Washington, D.C.

United Steelworkers of America, Pittsburgh.

DATA SOURCES AND DIRECTORIES

Annual Statistical Report and *Directory of Iron and Steel Works of the United States and Canada,* issued every few years (Washington, D.C.: American Iron and Steel Institute).

The Iron and Steel Industry, published annually (Paris: Organisation for Economic Co-Operation and Development).

Metal Statistics, an annual volume of data by the publisher of *American Metal Market* (New York: Fairchild Publications).

TRADE PUBLICATIONS

American Metal Market, daily.

Iron Age, biweekly.

33 Metal Producing, monthly.

BOOKS AND REPORTS

Barnett, Donald F., and Robert W. Crandall. *Up from the Ashes: The Rise of the Steel Minimill in the United States.* Washington, D.C.: Brookings Institution, 1986.

Barnett, Donald F., and Louis Schorsch. *Steel: Upheaval in a Basic Industry.* Cambridge, Mass.: Ballinger, 1983.

Crandall, Robert W. *The U.S. Steel Industry in Recurrent Crisis.* Washington, D.C.: Brookings Institution, 1981.

Hogan, William T. *Economic History of the Iron and Steel Industry in the United States.* 5 vols. Lexington, Mass.: Lexington Books, 1971.

————— . *Steel in the United States: Restructuring to Compete.* Lexington, Mass.: Lexington Books, 1984.

National Research Council. *The Competitive Status of the U.S. Steel Industry.* Washington, D.C.: National Academy Press, 1985.

Strohmeyer, John. *Crisis in Bethlehem: Big Steel's Struggle to Survive.* Bethesda, Md.: Adler & Adler, 1986.

U.S. Congress, Congressional Budget Office. *The Effects of Import Quotas on the Steel Industry.* Washington, D.C., 1984.

U.S. Congress, Office of Technology Assessment. *Technology and Steel Industry Competitiveness.* Washington, D.C., 1980.

Note: The Source Guides and tables are not indexed. Entries in bold refer to listings in the Leading Companies sections.

VERITAS

MDCCCXL

CREDENTIALING EDUCATIONAL ACCOMPLISHMENT

TASK FORCE ON EDUCATIONAL CREDIT
AND CREDENTIALS

A. D. Albright, President, Northern Kentucky University

J. Douglas Conner, Executive Secretary, American Association of Collegiate Registrars and Admissions Officers

May N. Diaz, Provost, Kresge College, University of California, Santa Cruz

John F. Grede, Vice-Chancellor, Career and Manpower Programs, City Colleges of Chicago

Cyril O. Houle, Professor of Education, University of Chicago; Senior Program Consultant, W. K. Kellogg Foundation

Jack C. Merwin, Professor, College of Education, University of Minnesota

Peter Meyer, Educational Consultant, Route 1, Box 98A, Burnsville, North Carolina

J. Boyd Page, President, Council of Graduate Schools in the United States; *Chairman*

Kenneth E. Young, President, Council on Postsecondary Accreditation

Jerry W. Miller, Director, Office on Educational Credit, American Council on Education; ex officio

AUTHORS OF ANALYTICAL WORKING PAPERS

Richard L. Ferguson, Vice-President, Research and Development, American College Testing Program

John Folger, Policy Coordinator, Education Commission of the States

John Harris, Professor of Education, Middle Tennessee State University

Donald P. Hoyt, Director, Office of Educational Resources, Kansas State University

Robert Kirkwood, Executive Director, Commission on Higher Education, Middle States Association of Colleges and Schools

William Troutt, Assistant Project Director, Tennessee Higher Education Commission

Jonathan R. Warren, Research Psychologist, Educational Testing Service —Berkeley

CREDENTIALING EDUCATIONAL ACCOMPLISHMENT

Report and Recommendations of
The Task Force on Educational
Credit and Credentials

WITH ANALYSES BY
John Harris and William Troutt
Jonathan R. Warren
Richard L. Ferguson
Donald P. Hoyt
Robert Kirkwood
John Folger

Edited by Jerry W. Miller and Olive Mills

AMERICAN COUNCIL ON EDUCATION
WASHINGTON, D.C.

Library of Congress Cataloging in Publication Data

American Council on Education. Task Force on Educational
Credit and Credentials.
Credentialing educational accomplishment.

Bibliography: p.
1. School credits. 2. American Council on Education.
Task Force on Educational Credit and Credentials.
I. Miller, Jerry W. II. Mills, Olive. III. Title.
LB2360.A5 1978 378.1′68′0973 78-10361
ISBN 0-8268-1227-9

9 8 7 6 5 4 3 2 1

PRINTED IN THE UNITED STATES OF AMERICA

Contents

Foreword

Both educational and social problems with the credit and credential system in postsecondary education prompted the Commission on Educational Credit of the American Council on Education to initiate the two-year study, of which one result is this book. Socially, the growing use of educational credentials as qualification for employment has brought into focus a significant issue with respect to credit and credentials, that is, their applicability to the work setting and, therefore, the fairness of their use. Educationally, the postsecondary community needs to move forward in modifying the present credit and credential system to accommodate learning attained in a variety of settings and under a variety of sponsorships and, at the same time, to maintain academic standards. Moreover, in any action on these matters, it is important to social progress that, through the credit and credential system, society's members be encouraged to pursue non-job-related learning by receiving appropriate recognition for their educational accomplishment.

This book, then, has two principal purposes: (1) to bring employers and those concerned with postsecondary education to increased awareness of the educational and social significance of credentialing educational accomplishment, and (2) to recommend changes in the credit and credentialing system so as to improve the quality of information conveyed. To the latter end, the book includes recommendations that will help institutions, individually and collectively, to adopt policies and practices more effective and consistent than those prevailing.

The book is addressed primarily to three audiences. The first is leaders of institutions of postsecondary education. The second is policy makers in education associations, the federal and state governments, and foundations, as well as other opinion makers who influence postsecondary education. The third audience is users of educational credits and credentials, including employers, who should find the report and the analyses will help them examine their policies concerning educational accomplishment credentialed by postsecondary institutions.

An earlier publication of the Task Force, *Recommendations on Credentialing Educational Accomplishment,* including a brief explanatory report, was issued to encourage careful study by leaders who can stimulate actions to bring the recommendations to full consideration and implementation. Brevity had risks in dealing with so complex a subject as credit and credentials, for the many intricacies and nuances that lie behind the recommendations may not be widely understood. For that reason, the Council decided to publish this larger work containing the Task Force's analyses of the problems and issues as well as the extensive working papers which the Task Force considered during its deliberations. Readers will find this larger volume useful in gaining a deeper understanding of the basis for the recommendations.

The development of the book under the aegis of the American Council on Education signifies in itself that leaders in the postsecondary education community are willing to seek solutions to problems significant to society by bringing increased order and coherence to the credit and credentialing system. But the discussions and recommendations presented here are only a first step. Institutions and their organizations must follow through if others are to be convinced that primary responsibility for educational credit and credentials should remain with the postsecondary educational community.

Educational credit and credentials are too intrinsic to the academic enterprise and to social equity to be left unattended for prolonged periods of time. The ACE Commission on Educational Credit will therefore give continuing, systematic attention to credit and credentials for postsecondary education. The overall, long-term objective, consistent with one purpose of this publication, will be to improve the quality of information conveyed by credit and credentials, both for social and for educational purposes.

The Council is grateful to Carnegie Corporation of New York for its grant supporting this effort, to the Commission on Educational Credit for initiating and providing general oversight of the Task Force activities, and to the authors of the working papers.

Special gratitude is expressed to members of the Task Force who helped design the study before the grant was obtained and met several times over the next two years to deliberate the issues and to develop the report. Their willingness voluntarily to participate in such an activity, both lengthy and demanding, is an illustration of the Council's greatest resource.

The recommendations contained herein are commended for implementation by institutions and the pertinent agencies serving postsecondary education.

J. W. PELTASON, *President*
American Council on Education

Preface

Credentialing educational accomplishment is a function that should embody thoughtful answers to fundamental educational and social questions. An article in the *Washington Post* (November 25, 1977, page 1) on law school graduates and the job market at least partially supports that thesis. The article notes that graduates with the highest class standing from the most prestigious schools have multiple opportunities to work for highly respected law firms and to make big salaries. Students with low class standing from prestigious schools and students from "second" and "third" rank schools are lucky to obtain jobs in smaller firms or in less desirable cities. By Labor Department estimates, 30,000 June 1978 law graduates would compete for 21,000 positions. By 1985, as many as 100,000 law school graduates may not be able to find jobs in the legal profession.

The *Post* story emphasizes one of the stark realities of today's society. Educational credentials are used to label people according to educational accomplishment, thus dramatically affecting how far the door of opportunity opens, if it opens at all. Not only do educational credentials affect the image other people hold of a person, but they also affect that person's self-image. Consequently, the role of postsecondary education institutions in credentialing educational accomplishment is laden with troublesome, complex questions.

How relevant are educational credentials and class standing in qualifying for employment? Whose responsibility is it to dispel the notion reflected in the *Post* article that there are valid, formal means for determining "first," "second," or "third" rank schools? Whose responsibility is it to correct other improper inferences drawn by those outside the academic community who use college and university degrees as indications of specific competences and qualifications?

What can be done to improve the murky meaning of educational credentials? How can the great variation among institutions in standards for educational accomplishment be accurately measured and conveyed to third parties, such as employers? What procedures can be established that will permit graduates of less well known institutions to compete on the basis of merit with graduates of prestigious institutions?

How can the educational credentialing system, including the award of credit, be used to encourage learning as a lifelong process? What is its role in the broadening of cultural perspectives and the refinement of social and personal values? What barriers does the system present for people whose aspirations and educational objectives change? Do current problems in credits and credentials cause people to duplicate educational experiences and waste time and personal resources?

The Commission on Educational Credit of the American Council on Education was conscious of many of these questions in 1974 when it authorized the appointment of the ACE Task Force on Educational Credit and Credentials. As the Task Force pursued its deliberations, some of the questions and many others not listed arose for discussion and debate.

In the final report of the Task Force, presented to the Commission on Educational Credit in November 1977, the questions were addressed less specifically and directly than many had initially hoped. The early, ephemeral objective of designing and codifying a credit and credentialing system that would serve all postsecondary education programs and institutions in American society vanished. Instead, the Task Force settled on a strategy of making recommendations to improve the quality of information conveyed by the system of credit and credentials now prevailing.

Exploring into the philosophical and technical considerations in credentialing inevitably came back to the difficulty of describing, assessing, and quantifying educational accomplishment. There was general recognition that educational credit and credentials, at best, are but gross measures of competences and learning.

Throughout the deliberations, the need for educational credit and credentials to represent more precise measures of educational accomplishment was acknowledged. But, repeatedly, compelling arguments held that many of the important outcomes or experiences in postsecondary education cannot be quantified. Thus, striking a balance between broad social and cultural objectives of postsecondary education and the use of educational credentials as accurate indicators of qualification for employment was a continuing concern.

Out of the deliberations came many points of consensus, all reflected in the Task Force's recommendations: The traditional roles of administration, governing boards, faculty, and nongovernmental accreditation should be preserved to undergird the meaning of educational credentials. In information regarding educational accomplishment, quantification and generic labeling are insufficient to meet present-day needs; therefore, narrative descriptions will become increasingly important. All of the above considerations rest on improved evaluation of student achievement.

There was also consensus that the Task Force's recommendations are only a beginning. Interinstitutional developmental efforts and cooperation will be essential to modify and improve the current system of credit and credentials. The American Council on Education, through the Office on Educational Credit, plans to use its leadership to implement several developmental projects. The follow-up efforts should be as exhilarating and challenging as the development of the Task Force report itself.

The text of this book contains the report and recommendations of the Task Force on Educational Credit and Credentials and the analytical working papers prepared for the Task Force. Chapter 1 presents the context for the undertaking. Chapter 2 is the Task Force's analysis of credentialing in American society, with emphasis on the role of educational credentials as measures of educational accomplishment, the types and uses of credentials in the society, the credentialing process, and principles for credentialing.

Chapters 3–8 are working papers which the Task Force commissioned to assist it in reexamining educational credit and credentials in a comprehensive framework. The papers address the evolution and uses of educational credit and credentials in society, current practices in awarding credits and credentials, the central role of evaluation of student achievement in the award of credit and credentials, the relationship of credit and educational credentials to other forms of credentialing, student mobility and transfer, and the administrative uses of credit. The authors examined the literature and were encouraged to think broadly about the issues and problems for the benefit of the Task Force. The chapters were written to stand alone and, therefore, sometimes overlap. Each working paper represents the views of the respective authors and not necessarily those of the Task Force, the Commission on Educational Credit, or the American Council on Education.

Chapters 9 and 10 present the recommendations and comments of the members, with substantial reliance on the working papers as a resource. As noted at the start of that section, the Task Force report and recommendations were approved by the Commission on Educational Credit of the American Council on Education on November 22, 1977, and endorsed by the ACE Board of Directors on January 30, 1978.

My personal satisfaction in working with the Task Force on Educational Credit and Credentials can be attributed partly to provocative subject matter that goes to the very core of the educational process. It must also be attributed to members of the Task Force, named elsewhere in this book. Reflecting diverse backgrounds and responsibilities, they debated their points with vigor and unfailing good humor. The time and effort they donated to the undertaking over a three-year period was substantial, far beyond the sessions which, alone, occupied eighteen days. I shall always remain in their debt.

Similar expressions of gratitude are owed to the authors of the working papers, which constitute the heart of this book. Their contributions to the thinking of the Task Force are apparent throughout the recommendations. Special thanks are due the professional staff of the Office on Educational Credit who commented on the report, and especially to Leonard Boswell, Henry Spille, and Lorraine Lofthus who helped staff the Task Force's activities.

JERRY W. MILLER, *Director*
Office on Educational Credit
American Council on Education

A Note on Terminology

Changes that have come about in postsecondary education relatively recently have introduced new concepts and some new terms to describe them. To assure that readers have a common understanding of some basic terms used in the pages that follow, a few are here defined.

Credit unit: Official certification of a course completed satisfactorily, statements of competence, and other increments of verified educational accomplishment (theses, oral and written examinations, internships, etc.) accepted toward completion of requirements for certificates and degrees. Credit units are most often assigned semester or quarter hour values.

Degree: An honor bestowed by an educational institution for meeting its requirements through the satisfactory completion of a program of study or other verified educational accomplishment.

Educational credential: A certificate, diploma, or degree document (associate, baccalaureate, or graduate) certifying that the requirements therefor have been met through satisfactory completion of a program of study or other verified educational accomplishment.

External degree: An academic award earned through one or more of the following means: extrainstitutional learning, credit by examination, specially devised experiential learning programs, self-directed study, and satisfactory completion of campus or noncampus courses. In some programs, the learning is attained in circumstances outside the sponsorship or supervision of the awarding agency.

Extrainstitutional learning: Learning that is attained outside the sponsorship of legally authorized and accredited postsecondary institutions. The term applies to learning acquired from work and life experiences, independent reading and study, the mass media, and participation in formal courses sponsored by associations, business, government, industry, the military, unions, and other social institutions such as hospitals.

Higher education: The part of postsecondary education that leads to the award of a degree.

Postsecondary education: The array of educational opportunities available to post-high-school age adults, including educational programs of postsecondary education institutions and extrainstitutional learning experiences defined above.

PART I

THE TASK FORCE PERSPECTIVE

CHAPTER 1

Credits and Credentials in Today's Society

Postsecondary education's basic system for awarding educational credit and credentials should be retained, but it should be modified to serve more adequately present-day educational and social needs. That is the first recommendation and the basic premise of this book.

Modification is the strategy selected because designing and implementing a new system would have been neither practical nor warranted. The present system has the clear-cut advantage of being widely used and generally understood, both in its operation and its imperfections. Yet there are pressing needs that are not being met but that can be met if the present system is modified.

Socially, the growing use of educational credentials to qualify for employment has highlighted an important educational and social issue concerning credit and credentials— their relevance to the work setting and, therefore, the fairness of their use. Postsecondary education institutions are aware of, and many say have encouraged, the widespread use of the credentials they award. Encouraging the use of educational credentials or giving tacit approval to how they are used carries with it the responsibility for communicating their meaning adequately and accurately. Currently, substantial evidence indicates that employers are overrelying on degrees and certificates as devices to screen the qualified.

Educationally, there is a need to accelerate progress in modifying the present system of credentials to make it more comprehensive. A modified system should accommodate learning attained not only in different types of postsecondary education institutions and diverse curricula, but also in structured and nonstructured extrainstitutional learning. The system should permit learners to move as necessary among different types of institutions and extrainstitutional learning opportunities in achieving their educational objectives. The result would be more effective use of all educational resources, improved social equity of credentials, better placement of students in educational programs, and increased motivation of members of the society to learn.

The policies and procedures for awarding credit and credentials have not undergone major change since around the turn of the century, when Harvard completed its process of establishing the elective system. Other colleges and universities quickly followed Harvard's example, leading to the pattern prevalent in postsecondary education today—primary but not exclusive reliance on the completion of courses to fulfill degree requirements, particularly in the undergraduate years.

The present system served education and society reasonably well as long as institutions were relatively homogeneous in the characteristics of faculties, students, courses, modes of instruction, academic calendars, curricular and institutional structures, and graduation requirements. By mid-century, however, education beyond the high school began to change dramatically in size and scope. Enrollments increased greatly and student bodies became far more heterogeneous. Scores of new programs were added as institutions modified their curricula and objectives to meet needs created by changes in the society and in the educational objectives of students. Community colleges and postsecondary vocational institutions multiplied in number and became vital elements of the system of postsecondary education institutions, broadening access to learning and providing diverse educational opportunities. Interest in nontraditional education encouraged more flexible programming. Learning in extrainstitutional circumstances became more common.

As the changes developed, most people associated with public and nonprofit educational institutions have come to a sharpened awareness of the substantial educational programs of a postsecondary nature being offered by proprietary schools, government agencies, business, industry, the military, unions, voluntary and professional associations, and other organizations outside the formal education structure.

The years of rapid change gave rise to the more encompassing concept of postsecondary education that came into dominant use with the enactment of the Education Amendments of 1972. Although colleges and universities continue to be referred to as institutions of *higher* education, they are now considered part of *postsecondary* education. Moreover, most colleges and universities have broadened their curricula and the student clienteles they serve to include many programs that do not result in the award of a degree. As a consequence, the term "higher education" as an institutional descriptor is increasingly ambiguous. It is more accurately used, at least for purposes of credits and credentials, when it is limited to curricula leading to the award of degrees.

"Postsecondary education," the dominant term today, is appropriately used when it applies to the array of educational opportunities available to post-high-school age adults—programs of colleges and universities, other postsecondary education institutions, and other sponsors such as those noted above, as well as the media and self-directed study. Large numbers of students can be expected to have had learning experiences in two or more of the educational settings listed above or in two or more curricula offered by postsecondary education institutions.

The diversity of sponsors of, and the numbers of participants in, postsecondary education have important implications for credit and credentials. As students find their personal circumstances and educational objectives change, many seek to have their learning, wherever and however attained, incorporated into the credit and credentialing system in order to take advantage of subsequent educational opportunities without duplicating educational experiences and wasting personal resources.

Other recent social changes also carry important implications for policies and practices in credentialing educational accomplishment. Linkages between education and performance in the work setting are a growing concern and have become a dominant theme in public discussions on education. As a result, society has come to emphasize credits and credentials somewhat more as measures of a person's capabilities, competences, and learning and somewhat less as accolades for educational accomplishment.

A new socioeconomic factor is emerging that may make the function of credentialing educational accomplishment even more important. Until recently, the nation's economy was able to provide most college and university graduates with entry-level employment commensurate with their educational accomplishments and expectations. Today, growing evidence indicates that the job market cannot continue to absorb so high a proportion of graduates at a job level appropriate to their aspirations or their educational accomplishments. If the employment projections for future graduates prove accurate, increased tensions in the employment marketplace and heightened competition among institutions for students with strong work goals will be inevitable. In comparison with today, tomorrow's students will be more concerned with how the institution's credentials will help them get a job or pursue advanced study, and employers will be more concerned with the validity of credentials for the work place.

Along with the emphasis on preparation for employment has come a countervailing concern with general/liberal education as an important personal educational objective of students and as a component of programs leading to degrees in professional and technical fields. Additionally, recognition is spreading that for a person to be a contributing member of society and competent in the work setting, learning must be a lifelong process. Credentials for educational accomplishment have substantial social significance as well as important economic consequences, both for those who attain such status and those who do not.[1]

It should be noted that crediting and credentialing policies and practices in postsecondary education institutions have not been unresponsive to educational and social change. Credit by examination is used extensively; procedures for translating

1. For a discussion, see John Harris and William Troutt, "Educational Credentials: Past, Present, and Future," chapter 3 in the present volume.

extrainstitutional learning into credit recommendations that can be used by institutions are being expanded; and faculty evaluation of experiential learning as a process is advancing. There has also been limited experimentation with narrative descriptions of educational accomplishment and with statements of competences and educational outcomes.[2]

Despite these efforts, the present system of credit and credentials continues to draw criticism from many quarters. Some critics say that credits and credentials are antithetical to the teaching-learning process. Others disparage credits and credentials as major obstacles to the realization of a learning society. Still others suggest that awarding credit and credentials should not be a function of educational institutions but should be left to other agencies. Some would abolish credits and credentials.

To contemplate the void that would result from either action is to conclude that credit and credentials (for reasons developed in the next chapter) are essential for a system of postsecondary education that serves a complex, technological, and highly mobile society. Moreover, certification of educational accomplishment is an established and accepted social function of postsecondary institutions that should not be disavowed. Rather, institutions should seek to carry forward the responsibility for certification in a manner that will improve its educational and social usefulness.

This book, containing the analyses and recommendations of the Task Force on Educational Credit and Credentials and the working papers prepared for the Task Force, is directed to that objective.

2. For discussion, see Jonathan R. Warren, "Current Practices in Awarding Credits and Degrees," chapter 4 in the present volume.

CHAPTER 2

Credentialing: Types, Processes, and Functions

The credentialing function of postsecondary education institutions must be understood in the context of society's use of credentials and the relationships between educational credentials and credentials issued by other authorities.

Society's Credentials

A mobile, complex society supported by a technological economy is, by its nature, dependent on formal certification to identify the qualified, to protect against the incompetent and the fraudulent, and to encourage learning and competence. In the United States, licensure by government agencies, certification by voluntary associations, and credentialing by educational institutions combine to serve these social needs.

Formal credentials, then, fall into three categories:

1. *Documents of certification, licensure, or registration—most often known as licenses—issued by agencies of government to persons who meet specific requisites.* Such documents are evidence that the state has granted a person permission to engage in a specified activity; practice by the uncredentialed is often, but not always, prohibited. Thus, credentials issued by agencies of government may be mandatory for practice or they may be advisory in the sense that the holder, in the view of the state, is qualified to engage in certain activities. An example of this type of credential is a license issued by a state government to practice dentistry.

2. *Documents of certification or registration awarded by voluntary occupational and professional organizations attesting that the holder meets certain requisites or occupational standards.* The credential represents an advisory opinion by

the issuing agency that the holder is qualified to engage in specified practices. The credential involves the authority of government only in cases where such credentials may be specified in legislation as a requirement to qualify for practice. Occupational certification may duplicate, complement, supplement, or in some cases provide a higher level of certification than credentials issued by an agency of government and educational institutions.

3. *Diplomas attesting to degree or certificate status conferred by educational institutions for successful completion of an organized program of study or for equivalent educational accomplishment.* Educational credentials may be an award for educational accomplishment. They may also be advisory in the sense that the holder, in the view of the institution, is qualified to engage in certain occupational activities. In some cases, a degree from an accredited institution may be one requirement in qualifying for governmental or voluntary credentials. A bachelor's degree in electrical engineering is an example.

The Credentialing Process

The credentialing process is essentially the same for the three categories of certification. Credentialing involves three parties: (1) the authority issuing the credential, (2) the person to whom the credential is issued, and (3) the persons, groups, or agencies benefitting from or using the judgments of the credentialing authority. The process involves three principal steps: (1) definition of the attitudes, competences, knowledge, or skills to be certified, (2) assessment of each individual to determine whether he or she meets the requisites, and (3) issuance of a document to attest the individual's possession of the requisites. To an increasing extent, credentialing involves a fourth step: periodic recertification that the holder continues to possess the requisites for the credential or meets new ones made necessary by advances in the field.

The possession of a valid credential is evidence that the holder has qualifications which, in the view of the issuing source, entitle him to authority and confidence within the area certified. The credential is not a guarantee that every person credentialed will perform satisfactorily or that any credential holder will perform well in every situation. It merely indicates that those people who hold the credential tend to deliver adequate services with substantially more consistency than those who do not hold the credential. Given the difficulty of defining and assessing the requisites for delivery of complex and highly refined services, credentialing cannot be expected to provide absolute protection to society. It has social utility because it increases the likelihood that satisfactory services will be delivered.

Since credentialing is inherently a judgmental process, based as it is on professional views and group values, it should be regularly and systematically questioned in all its forms. Although society must continue to rely on credentialing as a means of identifying the qualified, it must always recognize the potential for the credentialing process to be abused. Thus, society should continually seek answers to three questions: (1) What capabilities, competences, and learning can be validly, reliably, and usefully credentialed? (2) When is it in the interest of society to award credentials? and (3) Who should be the credentialing authority? There are, of course, no universally accepted answers to these questions, but some principles can be identified which appear pertinent to all three categories of credentialing.

Principles of Credentialing

1. Credentialing should minimize risks to the public health, safety, and welfare by identifying the qualified.

2. Credentialing that recognizes and encourages pride in accomplishment and the mastery of knowledge and skills is in the public interest.

3. Mandatory credentialing should be exercised only where there is a demonstrable relationship to the public health, safety, and welfare.

4. Credentialing is substantially interlinked with economic and social rewards in the society. In order to assure social equity, then, all credentialing systems should recognize requisite competences and learning for a given credential regardless of how or where they are achieved.

5. Credentialing activities of agencies and institutions, whether controlled by agencies of government or sponsored by voluntary occupational and professional organizations, substantially intersect the public interest. The policy-making and governing boards of such agencies should therefore be representative of broad social interests.

6. The credentialing process in fields closely related to the public health, safety, and welfare should include provision that the credentialed be required periodically to prove that they still possess the requisites for acceptable practice and have kept pace with advances in the field.[1]

The pluralistic approach to credentialing in the United States—governmental licensure, voluntary certification, and educational awards—will probably continue, and perhaps appropriately so. All three types have been increasing in use. Despite persistent questions about the public benefits of licensure, more and more occupational groups have been successful in persuading state legislatures to enact licensure statutes. The tendency of occupational groups to organize and to institute voluntary certification programs continues. And the award of educational credentials by postsecondary education institutions is growing rapidly. In the years 1965–77, the number of baccalaureate and higher degrees awarded increased from 670,000 to more than 1.3 million. For the same years, the number of associate degrees awarded quadrupled— from 100,000 to 400,000.[2]

Government has the ultimate responsibility for protecting the public health and safety and the body politic from fraud. Only government can engage in mandatory credentialing and impose criminal sanctions for violations. In specialties where it is beneficial to society to identify the qualified but where such an extensive measure as licensure lacks social efficacy, government has allowed voluntary and educational credentialing to hold sway without government intervention.

When voluntary associations are properly sensitive to their

1. Adapted from Jerry W. Miller, "Credentials for Health Administration," in *Selected Papers of the Commission on Education for Health Administration* 2:261–62.

2. *A Fact Book on Higher Education*, Fourth issue, p. 76.213.

social responsibilities, they serve their members and society by identifying those attitudes, competences, knowledge, and skills that can be defined, communicated, learned, and assessed and that the associations believe are generally essential to delivery of adequate services. Their advisory credentialing functions are useful in establishing occupational identity, in promoting pride in accomplishment and advances in the field, and in encouraging self-regulation as an alternative to governmental control.

The role of educational credit and credentialing—the focus of this report—requires elaboration.

Educational Credit

Postsecondary institutions and the educational objectives of their students are amazingly diverse. Curricula cover a broad spectrum: the academic disciplines; preparation for professional practice; trade, vocational, and technical studies; continuing and basic adult education; and general studies. The objectives of students include acquiring broad cultural foundations, qualifying for employment and professional practice, improving occupational proficiencies, fulfilling avocational interests, and achieving personal development.

Two devices—units of credit and continuing education units—are the principal means being used to record the educational accomplishments and experiences of students participating in postsecondary education curricula.

Units of Credit

Credits awarded are assumed to represent modules of verified educational accomplishment that can be combined in a prescribed program of study or in a set of requirements to define a body of comprehensive and integrated learning worthy of the award of a degree or certificate. Units of credit reflect the diversity of academic programs and are used to state the requirements for degrees, such as those in general/liberal education, majors, minors, electives, and lower-division and upper-division instruction. Based on evaluation of educational accomplishment, credits also reflect—albeit imprecisely—the competences, capabilities, and learning of students.

When credits are appropriately combined, their collective value is assumed to be greater than their sum, by reason of synergistic educational outcomes inherent in the design of educational programs. To assure that a degree marks more than a collection of courses, some institutions follow practices at the undergraduate level that are characteristic in graduate education, such as requiring theses and oral and written comprehensive examinations.

Credits are usually assigned quantitative values and are the components used to measure progress toward a larger educational goal, usually a degree. The majority of institutions follow either the quarter or the semester hour system, both of which take as their point of departure time-based formal instruction but increasingly incorporate learning attained in extrainstitutional settings.[3]

Credits, because of their uses in designing and describing educational programs and stating instructional outcomes, then, reflect the essential characteristics and activities of postsecondary education. In a genuine sense, credits state the articles of faith of the academy.

A system of accounting for educational progress is essential for postsecondary education to serve present-day society. Postsecondary education could not offer diverse programs to masses of students without the convenience and flexibility of learning modules which correlate with credits without well-understood, functional means of accounting for educational accomplishment. Moreover, credits are the facilitative mechanisms which assist students in transferring from one institution to another, in receiving recognition for equivalent educational accomplishment, and in changing educational objectives with-

3. The most common practice uses the following guidelines: (1) one semester credit hour for each fifteen hours of classroom contact plus thirty hours of outside preparation or the equivalent; or (2) one semester credit hour for each thirty hours of laboratory work plus necessary outside preparation or its equivalent, normally expected to be fifteen hours; or (3) one semester credit hour for not fewer than forty-five hours of shop instruction (contact hours) or the equivalent. The general practice is to equate two semester hours with three quarter hours.

out total loss of standing.[4] Credits are also a critical factor in allocating educational resources.[5]

Continuing Education Units

The continuing education unit (CEU) has come into substantial use during the 1970s as a measure of participation in educational programs that are designed not to be part of degree programs. Such programs include short courses, workshops, seminars, conferences, institutes, and other forms of noncredit continuing education offered by institutions of postsecondary education and occupational organizations.

The concept was developed by the National Task Force on the Continuing Education Unit (appointed by the National University Extension Association) to record an individual's participation in noncredit courses and to provide sponsors with a means to account for resources expended in offering such educational programs. One continuing education unit is officially defined as "ten contact hours of participation in an organized continuing education experience under responsible sponsorship, capable direction, and qualified instruction."[6]

The CEU differs from units of credit in one critically significant way: it relies on *participation* in educational programs rather than *evaluation* of educational accomplishment.

Educational Credentials

Certificates and degrees conferred by postsecondary education institutions serve one or more of the following functions: (1) as qualification for advanced study, (2) as qualification for employment and delivery of services, or (3) as recognition for personal development.

4. While the above holds for institutions serving the majority of students in postsecondary education, a few institutions have abandoned traditional forms of credit or have added requirements such as honors papers and field experience. As their students transfer to other institutions or change their educational objectives, they experience more than the usual difficulty in getting their educational accomplishments recognized.

5. For discussion, see John Folger, "Administrative Uses of Credit," chapter 8 in the present volume.

6. National Task Force on the Continuing Education Unit, *The Continuing Education Unit: Criteria and Guidelines,* p. 3.

Credentials as Qualification
for Advanced Study

To benefit from advanced study, students must have mastered certain basic knowledge and academic skills. The academy, therefore, has tended to structure its credentials by level of educational accomplishment to reflect depth and breadth of study as well as the intellectual skills required. An educational credential at a specified level of accomplishment and in an appropriate field is normally a basic qualification to begin study at the next level. For such purposes, certificates and degrees serve as credentials for academic qualifications deemed essential for advanced study.

Credentials as Qualification for
Employment and Delivery of Services

The use of certificates or degrees to qualify for employment or independent practice varies by occupation. In some cases, educational credentials are the only certifications used in an occupational field (business administration, public librarianship); for others, they may be the primary credential but may also qualify the holder to seek nongovernmental, voluntary certification or registration (medical technology). In still other areas, they may qualify the holder to sit for government-administered mandatory licensure, certification, or registration examinations (medicine, dentistry, law).

The closer the relationship between the specialized learning represented by a certificate or degree and the right to practice an occupational specialty, the greater the utility of an institutional diploma as a credential qualifying the holder for employment. However, the pertinence of an educational credential as a qualification for employment often transcends the certification of competences and learning in specified fields and is based on the general attributes of those awarded degrees and certificates. Earning an educational credential, even in fields unrelated to specific occupations, is assumed to be indicative of, and ideally should certify, attributes and synergistic educational outcomes highly valued by employers. These include mastery of a specialized body of knowledge, ability to communicate and to analyze verbally and quantitatively at a high level; drive to accomplish a difficult task and to achieve a personal goal; sensitivity to social issues and problems; competence in interpersonal skills; and—highly important to many employers—intellectual curiosity and ability and willingness to learn and master a new situation quickly.

Credentials as Recognition of Personal Development

Throughout history, a principal role of the academy[7] has been to provide a place in society where contemplative, analytical, and scholarly activities could be encouraged and nourished. To advance the understanding of cultures, the environment, and the human condition and to transmit this knowledge to others has been an end in itself, establishing the life of the mind and education as a high calling. The academy, in general, has tenaciously pursued this function even though it has reflected values not always widely shared by all members of the society. Nonetheless, society has generally recognized that social dividends accrue from permitting the academy to maintain and advance values which it holds to be in the broad interests of society and which transcend qualification for employment and advanced study.

The social values held by the academy are most concisely reflected in the requirements it sets for the credentials it awards, particularly at the undergraduate level. Its credentials have come to be accepted as a hallmark of an educated person —an accolade for personal development. Those who possess the academy's credentials, in comparison with the uncredentialed, have generally commanded increased confidence and been shown greater deference in social and work settings.

Moreover, degree holders have been expected to be more than occupationally proficient. They have been expected to be effective members of society and above-average contributors to the commonweal through active, sensitive civic participation. Although postsecondary education collectively does not

7. As used in this section, "the academy" refers collectively to members of boards of control, administrations, and faculties who influence and determine the educational philosophy, curricula, and requirements of institutions of postsecondary education.

directly seek to prescribe or certify artistic, political, and spiritual values, it does design educational programs to help students advance their understanding of their culture and further develop and refine personal values that motivate them to exercise civil and social responsibilities. The meaning of this component of the degree is ambiguous, elusive, varied, and difficult to quantify as units of credit. It is more an accolade for personal development than a certification of educational accomplishment. But the attributes derived from this component of the degree are one reason the academy's credentials have been increasingly sought by members of the society. As a result, learning and intellectual activity have been encouraged, and knowledge of the social and natural environment advanced.

Meaning of Educational Credentials

Because educational credentials serve social functions, holders of formal recognition by postsecondary education institutions have enjoyed an advantage over the noncredentialed. Therein lies an important consideration—if not a problem—for educational institutions. Institutions must be concerned about the uses made of the recognition they confer. Appropriate uses must be determined in light of the variability, reliability, and validity of credit and credentials as symbols of learning and competence.

The credits and credentials awarded by postsecondary institutions, both numerous in numbers and varied in kinds, convey some commonality but no standard meaning. Contributing to the variation of meaning are diverse curricula, imprecise evaluation of educational accomplishment, pluralistic ownership and control of the academic enterprise, and other factors and forces in the academic community. Each merits discussion.

Diverse Curricula

Given the diversity of postsecondary education curricula, the credentials awarded for successful completion of a program of study require accompanying descriptors to elaborate the dimensions and characteristics of academic accomplishment. For credentials to be effective communication symbols, the descriptors need to include such elements as:

- Subject-matter specialization, e.g., chemistry, dentistry, electronics, general studies, history
- Level of accomplishment: certificate, associate, baccalaureate, master's, and doctor's
- Other types of accomplishment, such as analytical, communications, psychomotor, synthesizing, and quantitative skills; cognitive knowledge; and affective behavior

So varied are the types of educational accomplishment in postsecondary education that establishing a precise equivalence among institutions and programs would be an elusive goal. But what has been amply demonstrated through years of experience with students who have transferred among institutions and changed educational objectives is that types of educational accomplishment are describable and quantifiable within certain limits of precision.

Evaluation of Educational Accomplishment

If educational credit and credentials are to have meaning, educational accomplishment must be reliably and validly evaluated. That principle establishes the sine qua non of credit and credentials. Without evaluation, credit and credentials are of no value to third parties who look to them to certify qualification for employment, nor are they then adequate to the needs of educational institutions that use them as one consideration in admitting students to advanced study or those who transfer from other institutions. Evaluation currently occurs along four tracks:

Track 1. *Study sponsored by educational institutions.* Traditionally, members of the faculty have taught, evaluated, and certified educational accomplishment attained through study sponsored by the institution. This responsibility has included classroom and laboratory instruction, self-directed study, and educational accomplishment attained in other ways such as writing theses. Among the various evaluation techniques in use are faculty-developed quizzes and examinations, research papers, class participation measures, and class projects. Faculty members determine whether the student has met the institution's standards for achievement; the resulting certification is then recorded on the student's academic record.

Track 2. *Interinstitutional examination programs.* For reasons of economy and efficiency, the postsecondary education community has cooperated through its organizations to develop and administer national examination programs, the results of which are used by hundreds of institutions. Examples are the College-Level Examination Program of the College Entrance Examination Board and the College Proficiency Examination Program of the New York Board of Regents and the American College Testing Program.

Faculty members from a variety of institutions are integrally involved in the programs. Formed into committees, they determine the subject-matter domain to be evaluated and write the test items. Faculty members also participate in administering examinations to develop national norms and in establishing academic policy at their institutions regarding accepting the results and recording them on the student's academic record.

Track 3. *Credit recommendations for extrainstitutional learning.* Since World War II, academic institutions have awarded credit toward credentials for educational accomplishment attained in extrainstitutional settings. The best example is to be found in formal military training. In order to give due recognition for military training, the academic community in 1945 organized itself under the aegis of the American Council on Education to establish credit equivalencies for the military's formal courses and training programs. More recently, ACE has taken leadership responsibility for a national program to establish credit equivalencies for formal courses of other sponsors, such as business and industry.

As with the preceding tracks, faculty members play a central role. They participate in the establishment of the policies and procedures used to formulate the credit recommendations. In addition, teams of faculty members from different institutions conduct the evaluations and establish the credit recommendations. And at the institutional level, faculty members determine policy for accepting the recommendations and applying them toward the student's educational objective.

Track 4. *Prior experiential learning.* A great deal of non-sponsored learning attained by a student prior to regular matriculation is of a type that cannot appropriately or efficiently be evaluated under tracks two and three. The learning may have been gained on the job, in avocational pursuits, in nonsponsored, self-directed study, or in formal instructional programs not covered by credit recommendations.

In the area of evaluation of experiential learning, conceptual and procedural advances have been made under the aegis of an organization now known as the Council for the Advancement of Experiential Learning. CAEL has identified and refined, in institutional tryouts, methods and techniques for evaluating such learning. As with the other tracks, faculty participation is central in conducting the evaluations, in establishing institutional policies, and in applying credit toward a student's educational objective.

Because evaluation in each of the four tracks is imprecise, credit and credentials as measures of educational accomplishment should always be used with great care. Assessment techniques vary from the crude and simple to the refined and sophisticated and rely mainly on expert judgment rather than psychometrically valid instruments. Ambiguously stated educational objectives also contribute to the imprecision of credit and credentials as measures of educational accomplishment.

Further complications arise because standards for educational accomplishment are flexible and not standardized, varying as they do among institutions and among curricula within an institution. Standards also fluctuate according to faculty members and examination systems, the qualifications of students available to undertake study, and the state of development of a given occupational field at the time study is undertaken.

The problems in assessment and certification of educational accomplishment lie partly in the lack of agreement within the academic community about the role that postsecondary institutions should play in certification. Some people assert that the function of instruction and the function of certification are antithetical and that linking the two is an impediment to quality education. Others insist that effective pedagogy requires reliable and valid certification of educational accomplishment. There is also a great deal of uncertainty about the educational consequences of assigning the function of certifying educational accomplishment to other agencies in the society.

Evaluation of educational accomplishment, while essential, involves various mixes of objective and subjective measures, expert judgment, and differing academic values. Even so, evaluation of educational accomplishment across much of postsecondary education is sufficiently reliable and valid to establish some commonality of meaning. Otherwise, the transfer of students among institutions and programs would now be totally dysfunctional and society would have ceased to rely to the extent it does on educational credit and credentials.

Pluralistic Ownership and Control

Pluralistic ownership or sponsorship and control of the academic enterprise as well as the traditional roles of faculties and nongovernmental accreditation have had a bearing on the variations in meaning and in acceptance of credits and credentials. The pluralistic ownership and sponsorship of postsecondary institutions is both mandated and encouraged by public policy, which reflects political and social values of long duration. The pluralism of postsecondary education is evident in that chartered or licensed educational institutions are creatures of state and local governments, religious bodies, agencies of the federal government, eleemosynary organizations, profit and nonprofit corporations, and proprietorships. As a result, institutions have had a great deal of autonomy and latitude in defining their purposes and objectives and in designing educational programs.

The chartering and licensing of educational institutions by state governments and, on a limited basis, by the federal government legitimize the operations of institutions of postsecondary education. Although this function of government agencies is generally effective, it cannot be relied on as the sole external validation of the quality and integrity of postsecondary institutions and their programs. Therefore, the roles of faculties and of nongovernmental accreditation take on increased significance for the meaning and worth of credit and credentials.

Nongovernmental accreditation, the highest form of formal recognition educational institutions and their programs can attain, is often critical to the meaning and worth of credit and credentials. Accreditation of institutions and programs of study by nongovernmental agencies and associations recognized by the Council on Postsecondary Accreditation provides for the external validation of the quality and integrity of the institution and its programs by peer groups of experts. Institutional accreditation indicates that the institution is generally meeting its stated objectives, but it does not standardize curricula or educational outcomes. Specialized accreditation, such as that used for dentistry, social work, and engineering programs, provides additional in-depth evaluation and validation that programs of study within an institution are meeting specific standards of special concern to agencies, associations, and faculties in the disciplinary and professional practice fields. Specialized accreditation promotes a degree of commonality but does not standardize educational outcomes among educational programs in a given field.

The traditional role of faculties has been a major force in controlling credit and credentials. Working under authority delegated by lay boards of control, faculties have had the chief responsibility for the academic undertaking. This responsibility includes designing educational programs, establishing academic policy, setting requirements and standards for degrees, providing instruction and supervising learning, and certifying student accomplishment. Because faculty members inherently differ in their interests, values, and competences, additional variables are introduced into the meaning of credit and credentials.

Other Forces and Factors

Reputations of institutions and the influence of disciplinary and occupational organizations are other forces and factors that affect the meaning of credit and credentials. Both relate to the perceived quality of institutions and educational programs. Selective admissions have long contributed to perceptions of quality. Institutions that have practiced a policy of highly selective admissions have been perceived as producing graduates more capable than those from less selective institutions and thus have tended to create the coin-of-the-realm for credit and credentials. The educational outcomes achieved by students at such colleges and universities tend to be viewed as the standards of excellence by other institutions.

Other factors contribute to institutional reputation and affect how that institution is perceived. These include the educational credentials held by its faculty, its graduate programs and research publications, and the success of its graduates over a prolonged period of time—success that cannot always be directly attributed to educational accomplishment.

Institutions often continue to reap dividends from a reputation achieved long ago but unwarranted today. Conversely, institutions or programs which attain superior quality often find that recognition lags years behind their deserved reputation. Similarly, a specialized curriculum of low quality may benefit from the perceived high quality of its parent institution, or, conversely a high-quality curriculum may suffer because its parent institution is perceived as being of low quality.

Occupational groups exert strong influence on educational programs and standards for student accomplishment and thus become a factor in determining the meaning of credentials. As occupational groups mature and gain the social acceptance necessary to substantiate their claims to custody of a body of knowledge and expertise, education for professional practice tends to become institutionalized in colleges and universities. Strong professional and occupational organizations, which seek to influence educational programs through licensure or certification, emerge concurrently with the development of specialized curricula of colleges and universities. As an occupational group evolves, educational considerations may be unduly influenced by goals of economic and social parity with more successful occupational groups. At some point, further educational requirements are added which tend to equate the educational accomplishment with that at a given degree level; yet the learning achieved may be difficult to rationalize as qualification for employment or professional practice in the field. The foregoing holds to some degree for academic disciplinary organizations composed of faculty members of colleges and universities.

The uses and value of educational credit and credentials, then, are shaped by many forces, some positive and some negative. Analysis of the system initially creates a sense of hopelessness. That impression is soon tempered, however, by the realization that credits and credentials continue to provide essential information about educational accomplishment and that, despite their imperfections, they serve useful educational and social purposes.

Even so, with the exception of institutional and specialized accreditation, no broad-scale efforts have been undertaken to improve the accuracy, adequacy, or commonality of information conveyed by the credit and credentialing system. For reasons of social and educational need and equity, now seems a propitious time to attempt to modify the system to serve today's society.

Chapters 3–8 undertake to amplify the basis for understanding the recommendations contained in chapter 9.

PART II

ANALYSES FOR THE TASK FORCE

CHAPTER 3

Educational Credentials: Past, Present, and Future

John Harris and William Troutt

If one had asked a few centuries ago about the identity of a certain Englishman, a typical answer would have been, "He's a Smith from Sussex." The same question in America today might be phrased, "He's a systems analyst with General Manufacturing." In small towns and rural America, many of us have heard relatives identify a person by parentage and place rather than by work and employer. The shift in how a person understands who he or she is represents a momentous societal change. In large measure, industrial and postindustrial societies reward their members according to their work, and studies show Americans to be consistent in their rankings of occupational status. In contrast, medieval society emphasized service to God through a hierarchically organized church.

Today's societies—capitalist and communist—emphasize productivity and encourage workers to strengthen the materialistic culture. Powerful reinforcements to the merit attributed to productivity are evidenced in having people identify themselves by their work, their ranking some kinds of work as more prestigious than other kinds, and recognizing the differences through social status and money. Vocational choice affects ranking by others, life style, and socioeconomic and geographic mobility. Furthermore, many young Americans still have powerful incentives to rise higher than their parents in job rankings. One's work thus becomes one's life, and any threat to career success must be opposed with all one's resources. Most professional organizations, it is charged, operate, as did the medieval guilds, primarily to keep their economic frontiers open and to guard against competition[1] lest the work

1. Perry London, *The Modes and Morals of Psychotherapy*, p. 149.

be devalued by an oversupply of workers. If poor performance becomes characteristic for a field, the social and monetary rewards could diminish.

Vast numbers of people have no inherited land or wealth that might confer status; no new frontiers remain to offer a route to change of status. No New World or Old West exists to be pioneered, where the disfranchised may start anew on their own. Advanced cultures have established material rewards and penalties that force most people to contribute to an industrial-technological society in order to feel good about themselves. An incredible burden is placed on the world of work to provide people with opportunities for material fulfillment.

Frontiers have been replaced by a quasi-meritocracy. To oversimplify and overstate, securing a credential through some combination of prescribed training, supervised experience, or standardized tests replaces lineage. Increasingly, the opportunity to get even some of the glittering prizes of modern economics depends not only on occupational choice and hard work but also on admission to an occupation. In this sense, credentialing is critical in a society dominated by material rather than spiritual values and by optimal productivity rather than social stability.

Formal education has served as a principal means for giving people "a better chance" at the jobs which bring social and material rewards. Perhaps no other society has so committed itself to optimizing productivity by maximally rewarding the individual for his achievements. At the same time, commitments to justice and equity demand equality of opportunity for the limited number of status-conferring jobs. Rewarding achievers, it may be noted, is the best way to maintain a production- and service-oriented society.

Formal education, with its presumed potential to compensate for hereditary and environmental differences, serves two functions. First, formal education made available or even mandatory for everyone relieves the prickings of conscience about equity. Second, it conditions and encourages its participants to base their vocational aspirations on their respective interests and abilities rather than on a family trade or inheritance. Education and its credentials therefore become a critical component to a society committed to production and equity.

This chapter is a broad treatment of the uses of educational credits, degrees, and other awards as credentials in our society and explores the past, present, and likely future roles of credentials. In addition to the use of credentials as an accolade for educational accomplishment, a pervading issue is how and when educational credentials are appropriate, valid, and reliable as indications of special professional or technical expertise. Other chapters deal specifically and technically with the same issues.

Evolution of the Present System

In the United States, certification by colleges and universities of academic accomplishments is formalized through the award of credits and degrees. Academic credentials for college students are usually certified internally, that is, by the faculty members who taught the student. By contrast, in Great Britain, external examiners are responsible for the certification function. At Oxford and Cambridge, for example, the component colleges are each responsible for instruction, and the university is the examining and degree-granting body. The technical and teacher-training institutes are responsible for instruction, but do not grant academic degrees.

In both countries, liberal arts faculties and professional schools recognize accomplishment through the form of academic degrees. Higher education institutions grant degrees; but, as noted in the previous chapter, the granting of a degree is not the same thing as licensure by a government agency or certification by a voluntary professional association. The ties, however, are many. State-approved teacher-training programs at colleges and universities lead directly to state government certification as a teacher. Likewise, a professional association may accredit a professional program at a university and thereby bind itself to accept the institution's degree as qualifying program graduates for professional status.

American academic degrees are a special kind of credential, differing in function from similar degrees in other countries.

U.S. students usually pursue higher education to earn a degree, which certifies an accomplishment but not necessarily a competence. Degrees may serve as prerequisites for admission to graduate study, entrance into some professions, and the right to take licensing examinations for some occupations. Rarely are they certificates to professional practice, yet nearly always are prerequisite to reaching professional candidacy. In continental Europe, students often enter higher education, not to earn a degree, but to qualify for the state examination for a profession; professional certification from government, rather than a degree, marks the end of a student's education.[2]

Origins of Educational Credentialing

Our system of educational credentialing emerged during the Middle Ages with the founding of the first university at Bologna, Italy. University (*universitas*) represents a generic term describing guilds and all other types of collective associations. The foreign students of Bologna organized a *universitas*—or guild—for protection against the profiteering of townspeople on room and board, and, united, they brought townspeople to terms by threatening to depart as a body. Successful in that collective threat, students turned on their professors, whose economic dependence on student fees forced them to be responsive to student concerns.[3] Student guild regulations, which were designed to control both the quantity and quality of instruction, required faculty members to perform certain functions or pay a fine.

Excluded from the student *universitas*, professors formed their own guilds. Admission to the *universitas* of professors came only by direct examination. Like other guilds, professors could admit or reject candidates for membership. Taking the doctoral degree initially meant admission to the guild of doctors. (In the Middle Ages, the terms "doctor," "professor," and "master" were synonymous.) The faculty examined candidates and licensed them to "incept"—"begin"—by giving a

2. Stephen H. Spurr, *Academic Degree Structures*, p. 3.
3. Charles H. Haskins, *The Rise of Universities*, pp. 8–10.

public lecture. The faculty conferred in its own name the license to teach to those passing this examination.[4]

The titles "master" and "doctor" conveyed the full right to teach at any university without further examination. Once a university received papal approval to grant degrees, its graduates were internationally sanctioned.[5] The terms "master" and "doctor" implied titles to an office, a faculty position. As control of the early university shifted away from the faculty, such titles lost their original meaning and became honorary distinctions, that is, a degree. Only at Oxford and Cambridge does the term "master" continue to denote a faculty position.[6]

The title "bachelor" at that time signified the right of advanced students (known at Bologna as *bachalari*) to tutor in limited areas. Reaching the stage of bachelorship involved a formal disputation in grammar and logic with a master and examination by a faculty board. Over the years, the bachelor's degree disappeared in Germany whereas it became the dominant degree in England.[7]

American Higher Education Evolvement

The English college provided the initial model for American higher education. From Harvard's founding in 1636 until the Civil War, American colleges awarded only the bachelor's degree. The Bachelor of Arts (B.A.) initially represented the only degree signifying completion of a four-year curriculum. The Bachelor of Science (B.S.) emerged in the mid-nineteenth century to recognize completion of a three-year scientific curriculum. It remained a second-class degree, however, until the twentieth century.

Earned graduate degrees were not awarded in the United States until the last half of the nineteenth century. The Master of Arts (M.A.) was awarded earlier, but only as a matter

4. Hastings Rashdall, *The Universities of Europe in the Middle Ages,* 1:150, 223.

5. Henry Malden, *On the Origin of Universities and Academic Degrees,* p. 21.

6. Spurr, *Academic Degree Structures,* p. 10.

7. Ibid., pp. 10–11.

of course to all B.A. recipients paying fees and staying out of trouble for three years.[8] The founding of the Johns Hopkins University as an institution devoted to graduate education ushered in the development of the American university and the award of earned graduate degrees.

The Rise of Professional Education

Until late in the nineteenth century, professional education continued to emulate the apprentice model of the medieval guild. Candidates for a profession learned by imitation and observation while under the employ of a professional. The aspiring lawyer, minister, or physician might also read widely from the library of his employer, but the emphasis in professional training remained on learning by doing rather than on formal study at the university.[9]

Professionals eventually began to band together to teach apprentices collectively in schools. Lecturing replaced learning by doing. Low standards of admission and even lower expectations of student performance, however, marked these early professional schools. An upgrading of law and medical education occurred around the turn of the century with law and medical schools receiving university affiliation; simultaneously, admission and academic standards were raised. The Flexner Report, a 1910 study of medical education funded by the Carnegie Foundation for the Advancement of Teaching, proved to be an epoch-making force in improving professional education. By its emphasis on requiring medical education to be postbaccalaureate, the Flexner Report placed medical education at the forefront of professional education. Training in fields such as architecture, business, and education followed the trend of medicine and law by establishing graduate professional schools.[10]

The Elective and Credit Systems

The latter part of the nineteenth century also witnessed a radical curricular change in higher education with the intro-

8. Frederick Rudolph, *American College and University*, p. 336.
9. John S. Brubacher and Willis Rudy, *Higher Education in Transition*, pp. 198–99.
10. Ibid., pp. 205, 207–8.

duction of the elective and credit systems. Until the 1870s, American higher education followed a traditional classical curriculum that allowed no variation in student course selection. Such a system presented no need for a complex educational accounting system: the end product (the student at graduation) provided the only necessary measure.[11]

In 1872, Harvard initiated the elective system, by which students were offered a wide selection of courses. To Harvard's President Eliot, the classical curriculum represented routine recitation capable of producing only an average product while an elective system provided motivation for superior work.[12] Harvard's elective system flourished and eventually provided a model for most colleges and universities. The elective system did bring much needed flexibility to degree programs emphasizing the production of Christian gentlemen. It also enabled American higher education to embrace the German model of scientific study and to develop specialized curricula to meet the needs of the contemporary society.

The elective system replaced an educational anachronism, but it also eliminated a standard set of experiences associated with earning a college degree. Diverse and specialized curricula devoid of standardization (1) decreased the common points of reference among college graduates, and (2) made less valid the assumptions of minimum proficiencies or knowledge attained by degree holders.

The variety of courses offered students a choice, but it also created a need for a system of quantifying student progress within the educational process. Courses came to be measured in terms of classroom contact. By 1877, the University of Michigan catalog indicated "24 or 26 full courses are required for the bachelor's degree (full course equals five exercises per week per semester, whether in lab, recitation or lecture)."[13] By the 1880s Harvard measured progress toward a degree by the accumulated number of courses, for example, 18.4 courses,

11. Barbara Burn, "The American Academic Credit System," in *Structure of Studies and Place of Research in Mass Higher Education,* p. 119.

12. Brubacher and Rudy, *Higher Education in Transition,* p. 109.

13. Dietrich Gerhard, "Emergence of the Credit System in American Higher Education," *AAUP Bulletin* 41 (1955):654.

rather than completion of a total course of study. Such practices were soon adopted nationwide.[14]

The credit system emerged as a corollary to the elective system. President Eliot's system of electives brought about a well-defined structure of degrees and course-time units expressed in semester hours.[15] By the early 1900s the credit system also embraced graduate degree programs.[16] Colleges found the system offered a common measure for student progress toward a degree. The credit system, like the elective system, is flexible: it allows students a varied combination of learning experiences, some prescribed and some elective. Nevertheless, it has disadvantages. Typically, student performance is assessed course by course rather than through comprehensive appraisal. Hence, an earned degree may represent an accumulation of credits rather than a mastery of knowledge with little assurance of a body of integrated knowledge.

Credit hours enter decision making about institutions beyond the realm of student records. Costs per credit hour or credits produced per facility are components in institutional analyses. In state funding of higher education, the credit hour has in many instances been adopted as a principal unit, with funding formulas for public higher education based largely on the number of credit hours produced by an institution. Today more than half the states use funding formulas, and many states without formulas carefully consider student credit hour production in determining appropriations for colleges and universities.[17] Given this widespread usage, any departure from the credit hour system will not be easily or soon forthcoming.[18]

Continuing Education Unit

With the growth of interest in continuing education, one writer noted some twenty years ago that "a stage was to be

14. Burn, "American Academic Credit System," p. 119.
15. James M. Heffernan, "The Credibility of the Credit Hour," *Journal of Higher Education* 44 (1973):61–72.
16. Burn, "American Academic Credit System," p. 119.
17. Heffernan, "Credibility of the Credit Hour," p. 65.
18. For discussion, see John Folger, "The Administrative Uses of Credit," chapter 8 in the present volume.

reached where the credit system would know of no time or age limit, where the 'earning' of additional credits, for some practical reason or other . . . would stop short only of the deathbed."[19] With the advent of the continuing education unit, recognition for continuing education, as with degree credits, can be earned at any point in life for a variety of non-degree-related educational activities.

The product of a National Task Force appointed in 1968, the continuing education unit (CEU) is defined as "ten contact hours of participation in an organized continuing education experience under responsible sponsorship, capable direction, and qualified instruction."[20] It was designed to recognize and record individual and institutional participation in adult education activities, and is gaining recognition as a standard unit of measurement in continuing education.

Under the system, an adult learner receives CEU's for satisfactory completion of a variety of approved experiences—training programs, workshops, conferences, in-service seminars, skill-upgrading courses, and the like. An adult participant may accumulate, update, and transfer information about noncredit continuing education experiences and in some cases may translate his CEU credentials into academic credits.[21] CEU's are used as building blocks in programs designed for continuing professional recognition and vocational competence or for meeting state relicensing requirements. They are often packaged to provide the type of recognition that students in academic credit programs receive in certificate or diploma programs. In fact, some community colleges such as Jefferson College in Missouri award a Continuing Education Diploma.[22]

19. Gerhard, "Emergence of the Credit System," p. 660.

20. Hazel G. Small, "The Continuing Education Unit," in *A Guide to Adult Education Programs in Area Vocational Centers*, pp. 85, 81.

21. See pp. 240–41 for Recommendation Fourteen and accompanying discussion by the Task Force on Educational Credit and Credentials with respect to proper uses of the continuing education unit, restrictions on its direct conversion to degree credit units, and criteria for individual evaluation of CEU's through assessment procedures appropriate for extrainstitutional learning.

22. Ronald W. Hoenninger and Joe W. Dyer, "Accrediting the New Clientele for Post-Secondary Education," p. 1.

Certificates

For post-high-school study, American higher education has normally not assigned degree status to programs that omit the accepted liberal arts component of the day. This tradition is of long standing; for example, early science students at Princeton who did not take Greek or Latin were awarded certificates rather than degrees.[23]

The award of certificates for post-high-school specialty study is most common at the vocational and technical field levels. Such awards recognize completion of a set of courses of less than two years of study or a set of requirements that do not include a general/liberal education component. Certificate-related study is usually designed to satisfy prerequisites for government licensing or voluntary professional certification examinations to meet minimum requirements for entry-level employment in the vocational and technical fields. For instance, course work for an associate degree in secretarial science takes about four semesters and includes studies in the subject-matter fields associated with general/liberal education requirements, whereas a certificate program of study in secretarial science is shorter and normally does not include the general/liberal education requirement.

At the postbaccalaureate levels, certificates are sometimes awarded for prescribed courses of study that do not fit the usual nomenclature or requirements for graduate degrees. An example is the Specialist in Education, usually an award for post-master's-degree study of less than the doctoral level.

Professional Degrees and the Professions

Baccalaureate and graduate degrees in professional practice fields, like associate degrees and certificates awarded in vocational and technical fields, reflect a close alignment between classroom study and actual practice. In the professional degree fields, specific expectations of competence are higher than in the academic disciplines. The award of the professional degree is one indication of competence to perform in a given field. Its meaning, however, is not the same as licensure

23. Rudolph, *American College and University*, p. 113.

or voluntary certification in that field. The professional degree includes additional requirements that reflect the values of the academy, particularly those associated with general/liberal arts education. Licensure and voluntary certification are intended to focus more narrowly on competence to practice, and required formal education—certified by the award of a degree —is often a prerequisite to sit for the examinations.

The linkages between formal college and university education and qualification to work at a level considered professional are untidy and intricate. While some professional-level work is tied to mandatory government licensure or voluntary professional certification, other fields such as management are not and the degree may be accepted by the employer as evidence—but not necessarily assurance—of competence.

Linkages between work and degrees are ever-evolving and appear to be growing more direct. According to one observer, the practice of linking jobs to degrees has become "so entrenched and has enough plausibility and practical convenience that it will not soon be eradicated."[24] The development of a profession appears to be accompanied by tightening ties between an occupational group and the professional schools in the field. This relationship to some extent expresses the economic self-interest of the profession. It also grows out of the joint need to define curriculum content and a need on the part of professional schools to transmit attitudes as well as skills and knowledge.[25]

Given the link between professional degrees and entry into the professions, the recent growth in the kinds and numbers of professional schools is unsurprising. Until the turn of the century, professional study was limited to law, medicine, and theology. Today a wide variety of professional specialties can be studied at a variety of degree levels. Although the doctorate continues to be a first professional degree in some fields, an increasing number of professions are utilizing a professional

24. Harold Orlans, "The Fatuity of Credentialing Everyone and Everything," in *Formulating Policy in Postsecondary Education*, ed. John F. Hughes and Olive Mills, p. 273.

25. Christopher Jencks and David Riesman, *The Academic Revolution*, p. 251.

bachelor's degree. Professional degrees at the baccalaureate and graduate levels tend to be identified by a modified use of their generic term, Bachelor of Nursing, Master of Social Work, or Doctor of Education. Professional degrees at the associate and bachelor's levels have not been universally successful in gaining esteem of students; a major handicap may be the limited career options they offer and their limitation as qualifications for advanced levels of study.[26]

Professional education has been characterized as consisting of three parts: the basic arts and sciences, the professional sciences, and application.[27] A similar characterization helps distinguish professional degrees from academic and technical degrees. Academic degrees represent focus on subject matter in the arts and sciences rather than on application. Technical degree programs focus, not on the arts and sciences or the subject matter of the professional sciences, but on the direct application of knowledge.

Current Degree Structures

The associate degree represents the most recent addition to our ever-evolving, seven-hundred-year-old structure of academic degrees. The associate degree marks completion either of the first two years of a bachelor's degree program or a two-year technical or vocational course. The University of Chicago first awarded the associate degree in 1900, replacing certificates awarded for the first two years of undergraduate study in their "junior college." Junior colleges established as feeder colleges for the University of Chicago also adopted the associate degree. Virtually all junior and community colleges now confer the associate degree, as do many senior institutions. The Associate of Arts and the Associate of Science represent the most common associate degrees.[28]

The medieval beginnings of the bachelor's degree, like those of the master's and doctor's degrees, have been noted. Although the bachelor's degree no longer connotes completion of a prescribed curriculum, it is still almost universally based on four years of study. Attempts to shorten the time span have

26. Spurr, *Academic Degree Structures*, pp. 22–23.
27. William J. McClothlin, *The Professional Schools*, p. 36.
28. Spurr, *Academic Degree Structures*, pp. 41–42.

been generally unsuccessful. Besides the liberal arts degrees of Bachelor of Arts and Bachelor of Science, other established four-year degrees include Bachelor of Science in Education, Bachelor of Music, Bachelor of Business Administration, and Bachelor of Fine Arts.[29]

The master's degree is now recognized as the initial post-baccalaureate degree in both the liberal arts and professional fields. The period of study varies from one to two years. A liberal arts master's degree is identified as either a Master of Arts or a Master of Science; in professional fields the degree title may be modified by an addition such as Master of Arts in Library Science or by a separate professional designation such as Master of Public Administration.[30]

In recent years an intermediate academic award between the master's and doctor's has begun to emerge as recognition for academic programs that extend at least one year beyond the master's but do not qualify as doctoral programs. Such programs have gained importance, but no single designation has received widespread acceptance. Commonly used terms are "specialist" in education, "candidate" or Master of Philosophy in the arts and sciences, and "engineer."[31]

Although the doctorate no longer denotes an office or faculty-member status, it remains the pinnacle of formal academic awards. Today it usually requires three years of full-time graduate study and demonstrated capacity to do independent work. This demonstration of ability may take several forms. The Doctor of Philosophy recognizes completed research; the Doctor of Education, an applied research effort; the Doctor of Medicine, clinical competence; the Juris Doctor, the capacity to analyze legal problems.[32]

The most striking observation about our current degree structure is that today's degrees convey no standard meaning beyond being general statements of intellectual interests and time spent in study. The evolvement of our system of educational credentials reveals a gradual diffusion of what it means to be a college or university graduate. Degrees appear to be

29. Ibid., pp. 49–50.
30. Ibid., p. 65.
31. Ibid., pp. 14–15.
32. Ibid., p. 15.

functioning less and less as commonly understood indicators of individual academic accomplishment and competence. What, then, do today's educational credentials mean? What functions do they serve in American society? And how well do they perform those functions? Perhaps the best approach to answers is first to consider how all credentials—educational, government licensure, and professional certification—*should* function.

Role of Credentials

"Credentials" in this section means objective indices of merit of competence provided by educational institutions, government licensure agencies, or professional certification agencies. Where a modification is warranted, the terms "educational credentials," "licensure," or "professional certification" will be used.

In discussing credentials, it is difficult to avoid either the confident advocacy of the ideal public protection or the cynical denunciation of legalized or institutionalized self-interest. Miller, writing about credentialing in health care administration, presents a balanced set of principles for credentialing in all three of its generic manifestations and in all fields. The principles, paraphrased in some cases for general applicability, are as follows:

1. Credentialing should minimize risks for harm to the public and individual consumers by clearly identifying the competent and qualified.

2. Credentialing that recognizes and encourages pride in accomplishment and the mastery of knowledge and skills is in the public interest, because it contributes to the advancement of society and the improvement of the human condition.

3. Mandatory credentialing should be exercised only where there is a demonstrable relationship to the health, safety, and protection of the public.

4. Credentialing that is intimately related to the health and safety of the public and individuals should periodically require proof that those who are credentialed still possess the requisites and have kept pace with advances in the field.

5. Credentialing is substantially involved with the system of economic, professional, and social rewards in society.

Therefore, it is incumbent on the system to provide alternate ways of recognizing attitudes, competences, knowledge, and skills regardless of how or where they were achieved. To do less is to discriminate unjustly.

6. Credentialing activities of agencies and institutions, whether publicly controlled or sponsored by occupational and professional organizations, substantially intersect with the public interest. Such agencies' and institutions' policy-making and governing boards, therefore, should represent broad social interests rather than a single occupation or profession.[33]

Miller's principles are set forth here because they deal with credentialing in a positive way but guard against abuses. If these principles for the role of credentialing in general are valid, then educational credentials may be judged by their contribution to these principles. Even to begin to make such a judgment on the validity and effectiveness of educational credentials, however, requires an understanding of (1) the functions of credentialing in our industrial and technological society, (2) the role of educational credentials in the evolvement of a work specialty or profession, and (3) the unique role of educational credentials as accolades for individual accomplishment.

Credentialing's Vital Functions

Credentialing serves a number of society's needs. As one function, it serves to sanction a body of knowledge, techniques, and skills for a given work specialty. In the world of work, then, practice may be informed by theory and theory modified by experience. Coupling theory and experience with scientific inquiry advances the knowledge and practice related to the specialty. Sometimes, however, suspicion creeps in that some work specialties are artificially constructed more by jargon than by substantial knowledge and skill.

Credentialing also serves to maintain a specialty work force. The persons within a specialty acquire some group identity through their common educational or training experiences and through having met common entry requirements. Creden-

33. Jerry W. Miller, "Credentials for Health Administration," in *Selected Papers of the Commission on Education for Health Administration,* 2:261–62.

tialing is in a sense an initiation rite—an induction into a distinct work group. Given the diverse backgrounds of persons within occupations, fellow workers must, for the sake of communication, develop some common reference points. Further, initiation rites are especially important to people who derive much of their self-identity and social status from a group. By undergoing a common preparation and demonstrating their competence, credentialed workers identify themselves by their commonalities with fellow workers and their contrasts with other people.

Credentials also serve as passports. In an industrial-technological society, such a need exists for many people whose primary attachment is to their work, wherever the work is. A mobile work population is not new in this country but is accentuated by the range and sophistication of work specialties. Thus, credentials serve two basic needs. First, credentials provide valuable information to employers who have no opportunity to know the competences of people on a personal basis, as they might in other societies. Second, credentials provide managers of a specialized work force with third-party, presumably objective, judgments about the competences of potential employees. As such, credentials are supportive of a mobile, industrialized, technological society.

Particularly in technological pursuits, high value is placed on talent. Talent, skill, training, and ingenuity count heavily in an age when businesses and nations compete on the basis of the best techniques, the most efficient way of doing something, whether it be producing food or splitting atoms. In any case, credentials serve as proxies for competence and as some basis for evaluation. A given society often measures its human resources in terms of credentials and judges its investment in education by the yield in talent as assumed to be measured by educational credentials or license credentials awarded.

The role of credentials in the service sector of the world of work appears to be greater than in the production sector. The United States has more people employed in service jobs (government, education, law, medicine, recreation, welfare, etc.) than in production (manufacturing, agriculture, materials processing, etc.). Recipients of service work, it is generally assumed, are not equipped to judge directly the quality and efficiency of services, particularly professional services—medical advice, financial consultation, and the like. In contrast, the consumer is presumed to have some competence to judge the quality and relative cost of products (automobiles, houses, etc.). In services, therefore, the credentials of the renderer are thought to be critical evidence to consumer judgment. The more specialized the work, the less able the nonspecialist is presumed to be in evaluating competence.

The price people pay for services often is affected by supply, which, in turn, may be affected by credentials. At professional levels, the consumer's choices are often restricted to licensed or certified services or to no service. Service manpower supply is governed by the quality standards set within the restrictive credential system and so to some extent is pricing. First, in periods of low supply and high demand for certain services, society may gain increased supply and eventually lower prices if the credentialing system lowers the standards and thus increases the number of admissions into the field. As Riesman points out, "Conscientious mediocre service may be better than none at all; sloppy, 'lost weekend,' mediocre service may be worse."[34] Second, periods of oversupply afford opportunities to improve quality by raising entrance standards without denying reasonable availability of services. Manipulation of entrance standards may also be in the self-interest of occupational groups. In any case, credentialing of any kind can be a way of controlling prices of services and supply of persons authorized to sell services.[35]

Relicensure and professional recertification are becoming a

34. David Riesman, personal communication to John Harris, July 22, 1976.

35. Control over prices of services by professions may be lessening. A recent Supreme Court decision (*Goldfarb* v. *Virginia State Bar*) treated the minimum fee schedule enforced by a state bar association as a violation of the Sherman Antitrust Act. The Court, abandoning the historical presumption that the legal profession is immune from federal antitrust attack, termed enforcement of the fee schedule "a classic illustration of price fixing." The decision establishes the jurisdictional framework for future antitrust lawsuits against learned professions and signals an end for required fee schedules in other upper-level professions (Michael Sennet, "Antitrust—Goldfarb v. Virginia State Bar: Professional Legal Service Held To Be Within the Ambit of Federal Antitrust Laws," *Loyola University Law Journal*, Winter 1976, pp. 254–76).

significant practice. Practitioners in various professions are being required to complete a certain amount of continuing education within a given number of years and, often, to stand certain examinations in their specialty. Not only then does credentialing assure a minimum floor of proficiency at entry into the profession, but also thereafter may require assurances about upgrading and currency of knowledge and skill. This latter policy is expected to spread.

Our society depends heavily on meritocratic interpretations of people. Credentials are passports and currency for human talent and accomplishment. Admittedly, they are proxies for human achievement and capability, not direct reflections of them. The validity of the proxies has always been questioned. However, to reject credentialing outright, rather than question the validity and reliability of particular credentials under certain circumstances, is essentially to question or reject technological or industrial society as we know it.

Educational Credentials in the Work Place

Educational credentials have always carried their own significance, independent from occupational credentials or economic advancement. In order to understand the role of educational credentials, the role of credentialing in the society must be understood in the context of today's cultural values.

Today's commitment to social egalitarianism and the maintenance of a productive society is a continuing tension. Assuming that the maintenance of a productive society will continue to play a significant role in social policies, we may also assume that credentialing will remain. It will continue to be shaped by both sides of the tension.

The principal questioning about the use of educational credentials, which is now quite intense, lies in two areas. First, grades as a measure of educational attainment correlate minimally with larger work achievement and success. Hoyt, in a review of studies of college or professional school grades and success in business, teaching, engineering, medicine, and scientific research, found no to only very moderate relationships between grades and success in professional practice.[36] Even

36. Donald P. Hoyt, "College Grades and Adult Accomplishment: A Review of Research," *Educational Record* 47 (1966):70–75.

in highly intellectual jobs, like scientific research, Taylor, Smith, Ghiselin have shown superior on-the-job performance is unrelated to high college grades.[37] It should be emphasized that the relationship sought between collegiate performance in such studies dealt, not with the differences between college and no college, but with differences among college graduates. A study of differences in job performance between persons with no college work and graduates would be difficult to conduct, in part because college graduates typically have the better opportunities for entry-level employment. Thus, the undocumented assumption still prevails that college graduates perform better than nongraduates.

The second concern is the legality of requiring credentials that are not demonstrably related to the work to be performed. Given the materialistic values and the societal arrangement which makes work a contingency for the rewards of the economic system, access to work is tantamount to the opportunity to pursue life, liberty, and happiness. Any entry criterion to a given occupation not bearing a direct relation to work performance may be considered a threat to civil rights. The most important legal developments in this area are title VII of the 1964 Civil Rights Act, the 1971 *Willie S. Griggs et al.,* v. *Duke Power Company* class action suit, and the Equal Employment Opportunity Act of 1972. The central concern of the two laws and the Supreme Court decision is equitable treatment of racial minorities and women in the labor market. Any selection or screening criteria having a particular effect on a given group must be justified by a demonstrable relationship to work performance.

Many observers see, beyond the civil rights issues, some implications related to "affected classes."[38] One may speculate about the probability that direct legislation or litigation will demand that high school diplomas and college and university degrees have no role in personnel selection except where there is a significant correlation with the work.

Educational credentials function in connection with general

37. Quoted in David C. McClelland, "Testing for Competence Rather Than for 'Intelligence,'" *American Psychologist* 28 (1973):2.
38. See Sheila Huff, "Credentialing by Tests or by Degrees," *Harvard Educational Review* 44 (1974):246–69.

credentialing principally with respect to professional work, to limit those eligible to perform certain functions. As previously noted, voluntary associations and government agencies also function as credentialing authorities in ways that need to be delineated in order to understand the relationships between work and credentialing.

At first brush, it appears that voluntary associations and government agencies have discrete credentialing responsibilities. In actuality, voluntary associations and government agencies are involved at different stages in the evolvement of a work specialty into a profession.

Caplow delineates four steps in the transformation of a work specialty into a profession.[39] The first step is establishing a voluntary association, with membership criteria designed to exclude the unqualified. The second step is naming the work and the workers so as to lessen the identification with the occupational status being left behind. The name must (*a*) stake out claim to a definite piece of the world of work and (*b*) imply a monopoly for a given work specialty. The third step is to delineate and adopt a code of ethics which, aside from "certain hypocrises," limits competition within the group.

To this point, the voluntary association is the credentialing agent; but at the fourth step, one of its prime objectives becomes gaining public or governmental sanction to limit the chosen occupational title to persons who have met the requirements—registered engineers, public accountants. The final stage occurs when performing activities of the profession without the credentials becomes a crime.

Concurrent with the fourth step, when governmental sanctions are sought and obtained, are three other developments. One is the development of prerequisite training, which is controlled by the professional association. Setting admission and qualifying standards are especially important. Legal sanction is also established for particular privileges of confidence and, after some conflict, of working relations with related professional groups.

Caplow's four-step description of the typical evolution of a

39. Theodore Caplow, *Sociology of Work*, pp. 139–40.

work specialty into a profession is important for two reasons. One, it shows voluntary association credentialing usually is a precursor to governmental credentialing, that is, state sanction of the position of the voluntary association. Thus, voluntary association and state credentialing are not really distinct. Second, Caplow's analysis begins to reveal the role educational credentials play in general credentialing: the nearer an occupation is to the final stage of professionalization, the more "training" becomes "education" and the greater the general claim the occupation has on the multiversity.

Miller suggests that educational credentials are particularly helpful during a profession's evolvement into a distinct and consistent role. He also notes that educational institutions usually fall short of being responsive to job market demands at two points: early in the development of a profession, and later in the evolution, when the role of the profession is settled.[40]

Colleges and universities will probably continue a role in general credentialing because of their contributions to the professions. As noted, the evolvement of a profession includes laying claim to a special curriculum or even a separate school within universities or colleges. The closer an occupation is to being a profession, the more it is based on an aggregated body of theory and practice. Professional education, as the keeper and developer of this body, is expected to induct the students into the profession not only through teaching the theory and skills of practice but also through inculcating "professional" attitudes. Concerning the latter attribute, competence as the sole criterion for entering practice—even if it could be measured directly—would not assure the professional attitudes hoped for through extended professional education. In such manner are educational credentials intricately tied to general credentialing by the social dynamic of professionalization.

Related to this theme is Miller's suggestion that educational credentials, unlike other types of credentials, "are less likely to retard desirable evolution of the profession."[41] That is, as

40. Miller, "Credentials for Health Administration," p. 268.
41. Ibid.

an occupation shapes itself toward becoming a profession, so too the education component may well evolve and be adapted to changed needs. To the extent that the education and training are revised constructively to meet the evolving profession's needs, the greater the likelihood that general credentialing will include educational credentials as requirements. This point is pertinent inasmuch as most occupations continually seek professional status.

Beyond professional credentialing, educational credentials will continue to be important for several reasons, including tradition. At least since Plato, education has been viewed as a talent filter as well as a talent developer. Thus, higher education often creates demand by supply: with the availability of a new type of graduate, the society often becomes aware of new needs or needs previously ignored. A glance through the U.S. Civil Service Commission's handbook for white-collar jobs reveals that accredited college work is sought for many of the positions described.[42] It is distinctly possible that the enlarging service component of the work force and the bureaucratization of government and other institutions are related to the large supply of college and university graduates. College graduates often fit into service jobs in bureaus. It has been suggested, for example, that federal and state legislative staffs have been enlarged in part because numbers of social science postbaccalaureate students and degree holders are not being absorbed into teaching and research positions.

A society striving to carry forward both an egalitarian ethic and economic productivity will value judgments about a person's intellectual achievements and ability to persist toward conceptual, artistic, or technological goals. The relative freedom within the academic estate to make such judgments apart from political or economic considerations is advantageous to our society; that is, the more politicized our society becomes, the more it may value judgments relatively free of political and legal biases. The alternative is for business, industry, and government to make these judgments increasingly

42. *Handbook X-188, Qualifications Standards for White-Collar Positions under the General Schedule*, p. 15.

through direct measures of talent believed to be related to respective jobs. A logical extension would then appear to be a "bureau of human weights and dimensions."

The widespread use of educational credits to evaluate people for many purposes other than professional credentialing makes the public trust responsibility of the academy greater than ever before. The academic community would be acting irresponsibly if it turned to some other agency to make judgments about abilities to write logically, think critically, or carry out scientific experiments simply because the task is unpleasant. The world of work needs such judgments, and the academy is best equipped to render them. Faculties, administrators, and lay boards should remember that educational credits and degrees are in reality public credentials—as in general they always have been. Earlier, degrees served as credentials to practice only in a few fields—law, theology, and medicine. Now educational credits and credentials serve many fields.

In view of the questioning about the use of educational credentials and the ultimate possibility of a "bureau of human weights and dimensions," the best alternative for the society and the academic community would seem to be: (1) Retain within the academic estate the educational credentialing authority to make judgments about academic achievement. Those judgments should, in society's interests, be made where political pressures and fads have the least opportunity to affect standards and procedures of evaluation. (2) In turn, the academic community should delineate criteria for its judgments, making them as explicit and public as possible. For the most part, academic institutions are operationally ill-equipped and reluctant to assess and certify competence attained outside the academy through nontraditional means, though substantial progress is being made.

The values and effects of general credentialing will increasingly become a major social and political issue. The typical conservative-liberal dichotomy is not in perfect harmony with the varying views of credentialing. Higher education's role in general credentialing can be only partially influenced by purely educational considerations.

Educational Credentials as Accolades

The preceding discussion dealt with the use of educational credentials in the larger process of general credentialing in technological societies. In this respect, educational credentials are essentially means to other ends. In many ways, however, they represent ends in themselves.

The instrumental value of education is so deeply ingrained in us as members of industrial and technological cultures that it is difficult to value education as an end itself. A case can be made that all education represents a means to larger ends and should be judged as an instrumentality to effect those ends. An end may be greater self-understanding or a keener understanding of one's environment. The understanding gained may help one to accept oneself or to adapt to society; conversely, the understanding gained may be used in the hope of changing oneself or society.

Something less lofty is usually meant by the *value* of education. Typically, it means direct preparation for a job or professional task. Its instrumentality is manifested in how directly evidences (credentials) of preparation (education) transfer into the currency of professional credentials.

Higher education has another personal and social role not directly related to personal income and society's material advancement. As a young social scientist in the 1930s, Lyle Lanier pointed out that "progress" in human affairs is a relatively recent concept. Only in the last few centuries have some people perceived they could deliberately and steadily improve their lot.[43] Education is a primary agent in this concept of social progress; its value is then to be judged according to its success in facilitating large societal projects designed to bring about economic and social progress.

Academic credentials as accolades have a much longer history, and some of these earlier purposes still hold for many persons both in and outside the academy. The Socratic dialogues were apparently pursued for the understanding they engendered. The great Rabbinic tradition was intended to

43. Lyle H. Lanier, "A Critique of the Philosophy of Progress," in *I'll Take My Stand,* by Twelve Southerners, pp. 122–54.

develop religious and moral clarity and behavior consistent with those common understandings. The medieval university provided some sanctuary from the fixed conceptions of the contemporary church. These examples point to the academy as an estate which serves best when it serves independently of the social agenda of the moment.

The academy's relative independence is manifested by the less than perfect match between its accolades and awards in the general culture. The university's highest accolades presumably go to the contemplative, analytical, and scholarly. Those who persist in objective inquiry are the academy's exemplars. In contrast, religious leaders and social reformers are expected to be advocates. Business people and public administrators are expected to make things happen. These differences, although more real in theory than in practice, illustrate underlying differences between the reward systems of a culture's major estates. It should be no surprise then that college grades do not match precisely with recognition and advancement in the nonacademic world.

In fact, many persons have done well in school but have made little money and achieved little or no social status. Is it proper to judge the academic credentials as faulty because they are not consistent with the values or standards outside the academy? Why not judge the world's values and standards by the academy's? Is there evidence that people stand on their own merit more in the give and take of business, industry, and government than in the academy?

Take the case of the seventy-year-old man who wanted a degree in classical Greek at the University of Georgia. As some people wish to paint, climb mountains, or become accomplished musicians, some wish to master a body of knowledge. In such cases, job relatedness is of no concern.

Even with such nonutilitarian motives, educational credentials as accolades of achievement are useful. First, credits earned toward the degree and the accompanying grades confirm progress and recognize achievement. The conferring of the degree through academic ceremony is essentially a rite of the academic estate confirming its own values—a way of saying to itself and society what it is that the academic world counts as important. Consistent with tradition, it so inducts graduates into the fraternity of learned persons.

All of this sounds a bit idyllic in a world bent on reductionist explanations. Nevertheless, the preservation of an estate free for unhindered analysis, research, and reflection is important to a society that would make deliberate effort to renew itself through improved understanding. The rites, privileges, and accolades of an estate celebrating its fundamental purposes are important to preserve and enhance. In the last analysis, as the academy is true to its purposes and traditions, the less it should be compelled to justify its accolades in terms of those of the larger society.

Although educational credentials may serve larger socioeconomic purposes, they should not lose their "academic" significance. But how well do they perform these different purposes? Do they serve all purposes equally well? Do they serve some at the expense of others? In short, what are the advantages and disadvantages of using educational credentials to serve such a wide variety of purposes?

Advantages and Disadvantages of Educational Credentials

While educational credit and credentials are being criticized, they continue to be awarded and used in conventional ways. Like any other social device that is widely adopted and deeply resistant to change, educational credentials serve our society in ways not to be lightly dismissed. Their assets and liabilities must be considered from both the socioeconomic and the academic perspectives.

Talent Scout

Educational credentialing and in a larger sense the entire educational system have enabled many people to improve their status over that of their parents. By giving people opportunities to demonstrate their abilities without regard to family background, racial identity, or socioeconomic condition, schooling has been a major way up. A college diploma has often been an earned ticket to improved socioeconomic status and personal enrichment. Perhaps, the United States, through its educational system, has come closer than any other society to allotting rewards to its members on the basis of their own efforts and abilities.

The phenomenal growth in the American economy since the Great Depression has created vast numbers of jobs, particularly service jobs, which have absorbed highly educated entrants into the job market. Now, according to the Bureau of Labor Statistics, we face a serious overproduction of college graduates for the job demand,[44] and advanced education may become a much less direct route to improved earning power. The significance of educational credentials as means to social and economic advancement may be changed dramatically by a tightened job market for college graduates.

What effects an oversupply of qualified people for jobs may have on the worth of the college degree are far from clear. One result may be that fewer people will seek degrees because they are not a certain route to a good job. Another possibility is that degrees will continue to be sought by a large proportion of the population because a degree will be essential even for job consideration.

Insularity from Politics

Colleges and universities, it was noted, not only account for student effort through units of time—credit hours—but also are often funded and managed on the basis of time measures. Institutions are to some extent funded to be themselves rather than direct agencies of the state. With respect to public institutions, it has been observed that a state may support a university, but it cannot own one. A university is not a university when it is a direct agency of the state. Instead the institutions have lay governing boards which are responsible for assuring that their respective institutions are operated in the public interest. If a political unit were to fund higher education strictly by buying products—so much competence in written English, so many chemists trained to specifications, etc.—it could directly select those outcomes it wanted at the moment.

44. U.S. Department of Labor, Department of Labor Statistics, *Occupational Manpower and Training Needs*, pp. 26–27.

In so doing, the state would directly shape the curricula of institutions. The credit hour, therefore, provides a way to fund colleges and universities in some proportion to their instructional loads without directly shaping the missions and means of their programs.

Two bulwarks protect American higher education from direct political interference. The most important in terms of number of institutions is the private sector. The other is the constitutionally established state universities. These traditions, undergirded by a lay board of control responsible for operating institutions in the public interest, reflect prevailing political and social values that colleges and universities operate best when they are protected to a degree from the lurches of the passions associated with social and political movements of a given time. The autonomy afforded private institutions and constitutionally established state universities stands as a model for all institutions of higher education. This degree of autonomy tends to keep political interference in the affairs of all institutions at a tolerable level. Thus, boards of control, administrations, and faculties remain reasonably free from external dicta in setting requirements for credentials.

Pluralism and Diversity

The credit system, which expresses educational attainment principally in terms of time spent (credit hours), has relieved educators of the awesome burden of developing national standards for minimum achievement, especially at the collegiate level. Our nation has a diversity of public and private institutions with varied regional, ethnic, religious, and class identities. This rich educational fabric, both the consequence and the reinforcer of a pluralistic culture, represents a great social strength. Conversely, an academic accounting system based on nationwide, common, explicit achievement units would probably diminish the diversity among institutions. The credit hour accommodates both educational diversity and a commonality for expressing educational attainment.

Historically, the prescribed college curriculum called for little accounting for educational progress other than by broad courses of study. The elective system created the need to account for educational progress in terms other than fixed programs of study. Furthermore, as student transfer among institutions increased, a common currency to credit students for work completed elsewhere became essential. Given the diversity among institutions and of programs within institutions, the time unit measure was the only way to bring standardization to higher education.

Misuse

The uncritical adoption of educational awards (grades, credits, degrees, and honors) as proxies in the sorting and rewarding of people in the world of work constitutes a serious problem. The evolution of this situation is understandable. A society in search of ways to recognize talent and initiative saw education as a relatively independent assessor. In many cases, therefore, educational credentials simply gave basically talented people a chance by lending credence to their implicit claims of competence and initiative.

Employers could and do use education as a first-line screening or filter system. Where "acceptable work performance" is ill-defined and reliable predictors of work performance have not been found, screening-by-credentials may be particularly attractive. Under such circumstances, it is considered, some minimum level of educational attainment may provide a base for communication among employees and employers. The ability to persist in higher education and adapt to social systems typical of our society may also be considered favorably.

Any selection criterion is ultimately judged by its "hits" and "misses." "Hits" occur when employees who have been selected on the basis of their educational credentials perform well and those without the requisite education consistently do less well. "Misses" occur when those selected by educational credentials do poorly and there is evidence that those rejected would have succeeded if given the chance. In too many situations, educational credentials as criteria "miss" as often as they "hit."

Even when the hits significantly exceed the misses, the case is made that education serves more as a filter than as a developer. As a free and affluent society reduces arbitrary inequities, the educational system may inherit a sorting function, and, to the extent that it sorts well, it will probably become the object of egalitarian criticism. To the extent it gives up the sorting function, either directly or indirectly by doing it poorly, other means of sorting will be called upon by a talent-conscious economy.

Definition and Integration of Learning

Whatever the problems with the medieval and early American curricula, most of the people interested in collegiate credentials knew their meaning. With the elective system came a phenomenal increase in types of degrees. Today, the development of a wide spectrum of institutions and programs under the rubric "postsecondary education," coupled with evolving modes of instructional delivery and assignment of credit, have left students, employers, sponsors, and even educators unsure about what is creditable as higher learning.

Aggregating separate course credits over a period of years to earn a degree does little to encourage or constrain integration of learning. Credits earned can easily mean subjects forgotten. Separate courses of study in related disciplines often do not lead students to understand, much less become proficient in, modes of inquiry and analysis common to most scholarly work. In brief, the credit hour system encourages a variety of educational sins and practices not conducive to integrated understanding. It becomes quite possible for students not to encounter the techniques and style of creative and analytical work that transcend subject-matter boundaries.

Inflation

Two types of inflation are affecting higher education credentials. One is grade inflation. The other is the increasing number of credit hours required, particularly for graduate degrees. Grade inflation is apparent on several counts. Nationally, while college aptitude test scores have declined, the average college grade appears to be nearer a *B* than a *C*. In the last decade the percentage of students graduating with honors has increased from about 10–15 percent to about 40 percent in some institutions. A contributing factor to grade inflation may be a similarity to dollar inflation—more academic credit-granting capability than academically capable students. For example, many private liberal arts colleges traditionally known for their selective admissions standards now recruit and admit less able students. Academics and their institutions respond to "economic realities." Discussions about maximizing access to higher education and minimizing attrition rates are mixed with idealism and economic self-interest. In some cases, faculty members understand that administrative admonitions to consider attrition rates are really cautions about rigorous grading.

In this country, higher education's capacity and capabilities in the aggregate may exceed the need or market for credits. The situation will likely be exacerbated in the 1980s when the 18–24-year-old population declines. Furthermore, higher education's interest in nontraditional students to some extent manifests its hope to create an additional clientele. If college and university enrollments are not to decline dramatically in the 1980s, the percentage of 18–24-year-olds going to college must increase, and far more older, nontraditional students must enroll.

The developing demographic and economic climate is likely to stimulate an unhealthy competition among institutions over which ones can grant the most credit for the least effort or achievement. The present serious grade inflation represents the edge of a more serious problem directly related to the funding of American higher education. The problem is particularly applicable in the public sector, which constitutes 75–80 percent of all enrollments. The more students enrolled and the more credit hours required, the more funds institutions draw from the state treasury. It is as if an automobile factory were financed by how many hours it took to make a car rather than what a car would bring on the market. The "academic factory" gets more money, not by turning out either a better product or more products with corresponding savings in costs per unit, but by enrolling more students and requiring them to stay longer regardless of their differing abilities.

The credit hour, which has been used to fund the processes of universities to be themselves, under changed circumstances has become the means of higher education's getting bigger without getting better or more efficient. For state governments, the problem has become acute, and one legislature recently set maximum limits on the number of credit hours fundable for various degrees.

Unbundling

In a legal critique of higher education's current structure, Wang argues that American higher education ties together separate educational services that may not be purchased separately. For example, he suggests the bundling of services such as instruction and assessment violates section 1 of the Sherman Antitrust Act. The act condemns agreements by a party to sell a product or service on the condition that the buyer also purchase a second product or service.

Regardless of the strength of any legal argument, the most compelling reasons for unbundling higher education, or separating instruction from the assessment function, remains educational. Students desiring assessment of educational achievement from a college may or may not need instruction. Unbundling higher education along functional lines offers the potential for improving the quality of lectures, making instruction more individualized, changing education into a lifelong process, and offering students more freedom in choosing when, where, and what they will study. Most important, higher education might be made available to more persons at a lower cost.[45]

These are all debatable points, of course, and if Wang's admonition to unbundle were heeded, major shifts in how American higher education establishes degree requirements, instructs, and certifies would occur. Embodied in his proposals are considerations worthy of serious thought and analysis as American higher education seeks to improve its credit and credentialing system.

The Future of Educational Credentialing

The present system of educational credentials is not the product of a single, reasoned design. Rather, the credentials

45. William K. S. Wang, "The Unbundling of Higher Education," *Duke Law Journal* 53 (1975): 53–90.

are evolved compromises to meet certain social and educational needs: (1) hope to help people achieve their social and economic potential regardless of inherited advantages and disadvantages; (2) belief that education could be an independent facilitator and sorter of individual aspirations and attainment; (3) need for proxies for human merit because, for most jobs, the distinctions between competent and incompetent work performance are difficult to establish; and (4) need to fund colleges and universities without directly manipulating their goals and functions.

The major social and economic projects we undertake as a culture will significantly affect higher education. Hence, they will affect educational credentialing. Among many possible social changes, society's reactions to the following matters may significantly affect educational credentialing:

- Realization of limits to material growth with a resultant turning to introspective pursuits and non-income-producing avocations
- In some sectors of the economy, partial return to labor— rather than capital-intensive modes of production
- Further seesawing between productivity and efficiency in a world with great appetites and scarce resources concomitant with further implementation of the egalitarian ethic
- Further seesawing between the freedom and opportunities associated with individualism and the need to belong to lasting groups—families, races, regions, and the like
- Further diffusion of knowledge—from paperbacks to computer-based instructional systems
- As the mobile society's pace quickens and its agenda become more chaotic, the increasing appeal of structured retreats to study and reflect
- The continuation or abatement of the present migration from metropolitan areas to towns and the countryside
- The demographic shift from a young to an older population —from greening to graying
- Enough affluence to sustain a relaxed, self-indulgent life style or serious, sustained study
- Changes in policies and procedures for professional credentialing and job selection may diminish the importance

of education prerequisites; that is, there may be more direct ways to evaluate human performance without the proxies of educational attainment

Higher education has been primarily a youth-oriented undertaking. Students have typically been full time, pursuing their education for its future value. Under these circumstances, credentials become driving ends. As America demographically grays, retirees might become a significant proportion of student bodies. These people would probably be less interested in credentials as educational currency and value them more as representations of achievements.

Nothing could affect education so dramatically as across-the-board outlawing of educational requirements for licensure and job selection except where education and training are demonstrably related to job performance. The performance criteria of job success are so persistently difficult to identify—much less measure—that in many instances there is little hope of showing a direct relationship to any predictors. In the absence of such criteria, two problems arise. On the one hand, do we settle the criterion as being first-job performance? Or do we make the criterion endurance in the vocation and/or monetary success? Advocates for a social order of full employment in which employees are rewarded on the basis of explicit job performance (regardless of seniority, background, education, etc.) hope for something that is now technically impossible, much less politically likely.

Nevertheless, the pressures and tensions will surely compel that educational credentials be based more on explicit attainments, more objectively assessed than they now are. Educational institutions need to reestablish the integrity of their own philosophy and procedures for awarding academic credentials. The academic estate, for its own good, needs to give critical attention to the awarding of academic credit. The more sure it is of its own integrity, the less vulnerable it will be to pressures to make its awards correlate more directly with the rewards of the nonacademic world.

CHAPTER 4

Current Practices in Awarding Credits and Degrees
Jonathan R. Warren

For about the first two hundred fifty years of American higher education, the bachelor's degree was awarded as recognition and certification for academic accomplishment and had little importance as an occupational credential. In the present century, degrees have taken on an occupational importance that permits their holders access to positions in employment and professional activities that are closed to those without degrees. These two functions of degrees—certifying academic accomplishment and qualifying a person for entry into future activities—will here be treated separately.

Structure of the Degree System

Until about a hundred years ago, degrees were awarded at two levels. The bachelor's degree, awarded after four years, was dominant. The master's degree, awarded after two or three additional years of unstructured, often inconsequential study, was the other. In roughly the last hundred years, the master's degree has been given greater substance and respectability, the two-year associate degree has been established, the Ph.D. has become the requisite for advanced scholarship and research, and a great variety of professional degrees have been established.

There are currently more than a thousand different designations for the earned degrees being awarded in the United States,[1] many with insignificant distinctions. For example, the Bachelor of Science in Electrical Engineering (B.S.E.E.) and the Bachelor of Science (B.S.) with a major in electrical engineering are virtually indistinguishable, and the distinctions

1. Stephen H. Spurr, *Academic Degree Structures*, p. 14.

between the Bachelor of Arts (B.A.) and Bachelor of Science (B.S.) are often no greater than differences between two B.A. or two B.S. programs.

A scheme that classifies degrees into two useful categories —period of study and type of degree—is shown in Table 1. The degrees listed are illustrative only, for there are many others in each category except the three- to four-year post-baccalaureate academic degree. Some recently established programs leading to the Doctor of Arts might be placed in the three-years-or-more category inasmuch as the period of study is open-ended.

Professional or occupational degrees differ from academic degrees primarily in being based on narrower, more detailed specifications of curricula and in having the field of specialization designated in the degree title. Examples are Bachelor of Fine Arts (B.F.A.) and Bachelor of Music (B.M.)—professional degrees usually awarded after completion of fairly rigorously specified programs. In contrast, the B.A. in art or music usually applies to patterns of courses that are broad in scope, extend outside the field of specialization, and allow students greater latitude in designing their programs. Some exceptions exist to both these distinctions. The Associate in Applied Science (A.A.S.) and Associate in Industrial Technology (A.I.T.) are typically awarded for completion of highly prescribed programs but do not designate the field of study.

Classification by duration of program shows at least two major distinctions. The first three levels, through the master's degrees, are defined by prescribed time periods, either accord-

TABLE 1: *Periods of Study Typical for Academic and Professional Degrees*

Years of Study	Degrees	
	Academic	Professional or Occupational
Two	A.A., A.S.	A.A.S., A.I.T.
Four	B.A., B.S.	B.F.A., B.M.
Postbaccalaureate		
One-two	M.A., M.S.	M.F.A., M.B.A., M.S.W.
Three-four	—	J.D., M.D., D.V.M., D.D.S.
Three or more	Ph.D.	D.Eng., Ed.D., D.B.A.

ing to numbers of credits earned or numbers of academic terms spent in full-time residence. The actual calendar time may be stretched by students who drop out intermittently or compressed by students who carry an overload or attend summer sessions; nevertheless, the period of academic time is fixed.

For the fourth level, which includes only professional degrees, both calendar and academic times are usually fixed. Students in law or medical programs take an almost completely prescribed course of studies which they complete in a specified three or four years. This type of program thus resembles bachelor's degree programs about a hundred years ago, before elective courses were introduced. Students enter as a class, take the same courses as a class, and graduate as a class. Although modifications are being tried, this fixed type of program still dominates in both medicine and law.

The fifth level departs markedly from the others. Program duration in either calendar or academic units is unspecified except for minimum requirements that have little effect because they are almost always exceeded. Progress through the programs is based on the satisfactory negotiation of a sequence of academic hurdles. When the final hurdle has been cleared, the degree is awarded. The time to be spent between hurdles has frequently not been designated, but the trend is toward specifying maximum periods, usually quite generous, after which the prior hurdles must be renegotiated. Because the time requirements for degrees at the fifth level are open-ended, the time actually taken to complete these programs is typically substantially longer than the nominal three or four years. The average enrolled time for the Ph.D. in all fields is six years beyond the bachelor's degree, and the average calendar time is about eight and a half years.[2]

In brief, the Table 1 classification of degree types by level and by academic or professional orientation also distinguishes among types of degree programs according to the form of the time requirements and the extent to which course requirements are specified.

2. *A Fact Book on Higher Education* 1976, Fourth issue: 76.258.

Credits

For roughly the first two and a quarter centuries of American higher education, all students in a college took the same series of courses, each class entering and progressing as a group through a common curriculum and all graduating at the end of the fourth year. About a hundred years ago the elective system was widely adopted in some form. Students were allowed options and no longer moved through college in a common program. A system then had to be devised to provide comparability among the different programs and courses, all of which led to a common degree. Initially, all students simply took the same number of courses: whatever combination of courses a student elected, the total number completed by the end of the fourth year was constant. At Harvard in about 1900, for example, the completion of sixteen full-year courses constituted completion of the degree.[3]

When some courses began to require more extensive study than others, they could no longer be treated as though all were equivalent, and the course credit or course hour or credit hour was devised. The number of hours per week of class meetings, with departures from the standard class procedure, became the basis on which different numbers of units or credit hours were associated with different courses.[4] The award of the degree was then based on completion of a prescribed number of units rather than courses. Current practice typically requires the completion of 120–130 semester hours or credits based on courses extending over about a fifteen-week period. Colleges and universities on the quarter system, in which courses typically last about ten weeks, have equivalent requirements— 180–190 quarter hours.

Credits therefore derive from degrees. Although they have taken on additional functions, their initial purpose was to mark students' progress toward a degree. If two students pursue different courses, their progress toward a degree can be compared only when comparable increments of progress

3. John S. Brubacher and Willis Rudy, *Higher Education in Transition*, p. 115.
4. James M. Heffernan, "The Credibility of the Credit Hour," *Journal of Higher Education* 44 (1973):61.

can be defined. The credit hour or course credit has served that function to the benefit of both students and institutions.

For students, the accumulation of credits gives them satisfaction by providing a continual measure of progress toward the long-range goal—a degree. The completion of courses or of academic terms serves the same function, but the generality of credits allows different course loads or courses differing in intensity to be weighted appropriately in marking progress toward a degree. Labeling a student as a sophomore or a junior is no longer as informative as reporting the number of credits accumulated. Marking progress with credits rather than courses also permits learning experiences other than those in traditional courses to be credited toward a degree. For almost as long as credits have been in use, less credit has been assigned to laboratory work and other activities that require less collateral work than does classroom study. Independent study, thesis research at the graduate level, and work on honors papers at the undergraduate level have been assigned credit in varying amounts, depending on the number of hours presumably spent in the activity. Field work, undergraduate and graduate internships, and other nonclassroom activities have also been credited according to the time they required. The use of credits thus permits great flexibility in the kinds of student activity that can be counted in the march toward a degree.

Credits are defined in terms of time but are intended to be measures of learning. A credit is implicitly calibrated to the learning an average student would acquire in an hour of class time plus outside study. But every class hour is not equally productive, and most students depart one way or another from the average. Thus Merwin regards the basic issue in credits as the conflict between whether credits measure time or learning or a combination of the two.[5] He suggests, with Elton,[6] that above-average and below-average students might be awarded more or fewer credits for the same number of class

5. Jack C. Merwin, "Uses of College Credit—Evolution and Current Problems," *Minnesota Education* 1, no. 4 (1974):1.

6. L. R. B. Elton, "The Assessment of Students—A New Approach," *Universities Quarterly* 22 (1968):291.

hours. In Elton's proposal, credits would be tied to grades, with average grades earning the standard number of credits, above-average grades earning bonus credits, and below-average grades earning fewer credits than the standard numbers. The proposal has attracted little support, perhaps because it would confuse level of learning with scope of learning. Faculty members seem more comfortable having credits indicate the scope of coverage of the student's learning rather than how well the material was learned.

Although credits were initially devised to indicate comparability of accomplishment in students' progress toward degrees—that is, learning completed—they now also function to measure the current level of effort of both students and faculty. Level of effort is associated with cost; thus credits are used as primary determinants of tuition, faculty compensation, and legislative appropriations. The number of course credits or units a student is carrying determines whether he or she is full time or part time. In many institutions credit load sets the student's tuition. A normal faculty work load is defined in credit hours taught. Faculty personnel are allocated to departments according to student credit hours "produced" by each department. Enrollment figures, on which central offices of multicampus systems and state legislatures base the apportionment of staff and dollars, are weighted according to the numbers of credit hours students carry. Since the number of credits carried or taught defines respectively a full-time student and a full-time faculty member, credits affect the student-faculty ratio and judgments about the eduactional efficiency of the institution. Redefining a full-time student from one carrying twelve units to one carrying eleven units will in one simple stroke sharply increase an institution's apparent efficiency.

The use of course credits as measures of faculty work load and the use of student credit hours produced as a measure of educational output and therefore as a determinant of educational efficiency have both been criticized.[7] In both student

7. Sidney Suslow, "Course Credits as Measures of Faculty/Student Effort—An Evaluation," *Minnesota Education* 1 (1974):12. See also Heffernan, "Credibility of the Credit Hour."

and faculty effort—particularly the latter—wide variability and varied circumstances that produce a student credit hour make questionable any common interpretation of what a credit hour means. As students move from the lower division to the upper division to graduate school, the cost of a credit hour becomes greater, and proposals have been made to charge more tuition for upper-division than for lower-division courses. But at a gross level, over an entire institution, the variations may offset each other sufficiently to give credence to a concern for the total number of students who have been moved a measured distance toward a degree by a given number of faculty members. Again, the anchor to which the measure of educational progress or accomplishment is attached, for both faculty and students, is the bachelor's degree.

The Role of Student Persistence

The all-or-none nature of the award of credit is an aspect of the degree-credit system that has received little attention. Students at every level of performance higher than complete failure receive the full credit the course carries, and failure is rare (a point developed in the discussion on academic standards, below). Thus progress toward a degree is largely mechanical, requiring only that the student persevere through a sequence of experiences that he or she finds manageable. Even without a concern for level of performance, however, completion of a program of fixed duration is no trivial requirement. It is dominant in determining the award of degrees. Its relative neglect in discussions of standards while grades get all the attention is therefore surprising. The combination of course requirements and students' reactions to those requirements determines persistence. Since unacceptably low persistence will cause requirements to be reduced, the same interplay between course requirements and student behavior sets standards.

Students engage in a wide variety of course patterns and a still wider variety of associated experiences—lectures, seminars, laboratory work, field experiences, papers, and examinations. Yet all are intended to lead to a level of intellectual competence that merits the award of a bachelor's degree. The diversity of programs, courses, and levels of performance available in higher education—and even within institutions— assures that almost anyone who so desires can achieve a college degree. In essence, the decisions to continue through the full set of experiences and receive a degree are made by the students. When they see they are not keeping pace with other students or find the content too unrewarding to justify continued effort, they decide not to continue or to continue in a less difficult or more interesting program or institution. Thus the nature of the academic experiences, both their content and difficulty, determines which students persist to a bachelor's degree and therefore what the degree represents. Stretching the process over approximately four years gives students an extended set of experiences on which to base the decision to persist or withdraw and sets the cost of persisting for students who find few intrinsic rewards in the process.

The student decision process—about entry, courses and programs, and withdrawal or persistence—and the few formal constraints imposed on persistent, minimally performing students have produced each year an unprecedented number of bachelor's degrees and great confusion over what they represent. Between 1964 and 1974, the annual number of bachelor's degrees awarded doubled, from slightly less than half a million to almost a million. Between 1960 and 1970, new high school graduates, the source of about half the college graduates four years later, increased by only 55 percent. Much of the growth in degrees awarded was therefore due to returning students. In the last few years the proportions of students continuing at each level have stabilized, with about three-fourths of the eighteen-year-old population finishing high school, about 60 percent of the high school graduates entering college, and slightly more than half of the college entrants eventually receiving a bachelor's degree.[8] In 1970 about 15 percent of men in the labor force had college degrees. If present trends continue, that percentage will slowly climb to 25–30 percent over the next two or three decades, and the

8. *A Fact Book on Higher Education* 1976, First issue:76.79 and Fourth issue:76.213. U.S. Bureau of the Census, *Census of Population, 1970: Subject Reports; Occupational Characteristics.*

occupational role of the bachelor's degree will have changed substantially.

Beyond the master's degree, credits are of little importance to students. Medical and law students do not need credits to mark their progress inasmuch as they usually follow fixed curricula. In other doctoral programs the minimum credit requirements are usually so far exceeded that, again, they have little importance to the students. Credits are important at the graduate level, however, in measuring faculty work loads, differentiating full-time from part-time students, and determining tuition.

Nontraditional Credits

The traditional credit is based on the number of hours per week a student spends in class, with the assumption that about twice that number of hours is spent in out-of-class preparation. As already noted, allowances are made for forms of instruction, such as laboratory courses and field work, that do not match the usual classroom experience. Independent study, practicum experiences such as student teaching for education majors, study abroad, work experience, and other out-of-class experiences have all come to be used educationally and to be assigned credits equivalent to those earned in the classroom. The reasoning is that credits in fact measure learning, that learning can occur in a variety of settings and through a variety of procedures, and that learning from any source that is equivalent to the learning associated with a semester or quarter hour of classroom experience merits the award of one credit.[9] Most of the controversy over nontraditional credit concerns how the equivalence between classroom and nonclassroom learning is to be determined.

Two forms of nontraditional credit with moderately long but modest histories have recently attracted interest—credit by examination and credit for experience not supervised by a collegiate institution. The award of credit equivalent to that of specified courses, usually lower-division courses, through passing a standardized examination is widespread and still grow-

9. Peter Meyer, *Awarding College Credit for Non-College Learning,* pp. 11–15.

ing.[10] Awarding credit for experience acquired outside traditional educational settings is comparatively rare but also growing. Usually such credit reduces the number of degree credits still to be earned but often does not specify the particular courses that are to be bypassed.

A form of learning intermediate between traditional classroom learning and nontraditional learning is learning acquired in classes that may be operated in traditional ways but in noncollegiate settings. In 1974, the American Council on Education and the New York Board of Regents established a Project on Noncollegiate Sponsored Instruction as a mechanism to evaluate the credit equivalency of such formal courses. The project based its evaluation techniques on those used by ACE to evaluate formal military courses and on guidelines developed by the ACE Commission on Educational Credit. At the request of a noncollegiate agency offering what it considers college-level courses, the program sends a team of subject-matter specialists to judge the quality of each course offered. The team produces a course description and recommends the number and type of credits the course merits. The description and recommendation are then published in an annual guide to noncollegiate educational programs.[11]

The recent interest in nontraditional forms of postsecondary education has focused new attention on the meaning of the bachelor's degree. As educators have struggled to attach academic credit to nonacademic experiences, they have had to examine the consequences of traditional academic experiences and clarify purposes that had never been explicit but about which agreement had been assumed.

The traditional baccalaureate consists of full-time study for four academic years, with a third to a half of that study concentrated in a selected academic field and the rest scattered over the humanities, social sciences, and natural sciences. (A great variety of programs depart to greater or lesser extent

10. Janet Ruyle and Lucy Ann Geiselman, "Non-Traditional Opportunities and Programs," in *Planning Non-Traditional Programs*, by K. Patricia Cross, John R. Valley, and associates, pp. 53–94.

11. *The National Guide to Credit Recommendations for Noncollegiate Courses, 1978 Edition.*

from this practice.) The learning expected to result from this modal pattern—the learning associated with the award of a bachelor's degree—acts as a standard against which learning acquired through other kinds of activities is compared.

Two fundamentally different methods are available, in principle, to make comparisons of achievement and therefore of program effectiveness. Under one method, students who complete the traditional program are administered various tests that measure each of the kinds of accomplishment expected; thus formal standards are established against which students coming from any program, traditional or nontraditional, can be tested. A comprehensive process of this kind is neither practical nor economically feasible: to test learning in the scope and variety that college programs are expected to produce would swamp faculty resources and student time. Yet if anything is to be known with confidence about the effectiveness of educational practice, some limited form of that process, using a variety of assessment procedures, must be employed.

The second method is both practical and economically feasible and has been used to some extent, though rarely completely, throughout educational history. It is based on planning a set of educational experiences presumed by an expert in the field to be productive. When a student has gone through the planned experiences with sufficient commitment of energy, he or she is presumed to have acquired the expected learning.

Essentially the above procedure has been used to determine the value of the learning students acquire in virtually every course taught today. The step that would complete the process (a step almost never taken explicitly, but that does occur informally and haphazardly) is to assess comprehensively the capabilities of a sample of students who have been through a course to determine whether they have in fact learned what the course is presumed to have taught. If such a comprehensive assessment were done thoroughly once for a course, then the assumptions about what is learned by later students in the same course could be made with some confidence. Final examinations are thought to perform this function and do so to some extent, but limitations in testing time mean that only samples of what the course was intended to produce can be tested. In essence, tests measure the student's commitment to the course. Students who perform well on the sample of learning tested are assumed to have committed enough effort to the course to have learned most of what was intended to be taught, even those capabilities that faculty members acknowledge they cannot test. If the current move to credit nontraditional forms of learning leads to the validation of traditional forms of learning, it will have accomplished much.

The Continuing Education Unit

A form of recognition for educational experiences that has some paradoxical qualities has recently been established by the National University Extension Association. This formal recognition is accorded persons for educational activities in which the participants are not concerned about credits toward a degree. One "continuing education unit," or CEU, is awarded for every ten hours of participation in an organized educational program provided, among other qualifications, the activity is not eligible for academic credits.[12] The CEU satisfies the desire of many persons to receive formal recognition for what they learn regardless of whether the recognition carries any practical consequence.[13] In its initial uses, it seems to be primarily a device for institutional record keeping, a way to account for the amount of educational effort expended by an agency and the educational results produced. It is patterned after the academic credit in its accounting functions but is severed from the degree, on which the meaning of the academic credit for accounting purposes rests. The American Nurses' Association and the National Association of Boards of Pharmacy have both adopted the CEU to record the noncollege-based, noncredited learning of nurses and pharmacists.

Current Degree Requirements

Degree requirements vary across the different categories of degrees described earlier. Almost all degrees, however, include

12. National Task Force on the Continuing Education Unit, *The Continuing Education Unit,* pp. vi, 3.

13. Abraham Carp, Richard Peterson, and Pamela Roelfs, "Adult Learning Interests and Experiences," in *Planning Non-Traditional Programs,* by Cross, Valley, and associates, pp. 11–52.

requirements based on (1) the duration of study, (2) curricular organization, (3) academic standards, and (4) residence. These requirements structure the students' academic experiences; certification of completion of those experiences is the older of the two functions served by degrees. In this function, degrees are backward-looking, reflecting whatever accomplishments have been acquired or demonstrated by students in satisfying the degree requirements. For the last hundred years, but especially in the last twenty-five, the accomplishments reflected by degrees have been considered important indicators of capabilities likely to lead to future accomplishment. As such, degrees have taken on the forward-looking function of qualifying their recipients for future activities.

Duration of Study

The most obvious requirement of academic programs is the amount of time students are required to commit to them. Thus the earliest distinction among degrees in the United States was between bachelor's and master's degrees, a distinction based solely on the additional time required for the master's. Today, even though the time period specified fluctuates, the time under instruction continues to be a major characteristic of degrees.

Attempts—largely unsuccessful—have been made to modify the four-year period required for the bachelor's degree. Early in the present century, efforts to trim the study period to three years were abandoned, principally because students were reluctant to cut short an enjoyable interlude in their lives. More recent efforts at contraction have kept the curriculum intact while shortening the elapsed time by extending the academic year, increasing the students' study load, or moving parts of the first year into the high school. A few programs have stretched the time to five years to accommodate combinations such as a technical field, like engineering, with the humanities. Master's degree programs have been more variable, ranging from one to three years.

That study between matriculation and completion of the undergraduate course should have remained fixed at four years while so much else in higher education has changed substantially is notable but not dysfunctional. Programs have been designed to fit the four-year time frame, and few educational goals are so precisely defined that their nature specifies the time required for completion. One time span is as defensible, in general, as any other. The important change in the last hundred years has been to sanction variations from the standard four-year period. The two-year associate degrees have made withdrawal after two years, even from nominally four-year programs, more acceptable than it had been. And the growing graduate school enrollments indicate the tendency of students to extend their formal learning beyond the traditional four years. The four-year period for a college education, for three hundred years a rigid aspect of higher education, is being relaxed, not only through formal changes in program structure as advocated by the Carnegie Commission on Higher Education, but also through student decisions to stop short of or go beyond the four-year degree.

The Carnegie Commission recognized that if higher education is to be available to more than half of the traditional college-age population, four years under instruction to the primary degree is often awkward.[14] For the moderately affluent, four years for transition from total dependence on parents to total independence is acceptable. For the less well-to-do, the time spent as a student must have strong justification, and provisions must be available for it to end at intervals shorter than four years. The Carnegie Commission recommended that the completion of an educational experience be certified with the award of a degree every two years. The associate degree would be awarded at the end of the sophomore year in four-year as well as two-year colleges. Beyond the four-year bachelor's degree, a master's degree would be awarded after two years of graduate study, and the Ph.D. or other doctoral-level degree would normally take four years beyond the B.A.

The award of a degree every two years might have been valuable twenty years or more ago. College was still seen as a four-year commitment, and students who might profitably

14. Carnegie Commission on Higher Education, *Less Time, More Options*, pp. 8–9.

have spent a year or two in college were deterred by the prospect of four years of study before any formal recognition of accomplishment was received. Two-year college enrollments were growing at a rate even faster than that in four-year colleges, but withdrawal short of a bachelor's degree was still commonly seen as some measure of failure.

Students today are more ready to take whatever amount of education they consider appropriate, regardless of degree formalities. The problem with degrees today no longer concerns locking students into a four-year program without regard for the wide variations in student competences, inclinations, and educational purposes. Instead, the problem is to establish some set of meanings for the million bachelor's degrees awarded each year that will permit them to carry information concerning the level and content of the competences they are to represent. This problem is two-faceted, involving both level and content, and will be discussed below under external implications of degrees.

Despite variations in the length of time specified, almost all degrees except the Ph.D. and other nonmedical doctorates are awarded on completion of a fixed period of study. Currently, medical education is under pressure to reduce the four-year span between entry and the M.D. degree.[15] Most degrees, in certifying completion of a specified program of fixed duration, imply that the recipient has acquired the knowledge and capabilities typical of those who have completed the same or similar programs. The fixed time period presumably provides some assurance that the student's learning has not been skimped.

A few programs at the bachelor's and master's levels are not held to a fixed duration or number of credits. For them, satisfactory completion is based on student demonstrations of the kinds and levels of competence considered typical of students who have completed degree programs. These nontraditional programs face the same problems in establishing comparability of student achievement that are encountered in equating

15. Barrie Thorne, "Professional Education in Medicine," in *Education for the Professions of Medicine, Law, Theology, and Social Welfare*, ed. Everett C. Hughes, pp. 17–99.

nontraditional with traditional forms of credit. One difficult problem is defining the achievement reached in traditional programs in sufficient detail to permit a feasible determination of equivalence.

Curricular Organization

When electives were introduced and flexibility and student options were added to the traditional bachelor's degree program, a major objection to the new system was that students would choose haphazard collections of courses which would lack the coherence and structure of a fully prescribed curriculum. A 1903 survey at Harvard by a faculty committee found that students were studying less than presumed and were choosing courses on the basis of their ease and the class meeting hour. In 1909, therefore, "concentration and distribution" requirements were instituted, specifying that six of a student's sixteen year-long courses were to be in a single major field and six more were to be distributed over three other fields.[16]

Similar requirements are almost universal today. For bachelor's degrees, most colleges and universities require some minimum number of course credits to be taken in a single field which the students designate as their "major." Typically from twenty-four to thirty-six semester hours are required in majors in the arts and sciences. Schools of engineering, business, and architecture frequently require more study in the selected field, up to 75 percent in engineering and architecture. Thus, from one-quarter to three-quarters of a student's undergraduate program today may be determined by his or her choice of major field. Most students, however, exceed substantially the minimum number of units required in their field of specialization.[17] In the major field, among the required courses, up to half may be designated courses required of all students in that field; the other half are selected by the student from the many course offerings in that field. The propor-

16. Brubacher and Rudy, *Higher Education in Transition*, p. 115.
17. Robert Blackburn et al., *Changing Practices in Undergraduate Education*, p. 29.

tion of designated or optional courses varies with the field and institution.

Distribution, or breadth, requirements—almost universally prescribed in bachelor's degree programs—vary more widely than do concentration requirements. In their most common form, each student is required to complete a minimum number of units, usually six to eight, in each of three broad areas —the humanities, the social sciences, and the physical sciences—but is free to choose among the courses available in each area. In a second common form each student is required to complete one or two courses from each of three to six course groups containing three to eight courses per group. Here the students' freedom of choice is more restricted. A third form of curricular organization provides for distribution of learning but allows the students no freedom of choice. In this form several courses, such as The History of Western Civilization, are organized to provide a broad overview of the current structure of knowledge, and every student is required to take that group of courses. Whatever form the distribution requirements take, they typically account for about a third of a student's total program.[18]

A few additional requirements are common but demand relatively little investment of student time. Among these are physical education and, particularly in public institutions, a course in American government or history or both. Foreign language requirements still exist in some fields but are declining.

The concentration and distribution requirements usually amount to 50–70 percent of bachelor's degree programs except in specialized fields such as engineering, where they are most extensive. For the remaining 30–50 percent, students choose their courses from among the large selection usually available. In practice, the students' free choice portion is frequently heavily filled with additional courses in their major fields.[19] In the most common curricular organization, half or more of a bachelor's program is committed to a specialized

18. Ibid., p. 11.
19. Ibid., p. 35.

field, about a third is directed over broad areas of knowledge, and the remainder is made up of whatever the students fancy from among the institution's offerings.

Associate degrees follow the pattern of bachelor's degrees. Associate in Arts (A.A.) and Associate in Science (A.S.) degrees are usually substitutes for the first two years of a bachelor's degree program and are often so planned. Concentration and distribution requirements are similar to those of the lower division of four-year programs. Two-year programs not intended to be a stage toward bachelor's degrees often lead to the Associate in Applied Science (A.A.S.), Associate in Industrial Technology (A.I.T.), or similar degree designations that distinguish them from A.A. and A.S. degrees. These two-year terminal programs may have an English composition or other minor nontechnical requirement, but they are essentially occupational. Distribution requirements are not applied. In addition, two-year colleges offer specialized programs of less than two years that lead to certificates of completion.

Master's degrees in the liberal arts and in professional fields are based on concentrated study in the major field. They may require one or two years, depending on the student's undergraduate preparation. About half of the typical master's program is committed to required core courses in the field. Study outside the major field is not normally required, but about one-fourth of a two-year program may allow for outside electives that have some supportive relationship to the field. One-year programs typically have no room for outside electives.

Degrees in medicine and law—the M.D. and J.D. degrees, with the J.D. having almost replaced the LL.B. degree—still follow fixed curricular patterns, although efforts are being made to diversify the curriculum in both fields and allow students some choice in specialties before completion of the program.[20]

Doctor's degrees other than those in law and the medical fields typically require a set of core graduate courses or sem-

20. Thorne, "Professional Education in Law," in *Education for the Professions,* ed. Hughes, pp. 101–68; see also Thorne, "Professional Education in Medicine."

inars followed by individually tailored programs of seminars, independent study, and research. Sometime in the program, competence in two foreign languages must be demonstrated, although that requirement is being increasingly modified, with competence in statistics, computer programming, or other supportive areas being substituted for one foreign language. In some fields—psychology, for example—a year-long paid internship may be required. Other requirements for practical experience for the Ph.D. or professional highest earned degrees sometimes exist in a less extensive form. The final requirement is a dissertation. As noted earlier, time and credit requirements at this level are less important than completion of academic hurdles, usually in a fixed sequence (discussed more fully in the next section).

Academic Standards

Many institutions, probably all but a handful, require undergraduates to maintain an overall grade average of C. This requirement seems to be a fairly rigorous standard that should reserve associate and bachelor's degrees to those who have demonstrated at least a moderate level of academic accomplishment. In actuality, little is known about the screening effect of that requirement, but a strong presumption can be made that it is small. The bases for that presumption are the small percentage of below C grades awarded, the much smaller proportion of below C grades that would not be balanced by above C grades to permit the student to graduate, and the availability within most institutions of less demanding courses and programs to which students may transfer.

The percentages of below C grades awarded throughout the country have not been summarized, although they are available in a disaggregated state somewhere in the administrative offices of most institutions. Selected data illustrate their probable range. At the nineteen-campus California State University and Colleges System in the spring term of 1972, 2.5 percent of the approximately one million grades awarded were F's. Another 4.4 percent were D's. More than 90 percent were C's or better, and 68 percent were A's or B's, giving weight to the assumption that many of the *D*'s and *F*'s would be balanced by grades above *C*. The percentage of *F*'s at individual institutions ranged from 1.1 to 5.9.[21]

During the same spring 1972 term, the seven senior colleges in the City University of New York awarded more than 200,000 grades, of which 5.5 percent were *F*'s, with a range among the institutions of 2.7 percent to 10.5 percent.[22] The percentage of *F*'s at CUNY institutions may be higher than that typically found nationwide because its liberal open admissions policy had been in effect for several years. A comparison of grades at the City College campus in 1972 and 1967, before the open admissions policy was introduced, showed that over that period freshman grades dropped while sophomore, junior, and senior grades rose.[23] It seems likely that *F*'s were disproportionately awarded to an unusually large number of entering freshmen who were poorly prepared, with the result that a larger proportion of *F*'s than usual were awarded.

A final illustration comes from the University of California, Berkeley, in the spring term of 1974. Of almost 70,000 grades awarded, 2.1 percent were *D*'s and 2.4 percent *F*'s. Almost 60 percent were *A*'s or *B*'s (29.7 percent *A*'s and 29.8 percent *B*'s). If grades of Pass are excluded, the *A*'s and *B*'s combined outnumbered the *C*'s by four to one. The distributions were not appreciably different during the fall and winter quarters of the same academic year or for upper-division compared with lower-division courses.[24]

These three sets of data suggest that grading standards are not an important factor in screening students who earn bachelor's degrees from those who do not. Too few disqualifying grades and too many counterbalancing high grades are awarded for academic disqualification to be common. Additionally, students have many options available with respect to

21. J. G. Safarik, "1972–1973 Grade Distributions and Analyses at California State University, Chico," p. 30.

22. Rena Kramer, Barry Kaufman, and Lawrence Podell, *Distribution of Grades: 1972*, p. 2.

23. Ibid., p. 9.

24. "A Report on Scholarship Grades: University of California, Berkeley," p. 28.

level of study demanded if they are willing to stay long enough in an academic setting to finish a degree program.

Yet standards of academic performance exist, even though they span a wide range over the three thousand institutions in the country. They are enforced not so much by grades as by the requirement that students persist for an extended period of time in an academic setting. Even in the least selective colleges the academic nature of most of the tasks students engage in requires some facility in, and tolerance for dealing with, verbal abstractions. Students without those qualities do not often remain in college long enough to graduate. Personal predilections toward other than intellectual or academic pursuits, probably more than limited intellectual competence or performance, keep the population of college graduates from growing more rapidly. Further, because stringent standards are absent in higher education collectively, student fatigue and lack of interest are important factors in limiting the numbers of degrees awarded.

Despite the broad intellectual tolerance within higher education generally, standards are not uniformly lax. The wide range of performance standards among institutions was first documented about forty-five years ago by Learned and Wood's demonstration that seniors at some institutions were, on the average, less knowledgeable than sophomores at others.[25] Today, the range in student competence across institutions is even greater. The more selective institutions maintain quite rigorous standards, not wholly through faculty conviction, but through an accommodation between faculty and students. Faculties adjust their expectations upward or downward depending on the degree of academic rigor the students can handle. If the students attracted to a college tend to be brighter than in the past, faculty expectations rise. If the reverse occurs, expectations are lowered. Occasional exceptions occur, as noted by a knowledgeable observer at one midwestern college who found its students to be generally brighter than the faculty and enjoying the relaxed atmosphere the

25. W. S. Learned and Ben D. Wood, *The Student and His Knowledge,* p. 18.

situation permitted. In that instance an upward adjustment of standards was not possible.

In particular institutions, the standards of a course and of the institution—through the collective standards of its courses—are set jointly by the faculty and students. Although grades are often regarded as the mechanism for maintaining institutional standards, they are in fact only the formal expression of a process that occurs with or without grades. Courses are designed for students who fall within a moderate range of competence, with upper and lower limits set by the prior knowledge brought by most of the students entering the course. Instructors set standards low enough so that most students who enter the course succeed, provided they have the prerequisite knowledge and give moderate effort to it, yet high enough to challenge the better students. The range of competence may be wide or narrow, high or low, depending on the institution, the department, and the nature of the course. The occasional failure is apparent to students and instructor well before the formal grade statement to that effect is made.

The various experiences of success or its lack that students encounter through all the activities of all their courses produce the decisions to drop out, to change fields, to plan on graduate school, to raise or lower expectations. Grades assist those decisions by contributing formal, definitive statements of faculty members' judgments about student performance. In such a situation, most students so inclined will successfully complete all their courses, accumulate the requisite credits, and be awarded a degree. Attrition between matriculation and graduation is therefore more plausibly attributable, not to academic failure itself, but to the disinclination of many students to remain in an academic setting at any level of rigor.

The academic qualifications of entering students and faculty expectations combine to produce an achievement level that the students can reach and the faculty can accept. This interplay has permitted higher education in this country to be extended to more than half the high school graduates without loss of quality in the education received by the most competent students. During the past decade, as the numbers of seniors taking the Graduate Record Examinations in selected fields have increased, in most of the fields the percentages of students with high scores—over 700 on a scale of 990, with mean scores from about 550 to 600—have held constant or increased. The absolute numbers of high-achieving students have risen. Since 1964, only in English and history have the absolute numbers of scores over 700 declined. If high scores on the GRE achievement tests are an indicator of successful education, the doubled number of college graduates in the 1964–74 decade indicates that, for the most able students, the quality of education received has not declined through dilution of the academic talent pool.

The mechanism through which students find instructional programs appropriate to their capabilities and faculty members learn what levels of performance they can reasonably expect, while allowing some errors, generally works. Some faculty members feel frustrated at the slow pace forced on them by the obtuseness of their students. Some students find themselves hopelessly over their heads; others are bored by the tedious pace of the class. But self-corrective mechanisms are available, at least for the students. The overburdened student shifts to a less demanding program, transfers to a college where the students are less competent and therefore keep the pace slower, or drops out if the degree seems not worth the struggle or if the satisfactions in the college experience are too scant. The result is a multitude of educational programs or complex sets of experiences that fit a fairly standard, extensive time frame but vary enormously in content and level of expected performance.

At the graduate level the attention to standards differs from that described above. At the master's degree level, grade distributions are narrower, often consisting dominantly of *A*'s and *B*'s, with a few *C*'s accounting for all marginal grades. Some graduate departments that award only master's degrees, particularly in professional fields, grade entirely on a Pass-Fail basis and award *F*'s only in unusual circumstances; students competent enough to be admitted are assumed competent enough to pass all their courses.

At the master's level, the thesis or a comprehensive examination is often an added device for assuring competence.

While comprehensive examinations and senior theses are occasionally used at the undergraduate level, they are rare in comparison with their use at the master's level. Some master's degrees are awarded after the completion of appropriate courses, without further examination.

Data on the nature or extent of attrition at the master's level that would indicate how rigorously standards are maintained are not readily available and would be difficult to generalize across many master's degree programs. Even if attrition figures were available, the differences between master's degrees earned by students who do not intend to pursue a doctorate, as in many engineering programs, and those offered as a gentle way out for unsuccessful doctoral aspirants would be difficult to interpret.

Attrition in medical and law schools is low, the assumption again being made (with considerable justification) that any student admitted is capable of finishing. Control of standards rests with frequent course examinations. Additionally for medical students, a licensing examination is administered by the National Board of Medical Examiners, part of which is commonly taken at the end of the second year of medical school. Neither the law nor the medical degree entitles its recipients to practice. Each state administers a licensing examination, many of them relying for medical licensure on the National Board examinations. A few states still admit to the bar examination candidates who have clerked with a law firm rather than completing a law degree, but, in general, completion of either a law or medical degree is one step in a continuing process to licensure as a lawyer or physician.

For the Ph.D. and professional doctorates in fields other than law and medicine, standards are controlled through a sequence of hurdles to be negotiated by the students rather than through numbers of courses or credits completed. A qualifying examination and foreign language examinations or their equivalent typically follow completion of the core set of courses or seminars. Specialized study or research or both are then undertaken and followed by a written or oral comprehensive examination. Completion of a dissertation, which is reviewed at several points by the student's major professor and doctoral committee, is followed by a formal, oral defense of the dissertation.[26] This series of examinations plus close contact with at least one faculty member replaces the accumulation of grades and credits that controls standards to some extent at the bachelor's and master's levels. Grades are usually either *A* or *B*, with a handful of *C*'s to act as warning flags to students and faculty that a student is floundering. At the University of California, Berkeley, for example, in the 1973–74 academic year, barely more than 1 percent of the 45,000 graduate grades assigned were *C*'s, *D*'s, or *F*'s; the rest were *A*'s, *B*'s, or *P*'s.[27]

Residence

A final requirement usually has students complete their last year of study through regular courses offered by the institution awarding the degree. The first three-fourths of a bachelor's degree program and smaller portions of other programs except those in law and the medical fields may be completed at another accredited institution, through limited amounts of extension or correspondence work, or through other experiences considered equivalent to the academic learning expected to occur at the degree-granting institution. The "crediting" of equivalent forms of learning (as noted in the section on non-traditional credits) is a growing practice. Particularly at the graduate level, degree requirements are set to assure that major parts, or at least critical parts, of a student's program are spent in close contact with the faculty. For the academic degrees, experience on the campus is an important part of socialization into teaching and research activities. For the professional degrees, on-campus contact with the faculty is part of the professional socialization process. In advanced professional degrees, internships or other kinds of field experience provide another part of the socialization process.

External Implications of Degrees

The degree requirements discussed above indicate what degrees imply about the academic accomplishments of the

26. Spurr, *Academic Degree Structures,* p. 120.
27. "A Report on Scholarship Grades," p. 42.

degree holder. Degrees symbolize completion of a program, and the program requirements specify its substance. Particularly since World War II, but to some extent for the past century, degrees have functioned additionally to certify eligibility for entrance to professional occupations or to advanced educational programs. The successful performance of this function requires that the academic accomplishments implied by possession of a degree be pertinent or requisite to the activities to which the degree provides entry. This function of degrees is external in the sense that it applies outside the institution that administered the educational program and awarded the degree. Two sources of many of the current problems surrounding degrees are the involvement of more than one institution in a process utilizing degrees, and the position of the degree as a link between two independent sets of activities in which the degree holder engages.

Treating degrees as a link between two sets of activities, usually carried out in different settings, suggests viewing them as part of an information system. To the agencies in which the more advanced activities occur, whether educational or occupational, degrees convey information about the prior activities of the degree holders and indicate something about levels of accomplishment or competence. And although undergraduate colleges value their independence, some information flows back to them to bring degree programs closer in line with the requirements of the positions into which their graduates move. Two problems with degrees as carriers of information are (1) the lack of discrimination in degrees themselves concerning level of accomplishment and (2) the variation in both the level of accomplishment reached and the content of the studies completed by graduates who are awarded nominally comparable degrees.

Certification of Quality and Level of Learning

The mechanical accumulation of enough credits to meet degree requirements and the almost automatic award of full credit for each course completed regardless of level of accomplishment mean that degrees themselves do not reveal the competence levels of the degree holders. Two kinds of information sometimes supplement a degree to indicate level of accomplishment. One is the reputation of the institution awarding the degree; the other is the student's grade-point average.

In a crude way, degrees from well-known and well-regarded colleges and universities are thought to indicate superior education or their degrees are considered superior to those from lesser institutions. Those who make employment or selection decisions that take into account the applicant's educational background tend to learn what to expect from graduates of the institutions they encounter most frequently, and a small number of institutions are widely known by reputation. But reputations are based on various kinds of information, and many small, little-known liberal arts colleges turn out graduates who score higher on achievement tests than do the graduates of many larger, better-known universities.

To the extent that knowledge about institutional quality is reasonably accurate and the quality among departments does not vary widely, the achievement level associated with a degree can be judged moderately well by identifying the awarding institution. Degrees from the Ivy League institutions, from other major universities, and from highly selective liberal arts colleges and technical institutes—Swarthmore, Pomona, Oberlin, MIT, for example—in general represent intellectual accomplishment of a higher order than those from colleges and universities that admit almost any high school graduate. Yet many decisions that rest on the possession of a degree are blanket decisions that ignore degree origin as long as the institution is accredited. Many civil service examinations include a degree as a prerequisite, but any degree will do. In instances where the quality of the awarding institution is considered—that is, when a decision is made about a given person—other considerations enter the process and the degree itself assumes a less dominant role. But when a million bachelor's degrees are awarded each year and when the proportion of the labor force holding degrees is climbing toward 25 percent, the degree itself, without elaboration, becomes a major consideration in employment. Whether degrees will maintain their occupational importance as they become more common is an open question.

The second kind of information often used with the degree is the overall grade-point average (GPA). Designation for honors at graduation derives from the GPA and the same considerations apply. The GPA summarizes from forty to fifty judgments made by almost as many faculty members over a four-year period about the student's academic competence. That many judgments, made over time and usually with considerable care, when averaged, constitute a quite reliable, definitive statement about the student's general academic competence relative to that of other graduates of the institution. The GPA in combination with knowledge about the quality of the awarding institution carries appreciable information. Yet the summary nature of that information, which gives it its reliability, is also its weakness. Where general information about a student's academic skills can be used, the GPA is most useful. Where more specific kinds of information are desired, its use is questionable. Determining which situation applies is difficult. Despite numerous studies on the relation between undergraduate GPA and variables external to the undergraduate college, little is known about the linkages or mechanisms that mediate such relationships as are found.

The kind of information that would most usefully supplement degrees and GPA's concerns the specific experiences or competences of particular interest to the person or agency deciding whether to admit the graduate. Graduate schools and departments differ in the capabilities they want in their students. Graduate programs in clinical and experimental psychology, for example, should to some extent select students with different kinds of competences; yet in most instances they use the same criteria. Law schools too differ in their goals and should therefore admit different kinds of applicants even though the general academic competence of their students may be comparable. More extensive information about the nature of the undergraduate academic experiences of the students would permit the selecting agencies to identify the competences most important to them.

An accounting firm, let us say, is hiring a recent graduate in accounting. It might consider significant the fact that one candidate had approached a study of the Civil War by documenting changes during the war in the nature and quantity of trade between the Southern states and Europe and the relationships between those changes and changes in military strategy. On the other hand, the same company might be more interested in the applicant who studied the Civil War through analyzing the personal qualities of the successive Union commanding generals in contrast to Lee. While these pieces of information may not be telling in isolation, their combination with related kinds of information about other experiences may indicate important differences in the kinds of learning implied by the degrees of the two graduates. If degrees are considered as elements in an information system, methods are available for extending the system to accommodate other kinds of information.

Equivalence

When electives and major fields were introduced into the organization of students' programs, they produced the necessity for assuring and recognizing some sort of equivalence among those programs. The primary basis for equivalence continues to be time under instruction—hours per week in class, number of weeks in an academic term, and number of terms completed. Concentration and distribution requirements, which developed fairly quickly after the elective system was adopted, are reasonably similar across institutions and constitute a second device that assures some comparability among degree programs. A bachelor's degree from almost any institution in the United States indicates about 1,800 hours of classroom instruction plus perhaps twice that number of hours in out-of-class study spread broadly over several fields of knowledge but with 25–75 percent of the effort concentrated in a single field. Equivalence of competence among students is not implied by the degree itself, but can be crudely estimated from the reputation of the awarding institution and the student's GPA, as described above.

Judgments of equivalence and the information on which

they are based are important only when students or graduates desire to enter new situations that require competences presumed to have been achieved by virtue of the students' experiences. Transferring to a new college or university and taking upper-division courses requires an assumption of some degree of equivalence between the preparatory lower-division courses at the new and the prior institutions. The growing proportion of lower-division work taken in two-year colleges—40 percent of the new freshmen in 1975 entered two-year colleges compared with 28 percent in 1965—gives growing importance to the interinstitutional equivalence of lower-division studies. At the graduate level, the same problem in transition from one level at one institution to a higher level at another has been growing but more slowly. Between 1965 and 1975, graduate enrollment grew by 77 percent compared with a 68 percent growth rate for undergraduate enrollment. With enrollment increasing at both ends of higher education more rapidly than in the middle, the question of equivalent preparation in moving from one level to the next assumes an additional dimension.

Information Function of Degrees

The value of a degree must be differentiated from the value of the education it symbolizes. The value of an education is properly judged by the people directly involved—students and faculty. The faculty offers what it considers appropriate, and the students accept it or not. If students doubt the value of their current programs, they may try other educational experiences. The value of a program is what the faculty builds into it. If the faculty fails to offer something that society will value, their role in society will no longer be supported.

The degree is a device intended to assert to persons and agencies outside the educational process that the student has acquired something valuable to them. The degree, therefore, both is justified by, and needs to be validated for, the value the outside agencies attribute to it. A great variety of agencies, from graduate departments of philosophy to AT&T, are interested in some of the academic and personal qualifications that degrees are thought to represent. Thus, if degrees are to function effectively, they must carry a large, diverse body of information. Different parts of that information will be important to different agencies, but present procedures make it difficult to distinguish among them.

Degrees themselves represent an extended period of academic experiences at a level roughly indicated by the degree level. As noted, additional information about content is specified by the field of study. Further information about level of accomplishment is carried by the identity of the awarding institution and—for associate, bachelor's, medical, and law degrees—by the degree holder's grade-point average.

These elaborations of degrees still fall short of exhausting the potentially valuable information conveyed by descriptions of the educational experiences that led to the degrees. Holders of bachelor's degrees in mathematics, for example—whatever their college and grade-point average—will invariably have studied the real number system. But their approach to and understanding of the real number system will depend on their undergraduate program, in particular on whether it was oriented toward theoretical mathematics, applied mathematics, or public school teaching of mathematics. Further distinctions may involve differences in experience with computers, with statistics, and with the variety of other directions mathematics programs can take.

The nature of a degree holder's educational experiences could be conveyed through a document similar to a transcript which would list a series of descriptors characterizing the person's program in detail. Present transcripts list course titles, but course titles are often less than completely informative. They may fail to convey correct information as well as convey incorrect information. As illustration, a course in electrical engineering at one university is titled "Advanced Engineering Computation." A course in physics at another institution is titled "Introduction to Electromagnetic Theory." Despite the different titles, different departments, and apparently different levels as indicated by the terms "advanced" and "introduction," the two catalog descriptions are almost identical. The association of three or four descriptors with these two courses, among them "Fourier series" and "electromagnetic radiation," would carry information about possible academic competences held by graduates whose program had included one of those courses. Approximately one hundred such descriptors would convey reasonably well the content of a degree program.

The level at which an element of content is treated also affords a valuable elaboration on the information conveyed by degrees. "Level" in this sense differs from level of achievement indicated by grades. Fourier series may appear at various levels. They usually are treated briefly in lower-division calculus courses, appear more extensively in a variety of engineering and science courses, and may constitute the primary focus of an advanced mathematics course. Additional descriptors that indicate level of complexity and intensity can be added to the content descriptors.

A final descriptor for adding to the degree information would characterize the medium through which the content at a particular level was studied. Something about the nature of the learning would be revealed by whether a person's knowledge had been acquired from a lecture course, an advanced seminar, independent work in the library, a laboratory project, an internship or other field experience, an experience as a research assistant, or any other learning experience.

The use of descriptors to convey information about any educational program has been discussed elsewhere.[28] A document of about one hundred entries, each entry containing three descriptors denoting content, level, and nature of the learning experience, would serve an information function that the degree itself performs inadequately but that external agencies need and want. Problems of equivalence between educational programs and certificates would also be reduced by the detailed information carried by a body of descriptors. If two or more programs were being examined, the common portions and distinct portions would be revealed by comparing the sets of descriptors. An agency would select for special attention those pieces of information most pertinent to its interests.

28. Jonathan R. Warren, "Awarding Credit," in *Planning Non-Traditional Programs*, by Cross, Valley, and associates, pp. 116–47.

Some agencies would, as today, be concerned only that a person had successfully completed a four-year or other period of learning. Other agencies would focus on particular aspects of the educational experience described and vary in the specificity of the information they selected. The point is that the external agency would have options, choosing those aspects of an educational experience at a level of specificity that best suited its purposes.

Still unresolved by an information system are some troublesome matters presented by degrees and credits. Whether a degree in a stated field plus a relatively high grade-point average from a highly regarded university does in fact constitute a valid indicator of how well the degree holder might perform in some future set of activities remains a question. The predictive implications of that information have yet to be determined.

Present uses of degrees as indicators of future performance rest on untested inferences about the effects of present educational practices. Engineering and law faculties, for example, often consider one important task to be that of teaching students to think like practitioners in the field. Their educational procedures may accomplish that purpose, but whether they do or not and whether different procedures might be more effective or more efficient are rarely examined. A law firm hiring new law graduates may assume that because the new employees have been through a well-regarded law school's program, they do in fact think like lawyers. But whether thinking like lawyers has similar meanings for the law firm, the law school, and the law graduates, or, given the same meaning, whether everyone who successfully completes a law degree has in fact learned to think like a lawyer may not be defensible assumptions.

The way out of the uncertainty over the inferences that legitimately follow from knowledge of a person's educational experiences is to examine the connections between experiences and competences. If some of the effort now spent in assessing students individually were shifted to assessing the effectiveness of identifiable sets of experiences, students' accomplishments could then justifiably be inferred, without further assessment, from the fact of their having engaged in the identified experiences.

Better, more detailed information and knowledge about the inferences to which the information justifiably points, that is, a sound understanding of the meaning of the information, would represent a substantial advance over the present degree and credit system.

CHAPTER 5

Assessing Learning for Credit and Credentials

Richard L. Ferguson

Nearly all purposes attributed to educational credentials and nearly all persons interested in or using the credentials make a common assumption: that a credential holder has achieved skills and knowledge at a level acceptable in some prescribed educational program. Conversely, an institution, by awarding a credential, implies it has verified that the learning requisite to the credential has indeed occurred. From this perspective, awarding credit and a credential can be regarded as a transaction between student and institution in which the student receives recognition that he has demonstrated proficiency in some prescribed set of competences or that he has satisfied the criteria to be met. Neither of these assumptions is tenable without reliable and valid measurement of student achievement. Accordingly, as part of the crediting and credentialing processes, most institutions have developed a variety of mechanisms—examinations, grades, academic requirements (minimum number of credit hours, distribution requirements, etc.), and residency requirements—to facilitate the evaluation.

The measurement instruments and procedures used to evaluate student attainment of educational program objectives vary across institutions. Differences in educational philosophies, in student background characteristics, and in institutional resources all influence evaluation policies and practices. How evaluation proceeds is illustrated by a simple evaluation model which covers several key steps: (1) identification of the specific knowledge and skills to be evaluated, (2) development, or selection, and use of assessment instruments and procedures for measuring the specified knowledge and skills, and (3) application of rules (based on the outcomes of the assessment process) to judge whether the student has attained both the required knowledge and sufficient proficiency in the skills to warrant the award of credit or a credential.

In step one, identifying the knowledge and skills to be measured, thoroughness significantly affects the quality of the evaluation process and its outcomes. Institutions differ markedly in how they go about the task. Most institutions invest little time and energy in defining explicitly the intended outcomes of their educational programs but, rather, rely on the faculty, who, by their expertise, training, and experience, are presumed to make formal specification of program objectives needless. At the other extreme are institutions with competence- or objectives-based programs, for which systematic evaluation of students' learning is viewed as an imperative. Such institutions are thorough in specifying formally the knowledge and skills that constitute the requirements of given courses or units of learning and, by extension, of the entire educational program.

Variations also arise at stage two, developing and selecting procedures for evaluating student learning. In most educational programs, evaluation of achievement is accomplished solely by traditional methods such as teacher evaluations (grades), credit-hour requirements, and residency requirements. In general such programs are tied to time-bound credit and credentialing systems; that is, they require directly or indirectly that students participate in a sequence of activities which occur over some relatively fixed period of time. In other institutions, less restriction is placed on the time frame for learning. These latter institutions are usually receptive to procedures for recognizing extrainstitutional learning (learning acquired outside the control of the institution and its faculty members), as well as to less traditional procedures for evaluating student learning (proficiency testing, performance testing, simulation techniques, checklists, jury or committee ratings). They are also generally more flexible about residency requirements and seldom set artificial time barriers for graduation.

Because institutions differ in how they identify educational program objectives and in the types of assessment instruments and procedures they employ, they also differ in the quality of the evaluative judgments reached. The variation may impede students who want to transfer credit across institutions. Within institutions, similar problems may arise in that a common approach to evaluating student achievement does not guarantee common meaning or interpretation of results. In typical practice, responsibility for defining the credit hour lies with the individual departments; thus the meaning of the credit hour and, more specifically, the knowledge and skills represented by the credit hour may vary substantially across departments.[1] The substantial differences in evaluation practices and standards are attested by the reputations of some institutions and of some departments as being extremely rigorous, whereas others are known to be less demanding.

The problems related to awarding credits and awarding credentials are of different orders of magnitude and must be examined separately.

Evaluating Achievement for the Award of Credit

Traditionally, students have received credit when they satisfactorily completed a course or other specified block of instruction. The process for awarding credit has required that students complete assigned tasks (e.g., writing papers, writing problem sets, completing laboratory or field assignments), that they perform satisfactorily on prescribed tests, and that they faithfully attend class.[2] The disadvantages inherent in such requirements for awarding credit (e.g., disregard for differences in students' background skills and abilities and the resulting lockstep approaches to education) have long been recognized, and other approaches have been developed.

As early as the 1930s, the University of Chicago tackled

1. Margaret F. Lorimer, "How Much Is a Credit Hour?" *Journal of Higher Education* 33 (1962):302.
2. Jonathan R. Warren, "Awarding Credit," in *Planning Non-Traditional Programs*, by K. Patricia Cross, John R. Valley, and associates, p. 127.

these problems by stating the requirements of its College in terms of educational attainments and by giving students the option to earn credit by demonstrating their proficiencies through written examinations.[3] The Chicago College effort called attention to the constraints of time-based curricula, especially the negative effects that the lockstep system had on students.

Pursuant to the Chicago College approach, many institutions, often without much fanfare, began awarding credit for extrainstitutional learning. At the close of World War II, colleges began to recognize and award credit for experiences in the armed forces and for successful performance in high school advanced placement programs. In addition, they experimented with course options such as independent study, workshops, and field practicums. More recently, examination programs like the College-Level Examination Program (CLEP) of the College Entrance Examination Board and the College Proficiency and Regents External Degree Examination Programs of the University of the State of New York have been developed and are being widely used by postsecondary institutions throughout the country as a basis for awarding credit. Since the two New York programs were first introduced, they have been used primarily by institutions in New York State; however, most of the examinations in the two programs are now also administered nationally by the American College Testing Program through its Proficiency Examination Program (PEP).

The procedures for evaluating student achievement are closely related to institutional philosophy and goals. The current flux in practices related to credit and credentialing speaks against any attempt to classify institutions by their philosophies, thus to draw contrast between their evaluation practices. For the remaining discussion, a somewhat artificial but useful two-pronged approach to evaluation procedures is adopted: (1) procedures typically used for evaluating formal learning acquired in institutions, and (2) procedures used for

3. Chauncey Samuel Boucher, *The Chicago College Plan*, p. 19.

evaluating extrainstitutional learning. Even though the two types overlap in many respects, they are used in different contexts, each of which presents its own problems.

Evaluating Institutional Learning

Grades and hour requirements are the two most common criteria for awarding credit for learning in formal institutional programs. "Grades," as used here, refers to the evaluation system which instructors use (1) to communicate satisfactory or unsatisfactory completion of a course, or (2) to document the specific competences in which students have attained proficiency. In the first procedure, grades are usually letters (*A, B, C, D,* and *E,* or *P/F*). The second system is most often associated with competence- or objectives-based courses and programs for which "grades" are likely to be reported in narrative or checklist form.

The term "hour requirements" refers to the number of clock hours per week of classroom instruction in a course and, by extension, the number of hours of concentrated, but independent, study required of the student. Because both grades and hour requirements are routinely used as criteria in awarding credit, and because they are based on different presumptions of what contributes to accurate and fair evaluation of student achievement, they must be considered separately.

Grades. Letter-grade systems typically include at least two potentially significant pieces of information about students' level of achievement. First, they provide an index to the level of achievement—for example, whether a student achieved at an above-average level (*A* or *B*), an average level (*C*), or a below-average level (*D* or *F*). Second, they indicate whether a student achieved the minimum level of proficiency required to "pass"—whether the student earned a *D* grade or better—and therefore is entitled to credit.

The credit awarded by an institution for a course or an instructional unit completed by a student essentially depends on the judgment of an instructor. Instructors are relatively free to design and use almost any reasonable set of procedures for evaluating students' achievement and assigning grades. The instructor, as the person who submits a passing or failing grade for a student's work, has great influence on whether the institution does or does not award credit for the work.

Because the instructor is given so much discretion in selecting evaluation procedures, many educators consider grading practices to be highly arbitrary and therefore problematic. The current opposing trends toward inflated high school and college grades and declining achievement test scores and the absence of hard evidence that today's students are more able than those of five or ten years ago serve to emphasize the general inconsistency and subjectivity in instructor grading practices.[4] This concern among educators is underscored by the many studies which show that college grades exhibit little relationship to postgraduation job performance.[5] A conclusion is not entirely warranted, on the basis of data collected to date, that what is learned in college and how well it is learned are unrelated to job success. To the extent that the conclusion may be warranted, however, grades and ultimately educational credit and credentials would eventually become a "false currency" in the employment market, providing little information about individual probability of job success.[6]

Proponents of instructor-based grades as evidence of student achievement and as the basis for awarding credit argue that the accrediting procedures applied to most educational institutions militate against extreme grading practices, which ignore academic standards. In their view, the periodic review of faculty—part of the accrediting process—is designed to ensure that institutions employ academically qualified instructors who will insist that minimum standards be maintained.[7] Proponents further assert that courses taught in traditional modes have yielded outcomes sufficiently standardized to

4. Richard L. Ferguson and E. James Maxey, *Trends in the Academic Performance of High School and College Students,* pp. 1–2. Arvo E. Joula, "Grade Inflation (1960–1973)," pp. 1–4.

5. Ivar E. Berg, *Education and Jobs,* p. 104; Donald P. Hoyt, "College Grades and Adult Accomplishment," *Educational Record* 47 (1966):70–75.

6. Frank Newman et al., *Report on Higher Education,* p. 40.

7. Donald P. Hoyt, "Evaluating Learning from Nontraditional Contexts," p. 3.

justify the grading procedures and that the grading and credit systems have functioned quite adequately for more than fifty years. Nevertheless, there are difficulties with articulation both among institutions (difficulties in equating grades when credit is to be transferred) and within institutions (differences in standards among programs and in procedures for awarding grades).

The recent competence- or objectives-based education programs—with emphasis on specification and precise measurement of well-defined competences (knowledge and skills)— have introduced another kind of "grading." Some educational institutions already have or are considering procedures for reporting the results of achievement evaluations in a narrative form. Narrative reports are typically more elaborate and detailed than a single grade. Some reports include detail about students' strengths and weaknesses, the nature of their learning activities and resulting competences, and how their achievement was evaluated.[8] All these information elements are presumably of greater value to the prospective user than are traditional grades alone.

Whatever the type of grading system—letter, narrative, or some combination of the two—a system is fundamental to the effective evaluation of students' activities and the subsequent award or withholding of credit or a credential.

Hour requirements. Most postsecondary institutions also use a second criterion, course-hour requirements, for the award of credit. Like the grade criterion, the course-hour criterion is used for many different reasons, including all the presumed advantages it offers for the standardization of credit practices within and among institutions. For example, the credit-hour system, which is a by-product of course-hour requirements, implicitly suggests that each credit hour stands for a specific and equal amount of work for all students. The credit-hour requirement also appears to have been based, in part, on the assumption that a common number of hours of instruction enhances the probability that students will achieve at least some minimal level of proficiency.

8. Aubrey Forrest, Richard L. Ferguson, and Nancy S. Cole, "The Narrative Transcript," *Educational Record* 56 (1975):59–65.

Hour requirements are also used because they are highly functional at the institutional level. They both provide a mechanism for keeping track of students' progress toward a credential or other educational goal and facilitate program administration. The latter use occurs, for example, in institutional budgeting. The department budget is often determined by first determining faculty load, and faculty load is usually based on the total number of credit hours being taught by the department's faculty members.[9]

Despite their practical value, course-hour requirements have, in recent years, been the target of substantial criticism from several sources. First, among educators, there is a growing awareness that a time-based credit-hour system ensures only that students will be exposed to a certain amount of instruction, not that they will acquire the knowledge and skills associated with a particular course or credential. In fact, emphasis on time as a criterion in itself has, in many instances, made persistence the major requirement for attainment of a degree. Substandard practices can only lead to erosion of the confidence placed in credits and credentials.

Second, many critics argue that requiring all students to spend the same number of hours in class engaged in essentially the same instructional activity is counterproductive to learning and wastes the resources of both students and institutions. The proposed solution relies on adopting mechanisms that permit students to learn at their own pace, that allow them to demonstrate achievement attained independently of formal course work, and that result in their receiving credit for that achievement.

The third, perhaps most significant criticism of the credit-hour system is that the system fails to respond to the wide diversity of student needs. The diversity arises from both greater access to postsecondary education by students who have traditionally not enrolled (e.g., students from families of low socioeconomic status) and from the increased number of adult students who are returning to postsecondary institutions after many years' absence. Many returning students

9. Ernest A. Vargas, "The Credit Hour: An Anachronism" (MS), p. 1.

have had experiences in which they acquired knowledge and developed skills comparable to those taught in the classroom and for which credit is typically awarded. As a result, institutions enrolling adult students need procedures for evaluating and, where appropriate, awarding credit for the nontraditional learning.

Given the many criticisms addressed to hour requirements as a criterion for the award of credit, why have postsecondary institutions continued to use them? The principal reason, of course, is the need for measures that are interchangeable across institutions.[10] Additionally, despite the faults with hour requirements, institutions lack other acceptable criteria. Over the years, institutions have investigated and tried a variety of procedures aimed at resolving the problems associated with hours requirements. Honors programs, independent study, and examinations have been used to this end with varying degrees of success. Most devices have proved inadequate because they have failed to address the problem of interchangeability and because usually they are appropriate in relatively few institutions.

College-level proficiency examinations and other procedures for evaluating learning do promise to provide significant alternatives to the present time-bound credit-hour system. By using such national examination programs as the College-Level Examination Program (CLEP) of the College Entrance Examination Board and the Proficiency Examination Program (PEP) of the American College Testing Program (PEP consisting of most of the examinations contained in the New York Regents College Proficiency and External Degree Examination Programs), institutions can institute more enlightened credit practices and at the same time ensure that the results will be accepted by institutions throughout the country.

Evaluating Extrainstitutional Learning

Although the traditional approach to earning educational credit (and credentials) may be appropriate for large numbers of students, it is not completely satisfactory for students

10. Lanora Lewis, *The Credit System in Colleges and Universities*, p. 9.

who want to receive credit for the knowledge and skills they have acquired in settings outside the formal classroom. These students need a more suitable method for demonstrating their competences and receiving educational credit for them. In response, more institutions are seeking means for recognizing and awarding credit for extrainstitutional learning, whether acquired through informal activities such as independent study and reading, work, and life experiences, or formal training provided by associations, business, government, industry, the military, or unions. In order for institutions to credit pertinent extrainstitutional learning, however, procedures for effective evaluation of achievement must be developed. This is no small matter inasmuch as the development and implementation of such evaluative procedures is a complex and difficult task. Several factors contribute to the complexity and argue for caution in the crediting process.

First, the award of credit for extrainstitutional learning is most meaningful when it permits a student, through an alternate way, to satisfy the credit requirements for a course offered by the institution. The institution, on its side, must exercise considerable care in the evaluation process to assure that the important knowledge and skill outcomes of the course are adequately covered. If the evaluation process employs a written examination, the matching process is somewhat facilitated. Other types of measures, because they are less likely to be highly systematic, present a greater challenge. The problem can be larger than simple comparison of what the evaluation instrument measures with the intended program outcomes. It may also entail administrative matters such as cutoff scores and how much, if any, credit should be awarded.

In the crediting of extrainstitutional learning, some critics argue that the difficulty both in adequately specifying what is to be evaluated and then in measuring it make the task hopeless. The criticism seems unwarranted, for it conveniently overlooks the same problem when the evaluation process focuses on student achievement in traditional learning environments. In either situation, the problem is challenging and deserves earnest attention from educators concerned with instruction and evaluation.

A second factor contributing to the complexity of evaluating extrainstitutional learning is the limited availability of reliable and valid instruments for measuring student achievement. Traditional paper-and-pencil instruments are frequently inadequate especially for measuring the types of skills acquired through work or life experiences. As a result, many institutions which are committed to providing alternative routes to earning credit have found that, to do so, they must develop their own formal evaluation devices. Yet few institutions have either staff members competent to develop the needed assessment tools or the resources to obtain them. In the absence of reliable and valid measurement instruments and procedures, the commitment cannot be met.

A partial solution to evaluating extrainstitutional learning is offered by programs like CLEP, PEP, and the College Proficiency and Regents External Degree Examination Programs of the University of the State of New York. Also contributing are the materials and procedures emerging from national efforts such as the Cooperative Assessment of Experiential Learning (described in more detail later in this paper). The problem is far from solved, and its solution will probably require the investment of significant amounts of energy and resources.

A final factor which has influenced educators' attitudes toward awarding credit for extrainstitutional learning is uneasiness about using a single examination or assessment procedure. Many faculty members doubt that a single measure administered in a relatively brief session can possibly produce as adequate an evaluation of the knowledge and skills as that obtained from traditional classroom measures. Although this perspective has some merit, it runs counter to the concept of credit as recognition for demonstrated student achievement; that is, credit is awarded, not merely for exposure to knowledge or skills or for educational activity, but only for competences demonstrated through systematic evaluation. If the single instrument adequately measures the competences, then a single measure ought to be considered sufficient.

Collectively, the complicating factors present educators with a challenging, though not unsolvable, task. Hundreds of postsecondary institutions are awarding credit for extrainstitutional learning, evidence that the challenge has been accepted, if not overcome.

Locally developed evaluation procedures. Written examinations as a basis for awarding credit are by no means new to postsecondary education. An early, prominent program of credit by examination, adopted in 1932 at the University of Buffalo, was designed for superior high school seniors.[11] Under the Buffalo program, students could receive credit through successful performance on examinations that paralleled the end-of-course examinations of specific college courses. To discourage all but the most able high school students from participating, eligibility requirements were relatively rigorous. The institution's enrolled students also could take the examinations, but only if they could satisfy the high academic criteria. The examinations covered mathematics, languages, English, history, chemistry, physics, accounting, psychology, philosophy, and economics. The most heavily used tests were those in which there was considerable overlap between high school and college work. The credit awarded by Buffalo was widely accepted for transfer by other accredited colleges and universities.

Locally constructed credit-by-examination programs similar to the Buffalo program are being administered extensively at colleges across the nation, with two of the largest programs at Ohio State University and the University of Illinois. A survey of credit-by-examination practices, conducted by the American College Testing Program in May 1976, revealed that, of the approximately 1,700 two-year and four-year institutions responding, some 60 percent were administering locally developed written examinations for credit purposes, with the award of credit dependent on the examination results. Although the examinations could be used with any student seeking college credit for noncollege learning, most programs are better suited for use by recent high school graduates inasmuch as the tests typically emphasize knowledge and skills taught in the classroom. As noted earlier, the knowledge and abilities that the adult student has acquired after years of work or life

11. Hannah Kreplin, *Credit by Examination*, pp. 15–16.

experience are frequently of a practical character that require measurement procedures different from the types traditionally used.

Since adult enrollments in postsecondary education are increasing, local institutions are trying to provide mechanisms to enable adults to receive credit for work and life experiences. Educational programs such as those of Empire State College, Metropolitan State University, and the University Without Walls typify the progress in this area.[12] The types of measures developed for use in such programs include interviews with students, performance tests, situational observations, simulations, and product assessment (e.g., evaluation of students' paintings by professional artists).[13]

Whatever type of locally developed instruments postsecondary institutions employ to evaluate students' extrainstitutional achievement, a prime condition for using the results is that the measurement tools or procedures be technically adequate. Technical adequacy implies that the tools both be comprehensive in coverage of the knowledge and skills to be credited and be psychometrically sound—reliable and valid. The first criterion, comprehensiveness, might well be satisfied by adherence to a guideline recommended by the Office on Educational Credit of the American Council on Education:

Institutions should evaluate extrainstitutional learning and award credit only in subject-matter fields in which they have available faculty expertise or where they can rely on nationally validated examinations or other procedures for establishing credit equivalencies. Normally, institutions should evaluate learning and award credit only in subject fields in which they offer comparable courses or curricula; however, elective credit appropriately may be excepted.[14]

12. John R. Valley, "External Degree Programs," in *Explorations in Non-Traditional Study*, by Cross, Valley, and associates, pp. 95–125.

13. Aubrey Forrest, Miriam Meyers, and Catherine Tisinger, "Assessment Handbook" (MS), pp. 8–9.

14. "Awarding Credit for Extrainstitutional Learning," statement by the Commission on Educational Credit of the American Council on Education, approved by the ACE Board of Directors and endorsed by the Council on Postsecondary Accreditation (Washington: ACE, Office on Educational Credit, January 1977), p. 1. See also Recommendation Ten of the Task Force on Educational Credit and Credentials and the ensuing discussion in the present volume.

The second criterion for locally developed instruments or procedures is technical adequacy of the evaluation tools. Appropriate standards for written examinations are available in *Standards for Educational and Psychological Tests,* prepared by the American Psychological Association, and need only be applied by the institutions to the examinations used for awarding credit. Postsecondary institutions should encounter no serious problems in implementing these standards, given the availability of a captive audience to provide the data necessary for the various technical studies, especially those related to test reliability, content validity, and criterion-related validity (e.g., the relationship between students' test performance and their actual performance in the courses). Another important technical determination to be addressed in such studies is cut-off scores for the award of credit.

Evaluation of the technical adequacy of nontraditional measures and procedures is quite a different matter, however. Measurement methodology for this type of assessment is less firmly established, and consequently, results must be interpreted and used more cautiously. The criteria to be applied when student achievement in the performance type of skill is being evaluated for the possible award of credit should include: (1) selection of an assessment technique which, as nearly as possible, directly measures the skill or performance to be evaluated, (2) if the skill calls for a subjective judgment, participation by more than one evaluator, and (3) current testimonial from experts with whom the student has worked, supplemented by additional objective evaluations. Where appropriate, traditional standards should also be applied to such evaluation procedures; for example, whenever possible, reliability and validity data in some form should be routinely collected.

Evidence on the technical adequacy of the assessment instruments and procedures is desirable in order that the institution may reach accurate evaluation and credit decisions. For students who wish to transfer credits to other institutions, such evidence is imperative. If data about the content and technical adequacy of the examinations are not available, the credit involved may well be meaningless to the receiving institution and hence not accepted.

National examination programs. State and national testing groups and agencies have been motivated, through agreement with the principles of credit for extrainstitutional learning, to respond to the challenges posed by the development and large-scale implementation of assessment devices designed to serve those principles. To do so, they have experimented with a variety of innovative assessment procedures and instruments. Additionally, they have developed mechanisms to expand the use of examinations for credit purposes and to facilitate transfer of credit.

The first credit-by-examination program to be widely used by educational institutions was the College Proficiency Program (CPEP) of the Board of Regents of the State of New York. Established in 1961, CPEP was designed to help postsecondary institutions evaluate extrainstitutional student achievement for the award of college credit. Thus far, colleges and universities in New York and other states have awarded more than 100,000 credits on the basis of performance on the CPEP subject examinations.[15] The CPE's are developed jointly by content specialists from colleges and universities and the Board of Regents testing staff. Currently, some twenty-nine examinations cover college subjects in the arts and sciences, health, education, criminal justice, and nursing.[16]

Because the CPEP was well received by the education community and by the students it was designed to help, the Board of Regents in 1970 introduced a second program for extra-institutional learning—the Regents External Degree (RED) Program. It is designed to permit a person who demonstrates knowledge and skills equivalent to those of the graduate of a traditional baccalaureate program to earn an undergraduate degree, regardless of how the knowledge and skills were acquired. RED examinations are being offered in the fields of business, nursing, and modern foreign languages, the latest being the Foreign Language Proficiency Tests for Teachers and Advanced Students, prepared by the Modern Language Association.

Until recently the CPEP and RED examinations were of-

15. *College Proficiency Examinations/Regents External Degrees,* p. 177.
16. Ibid., p. 183.

fered four times a year, primarily in New York, Connecticut, Idaho, Illinois, Oregon, and California. Since fall 1976, nearly all the examinations have been administered nationally by the American College Testing Program through its Proficiency Examination Program (PEP). The PEP examinations are offered at test centers principally on college campuses and through military test centers sponsored by the Defense Activity for Non-Traditional Education Support (DANTES).

A second program, the College-Level Examination Program (CLEP), was designed originally for postsecondary students who had acquired certain knowledge and skills in extrainstitutional settings. Introduced by the College Entrance Examination Board (CEEB) on a national basis in 1966, CLEP now serves extensively as a means for both adults and entering college students, primarily recent high school graduates, to obtain credit for college-level courses.[17]

CLEP examinations are of two types, General Examinations and Subject Examinations, both of which are based on typical courses in a variety of colleges across the country. Because the examinations sample content from college courses, they are as applicable for measuring knowledge and skills acquired through the formal college curriculum as through nontraditional methods of study. The five General Examinations cover respectively English composition, mathematics, natural sciences, social sciences, and humanities. Originally each examination consisted entirely of multiple-choice items. The English General Examination is being revised to include a written section. Forty-two Subject Examinations are currently being offered in business, education, humanities, mathematics, medical technology, nursing, sciences, and social sciences. Each of the Subject Examinations consists of multiple-choice items, to which, for most of the examinations, interested postsecondary institutions may add an optional essay section.[18]

Although CLEP cannot itself award credit, institutions across the country do award credit for successful performance

17. *CLEP May Be for You,* p. 3.
18. Ibid., pp. 4–8. See also "There's More Than One Way to Earn a College Degree," *Carnegie Quarterly* 23 (1975):2–4.

on the examinations. Students seeking such credit take the examinations at test centers located primarily on college campuses, at military test centers sponsored by DANTES, or through the Testing Academic Achievement Program of CEEB, under which some institutions administer retired forms of the General Examinations.[19]

Each of these examination programs intentionally challenged the traditions inherent in the course-hour approach to educational crediting. Each acknowledged the need for alternatives to a time-bound system of crediting which failed to take into account the vast differences in the educational backgrounds and experiences of postsecondary students and would-be students; each attempted to provide alternatives. Other national assessment programs used in awarding college credit were not designed to challenge these assumptions.

The Advanced Placement (AP) Program of CEEB, for example, grew out of two projects sponsored by the Ford Foundation which investigated integration of high school and college curricula and acceleration through early admission to college.[20] Because the AP program emphasizes articulation, it does not challenge the time-bound system of crediting; it does not presume, as do the CLEP, PEP, and the New York programs, that credit can be awarded for learning acquired outside the institution. Typically, high school students enroll in AP courses to acquire the specified college-level knowledge and skills. The present AP Subject Examinations each include essay and objective components and are, of course, at the college level. Development of the examinations has oversight from examining committees consisting of high school and college teachers and professional testing staff. Because only those colleges and universities participating in the AP program can award credit, each institution decides for itself the subject areas in which credit is awarded, the amount of credit awarded, and the scores required to earn credit. As a consequence, credit award policies and practices for the AP program vary widely among the institutions.

19. Jerilee Grandy and Walter M. Shea, *CLEP General Examinations in American Colleges and Universities*, p. 6.
20. Kreplin, *Credit by Examination*, p. 10.

Other national programs not specifically designed for the award of credit but frequently so used by educational institutions include the Assessment Program of the American College Testing Program and the Achievement Tests component of the CEEB Admissions Testing Program (ATP). The 1976 ACT survey on credit-by-examination practices, cited earlier, indicated that 175, or more than 9 percent of the approximately 1,700 responding colleges, award credit to students on the basis of performance on the ACT tests. The academic portion of the ACT Assessment Program consists of four subtests, in English, mathematics, social studies, and natural sciences. Unpublished data from ACT surveys made in the fall and winter of 1973 indicated that credit is most typically awarded for entrance-level courses in English and mathematics. These findings seem reasonable inasmuch as the scope and content of the English and mathematics subtests are easily equated to entering-level college courses.

Approximately 10 percent of the institutions responding to the ACT 1976 survey indicated they use the Achievement Tests of the CEEB Admissions Testing Program for the award of credit. These examinations sample the domain of specific subject-matter areas and are administered independently of, but in conjunction with, the Scholastic Aptitude Test.

Criticisms of written examinations. The use of examinations as the basis for evaluating student achievement to award credit for extrainstitutional learning has clearly gained in acceptance among postsecondary institutions over the past ten years. Although credit by examination has become legitimated, so to speak, possibly through its increased use by colleges and universities, all the problems related to the award of credit have by no means been resolved. The fundamental concern of most educators about credit by examination is whether the knowledge and skills measured by a two- or three-hour examination can possibly be equated to the learning which occurs in a course that typically involves thirty to fifty hours of formal instruction. A corollary concern is whether credit can be awarded on the basis of such measures without diluting academic standards.

Most critics of credit by examination generally concede the

examinations are effective for evaluating students' cognitive-level achievement. Their doubts usually pertain to the inadequacy of such examinations to assess accurately whether a student has acquired the cultural and moral values that faculties of liberal arts colleges and liberal arts components of most baccalaureate programs attempt to inculcate. The criticism seems justified. Significantly, however, the criticism applies equally to the evaluation processes in traditional procedures for awarding credit. For example, there are relatively few documented accounts of successful attempts by institutions to evaluate students' attainment of noncognitive objectives. The problem is not entirely that of the mechanisms for evaluating achievement, but lies also in the inability of educators to specify the values they seek to foster and in their inability to describe adequately the behaviors which, if properly measured, would verify that the values have been communicated by the institution and acquired by students.

Another problem in written examinations for the award of credit concerns the assumptions which underlie their development. Typically, the scope and content of the examinations sample the curricula of many institutions, the goal being examinations that reflect, as much as possible, the common core of all these programs. Some educators question the viability of this approach to examination development and express concern that institutions may use the results to evaluate achievement and award credit even when the examinations do not adequately sample the content domain of the educational program. Yet institutions can take the steps to determine whether the scope and content of an examination does adequately sample the course, knowledge, and skills for which credit is to be awarded. The steps imply careful study both of the examination itself and of the learning objectives of the educational program. The developers of the examinations have responsibilities to make available to institutions materials which facilitate accurate judgments in this regard. These procedures, if followed, should help eliminate inappropriate uses of examinations for awarding credit.

Another matter deserving educators' attention concerns the technical adequacy of the examinations, especially those receiving widespread use. Most agencies responsible for national testing programs recognize the need for reliable, valid measures of learning and will probably continue to provide, at their own initiative, adequate documentation of the technical characteristics of their programs. Still, as the use of such programs increases and additional programs are developed, the need for scientific objectivity and the concern for the rights of the persons most affected by the crediting and credentialing process will also grow.

One approach to the evaluation of examinations used to award credit is to involve an objective third party.[21] The Office on Educational Credit (OEC) of the American Council on Education is entering this third-party role by extending its current function of making credit recommendations to colleges and universities for CLEP and the military Subject Standardized Tests to include other testing programs.[22] In this role, OEC will accomplish two important functions. First, it will assist institutions using the examination programs by certifying their technical adequacy (e.g., reliability and validity)— a considerable service, given the many examinations available. Second, if OEC provides credit recommendations to colleges, some consistency may be introduced into the use made of the examinations. The challenge facing OEC is formidable and also highly worthwhile.

Innovations in assessment procedures. The traditional paper-and-pencil examinations used as assessment instruments tend, as previously noted, to be inappropriate to extrainstitutional noncognitive learning and to many types of life and work experience, especially those which include performance. An effort to fill the gap is being made by CAEL. CAEL started as a project known as the Cooperative Assessment of Experiential Learning, involving the Educational Testing Service and ten collaborating institutions. It has evolved into the Council for the Advancement of Experiential Learning, an association of approximately three hundred in-

21. Hoyt, "Evaluating Learning from Nontraditional Contexts."
22. "Guidelines for Appraising the Technical Quality of Achievement Examinations," duplicated (Washington: American Council on Education, Office on Educational Credit, November 1977).

stitutions. A principal objective of the CAEL project is to determine how best to fix the worth, in academic credit, of extrainstitutional learning, especially learning associated with work and life experience.

CAEL was initiated because of the obvious complexity of the problem and the futility of institutions duplicating their research efforts aimed at developing new types of assessment techniques. As an initial goal, the project attempted to bring together a large number of institutions which were having common measurement problems in order to compare and research the assessment techniques different members had developed. An initial outcome was the identification of a six-stage taxonomy for assessment techniques in experiential education. Those stages involve: (1) identifying what has been learned, (2) specifying how what has been learned relates to the person's educational goals, (3) documenting the learning experience(s), (4) determining how much has been learned, (5) determining whether what has been learned, for which the person seeks credit, meets an acceptable standard, and, if so, how much credit should be awarded, and, finally, (6) describing the credit awarded by means of a transcript (usually narrative in type).[23]

During the four years since CAEL was initiated, an extensive inventory of the assessment procedures and techniques being used by its members has been completed. In addition, numerous projects related to assessing experiential learning have been carried out by individual institutions as well as groups of institutions. Most activities have included collecting data on the actual use of the new assessment techniques and procedures to evaluate how well they function in practical settings.[24] The major efforts currently include dissemination of information about good assessment practices through a series of guidebooks and workshops.

The College Outcomes Measures Project (COMP) has goals complementary to those of the CAEL project. COMP is a joint

23. Joan E. Knapp, *A Guide for Assessing Prior Experience through Portfolios.*" Aubrey Forrest, *A Student Handbook on Preparing a Portfolio for the Assessment of Prior Experiential Learning.*
24. "There's More than One Way to Earn a College Degree," pp. 4–7.

effort by the American College Testing Program (ACT), ten postsecondary institutions, and two state agencies. Here, the attempt is to develop a variety of types of assessment instruments and procedures, traditional and nontraditional, to measure competences common to the liberal arts or general education components of the baccalaureate programs of the participating institutions. The project will build on work under way at the institutions to define program competences and on work of other projects with similar purposes, such as CAEL.[25]

Both CAEL and COMP focus on measures for evaluating the outcomes of learning activities and not on the nature of the activity that led to the learning. Moreover, they are committed to seeking reasonable alternatives to traditional forms of assessment for evaluating those outcomes. To observe that the road to achieving such ambitious goals is paved with thorns is to state the obvious. Nonetheless, the projects represent a reasonable first step in responding to the challenge posed by Virginia Smith, as director of the Fund for the Improvement of Postsecondary Education:

> The desire to recognize learning wherever and whenever it occurs will not be defeated by any prejudice against experiential learning, but by the primitive state of the art for assessing various types of learning outcomes. That art will not progress until our focus is shifted from the nature and length of the educational activity to the type of learning outcome desired.[26]

The above innovative moves in evaluating extrainstitutional learning all, directly or indirectly, involve educational institutions in the actual evaluation of students' achievement. CLEP and PEP and the College Proficiency and Regents External Degree Examination Programs of the University of the State of New York, on the other hand, are simply mechanisms whereby an institution evaluates the students' level of proficiency in certain knowledge and skills and then decides whether to award credit and how much credit to award. CAEL and COMP turn to nontraditional types of assessment procedures administered directly by the institutions.

25. "Development and Use of College Outcome Measures."
26. "Assessing Experiential Learning," in *Reflections on Experiential Learning and Its Uses*, p. 20.

Formal courses of nonacademic sponsors. Three efforts of the American Council on Education (ACE), through its Office on Educational Credit (OEC), present a different approach to the award of credit for extrainstitutional learning. The first program is concerned with learning acquired in formal military training; the second, learning acquired in courses taught by other nonacademic sponsors, for example, business and industry; and the third, learning acquired for occupational competence. In the first two programs, student achievement is measured and evaluated directly by evaluating the training program and the courses, including the procedures used to evaluate student learning, and then recommending whether educational institutions should award credit for the course and, if so, how much.

For more than thirty years, ACE, through the Office on Educational Credit and its predecessor Commission on the Accreditation of Service Experiences, has been evaluating formal educational programs and courses sponsored by the military for the purpose of preparing credit recommendations to colleges and universities. During that time, hundreds of thousands of service men and women have, in fact, been awarded credit on the basis of the ACE recommendations published in *Guide to the Evaluation of Educational Experiences in the Armed Services.*[27]

In 1974, ACE extended its evaluation activities to include formal programs and courses offered by other nonacademic sponsors such as businesses, government agencies, and professional and voluntary associations. The program—Program on Noncollegiate-Sponsored Instruction—is carried on with cooperating state education agencies to evaluate such courses, and the resulting recommendations are issued by ACE in *The National Guide to Credit Recommendations for Noncollegiate Courses,*[28] a companion volume to the military guide. ACE coordinates the program at the national level, provides the policy leadership, and evaluates courses and programs offered in states not yet participating in the program. As of October 1977, the cooperating state agencies included the Consortium

27. *Guide, 1976* is the latest of four editions.
28. The first edition is to be issued in 1978.

of the California State University and Colleges, the Commonwealth of Pennsylvania Department of Education, and the Tennessee Higher Education Commission.

A third ACE program concerns the evaluation of learning associated with occupational competence. The success of the program depends on occupations being properly defined within an occupational classification system and on individual occupational competence being adequately verified. The occupational assessment approach was first used in 1975 when Army enlisted military occupational specialties (MOS's) were evaluated.[29] The procedures developed for, and used in, the MOS evaluations were then applied to other occupational classification systems, including Army warrant officer occupations, Navy enlisted occupations, and nationally registered apprentice training programs.

Before a given occupational classification system can be evaluated, four criteria must be met. First, the occupations must be adequately codified within the classification system; that is, they must be defined in such a way as to distinguish one occupation clearly from another. Second, the occupations must be described in terms of the specific tasks, responsibilities, skills, competences, and knowledge required by each occupational designation. Third, there must be a valid and reliable method of verifying that a given person in a given occupation has indeed acquired the learning required for the job, and normally the verification method must include an objective measurement component. Fourth, individual occupational proficiency must be accurately recorded so that postsecondary institutions can be furnished with a reliable record of that person's achievement.

Once these four criteria have been satisfied, ACE evaluates the occupations within the classification system. Credit recommendations for military occupations are published in the *Guide to the Evaluation of Educational Experiences in the Armed Services.* Credit recommendations for nationally reg-

29. "Project to Study the Feasibility of Using the Army Enlisted Military Occupational Specialty Classification System as a Means of Recognizing Learning," duplicated (Washington: American Council on Education, Commission on Educational Credit, May 1975).

istered apprentice training programs will be published by ACE in 1978.

Whether the credit recommendations made by ACE for learning offered by nonacademic sponsors or agencies are appropriate depends on the adequacy of the procedures for establishing both the merit of the educational program and the reliability and validity of the evaluation of achievement. The formal military courses have been successfully evaluated for many years. The expansion of the role of ACE to include the evaluation of occupations and noncollege, nonmilitary courses will both enlarge the evaluation process and introduce complexities. Indeed, the rigorous procedures for evaluation will have to be faultlessly maintained: systematic reevaluations will have to be conducted not only to assess revisions in content and evaluation procedures, but also to reassess the appropriateness of credit recommendations to the evolving educational programs of the crediting institutions.

Continuing education unit. Millions of people in the United States engage in a variety of noncredit continuing education programs—institutes, workshops, conferences, seminars, adult education classes, and many other organized activities. Their reasons for participating are various: some do so purely for pleasure and relaxation; others, to update their knowledge and skills for personal recognition and job advancement; and others, to meet certification and licensing requirements. Completion of these programs will not lead to the award of educational credit on some automatic formula basis.

The continuing education unit (CEU) was developed by the National Task Force on the Continuing Education Unit (a group representing a cross section of interests and organizations in continuing education) as a mechanism for measuring and recording institutional or organizational output from *noncredit* educational activities. One CEU is defined as a unit of measurement representing "ten contact hours of participation in an organized continuing education experience under responsible sponsorship, capable direction, and qualified instruction."[30]

30. National Task Force on the Continuing Education Unit, *The Continuing Education Unit,* see especially pp. vi, 3.

The activities in which participants engage to obtain CEU's are similar in many respects to the activities pursued by persons who are awarded credits. The basis for award of CEU's and credit, however, differ fundamentally. When an institution or organization awards a CEU, it is required only to attest to a prescribed amount of educational activity. In awarding credit, an institution presumably confirms both that the person has completed a prescribed amount of educational activity *and* that he or she has attained the knowledge and skills associated with that activity.[31] A requirement for the award of credit is that the institution conduct a reliable and valid evaluation of student achievement. This difference between CEU's and educational credit thus argues strongly against any attempt to equate the two.

The educational activity that leads to credit may or may not be of greater value than one which leads to the CEU. The student seeking a master's degree would undoubtedly choose a course that yields educational credit. However, if a short, intensive CEU course helps the participant to perform better in a job, then that course may be far more appropriate than one that yields credit but requires a semester.[32] The CEU is well suited to recognizing educational activity which has self-improvement and avocational objectives, objectives that tend to be general in nature and call for attainment of skills and knowledge which can be acquired in a relatively short time. Neither objective implies study prerequisites; the learning is typically not directly related to occupational competence or pursued for job qualifications, so that evaluation of skill achievement is usually not crucial.

The CEU, when used to recognize continuing education in the professions, especially medicine, is far more controversial. The problem derives, not from its use to acknowledge educational activity, but from its potential use as evidence that

31. Jerry W. Miller, "The CEU and Educational Alternatives" (Paper read at the Continuing Education Unit in Business, Industry, Government and Associations, December 8, 1975, at Statler Hilton Hotel, Washington, D.C.), duplicated.

32. John W. Enell, "The CEU Comes of Age," *Engineering Education* 66 (1975):150.

practitioners have kept up with knowledge and developments in their field. Such use of the CEU is completely without merit: verification that the practitioner has acquired, not merely been exposed to, the important competences is essential to the entire purpose of recertification and relicensure activities.

Because CEU's and credits serve different purposes in education, any interest in developing a standard formula for converting CEU's to credit lacks foundation. Educators should, however, be willing to acknowledge that CEU activities represent legitimate opportunities for learning and that, collectively, such a set of activities could easily result in learning equivalent to that acquired in a credit course. In this sense, the learning derived from CEU activities may be viewed as another form of experiential learning which the institution is prepared to acknowledge with credit after appropriate evaluation of achievement.

Evaluating Achievement for the Award of Credentials

Although the crediting process and the credentialing process clearly have many points in common, they also have significant differences: differences in the objectives of the evaluation process, and differences in the evaluation methods. Credits are awarded to students as recognition for academic achievement. Credentials are awarded by an institution once a specified number of credits, distributed in an approved manner, have been accumulated. Usually, to attain the required number of credits, students must enroll in courses at the institution for some fixed period of time. For most baccalaureate degrees, the number of credit hours that students must earn translates into a program of approximately four years. A time-fixed process also assumes some limit on the maximum number of credit hours a student may achieve each term. Credits and credentials are, then, interdependent.

Because credits recognize student achievement of proficiency in the knowledge and skills identified with a course or some small unit of instruction, they often have little utility beyond contributing to the requirements for the credential. As a result, achievement at the credit or course level is seldom scrutinized by sources external to the institution. An educational credential, however, is perceived by the public, business, and industry as identifying a person who has attained some specific level of achievement in the field associated with his or her educational program. Therefore, the evaluation of student achievement for credentialing plays a highly significant role. Indeed, if an institution fails to use adequate evaluation procedures to measure and certify student achievement, and if, as a consequence, it grants credentials to students who lack the competences generally attributed to holders of such credentials, eventually the credibility and viability of that institution will be jeopardized.

In general, students must satisfy two criteria to become eligible for the credentials awarded by most postsecondary institutions. First, they must show evidence that they have achieved the knowledge and skills which define the area in which they seek the credential. This evidence is typically provided by histories of grades and credit hours earned in the program (e.g., a transcript) and in some instances through theses, results on comprehensive examinations, or some other form of assessment. Histories include data specific to individual students. The second criterion, the residency requirement, is not directly evaluative but rather has the objective of ensuring that a student receives a certain minimum exposure to the knowledge and skills that define a particular program. The two criteria are fundamental to the evaluation of student achievement in most educational credentialing.

Achievement Requirements

The process of earning a credential primarily calls for students to obtain a specified number of credits over a given time period; credits are usually earned incrementally through completion of courses or small blocks of instruction. The data used in the evaluation of student achievement for credentialing are generally the sum of the individual evaluations which result from each course. The adequacy of this "overall" evaluation of achievement thus depends heavily on the reliability and validity of the individual evaluations made throughout a student's program.

The above procedures for credentialing collectively describe the method most frequently used by postsecondary institutions for the past fifty years. That approach has its critics. The greatest criticism has been aimed at one assumption in the approach: that the level of achievement recognized by a credential can be represented by the simple addition of course credits. The critics typically argue for a synergistic interpretation of the education process that leads to a credential. As a result, several alternative models of evaluation have been developed. In all cases, the alternatives begin with the evaluative information derived from the crediting process and augment it with information obtained from other types of assessment instruments and techniques. Comprehensive examinations and theses are examples of mechanisms that many institutions have added to improve the quality of the student evaluation process for credentialing.

A comprehensive examination is any form of measurement of student learning intended to survey a major portion of the knowledge and skills acquired throughout a student's educational program. Such examinations are typically administered for two purposes. First, in principle, they provide a vehicle for measuring the knowledge and skills as a unified body of attainment and also presumably assess that added element of the educational process—the synergistic outcome of the educational program. Second, in many instances, the comprehensive examination is used simply as a further check on the evaluation outcomes of the individual courses through a practical check on the differences among faculty members in the quality of instruction provided and on the standards applied in the evaluation process. The comprehensive examination serves as an equalizer in the evaluation process.

The types and levels of comprehensive examinations used by postsecondary institutions vary according to needs. Many institutions administer locally developed comprehensives as quality control devices at the end of the sophomore year in order to identify areas of deficiency which students must correct before being admitted to junior-level standing. Some institutions also administer them at the end of the educational programs in order to identify students who have not yet achieved the standards required for a credential. For some students, performance on these examinations may be used to decide their eligibility for admission to an advanced program of study (e.g., a higher level degree program).

Many comprehensive examinations used in evaluating overall achievement are weak in that they emphasize factual knowledge rather than the skills which demonstrate students' ability to use that knowledge effectively. Such an approach to evaluation lends little hope that students' performance on such measures will be highly related to their performances in adult roles. Unless institutions and the developers of comprehensive examinations devote major effort to assuring accurate measurement of the essential outcomes of educational programs, the value of such examinations will be limited; the results are unlikely to offer much new information about students' proficiencies beyond that already available through the individual course evaluations.

Efforts by postsecondary institutions to improve the quality of comprehensive examinations and make them more useful are illustrated by the increasing interest in proficiency tests that measure students' competence in the "basic" knowledge and skill areas. Some institutions are considering as a requirement for graduation that students pass an examination demonstrating their writing proficiency.

A second evaluation tool, which supplements instructor evaluations of students' proficiencies, especially those associated with upper level programs, is the thesis. The thesis, used primarily in graduate programs, is intended to measure a type of proficiency not easily assessed in a single course. The thesis is presumed to provide the basis for evaluating the student's initiative and ability to carry through on a significant project, and, perhaps more important, ability to apply in a dynamic and meaningful way the knowledge and skills acquired through the classroom.

Some critics identify two frequent drawbacks to the thesis as an indicator of student achievement. First, the thesis is too specialized: it frequently permits and may encourage such a high degree of specialization that the results cannot serve as an effective measure of students' overall educational development. Given the time and energy that students and faculty members invest in a thesis, the payoff in quality and quantity of information gained may prove too small. A second weakness attributed to the thesis as an evaluation device is that the finished document often fails to represent original work by the student. Often it reflects the philosophy of, and major input from, the student's advisers and committee members.

Unless the purposes for the thesis and the criteria for its evaluation are carefully defined at the outset, the results of the process are likely to be ambiguous and to shed little light on students' competences. Institutions requiring theses are well advised to give heed to the precise kinds of evaluative information required and to whether some other form of assessment might prove more productive and efficient.

Residency Requirements

Probably no single policy of postsecondary institutions related to the credentialing process has been more maligned by educators than the residency requirement. In the early 1920s, the credit-hour system and companion residency requirements as measures for earned degrees were reaching the peak of acceptance by educational institutions. But resistance to their inflexibility was already evident, and attacks on them have continued. Occasionally there has been great furor, but eventually to little avail.

The attacks on the system were futile for reasons mostly related to the original influences which led to the residency requirement. (1) Little trust was placed in final course examinations as evidence of student achievement. No tradition prevailed in this country for external testing to verify learning. Therefore, the amount of time spent on the college campus became a convenient measure. (2) Accrediting agencies, in order to have a common standard, promoted the idea that all students should do a fixed amount of work in a specified fashion. (3) State universities or education departments, by controlling procedures for awarding credentials, were able to regulate college practices. (4) Educators and students came to associate the four years of college with the social and intellectual life on campus, although the two were quite independent of the pronounced educational purposes of the college. (5) Preprofessional requirements tended to stipulate a four-year curriculum. (6) Some institutions needed the income generated by four years' tuition and other fees to meet their budgets.[33]

Not all these factors are as influential in maintaining the system as they were in institutionalizing it more than a half-century ago, but many retain their raison d'être. Policies and practices concerning residency affect the entire postsecondary student population—full-time residents, full-time commuters, part-time commuters, and students who earn their degrees away from the institution. Many institutions' policies specify fixed amounts of time that all students—undergraduates, graduates—must spend in full-time residency as a condition to eligibility for a degree.

Proponents for residency requirements offer strong arguments that unless students engage in full-time educational activities at the institution, certain outcomes of the educational process are diminished. They also emphasize benefits which they believe derive from students' exposure to points of view, attitudes, and philosophies of teachers and fellow students. For example, many institutions, both secular and religious, include the inculcation of values and ethics among the intended outcomes of their programs. It is difficult to see how such outcomes could be seriously regarded as program objectives if students had only limited direct contact with the institution.

Another argument supporting residency requirements is that they assure at least a minimum level of commonality in the educational experiences of students. Although four years invested in on-campus college-level study is not evidence that students have achieved the knowledge and skills identified with the educational program, it does ensure that they have been exposed to a supportive educational environment and some specific course of instruction.

Opponents of residency requirements hold a different per-

33. Kreplin, *Credit by Examination,* p. 3.

spective. They view policies which require all students to take essentially the same number of courses and spend the same number of hours in the classroom as logically and educationally indefensible. Further, they believe that students' educational process should not be hindered by artificial time barriers and that institutions should instead focus on determining whether students have attained, rather than merely been exposed to, the skills and abilities identified by the institution as necessary and sufficient for the degree or credential. They hold that inasmuch as residence in no way guarantees that students have achieved some minimum set of competences or even shared a common educational experience, the educational and social shortcomings speak forcefully for institutional policies and practices on residency requirements to be reexamined.

For institutions that value flexibility for students, the adoption of less restrictive residency requirements poses an essential responsibility: to be able to demonstrate that academic standards are not diluted in the process. Thus, if residency requirements are eased, at the same time reliable and valid assessment procedures must be instituted to assure that students are achieving the objectives of the educational programs.

There are encouraging signs that many institutions are facing this issue squarely by developing instruments and procedures for evaluating student attainments. The approach seems more consistent with the role of the credential as an indicator of the students' level of competence than does the residency requirement which, even at best, attests only to the students' adherence to a prescribed program carried out in a prescribed manner. A major condition of such measurement is that the intended outcomes of the educational programs on which they are based be well specified. For most institutions, this task requires a significant effort because few of them have yet invested the time and resources to formally document their objectives at either the course or the program level. The effort is desirable, however, to serve both curricular and evaluative purposes: it defines the minimum proficiences which represent individual objectives in the program, and it delineates the general knowledge and skill areas which should be measured in evaluating students' achievements for credentialing.

One final point about the residency requirement is necessary. Even critics acknowledge its appropriateness in some credentialing situations. The residency requirement for a medical degree, for example, is crucial, since such programs include the development of knowledge and skills which are not strictly academic in character and which are best learned and evaluated in a supervised clinical environment.

External Degree Programs

Discussion of the appropriateness of residency requirements in the award of a credential inevitably leads to a corollary concern—the appropriateness of removing all time and residency requirements as criteria for a credential. A few major programs of national scope already provide for the award of degrees solely on the basis of examinations. The New York Regents External Degree (RED) Program is one example. RED undergraduate programs in which degrees can be earned by successful results on a comprehensive battery of proficiency examinations currently include business administration and nursing.

Educators differ in their views about the appropriateness of external degree programs. Some thoroughly oppose the concept, believing that certain unmeasurable but important outcomes of college education can accrue only to students who participate in the traditional on-campus program. Others argue forcefully that if institutions are either unable to specify these intangible outcomes or to measure students' achievement of them, then the credential earned through the traditional program cannot attest to the achievement of such outcomes. In short, it is possible to credential only that which can be measured.

The disparity in views among educators on the appropriateness of the external degree will not be readily resolved. In all likelihood, the future of the external degree will rest largely on whether or not graduates from such programs demonstrate that they can perform as well in their jobs and enjoy the same measure of success, however broadly defined, as do graduates of traditional programs. Such a perspective argues against sweeping generalizations about external degree programs and favors judgment of individual programs on the basis of their quality and the quality of their graduates.

That evaluation of student achievement should play a significant role in the award of credit and credentials by postsecondary institutions is a truism. Yet the obvious is not always common practice. For decades, postsecondary education, structured on credits and credentials, has focused on time rather than on achievement. Consequently, reliable and valid assessment techniques have only infrequently been applied systematically to evaluate student achievement for the award of credit and credentials. Recent developments in postsecondary education portend significant changes in the future. It may well be that postsecondary institutions, as they face up to the needs and demands of their students and potential students, will also increase their attention to evaluation of student achievement of intended outcomes of their educational programs. The surge in numbers of adult students, many of whom are seeking, not degrees, but rather opportunities for self-advancement or development, will almost certainly cause institutions to offer or emphasize programs that are appropriate to those objectives. As they do so, they are likely to reexamine the relationship of the knowledge and skills acquired in the educational program to students' needs beyond their formal schooling. Such relationships can be demonstrated, of course, only if reliable and valid assessment of students' achievement is a systematically applied component of the educational program. A challenge to educators is to make this goal a reality.

CHAPTER 6

Competence as a Basis for Credit and Credentialing

Donald P. Hoyt

Of the unresolved questions in education, some of the most perplexing concern measuring "what" and "how much" learning occurred. The problem arises in various contexts: The student typically desires a reading on his or her progress and current status. Educational institutions need to know the extent to which students and prospective transfer students have met requirements according to the institutional "standards" adopted. And various people and agencies in the society—especially employers and representatives of postbaccalaureate programs—are eager to know as much as possible about the person's educational development in order to judge the appropriateness of the opportunities they offer. Thus, there has been considerable pressure to invent measures of learning suited to use in various settings and for various purposes.

Responses to assessment needs, traditional and recent, are here described briefly. Examined in greater detail is "competence-based learning," a response formulated in the last few years. In this concept, competences serve as a means to establish functional goals for learning and as guides for assessing the level of competence attained through the learning experiences. Because assessment is an integral part of the concept and process, unusual emphasis is given to the consequences of the learning as compared with results obtained from traditional measures.

From the early 1900s until about 1970, nearly all colleges and universities have used "courses," "credits," "grades," and "degrees" to describe the educational attainment of their students. Manageable units of knowledge or skill have been separated into discrete *courses*. Each course makes its own demands for effort needed to achieve mastery of its content; this effort is reflected in the *credit* awarded for satisfactory completion of the course. The level of mastery is indicated by a *grade* in the course. Institutional authorities establish the number of credits, their distribution by discipline, and minimum average grades required for the award of a *degree.*

Although these terms were used to describe educational programs and progress, they were never intended to have identical meanings at all institutions. In fact, American higher education has prided itself on its diversity, a characteristic that has presumably stimulated innovation and enabled institutions collectively to provide educational experiences that were responsive to a wide range of interests and talents. Furthermore, the tradition of academic freedom and the pride most educators take in their intellectual independence have reduced the probability that two courses with the same name will have identical content, that the same grade in two different courses will have an identical meaning, or that the same degree from different institutions will have the same implications. These two traditional freedoms—of the institution to pursue its own mission and of the professor to define course content, processes, and standards—have severely restricted the accuracy with which credits, grades, and degrees can be used as "common currency" for communicating educational status.

A number of pressures are being exerted to make these measures more "exchangeable" if not precisely uniform. One pressure is the need to accommodate transfer students. Another stems from the implications that being "different" carries not only the potential for being superior, but also the fear of being inferior. The latter has provided strong motivation toward uniformity.[1]

In part to guard against charges or implications that a given educational process or experience is inherently inferior or superior, institutions have established and affiliated with accrediting agencies or associations. These voluntary groups

1. See, for example, Frank Newman et al., *Report on Higher Education,* and C. Robert Pace, *The Demise of Diversity?*

serve to assure the public that educational opportunities provided by the institution are of an acceptable quality. The assurance is based in large part on a detailed review of the institution's resources and processes in the light of its publicly stated purposes and objectives. Thus, the educational qualifications of the faculty are considered, as are classroom and laboratory facilities, support facilities (libraries, computer services, student services), the educational process (typical course arrangements, including classroom hours per credit, textbooks and other educational materials, student appraisal devices), and mechanisms for establishing educational policies.

The availability of accreditation information, both institutional and professional, has facilitated the transfer process. Most institutions have willingly adopted policies to accept credit earned at regionally accredited institutions and, within reasonable limits, to apply this credit toward a degree.

Shortcomings of Traditional Measures of Educational Attainments

In recent years, discontent with the "common currency" of educational attainment has increased. There are several bases for this discontent.

First, degrees, credits, and grades awarded have such diverse meanings that they cannot be validly interchanged or meaningfully interpreted without detailed knowledge of particular circumstances. At one institution, the course in general psychology may focus on the development of personal values and self-understanding, and at another institution, will emphasize the content of psychology as a discipline and its chief methods of inquiry. Both may offer quality educational experiences, but their purposes and expected outcomes are so different that it is misleading to give them the same title or to imply that they are equivalent.

Similarly, a degree in computer science at one institution may reflect an emphasis on the applied aspects of programming and systems analysis; at another, it may mean that the student has satisfactorily mastered formal language theory or theory of automata. A grade *A* may represent the modal performance in one course and a superior performance in another.

Second, grades have no established value for predicting success beyond the formal educational structure. The problem of establishing the relationship between college grades and postcollege success is fraught with technical and practical problems; there have been no totally conclusive studies. The bulk of the evidence supports the proposition that college grades and adult accomplishment are relatively independent variables.[2] From what is now known, those who claim that "book learning" (college grades) and "adult competence" (job performance; community participation; achieving a satisfying and enriching family and personal life) are different characteristics have more data on their side than those who make the opposite claim.

The absence of an established relationship between educational success and other types of success is a matter of concern for two reasons. (1) For the individual, there is a direct tie between his or her educational background and the range and quality of opportunities available. (2) Many elements in society have used degrees, credits, and grades as credentialing measures, that is, as assurance that the person has competences related to a given opportunity. Thus, critics claim that the traditional grading system acts irrationally to deny opportunity to some and at the same time to mislead those who expect the transcript to represent competences and skills that the student has attained.

Third, no generally accepted mechanisms have been devised for translating attainments from some postsecondary educational experiences into educational equivalents in a different type of educational institution. For example, vocational-technical educational attainments acquired in public or proprietary trade schools are seldom recognized (awarded credit) by colleges and universities in which the student may later enroll.

Fourth, traditional measures of educational progress and attainment are not suited for use in recognizing learning from

2. Donald P. Hoyt, "College Grades and Adult Accomplishment, *Educational Record* 47 (1966): 70–75.

nontraditional sources. It is no new insight that learning is a lifelong process and, for many persons, is acquired outside formal educational settings—on jobs, in homes, through independent reading, in other types of experience. What is new is the insistence that mechanisms be found for translating educational attainments gained in nontraditional settings into an educational currency that will permit recognition of achievement and facilitate articulation between informal and formal learning.[3]

Pressure to develop such mechanisms is related to the concept of equal opportunity. Increasingly, formal educational credentials are being used as screens that permit or deny access to various educational, occupational, and social opportunities. Because of other complex factors, high percentages of some groups have attained significant portions of their learning through experiences outside educational institutions. They want this learning to be recognized so that they may qualify for a broader range of opportunities—personal, social, employment, educational.

Some Responses

A number of attempts have been made to respond to the shortcomings in traditional measures of attainment. For example, several institutions have instituted "narrative transcripts" or have supplemented the traditional transcript of courses and grades with a narrative elaboration of the educational experiences provided and the outcomes observed. Goddard College, for example, evaluates student progress through detailed reports written by the student and the student's instructors; abstracts of these reports appear on the transcript. Similarly, institutions that base their programs on "learning contracts" (Empire State, Evergreen State) often describe the contracts and the outcomes required from the activity.[4]

Several other mechanisms have been devised to respond to the need to evaluate educational experiences offered in non-

3. See, for example, Cyril O. Houle, *The External Degree*, and Peter Meyer, *Awarding College Credit for Non-College Learning.*

4. American College Testing Program, "Background Materials for the Workshop on Narrative Evaluation, Documentation, and Reporting."

traditional or informal settings. For example, the American Council on Education has, since 1945, evaluated formal military programs and courses and, on the basis of the findings, made credit recommendations to colleges and universities.[5] Recently, the Council initiated review of Army military occupational specialties (MOS's) to determine whether successful performance in these programs permitted reasonable inferences about skills, competences, and knowledge appropriate for credit. As a result, recommendations for the amount, level, and type of credit to be granted for a given MOS have been released to postsecondary institutions.[6]

The problem of assessing the educational outcomes and credit equivalencies of unique learning experiences which occur outside any formal educational structure is being addressed by the Council for the Advancement of Experiential Learning (CAEL) and its predecessor, the Cooperative Assessment of Experiential Learning project.[7] Participating institutions meet with educational measurement specialists to design and develop means for evaluating experiential learning in terms of credit and degree equivalents.

Credit by examination, especially through the mechanism of nationally standardized achievement tests, has gained increased use; the College-Level Examination Program (CLEP) of the College Entrance Examination Board is, perhaps, the best-known example. Several other examinations, ranging from coverage of general education to highly specialized competences, have been developed and will probably gain in use for credit purposes.[8]

5. *Guide to the Evaluation of Educational Experiences in the Armed Services, 76.*
6. *Guide to the Evaluation of Educational Experiences in the Armed Services, 1975 Supplement.*
7. To support this program, the Educational Testing Service has published a series of CAEL Institutional Reports which address specific measurement problems. Report no. 5, *Guidelines and Procedures for the Assessment of Experiential Learning and for the Selection and Training of Field Experts* is pertinent.
8. See, for example, J. Grandy and W. M. Shea, *The CLEP General Examinations in American Colleges and Universities;* New York Regents, *Regents External Degrees/College Proficiency Examinations; Placement and Proficiency Examinations, 1975–76;* Edward M. White, *Comparison and Contrast: The 1975 California State University and Colleges Freshman English Equivalency Examination.*

Competence-based Education as a Response

In addition to the responses described above, an innovation called "competence-based education" merits attention. The assessment procedures, which constitute a significant element of this movement, appear to have potential as a mechanism for expanding the currency of educational attainment. The competence movement is a direct response to some short-comings in the currencies of educational achievement previously discussed.[9] Its leaders have claimed that the meaning of credits, grades, and degrees is either obscure or trivial and, therefore, a new currency should be provided. Their views, in brief, are as follows.

A *credit* generally signifies a certain amount of exposure to educational materials, processes, and personnel which the institution believes will stimulate desirable educational outcomes. Typically, an appropriate authority (usually the teacher) is required to certify that a satisfactory level of achievement was reached. The record noting this credit does not include what the educational objectives of the course were, nor does it specify what knowledge, skills, or competences were achieved by the student. A competence-based learning experience, in contrast, specifies the objectives and the assessment procedures. Official records note the type and level of achievement which the student demonstrated.

A *degree* traditionally means that a specified number of credits have been accumulated with at least a minimum average grade. Further, some distribution of credits is usually required (a minimum number in social sciences, natural sciences, humanities, communications, and so on, as well as a minimum or a maximum in the major field). Although the college's catalog usually describes the educational objectives, the statements often lack the specificity needed to make inferences about the graduate's skills or competences. Similarly, the achievement record (transcript) does not certify that the student attained all objectives or attained a given level of accomplishment on any one objective. Graduation from a

9. For introduction to competence-based education programs, see William R. O'Connell and W. Edmund Moomaw, eds., *A CBC Primer*, and David A. Trivett, *Competency Programs in Higher Education*.

competence-based program, in contrast, is tantamount to certifying that the student achieved a given level of competence on carefully defined objectives.

In traditional programs, *grades* are ambiguous summaries of achievement. Generally they indicate the achievement of the student in relation to that of all students in the course (norm-referenced assessment). In courses that use contract grading or criterion-referenced assessment (competence with respect to a specified performance task), grades represent a prescribed level of achievement. Again, the achievement domain or domains are frequently undefined; attempts to make them more specific and uniform are typically resisted on the grounds of unwarranted intrusion upon academic freedom. As indicated earlier, a sizable body of literature suggests that grades can forecast other grades, but they have not been shown to be related to meaningful measures of adult accomplishment. Competence assessment appears to be decidely less ambiguous. Competences are clearly stated, and levels of achievement are typically given operational definitions. Although no evidence has been produced to relate competence achievement to measures of adult success, there is at least a firm rationale for conducting such studies.

The Competence Approach

Before some principles and procedures of competence assessment are described, it is desirable to elaborate the competence-based approach to education. There are five distinct tasks.

1. *Developing competence goals.* The initial task is the development of a set of purposes stated in terms of competences. Inasmuch as this work will produce the foundation on which the entire program rests, it is important that provision be made for wide-scale participation in the effort and that representatives of the various components of the institution overtly accept and endorse the end product.

The task is not an easy one. It requires an in-depth analysis of challenging educational questions. The issues that must be resolved are frequently those which either divide thoughtful people or resist rational analysis. For liberal arts programs, participants must develop their conception of a liberally educated person. For professional programs, a consensus of the qualities needed for effective professional functioning is required.

One established competence-based program in liberal arts is that at Alverno College in Milwaukee.[10] In that program, a set of eight competence goals has been constructed:

1. Develop effective communication skill
2. Sharpen analytical capabilities
3. Develop workable problem-solving skill
4. Develop a facility for making value judgments and independent decisions
5. Develop facility for social interaction
6. Achieve understanding of the relationship of the individual and the environment
7. Develop awareness and understanding of the world in which the individual lives
8. Develop knowledge, understanding, and responsiveness to the arts and knowledge and understanding of the humanities

2. *Identifying components of each competence.* To clarify the meaning of each competence and to explicate its complexities, a detailed analysis of its components is undertaken. Alverno College approached this task by identifying six levels for each competence. These are arranged in a hierarchy of complexity, with the clear assumption that, within any given competence, success at one level depends upon the achievement of competence at all preceding levels. The six levels of Competence 1 are:

Level 1—Identify own strengths and weaknesses as initiator and responder in communication situations of the following types, including a variety of audiences: reading, writing, listening, speaking, graphing and reading graphs
Level 2—Analyze written and oral communication situations
Level 3—Communicate with clarity of message-exchange in communication situations of the following types, including a variety of audiences: reading, writing, listening, speaking, graphing and reading graphs

10. *Competence-based Learning at Alverno College.* See also Sister Joel Read, "A Degree by Any Other Name . . . The Alverno Plan."

Level 4—Demonstrate sufficient understanding of basic concepts of at least 3 major areas of knowledge to communicate in terms of them

Level 5—Demonstrate understanding of communication as historical process involving development of meaning and form in relation to technological and cultural forces

Level 6—Communicate effectively through coordinated use of 3 different media that represent contemporary technological advancement in the communications field

The process is illustrated by a comparison with the components specified at Our Lady of the Lake University of San Antonio, which is on an ostensibly similar competence program.

Competency I: Graduates of Our Lady of the Lake University have developed effective communication skills:

1.1 Understand communication theory and its implications for effective communication

    1.1.a. Explain the basic nature and aims of communication

    1.1.b. Explain the purpose and process of human communication

1.2 Understand and use effective verbal communication

    1.2.a. Evidence an undertanding of the nature of language

    1.2.b. Be able to gather information

    1.2.c. Communicate effectively orally and in writing

    1.2.d. Evaluate verbal communication according to logical and rhetorical principles

    1.2.e. Formulate, express, and support reasoned judgments

1.3 Use effective nonverbal symbolic communication

    1.3.a. Recognize and use correctly mathematical symbols for operations within the real number system

    1.3.b. Translate verbal problems into symbolic form

    1.3.c. Represent information graphically and use graphic representations to obtain information

    1.3.d. Demonstrate effective use of one of the following computational devices; electronic digital computer, electronic calculator, slide rule, logarithmic tables, abacus

    1.3.f. Use statistical characteristics to evaluate data and make proper inferences therefrom

1.4 Understand the importance and impact of psychological processes for effective communication, and apply those processes

    1.4.a. Discuss the importance of psychological factors in communication

    1.4.b. Analyze communication events and stipulate how psychological factors influence the communication

 1.4.c. Understand behavioral systems (body language, etc.) and their relationship to message effectiveness

1.5 Understand the impact and processes of the mixed media as channels of communication

 1.5.a. Evidence understanding of the following media in terms of forms and content: television, radio, newspaper, magazines, popular books

 1.5.b. Demonstrate awareness of the impact and influence of the mass media in the shaping of human values and behavior[11]

Clearly, these two liberal arts programs have developed quite different conceptions of "effective communication skills." If the component specifications were excluded, it might erroneously be concluded that Competency 1, effective communication skill, represented a common goal for the two institutions.

One further example is found at the Antioch College School of Law in Washington, D.C.[12] This professionally oriented competence program has identified general "lawyering skills": interviewing, legal analysis, negotiating, counseling, fact verification/investigation, and so on. Each of these contains subcategories, and each subcategory contains general performance objectives (GPO's). Each GPO contains several specific performance objectives (SPO's). Thus, "intake interviewing" is a subcategory under interviewing. Some of its GPO's are "Knows objectives of intake interviews," "Knows role of the context and situational variables." The SPO's convert the meaning of the GPO's into goals for learning activities. Examples of SPO's include, "The student can list from memory the basic objectives of the intake interview," "The student can list 6 of 8 principles of intake interviewing."

 3. *Diagnosing status.* Some programs assume that students enter with none of the desired competences. But most pro-

---

11. "Competency Statements for General Education," Working papers for task forces at Our Lady of the Lake University of San Antonio, February 1976. For a general description of the Our Lady of the Lake program, see Sister Virginia Clare Duncan et al., *Competency Alternatives for Achievement.*

12. Acknowledgment is owed to Thomas Corcoran of the Fund for the Improvement of Postsecondary Education, who made basic materials for FIPSE-supported programs available to the author.

grams assume that previous learning experiences have had different effects on the status of enrollees. Hence, some attempt at initial assessment is generally made. This step, like step 5 (assessment) below, requires that the assessment procedures devised be based on the competences defined in steps 1 and 2. At this diagnostic stage, considerable reliance may be placed on a "guided self-analysis"—an inventory of personal characteristics (strengths, weaknesses, interests, goals, obstacles) developed by the student with the aid of a skilled adviser-monitor.

4. *Program development and selection.* The list of goals developed in steps 1 and 2 is closely related to program development. Sometimes faculty members are asked to identify the particular competences and competence components which their courses are designed to develop. But experience indicates that the most effective program development is done in the reverse order; that is, with certain goals (competences) in mind, what would be the most effective learning experiences that could be devised within my discipline? By approaching the question this way, faculty members are more likely to revise their courses drastically and to suggest alternative learning experiences or approaches (e.g., experimental or project learning, modular designs, guided independent study).

Within the limits set by institutional goals, students are typically encouraged to design their own learning program. Thus, Alverno is concerned that students develop "workable problem-solving skills" (Competence 3); but the student may elect any of several learning experiences that have been designed to facilitate the achievement of such skills.

5. *Competence assessment.* After the learning experiences have been selected on the basis of diagnosed deficiencies and personal predilections, the effectiveness of the respective experiences must be assessed. Again, the highly detailed specification of competence goals (steps 1 and 2) serves to guide the development of measuring devices.

Among institutions, there is considerable diversity in the mechanisms selected for developing assessment devices. Experience suggests that (*a*) it is desirable to have some professional expertise in an assessment center to coordinate assessment activities, consult on specific procedures, and maintain assessment records, and (*b*) the responsibility for making judgments of competence attainment should be assumed by a team which represents a diversity of perspectives and whose members have been trained in the evaluation task. Reliance on individual advisers, mentors, or teachers has not been a generally satisfactory solution.

Competence Measurement:
Principles and Practices

As in any other type of measurement, the initial step in developing devices for appraising competence is to identify and define the attributes to be "measured." The process is both complex and crucial. This step assumes an understanding of the institution's mission and educational goals, and frequently necessitates an extended period of clarification and consensus building. It also requires sensitive differentiation between the characteristics that the institution can realistically hope to affect and those that are unlikely to change under any educational arrangements. Considerable conceptual and semantic skill is needed to identify an array of competences which is both comprehensive and nonredundant.

Typically, these "goal competences" reflect more than one achievement domain. Some may be purely cognitive (development of factual knowledge, problem-solving ability), some may be affective (appreciation of a cultural expression, "enthusiasm" for a given intellectual activity), and some may be psychomotor (performance in a musical or technical arena, leading a group discussion). Whatever the achievement domain, the assessment process requires the specification of how a given level of competence can be displayed. Assuming that student A has developed Competence Alpha at Level 1 and student B has not, how do the two students differ?

The conceptual effort at this stage is normally merged with the pragmatic problem of inventing ways to observe and verify that the student possesses the competence. To this end, a variety of nontraditional approaches to assessment have been made. Advocates of competence-based education apparently agree that the multiple-choice, short-answer, and essay examinations, which have dominated appraisal procedures in education, are of limited value in competence assessment. One reason for rejecting traditional appraisal methods is that these have usually been norm-referenced. That is, student progress has been considered a relative matter; high grades have gone to the best x percent, and the lowest y percent have been failed. In competence appraisal, a criterion-referenced approach is required. The question is not, Where does the student stand with reference to others in the class? but rather, Has a given level of a particular competence been attained?

Practices vary widely among institutions. Competence assessment is one of the most obvious areas where workable procedures and practices are still being sought. Alternative approaches are derived from policies allocating responsibilities for designing assessment tasks and for observing and judging performance on such tasks. Although assessments of progress may be used as an instructional tool, the trend has been to relieve the instructor from responsibility for being the final judge. In some institutions, a specially appointed mentor serves as evaluator; in others, there are special administrative units (assessment centers); or ad hoc committees may be appointed to guide assessment procedures in a given competence area.

Regardless of who assumes responsibility for devising the assessment procedures, there remain the problems of what vehicles can be used to provide assessment data and who can interpret student performance in terms of competence. The vehicles used thus far include the relatively traditional background or research paper; a portfolio of activities, accomplishments, and reactions summarizing an integrated learning experience; participation in free or focused group discussions; performance in "real life" or simulated experiences such as interviewing a client or teaching others how to play a game.

Because competences are expected to be relevant to life functioning, it is common practice to establish teams of evaluators who can make judgments from perspectives broader than those of a single faculty member. Thus, a team may include a business or professional person from the community, a recent graduate, and faculty members from two different disciplines. The particular combinations vary but most competence-based programs insist on a team approach to guarantee a broad perspective for judging performance.

As noted earlier, one step in building a competence-based program is the development of the components and subcomponents of each competence. The process proceeds from an abstract description of the ideal graduate to the specific types of accomplishment that are accepted as indicating that the competence has been attained.

To illustrate, at Our Lady of the Lake University, Competence I is "Effective Communication Skills."[13] One component is "Understand and use effective verbal communication," for which a subcomponent is "Evaluate verbal communication according to logical and rhetorical purposes." A sample task for assessing the attainment of this subcomponent competence and the standards for evaluating performance are as follows:

A component 1.2 sample task: Given a verbal communication containing an explicit argument and implicit elements:
    a. abstract and state the given argument
    b. evaluate the validity of the argument
    c. identify the implicit elements and their effect on the validity of the argument
    d. evaluate the rhetorical effectiveness of the communication and its contribution to the effectiveness of the argument

Standards: —accurate statement of the argument　(20%)
             —accurate evaluation of the argument　(20%)
             —identification of implicit elements and their effect on validity of argument　(35%)
             —evaluation of rhetorical effectiveness　(25%)
    Average of evaluation by 3 judges to be 70%.

Much of the support for the competence movement has come from the Fund for the Improvement of Postsecondary Education (FIPSE). The fund has been especially helpful in developing competence-based liberal arts programs. It has also supported some professionally oriented programs concerned with human services (the Antioch law program; the College for Human Services, New York; the College of Public

13. See "Competency Statements for General Education."

and Community Service, University of Massachusetts).[14] The prime interest has been to promote the competence approach to education as a rational way to integrate educational objectives, educational process, and educational assessment. As such, assessment procedures constitute only one segment of a complex innovation.

In some occupational-technical fields, competence measurement has been pursued as such, without regard to educational objectives and processes. For example, under a contract with the National Institute for Automotive Service Excellence, the Educational Testing Service has developed a series of paper-and-pencil competence examinations for automobile and truck mechanics.[15] Similarly, the National Occupational Competency Testing Institute (NOCTI) has developed written and performance tests to access competence in more than thirty technical areas (auto mechanic, electrical installation, carpenter, etc.); although these tests were originally designed to certify the occupational competences of technical teachers, active exploration of their use for establishing credit equivalency in vocational-technical programs is under way.[16]

A promising development in this area is the work being done by the Vocational-Technical Education Consortium of States (V-TECS) in the Southern Association of Colleges and Schools.[17] That group has developed a twelve-stage process to produce "catalogs" for assessing competences in a variety of occupations. As of June 1976, eighteen catalogs were available for use, nine were nearing completion, and thirty more were expected during 1977.

The V-TECS system standardizes data collected from workers employed in a given job classification. Analysis of these

14. A complete listing of FIPSE-sponsored competence-based programs is available from the Fund.

15. National Institute for Automotive Service Excellence, *Bulletin of Information*.

16. Materials describing this program are available from National Occupational Competency Testing Institute, 35 Colvin Ave., Albany, N.Y. 12206.

17. See Ben Hirst, *V-TECS: The Vocational-Technical Education Consortium of States*; Billy J. Koscheski, "V-TECS as a Servant of the Curriculum"; "V-TECS Progress Report."

data reveals the major duties of the workers, the particular tasks associated with each duty, the tools and equipment needed to accomplish each task, and the relative frequency with which each task is encountered by workers with different amounts of experience. Performance objectives are written for each task. From these, measures of the ability to perform are derived. A team of experts establishes the standards against which performance is measured. These criterion-referenced measures are exclusively *performance* tests; the program does not include cognitive testing inasmuch as its sole concern is terminal performance.

The V-TECS project is relatively new. Although its rationale and procedures appear exemplary, it is too early to judge its products and their effectiveness. The catalogs are intended to guide curriculum and program development as well as to evaluate the competence of applicants, trainees, and graduates. The direct correspondence between the realities of the world of work and the criterion-referenced measures provides reason for optimism about the ultimate value of competence assessment in this area.

A Critique of Competence Assessment

The competence movement has contributed some useful educational innovations. To most observers, the serious effort to define goals in terms of competences whose meanings are converted to learning activities represents a solid advance over the continued acceptance of the platitudinous goal statements characteristic in many traditional programs. Similarly, competence-based programs deserve commendation for placing the educational program in perspective: the program should be the servant of goals and not an end unto itself. The development of options and potentially more significant educational experiences is undoubtedly facilitated when the question is, How can we accomplish our goals? rather than, Given this curriculum or course, what goals seem appropriate? It would be unfortunate if the philosophical stimulation and educational reforms initiated by the competence movement were diminished by a critique of one of its features.

Nonetheless, this paper must ask whether the competence

movement has made a serious contribution to assessment which can help resolve some difficult problems involving credits and credentialing. The measurement procedures employed are more diverse and flexible than those typically used in traditional programs. But being different doesn't necessarily mean being better.

1. *Is there reason to believe that competence measurement is performed with acceptable reliability?* No dependable data have been found on this question. However, in general it has been difficult to obtain high reliabilities in judging human performance, even when judges have had considerable explicit instruction or training in the judging process. Since characteristically competence assessment requires such judgments from three or four raters, there is little reason to be optimistic about reliability. Perhaps one reason reliability figures have not generally been reported is that independent judgments are rarely used. Typical practice is to seek a consensus among the raters. Such a process has the virtue of introducing diverse ideas, thoughts, and observations, but is subject to the criticism that the views of a single charismatic or persuasive rater may exercise undue influence on the outcome.

It may seem unfair to criticize competence assessment for its suspected unreliability when unreliability is characteristic of many traditional assessment procedures. The criticism is just in the sense that, under present circumstances, interpretations of competence assessments are likely to reflect the particular questions chosen and the judgments made by the particular persons on the assessment team.

2. *Is competence assessment more valid than traditional assessment?* In view of the typical process of specifying the meaning of each competence, there is reason to believe that the *content validity* of the average competence measure will exceed the content validity of most traditional measures. The specification process should provide a reasonable guarantee that the appraisal will focus on applicable achievement domains.

Whether or not competence assessment possesses other types of validity to a greater degree than do traditional measures is an unanswered empirical question. Studies of *construct validity* (attributes measured) and of *criterion-related validity* (concurrent, predictive) simply have not been reported; their absence is not surprising inasmuch as competence-based education has been an active movement for only a few years.

In the occupational-technical area, competence measures have specific and limited purposes. Even without formal validation studies, it seems certain that competence measures will possess considerable predictive validity. They typically require the demonstration of a skill or an understanding whose importance for the field of work has been empirically established.

3. *Is the rationale defensible?* Again, some reservations are in order. They relate to problems in criterion-referenced measurement as well as to human nature. In theory, a criterion-referenced measure is concerned with one simple question: Was the performance displayed at the level which was initially designated as "success"? Whether others performed as well or better is irrelevant to this concept.

Two problems arise in criterion-referenced assessment. First, the performance standard is frequently less precise than its advocates imply. For example, at Alverno, the assessment team, in assessing level 1 of Competence 7, will observe a group of four to six students who, under the direction of a trained leader, are discussing international, national, and local events. After recording their observations of each student's performance, the team comes to a consensus on whether or not the students have each met the specified criteria. (For two international, two national, and two local events, the student should be able to identify issues and significant personnel, to state for a given event its short- and long-range implications for a related area, and to identify aspects of a given local event that account for its significance.) Such standards leave much to the discretion of the assessment team. Does identifying two of ten key figures in an international event satisfy the criteria? How should a team regard the performance of a student who properly recognizes that a given political decision will have important economic effects but then makes erroneous or superficial assumptions about such effects? How does a team judge the performance of a student who initially offered a promising analysis of an affair but ultimately was led into serious errors by misguided suggestions from another participant?

Similar kinds of questions apply to the assessment procedures used in other settings. At some point, a subjective judgment about the quality of the performance is required. Despite the detailed definitions of competences and their components, the standards ultimately are those of the assessment team. While this outcome is not necessarily bad, it is quite different from the position that criterion-referenced measures are fairer than grades and credits because they are based on bias-free standards.

A related problem with competence assessment concerns the "all or nothing" nature of the evaluation decision. The individual either *has* or *has not* reached the required standard. It permits no observations that distinguish among those who have attained some prescribed minimal performance. But such individual differences may be of vital importance to the examinee and to society. We may, for example, establish fourteen seconds as a reasonable standard for the hundred-yard dash for physically healthy eighteen-year-olds. While there is value in attesting that a given individual reached that level of competence, there is much additional value in knowing that that person made the run in nine seconds.

The concept of excellence appears to be in conflict with criterion-referenced standards in some practical ways. By nature, people are extremely diverse in their capacities and their interests. If a single standard of acceptability is established such that most of those who make a reasonable effort in appropriate learning situations could reach it, then that standard will probably be far below the level of excellence which the most proficient can display. It is precisely these points of excellence which are most valuable in building a personal identity as well as in gaining society's recognition and rewards.

Competence-based programs share a related problem with traditional curricula: they assume that the distribution of talents and interests is such that it is reasonable to expect large numbers of students to achieve a fairly high level of competence or development on a broad array of objectives. Thus, curriculum builders begin with some conception of the "ideal graduate" and prescribe "expectations," "goals," or "requirements" accordingly. One cannot help but be impressed by the heroic images conveyed by the goals listed in the typical college catalog or by the competence lists prepared by institutions like Alverno. But one may ask if wishing will make it so.

There are people who exemplify "the educated person"— persons who accept community responsibilities and execute them with wisdom and compassion, who support and enjoy artistic and cultural experiences, who lend intellectual authority and open-mindedness to discussions of the day's issues and events, who provide responsible and creative leadership to their profession, who convey warmth and affection to family and friends, and who lead rich spiritual lives while demonstrating impeccable moral virtues. Any college or university would gladly acknowledge such an alumnus as representing the epitome of their educational ideals.

But the fact that such persons are so rare deserves careful consideration. Does it mean that, by and large, colleges and universities have failed to achieve worthwhile educational goals? Or does it mean that the ideals expressed by such goals are essentially unattainable for most people? (Without digressing too far, it can be noted that a sizable body of literature suggests normal human development may be more in the direction of lopsidedness than well-roundedness.) The values, capacities, interests, experiences, and personal styles of people are obviously diverse. If an institution establishes common objectives for all students, it appears to be endorsing similarity as a virtue. Granted, most institutions provide for individual differences by establishing majors (emphases) and electives (choices). But questions remain: Is it realistic to seek significant levels of development on common dimensions, no matter how virtuous these dimensions may be? Do the different backgrounds, experiences, and constitutions of students erect barriers that doom such aspirations to failure?

If so, what choices must educational institutions confront?

This is not the place for a detailed analysis. But it is worthwhile, as one considers competence measurement as a method of credentialing, to ponder the possibility of individualizing educational goals to a much greater extent than has been done heretofore. Standards that connote excellence, whether in a competence framework or in more traditional language, will probably have more meaning than scaled interpretations would, both to the individual and to society. Institutions will need to take care that the number of standards against which high achievement is judged is not so great that few can succeed or so uniform that individuality and personal identity are submerged.

Competence Assessment, Consequences, and Credentials

Conclusions about the role of competence measurement in the credit and credentialing process are contingent on the type of competence measure involved and the purpose to which the measurement is applied.

An initial distinction should be made between competence measures that have direct consequences and those for which consequences are merely assumed or expected. Consider the criterion, "From a printed manuscript, types an average of 60 words or more per minute for five minutes with five or fewer errors." This "typing competence" measure has direct implications for the work of typing manuscripts. A person who can demonstrate competence at the criterion level can be certified as a rapid and accurate typist. Similarly, a person who can, in five minutes or less, discover the reason why four out of five cars with specific electrical malfunctions will not start can be certified as capable of making this kind of auto repair diagnosis. Many of the occupational competence tests noted earlier do have direct application to job performance.

But the kinds of competence employed in liberal arts or professional programs do not generally have such direct consequences. For example, the University of Houston's competence-based teacher education program seeks to develop sixteen general teaching competences. The first competence is "Diagnoses the learner's emotional, social, physical, and intellectual needs. Draws upon knowledge of human growth and development, learning theories, social/cultural foundations, assessment techniques, curriculum goals and content to gather information about the learner and to identify instructional needs."[18] The statement clearly implies that persons who have this competence will be better teachers than those who do not. But the goal statement is only an assumption; there is no compelling evidence, for example, that pupil learning is a direct function of the teacher's competence in this area. Similarly, graduates of Mars Hill College must demonstrate competence in seven areas, one of which is ". . . understands the nature of aesthetic perception and is aware of the significance of creative and aesthetic dimensions of his own experience which he can compare to other cultures."[19] Again, the statement assumes that this competence will be directly related to an active and rich aesthetic life. But no evidence confirms that those who demonstrate the competence differ from those who do not on the basis of such postcollege measures as frequency of going to art galleries, museums, symphonic concerts, operas, and the theater; purchasing art objects; reading books that describe art and artists; or expressing oneself in some artistic form.

When a given competence has an obvious and direct connection with a consequence, then its certification serves as a public service credential. An institution which certifies that the student has achieved such a competence assures the public that he or she can produce the consequence in question. If the connection with the consequence is not direct, but only assumed, then certification of the competence cannot serve the public in this way until a firm connection between competence and consequence has been established empirically.

Having made the distinction between competences tied to consequences and those for which no tie has been established, it is appropriate to ask, Are such ties necessary? More simply, Is the only reason for developing competences to confirm that

18. W. Robert Houston and Howard L. Jones, *Three Views of Competency-based Teacher Education, II: University of Houston,* p. 20.
19. Richard Hoffman, "Introduction to Mars Hill," in *A CBC Primer,* ed. O'Connell and Moomaw, p. 49.

they have identifiable consequences? Some education philosophers have argued that educational outcomes need not be instrumental, and many writers have defended learning for the sake of learning as a viable educational goal. And to many, *private* credentialing (recognizing a person's personal development and certifying his or her right to claim successful pursuit of a legitimate set of educational objectives) is much more important than assurances to employers or others. Therefore, it should not be presupposed that a competence which has no direct or assumed consequence is inferior to one which does.

An established consequential tie does, however, have implications for purposes which the assessment can serve. If *public service credentialing* is held as a means for verifying performance capabilities to the public, then competence assessment can be used for such credentialing only when the tie to consequences is either directly apparent or empirically established.

The preceding discussion has focused on a special kind of credentialing—advising the public what it can expect from the person holding the credential. Although competence assessment offers promise for improving this process, most of the measures thus far employed have not been validated for credentialing purposes. The rationale and process of competence assessment should result in assessments that bear closer relationships to posteducation functioning than have been found for traditional college grades. It is important, however, that this assumption be tested before suggesting to the public that such a relationship exists.

Institutional Transfer

A second general problem with competence assessment is establishing means for facilitating the transfer process in a meaningful, defensible way. The elaborate specification of competences, their components, and subcomponents should convey to receiving institutions the nature of educational growth certified by the sending institution. The specificity will be helpful when the certified competences have easily identified counterparts in the receiving institution's curriculum.

There's the rub! Receiving institutions with traditional programs will be hard pressed to translate "Level 4, Competency 3" into specific credits or courses. Is such an accomplishment pertinent to any of the institution's graduation requirements? Receiving institutions with competence-based programs will face the problem of translating the sending institution's conception of competence into their own; the earlier illustration of two institutions which have conceptualized "effective communication" in very different ways suggests that the conversion presents more than a minor semantic hurdle.

Typically. credits earned at one accredited institution are transferred to another with little difficulty. Some assumption of "equivalence" is clearly made. But what is assumed to be equivalent? If it is specific content and emphases, then, except for fundamental courses in single paradigm disciplines (mathematics, natural sciences), the assumption will not often be tenable. That the transfer process "works" (students move from one institution to the next without severely disrupting their educational progress) suggests that other types of equivalence are at work. Although these latter have not been empirically established, they probably include rough equivalences in qualifications of instructors, academic effort required of the student, and level of academic challenge encountered by the student with at least minimal success. These types of equivalences can be judged without the aid of competence assessment.

In programs that are tightly organized around the attainment of specified competences, the only equivalence that counts is competence attainment. In such cases, receiving institutions offering competence-based programs will probably require that transfer credits be awarded only after the competence development has been assessed. The transfer process then will probably become more cumbersome for competence-based programs than for traditional programs.

Just how competence assessment will facilitate the transfer process is difficult to see. It may enable competence-based programs to help transfer students choose learning activities appropriate to their current educational development.

Assessment, Nontraditional Learning,
and Accountability

Does competence measurement contribute solutions to the problems in recognizing experiential learning or, more generally, learning from nonformal educational settings? Of course, institutions with competence-based programs will have assessment procedures for any applicant inasmuch as they assess *all* entering students (including adults with extensive nontraditional learning experiences) in order to determine current competences and then to plan and select learning experiences.

Typically, institutions with traditional educational programs also offer new students (including the older adult) opportunities to earn advanced standing by providing appropriate evidence. This evidence may come from locally constructed examinations, CLEP or other nationally standardized examinations, or through some special administrative-assessment mechanism (including CAEL). Competence assessment as a mechanism for granting credit for learning attained outside the formal educational structure does not establish a precedent.

Does competence assessment offer something different? Of course, some advocates of competence-based programs contend seriously that it does. Competence assessment is said to examine characteristics beyond those tested in traditional programs. Such characteristics are believed to be especially important in assessing the status of adults since the type of learning they can exhibit may be less obvious on purely academic criteria than on more practical and applied criteria.

To the degree that this view is correct, then institutions that offer competence-based programs may be more responsive to the needs of applicants whose learning experiences were outside formal educational channels. But the institution can be responsive only to the degree that the competences for which it has developed assessment procedures match the competences the applicant has developed. In brief, the problem of recognizing experience-based learning is one of articulating the prospective student's verifiable knowledge, skills, and understanding with the institution's conception of an "education" or an "educational program." Competence assessment appears to enlarge the prospect that a given prospective student can find an institution which will verify his or her previous learning and credit it toward a degree. But it does not guarantee that all adult learning has a legitimate equivalence in some type of postsecondary educational institution.

Finally, the role of competence assessment in institutional accountability requires brief attention. Are institutions which pursue competence-based programs more accountable to their clienteles than those which offer traditional programs? In principle, they may be. The highly detailed specification of goals and expectations does communicate institutional intentions more clearly than do the traditional statements of purpose. And the elaborate attempts to assess progress in relation to goals seems to offer assurance to the public that graduates have reached the established goals.

It is regrettable that the assessment procedures developed thus far have yet to merit outsiders' assurance about the results. As already noted, there are reservations about the technical quality of competence assessments. Beyond are questions of "standards," of identifying excellence, and of establishing meaning in relation to consequences. For these reasons, competence-based education cannot be regarded as more "accountable" than other forms of education, but its potential for achieving such status is promising.

On Balance

As a replacement currency for use in the credit and credentialing process, competence assessment appears not to be a practical alternative. Its use as a means to communicate information about educational progress and attainment and to translate learning outcomes gained in one setting into educational status in another is contraindicated by several considerations:

1. For most types of programs, no taxonomy of competences has been developed. The careful work on assessment of occupational competences being done by V-TECS in the Southern Association is a noteworthy exception. Typically,

however, each competence-based program develops its own list of competences. The degree to which competences within one system overlap or the degree to which each is equivalent to a competence in some other system is unknown. If "measured competence" is to serve as a common currency, there must be an acceptable taxonomy of competences from which individual institutions may select their own emphases.

2. In general, while competence assessment processes have been more creative and better integrated than have traditional achievement examinations, the subjectivity of observer judgment based on observer standards has not been removed. Thus, the evaluation of a given student's performance still depends on the evaluator's standards and biases.

3. Except for relatively straightforward technical performance, competence measurement has assumed, but not established, a direct link with "real life" consequences. Such assumptions are also characteristic in traditional programs, though many of them have been nullified by empirical research (the classics provide students with mental discipline; mathematical training produces persons who characteristically think clearly and behave rationally).

4. The tendency to place competence assessment in a criterion-referenced format has the regrettable effect of ignoring the individual differences that provide the basis for personal identity and life planning. By establishing competence goals applicable to all, the movement reduces its capacity for communicating individual uniqueness.

5. Those who use the academic record to make judgments about the suitability of a given person to a new opportunity (employers, graduate or professional school committees) are not likely to find that a comprehensive listing of the competences attained provides a helpful comparison of the candidate with candidates from other institutions.

Conceivably, future developments in competence assessment will alter this verdict. Its reliability as a common currency in the credit and credentialing process would seem to depend on:

1. Standardizing the definitions and developing a taxonomy of competences. This problem has been recognized: the

Fund for the Improvement of Postsecondary Education awarded the American College Testing Program a contract to coordinate efforts to construct such a taxonomy and some measures to support it.[20] If the project succeeds, the resulting taxonomy could provide an important stimulus to overcoming this serious deficiency.

2. Creating measurement processes which produce technically satisfactory assessments and unequivocal appraisals of the level of individual development.

3. Establishing the relationship between competence status and consequences of importance to the individual and to society, including employers and those concerned with post-baccalaureate programs.

20. Assessment of College Outcomes, a project sponsored by the Fund for the Improvement of Postsecondary Education and directed by Richard L. Ferguson of the ACTP, was initiated in July 1976.

CHAPTER 7

Student Mobility and Transfer

Robert Kirkwood

As much as any issue in higher education, the subject of student transfer has received its share of attention and discussion in recent years. Appropriately so, for it tends to epitomize much of the current concern and controversy about academic standards, access to higher education, and even the very meaning of a college degree.

The growing mobility of learners challenges the traditional concept of high school graduates dutifully enrolling in a particular college and following a prescribed and continuous path to a bachelor's degree. An emerging range of alternative approaches to postsecondary education caters more fully and flexibly to the needs and interests of individual students. Perhaps most important for the long-range future of higher education, a whole spectrum of students heretofore viewed at best only as peripheral to the academic enterprise now demands and receives serious consideration. Inevitably, these developments relate to student transfer and add to its complexities.

Of course, all that is sound in academia is not about to collapse, and traditional patterns persist more often than not. But the evidence abundantly testifies that students are finding an expanding variety of ways to piece together what is loosely labeled a "college education" in the United States. They are also more likely to be aided than thwarted in doing so. The educational system is becoming increasingly responsive in its efforts to cope with the diverse educational needs of more and more Americans.[1] How to do so without destroying the in-

1. James R. Davis, "The Search for Standards," *Journal of Higher Education* 45 (1974):145–51.

tegrity of the academic degree or diminishing the quality of higher education is at once the dilemma and the opportunity.

The Social and Educational Context of Academic Transfer

Transience has long been a characteristic of American life. From the days of the Pilgrims, through the lumbering journeys of Conestoga wagons, and on into the jet age, the periodic peregrinations of families have resulted in the statistic that 20 percent of U.S. households relocate every year. The most dramatic recent statement of this phenomenon is provided by Sale in a provocative and timely analysis of restless Americans seeking new locations for the pursuit of happiness and personal success.[2] The multiple implications of transience—social, political, economic—are fascinating, but here we shall touch on only a few implications for education.

Until recently, the migration of America's college population closely paralleled family mobility. From 1938 through 1968 approximately 19 percent of students enrolled in colleges and universities were from out of state.[3] In 1972 the total figure including foreign students was down to 16.2 percent, but because enrollments rose during the interim, this proportion represented an almost fivefold increase in numbers —1,041,076 out-of-state students in 1972 against 236,444 in 1938, and 151,344 from foreign countries.[4] Indications are that interstate migration may be diminishing,[5] but the decline could possibly be offset by larger numbers of foreign students, particularly from the oil-producing countries. While migration

2. Kirkpatrick Sale, *Power Shift*. See also "Americans on the Move," *Time*, March 16, 1976, pp. 54–64.

3. Thomas E. Steahr and Calvin F. Schmid, "College Student Migration in the United States," *Journal of Higher Education* 43 (1972): 445.

4. U.S. Department of Health, Education, and Welfare, National Center for Educational Statistics, *Residence and Migration of College Students, Fall 1968,* p. 4; also unpublished data from the survey of residence and migration of college students, fall 1972, p. 77.

5. Robert H. Fenske, Craig S. Scott, and James F. Carmody, "Recent Trends in Studies of Student Migration," *Journal of Higher Education* 45 (1974):61–74; also Steahr and Schmid, "College Student Migration."

itself is not the transfer problem, it is related, as we shall see later. For the moment, it serves to underscore the transient character of significant numbers of students across the United States.

Of more direct concern, and intimately related to the transfer problem, is the increasing tendency of younger students to stop out of the educational process and of older persons to stop in. There was a time, and not so long ago, when any student who dropped out of college was counted in the attrition statistics and generally lamented as a failure and a loss to the academic world. Not so any longer. As Davis accurately observes:

> It is not unusual today for a student to begin college with "advanced standing" credits earned in his home town high school, to "test out" of a few courses by taking exams standardized in Princeton, N.J., to spend a term during his second year in a work or service experience, to study in a foreign country for one year and spend a term in the final year in student teaching or in an internship in a hospital or social service agency. Many students live out of a suitcase (more likely out of a pack), travel about all over the world on youth fares and rail passes, and use the "campus" as a home base to arrange and certify a vast array of educational (and not so educational) experiences. Faculty members are only less mobile, and students rejoice in meeting one of their "own professors" in London or Tokyo. The concept of "campus" is almost meaningless, and there are no meaningful standards to determine where, geographically, a college education might best take place or what portions of it should take place on a campus.[6]

Certainly not every student fits Davis's profile, but the numbers are now of sufficient magnitude to be taken seriously. Many of the peripatetic scholars do their stopping-in-or-out at the same institution, but each year, for a variety of reasons virtually as large as their numbers, approximately half a million students are in the process of transferring to other institutions.[7]

The stop-in is a relatively recent phenomenon, although the circumstances rather than the numbers may represent the

6. Davis, "The Search for Standards," p. 147.
7. Frederick C. Kintzer, "The Transfer Student Dimension of Articulation," in *College Transfer: Working Papers and Recommendations,* p. 78.

greater change. Adult education has met the needs of countless thousands in this century, and the university extension movement has been a long-established if not always integrated part of higher education. Although many degrees were earned through the evening and extension route, a great deal more of the work was classified as nondegree level. Even when the work was taken at the same institution, much of it was unacceptable for traditional degree programs—when it wasn't actually disdained. This situation has been changing as the credential consciousness of society has heightened and particularly as the needs for continuing and recurrent education have grown. The idea of midcareer changes is also catching on, and further education is frequently the means to their facilitation. Social mobility has played its part in the process, along with a rootlessness and restlessness which have always been present but now seem more pervasive in the American way of life. So the stop-in has emerged, the older adults who find that professional advancement and even personal satisfaction hinge on updating their academic qualifications with authentic credits and degrees. And the opportunities for doing so are no longer confined to evening or extension programs as a steadily rising number of colleges and universities modify their curricula and calendars to accommodate and, indeed, to compete for the new clientele.

The traffic is not entirely of people, however. Institutions have become highly mobile too, in effect transferring themselves to the students. While it taxes the credulity and cherished concepts of traditional academicians, the University Without Walls is not alone in breaking the confines of geographically identified settings. The University of Southern California, Northern Colorado, and Upper Iowa may be found offering credit programs in Washington, D.C., or the surrounding suburbs. Kansas City's tiny Park College conducts degree programs in four fields on sixteen military bases as far as 2,000 miles from the home campus. And the external degree has proliferated steadily since 1973 when Houle published his excellent treatise on the subject for the Commission on Non-Traditional Study.[8]

8. Cyril O. Houle, *The External Degree*.

In simple fact, some institutions have become as peripatetic as students, following them to the proverbial four corners of the globe to provide for their educational needs and aspirations. Nevertheless, institutional mobility has clearly been a serious attempt to respond to individual mobility in recent years and, in the process, has further emphasized the transient character of American society. That serious problems are connected with the proliferation of satellite operations and remote campuses is abundantly reflected in the files of the regional accrediting commissions of higher education. Such movement has also exacerbated the problems of controlling quality and safeguarding the integrity of academic degrees, while simultaneously further complicating the nature and scope of the transfer problem.

Changing Educational Objectives

The mobility of students and institutions appears to result in part from profoundly changing educational objectives among Americans of widely varying ages and expectations. As London writes,

emerging from the turbulent university days of the late sixties was a new language, a language that assumed ritualistic uses. Terms such as "change," "innovation," "reform," "restructuring," "experimentation," and "nontraditional" were eulogized. They were words pegged into the timetable of recent history. They represented moods and needs. For many the words became policies. Acting out of fear, ideological predilection, a genuine concern for improvement of academic conditions, or simply not knowing what else to do, university administrators bureaucratized student demands into nontraditional educational enterprises. What students sought— and generally received—was a style of education different from the lecture/classroom/exam mode, one that had the glow of "relevance."[9]

For many reasons, the purposes and uses of postsecondary education are undergoing a scrutiny and questioning unparalleled in many years. Yarmolinsky somberly states that

even in those parts of the world where the cultural revolution has not been formalized, established institutions are under siege, including the once sacrosanct institutions of higher learning. The

9. Herbert I. London, "The Case for Nontraditional Learning," *Change*, June 1976, p. 25.

ultimate destinies of the latter, no less than other major social institutions, are subject now to large and global forces. Their future must be examined in that context rather than in the barometric ups and downs of public skepticism and support.

There are elemental forces at work, and to understand the major underlying causes of the growing divergence of public sentiment and our colleges and universities is also to begin determining some appropriate institutional responses. Without them, the central institutional purpose may not long remain.[10]

If the foregoing statements do not characterize the entire educational establishment, they are representative of issues that have been posed and earnestly discussed at recent meetings of major educational organizations and lesser groups of academically oriented and other concerned persons.

Unfortunately, much of the debate degenerates into often absurd arguments about whether higher education should be vocational or humanistic, thus perpetuating a dichotomy that is more myth than fact.[11] Because the case for education as a major public priority can no longer be assumed as it was during the 1960s, the debate is ill-timed and seriously undermines the public credibility of all education. Significant social changes occurred during the past decade, and inevitably they have implications for the campus. In a searching analysis, Stickgold writes:

> The new demands on academia resulting from changes in students, and society as a whole, are in part legitimate and in part illegitimate. They extend from the trivial to the fundamental. Some would allow academia to continue the educational process of the past. Others . . . that the educational process be altered. Some have the latent function of preserving the intellectual tradition of academia, others have the manifest function of eliminating it. Some . . . [insist] that academia lead in the reconstruction of society; others . . . that academia compensate for the deficiencies of society.[12]

The result of the current flux in educational patterns and processes may simply be wider acknowledgment and accep-

10. Adam Yarmolinsky, "Challenges to Legitimacy: Dilemmas and Directions," *Change*, April 1976, p. 18.

11. Stephen K. Bailey, "Career Education and Higher Education," *Educational Record* 54 (1973):256.

12. Arthur Stickgold, "Policy Implications of Changing Student Values in the Collegiate Culture," *Liberal Education* 61 (1975):180.

tance of a diversity that in the past academia has professed more often than practiced. In any event, the context in which academic transfer must be considered today is greatly enlarged and infinitely more complex than it was less than a decade ago.

Who Are the Transfer Students?

The thought that transfer students would require their own taxonomy, had it occurred a few years ago, would have been hastily dismissed. They were, after all, a handful of students who couldn't make it in one institution and moved to a similar but less selective college to improve their chances. If that description was ever true, it isn't today, and indeed there is a taxonomy of transfer students.

1. *Articulated Vertical Transfer.* Students moving directly from junior college transfer programs to four-year institutions.
2. *Traditional Horizontal Transfer.* Students moving from one four-year institution to another.
3. *Nontraditional Transfer.* Adults who may not have attended college for some years, students with unusual records including heavy representation of odd grades or credit awards, and transfers from innovative programs that do not conform with familiar lower division course work.
4. *Reverse Transfer.* Students moving from four- to two-year institutions.
5. *Open Door Transfers.* Students moving from two-year to two-year institutions.
6. *Double Reverse Transfer.* Students who transfer from four-year to two-year and then back to four-year institutions.
7. *Vocational Transfer.* Students in occupational programs transferring to four-year degree programs.[13]

Without stretching the case or being overly inventive, other categories could be added, for example:

8. *Lateral Graduate School Transfer.* Graduate students moving from one graduate program to another, or from a master's-level to a doctoral-level institution.
9. *Up and Down Escalator Transfers.* Students who transfer from graduate to professional school or vice versa.

13. Warren W. Willingham, "Transfer Standards and the Public Interest," in *College Transfer*, pp. 39–45.

10. *Advanced Articulated Vertical Transfer.* Undergraduates entering graduate or professional schools. This move may be seen as more strictly an admissions than a transfer problem, but the similarities for the student are greater than the differences.
11. *Extrainstitutional Learner Transfer.* Students who, through noncollegiate-sponsored educational activities, acquire learning for which they then seek credit in established institutions.

There is also a group of students attending proprietary institutions who, like their community college cousins in non-transfer programs, decide to continue their education toward a degree and seek admission with credit for work already completed. In a few states authorization has been extended to proprietary schools to permit certain types of degrees to be awarded, but most proprietaries do not grant degrees. The point is that problems of educational articulation occur at many levels, involving a variety of institutions (and even non-institutions), with abundant and often profound implications for the sizable numbers of people they affect.

Until the spread of community colleges in the 1960s, student movement was predominantly a matter of transferring between similar institutions with essentially identical programs. For a variety of causes ranging from family migration through economics and a whole congeries of personal reasons (including plain old homesickness), students elected to transfer from one campus to another. But transfer was by and large an aberration, not an inherent or integral part of the system, and therefore usually discouraged. Such was the case until two-year colleges began to absorb rapidly growing numbers of entering freshmen whose ultimate objective was a baccalaureate degree. Suddenly, articulation, which for years had connoted the relationship between high school and college, now embraced college-to-college relationships as well. And while personal reasons continue to affect transfer decisions, *the educational structure itself has become a prime cause of student transfers.*

With a slowness and even reluctance that academics would denounce in any other social institution, the academy has gradually awakened to the dimensions and ramifications of the transfer situation. The data are beginning to accumulate and the research is increasingly productive, but we are a long way from a comprehensive and current picture of student transfer in the United States. One of the most useful early studies illustrates the complexities and varieties of transfer and bears out the aptness of Willingham's taxonomy. In analyzing the mobility patterns of Illinois transfer students in 1967–68, the Illinois Council on Articulation found that the patterns of movement were all there, with significant numbers of students in all except the vocational and technical areas transferring in and out of the various types and levels of colleges and universities.[14] The study did not include graduate and professional schools, but the statistics were especially surprising with respect to the movement of students from four-year institutions: a notably larger number moved from four-year than from two-year colleges. By 1973, however, there had been a 70 percent increase in transfer students, most of them moving from community colleges to public senior colleges.[15] In the State University of New York, transfer enrollments rose from 21,697 in fall 1972 to 27,745 in fall 1974, almost 28 percent in two years, with the largest numbers again in the Articulated Vertical Transfer category, those moving from a two-year to a senior institution.[16]

As the community and junior colleges become an increasingly integrated segment of the educational structure, there is little question about where the preponderance of transfer students will continue to come from. At present it seems that the stereotype of transfer students as restless, unmotivated dummies is an absurd vestige of wrong-headed elitism. The growing evidence on ability and attainment shows transfer students comparing favorably with native students, that is, with those who continue to a degree within a single institu-

14. Illinois Council on Articulation, "Transfer Students in Illinois," *North Central Quarterly* 46 (1971):297.
15. Illinois Community College Board, "A Statewide Follow-up Study of Fall 1973 Transfer Students from Illinois Public Community Colleges," p. 3.
16. State University of New York, "Application and Enrollment Patterns of Transfer Students, Fall 1972," p. ix; "Application and Enrollment Patterns of Transfer Students, Fall 1974," pp. xi, 3.

tion.[17] One point must be emphasized: the statement applies to transfer students, *not* to comparisons of total student bodies among various types of institutions.

Demographic data on transfers are hard to come by. Moughamian's study of City Colleges of Chicago transfers indicated a two-to-one male-female ratio, 66.3 percent against 33.7 percent, although the male enrollment in CCC was only 54 percent.[18] There is no explanation for the differences. The socioeconomic background of community college students has tended to be lower than that in senior colleges and universities, but there are no easy generalizations about the other types of transfer students. Age spread among transfer students has widened, in part because 20 percent of community college students are twenty-five or over,[19] and also because the stop-in students range from the twenties to the seventies. Adult students constitute as much as 50 percent of the enrollments at some community colleges[20] and are filtering into senior institutions as well, through either the Articulated Vertical Transfer or the Nontraditional Transfer route. A significant proportion of the adults are mature women for whom dozens of imaginative programs have been devised to help bridge the gap between their child-rearing years and their last formal education.

Still other kinds of students are entering the transfer mainstream, each bringing needs requiring special attention or arrangements. An estimated 165,000 service personnel are potential transfers, already earning college credits through

17. See Dorothy M. Knoell and Leland L. Medsker, *From Junior to Senior College*; Illinois Community College Board, "A Statewide Follow-up Study of Fall 1973 Transfer Students"; Henry Moughamian, "A Five Year Longitudinal Study of City Colleges of Chicago Transfer Students, September 1967–June 1972"; Ben K. Gold, "Academic Performance of L.A.C.C. Transfers Entering the University of California during the Academic Year 1971–72"; and "Academic Performance of L.A.C.C. Transfers to UCLA through the Special Services Program, 1971–72."

18. Moughamian, "A Five Year Longitudinal Study," p. 12.

19. Frederick C. Kintzer, "The Community College Transfer Student," in *Understanding Diverse Students*, p. 5.

20. Mildred Bulpitt, "The Adult Student," in *Understanding Diverse Students*, p. 56.

such programs as the Servicemen's Opportunity College, Community College of the Air Force, Navy's Program for Afloat College Education, the Army's Project AHEAD, and the Defense Activity for Non-Traditional Education Support (DANTES).[21] The Servicemen's Opportunity College is the most extensive effort yet to facilitate the educational progress of military personnel and reduce the problems of transfer peculiar to the transiency of service life. More than 350 institutions are committed to SOC, roughly divided evenly between two-year and four-year institutions, with approximately 20 percent being private and the remainder public colleges and universities.[22] The military emphasis on education increased enormously with the advent of the all-volunteer armed forces, and the total effects are yet to be felt on the campuses. Nevertheless, another contingent of potential transfer students has been identified, and its diversity alone will tax the inventiveness of many an academic institution.

Perhaps even more taxing will be the problems of dealing with rising numbers of prisoners who are pursuing educational programs in most federal penitentiaries and some state prisons. Approximately 22,000 are federal inmates, and more than 400,000 are prisoners in state and county systems. Among the significant educational programs under way on the federal level, GED and high school courses leading to diplomas engage more than 6,000 persons, and nearly another 2,000 are pursuing college programs. The completion rate is better than 50 percent in the high school group and over 70 percent in the college group.[23] It is reasonable to expect that prisoners who have succeeded in college-level work or who have completed high school will want further opportunities upon release and, indeed, are beginning to find them. The seriousness of society's commitment to rehabilitation is in-

21. Kintzer, "Community College Transfer Student," p. 1.

22. American Association of State Colleges and Universities and American Association of Community and Junior Colleges, "Servicemen's Opportunity College," p. 5.

23. U.S. Department of Justice, Bureau of Prisons, Education Branch, *Education and Vocational Training of Incarcerated Federal Offenders,* Annual Report FY-72, pp. 3, 11.

volved, and another dimension is added to the diversity of the transfer population.

Foreign students constitute still another group of transfer students, although they do not entirely fit the taxonomy until after they are accepted in an American institution. British, French, and German as well as American influences have shaped the educational patterns of many formerly colonial countries or nations. Asian, African, and Middle Eastern countries have sent thousands of students to the United States, along with lesser numbers from Latin America and other parts of the globe. Virtually every race and nationality have been represented, and not a few of the students have encountered difficulties in adapting their previous educational backgrounds to the idiosyncratic nature of American colleges and universities. Although foreign students as a proportion of total U.S. enrollment declined from 1.75 percent in 1958 to 1.64 percent in 1968, the figure rose sharply in 1972 to 1.9 percent. This last percentage represented an increase from 110,263 in 1968 to 151,344 in 1972, and it also included attendance at a larger variety and number of institutions than in earlier years. Of the total, 75.5 percent were men; 55.2 percent attended public institutions; 7.6 percent enrolled in two-year colleges; and 54.4 percent were undergraduates, 3.1 percent were first-professional students, and 42.5 percent were in graduate school.[24] Foreign students have enhanced the cosmopolitanism of many American campuses, but they have also added to the multiplicity of transfer types. Their numbers are sufficient to warrant the concerted efforts of five national organizations working together in the National Liaison Committee on foreign student admissions to U.S. graduate schools.[25]

24. HEW, NCES, *Residence and Migration of College Students, Fall 1968*, note 4, p. 18, and unpublished data from fall 1972 survey.

25. The organizations on the National Liaison Committee on Foreign Student Admissions are: American Association of Collegiate Registrars and Admissions Officers, Institute of International Education, College Entrance Examination Board, Council of Graduate Schools, and National Association for Foreign Student Affairs. For a report on the committee's work see Council of Graduate Schools in the United States, *Proceedings of the Fifteenth Annual Meeting*, December 1975, pp. 43–46.

A final group to identify as transfer students, at least for purposes of this paper, are the graduate students who transfer from one graduate school to another or to or from a professional school. A task force on the transfer problem in graduate schools delivered a major report, "Graduate Credit: Its Recognition and Transfer," at the annual meeting of the Council of Graduate Schools in December 1976.[26] That report is now a policy statement of CGS, and another classification has been added to the Willingham transfer taxonomy.

In sum, transfer students are a far more heterogeneous lot than most people suspect, and their numbers are growing. Even more remarkable are the expanding opportunities for mobility within the educational structure as institutions increase their efforts to be responsive and flexible in accommodating the heterogeneity.

The Transfer Process

A cursory review of several randomly selected college and university catalogs suggests that academic transfer is a relatively uncomplicated process. Students are advised to apply early, to submit an official transcript of previous college work, perhaps a letter or two of recommendation, and usually the high school record and evidence of SAT or ACT scores. They are cautioned in some cases that *D* grades may not be accepted, that they may have to meet certain residency and distribution requirements, and that their chances for financial aid may not be high. At least that is the way it seems, and even a closer reading of the catalog will not greatly alter the impression. Only reality will, and despite notable progress in simplifying the process in recent years, transferring from one educational institution to another will often test the prospective student's persistence and, occasionally, sporting blood.

Barriers to Transfer

Among the cherished institutional prerogatives in American higher education, few are as jealously regarded as the authority to establish admission and graduation standards. The

---

26. Council of Graduate Schools in the United States, *Proceedings of the Sixteenth Annual Meeting,* December 1976, pp. 12–19.

principle is sound, but it is exercised variously under an array of pressures, precedents, and prejudices which rarely add up to a rational whole. At the undergraduate level, the faculty faces the twofold problem of determining the general education requirements for a degree, whether two year or four, as well as the requirements for majors or specialized programs. The latter usually become a departmental determination, and more absolutely so at the graduate level; but within a given institution, the breadth and depth and rigor of the specifications are rarely consistent from one major or discipline to another. Professional schools are more standardized but, again, practice many variations on the theme of an optimal path to a degree.

There is no quarrel with the principles of institutional determination and diversity when they are sensibly and substantively determined. However, perceptions of what constitutes college- or graduate-level work depend heavily on personal experience and subjective criteria, if only because no universal bases are available for determining such matters. Attitudes thus become controlling factors in what may or may not be acceptable as transfer credit, and the student is often sacrificed to "institutional sanctity." Elitists argue that the *integrity* of the academic degree must be preserved, but they are really arguing for the *purity* of the degree. The distinction lies between what is rationally defined to be a thoughtfully and carefully determined curriculum that combines the best of historically demonstrated educational values with appropriate preparation for contemporary needs, and what is traditionally conceived to be the classically educated person. Even that differentiation is an oversimplification, for it suggests that the advocates of the alternatives basically are in agreement. Still, the capsulation is reasonably close to the mark and characterizes the schism that divides academicians and sunders their institutions.

The debate is intensified by those who conceive of democracy as an egalitarian system in which all citizens must be treated equally regardless of genetically or environmentally conditioned differences. In their eyes, to distinguish between students on such grounds is to visit the sins of the fathers on sons and daughters unto the nth generation, and this penalty is simply unacceptable. So the debate rages, but meanwhile it shapes practices that determine the educational fate of persons who may well wonder about the justice or logic of the system. In short, such arguments have thwarted the promulgation of internally consistent and accepted transfer criteria in many of the nation's colleges and universities.

There are less ethereal or esoteric barriers to a rational transfer process, those which are essentially paper-bound. They relate to problems of documentation in transcripts, catalogs, and grading practices. Education has no Linnaean system nor even a lingua franca for communicating the nature and content of academic courses. A casual reading of college catalogs leaves one wondering why English composition or Western civilization must be subsumed (or is it disguised?) under so many captions, and where the titles and descriptions agree, why the disparities in the value of credits granted. Some persons suggest that these "bookkeeping problems" are "symptoms of much more deep seated philosophical positions . . . centered around questions of institutional integrity, faculty competencies, restricted admissions policies, equivalency of courses, planning of programs, individual counseling procedures, student activities, and occupational objectives."[27] The effect, however, is to pose obstacles for mostly earnest students seeking to move from one educational setting to another.

Grading practices further complicate the paper-bound problems of the transfer process. Although the traditional pattern of *A-F* grading may be making a comeback, numerous experiments with grading practices have been carried on, not all confined to experimental institutions. In consequence, institutions receiving transfer applications face a vastly complicated task in evaluating student performance. The effect on the student increases greatly with the level of transfer sought, and here the similarity between the undergraduate transfer stu-

27. Frederick C. Kintzer, *Middleman in Higher Education*, p. 28.

dent and the college graduate seeking admission to graduate
or professional school becomes especially acute. In a study of
grading systems and student mobility, Stevens concluded that

> if a less than highly prestigious institution adopts a nonstandard
> grading system, it should plan to assist a significant number of its
> students who attempt to transfer or gain admission to graduate
> or professional schools with especially comprehensive letters, an-
> notated grade reports, and other devices. Students should recognize
> the added weight other institutions will give to their scores on
> standardized tests. One cannot predict precisely who will have
> what difficulties where, but it is clear that many students will have
> many difficulties in many places. The very uncertainty regarding
> individual situations and problems will, no doubt, make dealing
> with them even more difficult.[28]

To the effects of unorthodox grading practices on a student's prospects for easy mobility may be added grade inflation, which further undermines the transcript as a credible
testimonial to the merits or achievements of a student.

Far as higher education is from achieving generally acceptable guidelines on grading and credit (guidelines rather than
uniform, monolithic standards are the desiderata), new forms
of credit complicate the process still further. There have long
been vehement disagreements over the validity of the semester
or credit hour as a measure of educational activity, either
teaching or learning.[29] A major thrust of the nontraditional
movement has been toward outcome assessment as the means
for measuring effective learning. Although a variety of approaches are being tried, their effect appears to have added
variables without diminishing old problems. Consequently,
the student whose transcript is anecdotal, or one who has
earned credit through experiential learning, or one whose performance is described in terms of competences, or one who
has completed a battery of College-Level Examinations
(CLEP), or a recent veteran, or (the possibilities proliferate
steadily)—any of these students may have to shop around be-

28. Edward I. Stevens, "Grading Systems and Student Mobility,"
Educational Record 54 (1973):312.

29. James M. Heffernan, "The Credibility of the Credit Hour," *Journal of Higher Education* 44 (1973):66.

fore finding an institution that will accept at face value any documentation reflecting measures other than the traditional credit hour.

Still other barriers to transfer may not be readily apparent in the ordinary college catalog. Residency requirements for degrees are usually stated, but not always as clearly and completely as needed by a prospective transfer student. In addition, departments may impose residency qualifications for satisfying majors or prerequisite courses. Thus, a student may find that all the credits previously earned are *acceptable* for recording at the receiving institution, but they may not all be *applicable* toward fulfilling the degree requirements. Residency requirements are ostensibly designed to assure the integrity of the degree; they are also a means of preserving an institution's "self-image" and of holding on to currently enrolled students.[30] Whatever their intent, they are barriers to students seeking to transfer either in or out and they often lengthen the time for completing a degree.

Political residency requirements are similarly thwarting to prospective transfers. Some of their implications are evident at the outset; others may appear only years later. Quotas on out-of-state students, higher tuition for nonresidents, and ineligibility for financial aid are common obstacles to transferring to public institutions in another state. Of sixty-one various state student incentive grant programs offered by thirty-nine states in 1974–75, only fourteen programs permitted students to use the grants at out-of-state institutions.[31] What the unsuspecting student may learn later, perhaps too late, is that some types of licensure or certification may be available only if the degree is earned within the state where the occupational credential is sought.[32] While reciprocity agreements have diminished these barriers, most notably in

30. W. Todd Furniss and Marie Y. Martin, "Toward Solving Transfer Problems," in *College Transfer*, pp. 14–15.

31. Joseph D. Boyd, "1974–75 Undergraduate State Scholarship/ Grant Programs."

32. Council of State Governments, *Occupational Licensing Legislation in the States*, pp. 49, 56.

teacher certification,[33] preprofessional students contemplating transfer across state lines are well advised to inquire thoroughly before rather than after the fact.

Last in this catalog of barriers to transfer is the use and misuse of accreditation. Clearly, institutional autonomy lies at the root of many of the barriers to transfer here described. Equally clearly, the regional accrediting agencies have by and large respected and often abetted that autonomy. Yet accreditation has often been used as a crutch (and occasionally as a club) to legitimize institutional policies designed to ward off undesirable transfer applicants. As this author has written:

> The regional commissions accredit educational institutions, not students. There is no *guarantee*, therefore, that a student seeking transfer from an accredited college or university is any better risk than one from an unaccredited unit. Admissions officers and registrars are urged to evaluate each applicant on individual merit, perhaps attaching provisional status or other conditions where necessary, but *automatic* rejection of an applicant from an unaccredited institution is inappropriate and grossly unfair. Any institution whose quality or integrity would be endangered by such admission hardly deserves accreditation; the rest can act without fear of jeopardizing their status. . . .
>
> [Accreditation may guarantee transferability of credit, albeit not in every case, and] the fact remains that the receiving institution determines its own criteria for accepting credit from another campus. Even within systems where all units are accredited, credits are not always accepted at face value, and some hard negotiations have been necessary to change existing policies. The regional accrediting commissions urge that every decision on transfers be based on judicious weighing of evidence and not on outmoded prejudices or ill-founded fears.[34]

Generally, the relationship between accreditation and transfer is not wholly understood. The difficulty is compounded by

33. Only five states—Louisiana, Michigan, Montana, Nevada, and Wyoming—have no form of reciprocity or other basis for recognizing out-of-state teaching preparation. Thirty-one states participate in the Interstate Certification Project, a reciprocity arrangement, and others have some basis for recognition (National Education Association, *A Manual on Standards Affecting School Personnel in the United States*, ed. T. M. Stinnett, 1974 ed., p. 25).

34. Robert Kirkwood, "The Myths of Accreditation," *Educational Record* 54 (1973):213–14.

some of the professional and specialized accrediting agencies that approve particular programs within institutions. Because many of them deal with occupations and professions requiring licensure, the tendency is to be prescriptive in detailing acceptable curricula and performance standards. Thus a student seeking to transfer into a specialized program may find that previous education, whatever its merits or relevance, may be unacceptable in fulfilling degree requirements.[35] The Council on Postsecondary Accreditation has declared among its purposes "to insure that learners of any age and in whatever learning situation receive due recognition for accomplishment . . ."[36] Initially, COPA confined its interest to cooperation with the Office on Educational Credit of the American Council on Education in promoting acceptances of credit equivalencies for military courses. COPA has recently extended its concern to the gamut of postsecondary educational endeavor, and a task force jointly appointed by the American Association of Collegiate Registrars and Admissions Officers, ACE, and COPA will issue a statement on transfer which represents the most serious effort in more than a decade to address a number of the key problems discussed in this chapter.

Problems of Transfer Students

When a student has surmounted the barriers to transfer, life is still unlikely to be a bowl of cherries. In a world where second-class citizenship is common, transfer students might welcome that dubious honor over their actual status. Despite their growing numbers, transfers are often strangers in an alien land. Where they have entered a senior institution at the junior-class level, they find the social structure already tightly knit, based on groupings shaped by two years' prior residence among students who began and remained on the campus. Clubs, fraternities, activities, teams—the extracurricular program has its own seniority system, and, like all other such

---

35. Kintzer, *Middleman in Higher Education,* p. 29. Also James Wattenbarger, "Problems of Articulation," *Toward Solving Transfer Problems in Southern Colleges and Universities,* p. 43.

36. "The Balance Wheel for Accreditation," information leaflet, p. 5.

systems, the tendency is to look askance at newcomers if not straightaway reject them.

Counseling and orientation programs rarely compensate for the alienation experienced by transfer students. What's worse, they fail to provide the newcomer with a coherent plan conducive to adapting to the new educational setting.[37] Most orientation programs are geared to first-time entering students, and few colleges recognize the different and often unique requirements of the transfer student. The problem is exacerbated when the adviser is a faculty member not wholly conversant with the vagaries of the curricula or the mechanics of the registrar's office. In the words of one study, "As many of the transfer students see it, if the goals of the university are to develop and test their initiative, persistence and tolerance of uncertainty, the processes of transfer student intake, orientation, advisement, and classification do an outstanding job. If, on the other hand, the university purposes to facilitate their transfer and adjustment to student life at MSU, present practices leave much room for improvement."[38]

Then there is the hassle of registration, frustrating to almost any student. Infinitely greater is the frustration to the transfer student who finds that registration for resident students was held during the previous semester and that a number of the courses he needs are already filled. And if a community college freshman plans to transfer and bases a program on the senior institution's current catalog, said student may find two years later that the requirements have been changed. Native students are usually protected when such changes occur; transfer students are not.

The distinction between acceptability of credits for transfer and their applicability in specific programs has been noted. In some cases the distinction is valid and reflects an appropriate exercise of institutional control over the content of its

37. Kintzer, *Middleman in Higher Education*, n. 39, p. 7. Also Wattenbarger, "Problems of Articulation," n. 39, p. 45.

38. Paul K. Preus, "Report of an Investigation of Student's Perception of the Process of Transferring to MSU," p. 14. Also Glen A. Rose, Abstract of a major applied research project "Relationships of Student and Faculty Perceptions of Transfer Barriers Faced by Students at Broward Community College," pp. i–xv.

programs, but in other cases prejudice or occasionally whimsy are the determinants. The acceptance or rejection of *D* grades has been widely discussed, but the problem remains of explaining why native students may be permitted to graduate with several *D*'s on their records whereas transfer students may have none. Transfer students with excellent records may encounter none of these problems yet find that, despite their brilliance, they cannot qualify for honors or special awards because they have not been on campus long enough. The same generalities hold for membership in campus organizations or opportunities for jobs or class offices. The most serious exclusion for transfer students is from institutional financial aid. While this information may be known beforehand, the effect is severe, and one has to wonder about the equity of it all. Indeed, in the transfer story, inequity is only one of many details which reveal it to be less than a glorious chapter in the history of American education.

Trends in Transfer Practices

We began by saying that student transfer has received a good deal of attention in recent years. Though some of that attention has resulted in action, the action has not always been of the most desirable kind: some of it is perceived as being properly responsive to the educational needs of a democratic society or, again, as further demeaning the quality and integrity of American higher education.

As noted, the academic community has been slow and often reluctant to respond to the transfer problem, even after its dimension grew from hundreds to hundreds of thousands of students. In consequence, legislatures and state boards have tended to prod at least the public institutions into more positive articulation efforts. Kintzer, in reporting state-by-state surveys of the transfer situation in 1973 and 1976[39] has focused attention on the most important current trend in transfer practices—the effort to rationalize the process. One danger, of course, is that the states may go too far in their zeal and preempt what are properly institutional prerogatives.

39. Kintzer, *Middleman in Higher Education*, n. 39, p. 7, and "'Articulation' Comes of Age," *Compact* 10, no. 2 (1976):13–16.

While the states are variously active, the federal government too is in the picture, in part because the Congress is worried about how federal dollars are being spent in education and also because of emergent consumerism. Willett, an enthusiastic supporter of federal consumer protection, speaking of government attitudes and actions concerned with educational problems, stated before the 1975 annual meeting of the Association of American Colleges that "two philosophical shifts are taking place: a) the student is defined, and more and more accepted, as the direct consumer of educational services; and b) educational abuse is viewed as the responsibility to a large extent of the federal government, no longer primarily of the states."[40] Many of the "abuses" in higher education cited by Willett are clearly related to the transfer problem. Consumer protection is an appropriate concern of government, but it could also be used to justify an insidious invasion of institutional prerogatives. The initiative is still within the grasp of the educational community, and we simply have no choice but to keep it there.

Not all of the trends result from external pressures. Many academicians and academic administrators are evidencing a new awareness of respectable alternative routes to associate, bachelor's, and even graduate degrees. When the Cooperative Assessment of Experiential Learning (CAEL) reorganized as the Council for the Advancement of Experiential Learning in 1977, it reported a membership in excess of 240 institutions, with even larger numbers of persons participating in the project's activities.[41] Other working papers in the present volume deal with an array of alternative programs in higher education, means for earning and measuring credit, the New York State Regents External Degree Program, and other efforts to examine the problems and opportunities in meeting the needs of a learning society.

Since 1967, more than one and a half million people have taken nearly three million General Examinations in the College-Level Examination Program, over 300,000 in the 1973–

40. Sandra L. Willett, "Consumer Protection in Higher Education: Why? For Whom? How?" *Liberal Education* 61 (1975):163.

41. Cooperative Assessment of Experiential Learning, *CAEL Newsletter* 3, no. 2 (1977):1.

74 academic year alone.[42] Moreover, three-fourths of the students submitting CLEP scores received credit in some area, a clear indication of new flexibility in academic institutions. The Office on Educational Credit of the American Council on Education finds increasing interest in *and* use of its revised and updated *Guide to the Evaluation of Educational Experiences in the Armed Services.*[43] More recently, the OEC has published *The National Guide to Credit Recommendations for Noncollegiate Courses,* parallelling its credit recommendations for the military with similar assessments of courses sponsored by employer and professional groups.[44]

Activities like these under such eminent auspices indicate more than merely academic exercises and desperation moves motivated by frantic fears about survival. To be sure, the specter of shrinking enrollments in the 18–22 age group has driven some colleges to radically revised admission practices and to search for new constituencies. In their zeal, some institutions have made compromises with traditions that would have been unthinkable in the halcyon days of the 1960s or before. But the increasing preponderance of evidence reflects a changing mood toward openness in the learning process, and inevitably transfer students will benefit.

Voluntary interinstitutional cooperation is obviously preferable to government-decreed practices, and it is happening. The Committee on Institutional Cooperation, comprising the Big Ten universities and the University of Chicago, has produced a massive document on the itinerant student, covering opportunities for movement among or between the cooperating universities.[45] In Massachusetts, a state committee, which included two- and four-year colleges and universities, collaborated to produce guidelines for receiving institutions.[46] Those who would scoff that institutions are making a virtue of neces-

42. Jerilee Grandy and Walter M. Shea, *CLEP General Examinations in American Colleges and Universities,* p. 3.

43. The latest edition was published in 1978.

44. Program on Noncollegiate Sponsored Instruction, *The National Guide to Credit Recommendations for Noncollegiate Courses,* 1978 ed.

45. Patricia Ann McFate, *Education for the Itinerant Student: A Guide to Opportunities in Liberal Arts and Sciences at CIC Universities.*

46. Massachusetts State Transfer Articulation Committee, *Guidelines for Articulation for Receiving Institutions.*

sity exhibit a cynicism that ignores the genuine, spreading concern in the academic world for removing some serious causes of injustice and inequity—a healthy trend at any time.

The need for research on transfer students is also receiving attention. Although the efforts are fragmented and sometimes duplicative, they are beginning to produce data that will be essential in the ongoing planning and replanning of the nation's educational activities. On the subject of "Reverse Transfers," for example, three recent studies do much to dispel the notion that only flunk-outs transfer from senior to junior colleges and that such people should never have been admitted in the first place.[47] There is much to learn about all students, but now that mobility is becoming a pronounced characteristic of the student population, this trend in research activity is especially encouraging.

Certain developments in transfer can hardly be labeled trends, but they may be adumbrations of things to come. Grieder and Cassady observe "the ubiquitous pressures within our culture to seek degrees or to advance one's self as far as possible in formal education." The result, they say, is that more students who are enrolled in "terminal" programs are looking toward transfer into a baccalaureate institution.[48] Southern Illinois University has a program offering a B.S. in Occupational Teaching "which accommodates all manner of post- and extra-secondary, pre- and in-service occupational education professionals.[49] Northwestern Electronics Institute, a private technical school, arranged an agreement with the General College of the University of Minnesota for a joint associate degree program in electronics several years ago, and NEI's graduates have transferred with credit to a number of

47. Charles E. McCandless and Henry D. Pope, "Transfer Practices of Junior Colleges Affecting Students on Suspension from Senior Colleges," *College and University* 51 (1974):178–85; Glen A. Rose, "A Follow-up Study of the Broward Community College Reverse Transfer Student Questionnaire"; Glenda E. Lee, "Reverse Transfer: The 'Retread Function' of Community Colleges."

48. T. M. Grieder and Royce W. Cassady, "Transferring the Non-Transfer Program," *College and University* 50 (1974):76.

49. Mimeographed letter from Ronald W. Stadt, chairman, Department of Occupational Education, Southern Illinois University (n.d.).

state universities and community colleges.[50] At Culver-Stockton College, a small church-related liberal arts college in Missouri, an experimental "Bachelor of Science with the Proficiency Major Gained by Life Experiences" degree program has been successful enough to be approved by the faculty for continuation as one of the college's offerings.[51] And in March 1976, the National Center for Higher Education Management Systems convened a meeting of an Ad Hoc Committee on Vocational-Technical Outcomes to discuss more effective means for measuring and documenting vocational and technical education.[52]

Such a development, however, carries dangers, and two-year colleges and vocational-technical institutes, whether public or proprietary, are cautioned to be on guard against them. While "terminal" may have been an ill-chosen term to describe certain types of postsecondary programs—no one's educational experience should ever be seen as final—its implications were clear. At the end of a prescribed program, the student is expected to have developed certain skills which qualify the holder for employment. This function is entirely appropriate to the teaching and learning process and certainly belongs in the total scheme of educational opportunities. It would be unfortunate and even undesirable, therefore, if the concept of self-contained programs designed within a limited framework were to be subordinated or in any way denigrated by shifting the focus to longer range degree-potential programs as preferable or more prestigious. Preferable they may be for some students, but surely not more prestigious in relation to the career needs and objectives of many people. The chance to continue toward a degree from programs that are

50. Letter from C. L. Larson, president, Northwestern Electronics Institute, to Henry A. Spille, American Council on Education, Feb. 11, 1976.

51. "Report to the Faculty from the Committee for the Assessment of Experiential Learning," Culver-Stockton College, Canton, Mo., February 1, 1976.

52. Minutes of the Ad Hoc Committee on Vocational-Technical Education, March 15, 1976 (Boulder, Colo.: National Center for Higher Educational Management Systems).

occupation-oriented should not be foreclosed, but neither should this objective become their primary function.

Related to this development are some findings and recommendations of the staff of the California Postsecondary Education Commission resulting from a study directed by Dorothy Knoell. In observing that "continuing education for part-time, adult students has become the dominant function of Community Colleges [at least in California], with no resultant neglect of the occupational, transfer, and general education functions for more traditional students," the report goes on to recommend that:

Community Colleges should be recognized as "less than baccalaureate" institutions of postsecondary education . . . with statements of function refined so as to give proper emphasis to the mission of serving community needs and providing opportunities for continuing education for local residents. This redefinition of function should not be construed as authorization for offering upper division courses and programs.[53]

The report simply emphasizes the importance of *not* compartmentalizing all educational programs and opportunities in terms of academic degrees. As a first-class piece of research, the California study deserves to be emulated in the other forty-nine states.

Another development that would bear emulation is found in Florida. As of 1974, Florida was the only state to have an Articulation Counseling Office in each of the nine public universities, and the situation nationally has not changed significantly since. The need is obvious: "in eight of the nine institutions, transfer students accounted for over 60 percent of the upper division enrollment, with an average of 65 percent of the transferring students coming from Florida community colleges."[54] From campus to campus, the titles of the officers for articulation counseling vary, as do their administrative status and responsibilities. However, the concept of a

53. California Postsecondary Education Commission, *Through the Open Door: A Study of Patterns and Performance in California's Community Colleges*, pp. i, ii.

54. Suzan Schafer, *A New Position in Higher Education: Liaison Officer for Articulation*, pp. 10, 14.

specific office and staff directly related to the transfer situation is one of the more constructive steps yet taken in the slow-moving response to a steadily growing phenomenon at the undergraduate level.

Even at the graduate level the earth is beginning to shake a little in response to the report of the Panel on Alternate Approaches to Graduate Education.[55] At the 1975 annual meeting of the Council of Graduate Schools in the United States, a session, "Admissions Criteria," listened to three deans and a member of graduate faculties describing their involvement with external degrees, new criteria and procedures in processing applications, a graduate program for nonbaccalaureate students, and minority recruitment. Dean David S. Sparks of the University of Maryland Graduate School observed, "Several current graduate catalogs describe broadened criteria for admissions including recognition of nontraditional study, external baccalaureate degrees, and [experiential] learning. The number and variety of institutions embracing these new criteria remains, however, relatively small."[56] What is remarkable is not that the number is small but, given the nature of graduate department autonomy, that any institutions have acted at all.

Time and further inquiry will probably uncover other developments and incipient trends. In many instances, what started as an effort to assist transfer students or at least to diminish their problems has already begun to affect the fundamental fabric of higher education.

Present Status

As long as the structure of higher education was such that student transfer was only a chance occurrence at many colleges and universities, little was done about it. The higher education system was defined as four years of continuous study on the same campus by 18–22-year-olds, and the student simply conformed to it. When veterans invaded the

55. Panel on Alternate Approaches to Graduate Education, *Scholarship for Society.*
56. Council of Graduate Schools in the United States, *Proceedings of the Fifteenth Annual Meeting,* 1975, p. 73.

colleges following World War II, regardless of their age or experience they did just that. The numerous two-year colleges created in the late fifties and early sixties also conformed to the pattern, borrowing their curricula almost entirely from the lower division of their senior models.

So complacent was the academy that few people anticipated the implications of the two-year colleges for student mobility. Unfortunately, part of the indifference was a result of the same kind of snobbery academics manifested toward the high schools. It was also owed to the preoccupation of faculties with their disciplines to the exclusion of involvement with broader educational issues. When public support for education surged after the shock of Sputnik, educators limited their responses largely to providing more of the same. Then, and again when the students challenged the establishment in the 1960s, great opportunities were missed to reexamine the rationale and rationality of American higher education and to reorder it in light of the contemporary and future needs of society.

Like the tip of an iceberg, this paper focuses on only one issue which our neglect has allowed to become a problem whose magnitude can no longer be ignored or casually treated. The message is plain: either the academic community must handle such problems internally, or solutions will be imposed externally and not necessarily in public institutions alone. Student mobility and transfer deserve the priority attention they are getting on some campuses; they require it everywhere else.

That transfer should emerge as a major issue now is somewhat ironic. During all those years when academic life was simpler, it would have been much easier to address and solve the transfer problem. But inertia and the concatenation of events decreed otherwise, and now transfer is enmeshed in a web of serious problems. Institutions should see the situation, not as one for lamentation, but rather as the opportunity it is to reexamine their reasons for being in order to reaffirm or redefine their respective missions and goals.

The diversity of America's educational institutions has been a matter of national pride, but the past few years have blurred the clarity of that diversity. One danger in the current scramble for students is the temptation to obscure institutional differences still further. Even were it desirable, no college or university can be all things to all people. Recruiting and retaining students are essential to the existence of any institution, but what ends are served if expectations are generated that cannot be fulfilled, or students enrolled whose needs cannot be met?

To call for a reexamination of institutional transfer policies, then, is far from suggesting that every college or university is errant if it chooses not to admit certain students. In the past, institutional diversity derived in considerable measure from homogeneity of their respective constituencies; that principle appears to be no less valid today. The need is not to abandon principles and standards in the treatment of transfer students, but rather to abolish absurd, irrational practices. Of course transfer is a complex matter, but the evidence indicts the process for being unnecessarily eccentric and obstructive.

One serious cause of transfer problems is the gap between institutional statements and departmental practices, particularly in larger institutions. Catalogs and recruitment officers usually speak in general, often ambiguous terms, perhaps for understandable reasons. But when a student transfers in good faith that his or her degree interests can be pursued in sequence without delay, it comes as a blow (and the credibility of the system suffers) to learn that departmental prerequisites for majors differ in specification or content from what the community college provided. The burden of responsibility rests with the departments for demonstrating the validity of their position.

The premise of this paper is that the interests of both the society and the individual are best served by facilitating student mobility in the educational process. Excessive mobility may, of course, jeopardize the stability and continuity of society and its institutions, but improved articulation among colleges and universities can hardly be viewed so ominously. To address the issue of transfer policy will require treating it in light of other issues confronting American higher education. The issues collectively present another opportunity to clarify and consolidate the strengths and purposes of higher education and to reestablish its credibility with the American people.

How the higher education community responds to that opportunity will be critical. If we believe that institutional integrity is the keystone of the educational structure, that integrity must be reflected in every facet of the academic enterprise, certainly in the policies and procedures intended to shape the learning experience. As I have written elsewhere,

> it is not my purpose to rehash the debate about either the desirability or the attainability of universal standards, although I confess to a strong skepticism on both counts. What *is* important is the integrity of the *process* whereby we establish standards—the extent to which honesty and objectivity, care and thoroughness, equity and due process, characterize the determination of educational objectives and any assessment of their attainment.[57]

It is time, then, to get on with the job.

Matters for Attention

Educators frequently object to the inefficiency of reinventing the wheel and then proceed to do so themselves. Two major statements on student transfer have been formulated in recent years, one in 1966 and the other in 1973.[58] Each of the statements is still fundamentally sound and sufficiently broad to warrant further consideration. The following discussion concentrates on points that have not been adequately emphasized before or else are of such importance that they deserve further stress.

Transfer is an educational rather than a political issue, but it will remain so only if educators retain the initiative. Consumer, governmental, and political pressures are building steadily, and in some states it may already be too late. The

57. Robert Kirkwood, "Importance of Assessing Learning," in *Experiential Learning,* by Morris T. Keeton and associates, p. 158.

58. Joint Committee on Junior and Senior Colleges of the Association of American Colleges, American Association of Junior Colleges, and American Association of Collegiate Registrars and Admissions Officers, *Guidelines for Improving Articulation Between Junior and Senior Colleges,* 1966, 17 pp.; *College Transfer: Recommendations from Airlie House Conference,* 1973, 6 pp.

academic community must be made aware that a major prerogative of institutional policy making may soon be lost by default unless the weaknesses and contradictions of present policies are eliminated.

The subject of student transfer must be viewed in the larger context of institutional purposes and goals. Until an institution has defined precisely the nature of its educational mission, it is simply irresponsible in trying to attract new constituencies or qualify for increased financial support.

The student's responsibility in the transfer process is frequently overlooked. A more careful reading of the catalog or the use of counseling and advisory services by students could often reduce or even eliminate the seriousness of some transfer problems. It is incumbent on institutions to keep this point to the fore in all literature and discussions related to transfer planning.

Independent colleges and universities continue to be a vital aspect of educational diversity and opportunity in the United States. When they are not invited to participate in articulation planning and agreements, they should insist on being included.

Interstate and regional arrangements in many cases would be preferable to single state plans. Educational opportunities may be more accessible just across the border than within a state. The WICHE Student Exchange Programs and the compact between Wisconsin and Minnesota are illustrative.

The meaning of residency should be reexamined. Where an institution can demonstrate that residency is explicitly related to its educational program, let it do so and recruit its students accordingly. Where not, residency should be abolished.

Institutions vary in their ability to define their clientele. Certain types of public institutions have their student bodies decreed by public edict, while others have some options. Private institutions have considerably more leeway. Whatever the situation, there is considerable opportunity to establish reasonably precise guidelines for determining which students are most desirable or may potentially achieve the maximum educational benefits in a particular institution. The need for students should be no justification for playing loosely with human lives.

Counseling and orientation continue as major institutional weaknesses, despite persistent criticism. The problem is especially serious for transfer students whose particular needs are rarely provided for even in the best of programs. It is time to consider other approaches to counseling, for example the possibility of installing educational counseling centers in state employment offices or Social Security centers. If the adult population is to be fully served educationally, they must have better access to information and advice than is now possible. Better orientation programs for transfer students will develop only when institutions give greater recognition to transfer students and acknowledge their peculiar needs.

There is a continuing need for improved documentation of educational records. Diplomas and transcripts must be more integrally related, diplomas containing a substantive statement in plain English of what the degree signifies, and transcripts providing the qualitative and quantitative details. Transfer is complicated for many students because of the inadequacy or the incoherence of a transcript.

The inequity of making institutional financial aid virtually unavailable to transfer students is unconscionable. Discriminatory practices in eligibility of transfer students, as opposed to resident or continuing students, are also dubious. New effort is needed to redress the imbalance between funds available to transfer and nontransfer students.

As institutions reexamine their purposes and goals, careful attention should be paid to the compatibility between institutional statements and departmental policies. In complex universities especially, internal inconsistencies are among the most frequent causes of problems for transfer students.

The outcomes of the educational process are at best inadequately measured; thus the tendency continues to judge the quality of an institution by the caliber of the entering students rather than the attainments of its graduates. New emphasis on research and follow-up studies are needed to develop more substantive evidence about educational effectiveness and sounder bases for articulation arrangements.

A major effort should be undertaken by national and regional education organizations to focus immediately on the subject of student transfer to alert their constituents to the nature and magnitude of the transfer problem, the dangers of inaction, and the opportunity at hand to restore public confidence in higher education in America.

CHAPTER 8

The Administrative Uses of Credit
John Folger

Credit measures of some kind are essential in an educational system that permits students to transfer between institutions in the middle of a degree program, allows students to choose electives, and subdivides educational programs into parts or units. Standardized units of performance are necessary in order to keep records on the large numbers of students in big institutions and state systems. As the number and varieties of institutions and programs in postsecondary education in America have increased, credit has become part of the administrative process.

Although credits function primarily in the administration of student educational records, they are also used as a measure in the budget process and in personnel management of faculty. Credit provides a legitimating function for the full range of postsecondary institutions: if an institution's credits are acceptable, the institution can claim a place in higher education.

Historically, the administration of instruction has been highly decentralized and personal. Growth during the last quarter century has brought more multicampus systems, state-level controls, and formal, bureaucratic forms of administration, including greater dependence on formal credit measures. The traditional colleges and universities have provided the main route to a credential, but are now under pressure to recognize new types of activities for credit, including certain experiences outside higher education. Changes in administrative processes in higher education and the increasing diversity of institutions involved in the credentialing process have brought pressures for change in the ways credit is determined and awarded.

This chapter examines the part credit plays in current administrative processes and explores the adaptation of credentialing to new ways of awarding credit that may be educationally desirable.

Operation of the Credit System

When Mark Hopkins was on one end of the log, and the student on the other, credit was unnecessary; evaluation of learning was direct. In highly individualized educational settings, such as the American graduate schools before World War I, the award of degrees was based on evaluation of the candidates by the departmental faculty; when they said a candidate was ready, he received a degree.

More formal measures of progress and accomplishment were called for when the system grew, the curriculum became diversified and included electives, and students prepared for specific professions, and when students began to transfer between different, largely autonomous institutions en route to a degree. Under these conditions—characteristic in American higher education in the twentieth century—a system of credits for parts of a program en route to a degree or other educational credential has become a necessity. For administrative purposes, a credit system needs to be based on fairly uniform units, which represent generally agreed upon parts or subdivisions of a total program of work for a degree.[1]

The most obvious possibilities for measuring educational progress are the amount of time spent in studying a particular subject or the amount of learning achieved. A credit system could represent both time spent and level of accomplishment, but, administratively, a single standard is simpler. Time spent, counted in semester or quarter hour credits, has become the generally accepted unit of measurement. Student progress is so recorded, and quarter hour and semester credits can be directly converted as necessary to fit into a particular institution's system.

1. For detailed discussions, see Jonathan R. Warren, "Current Practices in Awarding Credits and Degrees" in the present volume, and Sidney Suslow, "Course Credits as Measures of Faculty/Student Effort," *Minnesota Education* 1, no. 4 (1974):12–25.

Why did higher education not use the *amount* of learning achieved as the credit unit for administration purposes? Achievement measures have a more direct relationship to the stated purposes of education and to what should be the meaning of the degree or other educational credential. The credit system does take into consideration the quality of work, but only to a limited extent. The first limitation is accreditation: if an institution is not accredited, its credits cannot be accepted for transfer; other institutions will not recognize either the credits or the credential it awards. Accreditation, however, is not uniform because there are several accrediting agencies and several routes to approval. Moreover, for institutions that have been accepted as candidates for accreditation and are going through the accrediting processes, a variety of arrangements have been worked out so that their students may not be penalized. The requirements for accreditation, thus, represent an important but limited application of quality control in the operation of the credit system.

A second limitation is the requirement by most institutions that only *C* or better work may be accepted for transfer. This policy rules some ineffective work out of the credit system; it also is a limited application of quality control.

Within these minor limitations, an *A* from a highly selective institution has the same credit value as a *C* from an unselective one. The actual performance and knowledge acquired as represented by credits from different institutions is highly variable.[2]

From both an educational and administrative perspective, the interesting question is why the "time spent" choice came about. How could higher education adopt a standard so variable, and, because of that variability, why did it not shift long ago to a performance standard? Two reasons, which have their roots in the social environment, are principally responsible.

2. The variability in the meaning of grades in relation to test score performance is illustrated in John Folger, "Some Relationships Between Ability and Self Reported Grades," *Sociology of Education* 40 (1967): 270–74. See also Alexander W. Astin, "Academic Credit as Achievement," *Minnesota Education* 1, no. 4 (1974):26–34, and James M. Heffernan, "The Credibility of the Credit Hour," *Journal of Higher Education* 44 (1973):61–72.

First, the job market for college graduates did not require a more uniform measuring of an educational credential than that provided. In most fields, the possession of a college degree was sufficient to assure consideration in the job market. Employers recognized that the content and quality of programs with the same label varied substantially and, in considering job applicants, made their own adjustments for program differences. Applicants varied greatly in personality and motivation as well as in their educational backgrounds, and frequently employers considered the nonacademic characteristics to be more important to job success than their educational credentials. As employers performed the complex task of assessing the potential of the applicants, they used the educational credential as a "threshold factor" and supplemented it with other factors in the choice process.

The second principal reason the credit measure did not become performance-based was the decentralized and autonomous nature of American higher education. At the time the credit system developed, small private institutions were in the majority. In the public sector, the states provided most of the funding but exercised only limited control. At the same time, there was a strong belief that a federal or national system of education was politically unwise and educationally undesirable. In this situation, institutions established their own standards (which varied both within and among institutions) of performance and, within broad limits, content of courses. If the institutions had had to develop a uniform curriculum and use standardized testing of achievements, they would have had to give up a substantial part of their autonomy in instructional matters. Furthermore, a performance standard requires a central method of establishing and maintaining the standards. Autonomous institutions did not see advantages in this approach, and no group or agency external to higher education was either able to, or interested in, imposing such standards.

The model of the College Entrance Examination Board, which had been created to deal with the variable quality and content of secondary school programs, was available to deal with the differences in collegiate standards. It is one thing to provide an appraisal of achievement as *part* of an admissions process, but quite another to provide a measure that *determines* the credit and ultimately the credential that will be awarded. Standardized testing for graduate and professional school admissions has long been in use and has helped graduate and professional schools to determine who shall be admitted and to make adjustments for the variability of undergraduate grading standards. But higher education institutions were neither motivated nor pressured to develop a performance system for awarding credits. The standardization of the credit system on the basis of the amount of time spent in courses was easier, met the need for a uniform basis for equating the work done in one institution with that done in another, and also fitted the decentralized and autonomous nature of the higher educational system. Even though what the credits represented differed from one institution to another, informal and formal ways of adjusting for the differences were found, and the system could tolerate a good deal of imprecision.

The credit system and the administrative procedures for awarding credit developed when the institutions were fewer and smaller and had more full-time students, fewer transfers, a less varied curriculum, and a more homogeneous student clientele. In the last quarter century, these characteristics have undergone great change. Nearly a thousand institutions have been created, enrollments have more than quadrupled, and a much more diverse clientele is being served with a much greater variety of programs. These changes have put strains on a credit system that is based on the time students spent in courses. Some of the problems identified fall into three broad categories: (1) variable standards—credit from one institution may mean something quite different from credit awarded by another institution—essentially an educational problem but with administrative implications; (2) the problem of giving a common credit definition to increasingly diverse educational activities; and (3) the problems of using credit for administrative functions not closely related to the administration of student programs, such as measuring faculty activity, justifying budget requests, and distributing student assistance funds.

Variable Standards of Credit

Should an institution give full credit to a student seeking transfer for work done at an institution which has much lower standards? Institutions have developed various means for dealing with this matter. In practical terms, transfer of credit can be an especially delicate subject when the two unequal institutions are part of the same state system. One resolution is to give the student elective credit for work completed, but require that he or she take most or all of the required courses at the second institution. Another means is to require the student to validate some parts of his educational experience by taking examinations given by the institution to which he is transferring. A third variation is to make the validation of the earlier work dependent in part on the quality of performance at the second institution.

The transfer of credit is administratively not too difficult; it is a difficult problem for the student who may have to take additional work at additional cost and time.

The increase in number of institutions in the last two decades and the development of state systems of community colleges with a function of preparing students to transfer to universities and four-year colleges has highlighted the problems inherent in differing standards. Administratively, the problems have been manageable but increasingly troublesome.

Credit for Diverse Educational Activities

As educational programs became more complex and as practical and clinical experiences were added to the curriculum, particularly in professional programs, credit was assigned to these nonclassroom activities and was generally converted into academic credits. Most of this work was fitted into the academic calendar, had definite time requirements, and was supervised by the faculty. It could, with relative ease, be integrated into the credit system.

In recent years, even more diverse programs have been developed to extend education to new clienteles in new ways. These include programs organized on an achievement basis, with no definite time for completion. Other programs take place entirely off campus and provide for limited contact with the faculty. Such programs are harder to fit into the conventional conception of a credit system, particularly when they may not be organized as conventional courses.

When unconventional programs are offered by a new institution established to provide a new type of learning experience —as in the case of Empire State College and Thomas A. Edison College—the conventional credit system is strained even further. How can experiential learning, validated by a unique examination, be equated in the credit system? A principal difficulty is that the performance standards for the unconventional program may be specific, but the conventional program, with which it is being compared, has unclear performance requirements.

Credit as a Measure of Other Administrative Activities

Although the credit system was developed to account for student progress, it has become significant in the accounting for faculty work loads and as a measure of the need for funds both in presenting and in justifying budgets.

Colleges and universities, unlike most public bureaucracies, operate internally largely on a collegial principle, with faculty members acting as independent professionals within the limits of the academic calendar and schedule of courses. When institutions were small, administration could be minimal and the administration's expectations and requirements were transmitted informally to the faculty members and staff. As institutions expanded, the pressure grew to institute formal faculty work load requirements and other administrative rules. The number of hours of formal classroom instruction was the easiest way to express work load expectations. This formulation became the most widely used standard even though it covered only part of the institutions' expectations about faculty activity. Responsibilities for research, public service activities, and non-course-related instructional activities, such as counseling and advisement of students, are not measured by a "contact hour" load.

To the extent that faculty members carry on the related activities as an aid to professional advancement, a faculty record keeping system limited to contact hours of formal instruction may be adequate for administrative purposes. As institutions grow and state systems of institutions develop, the informal, simple administrative systems are replaced by more formal and complex rules, work standards, and measurement procedures. The twelve-hour teaching load is replaced by a different, more quantitative measure, for example, "250 semester credit hour production during each term." This latter measure accounts for average size of class as well as number of formal preparations. Measures are added for number of students being advised, for time spent with graduate students on research problems, and the like. The National Center for Higher Education Management Systems (NCHEMS) has developed definitions, guidelines, and procedures for conducting faculty activity analysis [3]

As work load rules and accounting procedures increase and become more bureaucratically established, difficulties in applying teaching activity measures to other instructional modes will arise and lead to still more rules. For example, if the faculty role in a self-instructional program is limited primarily to developing curricular materials and examining students who have essentially taught themselves by using the instructional packages provided, the faculty work load cannot be assessed in credit hours of formal instruction. Other methods for measuring faculty contribution are required.[4]

In budget requests, credit hours have become a principal factor in measuring instructional effort. Among public higher education systems, the method for making the calculation varies. In some, credit hours are expressed as full-time equivalent students, and funds are provided for instruction on the basis of number of FTE students enrolled. In others, credit hours to be produced are divided by the average or expected faculty teaching loads, to arrive at the number of faculty members required for instruction; faculty positions are translated into an instructional budget request by multiplying num-

3. NCHEMS, *Faculty Activity Analysis: Overview and Major Issues* provides an introduction to the approach and problems in measuring faculty work load.

4. Charles W. Manning and Leonard C. Romney, *Faculty Activity Analysis: Procedures Manual.*

ber of faculty members needed by an average faculty salary and then adding amounts for other instructional expenses. In still other systems, different money amounts are provided per credit hour for different levels and fields of instruction: the budget request for the cost of instruction is adjusted for different kinds of programs (graduate, undergraduate, science, humanities, etc.).[5]

These approaches to faculty work load and costs exert strong pressure to translate *all* instructional activities into terms of credit hours to be included in the budget request. In some instances special instructional activities must be separately identified and justified, a process that makes them more visible—and perhaps more vulnerable—during the budget review process. About two-thirds of the states now employ a budget formula in developing legislative appropriations requests, and most of the formulas use credit measures in the budget process. The "formula" or objective measure, however, covers only 50–70 percent of the budget request,[6] and in no case is the entire budget request determined by an objective formula. Although credit measures are important, most state budgeting systems include considerable leeway for items and programs that are not in the formula portion of the appropriations request.

In most states, the budget request and actual budget management of appropriated funds are separate processes. In state systems, after the level of funding has been determined, the institutions are given varying degrees of flexibility in administering the budget. In several states, an objective formula employing credit hours is the basis for the request, but the public institutions each get a lump sum appropriation and have considerable flexibility in their use of funds to support both conventional and unconventional instruction.

Credit measures are widely used in institutional accounting and record keeping partly because more appropriate measures for budgeting needs and for faculty activity are not available.

5. Francis Gross, *A Comparative Analysis of Existing Budget Formulas.*
6. Lyman Glenny et al., *State Budgeting for Higher Education.*

Partly they are used because instruction is the central function in higher education and credit has become its basic accounting unit. Administratively, credit measures are often used in determining need for classrooms and laboratories in capital building programs. The concept is that a classroom is needed to accommodate the addition of an average number of credit hours of work. Laboratory requirements can also be expressed in terms of credit hours. The instructional level of credit may determine students eligibility for campus housing, participation in athletics, parking privileges, and so on.

Managing and Accounting for Student's Educational Experience

In general, the variability in the meaning of a credit is greater between institutions than within an institution.[7] The most frequent administrative problems arise in equating credits from one institution to another, and, as noted, a variety of administrative procedures have been developed for handling transfer students. To the institutional administrator, these arrangements are reasonable and fairly simple to handle. To the student who is required to take additional work and whose transferred credits are counted only partially toward a credential, the arrangement is less satisfactory. Legislators are beginning to question transfer arrangements that lengthen students' programs and thus increase the cost of the education to the taxpayers.[8] Student and legislative concerns may change a fairly simple administrative process for transferring credits into a more complex concern for fairer and more uniform treatment of students who transfer.

Besides transfer, other matters are impinging on current administrative practices in awarding credit. Public concern about the quality of education coupled with the less evident value of many kinds of credentials in the job market is gen-

7. James R. Davis, *Great Aspirations*, Appendix 3: "Notes on the Validity of the Academic Performance Index." See also Astin, "Academic Credit as Achievement."

8. See Joint Legislative Audit and Review Commission, *Program Evaluation, The Virginia Community College System.*

erating pressures for improved evidence about the meaning of credits.[9] Again, as with transfer, pressures are exerted on and by legislators and state executives for performance-oriented credit measures. In fields where precise evidence of the meaning of credits is needed, such as admission to professional schools, performance measures (tests) were long ago added to the credit record, and the scores attained carry substantial weight in the selection process. In medical school admissions, where qualified applicants outnumber spaces, the amount of credit in required subjects, the quality of the work completed (grades), test scores on the Medical Admission Test, and the interview are determinants in the decision. The proper number of credits in the right courses will get the applicant into the selection process for medical school; the credits will not alone lead to selection.

Administratively, the addition of performance measures to a credit system introduces another element, but is quite feasible. Indeed, it seems likely that the system will be supplemented with additional performance measures and that candidates for degrees may be required to demonstrate specific competences beyond hours of course work completed. Administrators prefer the simplicity of a time-based credit system, but when the need is demonstrated, they can and will operate a multiple criterion system based both on credits completed and on performance measured.

Any given institution will find it is a big step from integrating performance requirements and credits received into a credentialing process and that it is an even greater step to comply with some standard of performance set for all credentials of a particular type awarded by all institutions. The latter step, if adopted, will require some procedure for agreeing on what performance is to be measured, how it is to be assessed, and what weight it shall carry for the award of the degree. Our present decentralized system of awarding educational credentials does not readily accommodate this kind of requirement, nor do most educators believe it is desirable.

9. See Jonathan R. Warren, "Awarding Credit," in *Planning Non-Traditional Programs,* by K. Patricia Cross, John R. Valley, and associates, pp. 125–26.

Unless higher education can develop some common meanings beyond number of credits required in diverse programs that lead to similar degrees (such as A.A. or B.S.), the heterogeneous characteristics of credentials will not only continue but also continue to be a big problem.

However, if an institution could say, This graduate can read at a specified level of speed and comprehension, or, This graduate has had a six months' internship in a job, or, This graduate has lived for a year in Germany as a part of his education—to use examples of three different kinds of performance measures—it would be adding to its credentials information useful to the public.

Performance measures can be a means of institutional accountability as well as indications of how well an individual student has performed. If the measures and levels of performance required by the institution for award of its credential are indicators which the public values (such as success in getting a job), then performance measures would be an effective accountability measure as well; that is, if an institution's students did well on the performance measure, the public would upgrade the institution's rating. If performance measures help demonstrate the value of an institution's degrees to potential students and to the public, then their use is likely to spread as a means to counteract public concern about the value or lack of value of a degree.

The other administrative problem with student credits is the increasing diversity of educational experiences that are being developed to meet the needs of an increasingly diverse student clientele.[10] Programs that are based, not on time, but on achievement of specified competences offer obvious difficulties in translating desired outcomes into conventional credit measures. In this sense, the credit system is seen as a problem or barrier to the new programs that don't "fit." Furthermore, among traditionalist colleges and universities, there

10. A survey of nontraditional programs (some of which use time-based credit measures) was made by the Center for Research and Development in Higher Education, University of California, Berkeley, for the ·Commission on Non-Traditional Study; see the commission report, *Diversity by Design*, pp. 29–31.

are enough traditionalist administrators—"business as usual"
—to create problems for innovations of all kinds. Yet the
rapid expansion of innovative programs suggests that in institutions motivated to try new approaches and to reach new
groups of students, the credit system and other administrative
procedures do not create major barriers.

During the next decade, leaders in postsecondary education
will encounter pressures that will predispose them to try new
things. Most institutions will need to: (1) compete effectively
for adult students by providing programs designed to meet
their learning needs and offered at times and places that are
attractive to the students; (2) provide programs that prepare
students more effectively for an increasingly tight job market;
(3) operate efficient programs; resources are unlikely to grow
faster than inflation; and (4) demonstrate the effectiveness
of their efforts to potential students, the public, and legislators.

These challenges will put a premium on innovation and
flexibility and will force the administrative process to be
adaptable to new ideas. Performance-based credit will be an
essential for many innovative programs. Inasmuch as there
is already a need for performance measures to help assess the
variability in the meaning of credit, it seems likely that performance-based credit will become a more widespread part of
the credit and credentialing system. Just as credit cards in
business have not driven out the use of money, conventional
time-based credits and performance-based activities will both
be used in accounting for student learning. Administrators
will have to make adjustments to accommodate the complexities of a dual system.

Credit as a Measure of Faculty Activity

Faculty performance in teaching can be thought of as the
other side of the coin of student performance in learning and
is the concept behind the credit hour as a measure for faculty
activity. This use developed, not from a conceptual model, but
because the credit hour was a readily available measure of
faculty effort in instruction. In most institutions, other measures were not available.

Faculty members view themselves as self-regulating professionals who conform to the minimum scheduling and supervisory activity essential for the school to function; in other respects, however, they feel they should be independent professionals. Administrators have adapted to the faculty view of how the work should be organized. This arrangement keeps peace in the family so long as administrators can obtain the resources needed without presenting detailed evidence about the amount, kind, or quality of each faculty member's work.

As budgets for higher education grow, criticism of education and other social institutions has increased. Partly in consequence, legislatures and state budget officers, sometimes assisted by the new state higher education agencies, are making more precise demands for accountability. State fiscal analysts are aware that personnel costs are the largest part of college and university budgets and that there is little information about what the faculty members do to earn their salaries.

Credit hour data on faculty, even when available, represent only a small part of the faculty activity picture. Public universities in many states have been required to develop faculty activity reports that cover all assigned duties and the average hours spent on each.[11] As comprehensive measurements of faculty activity become part of accountability requirements, credit hour measures of faculty activity are likely to decline in importance.

Collective bargaining often includes negotiations about conditions of work and faculty activity. In such instances, again, comprehensive reports will be required on whatever areas of duties the collective bargaining process is concerned with. Private higher education is under less external pressure to develop detailed faculty activity measurements except as they are used by the administration to determine costs, to allocate new positions, or otherwise to manage the institution.

Innovative educational programs that emphasize the role of faculty members in nonclassroom activities such as preparation of curriculum materials, evaluation, and counseling, also bring the inadequacies of faculty credit hour measures

11. See NCHEMS, *Faculty Activity Analysis: Interpretation and Uses of Data*; see also discussion in Suslow, "Course Credits as Measures of Faculty/Student Effort," pp. 20–21.

into focus. If credit hour productivity is the basis for budget allocations to the institution or to departments within the institution, there will be pressure on all innovative programs to translate their activities into credit hour terms. From the standpoint of an institution's administrators, it is just as easy to develop direct estimates of budget requirements for nontraditional programs as to translate the estimates into some kind of faculty credit hour equivalency, but the institution may be under external pressure to convert everything into the common denominator of "credits" to fit the budget-justification system.

More complex measures of faculty activity will come into use in more public institutions and systems and may include credit hour productivity as one part of the faculty activity accounting system. Administratively, the translation of all activities into credit hour equivalents will be cumbersome. The conversion to credit hours will probably occur principally in states where formulas require it for expressing needs for instructional funding or where minimum work loads, stated in credit hours, are specified by the legislature or the governor. In other states, direct measures of the various faculty activities will be developed as needed to justify budget requests, negotiate with unions, and complete a picture of what the faculty members are actually doing. Suslow quotes a faculty senate report at the University of California, Berkeley, which attacks the whole idea of refined analysis of faculty activities as a "fundamentally misleading way of approaching the problem of effectiveness."[12] Detailed activity analysis is inconsistent with faculty members' self-perception as independent professionals, and they are likely to resist it on both logical and political grounds.

Even when faculty activities are assessed comprehensively through a faculty activity report, the credit hour may continue to be the basic unit for reporting instructional activity. From the perspective of innovative program managers, this measure is gross. Credit hour measures of instructional activity imply that instruction is a unitary process, with the classroom

12. Suslow, "Course Credits as Measures of Faculty/Student Effort," p. 22.

contact between teacher and students at the center. "Instruction," however, includes many interrelated functions: academic advisement, career advisement, curriculum organization and revision, instruction, evaluation, and certification. Inasmuch as innovative programs often emphasize nonclassroom instructional activities, a faculty activity system that reports the various parts of the instructional process could properly account for both innovative and traditional instructional activities. There have been proposals to "unbundle" the instructional function into its components[13] so that programs could be adjusted to student needs (for example, not all students may need career counseling or classroom instruction). If education moves in this direction, credit hour measures of faculty activity will be replaced by a different set of faculty activity measures.

Faculty activity reports and credit hour measurement tell incompletely *what* the faculty members are doing or are assigned to do, but nothing about the effectiveness of their activities. As administrators in public institutions come under external pressure to provide accountability information about faculty, "credit hours produced" will probably become only one part of faculty activity reports that include more comprehensive procedures. Comprehensive measures of faculty activity are relatively easy to design. The NCHEMS products are an example of the broader approach; the more comprehensive procedures will help fit the realities of innovative programs. Their use will be resisted because they run counter to the concepts of faculty autonomy and of faculty members as self-regulating professionals. Despite faculty resistance, accountability requirements will lead to more administrative reporting about faculty activity.

The Credit Measure in Budget Requests and Allocations

The budget is the principal management tool in higher education. In institutions which deemphasize hierarchical administrative relationships, as colleges and universities do, the

13. George Weathersby, "The Unbudget," in *Ninth Biennial Legislative Work Conference*, p. 42.

budget assumes an even greater role. As indicated earlier, in a majority of states, credit measures have become a principal factor in the justification of instructional fund needs in the development of the budget requests for public institutions. In about two-thirds of the states, an objective formula is used to develop a part of the budget request.[14] The part of the formula pertaining to instruction employs credit hours as a measure of effort or as an indicator of funding needs either directly or indirectly by converting them into full-time equivalent faculty members. A few funding formulas also recognize noncredit activities, often translated into continuing education units (CEU's), as a part of instructional activity.

In no state is the total budget request based solely on objective factors. Glenny's study of state budgeting included a sample of nine states in which formulas were used. In three of the nine, less than half of the budget request was determined by formulas; in two, 50–80 percent of the request employed formula factors; and in the remaining four states, over 80 percent (but less than 100 percent) was set through objective factors.[15] Thus, in most states, the formulation for the budget request provides leeway for unusual programs and nonstandard situations. With respect to the use of credit measures in the budget process in the Glenny sample, only in six of the seventeen states was a formula used in the instructional area; in ten others, credit hours or full-time equivalent students were used as indicators to test the reasonableness of requests for instructional funding,[16] but not as direct elements in formula computations of fund requirements. These findings suggest considerable flexibility in how budget recommendations are developed and room in the process to accommodate nontraditional and innovative programs. However, in most states an incremental (last year's base budget plus improvements) approach to budgeting is still used, and in this budget process new programs of any kind—innovative instruction,

14. See Francis McK. Gross, "A Comparative Analysis of the Existing Budget Formulas Used for Justifying Budget Requests for Allocating Funds for the Operating Expenses of State-Supported Colleges and Universities."

15. Glenny, *State Budgeting,* table 40 (p. 160).

16. Ibid., table 38 (p. 156).

public service, library operations, or whatever—face greater difficulty in obtaining approval than do ongoing programs.

In many states the budget request process is separate from the budget management process that follows the appropriation. In the sample states studied by Glenny, in six states lump sums were appropriated to individual campuses or systems; in nine, the appropriation had no more than ten subdivisions (lines) in institutional budgets, and in only three were line items more detailed.[17] Thus even where the budget request is derived through a credit hour formula, the institution may receive a lump sum appropriation and have considerable flexibility in allocating and reallocating funds to special activities.

In general, a budget process using credit as a measure of instructional activity appears to include sufficient flexibility for innovation and nontraditional education. This generality is subject to two qualifications: (1) the overall level of funding and the percentage growth in the budget, and (2) the priorities of the institutional decision makers, who are mostly administrators but who are affected by faculty opinion. A flexible system with favorably inclined decision makers will not provide support for new programs if funding has been cut, and a flexible system with substantial fund increases will not provide funds for new and innovative programs if the decision makers' priorities are elsewhere.

The perceptions of administrators of nontraditionl programs differ considerably from the budget process described by Glenny. Meeth surveyed more than three hundred administrators of nontraditional programs to discover barriers to management of their programs. About 36 percent of the respondents reported serious difficulty with funding procedures. Meeth reports, "From this investigation, it became clear that frustration with state and federal funding policies runs high in nontraditional education."[18] Although no control measure of budget frustrations experienced by other administrators is available, it would be surprising if less than a third of

17. Ibid., table 74 (p. 228).
18. L. Richard Meeth, *Government Funding Policies and Nontraditional Programs*, specifically "Summary," p. 1.

any administrative group reported serious problems with the budget process. Nontraditional program administrators share the traditional administrative view of the budget process, that it seriously limits their freedom of action.

Meeth lists a number of problems that nontraditional program administrators encounter with budgets and fiscal procedures, only a couple of which concern the use of credit measures in the budget process. As for recommendations for improvements, the nontraditional program administrators suggest that a percentage in budgets be set aside for innovative and nontraditional programs; that budget requests include provision for nonformula items (this already occurs in all states); and that a formula be developed, based on competence achievement rather than credit hours.[19]

The last recommendation has some interesting possibilities. In no state do the budgeting practices now provide significant funding based on performance. Several states (Hawaii, Rhode Island, Tennessee, and Washington) are exploring the possibilities. None of these explorations, however, suggest that performance funding be limited to nontraditional or innovative programs. In Tennessee, the Higher Education Commission has received grants, from the Fund for the Improvement of Postsecondary Education and the W. K. Kellogg Foundation, to develop ways of introducing performance concepts into the budget process.[20] Even if only a small portion of the budget were used to fund the effective performance of educational functions, the effects on the educational process could be substantial.

The development of performance measures that reflect student learning has a parallel in the efforts to introduce performance measures into the budget process. The "productivity" approach to budgeting for service functions like education is fairly recent and raises a complex set of questions about the relation of resources to achievements and outputs, the measurement of outputs, and the application of performance concepts to a diverse set of institutions with a diversity of stu-

19. Ibid., pp. 10–12.
20. Tennessee Higher Education Commission, "Models for Higher Education Evaluation," a status report and plan of action.

dents.[21] These issues have not been resolved in practice, and the reward of achievements in the budget process is still in an experimental stage. If indicators of student learning were used as an element to allocate a small part of the budget (3–5 percent), institutions would have a strong incentive to improve student achievements and the measurement of achievement, and institutions also would be more likely to adopt performance measures for individual student records.

The criticism that the use of credit measures in the budget process deters innovation and nontraditional education seems misplaced. Even now, most budget request and budget management systems include enough flexibility to provide resources for innovative programs but only if institutional and state system administrators assign adequate priority to them. The problem is not so much the budget system but the decision makers who do not give the innovative programs enough priority to assure their funding.

The real criticism of the budget process is that, like the traditional credit system, it is based on activities rather than accomplishments, on last year's base rather than this year's outputs. Inasmuch as the budget is the principal educational management tool, budgeting reform should be a high priority for those concerned with development and support of innovative education. Reform should focus less on the rigidities of objective measures (including credit hour measures) than on the introduction of performance and achievement concepts into the budget process.

Use of Credits in Planning and Evaluation

Credit-based measures of instructional activity are the building blocks for most institutional and state plans and future projections of instructional activity, its costs, and its personnel requirements. Traditional credit measures exclude several important educational activities (noncredit programs, for example) and tend to focus on the activities of traditional

21. For a review of issues, see Richard J. Meisinger, Jr., Ralph Purves, and Frank Schmidtlein, "Productivity from an Interorganization Perspective," in *Measuring and Increasing Academic Productivity,* ed. Robert Wallhaus.

full-time students. There is danger, therefore, that planning will give insufficient attention to off-campus, adult, and non-traditional programs. This weakness characterized several state plans developed during the 1960s, which emphasized campus growth and the development and expansion of traditional programs. States have now become concerned about the delivery of educational programs and services to nontraditional students in off-campus settings. Besides the budgetary implications of excessive duplication of off-campus programs, there are the quality issues. Can nontraditional programs be as effective as traditional programs? These interrelated issues of new clienteles, new delivery mechanisms, and off-campus educational quality rank high among the planning concerns in the states today.

In a period of limited or no growth, state agencies are also concerned about approving new programs and reviewing existing programs. Credit measures play an important role in both program approval and program review. Meeth states: "In one form or another state program approval has curtailed more nontraditional education than any other single regulation."[22] He gives several examples. In teacher education, professional certification requirements are usually phrased in terms of credit hours completed; thus persons who complete competence-based programs or time-shortened programs may be prevented from meeting certification requirements. He also cites licensing boards in nursing, accounting, and engineering as often adhering to rigid traditional requirements, phrased in credit hour terms, which eliminate nontraditional paths to licensure. On the other hand, he points to the variability among state licensing boards, some of which are quite amenable to new approaches. For example, more than a third of the states are developing competence-based teacher certification programs, a move that indicates some sensitivity.

Licensing boards and state agencies that approve degree-granting institutions for operation in the state emphasize objective standards: they operate in a legal environment

22. Meeth, *Government Funding Policies*, p. 14.

where they must be able to justify their decisions—particularly the decision to prevent an institution from operating—against legal challenges. Subjective judgments may be attacked as arbitrary or political, and persons or institutions adversely affected will be quick to complain about possible bias. Thus, licensing boards are loath to accept deviations from their established procedures and unlikely to be receptive to innovative ways of meeting their requirements.

The voluntary accreditation by regional associations has moved away from primary dependence on objective measures as indicators of quality and toward emphasizing the assessment of programs in relation to the program's own goals and objectives. Credit hour measures may be examined as indicators of faculty overload or of an institution's achievement of its own goals and objectives, but credit measures play a limited role in the process. Some professional accrediting groups, by contrast, use more objective measurement, including standards about credit hour loads in the professional schools. Although some accreditation standards still are based on traditional credit measures, the trend among the regional accrediting associations has been toward greater flexibility in the application of standards and the adoption of procedures for considering and evaluating innovative and nontraditional programs as special cases.

A majority of state coordinating and governing agencies for higher education review and approve new programs, and almost half also have procedures for reviewing ongoing programs. In some of the reviews of ongoing programs, the volume of credits produced in each program are examined, and low-producing departments are identified for fuller review and study. The agencies use credit measures as indicators, but do not depend solely on credit production figures to determine whether a program will be continued. The new program review activities focus for the most part on the need for the program, its costs, its potential quality, and the relationship of the program to other programs in the state. Credit hour data enter the process, but are only one of many determinants in the review and approval process.

Making Credits More Useful

Credit and credentials are integral to the administrative process in American higher education. The accounting for the educational accomplishments of students is done largely with time-based credit units, and, like any other accounting procedure, it affects the administration of education. Credits are used as measures in the accounting for faculty activity and as measures of instructional activity in budget requests and in the management and administration of the budget.

There is congruence in the approach that institutions use to account for student educational activities, for faculty personnel, and for the allocation and use of resources. Student credits measure completion of a unit of education but they don't measure how much was learned; the actual achievement levels of students who have similar credits vary substantially. Faculty activity too is estimated quantitatively, using credit as a measure of instructional effort, but it tells little about how well the faculty members taught or how well the students learned. In budget management, the principle is similar: funds are allocated to activities measured by credits, but no measure of performance or outcomes is applied as a basis for allocating funds.

In none of these areas is quality of effort emphasized by measurement and accounting procedures.[23] Quality is judged by faculty peers and by administrators; students are graded and assessed by faculty judgmental procedures. The process is carried out separately within each department, school, and institution. The credit unit thus has a highly variable meaning. The concept of faculty members as independent professionals who are responsible for their own efforts and who should have the fewest restraints possible placed on their freedom is central to the way most colleges and universities are organized. The time unit measure used in the credit system is consistent with the university approach to the faculty role, and the procedures for developing and managing the

23. See S. S. Micek, *Outcome-Oriented Planning in Higher Education,* and S. S. Micek, A. L. Service, and Y. S. Lee, *Outcome Measures and Procedures Manual.*

budget are also consistent with the way the faculty is managed.

As external and internal pressures have grown for greater accountability and for better evidence about the quality of education, more competence-based programs which use outcome measures have been developed. Some of these are difficult to fit into the existing credit system, and it is likely that more performance-based credit measures will be developed, but that the basic unit of credit will still be time-based.

The same accountability pressures are likely to bring about detailed recording of faculty activities and to require more evidence about the effectiveness of those activities. The activity and effectiveness evidence is important for nontraditional programs which use faculty members in a variety of ways and which do not organize the learning experience around the course taught in the classroom. New kinds of student credit produced by new kinds of organization of the learning process lead to new faculty activities and new types of accounting for faculty effort.

Changes in the teaching and learning process and in faculty roles also will bring changes in the budget process and in the resource allocation priorities that are built into the budget process. If the budget process provides for allocating some resources according to how well the educational job is being done, there will be support for existing performance-based activities and incentive to start others. Innovative program managers report frustration with the standard budget process and with problems in adapting to conventional credit accounting for degrees. They question the basis for justifying the budget and the methods for allocating faculty time.

One virtue of our decentralized system of education is that individual institutions can adapt to the new approaches, and administrative changes can be made to accommodate new bases for credit and credentials, new ways of managing the educational process, and new roles for faculty members. Changes are under way, and the next decade will see additional internal and external pressures for educational programs that serve diverse student clienteles, emphasize outcomes rather than time spent, and require new roles for faculty members.

The budget process needs to give more emphasis to the funding of performance rather than activity. If such a change occurs, it will provide rewards to faculty members and motivate them to emphasize outcomes, which in turn will provide impetus to educational processes that produce favorable outcomes. The recognition of achievement through award of performance-based credit and credentials will complete the circle.

Institutional changes in requirements for credentials and in the measurement and accounting for performance will be difficult to standardize across institutions.[24] As long as the 3,000 colleges and 2,000–4,000 other postsecondary institutions that provide programs which may be accepted toward educational credentials are each responsible for their respective definitions of quality, quality will vary widely among institutions. If state funds are to be allocated in part on how well institutions educate students, in addition to the standard funding based on how many students are educated, then measures of quality will be needed as a part of the budget process.

The budget as a resource allocation plan is the key to changes in management, in faculty performance, and in ways to encourage student learning and to account for and credential that learning. The credit and credentialing system is, in essence, a means of accounting for student learning. To the extent that the educational system encourages and emphasizes achievements and competences, the credit system can and will reflect those attributes in its recognition of new credit measures.

Progress will not be rapid, because consensus must be developed about what is to be measured and how, and how the results will be fitted into the credentialing process. The key to progress probably lies in the budget process. If the budget

24. See Donald P. Hoyt, "Competence as a Basis for Credit and Credentialing" in the present volume for an assessment of the difficulties in implementing the competence concept.

process provides some funds that reward more effective performance, then it will also encourage recognition of achievement measures in the credit system. If the budget includes some performance-related funding, the accounting system for student learning is also likely to recognize accomplishments for credits.

PART III

TASK FORCE RECOMMENDATIONS

The recommendations and report of the Task Force on Educational Credit and Credentials were approved by the Commission on Educational Credit of the American Council on Education on November 22, 1977. The recommendations and a summary report by the Task Force were endorsed by the Council's Board of Directors on January 30, 1978.

CHAPTER 9

The Recommendations

The recommendations that follow have been formulated with the overriding purpose of improving the quality of information conveyed by educational credit and credentials. Other aims are:

- To encourage lifelong learning and the maximum use of all educational resources
- To recognize educational accomplishment, regardless of how or where that accomplishment is attained
- To improve the appreciation and understanding of the proper basis for awarding credit and credentials
- To encourage appropriate uses by all segments of society of the credentials conferred by institutions of postsecondary education
- To develop improved and expanded procedures for assessing educational accomplishment in order to increase flexibility for learners to meet educational requirements, particularly at the undergraduate level
- To reduce unnecessary barriers that restrict student mobility and access to educational programs
- To improve articulation among postsecondary institutions and programs and the extrainstitutional learning experiences available in society, including the improved placement of students in educational programs
- To improve educational credentials as alternatives to governmental and voluntary certification for identifying the qualified

The recommendations are intended to apply broadly across postsecondary education—to vocational, technical, professional, general/liberal education, and the disciplines; to pub-

221

lic, private nonprofit, and proprietary institutions; and to non-degree, undergraduate, and, less generally, graduate programs. Because curricula in postsecondary education are diverse and the educational objectives of students are wide-ranging, the extent to which the recommendations can be implemented will vary from program to program and from institution to institution.

RECOMMENDATION ONE

The basic system of credit and credentials for postsecondary education should be retained, but it should be modified to serve more adequately present-day educational and social needs.

Credit and credentials permeate postsecondary education and have substantial roots in the economic and social system. Funding formulas, salary and wage scales, qualification for employment, and social standing, for example, often make use of the present system. The credit and credential system has the decided advantage of being generally understood, both in its operation and its imperfections. That basis of understanding suggests that the present system should be modified to meet present-day needs rather than be replaced by a new system— assuming that a better system could be conceptualized and designed.

The system's shortcomings derive mainly from the inadequacy and inaccuracy of the information conveyed, from reluctance to deviate from commonly accepted time frames and places and modes of instruction, and from infrequent use of nonclassroom educational requirements (work-study, theses, comprehensive examinations, etc.), particularly at the undergraduate level. These shortcomings can be corrected by giving increased emphasis to assessing and communicating educational accomplishment and its implications for performance in work and social settings, to designing more-flexible educational programs, and to incorporating the results of varied educational experiences into the current system of credit and credentials.

The system has already shown considerable strength and flexibility in adapting to the changing needs of education and society. It is being used to some extent to record extrainstitutional learning, learning measured by examinations, experiential learning, independent study, and self-paced instruction. For many years, the system has been flexible enough to combine classroom and laboratory instruction with learning demonstrated by such means as writing theses and passing comprehensive examinations. This characteristic of the system has been especially evident at the graduate level.

The problems inherent in trying to conceptualize, design, and implement a new system and the probable educational and social repercussions strongly suggest that, at this time, adoption of a strategy aimed at accepting but modifying the current system is clearly the preferable and more promising course.

RECOMMENDATION TWO

A. The primary responsibility for awarding degrees should remain with the faculties, administrations, and boards of control of accredited institutions that are legally authorized to grant such formal recognition.

The widespread use and acceptance of degrees awarded by postsecondary education institutions can largely be attributed to the following: (1) faculties and administrations that have, by and large, performed in a socially responsible manner, (2) boards of control that have exercised general oversight of the academic enterprise for the public or for broadly based constituencies but that have delegated extensive responsibility to the faculty and administration of institutions, and (3) a system of peer review that has been exercised through nongovernmental accreditation. Degree-granting institutions that lack any one of the three components should be severely limited in number and in the total proportion of degrees awarded. Degree-granting arrangements that deviate from the norm should be authorized only for sound social reasons and should serve purposes that are primarily educational.[1]

Degrees will continue to be socially useful only if they retain their uniqueness. That uniqueness flows from the historical and central role of faculties in designing educational programs, in establishing requirements for degrees, and in certifying and setting standards for educational accomplishment.

Qualified faculties, with substantial academic independence, with their responsibility delegated to them by boards of control, and with peer review provided by nongovernmental accreditation, are the best sources in society for the expertise needed to exercise the degree-granting function. In a complex, technological society, education for work requirements must be balanced with cultural considerations in education. While the importance of education for work cannot be minimized, neither can the importance of education designed to advance the understanding and quality of cultural values, the environment, the human condition, and to develop analytical, communication, quantitative, and synthesizing skills. The composition and organization of faculties, though not guaranteeing the avoidance of narrow, self-seeking interests, tends to bring balance to these considerations.

External degree programs embodying the above characteristics for granting degrees are useful and valid means of certifying educational accomplishment and should be considered acceptable alternatives to traditional degree programs.

> *B. Institutions or organizations that lack the proper degree-granting structure described above should limit their awards to certificates or other credentials whose designations are clearly distinguishable from degrees. Undergraduate degrees should not be awarded by any institution for programs that lack a general/liberal education component.*

---

1. See "Statement of Principles Regarding Degree Granting by Federal Agencies," *Higher Education and National Affairs* (American Council on Education) October 29, 1976, p. 3.

The important educational role played by institutions which lack the characteristics necessary for the award of degrees is increasingly being recognized, particularly in the areas of preparation for employment and upgrading of employment skills. Appropriate recognition for educational accomplishment attained in these settings is in the interests of both society and the individual. However, inasmuch as the primary purpose of educational awards is to communicate the meaning and type of educational accomplishment, designations for credentials awarded for these programs should remain distinct from degrees.

For reasons discussed in Recommendation Three, awards by any institution for undergraduate-level programs that lack a general/liberal education component should not be designated as degrees.

RECOMMENDATION THREE

Associate degrees and bachelor's degrees should attest to at least the following three types of accomplishment:

1. *Accomplishment specified by the awarding institution as necessary for the development of a broadly educated person, including familiarity with general areas of knowledge;*
2. *Competence in analytical, communication, quantitative, and synthesizing skills;*
3. *Accomplishment in a specialized area of study covering a set of integrated learnings requiring analysis, understanding of principles that have judgmental application, and a theoretical knowledge base.*[2]

Requirements for credentials designated as degrees have broad social implications: The refinement of academic skills and the extension of opportunities for general/liberal education beyond the secondary school undergirds a democratic

2. Associate degrees designed primarily as the general/liberal education component of the baccalaureate degree may be appropriately excepted from this requirement. In such cases, specialization is required for the baccalaureate.

society and enhances personal development. These general but highly refined competences attained through arduous study are essential for an informed citizenry and to the individual and should be encouraged by formal recognition. Also essential to society and the individual is the recognition of specialized competences related to the work setting.

A credential designated as a "degree" has been the primary device used by colleges and universities to recognize learning of the depth, breadth, and rigor associated with college study. The meaning of the undergraduate degree should be protected to preserve its legitimacy as an accolade for educational accomplishment at higher and broader levels of learning. The learning which the degree certifies should extend beyond the narrower educational qualifications for employment to include as well knowledge and skills characteristic of a broadly educated person.

Determining what constitutes a broadly educated person is difficult, and distinctions between higher and other learning are admittedly abstract. But the impact on the social fabric of appropriately recognizing and rewarding learning makes it important for both concepts to be discussed.

Certain qualities of degree-level learning reduce the abstruseness. These qualities include the attainment of a working familiarity with general areas of knowledge that begins the lifelong process of broadening and deepening the understanding of culture and environment; further refinement of personal values which motivate assumption of civic and social responsibilities; and the development of skills essential to an independent and resourceful learner—ideally, the development of the ethos of lifelong learning. Those skills include the proficient use of an array of educational resources available in the society and the ability to learn in many settings and by means of a variety of instructional modes.

At the associate and baccalaureate levels of accomplishment, certain other factors should characterize the learning. The emphasis should be on acquiring competence in different modes of thought and in analytical, communication, quantitative, and synthesizing skills, including accomplishment in a wide range of subject matter. Particularly at the baccalaureate level, the learning should involve a body of theory and principles that have broad judgmental application.

The component of the degree covering accomplishment in a specialized area of study should generally conform to the characteristics of higher learning listed above, both for the academic disciplines and for learning related more directly to entry-level employment. The hallmark for occupational programs which use the degree as a credential should be a general/liberal education component that enhances competent judgment and application of knowledge in the work setting.

Stressing general/liberal education and in-depth, rigorous study in specialized areas does not denigrate or diminish, to either the individual or society, the importance of educational programs or institutions that focus solely on preparation for employment. But if recognizing and rewarding educational accomplishment are to be kept socially useful, the distinctions between awards for the completion of such programs and awards for the broader educational objectives associated with a degree should remain clear.

RECOMMENDATION FOUR

Each credential-granting institution should clearly define, to the extent possible, the meaning of the certificates and degrees it awards.

So diverse are the curricula and objectives of postsecondary education and so pluralistic are the forms of control that the meaning of students' educational accomplishments cannot be standardized with precision. Moreover, even if the art and science of assessing and describing educational accomplishment were to become such that a precise interinstitutional credit and credentialing system were possible, it probably would run counter to ingrained educational philosophy. Diverse, pluralistic postsecondary education, encompassing the concept of institutional autonomy, is a credo commanding wide allegiance.

That allegiance, however, should be tempered by careful assessment of how society uses educational credentials and how that use affects people, both those who hold such status and those who do not. Society's use of educational credentials, particularly for employment purposes, tends to assume standardization of meaning; in exception are the certificates and degrees of a limited number of colleges and universities which have attained and successfully perpetuated reputations for high quality.

Given the educational and social uses of educational credentials, institutions should seek to improve the quality of information conveyed by the credentials they confer. Degree designations and a transcript listing of course titles and grades fall short in meeting today's needs for accurate and adequate information on the qualifications of credential holders.

Narrative definitions would more adequately meet the needs of employers and other users and, over the long run, would be worth the effort and resources required to formulate the statements. If the certificate or the degree is directly related to qualification for employment, the definition should set forth, to the extent possible, the competences certified by the credential. All degree definitions should directly address the levels of the analytical, communication, quantitative, and synthesizing skills attained.

The specificity of definitions will, and should, vary by program. In some cases, an appropriate response may be a narrative description which defines a program of study that the holder successfully completed; in other cases, very specific statements regarding the student's competences may be possible and desirable.

RECOMMENDATION FIVE

Institutions should give careful attention to the use of degree designations, to include consistent use of the terms "arts" and "science."

Even with the availability of narrative definitions of degrees, degree designations—the most succinct communicators of educational accomplishment—will continue to be the only level of information considered by many users. Clarity, then, with respect to degree designations will continue to be important.

The terms "arts" and "science" have traditionally been used as part of degree designations to distinguish between broad types of educational programs. Practices among institutions as well as within institutions in using the terms have not always been consistent, with a resulting loss of clarity.

Where either term is used in the designation, its significance should be established in the narrative definition for the degree. The use of "arts" or "science" across an institution should be consistent and the terms should be used only to make substantive distinctions among programs. In general, the "arts" should be used for the arts, humanities, and letters, and the term "science" for the sciences and applied sciences. Moreover, the terms should be generally limited to degrees in broad academic programs as opposed to programs more occupationally and professionally oriented. In the latter case, degree designations of only two components—level of accomplishment (e.g., associate, baccalaureate) and area of specialization (e.g., nursing, business administration) will add clarity to the information communicated by a degree designation.[3]

RECOMMENDATION SIX

Each postsecondary education institution should clearly define the meaning of the credit units it awards. Statements of educational accomplishment, as explicit as possible, should be made for each credit unit.

Credit units, such as courses and other increments of verified learning, represent the most basic and detailed level of information conveyed by credits and credentials. At this level of detail, the present system provides useful but inadequate information. The course titles listed on transcripts and the

3. Recommendations on appropriate usage for graduate degrees have been made by the Council of Graduate Schools in *The Master's Degree: A Policy Statement*, pp. 5–6.

course descriptions in catalogs are often ambiguous and generate little confidence that they reflect with precision the desired or actual learning outcomes.

Accurate, adequate descriptions of credit units would be helpful to employers who need the additional detail in determining qualification for employment, to educational counselors in placing students who transfer or change educational objectives, to students in choosing courses, and to students and others who seek increased accountability for the instructional process. Accurate information would also greatly enhance the possibility that educational accomplishment attained in extrainstitutional circumstances could be matched with the requirements for certificates and degrees.

RECOMMENDATION SEVEN

Postsecondary education, through its organizations, should work toward common meanings for certificates and for degrees that are in the same area of specialization and at the same level of accomplishment. Such efforts should include improvement of the accuracy and adequacy of descriptions of educational accomplishment represented by credit units as well as interinstitutional experimentation with common assessment instruments as one means of measuring and certifying analytical, communication, quantitative, and synthesizing skills.

The similar or identical certificate and degree designations used by thousands of institutions has created expectations that the credentialed hold certain educational accomplishments and competences in common. Such expectations are especially noticeable with respect to the component of the degree used to qualify for employment and with respect to analytical, communication, quantitative, and synthesizing skills.

Organized efforts to provide common meanings for degrees on an interinstitutional basis have usually taken the form of specialized accreditation of curricula by occupational associations or organizations of components of institutions. Specialized accreditation is a defensible activity in some fields because it is related to protection of the public health and safety. However, specialized accreditation of all curricula would be chaotic and a grossly expensive way of approaching the problem.

Recent conceptual and technological advances in the design of information systems and in information processing have potential application on an interinstitutional basis for describing and reporting educational accomplishment. It is perhaps possible to design an information system that could be used throughout postsecondary education but that would leave with institutional faculty the primary responsibility for formulating descriptions for credit units and definitions of degrees. Such a system would not only enhance diversity by providing adequate and accurate descriptions of educational programs but would also facilitate standardization of minimum levels of educational outcomes where they may be desirable.

An agency representative of postsecondary education should assume responsibility for an *experimental effort* to design such an information system. The system should be developed cooperatively with academic disciplinary and professional associations, practitioners, and users of the information, and it should include suggested information components for degree definitions and descriptions of credit units. If such a system is deemed feasible, an agency should be designated to assume ongoing responsibility for developing the program and for maintaining its usefulness.

Development of such a system would be consistent with Recommendations Four, Five, and Six, and could (1) lessen the pressures that cause proliferation of specialized accrediting, (2) provide institutions and their faculties with additional means for demonstrating accountability, and (3) improve horizontal and vertical articulation among postsecondary education institutions and programs.

The most substantial body of agreement regarding the attributes of the broadly educated person centers on analytical, communication, quantitative, and synthesizing skills. Degree holders are in general expected to be at least minimally proficient in these areas, and graduates who are not reflect unfavorably on all colleges and universities. These skills are also the most susceptible to precise measurement through the use of common assessment instruments. Experimentation with interinstitutional assessment programs should be encouraged as one means for postsecondary education institutions to improve their accountability for this component of the degree.

The tests, or similar instruments, should also prove useful as a screening device for nondegree persons seeking to qualify for employment. For occupations requiring high-level analytical, communication, quantitative, and synthesizing skills, prospective employees could take the tests to establish whether they are comparably qualified to degree holders.

RECOMMENDATION EIGHT

Postsecondary education institutions should[4] develop alternative programs that (1) state requirements in terms of assessable educational accomplishment, and (2) permit students to demonstrate accomplishment without reference to time-bound and campus-bound instruction and learning.

Currently, the touchstone for credit and credentials is the learning achieved by qualified students during a specified period of formal instruction and study. But pedagogical theory, qualification for employment, and data on learning rates do not generally support rigid adherence to the quarter or semester time frames or the two-year and four-year time spans for earning associate and bachelor's degrees. Courses and degree programs within an institution vary significantly in rigor and difficulty, just as they do among postsecondary education institutions. Students, too, differ in academic aptitudes, inter-

---

4. This report frequently uses the wording "postsecondary education institutions should." The wording is addressed to postsecondary institutions collectively unless otherwise specified; it is not intended to mean "all postsecondary institutions should." The Task Force recognizes that, among institutions, purposes are diverse and that, for many institutions, some recommendations may be inappropriate. Each institution is, however, urged to consider each recommendation.

ests, and educational experiences, and therefore also differ in their learning abilities and rates. Intense competition for status among academic disciplines and professional programs exerts invalid but nonetheless real pressures on course structures, standardization of time frames, and methods for earning degrees.

For at least two reasons, the great bulk of learning and instruction probably must continue to be delivered in modular form despite its inherent pedagogical limitations: society must, of necessity, set limits on the resources it can devote to mass postsecondary education; and the use of courses and specified time frames for earning credentials is a comfortable, preferred, and productive learning style for many students.

On the other hand, educational programs that are not bounded by time or by places and types of instruction need to become more abundant for high achievers recently graduated from secondary schools, for highly motivated adults who return to formal study after considerable work experience and extrainstitutional learning, and for all students who, for sound educational reasons, can combine work with study. Flexible programs would encourage undergraduate learners to use self-directed study, correspondence and media instruction, internships, and other nonclassroom learning modes. Flexible programs and the learning modes cited above all contribute to inculcating the ethos of lifelong learning and lessening dependence on time-bound and place-bound instruction and learning.

RECOMMENDATION NINE

Postsecondary education institutions, individually and through interinstitutional efforts, should give high priority to developing improved, technically sound approaches for evaluating educational accomplishment attained under their sponsorship and for assessing equivalent learning attained in extrainstitutional settings.

Evaluation of educational accomplishment is the sine qua non of credit and credentials. Without verification of the competences, knowledge, and skills that mark educational accomplishment, certification is meaningless. The reason for technically reliable and valid evaluation of educational accomplishment goes beyond certification. Effective evaluation is also essential to sound pedagogy.

Because evaluation is dependent on expert judgment, qualified faculty must predominate in the evaluation of all educational accomplishment to assure that academic standards are maintained and that evaluation instruments are valid and reliable.

Despite the critical role of faculty members in the evaluation of educational accomplishment, few have been formally trained in evaluation, and only moderate effort has been devoted to improving their evaluation skills. Institutional faculty development programs on evaluation are one means for improving the evaluation of educational accomplishment. In addition, graduate programs for preparing new faculty members should include the development of competences in evaluation.

RECOMMENDATION TEN

Postsecondary education institutions should implement policies and procedures for awarding credit for educational accomplishment attained in extrainstitutional settings. Faculties of institutions, in accordance with the established framework of individual institutional authority and responsibility, should be directly responsible for assessing the equivalency of educational accomplishment attained in extrainstitutional circumstances and for formulating policy for accepting the results of nationally validated examinations or other procedures for establishing credit equivalencies.[5]

5. The Board of Directors of the American Council on Education adopted as ACE policy a statement initiated by the ACE Commission on Educational Credit and subsequently endorsed by the Council on Postsecondary Accreditation. The statement urges institutions to develop policies and procedures for awarding credit for extrainstitutional learning. The above recommendation and the supporting narrative are similar to the policy statement. See "Awarding Credit for Extra-institutional Learning," *OEC Newsletter*, no. 48 (Spring 1977), pp. 5, 8.

Assessing extrainstitutional learning and awarding appropriate credit toward the requirements for a certificate or a degree can serve two purposes: (1) improved social fairness of certificates and degrees used as credentials to qualify for employment, and (2) proper placement of students in educational programs. The latter purpose has received insufficient attention by most faculties. Teaching students what they already know is both stultifying to them and wasteful of educational and personal resources.

Awarding credit for extrainstitutional learning should be under the control of the faculty responsible for establishing requirements for degrees. In evaluating extrainstitutional learning and formulating policy for accepting credit equivalencies established through national programs, faculties should use the following guidelines:

1. Evaluation of educational accomplishment is essential. Experience, whether it be acquired at work, in social settings, in the library, at home, or in the formal classroom, is in itself an inadequate basis for awarding credit. Increased attention to evaluation procedures and techniques is necessary when learning has been attained without participation in a program of study prescribed by an educational institution.

2. In determining whether it is appropriate to accept a student's extrainstitutional learning for credit, the governing consideration should be the student's educational objective, including the requirements for graduation. Learning should be articulated, documented, and measured in the context of the institution's role and the student's educational objective.

3. Institutions should evaluate extrainstitutional learning and award credit only in subject-matter fields in which they have available faculty expertise or where they can rely on nationally validated examinations or other equally acceptable procedures for establishing credit equivalencies. Normally, institutions should evaluate learning and award credit only in subject fields in which they offer comparable courses or curricula; however, elective credit appropriately may be excepted.

4. Institutions awarding credit for extrainstitutional learning should develop clearly stated policies and other information related to administrative responsibility, student eligibility,

means of assessment, recording of results on transcripts, storage of documentation, student fees, and maximum number of credits allowable.

5. Institution policy should provide for the periodic reevaluation of all policies and procedures related to the awarding of credit for extrainstitutional learning.

On a broader scale, agencies engaged in interinstitutional efforts to establish credit equivalencies for extrainstitutional learning have an obligation to involve academicians from postsecondary education institutions in evaluation activities, in the development of assessment instruments, and in the establishment of policy. Faculties are likewise obligated to be informed about the policies and procedures that national agencies use for establishing credit equivalencies and also to assure themselves that the national assessment instruments they use in exercising the credentialing function are valid and reliable.

RECOMMENDATION ELEVEN

Postsecondary education institutions should consider the needs of mobile and older adult students, providing them with sufficient information, orientation, and counseling on the requirements for credentials and on the policies for the transfer of credit and for the award of credit for extrainstitutional learning.

Mobile and older adult students, many of whom attend part time, have become a major clientele for postsecondary education. They have needs, educational accomplishments, and educational objectives that differ from those of the traditional college-age student. As a result, they bring both new problems and new opportunities to the institutions that seek to serve them.

The mature student may have educational accomplishments attained in extrainstitutional settings or at other institutions which are equivalent to at least some of an institution's requirements for an educational credential. Clearly enunciated institutional procedures and decision rules for acceptance of such accomplishment, certified either by other institutions or by nationally validated examinations and procedures for establishing credit equivalencies, are essential.

Because the mature student often has family or other obligations that prohibit full-time attendance, an important element in educational programming is flexibility. Flexible programming may include counseling the mature student to take advantage of nonclassroom instruction and educational resources available in the work setting or elsewhere in the community in order to satisfy the institution's requirements for a credential.

Under such circumstances, the guidance and counseling role of the institution takes on increased importance. Institutions will probably continue to provide the bulk of instruction for such students, but, by exercising a counseling and credentialing function, they can also help students increase their self-reliance and resourcefulness as lifelong learners.

RECOMMENDATION TWELVE

Postsecondary education institutions should carefully define and evaluate existing and new requirements for residence study to assure that their requirements have educational validity.

Of all the requirements for educational credentials, residence requirements are perhaps the most in need of reevaluation as justifiable requirements for credentials. As barriers to the attainment of an educational credential, they have no equal. Residence requirements vary widely in application and meaning from institution to institution. One institution may require that the student live on campus. Another may stipulate that the student study at the institution for a specified number of terms, months, or years. Yet another may require that the student be engaged in full-time study for a certain period of time. Still others may require that a specified number of credits or courses be completed in "residence." These requirements may be valid at one institution and invalid at another, or may be valid for one program within an institution and invalid for another.

In assessing the validity of residence requirements, institutions should consider the following questions:

1. Is residence study essential to the unique meaning of the institution's degree?

2. Will residence study result in identifiable and measurable educational accomplishment that cannot otherwise be attained or assessed?

3. Are the residence requirements justified by differences in curricula or in the demographic attributes of students?

a) If the requirement is for maturation or socialization purposes, are students who will complete college without intervening or concomitant work experiences treated differently from the more broadly experienced student?

b) Do the requirements differ among curricula? For example, do curricula requiring development of clinical or laboratory skills require more extensive residence instruction than curricula in general studies?

4. Are the residence requirements justifiable as a means for assuring that transfer students meet the institution's standards for educational accomplishment; that is, is a period of residence required to validate previous educational accomplishment?

RECOMMENDATION THIRTEEN

National and regional organizations, including academic disciplinary and professional associations, and state agencies should give vigorous attention to transfer policies and should encourage interinstitutional efforts to develop articulation agreements and to eliminate arbitrary transfer barriers.

Transfer is an educational issue that is becoming political. There is no guarantee that it will remain primarily an educational issue unless institutions meet their responsibilities to eliminate arbitrary barriers that have little or no educational significance. Public institutions, consistent with their roles as part of state systems of postsecondary education, bear a special responsibility for developing articulation agreements and equitable policies for serving transfer students. Singling out public institutions is not meant to deemphasize the importance of private institutions taking similar steps.

Preceding recommendations that are directed to improving the quality of information regarding educational accomplishment, if implemented, can provide institutions with the basic data needed for transfer of credit and valid placement in educational programs. But that advance will not eliminate the need for institutions to assess their policies and attitudes on the transfer of credit and to remove barriers that cannot be justified. Assessment by institutions should consider the following:

1. Transfer must be viewed in the larger context of institutional purposes and goals. If an institutional purpose is to serve the transfer student or the mature adult who has had extrainstitutional learning experiences, essential to that purpose are policies that permit equitable transfer of credit and specially designed programs that accommodate the transfer and mature student.

2. Transfer-of-credit policies should encompass educational accomplishment attained at other accredited institutions of postsecondary education as well as equivalent educational accomplishment attained in extrainstitutional situations. Consideration should be given to the American Council on Education credit recommendations, the use of credit-by-examination programs, and faculty evaluation procedures as means of validating extrainstitutional learning for transfer purposes. Whether the learning has been attained in accredited institutions or from extrainstitutional sources, the following questions should apply to the learning being considered for transfer:

a) Is the learning comparable to that required by the receiving institution?

b) Is the quality of the learning comparable to that attained at the receiving institution?

c) Is the learning appropriate to the student's educational objective?

3. Departmental transfer practices should be reviewed to assure that they are consistent with institutional policies.

4. Successful intrastate transfer and articulation agreements should be extended to regional or interstate agreements in areas where there is high mobility of students. All such efforts should have as participants private institutions whose purposes include serving transfer students and mature adults.

5. Institutions should establish mechanisms for providing services to transfer students and mature adults who have had extrainstitutional learning, including guidance and counseling and the publication of appropriate information.

RECOMMENDATION FOURTEEN

Credit for continuing education courses, where standards, course objectives, and evaluation of educational accomplishment differ from regular credit courses, should be evaluated by methods appropriate for extra-institutional learning. Direct formula conversion of measures such as the continuing education unit (CEU) is not appropriate.

Confusion exists in the academic community regarding the proper use of the continuing education unit. The confusion has arisen, perhaps, because the concept of the CEU was introduced at about the same time that nontraditional education and educational alternatives gained prominence. Some people apparently assume that the CEU is an alternative to the credit hour and that it should be used for recognizing educational alternatives and converted to units of credit on a formula basis.

The continuing education unit concept is too new to draw firm conclusions about its educational and social utility. As a record of educational experiences, it differs from other forms of recognition that can be appropriately combined and lead to the award of degrees or certificates. CEU's are useful as: (1) a measure of effort and resources expended by an institution or organization in providing the educational program, (2) a measure for people who want a record of their non-degree-related but organized educational activity; and (3) a measure for third parties (i.e., professional groups, licensing agencies, employers) who need a record of a person's participation in organized educational activity but do not need a high degree of assurance that learning actually occurred.

Because education programs awarding continuing education units are extraordinarily diverse in objectives and do not require evaluation of student accomplishment, CEU's should never be directly converted to credit units on a formula basis. That restriction does not mean that educational accomplishment attained in continuing education classes cannot be applied toward the requirements for a degree. In instances where the accomplishment is applicable, the educational accomplishment must be articulated with the student's certificate or degree objective and individually evaluated through assessment procedures appropriate for extrainstitutional learning.

RECOMMENDATION FIFTEEN

Postsecondary education institutions should formulate their roles in recredentialing consistent with their function of providing educational programs.

Although recredentialing has not yet manifested itself as revalidation of educational credentials, it is becoming commonplace in licensure and voluntary certification. Rapid advances in knowledge are being made in most fields. Additionally, there is growing recognition that competence once attained is not necessarily indefinitely retained. Therefore, recredentialing for the purpose of identifying qualified persons for continuing employment is a rapidly growing phenomenon virtually certain to gain additional momentum.

Postsecondary education institutions, working with professional associations, should begin to explore the possibility of revalidating educational credentials consistent with the credential's use as a qualifier for employment. Where continuing education programs are designed to update holders' credentials or to assure their continuing competence, evaluation of a person's educational accomplishment should be required. In both cases, principles enunciated in this report will apply.

CHAPTER 10

Needed Next Steps

The fifteen recommendations in this report have implications that go far beyond the overall objective of improving
the quality of information conveyed by credit and credentials.
Their implementation can help institutions demonstrate their
accountability to all their constituencies—students, parents,
employers; external monitoring agencies, government, and
their peer institutions; and others who support them or have
an interest in their operations.

In the era of financial stringency, institutions are being
called on to justify their programs. Students are interested,
more than before, in specific educational outcomes and are involving institutions in litigation over whether their expectations
have been realized. Parents and employers are seeking specific
information about educational programs and outcomes as the
competition intensifies among institutions for students and
among college graduates for jobs.

Inasmuch as credit and credentials reflect the programs, the
requirements, and outcomes of postsecondary education, the
recommendations, if successfully implemented, should help institutions with their external communications. Internally, the
recommendations will assist in the formulation of more con-
crete and measurable educational objectives, in the improvement of the design of educational programs and the evaluation
of their effectiveness, and in the wiser use of educational resources.

Implementing the recommendations need not be the onerous
chore that a first reading may suggest. To the contrary, many
of the recommendations point first to collective developmental
efforts by the postsecondary educational community. The results will make implementation by institutions much easier

and cost effective. Examples are the development of an information system for defining degrees and credit units and the construction of common assessment instruments to measure analytical, communication, quantitative, and synthesizing skills.

The implications noted here are by no means exhaustive. In considering the recommendations, leaders of institutions and the postsecondary educational community should ponder the implications for themselves, both for what will happen if they are implemented and what will happen if they are not.

References

American Association of State Colleges and Universities and American Association of Community and Junior Colleges. "Servicemen's Opportunity College: A Summary Report to the Carnegie Corporation of New York, October 1, 1974, through September 30, 1975." Washington: The Associations.

American College Testing Program. "Background Materials for the Workshop on Narrative Evaluation, Documentation, and Reporting." Iowa City: ACTP, 1974.

American Council on Education. Commission on Educational Credit. "Awarding Credit for Extra-institutional Learning." MS. Washington: ACE, Office on Educational Credit, 1977.

American Psychological Association. *Standards for Educational and Psychological Tests.* Washington: The Association, 1974.

"Americans on the Move." *Time,* March 16, 1976, pp. 54–64.

"Assessing Experiential Learning." In *Reflections on Experiential Learning and Its Uses.* CAEL Working Paper no. 3. Princeton, N.J.: Educational Testing Service, 1975.

Astin, Alexander W. "Academic Credit as Achievement: A Critique." *Minnesota Education* 1, no. 4 (1974):26–34.

"Awarding Credit for Extra-institutional Learning." *OEC Newsletter,* no. 48 (Spring 1977), pp. 5, 8. (Washington: American Council on Education, Office on Educational Credit.)

Bailey, Stephen K. "Career Education and Higher Education." *Educational Record* 54 (1973):255–59.

Berg, Ivar E. *Education and Jobs: The Great Training Robbery.* New York: Praeger, 1970.

Blackburn, Robert, et al. *Changing Practices in Undergraduate Education.* Berkeley, Calif.: Carnegie Council on Policy Studies in Higher Education, 1976.

Boucher, Chauncey Samuel. *The Chicago College Plan.* Chicago: University of Chicago Press, 1935.

Boyd, Joseph D. "1974–75 Undergraduate State Scholarship/Grant Programs." Deerfield, Ill.: Illinois State Scholarship Commission, 1974.

Brubacher, John S., and Rudy, Willis. *Higher Education in Transition: A History of American Colleges and Universities, 1936–1976.* 3d ed. New York: Harper & Row, 1976.

Bulpitt, Mildred. "The Adult Student." In *Understanding Diverse Students. New Directions for Community Colleges,* no. 3, Autumn 1973. San Francisco: Jossey-Bass, 1973.

Burn, Barbara. "The American Academic Credit System." In *Structure of Studies and Place of Research in Mass Higher Education.* Paris: Organization for Economic Development, 1974.

California Postsecondary Education Commission. *Through the Open Door: A Study of Patterns and Performance in California's Community Colleges.* Commission Report 76-1. Sacramento: The Commission, February 1976.

Caplow, Theodore. *Sociology of Work.* Minneapolis: University of Minnesota Press, 1954. Reprinted in *Professionalization,* ed. Howard Vollmer and Donald Mills. Englewood Cliffs, N.J.: Prentice-Hall, 1966.

Carnegie Commission on Higher Education. *Less Time, More Options: Education Beyond the High School.* New York: McGraw-Hill, 1971.

Carp, Abraham; Peterson, Richard; and Roelfs, Pamela. "Adult Learning Interests and Experiences." In *Planning Non-Traditional Programs,* by K. Patricia Cross, John R. Valley, and associates. San Francisco: Jossey-Bass, 1974.

CLEP May Be for You. New York: College Entrance Examination Board, 1975.

College Proficiency Examinations/Regents External Degrees. Albany: University of the State of New York, 1975.

College Transfer: Recommendations from Airlie House Conference [2–4 December 1973]. Washington: Association Transfer Group [1974]. ERIC ED 090904.

Commission on Non-Traditional Study. *Diversity by Design.* San Francisco: Jossey-Bass, 1973.

Competence-based Learning at Alverno College. Milwaukee, Wis.: Alverno College, n.d.

"Competency Statements for General Education." Working papers for task forces at Our Lady of the Lake University of San Antonio, February 1976.

Cooperative Assessment of Experiential Learning. *CAEL Newsletter* 3, no. 2 (1977):1.

Council of Graduate Schools in the United States. *The Master's Degree: A Policy Statement.* Washington: Council of Graduate Schools in the United States, 1976.

————. *Proceedings of the Fifteenth Annual Meeting, December 1975.* Washington: The Council.

————. *Proceedings of the Sixteenth Annual Meeting, December 1976.* Washington: The Council.

Council of State Governments. *Occupational Licensing Legislation in the States.* Chicago: The Council, 1952.

Council on Postsecondary Accreditation. "The Balance Wheel for Accreditation." Information leaflet, Washington: COPA, n.d.

Cross, K. Patricia; Valley, John R.; and associates. *Planning Non-Traditional Programs.* San Francisco: Jossey-Bass, 1974.

Davis, James R. *Great Aspirations: The Graduate School Plans of America's College Seniors.* National Opinion Research Center Monographs in Social Research, no. 1. Chicago: Aldine Publishing Co., 1946.

————. "The Search for Standards: Relativism and Emerging Pluralism in Higher Education." *Journal of Higher Education* 45 (1974):145–51.

"Development and Use of College Outcome Measures." MS. American College Testing Program, 1976.

Duncan, Sister Virginia Clare, et al. *Competency Alternatives for Achievement.* San Antonio, Tex.: Our Lady of the Lake University, Center for Educational Development, 1975.

Elton, L. R. B. "The Assessment of Students—A New Approach." *Universities Quarterly* 22 (1968):291–301.

Enell, John W. "The CEU Comes of Age." *Engineering Education* 66 (1975):150.

A Fact Book on Higher Education 1976: First and fourth issues. Washington: American Council on Education.

Fenske, Robert H.; Scott, Craig S.; and Carmody, James F. "Recent Trends in Studies of Student Migration." *Journal of Higher Education* 45 (1974):61–74.

Ferguson, Richard L., and Maxey, E. James. *Trends in the Academic Performance of High School and College Students.* ACT Research Report no. 70. Iowa City: American College Testing Program, 1976.

Folger, John. "Some Relationships Between Ability and Self Reported Grades." *Sociology of Education* 40 (1967):270–74.

Forrest, Aubrey. *A Student Handbook on Preparing a Portfolio for the Assessment of Prior Experiential Learning.* CAEL Working Paper no. 7. Princeton, N.J.: Educational Testing Service, 1975.

Forrest, Aubrey; Ferguson, Richard J.; and Cole, Nancy S. "The Narrative Transcript: An Overview." *Educational Record* 56 (1975):59–65.

Forrest, Aubrey; Meyers, Miriam; and Tisinger, Catherine. "Assessment Handbook." MS. Minnesota Metropolitan State College, 1974.

Furniss, W. Todd, and Martin, Marie Y. "Toward Solving Transfer Problems." In *College Transfer: Working Papers and Recommendations from the Airlie House Conference, 2–4 December 1973.* Washington: Association Transfer Group, 1974. ERIC ED 090904.

Gerhard, Dietrich. "The Emergence of the Credit System in American Education Considered as a Problem of Social and Intellectual History," *AAUP Bulletin* 41 (1955):645–68.

Glenny, Lyman, et al. *State Budgeting for Higher Education: Data Digest.* Berkeley: University of California, Berkeley, Center for Research and Development in Higher Education, 1975.

Gold, Ben K. "Academic Performance of L.A.C.C. Transfers Entering the University of California during the Academic Year 1971–72." Research Study no. 73–3. Los Angeles: Los Angeles City College, 1973.

———. "Academic Performance of L.A.C.C. Transfers to UCLA through the Special Services Program, 1971–72. Research Study no. 73–13. Los Angeles: Los Angeles City College, October 1972.

Gould, Samuel B., and Cross, K. Patricia, eds. *Explorations in Non-Traditional Study.* San Francisco: Jossey-Bass, 1972.

Grandy, Jerilee, and Shea, Walter M. *CLEP General Examinations in American Colleges and Universities.* New York: College Entrance Examination Board, 1976.

Grieder, Timothy M., and Cassady, Royce W. "Transferring the Non-Transfer Program." *College and University* 50 (1974):76–81.

Gross, Francis McK. *A Comparative Analysis of Existing Budget Formulas.* Office of Institutional Research, vol. 14, monograph 9. Knoxville: University of Tennessee, Office of Institutional Research, 1973.

———. "A Comparative Analysis of the Existing Budget Formulas Used for Justifying Budget Requests or Allocating Funds for the Operating Expenses of State-Supported Colleges and Universities." Ph.D. diss., University of Tennessee, 1973.

Guide to the Evaluation of Educational Experiences in the Armed Services, 1975 Supplement. Washington: American Council on Education, 1975.

Guide to the Evaluation of Educational Experiences in the Armed Services. 1976 ed. Washington: American Council on Education, 1976.

Guidelines and Procedures for the Assessment of Experiential Learning and for the Selection and Training of Field Experts.

Council for the Advancement of Experiential Learning Report no. 5. Princeton, N.J.: Educational Testing Service, 1976.

"Guidelines for Appraising the Technical Quality of Achievement Examinations." Duplicated. Washington: American Council on Education, Office on Educational Credit, November 1977.

Guidelines for Improving Articulation Between Junior and Senior Colleges: A Statement by the Joint Committee on Junior and Senior Colleges. Washington: Association of American Colleges, American Association of Junior Colleges, American Association of Collegiate Registrars and Admissions Officers [1966].

Handbook X-118, Qualifications Standards for White-Collar Positions Under the General Schedule. Washington: U.S. Civil Service Commission, Bureau of Policies and Standards, 1975 edition.

Haskins, Charles H. *The Rise of Universities.* Ithaca, N.Y.: Cornell University Press, 1957.

Heffernan, James M. "The Credibility of the Credit Hour: The History, Use, and Shortcomings of the Credit System." *Journal of Higher Education* 44 (1973):61–72.

Hirst, Ben. *V-TECS: The Vocational-Technical Educational Consortium of States.* Atlanta, Ga.: Southern Association of Colleges and Schools, n.d.

Hoenninger, Ronald W., and Dyer, Joe W. "Accrediting the New Clientele for Post-Secondary Education." 1974. ERIC ED 089801.

Hoffman, Richard. "Introduction to Mars Hill." In *A CBC Primer*, ed. William R. O'Connell and W. Edmund Moomaw. Atlanta, Ga.: Southern Regional Education Board, 1975.

Houle, Cyril O. *The External Degree.* San Francisco: Jossey-Bass, 1973.

Houston, W. Robert, and Jones, Howard L. *Three Views of Competency-based Teacher Education, II: University of Houston.* Bloomington, Ind.: Phi Delta Kappa Educational Foundation, 1974.

Hoyt, Donald P. "College Grades and Adult Accomplishment: A Review of Research." *Educational Record* 47 (1966):70–75.

———. "Evaluating Learning from Nontraditional Contexts." MS. American Council on Education, Office on Educational Credit, 1975.

Huff, Sheila. "Credentialing by Tests or by Degrees: Title VII of the Civil Rights Act and Griggs v. Duke Power Company." *Harvard Educational Review* 44 (1974):246–69.

Hughes, John F., and Mills, Olive, eds. *Formulating Policy in Postsecondary Education: The Search for Alternatives.* Washington: American Council on Education, 1975.

Illinois Community College Board, "A Statewide Follow-up Study of Fall 1973 Transfer Students from Illinois Public Community Colleges." Research Report no. 12. Springfield: The Board, April 1976.

Illinois Council on Articulation. "Transfer Students in Illinois: Where Do They Go and How Well Do They Succeed?" *North Central Quarterly* 46 (1971):295–306.

Jencks, Christopher, and Riesman, David. *The Academic Revolution.* Garden City, N.Y.: Doubleday, 1968.

Joint Legislative Audit and Review Commission. *Program Evaluation, The Virginia Community College System.* Richmond: Virginia General Assembly, The Commission, March 17, 1975.

Joula, Arvo E. "Grade Inflation (1960–1973): A Preliminary Report." MS. Michigan State University, August 1974.

Keeton, Morris T., and associates. *Experiential Learning: Rationale, Characteristics, and Assessment.* San Francisco: Jossey-Bass, 1976.

Kintzer, Frederick C. " 'Articulation' Comes of Age." *Compact* 10, no. 2 (1976):13–16.

―――. "The Community College Transfer Student." In *Understanding Diverse Students. New Directions for Community Colleges,* no. 3, Autumn 1973. San Francisco: Jossey-Bass, 1973.

―――. *Middleman in Higher Education.* San Francisco: Jossey-Bass, 1973.

―――. "The Transfer Student Dimension of Articulation." In *College Transfer: Working Papers and Recommendations from the Airlie House Conference, 2–4 December 1973.* Washington: Association Transfer Group, 1974. ERIC ED 088408.

Kirkwood, Robert. "Importance of Assessing Learning." In *Experiential Learning: Rationale, Characteristics, and Assessment,* by Morris T. Keeton and associates. San Francisco: Jossey-Bass, 1976.

―――. "The Myths of Accreditation." *Educational Record* 54 (1973):211–15.

Knapp, Joan E. *A Guide for Assessing Prior Experience through Portfolios.* CAEL Working Paper no. 6. Princeton, N.J.: Educational Testing Service, 1975.

Knoell, Dorothy M., and Medsker, Leland L. *From Junior to Senior College: A National Study of the Transfer Student.* Washington: American Council on Education, 1965.

Koscheski, Billy J. "V-TECS as a Servant of the Curriculum." Paper delivered to the Education Professions Development Act Workshop on Competency-based Vocational Education, Lexington, Ky., 1976.

Kramer, Rena; Kaufman, Barry; and Podell, Lawrence. *Distribution of Grades: 1972*. New York: City University of New York, Office of Program and Policy Research, 1974.

Kreplin, Hannah. *Credit by Examination: A Review and Analysis of the Literature*. New York: Ford Foundation, 1971.

Lanier, Lyle H. "A Critique of the Philosophy of Progress." In *I'll Take My Stand: The South and the Agrarian Tradition*, by Twelve Southerners. 1930. Reprint ed., New York: Harper Torch Books, 1962.

Learned, W. S., and Wood, Ben D. *The Student and His Knowledge*. New York: Carnegie Foundation for the Advancement of Teaching, 1938.

Lee, Glenda E. "Reverse Transfer: The 'Retread Function' of Community Colleges." Paper presented to the A.E.R.A./S.I.G. Community College Follow-up and Instructional Evaluation Studies Session, April 1, 1975.

Lewis, Lanora. *The Credit System in Colleges and Universities*. New Dimensions in Higher Education, no. 9. Washington: Department of Health, Education, and Welfare, 1961.

London, Herbert I. "The Case for Nontraditional Learning." *Change*, June 1976, pp. 25–29.

London, Perry. *The Modes and Morals of Psychotherapy*. New York: Holt, Rinehart & Winston, 1964.

Lorimer, Margaret F. "How Much Is a Credit Hour?" *Journal of Higher Education* 33 (1962):302–6.

McCandless, Charles E., and Pope, Henry D. "Transfer Practices of Junior Colleges Affecting Students on Academic Suspension from Senior Colleges." *College and University* 49 (1974):178–85.

McClelland, David C. "Testing for Competence Rather Than for 'Intelligence.'" *American Psychologist* 28 (1973):1–14.

McClothlin, William J. *The Professional Schools*. New York: Center for Applied Research, 1964.

McFate, Patricia Ann. *Education for the Itinerant Student: A Guide to Opportunities in Liberal Arts and Sciences at CIC Universities*. Evanston, Ill.: Committee on Institutional Cooperation, 1973.

Malden, Henry. *On the Origin of Universities and Academic Degrees*. London: John Taylor, 1835.

Manning, Charles W., and Romney, Leonard C. *Faculty Activity Analysis: Procedures Manual*. Technical Report no. 44. Boulder, Colo., National Center for Higher Education Management Systems, 1973.

Massachusetts State Transfer Articulation Committee. *Guidelines for Articulation for Receiving Institutions*. New York: College Entrance Examination Board, 1973.

Meeth, L. Richard. *Government Funding Policies and Nontraditional Programs.* Report no. 2. Washington: Institute for Educational Leadership, 1974.

Meisinger, Richard J., Jr.; Purvis, Ralph; and Schmidtlein, Frank. "Productivity from an Interorganization Perspective." In *Measuring and Increasing Academic Productivity,* ed. Robert A. Wallhaus. *New Directions for Institutional Research* 2, no. 4. San Francisco: Jossey-Bass, 1975.

Merwin, Jack C. "Uses of College Credit—Evolution and Current Problems." *Minnesota Education* 1, no. 4 (1974):1.

Meyer, Peter. *Awarding College Credit for Non-College Learning.* San Francisco: Jossey-Bass, 1975.

Micek, Sidney S. *Outcome-Oriented Planning in Higher Education: An Approach or an Impossibility?* Boulder, Colo.: National Center for Higher Education Management Systems, 1976.

——; Service, A. L.; and Lee, Y. S. *Outcome Measures and Procedures Manual.* Technical Report no. 70. Boulder, Colo.: National Center for Higher Education Management Systems, 1975.

Miller, Jerry W. "Credentials for Health Administration." In *Selected Papers of the Commission on Education for Health Administration,* vol. 2. Ann Arbor, Mich.: Health Administration Press, 1975.

Moughamian, Henry. "A Five Year Longitudinal Study of City Colleges of Chicago Transfer Students, September 1967–June 1972." MS. City Colleges of Chicago, November 1972.

National Center for Higher Education Management Systems. *Faculty Activity Analysis: Interpretation and Uses of Data.* Technical Report no. 54. Boulder, Colo.: NCHEMS.

——. *Faculty Activity Analysis: Overview and Major Issues.* Technical Report no. 24. Boulder, Colo.: NCHEMS, 1972.

National Education Association. *A Manual on Standards Affecting School Personnel in the United States,* 1974 ed., ed. T. M. Stinnett. Washington: The Association, 1974.

The National Guide to Credit Recommendations for Noncollegiate Courses, 1978 Edition. Washington: American Council on Education, 1978.

National Institute for Automotive Service Excellence. *Bulletin of Information.* Princeton, N.J.: Educational Testing Service, 1976.

National Task Force on the Continuing Education Unit. [William L. Turner, chairman.] *The Continuing Education Unit: Criteria and Guidelines.* Washington: National University Extension Association, 1974.

New York Regents. *Regents External Degrees/College Proficiency Examinations.* Albany: University of the State of New York, 1975.

Newman, Frank, et al. *Report on Higher Education.* Washington: Department of Health, Education, and Welfare, 1970.

O'Connell, William R., and Moomaw, W. Edmund, eds. *A CBC Primer.* Atlanta, Ga.: Southern Regional Education Board, 1975.

Orlans, Harold. "The Fatuity of Credentialing Everyone and Everything." In *Formulating Policy in Postsecondary Education: The Search for Alternatives,* ed. John F. Hughes and Olive Mills. Washington: American Council on Education, 1975.

Pace, C. Robert. *The Demise of Diversity?: A Comparative Profile of Eight Types of Institutions.* Berkeley, Calif.: Carnegie Commission on Higher Education, 1974.

Panel on Alternate Approaches to Graduate Education. *Scholarship for Society.* Princeton, N.J.: Educational Testing Service, 1973.

Placement and Proficiency Examinations, 1975–76. Urbana: University of Illinois, Office of Instructional Resources, 1975.

Preus, Paul K. "Report of an Investigation of Student's Perception of the Process of Transferring to MSU." MS. Center for the Study of Higher Education, Memphis State University, June 1973.

Rashdall, Hastings. *The Universities of Europe in the Middle Ages,* vol. 1. Oxford: Clarendon Press, 1895.

Read, Sister Joel. "A Degree by Any Other Name . . . The Alverno Plan." In *Formulating Policy in Postsecondary Education: The Search for Alternatives,* ed. John F. Hughes and Olive Mills. Washington: American Council on Education, 1975.

Reflections on Experiential Learning and Its Uses. CAEL Working Paper no. 3. Princeton, N.J.: Educational Testing Service, 1975.

"A Report on Scholarship Grades: University of California, Berkeley." MS. University of California, Berkeley, Office of Institutional Research, 1975.

"Report to the Faculty from the Committee for the Assessment of Experiential Learning." Canton, Mo.: Culver-Stockton College, 1 February 1976.

Rose, Glen A. "A Follow-up Study of the Broward Community College Reserve Transfer Student Questionnaire." MS. Nova University, Ft. Lauderdale, Fla.

———. "Relationships of Student and Faculty Perceptions of Transfer Barriers Faced by Students at Broward Community College." Abstract, pp. i–xv. MS. Nova University, Ft. Lauderdale, Fla.

Rudolph, Frederick. *The American College and University.* New York: Alfred A. Knopf, 1962.

Ruyle, Janet, and Geiselman, Lucy Ann. "Non-Traditional Opportunities and Programs." In *Planning Non-Traditional Programs,* by K. Patricia Cross, John R. Valley, and associates. San Francisco: Jossey-Bass, 1974.

Safarik, J. G., "1972–1973 Grade Distributions and Analyses at California State University, Chico." MS. California State University, Chico, 1974.

Sale, Kirkpatrick. *Power Shift: The Rise of the Southern Rim and Its Challenge to the Eastern Establishment.* New York: Random House, 1975.

Schafer, Suzan. *A New Position in Higher Education: Liaison Officer for Articulation.* Gainesville: University of Florida, Institute of Higher Education, 1974.

Sennet, Michael. "Antitrust—Goldfarb v. Virginia State Bar: Professional Legal Service Held To Be Within the Ambit of Federal Antitrust Laws." *Loyola University Law Journal,* Winter 1976, pp. 254–76.

Small, Hazel G. "The Continuing Education Unit." In *A Guide to Adult Education Programs in Area Vocational Centers.* Camden, S.C.: South Carolina Department of Education, Office of Vocational Education, 1973. ERIC ED 090438.

Smith, Virginia B. "Assessing Experiential Learning: The Search for an Integrating Logic." In *Reflections on Experiential Learning and Its Uses.* CAEL Working Paper no. 3. Princeton, N.J.: Educational Testing Service, 1975.

Spurr, Stephen H. *Academic Degree Structures: Innovative Approaches.* New York: McGraw-Hill, 1970.

State University of New York. "Application and Enrollment Patterns of Transfer Students, Fall 1972." Office of Institutional Research Report no. 41. Albany: SUNY, February 1974.

———. "Application and Enrollment Patterns of Transfer Students, Fall 1974." Office of Institutional Research Report no. 6–76. Albany: SUNY, March 1976.

"Statement of Principles Regarding Degree Granting by Federal Agencies." *Higher Education and National Affairs* (American Council on Education), October 29, 1976.

Steahr, Thomas E., and Schmid, Calvin F. "College Student Migration in the United States." *Journal of Higher Education* 43 (1972):441–63.

Stevens, Edward I. "Grading Systems and Student Mobility." *Educational Record* 54 (1973):308–12.

Stickgold, Arthur. "Policy Implications of Changing Student Values in the Collegiate Culture." *Liberal Education* 61 (1975): 173–86.

Suslow, Sidney. "Course Credits as Measures of Faculty/Student Effort—An Evaluation." *Minnesota Education* 1, no. 4 (1974): 12–25.

Tennessee Higher Education Commission. "Models for Higher Education Evaluation: Explorations in Policy Intent and Impact; Status Report and Plan of Action." Nashville, Tenn.: The Commission, 1976.

"There's More than One Way to Earn a College Degree." *Carnegie Quarterly* 23 (Fall 1975):1–8.

Thorne, Barrie, "Professional Education in Medicine." In *Education for the Professions of Medicine, Law, Theology, and Social Welfare,* ed. Everett C. Hughes. New York: McGraw-Hill, 1973.

Trivett, David A. *Competency Programs in Higher Education.* ERIC/Higher Education Research Report no. 7, 1975. Washington: American Association for Higher Education, 1975.

U.S. Bureau of the Census. *Census of Population, 1970: Subject Reports; Occupational Characteristics.* Washington: Government Printing Office.

U.S. Department of Health, Education, and Welfare. National Center for Educational Statistics. *Residence and Migration of College Students, Fall 1968: Analytic Report.* Washington: Government Printing Office, 1970.

U.S. Department of Justice. Bureau of Prisons. Education Branch. *Education and Vocational Training of Incarcerated Federal Offenders: Annual Report FY–72.* Washington: U.S. Department of Justice, Bureau of Prisons, Education Branch.

U.S. Department of Labor. Bureau of Labor Statistics. *Occupational Manpower and Training Needs, Revised 1975.* Washington: Government Printing Office, 1975.

Valley, John R. "External Degree Programs." *Explorations in Non-Traditional Study,* by K. Patricia Cross, John R. Valley, and associates. San Francisco: Jossey-Bass, 1974.

Vargas, Ernest A. "The Credit Hour: An Anachronism." MS. West Virginia University, 1975.

"V-TECS Progress Report." Atlanta, Ga.: Southern Association of Colleges and Schools, 1976.

Wang, William K. S. "The Unbundling of Higher Education." *Duke Law Journal* 53 (1975):53–90.

Warren, Jonathan R. "Awarding Credit." In *Planning Non-Traditional Programs,* by K. Patricia Cross, John R. Valley, and associates. San Francisco: Jossey-Bass, 1974.

Wattenbarger, James. "Problems of Articulation." In *Toward Solving Transfer Problems in Southern Colleges and Universities: Report of a Workshop.* Atlanta, Ga.: Southern Regional Education Board, 1975.

Weathersby, George. "The Unbudget: State Support for Postsecondary Education in Times of Fiscal Stringency." In *Ninth Biennial Legislative Work Conference.* Boulder, Colo.: Western Interstate Commission on Higher Education, March 1976.

White, Edward M. *Comparison and Contrast: The 1975 California State University and Colleges Freshman English Equivalency Examination.* Los Angeles: California State University and Colleges, 1976.

Willett, Sandra L. "Consumer Protection in Higher Education: Why? For Whom? How?" *Liberal Education* 61 (1975):161–72.

Willingham, Warren W. "Transfer Standards and the Public Interest." In *College Transfer: Working Papers and Recommendations from the Airlie House Conference* [2–4 December 1973]. Washington: Association Transfer Group [1974]. ERIC ED 088406.

Yarmolinsky, Adam. "Challenges to Legitimacy: Dilemmas and Directions." *Change,* April 1976, pp. 18–25.

AMERICAN COUNCIL ON EDUCATION

J. W. PELTASON, *President*

The American Council on Education, founded in 1918 and composed of institutions of higher education and national and regional education associations, is the nation's major coordinating body for postsecondary education. Through voluntary and cooperative action, the Council provides comprehensive leadership for improving educational standards, policies, procedures, and services.

The Office on Educational Credit is the Council's division concerned with credit and credentialing policies and practices in postsecondary education. The role of the office and its policy-making and advisory arm, the Commission on Educational Credit, is to give attention to educational credit and credentialing policies for postsecondary education; to foster high standards and sound practices for the evaluation and recognition of extrainstitutional learning; to foster and operate programs to establish and publish credit equivalencies for extrainstitutional learning, and to advise postsecondary education institutions on how these credit equivalencies can be used in placing students in academic programs and in credentialing educational accomplishment; to assist postsecondary education institutions in providing people with due recognition for competency, knowledge, and skills, wherever and however obtained; and to provide people with an alternative means of demonstrating high-school-graduation competences.

OEC makes credit recommendations for testing programs such as the College-Level Examination Program (CLEP) and administers the General Educational Development (GED) Testing Program. OEC also makes credit recommendations for formal courses offered by the military and other noncollegiate sponsors such as business, industry, government agencies, voluntary and professional associations, and labor unions; for Army military occupational specialties (MOS's) and Navy ratings; and for home study courses accredited by the National Home Study Council. In a new study for the U.S. Department of Labor, the Office will determine whether credit recommendations can be made for apprenticeship programs registered with the Bureau of Apprenticeship and Training. The office's Task Force on Educational Credit and Credentials has developed recommendations for improving the credit and credentialing system. The final report of the Task Force, *Credentialing Educational Accomplishment,* includes the recommendations and the analyses prepared as a resource for arriving at the recommendations.